THE LOEB CLASSICAL LIBRARY

EDITED BY

E. CAPPS. PH.D., LL.D.   T. E. PAGE, LITT.D.
W. H. D. ROUSE, LITT.D.

PLATO

PLATO

WITH AN ENGLISH TRANSLATION
X

LAWS

BY

R. G. BURY, Litt.D.

FORMERLY SCHOLAR OF TRINITY COLLEGE, CAMBRIDGE

IN TWO VOLUMES
II

LONDON : WILLIAM HEINEMANN
NEW YORK : G. P. PUTNAM'S SONS
MCMXXVI #192

CONTENTS

20263

V. 10

LAWS

ΝΟΜΟΙ

ΤΑ ΤΟΥ ΔΙΑΛΟΓΟΥ ΠΡΟΣΩΠΑ

ΑΘΗΝΑΙΟΣ ΞΕΝΟΣ, ΚΛΕΙΝΙΑΣ ΚΡΗΣ,
ΜΕΓΙΛΛΟΣ ΛΑΚΕΔΑΙΜΟΝΙΟΣ

Ζ

788 ΑΘ. Γενομένων δὲ παίδων ἀρρένων καὶ θηλειῶν
τροφὴν μέν που . καὶ παιδείαν τὸ μετὰ ταῦτα
λέγειν ὀρθότατ᾽ ἂν ¹ γίγνοιθ᾽ ἡμῖν, ἣν εἶναι μὲν
ἄρρητον πάντως ἀδύνατον, λεγομένη δὲ διδαχῇ
τινὶ καὶ νουθετήσει μᾶλλον ἢ νόμοις εἰκυῖ᾽ ἂν
ἡμῖν φαίνοιτο. ἰδίᾳ γὰρ καὶ κατ᾽ οἰκίας πολλὰ
καὶ σμικρὰ καὶ οὐκ ἐκφανῆ πᾶσι γιγνόμενα
ῥᾳδίως ὑπὸ τῆς ἑκάστων λύπης τε καὶ ἡδονῆς
Β καὶ ἐπιθυμίας, ἕτερα παρὰ τὰς τοῦ νομοθέτου
ξυμβουλὰς παραγενόμενα παντοδαπὰ καὶ οὐχ
ὅμοια ἀλλήλοις ἀπεργάζοιτ᾽ ἂν τὰ τῶν πολιτῶν
ἤθη· τοῦτο δὲ κακὸν ταῖς πόλεσι. καὶ γὰρ διὰ
σμικρότητα αὐτῶν καὶ πυκνότητα ἐπιζήμια τιθέντα ποιεῖν νόμους ἀπρεπὲς ἅμα καὶ ἄσχημον.
διαφθείρει δὲ καὶ τοὺς γραφῇ τεθέντας νόμους,
ἐν τοῖς σμικροῖς καὶ πυκνοῖς ἐθισθέντων τῶν
C ἀνθρώπων παρανομεῖν· ὥστε ἀπορία μὲν περὶ
αὐτὰ νομοθετεῖν, σιγᾶν δὲ ἀδύνατον. ἃ δὲ λέγω,

¹ ὀρθότατ᾽ ἂν Ast: ὀρθότατα MSS.

2

LAWS

[or ON LEGISLATION, political]

CHARACTERS

AN ATHENIAN STRANGER, CLINIAS OF CRETE,
MEGILLUS OF LACEDAEMON

BOOK VII

ATH. Now that our children, of both sexes, are
born, our proper course will be to deal in the next
place with their nurture and education. This is a
subject which it is wholly impossible to pass over;
but obviously it can be treated more suitably by way
of precept and exhortation than by legislation. For
in the private life of the family many trivial things
are apt to be done which escape general notice,—
things which are the result of individual feelings of
pain, pleasure, or desire, and which contravene the
instructions of the lawgiver; and these will produce
in the citizens a multiplicity of contradictory tendencies. This is bad for a State. For while, on the
one hand, it is improper and undignified to impose
penalties on these practices by law, because of their
triviality and the frequency of their occurrence, on
the other hand, it detracts from the authority of the
law which stands written when men grow used to
breaking the law in trivial matters repeatedly.
Hence, while it is impossible to pass over these
practices in silence, it is difficult to legislate concerning them. The practices I refer to I will try to

3

δηλῶσαι πειρατέον οἷον δείγματα ἐξενεγκόντα
εἰς φῶς· νῦν γὰρ λεγομένοις ἔοικε κατά τι σκότος.

ΚΛ. Ἀληθέστατα λέγεις.

ΑΘ. Οὐκοῦν ὅτι μὲν σώματα καὶ ψυχὰς τήν
γε ὀρθὴν πάντως δεῖ τροφὴν φαίνεσθαι δυναμένην
ὡς κάλλιστα καὶ ἄριστα ἐξεργάζεσθαι, τοῦτο μὲν
ὀρθῶς εἴρηταί που.

ΚΛ. Τί μήν;

D ΑΘ. Σώματα δὲ κάλλιστα, οἶμαι, τό γε ἁπλούστατον, ὡς ὀρθότατα δεῖ νέων ὄντων εὐθὺς φύεσθαι
τῶν παίδων.

ΚΛ. Πάνυ μὲν οὖν.

ΑΘ. Τί δέ; τόδε οὐκ ἐννοοῦμεν, ὡς ἡ πρώτη
βλάστη παντὸς ζῴου πολὺ μεγίστη καὶ πλείστη
φύεται, ὥστε καὶ ἔριν πολλοῖς παρέσχηκε μὴ
γίγνεσθαι τά γ' ἀνθρώπινα μήκη διπλάσια ἀπὸ
πέντε ἐτῶν ἐν τοῖς λοιποῖς εἴκοσιν ἔτεσιν
αὐξανόμενα;

ΚΛ. Ἀληθῆ.

ΑΘ. Τί οὖν; πολλὴ αὔξη ὅταν ἐπιρρέῃ πόνων
789 χωρὶς πολλῶν καὶ συμμέτρων, οὐκ ἴσμεν ὅτι
μυρία κακὰ ἐν τοῖς σώμασιν ἀποτελεῖ;

ΚΛ. Πάνυ γε.

ΑΘ. Οὐκοῦν τότε δεῖται πλείστων πόνων, ὅταν
ἡ πλείστη τροφὴ προσγίγνηται τοῖς σώμασιν.

ΚΛ. Τί δῆτα, ὦ ξένε; ἢ τοῖς ἄρτι γεγονόσι
καὶ νεωτάτοις πόνους πλείστους προστάξομεν;

ΑΘ. Οὐδαμῶς γε, ἀλλ' ἔτι καὶ πρότερον τοῖς
ἐντὸς τῶν αὐτῶν μητέρων τρεφομένοις.

ΚΛ. Πῶς λέγεις, ὦ λῷστε; ἢ τοῖς κυουμένοισι
φράζεις;

---

[1] 643D ff.

4

make clear by bringing some specimens, as it were, to the light; for at present my words rather resemble a "dark speech."

CLIN. That is quite true.

ATH. When we said[1] that right nurture must be manifestly capable of making both bodies and souls in all respects as beautiful and good as possible, we spoke, I presume, truly?

CLIN. Certainly we did.

ATH. And I suppose that (to take the simplest point) the most beautiful bodies must grow up from earliest infancy as straight as possible.

CLIN. Most certainly.

ATH. Well then, do we not observe that in every living creature the first shoot makes by far the largest and longest growth; so that many people stoutly maintain that in point of height men grow more in the first five years of life than in the next twenty?

CLIN. That is true.

ATH. But we know, don't we, that when growth occurs rapidly, without plenty of suitable exercise, it produces in the body countless evils?

CLIN. Certainly.

ATH. And when bodies receive most food, then they require most exercise?

CLIN. What is that, Stranger? Are we to prescribe most exercise for new-born babes and tiny infants?

ATH. Nay, even earlier than that,—we shall prescribe it for those nourished inside the bodies of their mothers.

CLIN. What do you mean, my dear sir? Is it unborn babes you are talking of?

5

B   ΑΘ.   Ναί. θαυμαστὸν δ᾽ οὐδέν ἐστιν ἀγνοεῖν
ὑμᾶς τὴν τῶν τηλικούτων γυμναστικήν, ἣν βου-
λοίμην ἂν ὑμῖν, καίπερ ἄτοπον οὖσαν, δηλῶσαι.

ΚΛ.   Πάνυ μὲν οὖν.

ΑΘ.   Ἔστι τοίνυν παρ᾽ ἡμῖν μᾶλλον τὸ τοιοῦτον
κατανοεῖν διὰ τὸ τὰς παιδιὰς αὐτόθι μειζόνως
τινὰς παίζειν ἢ δεῖ. τρέφουσι γὰρ δὴ παρ᾽ ἡμῖν
οὐ μόνον παῖδες ἀλλὰ καὶ πρεσβύτεροί τινες
ὀρνίθων θρέμματα, ἐπὶ τὰς μάχας τὰς πρὸς
ἄλληλα ἀσκοῦντες τὰ τοιαῦτα τῶν θηρίων.
C πολλοῦ δὴ δέουσιν ἡγεῖσθαι τοὺς πόνους αὐτοῖς
εἶναι τοὺς πρὸς ἄλληλα μετρίους, ἐν οἷς αὐτὰ
ἀνακινοῦσι γυμνάζοντες· πρὸς γὰρ τούτοις λαβόντες ὑπὸ μάλης ἕκαστος, τοὺς μὲν ἐλάττονας
εἰς τὰς χεῖρας, μείζους δ᾽ ὑπὸ τὴν ἀγκάλην ἐντός,
πορεύονται περιπατοῦντες σταδίους παμπόλλους
ἕνεκα τῆς εὐεξίας οὔ τι τῆς τῶν αὐτῶν σωμάτων,
ἀλλὰ τῆς τούτων τῶν θρεμμάτων. καὶ τό γε
τοσοῦτον δηλοῦσι τῷ δυναμένῳ καταμαθεῖν, ὅτι
τὰ σώματα πάντα ὑπὸ τῶν σεισμῶν τε καὶ
D κινήσεων κινούμενα ἄκοπα ὀνίναται πάντων ὅσα
τε ὑπὸ ἑαυτῶν ἢ καὶ ἐν αἰώραις ἢ καὶ κατὰ
θάλατταν ἢ καὶ ἐφ᾽ ἵππων ὀχούμενα [1] καὶ ὑπ᾽
ἄλλων ὁπωσοῦν δὴ φερομένων τῶν σωμάτων
κινεῖται, καὶ διὰ ταῦτα τὰς τῶν σίτων τροφὰς
καὶ ποτῶν κατακρατοῦντα ὑγίειαν καὶ κάλλος καὶ
τὴν ἄλλην ῥώμην ἡμῖν δυνατά ἐστι παραδιδόναι.
τί οὖν ἂν φαῖμεν ἐχόντων οὕτω τούτων τὸ μετὰ
τοῦτο ἡμᾶς δεῖν ποιεῖν; βούλεσθε ἅμα γέλωτι
E φράζωμεν, τιθέντες νόμους τὴν μὲν κύουσαν περι-
πατεῖν, τὸ γενόμενον δὲ πλάττειν τε οἷον κήρινον,
ἕως ὑγρόν, καὶ μέχρι δυοῖν ἐτοῖν σπαργανᾶν ; καὶ

6

ATH. It is. Still it is by no means surprising that you know nothing of this pre-natal gymnastic; but, strange though it is, I should like to explain it to you.

CLIN. By all means do so.

ATH. In our country it is easier to understand a practice of this kind, because there are people there who carry their sports to excess. At Athens we find not only boys but sometimes old men rearing birds and training such creatures to fight one another. But they are far from thinking that the training they give them by exciting their pugnacity provides sufficient exercise; in addition to this, each man takes up his bird and keeps it tucked away in his fist, if it is small, or under his arm, if it is large, and in this way they walk many a long mile in order to improve the condition, not of their own bodies, but of these creatures. Thus clearly do they show to any observant person that all bodies benefit, as by a tonic, when they are moved by any kind of shaking or motion, whether they are moved by their own action—as in a swing or in a rowing-boat—or are carried along on horseback or by any other rapidly moving bodies; and that this is the reason why bodies can deal successfully with their supplies of meat and drink and provide us with health and beauty, and strength as well. This being the state of the case, what does it behove us to do in the future? Shall we risk ridicule, and lay down a law that the pregnant woman shall walk, and that the child, while still soft, shall be moulded like wax, and be kept in swaddling clothes till it is two years

---

1 ὀχούμενα Ast : ὀχουμένων MSS.

δὴ καὶ τὰς τροφοὺς ἀναγκάζωμεν νόμῳ ζημιοῦντες
τὰ παιδία ἢ πρὸς ἀγροὺς ἢ πρὸς ἱερὰ ἢ πρὸς
οἰκείους ἀεί πῃ φέρειν, μέχριπερ ἂν ἱκανῶς
ἵστασθαι δυνατὰ γίγνηται, καὶ τότε διευλαβου-
μένας ἔτι νέων ὄντων μή πῃ βίᾳ ἐπερειδομένων
στρέφηται τὰ κῶλα ἐπιπονεῖν φερούσας, ἕως ἂν
τριετὲς ἀποτελεσθῇ τὸ γενόμενον ; εἰς δύναμιν δὲ
790 ἰσχυρὰς αὐτὰς εἶναι χρεὼν [καὶ μὴ μίαν] ;¹ ἐπὶ δὲ
τούτοις ἑκάστοις, ἂν μὴ γίγνηται, ζημίαν τοῖς μὴ
ποιοῦσι γράφωμεν ; ἢ πολλοῦ γε δεῖ ; τὸ γὰρ
ἄρτι ῥηθὲν γίγνοιτ' ἂν πολὺ καὶ ἄφθονον.

ΚΛ. Τὸ ποῖον ;

ΑΘ. Τὸ γέλωτα ἂν πολὺν ὀφλεῖν ἡμᾶς πρὸς τῷ
μὴ ἐθέλειν ἂν πείθεσθαι γυναικεῖά τε καὶ δούλεια
ἤθη τροφῶν.

ΚΛ. Ἀλλὰ τίνος δὴ χάριν ἔφαμεν αὐτὰ δεῖν
ῥηθῆναι ;

ΑΘ. Τοῦδε· τὰ τῶν δεσποτῶν τε καὶ ἐλευθέρων
Β ἐν ταῖς πόλεσιν ἤθη τάχ' ἂν ἀκούσαντα εἰς σύν-
νοιαν ἀφίκοιτ' ἂν τὴν ὀρθήν, ὅτι χωρὶς τῆς ἰδίας
διοικήσεως ἐν ταῖς πόλεσιν ὀρθῆς γιγνομένης μάτην
ἂν τὰ κοινά τις οἴοιτο ἕξειν τινὰ βεβαιότητα
θέσεως νόμων, καὶ ταῦτα ἐννοῶν αὐτὸς νόμοις ἂν
τοῖς νῦν ῥηθεῖσι χρῷτο, καὶ χρώμενος εὖ τήν τε
οἰκίαν καὶ πόλιν ἅμα τὴν αὑτοῦ διοικῶν εὐδαι-
μονοῖ.

ΚΛ. Καὶ μάλ' εἰκότως εἴρηκας.

ΑΘ. Τοιγαροῦν μήπω λήξωμεν τῆς τοιαύτης
νομοθεσίας, πρὶν ἂν καὶ τὰ περὶ τὰς ψυχὰς τῶν

¹ [καὶ μὴ μίαν] bracketed by W.-Möllendorff.

old? And shall we also compel the nurses by legal penalties to keep carrying the children somehow, either to the fields or to the temples or to their relatives, all the time until they are able to stand upright; and after that, still to persevere in carrying them until they are three years old, as a precaution against the danger of distorting their legs by over-pressure while they are still young? And that the nurses shall be as strong as possible? And shall we impose a written penalty for every failure to carry out these injunctions? Such a course is quite out of the question; for it would lead to a super-abundance of that consequence which we mentioned a moment ago.

CLIN. What was that?

ATH. The consequence of our incurring ridicule in abundance, in addition to meeting with a blank refusal to obey on the part of the nurses, with their womanish and servile minds.

CLIN. What reason, then, had we for saying that these rules ought to be stated?

ATH. The reason was this: the minds of the masters and of the freemen in the States may perhaps listen, and so come to the right conclusion that, unless private affairs in a State are rightly managed, it is vain to suppose that any stable code of laws can exist for public affairs; and when he perceives this, the individual citizen may of himself adopt as laws the rules we have now stated, and, by so doing and thus ordering aright both his household and his State, may achieve happiness.

CLIN. Such a result seems quite probable.

ATH. Consequently we must not desist from this kind of legislation until we have described in detail

9

C πάνυ νέων παίδων ἐπιτηδεύματα ἀποδῶμεν κατὰ
τὸν αὐτὸν τρόπον ὅνπερ ἠργμεθα τῶν περὶ τὰ
σώματα μύθων λεχθέντων διαπεραίνειν.

ΚΛ. Πάνυ μὲν οὖν ὀρθῶς.

ΑΘ. Λάβωμεν τοίνυν τοῦτο οἷον στοιχεῖον ἐπ'
ἀμφότερα, σώματός τε καὶ ψυχῆς τῶν πάνυ νέων
τὴν τιθήνησιν καὶ κίνησιν γιγνομένην ὅτι μάλιστα
διὰ πάσης νυκτός τε καὶ ἡμέρας, ὡς ἔστι ξύμφορος
ἅπασι μέν, οὐχ ἥκιστα δὲ τοῖς ὅτι νεωτάτοισι, καὶ
D οἰκεῖν, εἰ δυνατὸν ἦν, οἷον ἀεὶ πλέοντας· νῦν δ' ὡς
ἐγγύτατα τούτου ποιεῖν δεῖ περὶ τὰ νεογενῆ
παίδων θρέμματα. τεκμαίρεσθαι δὲ χρὴ καὶ ἀπὸ
τῶνδε ὡς ἐξ ἐμπειρίας αὐτὸ εἰλήφασι καὶ ἐγνώκα-
σιν ὂν χρήσιμον αἵ τε τροφοὶ τῶν σμικρῶν καὶ αἱ
περὶ τὰ τῶν Κορυβάντων ἰάματα τελοῦσαι· ἡνίκα
γὰρ ἄν που βουληθῶσι κατακοιμίζειν τὰ δυσυπ-
νοῦντα τῶν παιδίων αἱ μητέρες, οὐχ ἡσυχίαν
αὐτοῖς προσφέρουσιν ἀλλὰ τοὐναντίον κίνησιν, ἐν
ταῖς ἀγκάλαις ἀεὶ σείουσαι, καὶ οὐ σιγὴν ἀλλά
E τινα μελῳδίαν, καὶ ἀτεχνῶς οἷον καταυλοῦσι τῶν
παιδίων, καθαπερεὶ[1] τῶν ἐκφρόνων Βακχείων,
ἰάσει[2] ταύτῃ τῇ τῆς κινήσεως ἅμα χορείᾳ καὶ
μούσῃ χρώμεναι.

ΚΛ. Τίς οὖν αἰτία τούτων, ὦ ξένε, μάλιστ' ἔσθ'
ἡμῖν;

ΑΘ. Οὐ πάνυ χαλεπὴ γιγνώσκειν.

ΚΛ. Πῶς δή;

ΑΘ. Δειμαίνειν ἐστί που ταῦτ' ἀμφότερα τὰ

[1] καθαπερεὶ : καθάπερ ἡ MSS. ; καθάπερ αἱ Aldus, Zur.
[2] Βακχείων, ἰάσει: βακχειῶν ἰάσεις MSS. (βακχειῶν, ἰάσει
England).

the treatment suited for the souls of young children in the same manner as we commenced our advice regarding their bodies.

CLIN. You are quite right.

ATH. Let us take this, then, as a fundamental assumption in both cases,—that for both body and soul of the very young a process of nursing and moving, that is as continuous as possible both by day and by night, is in all cases salutary, and especially in the case of the youngest: it is like having them always rocked—if that were possible— on the sea. As it is, with new-born infants one should reproduce this condition as nearly as possible. Further evidence of this may be seen in the fact that this course is adopted and its usefulness recognized both by those who nurse small children and by those who administer remedies in cases of Corybantism.[1] Thus when mothers have children suffering from sleeplessness, and want to lull them to rest, the treatment they apply is to give them, not quiet, but motion, for they rock them constantly in their arms; and instead of silence, they use a kind of crooning noise; and thus they literally cast a spell upon the children (like the victims of Bacchic frenzy) by employing the combined movements of dance and song as a remedy.

CLIN. And what, Stranger, are we to suppose is the main cause of this?

ATH. It is easy enough to see.

CLIN. How so?

ATH. Both these affections are forms of fright;

[1] " Corybantism " is a technical term for a state of morbid mental excitement (cp. " tarantism ") derived from " Corybantes," the name given to the frenzied worshippers of Bacchus.

πάθη, καὶ ἔστι δείματα δι' ἕξιν φαύλην τῆς
ψυχῆς τινά. ὅταν οὖν ἔξωθέν τις προσφέρῃ τοῖς
791 τοιούτοις πάθεσι σεισμόν, ἡ τῶν ἔξωθεν κρατεῖ
κίνησις προσφερομένη τὴν ἐντὸς φοβερὰν οὖσαν
καὶ μανικὴν κίνησιν, κρατήσασα δὲ γαλήνην
ἡσυχίαν τε ἐν τῇ ψυχῇ φαίνεται ἀπεργασαμένη
τῆς περὶ τὰ τῆς καρδίας χαλεπῆς γενομένης
ἑκάστων πηδήσεως, παντάπασιν ἀγαπητόν τι
τοὺς μὲν ὕπνου λαγχάνειν ποιεῖ, τοὺς δ' ἐγρηγορότας ὀρχουμένους τε καὶ αὐλουμένους μετὰ θεῶν,
B οἷς ἂν καλλιεροῦντες ἕκαστοι θύωσι, κατειργάσατο
ἀντὶ μανικῶν ἡμῖν διαθέσεων ἕξεις ἔμφρονας ἔχειν.
καὶ ταῦτα, ὡς διὰ βραχέων γε οὕτως εἰπεῖν,
πιθανὸν λόγον ἔχει τινά.

ΚΛ. Πάνυ μὲν οὖν.

ΑΘ. Εἰ δέ γε οὕτω τοιαύτην τινὰ δύναμιν ἔχει
ταῦτα, ἐννοεῖν χρὴ τόδε παρ' αὐτοῖς, ὡς ἅπασα
ψυχὴ δείμασι ξυνοῦσα ἐκ νέων μᾶλλον ἂν διὰ
φόβων ἐθίζοιτο γίγνεσθαι. τοῦτο δέ που πᾶς ἂν
φαίη δειλίας ἄσκησιν, ἀλλ' οὐκ ἀνδρίας γίγνεσθαι.

ΚΛ. Πῶς γὰρ οὔ;

C ΑΘ. Τὸ δέ γε ἐναντίον ἀνδρίας ἂν φαῖμεν ἐκ
νέων εὐθὺς ἐπιτήδευμα εἶναι, τὸ νικᾶν τὰ προσ-
πίπτονθ' ἡμῖν δείματά τε καὶ φόβους.

ΚΛ. Ὀρθῶς.

ΑΘ. Ἕν δὴ καὶ τοῦτο εἰς ψυχῆς μόριον ἀρετῆς,
τὴν τῶν παντελῶς παίδων γυμναστικὴν ἐν ταῖς
κινήσεσι, μέγα ἡμῖν φῶμεν ξυμβάλλεσθαι.

ΚΛ. Πάνυ μὲν οὖν.

ΑΘ. Καὶ μὴν τό γε μὴ δύσκολον ἐν ψυχῇ καὶ
τὸ δύσκολον οὐ σμικρὸν μόριον εὐψυχίας καὶ
κακοψυχίας ἑκάτερον γιγνόμενον γίγνοιτ' ἄν.

and frights are due to a poor condition of soul. So whenever one applies an external shaking to affections of this kind, the external motion thus applied overpowers the internal motion of fear and frenzy, and by thus overpowering it, it brings about a manifest calm in the soul and a cessation of the grievous palpitation of the heart which had existed in each case. Thus it produces very satisfactory results. The children it puts to sleep; the Bacchants, who are awake, it brings into a sound state of mind instead of a frenzied condition, by means of dancing and playing, with the help of whatsoever gods they chance to be worshipping with sacrifice. This is—to put it shortly—quite a plausible account of the matter.

CLIN. Most plausible.

ATH. Seeing, then, that these causes produce the effects described, in the case of the people mentioned one should observe this point,—that every soul that is subjected to fright from youth will be specially liable to become timid : and this, as all would aver, is not to practise courage, but cowardice.

CLIN. Of course it is.

ATH. The opposite course, of practising courage from youth up, consists, we shall say, in the conquering of the frights and fears that assail us.

CLIN. That is true.

ATH. Let us say, then, that this factor—namely, the exercise of quite young children by the various motions—contributes greatly towards developing one part of the soul's virtue.

CLIN. Certainly.

ATH. Moreover, cheerfulness of soul and its opposite will constitute no small part of stoutheartedness and faintheartedness.

κλ. Πῶς δ' οὔ ;

D   αθ. Τίνα οὖν ἂν τρόπον εὐθὺς ἐμφύοιθ' ἡμῖν
ὁπότερον βουληθεῖμεν τῷ νεογενεῖ ; φράζειν δὴ
πειρατέον ὅπως τις καὶ καθ' ὅσον εὐπορεῖ τούτων.

κλ. Πῶς γὰρ οὔ ;

αθ. Λέγω δὴ τό γε παρ' ἡμῖν δόγμα, ὡς ἡ μὲν
τρυφὴ δύσκολα καὶ ἀκράχολα καὶ σφόδρα ἀπὸ
σμικρῶν κινούμενα τὰ τῶν νέων ἤθη ἀπεργάζεται,
τὸ δὲ τούτων ἐναντίον, ἥ τε σφοδρὰ καὶ ἀγρία
δούλωσις, ταπεινοὺς καὶ ἀνελευθέρους καὶ μισαν-
θρώπους ποιοῦσα ἀνεπιτηδείους ξυνοίκους ἀποτελεῖ.

E   κλ. Πῶς οὖν δὴ χρὴ τὰ μήπω φωνῆς ξυνιέντα
μηδὲ παιδείας τῆς ἄλλης δυνατὰ γεύεσθαί πω
τρέφειν τὴν πόλιν ἅπασαν ;

αθ. ῟Ωδέ πως· φθέγγεσθαί που μετὰ βοῆς
εὐθὺς πᾶν εἴωθε τὸ γεννώμενον, καὶ οὐχ ἥκιστα τὸ
τῶν ἀνθρώπων γένος· καὶ δὴ καὶ τῷ κλαίειν πρὸς
τῇ βοῇ μᾶλλον τῶν ἄλλων συνέχεται.

κλ. Πάνυ μὲν οὖν.

αθ. Οὐκοῦν αἱ τροφοὶ σκοποῦσαι τίνος ἐπιθυ-
μεῖ τούτοις αὐτοῖς ἐν τῇ προσφορᾷ τεκμαίρονται·
792 οὗ μὲν γὰρ ἂν προσφερομένου σιγᾷ, καλῶς οἴονται
προσφέρειν, οὗ δ' ἂν κλαίῃ καὶ βοᾷ, οὐ καλῶς.
τοῖς δὴ παιδίοις τὸ δήλωμα ὧν ἐρᾷ καὶ μισεῖ
κλαυμοναὶ καὶ βοαί, σημεῖα οὐδαμῶς εὐτυχῆ.
ἔστι δὲ ὁ χρόνος οὗτος τριῶν οὐκ ἐλάττων ἐτῶν,
μόριον οὐ σμικρὸν τοῦ βίου διαγαγεῖν χεῖρον ἢ μὴ
χεῖρον.

κλ. Ὀρθῶς λέγεις.

CLIN. Of course.

ATH. What way can we find, then, for implanting at once in the new-born child whichever of these qualities we desire? We must endeavour to indicate how and to what extent we have them at our command.

CLIN. By all means.

ATH. The doctrine held amongst us, I may explain, is this,—that whereas luxurious living renders the disposition of the young morose and irascible and too easily moved by trifles, its opposite (which is uttermost and cruel enslavement) makes them lowly and mean-spirited and misanthropic, and thus unfit to associate with others.

CLIN. In what way, then, should the State at large rear up infants that are still incapable of understanding speech or receiving other kinds of education?

ATH. In this way: it is usual for every creature that is born—and the human child as much as any—to utter at once a loud outcry; and, what is more, the child is the most liable of them all to be afflicted with tears as well as outcries.

CLIN. Quite true.

ATH. When nurses are trying to discover what a baby wants, they judge by these very same signs in offering it things. If it remains silent when the thing is offered, they conclude that it is the right thing, but the wrong thing if it weeps and cries out. Thus infants indicate what they like by means of weepings and outcries—truly no happy signals!—and this period of infancy lasts not less than three years, which is no small fraction of one's time to spend ill or well.

CLIN. You are right.

ΑΘ. Ὁ δὴ δύσκολος οὐδαμῶς τε ἵλεως ἆρ' οὐ
Β δοκεῖ σφῷν θρηνώδης τε εἶναι καὶ ὀδυρμῶν ὡς
ἐπὶ τὸ πολὺ πλήρης μᾶλλον ἢ χρεών ἐστι τὸν
ἀγαθόν ;

ΚΛ. Ἐμοὶ γοῦν δοκεῖ.

ΑΘ. Τί οὖν ; εἴ τις τὰ τρί' ἔτη πειρῷτο πᾶσαν
μηχανὴν προσφέρων ὅπως τὸ τρεφόμενον ἡμῖν ὡς
ὀλιγίστῃ προσχρήσεται ἀλγηδόνι καὶ φόβοις καὶ
λύπῃ πάσῃ κατὰ δύναμιν, ἆρ' οὐκ οἰόμεθα εὔθυμον
μᾶλλόν τε καὶ ἵλεων <ἂν>[1] ἀπεργάζεσθαι τηνι-
καῦτα τὴν ψυχὴν τοῦ τρεφομένου ;

ΚΛ. Δῆλον δή, καὶ μάλιστά γ' ἄν, ὦ ξένε, εἴ τις
Ϲ πολλὰς ἡδονὰς αὐτῷ παρασκευάζοι.

ΑΘ. Τοῦτ' οὐκέτ' ἂν ἐγὼ Κλεινίᾳ[2] ξυνακολου-
θήσαιμ' ἄν, ὦ θαυμάσιε. ἔστι γὰρ οὖν ἡμῖν ἡ
τοιαύτη πρᾶξις διαφθορὰ μεγίστη πασῶν· ἐν
ἀρχῇ γὰρ γίγνεται ἑκάστοτε τροφῆς. ὁρῶμεν δὲ
εἴ τι λέγομεν.

ΚΛ. Λέγε τί φῄς.

ΑΘ. Οὐ σμικροῦ πέρι νῦν εἶναι νῶν τὸν λόγον.
ὅρα δὲ καὶ σύ, ξυνεπίκρινέ τε ἡμᾶς, ὦ Μέγιλλε. ὁ
μὲν γὰρ ἐμὸς δὴ λόγος οὔθ' ἡδονάς φησι δεῖν
διώκειν τὸν ὀρθὸν βίον οὔτ' αὖ τὸ παράπαν φεύγειν
D τὰς λύπας, ἀλλ' αὐτὸ ἀσπάζεσθαι τὸ μέσον, ὃ νῦν
δὴ προσεῖπον ὡς ἵλεων ὀνομάσας, ἣν δὴ διάθεσιν
καὶ θεοῦ κατά τινα μαντείας φήμην εὐστόχως
πάντες προσαγορεύομεν. ταύτην τὴν ἕξιν διώκειν
φημὶ δεῖν ἡμῶν καὶ τὸν μέλλοντα ἔσεσθαι θεῖον·
μήτ' οὖν αὐτὸν προπετῆ πρὸς τὰς ἡδονὰς γιγνόμενον ὅλως, ὡς οὐδ' ἐκτὸς λυπῶν ἐσόμενον, μήτε

___

[1] ⟨ἂν⟩ added by H. Richards, England.
[2] Κλεινίᾳ MSS.: Κλεινία, Ast, Zur.

16

ATH.   When a man is peevish and not cheerful at all, do you not regard him as a doleful person and more full, as a rule, of complaints than a good man ought to be?

CLIN.   I certainly regard him as such.

ATH.   Well then, suppose one should try to secure by every available means that our nursling should experience the least possible amount of grief or fear or pain of any kind, may we not believe that by this means the soul of the nursling would be rendered more bright and cheerful?

CLIN.   Plainly it would, Stranger; and most of all if one should provide him with many pleasures.

ATH.   There, my good sir, I must part company with Clinias. For in our eyes such a proceeding is the worst possible form of corruption, for it occurs in every instance at the very beginning of the child's nurture.[1]   But let us consider whether I am right.

CLIN.   Explain your view.

ATH.   I believe that the issue before us is one of extreme importance. You also, Megillus, consider the matter, I pray, and lend us the aid of your judgment. What I maintain is this: that the right life ought neither to pursue pleasures nor to shun pains entirely; but it ought to embrace that middle state of cheerfulness (as I termed it a moment ago), which—as we all rightly suppose, on the strength of an inspired utterance—is the very condition of God himself. And I maintain that whosoever of us would be godlike must pursue this state of soul, neither becoming himself prone at all to pleasures, even as he will not be devoid of pain, not allowing

[1] Cp. *Rep.* 377 B.

ἄλλον, γέροντα ἢ νέον, ἐὰν πάσχειν ταὐτὸν
τοῦθ᾽ ἡμῖν, ἄρρενα ἢ θῆλυν, ἁπάντων δὲ ἥκιστα
Ε εἰς δύναμιν τὸν ἀρτίως νεογενῆ· κυριώτατον γὰρ
οὖν ἐμφύεται πᾶσι τότε τὸ πᾶν ἦθος διὰ ἔθος. ἔτι
δ᾽ ἔγωγ᾽, εἰ μὴ μέλλοιμι δόξειν παίζειν, φαίην ἂν
δεῖν καὶ τὰς φερούσας ἐν γαστρὶ πασῶν τῶν
γυναικῶν μάλιστα θεραπεύειν ἐκεῖνον τὸν ἐνιαυτόν,
ὅπως μήτε ἡδοναῖς τισὶ πολλαῖς ἅμα καὶ μάργοις
προσχρήσεται ἡ κύουσα μήτε αὖ λύπαις, τὸ δὲ
ἵλεων καὶ εὐμενὲς πρᾶόν τε τιμῶσα διαζήσει τὸν
τότε χρόνον.

ΚΛ. Οὐδὲν δεῖ σε, ὦ ξένε, Μέγιλλον ἀνερωτᾶν
793 πότερος ἡμῶν ὀρθότερον εἴρηκεν· ἐγὼ γὰρ αὐτός
σοι συγχωρῶ τὸν λύπης τε καὶ ἡδονῆς ἀκράτου
βίον φεύγειν δεῖν πάντας, μέσον δέ τινα τέμνειν
ἀεί. καλῶς τοίνυν εἴρηκάς τε καὶ ἀκήκοας ἅμα.

ΑΘ. Μάλα μὲν οὖν ὀρθῶς, ὦ Κλεινία. τόδε
τοίνυν ἐπὶ τούτοις τρεῖς ὄντες διανοηθῶμεν.

ΚΛ. Τὸ ποῖον;

ΑΘ. Ὅτι ταῦτ᾽ ἐστὶ πάντα, ὅσα νῦν διεξερ-
χόμεθα, τὰ καλούμενα ὑπὸ τῶν πολλῶν ἄγραφα
νόμιμα· καὶ οὓς πατρίους νόμους ἐπονομάζουσιν,
Β οὐκ ἄλλα ἐστὶν ἢ τὰ τοιαῦτα ξύμπαντα. καὶ ἔτι
γε ὁ νῦν δὴ λόγος ἡμῖν ἐπιχυθείς, ὡς οὔτε νόμους
δεῖ προσαγορεύειν αὐτὰ οὔτε ἄρρητα ἐᾶν, εἴρηται
καλῶς· δεσμοὶ γὰρ οὗτοι πάσης εἰσὶ πολιτείας,
μεταξὺ πάντων ὄντες τῶν ἐν γράμμασι τεθέντων
τε καὶ κειμένων καὶ τῶν ἔτι τεθησομένων, ἀτεχνῶς

---

¹ Cp. Ar. *Eth. N.* 1103ᵃ17: ἡ δὲ ἠθικὴ (ἀρετὴ) ἐξ ἔθους περι-
γίνεται, ὅθεν καὶ τοὔνομα ἔσχηκε μικρὸν παρεγκλῖνον ἀπὸ τοῦ

any other person—old or young, man or woman—
to be in this condition and least of all, so far as
possible, the new-born babe. For because of the
force of habit, it is in infancy that the whole
character is most effectually determined.[1] I should
assert further—were it not that it would be taken as
a jest—that women with child, above all others,
should be cared for during their years of pregnancy,
lest any of them should indulge in repeated and
intense pleasures or pains, instead of cultivating,
during the whole of that period, a cheerful, bright
and calm demeanour.

CLIN. There is no need for you, Stranger, to ask
Megillus which of us two has made the truer statement. For I myself grant you that all men ought
to shun the life of unmixed pain and pleasure, and
follow always a middle path. So all is well both
with your statement and with my reply.

ATH. You are perfectly right, Clinias. So then
let the three of us together consider this next point.

CLIN. What is that?

ATH. That all the regulations which we are now
expounding are what are commonly termed " unwritten laws." And these as a whole are just the
same as what men call " ancestral customs." Moreover, the view which was recently [2] impressed upon
us, that one should neither speak of these as " laws "
nor yet leave them without mention, was a right
view. For it is these that act as bonds in every
constitution, forming a link between all its laws (both
those already enacted in writing and those still to be

[1] ἔθους ("ethical virtue is the result of habit, and its name
'ethical' is also derived from 'ἔθος' (habit)").
[2] 788 B f.

οἷον πάτρια καὶ παντάπασιν ἀρχαῖα νόμιμα, ἃ
καλῶς μὲν τεθέντα καὶ ἐθισθέντα πάσῃ σωτηρίᾳ
περικαλύψαντα ἔχει τοὺς τότε γραφέντας νόμους,
C ἂν δ᾽ ἐκτὸς τοῦ καλοῦ βαίνῃ πλημμελῶς, οἷον
τεκτόνων ἐν οἰκοδομήμασιν ἐρείσματα ἐκ μέσου
ὑπορρέοντα, συμπίπτειν εἰς ταὐτὸν ποιεῖ τὰ
ξύμπαντα κεῖσθαί τε ἄλλα ὑφ᾽ ἑτέρων, αὐτά
τε καὶ τὰ καλῶς ὕστερον ἐποικοδομηθέντα, τῶν
ἀρχαίων ὑποπεσόντων. ἃ δὴ διανοουμένους
ἡμᾶς, ὦ Κλεινία, σοι δεῖ τὴν πόλιν καινὴν
οὖσαν πάντη ξυνδεῖν, μήτε μέγα μήτε σμικ-
D ρὸν παραλιπόντας εἰς δύναμιν ὅσα νόμους ἢ
ἔθη τις ἢ ἐπιτηδεύματα καλεῖ· πᾶσι γὰρ τοῖς
τοιούτοις πόλις ξυνδεῖται, ἄνευ δὲ ἀλλήλων
ἑκάτερα τούτων οὐκ ἔστι μόνιμα, ὥστε οὐ χρὴ
θαυμάζειν ἐὰν ἡμῖν πολλὰ ἅμα καὶ σμικρὰ δοκοῦντα εἶναι νόμιμα ἢ καὶ ἐθίσματα ἐπιρρέοντα
μακροτέρους ποιῇ τοὺς νόμους.

κλ. Ἀλλ᾽ ὀρθῶς σύ τε λέγεις ἡμεῖς τε οὕτω
διανοησόμεθα.

ΑΘ. Εἰς μὲν τοίνυν τὴν τοῦ τρὶ[1] ἔτη γεγονότος
E ἡλικίαν, κόρου καὶ κόρης, ταῦτα εἴ τις ἀκριβῶς
ἀποτελοῖ καὶ μὴ παρέργως τοῖς εἰρημένοις
χρῷτο, οὐ σμικρὰ εἰς ὠφέλειαν γίγνοιτ᾽ ἂν τοῖς
νεωστὶ τρεφομένοις· τριετεῖ δὲ δὴ καὶ τετραετεῖ
καὶ πενταετεῖ καὶ ἔτι ἑξετεῖ ἤθει ψυχῆς παιδιῶν
δέον ἂν εἴη, τρυφῆς δ᾽ ἤδη παραλυτέον κολάζοντα μὴ ἀτίμως, ἀλλ᾽ ὅπερ ἐπὶ τῶν δούλων
γ᾽ ἐλέγομεν, τὸ μὴ μεθ᾽ ὕβρεως κολάζοντας ὀργὴν
ἐμποιεῖν δεῖν τοῖς κολασθεῖσι μηδ᾽ ἀκολάστους
794 ἐῶντας τρυφήν, ταὐτὸν δραστέον τοῦτό γε καὶ

---

[1] Cp. 777 A ff.

enacted), exactly like ancestral customs of great antiquity, which, if well established and practised, serve to wrap up securely the laws already written, whereas if they perversely go aside from the right way, like builders' props that collapse under the middle of a house, they bring everything else tumbling down along with them, one thing buried under another, first the props themselves and then the fair superstructure, once the ancient supports have fallen down. Bearing this in mind, Clinias, we must clamp together this State of yours, which is a new one, by every possible means, omitting nothing great or small in the way of laws, customs and institutions ; for it is by all such means that a State is clamped together, and neither kind of law is permanent without the other. Consequently, we need not be surprised if the influx of a number of apparently trivial customs or usages should make our laws rather long.

CLIN. What you say is quite true, and we will bear it in mind.

ATH. If one could carry out these regulations methodically, and not merely apply them casually, in the case of girls and boys up to the age of three, they would conduce greatly to the benefit of our infant nurslings. To form the character of the child over three and up to six years old there will be need of games : by then punishment must be used to prevent their getting pampered,—not, however, punishment of a degrading kind, but just as we said before,[1] in the case of slaves, that one should avoid enraging the persons punished by using degrading punishments, or pampering them by leaving them unpunished, so in the case of the free-born the

ἐπ᾽ ἐλευθέροισι. παιδιαὶ δ᾽ εἰσὶ τοῖς τηλικούτοις
αὐτοφυεῖς τινές, ἃς ἐπειδὰν ξυνέλθωσιν αὐτοὶ
σχεδὸν ἀνευρίσκουσι. ξυνιέναι δὲ εἰς τὰ κατὰ
κώμας ἱερὰ δεῖ πάντα ἤδη τὰ τηλικαῦτα παιδία,
ἀπὸ τριετοῦς μέχρι τῶν ἐξ ἐτῶν, κοινῇ τὰ τῶν
κωμητῶν εἰς ταὐτὸν ἕκαστα· τὰς δὲ τροφοὺς ἔτι
τῶν τηλικούτων κοσμιότητός τε καὶ ἀκολασίας
ἐπιμελεῖσθαι, τῶν δὲ τροφῶν αὐτῶν καὶ τῆς
B ἀγέλης ξυμπάσης, τῶν δώδεκα γυναικῶν μίαν
ἐφ᾽ ἑκάστῃ τετάχθαι κοσμοῦσαν κατ᾽ ἐνιαυτὸν
τῶν προῃρημένων [1] ἃς ἂν τάξωσιν οἱ νομοφύλακες. ταύτας δὲ αἱρείσθωσαν μὲν αἱ τῶν
γάμων κύριαι τῆς ἐπιμελείας, ἐξ ἑκάστης τῆς
φυλῆς μίαν, ἥλικας αὐταῖς· ἡ δὲ καταστᾶσα
ἀρχέτω φοιτῶσα εἰς τὸ ἱερὸν ἑκάστης ἡμέρας
καὶ κολάζουσα ἀεὶ τὸν ἀδικοῦντα, δοῦλον μὲν
καὶ δούλην καὶ ξένον καὶ ξένην αὐτὴ διά τινων
τῆς πόλεως οἰκετῶν, πολίτην δὲ ἀμφισβητοῦντα
C μὲν τῇ κολάσει πρὸς τοὺς ἀστυνόμους ἐπὶ δίκην
ἄγουσα, ἀναμφισβήτητον δὲ ὄντα καὶ τὸν πολίτην αὐτὴ κολαζέτω. μετὰ δὲ τὸν ἑξέτη καὶ
τὴν ἑξέτιν διακρινέσθω μὲν ἤδη τὸ γένος ἑκατέρων·
κόροι μὲν μετὰ κόρων, παρθένοι δὲ ὡσαύτως
μετ᾽ ἀλλήλων τὴν διατριβὴν ποιείσθωσαν· πρὸς
δὲ τὰ μαθήματα τρέπεσθαι χρεὼν ἑκατέρους,
τοὺς μὲν ἄρρενας ἐφ᾽ ἵππων διδασκάλους καὶ
τόξων καὶ ἀκοντίων καὶ σφενδονήσεως, ἐὰν δέ
πῃ ξυγχωρῶσι μέχρι γε μαθήσεως καὶ τὰ θήλεα,
D καὶ δὴ τά γε μάλιστα πρὸς τὴν τῶν ὅπλων
χρείαν. τὸ γὰρ δὴ νῦν καθεστὸς περὶ τὰ τοιαῦτα
ἀγνοεῖται παρὰ τοῖς πᾶσιν ὀλίγου.

[1] προῃρημένων Badham : προειρημένων MSS.

same rule holds good. Children of this age have games which come by natural instinct; and they generally invent them of themselves whenever they meet together. As soon as they have reached the age of three, all the children from three to six must meet together at the village temples, those belonging to each village assembling at the same place. Moreover, the nurses of these children must watch over their behaviour, whether it be orderly or disorderly; and over the nurses themselves and the whole band of children one of the twelve women already elected must be appointed annually to take charge of each band, the appointment resting with the Law-wardens. These women shall be elected by the women who have charge of the supervision of marriage,[1] one out of each tribe and all of a like age. The woman thus appointed shall pay an official visit to the temple every day, and she shall employ a State servant and deal summarily with male or female slaves and strangers; but in the case of citizens, if the person protests against the punishment, she shall bring him for trial before the city-stewards; but if no protest is made, she shall inflict summary justice equally on citizens. After the age of six, each sex shall be kept separate, boys spending their time with boys, and likewise girls with girls; and when it is necessary for them to begin lessons, the boys must go to teachers of riding, archery, javelin-throwing and slinging, and the girls also, if they agree to it, must share in the lessons, and especially such as relate to the use of arms. For, as regards the view now prevalent regarding these matters, it is based on almost universal ignorance.

[1] Cp. 784 A.

ΚΛ. Τὸ ποῖον ;

ΑΘ. Ὡς ἄρα τὰ δεξιὰ καὶ τὰ ἀριστερὰ
διαφέροντά ἐσθ' ἡμῶν φύσει πρὸς τὰς χρείας
εἰς ἑκάστας τῶν πράξεων τὰ περὶ τὰς χεῖρας·
ἐπεὶ τά γε περὶ πόδας τε καὶ τὰ κάτω τῶν
μελῶν οὐδὲν διαφέροντα εἰς τοὺς πόνους φαίνεται,
Ε τὰ δὲ κατὰ χεῖρας ἀνοίᾳ τροφῶν καὶ μητέρων
οἷον χωλοὶ γεγόναμεν ἕκαστοι. τῆς φύσεως γὰρ
ἑκατέρων τῶν μελῶν σχεδὸν ἰσορροπούσης αὐτοὶ
διὰ τὰ ἔθη διάφορα αὐτὰ πεποιήκαμεν οὐκ
ὀρθῶς χρώμενοι. ἐν ὅσοις μὲν γὰρ τῶν ἔργων
μὴ μέγα διαφέρει, λύρᾳ μὲν ἐν ἀριστερᾷ χρωμένων,[1] πλήκτρῳ δὲ ἐν δεξιᾷ, πρᾶγμα οὐδέν, καὶ
ὅσα τοιαῦτα· τούτοις δὲ παραδείγμασι χρώμενον
καὶ εἰς ἄλλα μὴ δέον οὕτω χρῆσθαι σχεδὸν
795 ἄνοια. ἔδειξε δὲ ταῦτα ὁ τῶν Σκυθῶν νόμος,
οὐκ ἐν ἀριστερᾷ μὲν τόξον ἀπάγων, ἐν δεξιᾷ δὲ
οἰστὸν προσαγόμενος μόνον, ἀλλ' ὁμοίως ἑκατέ-
ραις ἐπ' ἀμφότερα χρώμενος. πάμπολλα δ'
ἕτερα τοιαῦτα παραδείγματα ἐν ἡνιοχείαις τ'
ἐστὶ καὶ ἐν ἑτέροις, ἐν οἷσι μαθεῖν δυνατὸν ὅτι
παρὰ φύσιν κατασκευάζουσιν οἱ ἀριστερὰ δεξιῶν
ἀσθενέστερα κατασκευάζοντες. ταῦτα δ', ὅπερ
εἴπομεν, ἐν μὲν κερατίνοις πλήκτροις καὶ ἐν
Β ὀργάνοις τοιούτοις οὐδὲν μέγα· σιδηροῖς δ' εἰς
τὸν πόλεμον ὅταν δέῃ χρῆσθαι, μέγα διαφέρει,
καὶ τόξοις καὶ ἀκοντίοις καὶ ἑκάστοις τούτων·
πολὺ δὲ μέγιστον ὅταν ὅπλοις δέῃ πρὸς ὅπλα
χρῆσθαι. διαφέρει δὲ πάμπολυ μαθὼν μὴ
μαθόντος καὶ ὁ γυμνασάμενος τοῦ μὴ γε-
γυμνασμένου. καθάπερ γὰρ ὁ τελέως παγκράτιον

---

[1] χρωμένων Apelt : χρώμενον MSS.

24

CLIN. What view?

ATH. The view that, in the case of hands, right and left are by nature different in respect of their utility for special acts; but, as a matter of fact, in the case of the feet and the lower limbs there is plainly no difference in working capacity; and it is due to the folly of nurses and mothers that we have all become limping, so to say, in our hands. For in natural ability the two limbs are almost equally balanced; but we ourselves by habitually using them in a wrong way have made them different. In actions of trifling importance this does not matter—as for example, whether a man uses the left hand for the fiddle and the right hand for the bow, and things of that sort; but to follow these precedents and to use the hands in this way on other occasions, when there is no necessity, is very like foolishness. This is shown by the Scythian custom not only of using the left hand to draw the bow and the right to fit the arrow to it, but also of using both hands alike for both actions. And there are countless other instances of a similar kind, in connexion with driving horses and other occupations, which teach us that those who treat the left hand as weaker than the right are confuted by nature. But this, as we have said, matters little in the case of fiddle-bows of horn and similar implements; but when it is a case of using iron instruments of war—bows, darts and the like—it matters a great deal, and most of all when weapon is to be used against weapon at close quarters. There is a vast difference here between the taught and the untaught, the trained and the untrained warrior. For just as the athlete who is thoroughly

ἠσκηκὼς ἢ πυγμὴν ἢ πάλην οὐκ ἀπὸ μὲν τῶν
ἀριστερῶν ἀδύνατός ἐστι μάχεσθαι, χωλαίνει δὲ
C καὶ ἐφέλκεται πλημμελῶν, ὁπόταν αὑτόν τις
μεταβιβάζων ἐπὶ θάτερα ἀναγκάζῃ διαπονεῖν,
ταὐτὸν δὴ τοῦτ᾽, οἶμαι, καὶ ἐν ὅπλοις καὶ ἐν
τοῖς ἄλλοις πᾶσι χρὴ προσδοκᾶν ὀρθόν, ὅτι
τὸν διττὰ δεῖ κεκτημένον οἷς ἀμύνοιτό τ᾽ ἂν καὶ
ἐπιτιθεῖτο ἄλλοις μηδὲν ἀργὸν τούτων μηδὲ
ἀνεπιστῆμον ἐᾶν εἶναι κατὰ δύναμιν· Γηρυόνου
δέ γε εἴ τις φύσιν ἔχων ἢ καὶ τὴν Βριάρεω φύοιτο,
ταῖς ἑκατὸν χερσὶν ἑκατὸν δεῖ βέλη ῥίπτειν
δυνατὸν εἶναι. τούτων δὴ πάντων τὴν ἐπιμέλειαν
D ἀρχούσαις τε καὶ ἄρχουσι δεῖ γίγνεσθαι, ταῖς μὲν
ἐν παιδιαῖς τε καὶ τροφαῖς ἐπισκόποις γιγνομέναις,
τοῖς δὲ περὶ μαθήματα, ὅπως ἀρτίποδές τε καὶ ἀρτί-
χειρες πάντες τε καὶ πᾶσαι γιγνόμενοι μηδὲν τοῖς
ἔθεσιν ἀποβλάπτωσι τὰς φύσεις εἰς τὸ δυνατόν.

Τὰ δὲ μαθήματά που διττά, ὥς γ᾽ εἰπεῖν,
χρήσασθαι ξυμβαίνοι ἄν, τὰ μὲν ὅσα περὶ τὸ
σῶμα γυμναστικῆς, τὰ δ᾽ εὐψυχίας χάριν μουσικῆς. τὰ δὲ γυμναστικῆς αὖ δύο, τὸ μὲν
E ὄρχησις, τὸ δὲ πάλη. τῆς ὀρχήσεως δὲ ἄλλη
μὲν Μούσης λέξιν μιμουμένων, τό τε μεγαλοπρεπὲς φυλάττουσα[1] ἅμα καὶ ἐλεύθερον· ἄλλη
δὲ εὐεξίας ἐλαφρότητός τε ἕνεκα καὶ κάλλους
τῶν τοῦ σώματος αὐτοῦ μελῶν καὶ μερῶν τὸ
προσῆκον καμπῆς τε καὶ ἐκτάσεως, καὶ ἀποδι-
δομένης ἑκάστοις αὐτοῖς αὑτῶν εὐρύθμου κινήσεως,
διασπειρομένης ἅμα καὶ ξυνακολουθούσης εἰς
796 πᾶσαν τὴν ὄρχησιν ἱκανῶς. καὶ δὴ τά γε κατὰ

[1] φυλάττουσα: φυλάττοντας MSS. (ἄλλο . . . φύλαττον
Badham).

26

practised in the pancratium or in boxing or wrestling is capable of fighting on his left side, and does not move that side as if it were numb or lame, whenever he is compelled to bring it into action through his opponent shifting to the other side,—in precisely the same way, I take it, in regard to the use of weapons of war and everything else, it ought to be considered the correct thing that the man who possesses two sets of limbs, fit both for offensive and defensive action, should, so far as possible, suffer neither of these to go unpractised or untaught. Indeed, if a man were gifted by nature with the frame of a Geryon or a Briareus, with his hundred hands he ought to be able to throw a hundred darts. So all these matters must be the care of the male and female officers, the women overseeing the games and the feeding of the children, and the men their lessons, to the intent that all the boys and girls may be sound of hand and foot, and may in no wise, if possible, get their natures warped by their habits.

The lessons may, for practical convenience, be divided under two heads—the gymnastical, which concern the body, and the musical, which aim at goodness of soul. Of gymnastic there are two kinds, dancing and wrestling. Of dancing there is one branch in which the style of the Muse is imitated, preserving both freedom and nobility, and another which aims at physical soundness, agility and beauty by securing for the various parts and members of the body the proper degree of flexibility and extension and bestowing also the rhythmical motion which belongs to each, and which accompanies the whole of dancing and is diffused throughout it completely. As to the

πάλην ἃ μὲν Ἀνταῖος ἢ Κερκύων ἐν τέχναις
ἑαυτῶν ξυνεστήσαντο φιλονεικίας ἀχρήστου
χάριν, ἢ πυγμῆς Ἐπειὸς ἢ Ἄμυκος, οὐδὲν χρήσιμα ἐπὶ πολέμου κοινωνίαν ὄντα, οὐκ ἄξια
λόγῳ κοσμεῖν· τὰ δὲ ἀπ᾽ ὀρθῆς πάλης, ἀπ᾽
αὐχένων καὶ χειρῶν καὶ πλευρῶν ἐξειλήσεως,
μετὰ φιλονεικίας τε καὶ καταστάσεως διαπονού-
μενα μετ᾽ εὐσχήμονος, ῥώμης τε καὶ ὑγιείας
ἕνεκα, ταῦτ᾽ εἰς πάντα ὄντα χρήσιμα οὐ παρετέον,
ἀλλὰ προστακτέον μαθηταῖς τε ἅμα καὶ τοῖς
B διδάξουσιν, ὅταν ἐνταῦθ᾽ ὦμεν τῶν νόμων, τοῖς
μὲν πάντα τὰ τοιαῦτα εὐμενῶς δωρεῖσθαι, τοῖς
δὲ παραλαμβάνειν ἐν χάρισιν. οὐδ᾽ ὅσα ἐν τοῖς
χοροῖς ἐστὶν αὖ μιμήματα προσήκοντα μιμεῖσθαι
παρετέον, κατὰ μὲν τὸν τόπον τόνδε Κουρήτων
ἐνόπλια παίγνια, κατὰ δὲ Λακεδαίμονα Διοσκό-
ρων. ἡ δὲ αὖ που παρ᾽ ἡμῖν κόρη καὶ δέσποινα,
εὐφρανθεῖσα τῇ τῆς χορείας παιδιᾷ, κεναῖς χερσὶν
C οὐκ ᾠήθη δεῖν ἀθύρειν, πανοπλίᾳ δὲ παντελεῖ
κοσμηθεῖσα οὕτω τὴν ὄρχησιν διαπεραίνειν· ἃ
δὴ πάντως μιμεῖσθαι πρέπον ἂν εἴη κόρους τε
ἅμα καὶ κόρας, τὴν τῆς θεοῦ χάριν τιμῶντας,
πολέμου τ᾽ ἐν χρείᾳ καὶ ἑορτῶν ἕνεκα. τοῖς δέ
που παισὶν εὐθύς τε καὶ ὅσον ἂν χρόνον μήπω
εἰς πόλεμον ἴωσι, πᾶσι θεοῖς προσόδους τε καὶ
πομπὰς ποιουμένους μεθ᾽ ὅπλων τε καὶ ἵππων
ἀεὶ κοσμεῖσθαι δέον ἂν εἴη, θάττους τε καὶ
βραδυτέρας ἐν ὀρχήσεσι καὶ ἐν πορείᾳ τὰς
ἱκετείας ποιουμένους πρὸς θεούς τε καὶ θεῶν

[1] Mythical giants and wrestlers, to whom were ascribed
such devices as the use of the legs in wrestling. Epeius

devices introduced by Antaeus or Cercyon[1] in the art
of wrestling for the sake of empty glory, or in boxing
by Epeius or Amycus, since they are useless in the
business of war, they merit no eulogy. But the
exercises of stand-up wrestling, with the twisting
free of neck, hands and sides, when practised with
ardour and with a firm and graceful pose, and
directed towards strength and health,—these must
not be omitted, since they are useful for all purposes; but we must charge both the pupils and
their teachers—when we reach this point in our
legislation—that the latter should impart these
lessons gently, and the former receive them grate-
fully. Nor should we omit such mimic dances as
are fitting for use by our choirs,—for instance, the
sword-dance of the Curetes[2] here in Crete, and that
of the Dioscori[3] in Lacedaemon ; and at Athens,
too, our Virgin-Lady[4] gladdened by the pastime of
the dance deemed it not seemly to sport with
empty hands, but rather to tread the measure vested
in full panoply. These examples it would well
become the boys and girls to copy, and so cultivate
the favour of the goddess, alike for service in war
and for use at festivals. It shall be the rule for
the children, from the age of six until they reach
military age, whenever they approach any god and
form processions, to be always equipped with arms
and horses, and with dance and march, now quick,
now slow, to make their supplications to the gods

is mentioned as a boxer in Homer, *Il.* 23. 668 ; and the
mythical Amycus is said to have invented the use of ἱμάντες
(boxing-gloves).

   [2] Priests of the Idaean Zeus.
   [3] Castor and Pollux.
   [4] Athenê.

D παῖδας. καὶ ἀγῶνας δὴ καὶ προαγῶνας, εἴ τινων, οὐκ ἄλλων ἢ τούτων ἕνεκα προαγωνιστέον· οὗτοι γὰρ καὶ ἐν εἰρήνῃ καὶ κατὰ πόλεμον χρήσιμοι εἴς τε πολιτείαν καὶ ἰδίους οἴκους, οἱ δὲ ἄλλοι πόνοι τε καὶ παιδιαὶ καὶ σπουδαὶ κατὰ σώματα οὐκ ἐλευθέρων.

Ὦ Μέγιλλέ τε καὶ Κλεινία, ἣν εἶπον γυμναστικὴν ἐν τοῖς πρώτοις λόγοις ὅτι δέοι διεξελθεῖν, σχεδὸν δὴ διελήλυθα τὰ νῦν καὶ ἔσθ᾽ αὕτη παντελής· εἰ δέ τινα ταύτης ὑμεῖς E ἔχετε βελτίω, θέντες εἰς κοινὸν λέγετε.

ΚΛ. Οὐ ῥᾴδιον, ὦ ξένε, παρέντας ταῦτα ἄλλα ἔχειν βελτίω τούτων περὶ γυμναστικῆς ἅμα καὶ ἀγωνίας εἰπεῖν.

ΑΘ. Τὸ τοίνυν τούτοις ἑξῆς περὶ τὰ τῶν Μουσῶν τε καὶ Ἀπόλλωνος δῶρα, τότε μέν, ὡς ἅπαντα εἰρηκότες, ᾠόμεθα καταλείπειν μόνα τὰ περὶ γυμναστικῆς· νῦν δ᾽ ἐστὶ δῆλα ἅ τ᾽ ἐστὶ καὶ ὅτι πρῶτα πᾶσι ῥητέα. λέγωμεν τοίνυν ἑξῆς αὐτά.

ΚΛ. Πάνυ μὲν οὖν λεκτέον.

797 ΑΘ. Ἀκούσατε δή[1] μου, προακηκοότες μὲν καὶ ἐν τοῖς πρόσθεν· ὅμως δὲ τό γε σφόδρα ἄτοπον καὶ ἄηθες διευλαβεῖσθαι δεῖ λέγοντα καὶ ἀκούοντα, καὶ δὴ καὶ νῦν. ἐρῶ μὲν γὰρ ἐγὼ λόγον οὐκ ἄφοβον εἰπεῖν, ὅμως δέ πῃ θαρρήσας οὐκ ἀποστήσομαι.

ΚΛ. Τίνα δὴ τοῦτον, ὦ ξένε, λέγεις;

ΑΘ. Φημὶ κατὰ πάσας πόλεις τὸ τῶν παιδιῶν

---

[1] δή H. Richards : δέ MSS.

---

[1] 672 D, 673 A ff.; cp. also 813 D ff.

and the children of gods. Contests, too, and preliminary trials must be carried out with a view to
the objects stated, if at all; for these objects are
useful both in peace and war, alike for the State
and for private families; but all other kinds of work
and play and bodily exercise are not worthy of
a gentleman.

And now, O Megillus and Clinias, I have pretty
fully described that gymnastic training which—as
I said [1] early in our discourse—requires description:
here it is in its full completeness. So if you know
of a better gymnastic than this, disclose it.

CLIN. It is no easy thing, Stranger, to reject your
account of gymnastic training and competition, and
produce a better one.

ATH. The subject which comes next to this, and
deals with the gifts of Apollo and the Muses, is
one which we previously [2] thought we had done
with, and that the only subject left was gymnastic;
but I plainly see now, not only what still remains to
be said to everybody, but also that it ought to come
first. Let us, then, state these points in order.

CLIN. By all means let us do so.

ATH. Give ear to me now, albeit ye have already
done so in the past. None the less, one must take
great heed, now as before, both in the telling and
in the hearing of a thing that is supremely strange
and novel. To make the statement that I am going
to make is an alarming task; yet I will summon up
my courage, and not shrink from it.

CLIN. What is the statement you refer to,
Stranger?

ATH. I assert that there exists in every State

[2] 673 B.

γένος ἠγνοῆσθαι ξύμπασιν ὅτι κυριώτατόν ἐστι
περὶ θέσεως νόμων, ἢ μονίμους εἶναι τοὺς τεθέντας
B ἢ μή. ταχθὲν μὲν γὰρ αὐτὸ καὶ μετασχὸν τοῦ
τὰ αὐτὰ κατὰ τὰ αὐτὰ καὶ ὡσαύτως ἀεὶ τοὺς
αὐτοὺς παίζειν τε καὶ εὐθυμεῖσθαι τοῖς αὐτοῖς
παιγνίοις ἐᾷ καὶ τὰ σπουδῇ κείμενα νόμιμα
μένειν ἡσυχῇ, κινούμενα δὲ ταῦτα[1] καὶ καινοτο-
μούμενα μεταβολαῖς τε ἄλλαις ἀεὶ χρώμενα, καὶ
μηδέποτε ταῦτα φίλα προσαγορευόντων τῶν νέων
μήτ' ἐν σχήμασι τοῖς τῶν αὐτῶν σωμάτων μήτε
ἐν τοῖς ἄλλοις σκεύεσιν ὁμολογουμένως αὐτοῖς
ἀεὶ κεῖσθαι τό τ' εὔσχημον καὶ ἄσχημον, ἀλλὰ
τόν τι νέον ἀεὶ καινοτομοῦντα καὶ εἰσφέροντα
C τῶν εἰωθότων ἕτερον κατά τε σχήματα καὶ
χρώματα καὶ πάντα ὅσα τοιαῦτα, τοῦτον τι-
μᾶσθαι διαφερόντως, τούτου πόλει λώβην οὐκ
εἶναι μείζω φαῖμεν ἂν ὀρθότατα λέγοντες· λανθάνειν γὰρ τῶν νέων τὰ ἤθη μεθιστάντα καὶ ποιεῖν
τὸ μὲν ἀρχαῖον παρ' αὐτοῖς ἄτιμον, τὸ δὲ νέον
ἔντιμον. τούτου δὲ πάλιν αὖ λέγω τοῦ τε
ῥήματος καὶ τοῦ δόγματος οὐκ εἶναι ζημίαν
μείζω πάσαις πόλεσιν· ἀκούσατε δὲ ὅσον φημὶ
αὐτ' εἶναι κακόν.

D ΚΛ. Ἦ τὸ ψέγεσθαι τὴν ἀρχαιότητα λέγεις ἐν
ταῖς πόλεσιν;

ΑΘ. Πάνυ μὲν οὖν.

ΚΛ. Οὐ φαύλους τοίνυν ἡμᾶς ἂν ἀκροατὰς
πρὸς αὐτὸν τὸν λόγον ἔχοις ἂν τοῦτον, ἀλλ' ὡς
δυνατὸν εὐμενεστάτους.

ΑΘ. Εἰκὸς γοῦν.

ΚΛ. Λέγε μόνον.

---

[1] ταῦτα England : τὰ αὐτὰ MSS.

a complete ignorance about children's games—how that they are of decisive importance for legislation, as determining whether the laws enacted are to be permanent or not. For when the programme of games is prescribed and secures that the same children always play the same games and delight in the same toys in the same way and under the same conditions, it allows the real and serious laws also to remain undisturbed; but when these games vary and suffer innovations, amongst other constant alterations the children are always shifting their fancy from one game to another, so that neither in respect of their own bodily gestures nor in respect of their equipment have they any fixed and acknowledged standard of propriety and impropriety; but the man they hold in special honour is he who is always innovating or introducing some novel device in the matter of form or colour or something of the sort; whereas it would be perfectly true to say that a State can have no worse pest than a man of that description, since he privily alters the characters of the young, and causes them to contemn what is old and esteem what is new. And I repeat again that there is no greater mischief a State can suffer than such a dictum and doctrine: just listen while I tell you how great an evil it is.

CLIN. Do you mean the way people rail at antiquity in States?

ATH. Precisely.

CLIN. That is a theme on which you will find us no grudging listeners, but the most sympathetic possible.

ATH. I should certainly expect it to be so.

CLIN. Only say on.

ΑΘ. Ἴτε δή, μειζόνως αὐτὸν ἀκούσωμέν τε
ἡμῶν αὐτῶν καὶ πρὸς ἀλλήλους οὕτως εἴπωμεν.
μεταβολὴν γὰρ δὴ πάντων πλὴν κακῶν πολὺ
σφαλερώτατον εὑρήσομεν ἐν ὥραις πάσαις, ἐν
πνεύμασιν, ἐν διαίταις σωμάτων, ἐν τρόποις
ψυχῶν, ἐν ὡς ἔπος εἰπεῖν <πᾶσιν>,[1] οὐ τοῖς μέν,
τοῖς δ' οὔ, πλήν, ὅ τί περ εἶπον νῦν δή, κακοῖς·
Ε ὥστε, εἴ τις ἀποβλέψειε πρὸς σώματα, ὡς πᾶσι
μὲν σιτίοις, πᾶσι δ' αὖ ποτοῖς καὶ πόνοις ξυνήθη
γιγνόμενα, καὶ τὸ πρῶτον ταραχθέντα ὑπ' αὐτῶν,
ἔπειτ' ἐξ αὐτῶν τούτων ὑπὸ χρόνου σάρκας
φύσαντα οἰκείας τούτοις, φίλα τε καὶ συνήθη
798 καὶ γνώριμα γενόμενα ἁπάσῃ ταύτῃ τῇ διαίτῃ
πρὸς ἡδονὴν καὶ ὑγίειαν ἄριστα διάγει· καὶ ἄν
ποτ' ἄρα ἀναγκασθῇ μεταβάλλειν αὖ τις[2] ἡντινοῦν τῶν εὐδοκίμων διαιτῶν, τό γε κατ' ἀρχὰς
συνταραχθεὶς ὑπὸ νόσων μόγις ποτὲ κατέστη
τὴν συνήθειαν τῇ τροφῇ πάλιν ἀπολαβών·
ταὐτὸν δὴ δεῖ νομίζειν τοῦτο γίγνεσθαι καὶ περὶ
τὰς τῶν ἀνθρώπων διανοίας τε ἅμα καὶ τὰς τῶν
ψυχῶν φύσεις. οἷς γὰρ ἂν ἐντραφῶσι νόμοις καὶ
κατά τινα θείαν εὐτυχίαν ἀκίνητοι γένωνται
Β μακρῶν καὶ πολλῶν χρόνων, ὡς μηδένα ἔχειν
μνείαν μηδὲ ἀκοὴν τοῦ ποτὲ ἄλλως αὐτὰ σχεῖν
ἢ καθάπερ νῦν ἔχει, σέβεται καὶ φοβεῖται πᾶσα
ἡ ψυχὴ τό τι κινεῖν τῶν τότε καθεστώτων.
μηχανὴν δὴ δεῖ τὸν νομοθέτην ἐννοεῖν ἀμόθεν
γέ ποθεν ὅντινα τρόπον τοῦτ' ἔσται τῇ πόλει.
τῇδ' οὖν ἔγωγε εὑρίσκω. τὰς παιδιὰς πάντες
διανοοῦνται κινουμένας τῶν νέων, ὅπερ ἔμπροσθεν

---

[1] <πᾶσιν>, added by H. Richards.
[2] αὖ τις Badham : αὖθις MSS., edd.

ATH. Come now, let us listen to one another and address one another on this subject with greater care than ever. Nothing, as we shall find, is more perilous than change in respect of everything, save only what is bad,— in respect of seasons, winds, bodily diet, mental disposition, everything in short with the solitary exception, as I said just now, of the bad. Accordingly, if one considers the human body, and sees how it grows used to all kinds of meats and drinks and exercises, even though at first upset by them, and how presently out of these very materials it grows flesh that is akin to them, and acquiring thus a familiar acquaintance with, and fondness for, all this diet, lives a most healthy and pleasant life ; and further, should a man be forced again to change back to one of the highly-reputed diets, how he is upset and ill at first, and recovers with difficulty as he gets used again to the food,—it is precisely the same, we must suppose, with the intellects of men and the nature of their souls. For if there exist laws under which men have been reared up and which (by the blessing of Heaven) have remained unaltered for many centuries, so that there exists no recollection or report of their ever having been different from what they now are,— then the whole soul is forbidden by reverence and fear to alter any of the things established of old. By hook or by crook, then, the lawgiver must devise a means whereby this shall be true of his State. Now here is where I discover the means desired :— Alterations in children's games are regarded by all lawgivers (as we said above [1]) as being mere matters

---

[1] 797 B, C.

ἐλέγομεν, παιδιὰς ὄντως εἶναι καὶ οὐ τὴν
μεγίστην ἐξ αὐτῶν σπουδὴν καὶ βλάβην ξυμβαί-
C νειν, ὥστε οὐκ ἀποτρέπουσιν ἀλλὰ ξυνέπονται
ὑπείκοντες· καὶ οὐ λογίζονται τόδε, ὅτι τούτους
ἀνάγκη τοὺς παῖδας τοὺς ἐν ταῖς παιδιαῖς
νεωτερίζοντας ἑτέρους ἄνδρας τῶν ἔμπροσθεν
γενέσθαι [παίδων],[1] γενομένους δὲ ἄλλους ἄλλον
βίον ζητεῖν, ζητήσαντας δὲ ἑτέρων ἐπιτηδευμάτων
καὶ νόμων ἐπιθυμῆσαι, καὶ μετὰ τοῦτο ὡς
ἥξοντος τοῦ νῦν δὴ λεγομένου μεγίστου κακοῦ
D πόλεσιν οὐδεὶς αὐτῶν φοβεῖται. τὰ μὲν οὖν
ἄλλα ἐλάττω μεταβαλλόμενα κακὰ διεξεργάζοιτ᾽
ἄν, ὅσα περὶ σχήματα πάσχει τὸ τοιοῦτον· ὅσα
δὲ περὶ τὰ τῶν ἠθῶν ἐπαίνου τε καὶ ψόγου πέρι
πυκνὰ μεταπίπτει, πάντων, οἴομαι, μέγιστά τε
καὶ πλείστης εὐλαβείας δεόμενα ἂν εἴη.

κλ. Πῶς γὰρ οὔ ;

αθ. Τί οὖν ; τοῖς ἔμπροσθεν λόγοις πιστεύομεν,
οἷς ἐλέγομεν ὡς τὰ περὶ τοὺς ῥυθμοὺς καὶ πᾶσαν
μουσικήν ἐστι τρόπων μιμήματα βελτιόνων καὶ
E χειρόνων ἀνθρώπων ; ἢ πῶς ;

κλ. Οὐδαμῶς ἄλλως πως τό γε παρ᾽ ἡμῖν
δόγμα ἔχον ἂν εἴη.

αθ. Οὐκοῦν, φαμέν, ἅπασαν μηχανητέον μηχανὴν ὅπως ἂν ἡμῖν οἱ παῖδες μήτε ἐπιθυμῶσιν
ἄλλων μιμημάτων ἅπτεσθαι κατὰ ὀρχήσεις ἢ
κατὰ μελωδίας, μήτε τις αὐτοὺς πείσῃ προσάγων
παντοίας ἡδονάς ;

κλ. Ὀρθότατα λέγεις.

799 αθ. Ἔχει τις οὖν ἡμῶν ἐπὶ τὰ τοιαῦτα βελτίω
τινὰ τέχνην τῆς τῶν Αἰγυπτίων ;

---

[1] παίδων] bracketed by Badham, England.

of play, and not as the causes of serious mischief; hence, instead of forbidding them, they give in to them and adopt them. They fail to reflect that those children who innovate in their games grow up into men different from their fathers; and being thus different themselves, they seek a different mode of life, and having sought this, they come to desire other institutions and laws; and none of them dreads the consequent approach of that result which we described just now as the greatest of all banes to a State. The evil wrought by changes in outward forms would be of less importance; but frequent changes in matters involving moral approval and disapproval are, as I maintain, of extreme importance, and require the utmost caution.

CLIN. Most certainly.

ATH. Well, then, do we still put our trust in those former statements of ours,[1] in which we said that matters of rhythm and music generally are imitations of the manners of good or bad men? Or how do we stand?

CLIN. Our view at least remains unaltered.

ATH. We assert, then, that every means must be employed, not only to prevent our children from desiring to copy different models in dancing or singing, but also to prevent anyone from tempting them by the inducement of pleasures of all sorts.

CLIN. Quite right.

ATH. To attain this end, can any one of us suggest a better device than that of the Egyptians?[2]

---

[1] 654 E ff., 668 A.
[2] Cp. 656 D ff.

ΚΛ. Ποίας δὴ λέγεις ;

ΑΘ. Τοῦ καθιερῶσαι πᾶσαν μὲν ὄρχησιν, πάντα
δὲ μέλη, τάξαντας πρῶτον μὲν τὰς ἑορτάς, συλλογισαμένους εἰς τὸν ἐνιαυτὸν ἄστινας ἐν οἷς χρόνοις
καὶ οἷστισιν ἑκάστοις τῶν θεῶν καὶ παισὶ
τούτων καὶ δαίμοσι γίγνεσθαι χρεών, μετὰ δὲ
τοῦτο, ἐπὶ τοῖς τῶν θεῶν θύμασιν ἑκάστοις ἣν
ᾠδὴν δεῖ ἐφυμνεῖσθαι, καὶ χορείαις ποίαισι
Β γεραίρειν τὴν τότε θυσίαν, τάξαι μὲν πρῶτόν
τινας, ἃ δ' ἂν ταχθῇ, Μοίραις καὶ τοῖς ἄλλοις
πᾶσι θεοῖς θύσαντας κοινῇ πάντας τοὺς πολίτας
σπένδοντας καθιεροῦν ἑκάστας τὰς ᾠδὰς ἑκάστοις τῶν θεῶν καὶ τῶν ἄλλων· ἂν δὲ παρ' αὐτά
τίς τῳ θεῶν ἄλλους ὕμνους ἢ χορείας προσάγῃ,
τοὺς ἱερέας τε καὶ τὰς ἱερείας μετὰ νομοφυλάκων
ἐξείργοντας ὁσίως ἐξείργειν καὶ κατὰ νόμον, τὸν
δὲ ἐξειργόμενον, ἂν μὴ ἑκὼν ἐξείργηται, δίκας
ἀσεβείας διὰ βίου παντὸς τῷ ἐθελήσαντι παρέχειν.

ΚΛ. Ὀρθῶς.

Γ ΑΘ. Πρὸς τούτῳ δὴ νῦν γενόμενοι τῷ λόγῳ
πάθωμεν τὸ πρέπον ἡμῖν αὐτοῖς.

ΚΛ. Τοῦ πέρι λέγεις ;

ΑΘ. Πᾶς που νέος, μὴ ὅτι πρεσβύτης, ἰδὼν ἂν
ἢ καὶ ἀκούσας ὁτιοῦν τῶν ἐκτόπων καὶ μηδαμῇ
πω [1] ξυνήθων, οὐκ ἄν ποτέ που τὸ ἀπορηθὲν περὶ
αὐτῶν συγχωρήσειεν ἐπιδραμὼν οὕτως εὐθύς,
στὰς δ' ἄν, καθάπερ ἐν τριόδῳ γενόμενος καὶ μὴ
σφόδρα κατειδὼς ὁδόν, εἴτε μόνος εἴτε μετ' ἄλλων
Δ τύχοι πορευόμενος, ἀνέροιτ' ἂν αὐτὸν καὶ τοὺς

---

[1] πω Bekker: πως MSS.

---

[1] i.e. with the caution proper to old men.

CLIN. What device is that?

ATH. The device of consecrating all dancing and all music. First, they should ordain the sacred feasts, by drawing up an annual list of what feasts are to be held, and on what dates, and in honour of what special gods and children of gods and daemons; and they should ordain next what hymn is to be sung at each of the religious sacrifices, and with what dances each such sacrifice is to be graced; these ordinances should be first made by certain persons, and then the whole body of citizens, after making a public sacrifice to the Fates and all the other deities, should consecrate with a libation these ordinances— dedicating each of the hymns to their respective gods and divinities. And if any man proposes other hymns or dances besides these for any god, the priests and priestesses will be acting in accordance with both religion and law when, with the help of the Law-wardens, they expel him from the feast; and if the man resists expulsion, he shall be liable, so long as he lives, to be prosecuted for impiety by anyone who chooses.

CLIN. That is right.

ATH. Since we find ourselves now dealing with this theme, let us behave as befits ourselves.[1]

CLIN. In what respect?

ATH. Every young man—not to speak of old men—on hearing or seeing anything unusual and strange, is likely to avoid jumping to a hasty and impulsive solution of his doubts about it, and to stand still; just as a man who has come to a crossroads and is not quite sure of his way, if he be travelling alone, will question himself, or if travelling with others, will question them too about

39

ἄλλους τὸ ἀπορούμενον, καὶ οὐκ ἂν πρότερον
ὁρμήσειε, πρίν πῃ βεβαιώσαιτο τὴν σκέψιν τῆς
πορείας, ὅπῃ ποτὲ φέρει. καὶ δὴ καὶ τὸ παρὸν
ἡμῖν ὡσαύτως ποιητέον· ἀτόπου γὰρ τὰ νῦν
ἐμπεπτωκότος λόγου περὶ νόμων ἀνάγκη που
σκέψιν πᾶσαν ποιήσασθαι καὶ μὴ ῥᾳδίως οὕτω
περὶ τοσούτων τηλικούτους ὄντας φάναι δι-
ισχυριζομένους ἐν τῷ παραχρῆμά τι σαφὲς ἂν
εἰπεῖν ἔχειν.

ΚΛ. Ἀληθέστατα λέγεις.

Ε ΑΘ. Οὐκοῦν τούτῳ μὲν χρόνον δώσομεν, βεβαι-
ώσομεν δὲ τότε αὐτὸ ὁπόταν σκεψώμεθα ἱκανῶς·
ἵνα δὲ μὴ τὴν ἑπομένην τάξιν τοῖς νόμοις τοῖς νῦν
ἡμῖν παροῦσι διαπεράνασθαι κωλυθῶμεν μάτην,
ἴωμεν πρὸς τὸ τέλος αὐτῶν. τάχα γὰρ ἴσως, εἰ
θεὸς ἐθέλοι, κἂν ἡ διέξοδος αὕτη ὅλη σχοῦσα
τέλος ἱκανῶς ἂν μηνύσειε καὶ τὸ νῦν διαπορού-
μενον.

ΚΛ. Ἄριστ᾽, ὦ ξένε, λέγεις, καὶ ποιῶμεν οὕτως
ὡς εἴρηκας.

ΑΘ. Δεδόχθω μὲν δή, φαμέν, τὸ ἄτοπον τοῦτο,
νόμους τὰς ᾠδὰς ἡμῖν γεγονέναι, καὶ καθάπερ οἱ
παλαιοὶ τό γε [1] περὶ κιθαρῳδίαν οὕτω πως, ὡς
800 ἔοικεν, ὠνόμασαν, ὥστε τάχ᾽ ἂν οὐδ᾽ ἐκεῖνοι
παντάπασί γ᾽ ἂν ἀφεστῶτες εἶεν τοῦ νῦν λεγομένου, καθ᾽ ὕπνον δὲ οἷόν πού τις ἢ καὶ ὕπαρ
ἐγρηγορὼς ὠνείρωξε μαντευόμενος αὐτό. τὸ δ᾽
οὖν δόγμα περὶ αὐτοῦ τοῦτ᾽ ἔστω· παρὰ τὰ
δημόσια μέλη τε καὶ ἱερὰ καὶ τὴν τῶν νέων
ξύμπασαν χορείαν μηδεὶς μᾶλλον ἢ παρ᾽ ὁντινοῦν

---

[1] τό γε Apelt, England : τότε MSS.

the matter in doubt, and refuse to proceed until he has made sure by investigation of the direction of his path. We must now do likewise. In our discourse about laws, the point which has now occurred to us being strange, we are bound to investigate it closely; and in a matter so weighty we, at our age, must not lightly assume or assert that we can make any reliable statement about it on the spur of the moment.

CLIN. That is very true.

ATH. We shall, therefore, devote some time to this subject, and only when we have investigated it thoroughly shall we regard our conclusions as certain. But lest we be uselessly hindered from completing the ordinance which accompanies the laws with which we are now concerned, let us proceed to their conclusion. For very probably (if Heaven so will) this exposition, when completely brought to its conclusion, may also clear up the problem now before us.

CLIN. Well said, Stranger: let us do just as you say.

ATH. Let the strange fact be granted, we say, that our hymns are now made into "nomes" (laws),[1] just as the men of old, it would seem, gave this name to harp-tunes,—so that they, too, perhaps, would not wholly disagree with our present suggestion, but one of them may have divined it vaguely, as in a dream by night or a waking vision: anyhow, let this be the decree on the matter:— In violation of public tunes and sacred songs and the whole choristry of the young, just as in violation

---

[1] A play on the double sense of νόμος,—"law" and "chant" or "tune": cp. 700 B, 722 D, 734 E.

PLATO

ἄλλον τῶν νόμων φθεγγέσθω μηδ' ἐν ὀρχήσει
κινείσθω. καὶ ὁ μὲν τοιοῦτος ἀζήμιος ἀπαλλαττέσθω, τὸν δὲ μὴ πειθόμενον, καθάπερ ἐρρήθη
νῦν δή, νομοφύλακές τε καὶ ἱέρειαι καὶ ἱερεῖς
B κολαζόντων. κείσθω δὲ νῦν ἡμῖν ταῦτα τῷ
λόγῳ ;

ΚΛ. Κείσθω.

ΑΘ. Τίνα δὴ τρόπον αὐτὰ νομοθετῶν τις μὴ
παντάπασι καταγέλαστος γίγνοιτ' ἄν ; ἴδωμεν δὴ
τὸ τοιόνδ' ἔτι περὶ αὐτά. ἀσφαλέστατον καθάπερ
ἐκμαγεῖ' ἄττ' αὐτοῖσι πρῶτον πλάσασθαι τῷ
λόγῳ, λέγω δὲ ἐν μὲν τῶν ἐκμαγείων εἶναι
τοιόνδε τι· θυσίας γενομένης καὶ ἱερῶν καυθέντων
κατὰ νόμον, εἴ τῷ τις, φαμέν, ἰδίᾳ παραστὰς τοῖς
C βωμοῖς τε καὶ ἱεροῖς, υἱὸς ἢ καὶ ἀδελφός, βλασφη-
μοῖ πᾶσαν βλασφημίαν, ἆρ' οὐκ ἂν φαῖμεν,
ἀθυμίαν καὶ κακὴν ὄτταν καὶ μαντείαν πατρὶ καὶ
τοῖς ἄλλοις ἂν οἰκείοις φθέγγοιτο ἐντιθείς ;

ΚΛ. Τί μήν ;

ΑΘ. Ἐν τοίνυν τοῖς παρ' ἡμῖν τόποις τοῦτ'
ἔστι ταῖς πόλεσι γιγνόμενον ὡς ἔπος εἰπεῖν σχεδὸν
ὀλίγου πάσαις· δημοσίᾳ γάρ τινα θυσίαν ὅταν ἀρχή
τις θύσῃ, μετὰ ταῦτα χορὸς οὐχ εἷς ἀλλὰ πλῆθος
χορῶν ἥκει, καὶ στάντες οὐ πόρρω τῶν βωμῶν
D ἀλλὰ παρ' αὐτοὺς ἐνίοτε πᾶσαν βλασφημίαν τῶν
ἱερῶν καταχέουσι, ῥήμασί τε καὶ ῥυθμοῖς καὶ
γοωδεστάταις ἁρμονίαις συντείνοντες τὰς τῶν
ἀκροωμένων ψυχάς, καὶ ὃς ἂν δακρῦσαι μάλιστα
τὴν θύσασαν παραχρῆμα ποιήσῃ πόλιν, οὗτος τὰ

42

of any other "nome" (law), no person shall utter a note or move a limb in the dance. He that obeys shall be free of all penalty; but he that disobeys shall (as we said just now) be punished by the Law-wardens, the priestesses and the priests. Shall we now lay down these enactments in our statement?

CLIN. Yes, lay them down.

ATH. How shall we enact these rules by law in such a way as to escape ridicule? Let us consider yet another point concerning them. The safest plan is to begin by framing in our discourse some typical cases,[1] so to call them; one such case I may describe in this way. Suppose that, when a sacrifice is being performed and the offerings duly burned, some private worshipper—a son or a brother —when standing beside the altar and the offering, should blaspheme most blasphemously, would not his voice bring upon his father and the rest of the family a feeling of despair and evil forebodings?

CLIN. It would.

ATH. Well, in our part of the world this is what happens, one may almost say, in nearly every one of the States. Whenever a magistrate holds a public sacrifice, the next thing is for a crowd of choirs— not merely one—to advance and take their stand, not at a distance from the altars, but often quite close to them; and then they let out a flood of blasphemy over the sacred offerings, racking the souls of their audience with words, rhythms and tunes most dolorous, and the man that succeeds at once in drawing most tears from the sacrificing city carries

---

[1] ἐκμαγεῖον ("mould" or "impression") is here used, much like εἶδος, of a class or "type" of cases needing legal regulation.

νικητήρια φέρει· τοῦτον δὴ τὸν νόμον ἆρ' οὐκ
ἀποψηφιζόμεθα; καὶ εἴ ποτ' ἄρα δεῖ τοιούτων
οἴκτων γίγνεσθαι τοὺς πολίτας ἐπηκόους, ὁπόταν
ἡμέραι μὴ καθαραί τινες ἀλλὰ ἀποφράδες ὦσι,
E τόθ' ἥκειν δέον ἂν εἴη μᾶλλον χορούς τινας ἔξωθεν
μεμισθωμένους ᾠδούς, οἷον οἱ περὶ τοὺς τελευτήσαντας μισθούμενοι Καρικῇ τινι Μούσῃ προπέμ-
πουσι [τοὺς τελευτήσαντας]; [1] τοιοῦτόν που
πρέπον ἂν εἴη καὶ περὶ τὰς τοιαύτας ᾠδὰς γιγνό-
μενον· καὶ δὴ καὶ στολή γέ που ταῖς ἐπικη-
δείοις ᾠδαῖς οὐ στέφανοι πρέποιεν ἂν οὐδ' ἐπί-
χρυσοι κόσμοι, πᾶν δὲ τοὐναντίον, ἵν' ὅτι τάχιστα
περὶ αὐτῶν λέγων ἀπαλλάττωμαι. τὸ δὲ τοσοῦτον ἡμᾶς αὐτοὺς ἐπανερωτῶ πάλιν, τῶν ἐκμαγείων
ταῖς ᾠδαῖς εἰ πρῶτον ἓν τοῦθ' ἡμῖν ἄρεσκον κείσθω.

κλ. Τὸ ποῖον;

αθ. Εὐφημία, καὶ δὴ καὶ τὸ τῆς ᾠδῆς γένος
801 εὔφημον ἡμῖν πάντη πάντως ὑπαρχέτω; ἢ μηδὲν
ἐπανερωτῶ, τιθῶ δὲ τοῦτο οὕτως;

κλ. Παντάπασι μὲν οὖν τίθει· νικᾷ γὰρ
πάσαισι ταῖς ψήφοις οὗτος ὁ νόμος.

αθ. Τίς δὴ μετ' εὐφημίαν δεύτερος ἂν εἴη νόμος
μουσικῆς; ἆρ' οὐκ εὐχὰς εἶναι τοῖς θεοῖς οἷς θύομεν
ἑκάστοτε;

κλ. Πῶς γὰρ οὔ;

αθ. Τρίτος δ', οἶμαι, νόμος, ὅτι γνόντας δεῖ
τοὺς ποιητὰς ὡς εὐχαὶ παρὰ θεῶν αἰτήσεις εἰσί,
δεῖ δὴ τὸν νοῦν αὐτοὺς σφόδρα προσέχειν μή ποτε

---

[1] [τοὺς τελευτήσαντας] bracketed by Burges, England.

44

off the palm of victory. Must we not reject[1] such a custom as this? For if it is ever really necessary that the citizens should listen to such doleful strains, it would be more fitting that the choirs that attend should be hired from abroad, and that not on holy days but only on fast-days—just as a corpse is escorted with Carian music by hired mourners. Such music would also form the fitting accompaniment for hymns of this kind; and the garb befitting these funeral hymns would not be any crowns nor gilded ornaments, but just the opposite,—for I want to get done with this subject as soon as I can. Only I would have us ask ourselves again[2] this single question,—are we satisfied to lay this down as our first typical rule for hymns?

CLIN. What rule?

ATH. That of auspicious speech; and must we have a kind of hymn that is altogether in all respects auspicious? Or shall I ordain that it shall be so, without further questioning?

CLIN. By all means ordain it so; for that is a law carried by a unanimous vote.

ATH. What then, next to auspicious speech, should be the second law of music? Is it not that prayers should be made on each occasion to those gods to whom offering is made?

CLIN. Certainly.

ATH. The third law, I suppose, will be this,— that the poets, knowing that prayers are requests addressed to gods, must take the utmost care lest

---

[1] Music should be used as an ennobling educational instrument, promoting self-control, not as a means of exciting vulgar sentiment and passion.

[2] Cp. 800 B.

B λάθωσι κακὸν ὡς ἀγαθὸν αἰτούμενοι· γελοῖον γὰρ
δὴ τὸ πάθος, οἶμαι, τοῦτ᾽ ἂν γίγνοιτο εὐχῆς
τοιαύτης γενομένης.

ΚΛ. Τί μήν;

ΑΘ. Οὐκοῦν ἡμεῖς ἔμπροσθεν σμικρὸν τῷ λόγῳ
ἐπείσθημεν ὡς οὔτε ἀργυροῦν δεῖ Πλοῦτον οὔτε
χρυσοῦν ἐν πόλει ἱδρυμένον ἐνοικεῖν;

ΚΛ. Πάνυ μὲν οὖν.

ΑΘ. Τίνος οὖν ποτὲ παράδειγμα εἰρῆσθαι
φῶμεν τοῦτον τὸν λόγον; ἆρ᾽ οὐ τοῦδε, ὅτι τὸ τῶν
ποιητῶν γένος οὐ πᾶν ἱκανόν ἐστι γιγνώσκειν
C σφόδρα τά τε ἀγαθὰ καὶ μή; ποιήσας οὖν δή πού
τις ποιητὴς ῥήμασιν ἢ καὶ κατὰ μέλος τοῦτο
ἡμαρτημένος[1] [εὐχὰς οὐκ ὀρθὰς][2] ἡμῖν τοὺς
πολίτας περὶ τῶν μεγίστων εὔχεσθαι τἀναντία
ποιήσει· καί τοι τούτου, καθάπερ ἐλέγομεν, οὐ
πολλὰ ἁμαρτήματα ἀνευρήσομεν μείζω. θῶμεν δὴ
καὶ τοῦτον τῶν περὶ Μοῦσαν νόμων καὶ τύπων
ἕνα;

ΚΛ. Τίνα; σαφέστερον εἰπὲ ἡμῖν.

ΑΘ. Τὸν ποιητὴν παρὰ τὰ τῆς πόλεως νόμιμα
καὶ δίκαια ἢ καλὰ ἢ ἀγαθὰ μηδὲν ποιεῖν ἄλλο, τὰ
D δὲ ποιηθέντα μὴ ἐξεῖναι τῶν ἰδιωτῶν μηδενὶ
πρότερον δεικνύναι, πρὶν ἂν αὐτοῖς τοῖς περὶ ταῦτα
ἀποδεδειγμένοις κριταῖς καὶ τοῖς νομοφύλαξι
δειχθῇ καὶ ἀρέσῃ. σχεδὸν δὲ ἀποδεδειγμένοι
εἰσὶν ἡμῖν οὓς εἱλόμεθα νομοθέτας περὶ τὰ μουσικὰ καὶ τὸν τῆς παιδείας ἐπιμελητήν. τί οὖν; ὃ
πολλάκις ἐρωτῶ, κείσθω νόμος ἡμῖν καὶ τύπος
ἐκμαγεῖόν τε τρίτον τοῦτο, ἢ πῶς δοκεῖ;

---

[1] ἡμαρτημένος : ἡμαρτημένον MSS., edd.
[2] [εὐχὰς οὐκ ὀρθὰς] bracketed by Badham.

46

unwittingly they request a bad thing as though it were a good thing; for if such a prayer were made, it would prove, I fancy, a ludicrous blunder.

CLIN. Of course.

ATH. Did not our argument convince us, a little while ago,[1] that no Plutus either in gold or in silver should dwell enshrined within the State?

CLIN. It did.

ATH. What then shall we say that this statement serves to illustrate? Is it not this,—that the tribe of poets is not wholly capable of discerning very well what is good and what not? For surely when a poet, suffering from this error, composes prayers either in speech or in song, he will be making our citizens contradict ourselves in their prayers for things of the greatest moment; yet this, as we have said,[2] is an error than which few are greater. So shall we also lay down this as one of our laws and typical cases regarding music?

CLIN. What law? Explain it to us more clearly.

ATH. The law that the poet shall compose nothing which goes beyond the limits of what the State holds to be legal and right, fair and good; nor shall he show his compositions to any private person until they have first been shown to the judges appointed to deal with these matters, and to the Law-wardens, and have been approved by them. And in fact we have judges appointed in those whom we selected to be the legislators of music and in the supervisor of education. Well then, I repeat my question,—is this to be laid down as our third law, typical case, and example? What think you?

[1] 742 D ff. Plutus is the god of wealth.
[2] 801 B.

κλ. Κείσθω· τί μήν;

αθ. Μετά γε μὴν ταῦτα ὕμνοι θεῶν καὶ
ἐγκώμια κεκοινωνημένα εὐχαῖς ᾄδοιτ᾽ ἂν ὀρθότατα,
καὶ μετὰ θεοὺς ὡσαύτως περὶ δαίμονάς τε καὶ
ἥρωας μετ᾽ ἐγκωμίων εὐχαὶ γίγνοιντ᾽ ἂν τούτοις
πᾶσι πρέπουσαι.

κλ. Πῶς γὰρ οὔ;

Ε   αθ. Μετά γε μὴν ταῦτ᾽ ἤδη νόμος ἄνευ φθόνων
εὐθὺς γίγνοιτ᾽ ἂν ὅδε· τῶν πολιτῶν ὁπόσοι τέλος
ἔχοιεν τοῦ βίου κατὰ σώματα ἢ κατὰ ψυχὰς
ἔργα ἐξειργασμένοι καλὰ καὶ ἐπίπονα καὶ τοῖς
νόμοις εὐπειθεῖς γεγονότες, ἐγκωμίων αὐτοὺς
τυγχάνειν πρέπον ἂν εἴη.

κλ. Πῶς δ᾽ οὔ;

802 αθ. Τούς γε μὴν ἔτι ζῶντας ἐγκωμίοις τε καὶ
ὕμνοις τιμᾶν οὐκ ἀσφαλές, πρὶν ἂν ἅπαντά τις
τὸν βίον διαδραμὼν τέλος ἐπιστήσηται καλόν.
ταῦτα δὲ πάντα ἡμῖν ἔστω κοινὰ ἀνδράσι τε καὶ
γυναιξὶν ἀγαθοῖς καὶ ἀγαθαῖς διαφανῶς γενομένοις. τὰς δὲ ᾠδάς τε καὶ ὀρχήσεις οὑτωσὶ χρὴ
καθίστασθαι· πολλά ἐστι παλαιῶν παλαιὰ περὶ
μουσικὴν καὶ καλὰ ποιήματα, καὶ δὴ καὶ τοῖς
σώμασιν ὀρχήσεις ὡσαύτως, ὧν οὐδεὶς φθόνος
ἐκλέξασθαι τῇ καθισταμένῃ πολιτείᾳ τὸ πρέπον
Β καὶ ἅρμοττον· δοκιμαστὰς δὲ τούτων ἑλομένους
τὴν ἐκλογὴν ποιεῖσθαι μὴ νεωτέρους πεντήκοντα
ἐτῶν, καὶ ὅ τι μὲν ἂν ἱκανὸν εἶναι δόξῃ τῶν
παλαιῶν ποιημάτων, ἐγκρίνειν, ὅ τι δ᾽ ἂν ἐνδεὲς ἢ
τὸ παράπαν ἀνεπιτήδειον, τὸ μὲν ἀποβάλλεσθαι
παντάπασι, τὸ δ᾽ ἐπαναιρόμενον [1] ἐπιρρυθμίζειν,
ποιητικοὺς ἅμα καὶ μουσικοὺς ἄνδρας παραλα-

LAWS, BOOK VII

CLIN. Be it laid down by all means.

ATH. Next to these, it will be most proper to sing hymns and praise to the gods, coupled with prayers; and after the gods will come prayers combined with praise to daemons and heroes, as is befitting to each.

CLIN. To be sure.

ATH. This done, we may proceed at once without scruple to formulate this law :—all citizens who have attained the goal of life and have wrought with body or soul noble works and toilsome, and have been obedient to the laws, shall be regarded as fitting objects for praise.

CLIN. Certainly.

ATH. But truly it is not safe to honour with hymns and praises those still living, before they have traversed the whole of life and reached a noble end. All such honours shall be equally shared by women as well as men who have been conspicuous for their excellence. As to the songs and the dances, this is the fashion in which they should be arranged. Among the compositions of the ancients there exist many fine old pieces of music, and likewise dances, from which we may select without scruple for the constitution we are founding such as are fitting and proper. To examine these and make the selection, we shall choose out men not under fifty years of age; and whichever of the ancient songs are approved we shall adopt, but whichever fail to reach our standard, or are altogether unsuitable, we shall either reject entirely or revise and remodel. For this purpose we shall call in the advice of poets and musicians,

---

[1] ἐπαναιρόμενον Hermann : ἐπανερόμενον MSS. ; ἐπανερομένους Stephens, Zur.

βόντας, χρωμένους αὐτῶν ταῖς δυνάμεσι τῆς
ποιήσεως, ταῖς δὲ ἡδοναῖς καὶ ἐπιθυμίαις μὴ
C ἐπιτρέποντας ἀλλ᾽ ἤ τισιν ὀλίγοις, ἐξηγουμένους
δὲ τὰ τοῦ νομοθέτου βουλήματα ὅτι μάλιστα
ὄρχησίν τε καὶ ᾠδὴν καὶ πᾶσαν χορείαν συστή-
σασθαι κατὰ τὸν αὑτοῦ[1] νοῦν. πᾶσα δ᾽ ἄτακτός
γε τάξιν λαβοῦσα περὶ Μοῦσαν διατριβὴ καὶ μὴ
παρατιθεμένης τῆς γλυκείας Μούσης ἀμείνων
μυρίῳ· τὸ δ᾽ ἡδὺ κοινὸν πάσαις. ἐν ᾗ γὰρ ἂν ἐκ
παίδων τις μέχρι τῆς ἑστηκυίας τε καὶ ἔμφρονος
ἡλικίας διαβιῷ, σώφρονι μὲν Μούσῃ καὶ τεταγμένῃ, ἀκούων ἀεὶ[2] τῆς ἐναντίας μισεῖ καὶ
D ἀνελεύθερον αὐτὴν προσαγορεύει, τραφεὶς δ᾽ ἐν
τῇ κοινῇ καὶ γλυκείᾳ ψυχρὰν καὶ ἀηδῆ τὴν ταύτῃ
ἐναντίαν εἶναί φησιν, ὥστε, ὅπερ ἐρρήθη νῦν δή,
τό γε τῆς ἡδονῆς ἢ ἀηδίας περὶ ἑκατέρας οὐδὲν
πεπλεονέκτηκεν, ἐκ περιττοῦ δὲ ἡ μὲν βελτίους, ἡ
δὲ χείρους τοὺς ἐν αὐτῇ τραφέντας ἑκάστοτε
παρέχεται.

ΚΛ. Καλῶς εἴρηκας.

ΑΘ. Ἔτι δὲ θηλείαις τε πρεπούσας ᾠδὰς ἄρρεσί
τε χωρίσαι που δέον ἂν εἴη τύπῳ τινὶ διορι-
σάμενον, καὶ ἁρμονίαισι δὴ καὶ ῥυθμοῖς προσαρ-
E μόττειν ἀναγκαῖον· δεινὸν γὰρ ὅλῃ γε ἁρμονίᾳ
ἀπᾴδειν ἢ ῥυθμῷ ἀρρυθμεῖν, μηδὲν προσήκοντα
τούτων ἑκάστοις ἀποδιδόντα τοῖς μέλεσιν. ἀναγκαῖον δὴ καὶ τούτων τὰ σχήματά γε νομοθετεῖν. ἔστι δὲ ἀμφοτέροις μὲν ἀμφότερα ἀνάγκη
κατεχόμενα ἀποδιδόναι, [τὰ δὲ τῶν θηλειῶν][3]

---

[1] αὐτοῦ: αὐτῶν MSS. ; αὑτῶν Zur.
[2] ἀεὶ W. R. Paton, England : δὲ MSS.
[3] τὰ . . . θηλειῶν I transpose, after W.-Möllendorff.

and make use of their poetical ability, without, however, trusting to their tastes or their wishes, except in rare instances; and by thus expounding the intentions of the lawgiver, we shall organise to his satisfaction dancing, singing, and the whole of choristry. In truth, every unregulated musical pursuit becomes, when brought under regulation, a thousand times better, even when no honeyed strains are served up: all alike provide pleasure.[1] For if a man has been reared from childhood up to the age of steadiness and sense in the use of music that is sober and regulated, then he detests the opposite kind whenever he hears it, and calls it "vulgar"; whereas if he has been reared in the common honeyed kind of music, he declares the opposite of this to be cold and unpleasing. Hence, as we said just now, in respect of the pleasure or displeasure they cause neither kind excels the other; where the superiority lies is in the fact that the one kind always makes those who are reared in it better, the other worse.

CLIN. Finely spoken!

ATH. Further, it will be right for the lawgiver to set apart suitable songs for males and females by making a rough division of them; and he must necessarily adapt them to harmonies and rhythms, for it would be a horrible thing for discord to exist between theme and tune, metre and rhythm, as a result of providing the songs with unsuitable accompaniments. So the lawgiver must of necessity ordain at least the outline of these. And while it is necessary for him to assign both words and music for both

---

[1] *i.e.* a "regulated" style of music pleases the educated just as much as the other sort pleases the uneducated. Cp. 658 E ff.

αὐτῷ τῷ τῆς φύσεως ἑκατέρου διαφέροντι, <τὰ
δὲ τῶν θηλειῶν> τούτῳ δεῖ καὶ διασαφεῖν. τὸ
δὴ μεγαλοπρεπὲς οὖν καὶ τὸ πρὸς τὴν ἀνδρίαν
ῥέπον ἀρρενωπὸν φατέον εἶναι, τὸ δὲ πρὸς τὸ
κόσμιον καὶ σῶφρον μᾶλλον ἀποκλῖνον θηλυγε-
νέστερον ὡς ὂν παραδοτέον ἔν τε τῷ νόμῳ καὶ
803 λόγῳ. τάξις μὲν δή τις αὕτη· τούτων δὲ αὐτῶν
διδασκαλία καὶ παράδοσις λεγέσθω τὸ μετὰ
τοῦτο, τίνα τρόπον χρὴ καὶ οἷστισι καὶ πότε
πράττειν ἕκαστα αὐτῶν· οἷον δή τις ναυπηγὸς
τὴν τῆς ναυπηγίας ἀρχὴν καταβαλλόμενος τὰ
τροπίδεια ὑπογράφεται τῶν πλοίων σχήματα,
ταὐτὸν δή μοι κἀγὼ φαίνομαι ἐμαυτῷ δρᾶν τὰ
τῶν βίων πειρώμενος σχήματα διαστήσασθαι
κατὰ τρόπους τοὺς τῶν ψυχῶν, ὄντως αὐτῶν τὰ
B τροπίδεια καταβάλλεσθαι, ποίᾳ μηχανῇ καὶ τίσι
ποτὲ τρόποις ξυνόντες τὸν βίον ἄριστα διὰ τοῦ
πλοῦ τούτου τῆς ζωῆς διακομισθησόμεθα, τοῦτο
σκοπῶν[1] ὀρθῶς. ἔστι δὴ τοίνυν τὰ τῶν ἀνθρώπων πράγματα μεγάλης μὲν σπουδῆς οὐκ ἄξια,
ἀναγκαῖόν γε μὴν σπουδάζειν· τοῦτο δὲ οὐκ
εὐτυχές. ἐπειδὴ δὲ ἐνταῦθά ἐσμεν, εἴ πως διὰ
προσήκοντός τινος αὐτὸ πράττοιμεν, ἴσως ἂν ἡμῖν
σύμμετρον ἂν εἴη. λέγω δὲ δὴ τί ποτε; ἴσως μέντ᾽
C ἄν τίς μοι τοῦτ᾽ αὐτὸ ὑπολαβὼν ὀρθῶς ὑπολάβοι.

ΚΛ. Πάνυ μὲν οὖν.

ΑΘ. Φημὶ χρῆναι τὸ μὲν σπουδαῖον σπουδάζειν,
τὸ δὲ μὴ σπουδαῖον μή· φύσει δὲ εἶναι θεὸν μὲν
πάσης μακαρίου σπουδῆς ἄξιον, ἄνθρωπον δέ,
ὅπερ εἴπομεν ἔμπροσθεν, θεοῦ τι παίγνιον εἶναι
μεμηχανημένον, καὶ ὄντως τοῦτο αὐτοῦ τὸ βέλτισ-

---

[1] σκοπῶν Peipers : σκοπεῖν MSS.

types of song as defined by the natural difference of the two sexes, he must also clearly declare wherein the feminine type consists. Now we may affirm that what is noble and of a manly tendency is masculine, while that which inclines rather to decorum and sedateness is to be regarded rather as feminine both in law and in discourse. Such then is our regulation of the matter. We have next to discuss the question of the teaching and imparting of these subjects—how, by whom, and when each of them should be practised. Just as a shipwright at the commencement of his building outlines the shape of his vessel by laying down her keel, so I appear to myself to be doing just the same—trying to frame, that is, the shapes of lives according to the modes of their souls, and thus literally laying down their keels, by rightly considering by what means and by what modes of living we shall best navigate our barque of life through this voyage of existence. And notwithstanding that human affairs are unworthy of earnest effort, necessity counsels us to be in earnest; and that is our misfortune. Yet, since we are where we are, it is no doubt becoming that we should show this earnestness in a suitable direction. But no doubt I may be faced—and rightly faced—with the question, " What do I mean by this? "

CLIN. Certainly.

ATH. What I assert is this,—that a man ought to be in serious earnest about serious things, and not about trifles; and that the object really worthy of all serious and blessed effort is God, while man is contrived, as we said above,[1] to be a plaything of God, and the best part of him is really just that; and

---

[1] 644 D.

τον γεγονέναι· τούτῳ δὴ δεῖν τῷ τρόπῳ ξυνεπόμενον καὶ παίζοντα ὅτι καλλίστας παιδιὰς πάντ᾽
ἄνδρα καὶ γυναῖκα οὕτω διαβιῶναι, τοὐναντίον ἢ
νῦν διανοηθέντας.

D ΚΛ. Πῶς ;

ΑΘ. Νῦν μέν που τὰς σπουδὰς οἴονται δεῖν
ἕνεκα τῶν παιδιῶν γίγνεσθαι· τὰ γὰρ περὶ τὸν
πόλεμον ἡγοῦνται σπουδαῖα ὄντα τῆς εἰρήνης
ἕνεκα δεῖν εὖ τίθεσθαι. τὸ δ᾽ ἦν ἐν πολέμῳ μὲν
ἄρα οὔτ᾽ οὖν παιδιὰ πεφυκυῖα οὔτ᾽ αὖ παιδεία
ποτὲ ἡμῖν ἀξιόλογος, οὔτε οὖσα οὔτ᾽ ἐσομένη, ὃ[1]
δή φαμεν ἡμῖν γε εἶναι σπουδαιότατον· δεῖ δὴ τὸν
κατ᾽ εἰρήνην βίον ἕκαστον πλεῖστόν τε καὶ ἄριστον διεξελθεῖν. τίς οὖν ὀρθότης ; παίζοντά[2] ἐστι
E διαβιωτέον τινὰς δὴ παιδιὰς θύοντα, καὶ ᾄδοντα
καὶ ὀρχούμενον, ὥστε τοὺς μὲν θεοὺς ἵλεως αὑτῷ
παρασκευάζειν δυνατὸν εἶναι, τοὺς δ᾽ ἐχθροὺς
ἀμύνεσθαι καὶ νικᾶν μαχόμενον. ὁποῖα δὲ ᾄδων
ἄν τις καὶ ὀρχούμενος ἀμφότερα ταῦτα πράττοι,
τὸ μὲν τῶν τύπων εἴρηται καὶ καθάπερ ὁδοὶ
τέτμηνται, καθ᾽ ἃς ἰτέον προσδοκῶντα καὶ τὸν
ποιητὴν εὖ λέγειν τὸ

804 Τηλέμαχ᾽, ἄλλα μὲν αὐτὸς ἐνὶ φρεσὶ σῇσι
      νοήσεις,
    ἄλλα δὲ καὶ δαίμων ὑποθήσεται· οὐ γὰρ οἴω
    οὔ σε θεῶν ἀέκητι γενέσθαι τε τραφέμεν τε.

ταὐτὸν δὴ καὶ τοὺς ἡμετέρους τροφίμους δεῖ διανοουμένους τὰ μὲν εἰρημένα ἀποχρώντως νομίζειν
εἰρῆσθαι, τὰ δὲ καὶ τὸν δαίμονά τε καὶ θεὸν

---

[1] ὃ Hermann : τὸ MSS.
[2] παίζοντά MSS. ; τί παίζοντά . . . διαβιωτέον ; τίνας δὴ Zur.

thus I say that every man and woman ought to pass through life in accordance with this character, playing at the noblest of pastimes, being otherwise minded than they now are.

CLIN. How so?

ATH. Now they imagine that serious work should be done for the sake of play; for they think that it is for the sake of peace that the serious work of war needs to be well conducted. But as a matter of fact we, it would seem, do not find in war, either as existing or likely to exist, either real play or education worthy of the name, which is what we assert to be in our eyes the most serious thing. It is the life of peace that everyone should live as much and as well as he can. What then is the right way? We should live out our lives playing at certain pastimes —sacrificing, singing and dancing—so as to be able to win Heaven's favour and to repel our foes and vanquish them in fight. By means of what kinds of song and dance both these aims may be effected,— this has been, in part, stated in outline, and the paths of procedure have been marked out, in the belief that the poet is right when he says [1]—

" Telemachus, thine own wit will in part
    Instruct thee, and the rest will Heaven supply ;
  For to the will of Heaven thou owest birth
    And all thy nurture, I would fain believe."

It behoves our nurslings also to be of this same mind, and to believe that what we have said is sufficient, and that the heavenly powers will suggest to them all

[1] *Odyss.* III. 26 ff.

αὐτοῖσιν ὑποθήσεσθαι θυσιῶν τε πέρι καὶ χορειῶν,
B οἶστισί τε καὶ ὁπότε ἕκαστα ἑκάστοις προσπαί-
ζοντές τε καὶ ἱλεούμενοι κατὰ τὸν τρόπον τῆς
φύσεως διαβιώσονται, θαύματα ὄντες τὸ πολύ,
σμικρὰ δὲ ἀληθείας ἄττα μετέχοντες.

ΜΕ. Παντάπασι τὸ τῶν ἀνθρώπων γένος ἡμῖν,
ὦ ξένε, διαφαυλίζεις.

ΑΘ. Μὴ θαυμάσῃς, ὦ Μέγιλλε, ἀλλὰ ξύγγνωθί
μοι· πρὸς γὰρ τὸν θεὸν ἀπιδὼν καὶ παθὼν εἶπον
ὅπερ εἴρηκα νῦν. ἔστω δ' οὖν τὸ γένος ἡμῶν μὴ
C φαῦλον, εἴ σοι φίλον, σπουδῆς δέ τινος ἄξιον.

Τὸ δ' ἐξῆς τούτοις, οἰκοδομίαι μὲν εἴρηνται
γυμνασίων ἅμα καὶ διδασκαλείων κοινῶν τριχῇ
κατὰ μέσην τὴν πόλιν, ἔξωθεν δὲ ἵππων αὖ τριχῇ
περὶ τὸ ἄστυ γυμνάσιά τε καὶ εὐρυχώρια, τοξικῆς
τε καὶ τῶν ἄλλων ἀκροβολισμῶν ἕνεκα διακεκοσμημένα, μαθήσεώς τε ἅμα καὶ μελέτης τῶν νέων.
εἰ δ' ἄρα μὴ τότε ἱκανῶς ἐρρήθησαν, νῦν εἰρήσθω
τῷ λόγῳ μετὰ νόμων. ἐν δὲ τούτοις πᾶσι διδασ-
D κάλους ἑκάστων πεπεισμένους μισθοῖς οἰκοῦντας
ξένους διδάσκειν τε πάντα ὅσα πρὸς τὸν πόλεμόν
ἐστι μαθήματα τοὺς φοιτῶντας ὅσα τε πρὸς
μουσικήν, οὐχ ὃν μὲν ἂν ὁ πατὴρ βούληται
φοιτῶντα, ὃν δ' ἂν μὴ ἐῶντα τὰς παιδείας, ἀλλὰ
τὸ λεγόμενον πάντ' ἄνδρα καὶ παῖδα κατὰ τὸ
δυνατόν, ὡς τῆς πόλεως μᾶλλον ἢ τῶν γεννητόρων
ὄντας, παιδευτέον ἐξ ἀνάγκης. τὰ αὐτὰ δὲ δὴ
καὶ περὶ θηλειῶν ὁ μὲν ἐμὸς νόμος ἂν εἴποι πάντα
ὅσαπερ καὶ περὶ τῶν ἀρρένων, ἴσα καὶ τὰς θηλείας
E ἀσκεῖν δεῖν· καὶ οὐδὲν φοβηθεὶς εἴποιμ' ἂν τοῦτον

---

[1] Cp. 644 D, E.   [2] 764 C, 779 D.

else that concerns sacrifice and the dance,—in honour of what gods and at what seasons respectively they are to play and win their favour, and thus mould their lives according to the shape of their nature, inasmuch as they are puppets [1] for the most part, yet share occasionally in truth.

MEG. You have a very mean opinion, Stranger, of the human race.

ATH. Marvel not, Megillus, but forgive me. For when I spoke thus, I had my mind set on God, and was feeling the emotion to which I gave utterance. Let us grant, however, if you wish, that the human race is not a mean thing, but worthy of serious attention.

To pursue our subject,—we have described [2] buildings for public gymnasia as well as schools in three divisions within the city, and also in three divisions round about the city training-grounds and race-courses for horses, arranged for archery and other long-distance shooting, and for the teaching and practising of the youth : if, however, our previous description of these was inadequate, let them now be described and legally regulated. In all these establishments there should reside teachers attracted by pay from abroad for each several subject, to instruct the pupils in all matters relating to war and to music ; and no father shall either send his son as a pupil or keep him away from the training-school at his own sweet will, but every " man jack " of them all (as the saying goes) must, so far as possible, be compelled to be educated, inasmuch as they are children of the State even more than children of their parents. For females, too, my law will lay down the same regulations as for men, and training of an identical kind. I will unhesitatingly affirm that

τὸν λόγον οὔτε ἱππικῆς οὔτε γυμναστικῆς, ὡς
ἀνδράσι μὲν πρέπον ἂν εἴη, γυναιξὶ δὲ οὐκ ἂν
πρέπον. ἀκούων μὲν γὰρ δὴ μύθους παλαιοὺς
πέπεισμαι, τὰ δὲ νῦν ὡς ἔπος εἰπεῖν οἶδα ὅτι
μυριάδες ἀναρίθμητοι γυναικῶν εἰσὶ τῶν περὶ τὸν
Πόντον, ἃς Σαυρομάτιδας καλοῦσιν, αἷς οὐχ
ἵππων μόνον ἀλλὰ καὶ τόξων καὶ τῶν ἄλλων
805 ὅπλων κοινωνία καὶ τοῖς ἀνδράσιν ἴση προστε-
ταγμένη ἴσως ἀσκεῖται. λογισμὸν δὲ πρὸς τούτοις
περὶ τούτων τοιόνδε τινὰ ἔχω· φημί, εἴπερ ταῦτα
οὕτω ξυμβαίνειν ἐστὶ δυνατά, πάντων ἀνοητότατα
τὰ νῦν ἐν τοῖς παρ' ἡμῖν τόποις γίγνεσθαι τὸ μὴ
πάσῃ ῥώμῃ πάντας ὁμοθυμαδὸν ἐπιτηδεύειν ἄνδρας
γυναιξὶ ταῦτά. σχεδὸν γὰρ ὀλίγου πᾶσα ἡμίσεια
πόλις ἀντὶ διπλασίας οὕτως ἐστί τε καὶ γίγνεται
ἐκ τῶν αὐτῶν τελῶν καὶ πόνων· καί τοι θαυμασ-
B τὸν ἂν ἁμάρτημα νομοθέτῃ τοῦτ' αὐτὸ γίγνοιτο.

ΚΛ. Ἔοικέ γε· ἔστι μέντοι πάμπολλα ἡμῖν,
ὦ ξένε, παρὰ τὰς εἰωθυίας πολιτείας τῶν νῦν
λεγομένων.

ΑΘ. Ἀλλὰ γὰρ εἶπον[1] τὸν μὲν λόγον ἐᾶσαι
διεξελθεῖν, εὖ διελθόντος δὲ οὕτω τὸ δοκοῦν
αἱρεῖσθαι δεῖν.

ΚΛ. Μάλα εἶπές τε ἐμμελῶς πεποίηκάς τ' ἐμὲ
τὰ νῦν αὐτὸν ἐμαυτῷ ἐπιπλήττειν ὅτι ταῦτα
εἴρηκα. λέγε οὖν τὸ μετὰ ταῦτα ὅ τί σοι
C κεχαρισμένον ἐστίν.

ΑΘ. Τόδε ἔμοιγε, ὦ Κλεινία, ὃ καὶ πρόσθεν
εἶπον, ὡς, εἰ μὲν ταῦτα ἦν μὴ ἱκανῶς ἔργοις
ἐληλεγμένα ὅτι δυνατά ἐστι γίγνεσθαι, τάχα ἦν
ἄν τι καὶ ἀντειπεῖν τῷ λόγῳ, νῦν δὲ ἄλλο τί που

---

[1] εἶπον Cornarius: εἰπὼν MSS., and some edd. (assigning
ἀλλὰ . . . δεῖν also to *Clin.*).

neither riding nor gymnastics, which are proper for men, are improper for women. I believe the old tales I have heard, and I know now of my own observation, that there are practically countless myriads of women called Sauromatides, in the district of Pontus, upon whom equally with men is imposed the duty of handling bows and other weapons, as well as horses, and who practise it equally. In addition to this I allege the following argument. Since this state of things can exist, I affirm that the practice which at present prevails in our districts is a most irrational one—namely, that men and women should not all follow the same pursuits with one accord and with all their might. For thus from the same taxation and trouble there arises and exists half a State only instead of a whole one, in nearly every instance; yet surely this would be a surprising blunder for a lawgiver to commit.

CLIN. So it would seem; yet truly a vast number of the things now mentioned, Stranger, are in conflict with our ordinary polities.

ATH. Well, but I said [1] that we should allow the argument to run its full course, and when this is done we should adopt the conclusion we approve.

CLIN. In this you spoke most reasonably; and you have made me now chide myself for what I said. So say on now what seems good to you.

ATH. What seems good to me, Clinias, as I said before,[2] is this,—that if the possibility of such a state of things taking place had not been sufficiently proved by facts, then it might have been possible to gainsay our statement; but as it is, the man who

---

[1] Cp. 746 C, 799 E.   [2] 805 A.

ζητητέον ἐκείνῳ τῷ τοῦτον τὸν νόμον μηδαμῇ
δεχομένῳ, τὸ δ' ἡμέτερον διακέλευμα ἐν τούτοις
οὐκ ἀποσβήσεται, τὸ μὴ οὐ λέγειν ὡς δεῖ παιδείας τε καὶ τῶν ἄλλων ὅτι μάλιστα κοινωνεῖν τὸ
D θῆλυ γένος ἡμῖν τῷ τῶν ἀρρένων γένει. καὶ γὰρ
οὖν οὑτωσί πως δεῖ περὶ αὐτῶν διανοηθῆναι.
φέρε, μὴ μετεχουσῶν ἀνδράσι γυναικῶν κοινῇ τῆς
ζωῆς πάσης μῶν οὐκ ἀνάγκη γενέσθαι γέ τινα
τάξιν ἑτέραν αὐταῖς ;

ΚΛ. Ἀνάγκη μὲν οὖν.

ΑΘ. Τίνα οὖν ἔμπροσθεν τῶν νῦν ἀποδεδειγ-
μένων θεῖμεν ἂν τῆς κοινωνίας ταύτης ἣν νῦν
αὐταῖς ἡμεῖς προστάττομεν ; πότερον ἣν Θρᾷκες
ταῖς γυναιξὶ χρῶνται καὶ πολλὰ ἕτερα γένη,
E γεωργεῖν τε καὶ βουκολεῖν καὶ ποιμαίνειν καὶ
διακονεῖν μηδὲν διαφερόντως τῶν δούλων ; ἢ
καθάπερ ἡμεῖς ἅπαντές τε οἱ περὶ τὸν τόπον
ἐκεῖνον ; νῦν γὰρ δὴ τό γε παρ' ἡμῖν ὧδέ ἐστι
περὶ τούτων γιγνόμενον· εἴς τινα μίαν οἴκησιν
ξυμφορήσαντες, τὸ λεγόμενον, πάντα χρήματα
παρέδομεν ταῖς γυναιξὶ διαταμιεύειν τε καὶ
κερκίδων ἄρχειν καὶ πάσης ταλασίας. ἢ τὸ
τούτων δὴ διὰ μέσου θῶμεν,[1] ὦ Μέγιλλε, τὸ
806 Λακωνικόν ; κόρας μὲν γυμνασίων μετόχους οὔσας
ἅμα καὶ μουσικῆς ζῆν δεῖν, γυναῖκας δὲ ἀργοὺς
μὲν ταλασίας, ἀσκητικὸν δέ τινα βίον καὶ οὐδαμῶς φαῦλον οὐδ' εὐτελῆ διαπλέκειν, θεραπείας
δὲ καὶ ταμιείας αὖ καὶ παιδοτροφίας εἴς τι μέσον
ἀφικνεῖσθαι, τῶν δὲ εἰς τὸν πόλεμον μὴ κοινω-
νούσας, ὥστ' οὐδ' εἴ τίς ποτε διαμάχεσθαι περὶ
πόλεώς τε καὶ παίδων ἀναγκαία τύχη γίγνοιτο,

---

[1] θῶμεν H. Richards : φῶμεν MSS.

rejects our law must try some other method, nor shall we be hereby precluded from asserting in our doctrine that the female sex must share with the male, to the greatest extent possible, both in education and in all else. For in truth we ought to conceive of the matter in this light. Suppose that women do not share with men in the whole of their mode of life, must they not have a different system of their own?

CLIN. They must.

ATH. Then which of the systems now in vogue shall we prescribe in preference to that fellowship which we are now imposing upon them? Shall it be that of the Thracians, and many other tribes, who employ their women in tilling the ground and minding oxen and sheep and toiling just like slaves? Or that which obtains with us and all the people of our district? The way women are treated with us at present is this—we huddle all our goods together, as the saying goes, within four walls, and then hand over the dispensing of them to the women, together with the control of the shuttles and all kinds of wool-work. Or again, shall we prescribe for them, Megillus, that midway system, the Laconian? Must the girls share in gymnastics and music, and the women abstain from wool-work, but weave themselves instead a life that is not trivial at all nor useless, but arduous, advancing as it were halfway in the path of domestic tendance and management and child-nurture, but taking no share in military service; so that, even if it should chance to be necessary for them to fight in defence of their city and their children, they will be unable to handle

B οὔτ' ἂν τόξων, ὥς τινες ᾿Αμαζόνες, οὔτ' ἄλλης
κοινωνῆσαί ποτε βολῆς μετὰ τέχνης δυνάμεναι,
οὐδὲ ἀσπίδα καὶ δόρυ λαβοῦσαι μιμήσασθαι
τὴν θεόν, ὡς πορθουμένης αὐταῖς τῆς πατρίδος
γενναίως ἀντιστάσας φόβον γε, εἰ μηδὲν μεῖζον,
πολεμίοισι δύνασθαι παρασχεῖν ἐν τάξει τινὶ
κατοφθεῖσας ; Σαυρομάτιδας δὲ οὐδ' ἂν τὸ παράπαν τολμήσειαν μιμήσασθαι τοῦτον τὸν τρόπον
διαβιοῦσαι, παρὰ γυναῖκας δὲ αὐτὰς ἄνδρες ἂν αἱ
ἐκείνων γυναῖκες φανεῖεν. ταῦτ' οὖν ὑμῶν τοὺς
νομοθέτας ὁ μὲν βουλόμενος ἐπαινεῖν ἐπαινείτω·
C τὸ δ' ἐμὸν οὐκ ἄλλως ἂν λεχθείη· τέλεον γὰρ καὶ
οὐ διήμισυν [1] δεῖν τὸν νομοθέτην εἶναι, τὸ θῆλυ μὲν
ἀφιέντα τρυφᾶν καὶ ἀναλίσκειν διαίταις ἀτάκτως
χρώμενον, τοῦ δὲ ἄρρενος ἐπιμεληθέντα, τελέως
σχεδὸν εὐδαίμονος ἥμισυ βίου καταλείπειν ἀντὶ
διπλασίου τῇ πόλει.

ΜΕ. Τί δράσομεν, ὦ Κλεινία ; τὸν ξένον
ἐάσομεν τὴν Σπάρτην ἡμῖν οὕτω καταδραμεῖν ;

D ΚΛ. Ναί· δεδομένης γὰρ αὐτῷ παρρησίας
ἐατέον, ἕως ἂν διεξέλθωμεν πάντῃ ἱκανῶς τοὺς
νόμους.

ΜΕ. ᾿Ορθῶς λέγεις.

ΑΘ. Οὐκοῦν τὰ μετὰ ταῦτα ἤδη σχεδὸν ἐμὸν
πειρᾶσθαι φράζειν ;

ΚΛ. Πῶς γὰρ οὔ ;

ΑΘ. Τίς δὴ τρόπος ἀνθρώποις γίγνοιτ' ἂν τοῦ
βίου, οἷσι τὰ μὲν ἀναγκαῖα εἴη κατεσκευασμένα
μέτρια, τὰ δὲ τῶν τεχνῶν ἄλλοις παραδεδομένα,
E γεωργίαι δὲ ἐκδεδομέναι δούλοις ἀπαρχὴν τῶν ἐκ
τῆς γῆς ἀποτελοῦσιν ἱκανὴν ἀνθρώποις ζῶσι

[1] οὐ διήμισυν Schneider : οὐ δι ἥμισυν MSS. : οὐδ' ἥμισυν Zur.

62

with skill either a bow (like the Amazons) or any other missile, nor could they take spear and shield, after the fashion of the Goddess,[1] so as to be able nobly to resist the wasting of their native land, and to strike terror—if nothing more—into the enemy at the sight of them marshalled in battle-array? If they lived in this manner, they certainly would not dare to adopt the fashion of the Sauromatides, whose women would seem like men beside them. So in regard to this matter, let who will commend your Laconian lawgivers: as to my view, it must stand as it is. The lawgiver ought to be whole-hearted, not half-hearted,—letting the female sex indulge in luxury and expense and disorderly ways of life,[2] while supervising the male sex ; for thus he is actually bequeathing to the State the half only, instead of the whole, of a life of complete prosperity.

MEG. What are we to do, Clinias? Shall we allow the Stranger to run down our Sparta in this fashion?

CLIN. Yes: now that we have granted him free speech we must let him be, until we have discussed the laws fully.

MEG. You are right.

ATH. May I, then, endeavour without more delay to proceed with my exposition?

CLIN. By all means.

ATH. What manner of life would men live, supposing that they possessed a moderate supply of all the necessaries, and that they had entrusted all the crafts to other hands, and that their farms were hired out to slaves, and yielded them produce

---

[1] For Athenê as a warrior, cp. 796 B.
[2] Cp. Ar. *Pol.* 1269[b] 12 ff.

κοσμίως· ξυσσίτια δὲ κατεσκευασμένα εἴη χωρὶς
μὲν τὰ τῶν ἀνδρῶν, ἐγγὺς δ' ἐχόμενα τὰ τῶν
αὑτοῖς οἰκείων, παίδων τε ἅμα θηλειῶν καὶ τῶν
μητέρων αὐταῖς· ἄρχουσι δὲ καὶ ἀρχούσαις εἴη
προστεταγμένα λύειν ταῦτα ἑκάστοις τὰ ξυσσίτια
πάντα καθ' ἑκάστην ἡμέραν θεασαμένους καὶ
ἰδόντας τὴν διαγωγὴν τὴν τῶν ξυσσίτων, μετὰ
δὲ ταῦτα σπείσαντας τόν τε ἄρχοντα καὶ τοὺς
807 ἄλλους, οἷς ἂν τυγχάνῃ θεοῖς ἡ τότε νύξ τε καὶ
ἡμέρα καθιερωμένη, κατὰ ταῦτα οὕτως οἴκαδε
πορεύεσθαι; τοῖς δὴ ταύτῃ κεκοσμημένοις ἆρα
οὐδὲν λειπόμενόν ἐστιν ἀναγκαῖόν τε ἔργον καὶ
παντάπασι προσῆκον, ἀλλ' ἐν τρόπῳ βοσκήματος
ἕκαστον πιαινόμενον αὐτῶν δεῖ ζῆν; οὔκουν τό
γε δίκαιόν φαμεν οὐδὲ καλόν, οὐδ' οἷόν τε τὸν
ζῶντα οὕτως ἀτυχῆσαι τοῦ προσήκοντος, προσήκει δὲ ἀργῷ καὶ ῥαθύμως καταπεπιασμένῳ ζῴῳ
B σχεδὸν ὑπ' ἄλλου διαρπασθῆναι ζῴου τῶν σφόδρα
τετρυχωμένων μετὰ ἀνδρίας τε ἅμα καὶ τῶν
πόνων. ταῦτα οὖν δὴ δι' ἀκριβείας μὲν ἱκανῆς
[ὡς καὶ νῦν] εἰ ζητοῖμεν [ἄν],[1] ἴσως οὐκ ἄν ποτε
γένοιτο, μέχριπερ ἂν γυναῖκές τε καὶ παῖδες
οἰκήσεις τε ἴδιαι καὶ ἰδίως ἅπαντ' ᾖ τὰ τοιαῦτα
ἑκάστοις ἡμῶν κατεσκευασμένα· τὰ δὲ μετ' ἐκεῖν'
αὖ δεύτερα τὰ νῦν λεγόμενα εἰ γίγνοιτο ἡμῖν,
C γίγνοιτο ἂν καὶ μάλα μετρίως. ἔργον δὲ δὴ τοῖς
οὕτω ζῶσι φαμεν οὐ τὸ σμικρότατον οὐδὲ τὸ
φαυλότατον λείπεσθαι, μέγιστον δὲ πάντων εἶναι
προστεταγμένον ὑπὸ δικαίου νόμου· τοῦ γὰρ
πᾶσαν τῶν ἄλλων πάντων ἔργων βίου ἀσχολίαν

---

[1] [ὡς καὶ νῦν] and [ἄν] I bracket (νυνὶ for νῦν εἰ Badham,
England : οὐ for εἰ Apelt).

64

enough for their modest needs? Let us further
suppose that they had public mess-rooms—separate
rooms for men, and others close by for their house-
holds, including the girls and their mothers—and
that each of these rooms was in charge of a master
or mistress, to dismiss the company and to watch over
their behaviour daily; and, at the close of the meal,
that the master and all the company poured a libation in honour of those gods to whom that night and
day were dedicated, and so finally retired home.
Supposing them to be thus organised, is there no
necessary work, of a really appropriate kind, left for
them, but must every one of them continue fatten-
ing himself like a beast?[1] That, we assert, is
neither right nor good; nor is it possible for one
who lives thus to miss his due reward; and the due
reward of an idle beast, fattened in sloth, is, as a
rule, to fall a prey to another beast—one of those
which are worn to skin and bone through toil
hardly endured. Now it is probable that if we
look to find this state of leisure fully realised exactly
as described, we shall be disappointed, so long as
women and children and houses remain private, and
all these things are established as the private property
of individuals; but if the second-best State,[2] as now
described, could exist, we might be well content
with it. And, we assert, there does remain for men
living this life a task that is by no means small or
trivial, but rather one that a just law imposes upon
them as the weightiest task of all. For as compared with the life that aims at a Pythian or

---

[1] Cp. Ar. *Pol.* 1334ª 13 ff.

[2] *i.e.* the (Magnesian) State described in the *Laws*, in con-
trast to the Ideal (communistic) State of the *Republic*.

παρασκευάζοντος, τοῦ Πυθιάδος τε καὶ Ὀλυμπι-
άδος νίκης ὀρεγομένου, διπλασίας τε καὶ ἔτι
πολλῷ πλέονος ἀσχολίας ἐστὶ γέμων ὁ περὶ τὴν
τοῦ σώματος πάντως καὶ ψυχῆς εἰς ἀρετὴν[1]
D ἐπιμέλειαν βίος εἰρημένος ὀρθότατα. πάρεργον
γὰρ οὐδὲν δεῖ τῶν ἄλλων ἔργων διακώλυμα
γίγνεσθαι τῶν τῷ σώματι προσηκόντων εἰς ἀπό-
δοσιν πόνων καὶ τροφῆς, οὐδ᾽ αὖ ψυχῇ μαθημάτων τε καὶ ἐθῶν· πᾶσα δὲ νύξ τε καὶ ἡμέρα
σχεδὸν οὐκ ἔστιν ἱκανὴ τοῦτ᾽ αὐτὸ πράττοντι, τὸ
τέλεόν τε καὶ ἱκανὸν αὐτῶν ἐκλαμβάνειν.

Οὕτω δὴ τούτων πεφυκότων τάξιν δεῖ γίγνεσθαι
πᾶσι τοῖς ἐλευθέροις τῆς διατριβῆς περὶ τὸν χρόνον
E ἅπαντα, σχεδὸν ἀρξάμενον ἐξ ἕω μέχρι τῆς ἑτέρας
ἀεὶ ξυνεχῶς ἕω τε καὶ ἡλίου ἀνατολῆς. πολλὰ
μὲν οὖν καὶ πυκνὰ καὶ σμικρὰ λέγων ἄν τις
νομοθέτης ἀσχήμων φαίνοιτο περὶ τῶν κατ᾽ οἰκίαν
διοικήσεων, τά τε ἄλλα καὶ ὅσα νύκτωρ ἀϋπνίας
πέρι πρέπει τοῖς μέλλουσι διὰ τέλους φυλάξειν
πᾶσαν πόλιν ἀκριβῶς. τὸ γὰρ ὅλην διατελεῖν
ἡντινοῦν νύκτα εὕδοντα καὶ ὁντινοῦν τῶν πολιτῶν,
καὶ μὴ φανερὸν εἶναι πᾶσι τοῖς οἰκέταις ἐγει-
808 ρόμενόν τε καὶ ἐξανιστάμενον ἀεὶ πρῶτον, τοῦτο
αἰσχρὸν δεῖ δεδόχθαι πᾶσι καὶ οὐκ ἐλευθέρου, εἴτ᾽
οὖν νόμον εἴτ᾽ ἐπιτήδευμα τὸ τοιοῦτον καλεῖν ἐστι
χρεών. καὶ δὴ καὶ δέσποιναν ἐν οἰκίᾳ ὑπὸ θερα-
παινίδων ἐγείρεσθαί τινων καὶ μὴ πρώτην αὐτὴν
ἐγείρειν τὰς ἄλλας, αἰσχρὸν λέγειν χρὴ πρὸς
αὐτοὺς δοῦλόν τε καὶ δούλην καὶ παῖδα, καὶ εἰ
πως ἦν οἷόν τε, ὅλην καὶ πᾶσαν τὴν οἰκίαν.
ἐγειρομένους δὲ νύκτωρ δεῖ πάντας πράττειν τῶν

[1] ἀρετὴν Ast, England: ἀρετῆς MSS.

Olympian victory and is wholly lacking in leisure
for other tasks, that life we speak of—which most
truly deserves the name of "life"—is doubly (nay,
far more than doubly) lacking in leisure, seeing that
it is occupied with the care of bodily and spiritual
excellence in general. For there ought to be no
other secondary task to hinder the work of supplying
the body with its proper exercise and nourishment,
or the soul with learning and moral training: nay,
every night and day is not sufficient for the man who
is occupied therein to win from them their fruit in
full and ample measure.

So this being nature's law, a programme must be
framed for all the freeborn men, prescribing how
they shall pass their time continuously, from dawn
to dawn and sunrise on each successive day. It
would be undignified for a lawgiver to mention a
host of petty matters connected with the domestic
arrangements—such as, in particular, the rules about
that wakefulness at night which is proper for men
who propose to guard a whole State adequately and
continuously. That any citizen, indeed, should spend
the whole of any night in sleep, instead of setting an
example to his household by being himself always
the first to awaken and rise—such a practice must be
counted by all a shameful one, unworthy of a free
man, whether it be called a custom or a law. Moreover, that the mistress of a house should be awakened
by maids, instead of being herself the first to wake up
all the others—this is a shameful practice; and that
it is so all the servants must declare to one another
—bondman and bondmaid and boy, yea, even (were
it possible) every stone in the house. And, when
awake by night, they must certainly transact a large

B τε πολιτικῶν μέρη πολλὰ καὶ τῶν οἰκονομικῶν, ἄρχοντας μὲν κατὰ πόλιν, δεσποίνας δὲ καὶ δεσπότας ἐν ἰδίαις οἰκίαις. ὕπνος γὰρ δὴ πολὺς οὔτε τοῖς σώμασιν οὔτε ταῖς ψυχαῖς ἡμῶν οὐδ' αὖ ταῖς πράξεσι ταῖς περὶ ταῦτα πάντα ἁρμόττων ἐστὶ κατὰ φύσιν. καθεύδων γὰρ οὐδεὶς οὐδενὸς ἄξιος, οὐδὲν μᾶλλον τοῦ μὴ ζῶντος· ἀλλ' ὅστις τοῦ ζῆν ἡμῶν καὶ τοῦ φρονεῖν μάλιστά ἐστι κηδεμών, ἐγρήγορε χρόνον ὡς πλεῖστον, τὸ πρὸς
C ὑγίειαν αὐτοῦ μόνον φυλάττων χρήσιμον· ἔστι δ' οὐ πολύ, καλῶς εἰς ἔθος ἰόν. ἐγρηγορότες δὲ ἄρχοντες ἐν πόλεσι νύκτωρ φοβεροὶ μὲν κακοῖς πολεμίοις τε ἅμα καὶ πολίταις, ἀγαστοὶ δὲ καὶ τίμιοι τοῖς δικαίοις τε καὶ σώφροσιν, ὠφέλιμοι δὲ αὐτοῖς τε καὶ ξυμπάσῃ τῇ πόλει.

Νὺξ μὲν δὴ διαγομένη τοιαύτη τις πρὸς πᾶσι τοῖς εἰρημένοις ἀνδρίαν ἄν τινα προσπαρέχοιτο ταῖς ψυχαῖς ἑκάστων τῶν ἐν ταῖς πόλεσιν· ἡμέρας δὲ ὄρθρου τε ἐπανιόντων παῖδας μὲν πρὸς
D διδασκάλους που τρέπεσθαι χρεών· ἄνευ ποιμένος δὲ οὔτε πρόβατα οὔτ' ἄλλο <ἄνουν>[1] οὐδέν πω βιωτέον, οὐδὲ δὴ παῖδας ἄνευ τινῶν παιδαγωγῶν οὐδὲ δούλους ἄνευ δεσποτῶν. ὁ δὲ παῖς πάντων θηρίων ἐστὶ δυσμεταχειριστότατον· ὅσῳ γὰρ μάλιστα ἔχει πηγὴν τοῦ φρονεῖν μήπω κατηρτυμένην, ἐπίβουλον καὶ δριμὺ καὶ ὑβριστότατον θηρίων γίγνεται. διὸ δὴ πολλοῖς αὐτὸ οἷον
E χαλινοῖς τισὶ δεῖ δεσμεύειν, πρῶτον μέν, τροφῶν καὶ μητέρων ὅταν ἀπαλλάττηται, παιδαγωγοῖς παιδίας καὶ νηπιότητος χάριν, ἔτι δ' αὖ τοῖς διδάσκουσι καὶ ὁτιοῦν καὶ μαθήμασιν, ὡς ἐλεύ-

---

[1] <ἄνουν> I add (πῶν for πω England).

share of business, both political and economical, the magistrates in the city, and the masters and mistresses in their own houses. For much sleep is not naturally suitable either to our bodies or souls, nor yet to employment on any such matters. For when asleep no man is worth anything, any more than if he were dead: on the contrary, every one of us who cares most greatly for life and thought keeps awake as long as possible, only reserving so much time for sleep as his health requires—and that is but little, once the habit is well formed. And rulers that are watchful by night in cities are a terror to evil-doers, be they citizens or enemies, but objects of respect and admiration to the just and temperate ; and they confer benefit alike on themselves and on the whole State.

The night, if spent in this way, will—in addition to all the other benefits described—lend greater fortitude to the souls of all who reside in these States. With the return of daylight the children should go to their teachers ; for just as no sheep or other witless creature ought to exist without a herdsman, so children cannot live without a tutor, nor slaves without a master. And, of all wild creatures, the child is the most intractable ; for in so far as it, above all others, possesses a fount of reason that is as yet uncurbed, it is a treacherous, sly and most insolent creature. Wherefore the child must be strapped up, as it were, with many bridles —first, when he leaves the care of nurse and mother, with tutors, to guide his childish ignorance, and after that with teachers of all sorts of subjects and lessons, treating him as becomes a freeborn child.

PLATO

θερον· ὡς δ᾽ αὖ δοῦλον, πᾶς ὁ προστυγχάνων τῶν
ἐλευθέρων ἀνδρῶν κολαζέτω τόν τε παῖδα αὐτὸν
καὶ τὸν παιδαγωγὸν καὶ τὸν διδάσκαλον, ἐὰν
ἐξαμαρτάνῃ τίς τι τούτων. ἂν δ᾽ αὖ προστυγχάνων
τις μὴ κολάζῃ τῇ δίκῃ, ὀνείδει μὲν ἐνεχέσθω
πρῶτον τῷ μεγίστῳ, ὁ δὲ τῶν νομοφυλάκων ἐπὶ
809 τὴν τῶν παίδων ἀρχὴν ᾑρημένος ἐπισκοπείτω
τοῦτον τὸν ἐντυγχάνοντα οἷς λέγομεν καὶ μὴ
κολάζοντα δέον κολάζειν, ἢ κολάζοντα μὴ κατὰ
τρόπον· βλέπων δὲ ἡμῖν ὀξὺ καὶ διαφερόντως
ἐπιμελούμενος τῆς τῶν παίδων τροφῆς κατευ-
θυνέτω τὰς φύσεις αὐτῶν, ἀεὶ τρέπων πρὸς
τἀγαθὸν κατὰ νόμους.

Τοῦτον δὲ αὐτὸν αὖ πῶς ἂν ἡμῖν ὁ νόμος αὐτὸς
παιδεύσειεν ἱκανῶς; νῦν μὲν γὰρ δὴ εἴρηκεν οὐδέν
B πω σαφὲς οὐδὲ ἱκανόν, ἀλλὰ τὰ μέν, τὰ δ᾽ οὔ· δεῖ
δὲ εἰς δύναμιν μηδὲν παραλείπειν αὐτῷ, πάντα δὲ
λόγον ἀφερμηνεύειν, ἵνα οὗτος τοῖς ἄλλοις μηνυτής
τε ἅμα καὶ τροφεὺς γίγνηται. τὰ μὲν οὖν δὴ χορείας
πέρι μελῶν τε καὶ ὀρχήσεως ἐρρήθη, τίνα τύπον
ἔχοντα ἐκλεκτέα τέ ἐστι καὶ ἐπανορθωτέα καὶ
καθιερωτέα· τὰ δὲ ἐν γράμμασι μὲν ὄντα, ἄνευ δὲ
μέτρων, ποῖα καὶ τίνα μεταχειρίζεσθαι χρή σοι
τρόπον, ὦ ἄριστε τῶν παίδων ἐπιμελητά, τοὺς ὑπὸ
C σοῦ τρεφομένους, οὐκ εἰρήκαμεν. καί τοι τὰ μὲν
περὶ τὸν πόλεμον, ἃ δεῖ μανθάνειν τε αὐτοὺς καὶ

---

[1] The child is of two-fold nature,—semi-rational; as such
he needs a double "bridle," that of instruction (proper to
free men), and that of chastisement (proper to slaves).

70

On the other hand, he must be treated as a slave; [1] and any free man that meets him shall punish both the child himself and his tutor or teacher, if any of them does wrong. And if anyone thus meets them and fails to punish them duly, he shall, in the first place, be liable to the deepest degradation; and the Law-warden who is chosen as president over the children shall keep his eye on the man who has met with the wrong-doings mentioned and has failed either to inflict the needed punishment at all, or else to inflict it rightly. Moreover, this Law-warden shall exercise special supervision, with a keen eye, over the rearing of the children, to keep their growing natures in the straight way, by turning them always towards goodness, as the laws direct.

But how is the law itself to give an adequate education to this Law-warden of ours? For, up to the present, the law has not as yet made any clear or adequate statement: it has mentioned some things, but omitted others. But in dealing with this warden it must omit nothing, but fully expound every ordinance that he may be both expositor and nurturer to the rest. Matters of choristry of tunes and dancing, and what types are to be selected, remodelled, and consecrated—all this has already been dealt with; [2] but with regard to the kind of literature that is written but without metre we have never put the question—O excellent supervisor of children, of what sort ought this prose to be, and in what fashion are your charges to deal with it? You know from our discourse [3] what are the military exercises they ought to learn and to practise, but the matters that

[2] 799 A ff., 802 A ff.
[3] Cp. 796 A ff.

71

μελετᾷν, ἔχεις τῷ λόγῳ, τὰ δὲ περὶ τὰ γράμματα
πρῶτον καὶ δεύτερον λύρας πέρι καὶ λογισμῶν, ὧν
ἔφαμεν δεῖν ὅσα τε πρὸς πόλεμον καὶ οἰκονομίαν
καὶ τὴν κατὰ πόλιν διοίκησιν χρῆναι ἑκάστους
λαβεῖν, καὶ πρὸς τὰ αὐτὰ ταῦτα ἔτι τὰ χρήσιμα
τῶν ἐν ταῖς περιόδοις τῶν θείων, ἄστρων τε πέρι
καὶ ἡλίου καὶ σελήνης, ὅσα διοικεῖν ἀναγκαῖόν ἐστι
D περὶ ταῦτα πάσῃ πόλει.   τίνων δὴ πέρι λέγομεν ;
ἡμερῶν τάξεως εἰς μηνῶν περιόδους καὶ μηνῶν εἰς
ἕκαστον τὸν ἐνιαυτόν, ἵνα ὧραι καὶ θυσίαι καὶ
ἑορταὶ τὰ προσήκοντ᾽ ἀπολαμβάνουσαι ἑαυταῖς
ἕκασται τῷ κατὰ φύσιν ἄγεσθαι, ζῶσαν τὴν πόλιν
καὶ ἐγρηγορυῖαν παρεχόμεναι, θεοῖς μὲν τὰς τιμὰς
ἀποδιδῶσι, τοὺς δὲ ἀνθρώπους περὶ αὐτὰ μᾶλλον
ἔμφρονας ἀπεργάζωνται.   ταῦτα οὔπω σοι πάντα
ἱκανῶς, ὦ φίλε, παρὰ τοῦ νομοθέτου διείρηται.
E προσέχε δὴ τὸν νοῦν τοῖς μετὰ ταῦτα μέλλουσι
ῥηθήσεσθαι.   γραμμάτων εἴπομεν ὡς οὐχ ἱκανῶς
ἔχεις πέρι τὸ πρῶτον, ἐπικαλοῦντές τί τῇ λέξει ;
τόδε, ὡς οὔπω διείρηκέ σοι πότερον εἰς ἀκρίβειαν
τοῦ μαθήματος ἰτέον τὸν μέλλοντα πολίτην
ἔσεσθαι μέτριον ἢ τὸ παράπαν οὐδὲ προσοιστέον·
ὡς δ᾽ αὔτως καὶ περὶ λύραν.   προσοιστέον μέντοι
νῦν φαμέν.   εἰς μὲν γράμματα παιδὶ δεκετεῖ
810 σχεδὸν ἐνιαυτοὶ τρεῖς, λύρας δὲ ἅψασθαι τρία
μὲν ἔτη καὶ δέκα γεγονόσιν ἄρχεσθαι μέτριος ὁ
χρόνος, ἐμμεῖναι δὲ ἕτερα τρία.   καὶ μήτε πλείω
τούτων μήτ᾽ ἐλάττω πατρὶ μηδ᾽ αὑτῷ, φιλομα-
θοῦντι μηδὲ μισοῦντι, περὶ ταῦτα ἐξέστω μείζω
72

have not as yet, my friend, been fully declared to you by the lawgiver are these—first, literature, next, lyre-playing; also arithmetic, of which I said that there ought to be as much as everyone needs to learn for purposes of war, house-management and civic administration; together with what it is useful for these same purposes to learn about the courses of the heavenly bodies—stars and sun and moon—in so far as every State is obliged to take them into account. What I allude to is this—the arranging of days into monthly periods, and of months into a year, in each instance, so that the seasons, with their respective sacrifices and feasts, may each be assigned its due position by being held as nature dictates, and that thus they may create fresh liveliness and alertness in the State, and may pay their due honours to the gods, and may render the citizens more intelligent about these matters. These points, my friend, have not all as yet been explained to you sufficiently by the lawgiver. Now attend carefully to what is next to be said. In the first place, you are, as we said, insufficiently instructed as yet concerning letters. The point we complain of is this—that the law has not yet told you clearly whether the man who is to be a good citizen must pursue this study with precision, or neglect it altogether; and so likewise with regard to the lyre. That he must not neglect them we now affirm. For the study of letters, about three years is a reasonable period for a child of ten years old; and for lyre-playing, he should begin at thirteen and continue at it for three years. And whether he likes or dislikes the study, neither the child nor his father shall be permitted either to cut short or to prolong the years

73

μηδ' ἐλάττω διατριβὴν ποιεῖσθαι παράνομον· ὁ
δὲ μὴ πειθόμενος ἄτιμος τῶν παιδείων ἔστω
τιμῶν, ἃς ὀλίγον ὕστερον ῥητέον. μανθάνειν δὲ
ἐν τούτοις τοῖς χρόνοις δὴ τί ποτε δεῖ τοὺς νέους
καὶ διδάσκειν αὖ τοὺς διδασκάλους, τοῦτο αὐτὸς[1]
B πρῶτον μάνθανε. γράμματα μὲν τοίνυν χρὴ τὸ
μέχρι τοῦ γράψαι τε καὶ ἀναγνῶναι δυνατὸν
εἶναι διαπονεῖν· πρὸς τάχος δὲ ἢ κάλλος ἀπηκρι-
βῶσθαί τισιν οἷς μὴ φύσις ἐπέσπευσεν ἐν τοῖς
τεταγμένοις ἔτεσι χαίρειν ἐᾶν. πρὸς δὲ δὴ
μαθήματα ἄλυρα ποιητῶν κείμενα ἐν γράμμασι,
τοῖς μὲν μετὰ μέτρων, τοῖς δ' ἄνευ ῥυθμῶν
τμημάτων, ἃ δὴ συγγράμματα κατὰ λόγον εἰρημένα μόνον, τητώμενα ῥυθμοῦ τε καὶ ἁρμονίας,
C σφαλερὰ γράμμαθ' ἡμῖν ἐστὶ παρά τινων τῶν
πολλῶν τοιούτων ἀνθρώπων καταλελειμμένα·
οἷς, ὦ πάντων βέλτιστοι νομοφύλακες, τί χρή-
σεσθε; ἢ τί ποθ' ὑμῖν ὁ νομοθέτης χρῆσθαι
προστάξας ὀρθῶς ἂν τάξειε; καὶ μάλα ἀπορήσειν
αὐτὸν προσδοκῶ.

ΚΛ. Τί ποτε τοῦτ', ὦ ξένε, φαίνει πρὸς σαυτὸν
ὄντως ἠπορηκὼς λέγειν;

ΑΘ. Ὀρθῶς ὑπέλαβες, ὦ Κλεινία. πρὸς δὲ
δὴ κοινωνοὺς ὑμᾶς ὄντας περὶ νόμων ἀνάγκη τό
τε φαινόμενον εὔπορον καὶ τὸ μὴ φράζειν.

D ΚΛ. Τί οὖν; τί περὶ τούτων νῦν καὶ ποῖόν τι
πεπονθὼς λέγεις;

ΑΘ. Ἐρῶ δή· στόμασι γὰρ πολλάκις μυρίοις
ἐναντία λέγειν οὐδαμῶς εὔπορον.

ΚΛ. Τί δαί; σμικρὰ καὶ ὀλίγα δοκεῖ σοι τὰ

---

[1] αὐτὸς Ritter; αὐτὸ MSS.

74

of study contrary to the law; and anyone who disobeys shall be disqualified for the school honours which we shall mention presently.[1] And, during these periods, what are the subjects which the children must learn and the teachers teach—this you yourself must learn first. They must work at letters sufficiently to be able to read and write. But superior speed or beauty of handwriting need not be required in the case of those whose progress within the appointed period is too slow. With regard to lessons in reading, there are written compositions not set to music, whether in metre or without rhythmical divisions—compositions merely uttered in prose, void of rhythm and harmony; and some of the many composers of this sort have bequeathed to us writings of a dangerous character. How will you deal with these, O my most excellent Law-wardens? Or what method of dealing with them will the lawgiver rightly ordain? He will be vastly perplexed, I verily believe.

CLIN. What does this mean, Stranger? Evidently you are addressing yourself, and are really perplexed.

ATH. You are right in your supposition, Clinias. As you are my partners in this investigation of laws, I am bound to explain to you both what seems easy and what hard.

CLIN. Well, what is it about them that you are now alluding to, and what has come over you?

ATH. I will tell you: it is no easy matter to gainsay tens of thousands of tongues.

CLIN. Come now,—do you believe that the points

---

[1] Cp. 832 E ff.

ἔμπροσθεν ἡμῖν εἰρημένα περὶ νόμων κεῖσθαι τοῖς
πολλοῖς ὑπεναντία ;

ΑΘ. Καὶ μάλα ἀληθὲς τοῦτό γε λέγεις· κελεύεις
γὰρ δή με, ὡς ἐμοὶ φαίνεται, τῆς αὐτῆς ὁδοῦ
ἐχθοδοποῦ γεγονυίας πολλοῖς, ἴσως δ᾽ οὐκ ἐλάτ-
Ε τοσιν ἑτέροις προσφιλοῦς, εἰ δὲ ἐλάττοσιν, οὔκουν
χείροσί γε, μεθ᾽ ὧν διακελεύει με παρακινδυ-
νεύοντά τε καὶ θαρροῦντα τὴν νῦν ἐκ τῶν
παρόντων λόγων τετμημένην ὁδὸν τῆς νομοθεσίας
πορεύεσθαι μηδὲν ἀνιέντα.

ΚΛ. Τί μήν ;

ΑΘ. Οὐ τοίνυν ἀνίημι. λέγω μὴν ὅτι ποιηταί
τε ἡμῖν εἰσί τινες ἐπῶν ἑξαμέτρων πάμπολλοι
καὶ τριμέτρων καὶ πάντων δὴ τῶν λεγομένων
μέτρων, οἱ μὲν ἐπὶ σπουδήν, οἱ δ᾽ ἐπὶ γέλωτα
ὡρμηκότες, ἐν οἷς φασὶ δεῖν οἱ πολλάκις μυρίοι
τοὺς ὀρθῶς παιδευομένους τῶν νέων τρέφειν καὶ
διακορεῖς ποιεῖν, πολυηκόους τ᾽ ἐν ταῖς ἀναγνώσεσι
811 ποιοῦντας καὶ πολυμαθεῖς, ὅλους ποιητὰς ἐκμαν-
θάνοντας· οἱ δὲ ἐκ πάντων κεφάλαια ἐκλέξαντες
καί τινας ὅλας ῥήσεις εἰς ταὐτὸ ξυναγαγόντες
ἐκμανθάνειν φασὶ δεῖν εἰς μνήμην τιθεμένους, εἰ
μέλλει τις ἀγαθὸς ἡμῖν καὶ σοφὸς ἐκ πολυπειρίας
καὶ πολυμαθίας γενέσθαι. τούτοις δὴ σὺ κελεύεις
ἐμὲ τὰ νῦν παρρησιαζόμενον ἀποφαίνεσθαι τί τε
καλῶς λέγουσι καὶ τί μή ;

ΚΛ. Πῶς γὰρ οὔ ;

ΑΘ. Τί δή ποτ᾽ ἂν οὖν περὶ ἁπάντων τούτων
Β ἑνὶ λόγῳ φράζων εἴποιμ᾽ ἂν ἱκανόν ; οἶμαι μὲν

---

[1] Cp. Heraclitus's saying (*Frag.* 16): πολυμαθίη νόον οὐ
διδάσκει; and the contempt shown for the versatile smatterer

in which our previous conclusions about laws con-
tradicted ordinary opinion were few and trifling ?

ATH. Your observation is most just. I take it
that you are bidding me, now that the path which
is abhorrent to many is attractive to others possibly
not less numerous (or if less numerous, certainly not
less competent),—you are, I say, bidding me adven-
ture myself with the latter company and proceed
boldly along the path of legislation marked out in
our present discourse, without flinching.

CLIN. Certainly.

ATH. Then I will not flinch. I verily affirm that
we have composers of verses innumerable—hexa-
meters, trimeters, and every metre you could mention,—some of whom aim at the serious, others at the
comic ; on whose writings, as we are told by our tens
of thousands of people, we ought to rear and soak the
young, if we are to give them a correct education,
making them, by means of recitations, lengthy
listeners and large learners, who learn off whole
poets by heart. Others there are who compile select
summaries of all the poets, and piece together whole
passages, telling us that a boy must commit these
to memory and learn them off if we are to have him
turn out good and wise as a result of a wide and
varied range of instruction.[1] Would you have me
now state frankly to these poets what is wrong about
their declarations and what right ?

CLIN. Of course.

ATH. What single statement can I make about
all these people that will be adequate ? This,

in *Phaedr.* 275 A (πολυήκοοι . . . δοξόσοφοι γεγονότες ἀντὶ
σοφῶι).

τὸ τοιόνδε σχεδόν, ὃ καὶ πᾶς ἄν μοι συγχωρήσειε,
πολλὰ μὲν ἕκαστον τούτων εἰρηκέναι καλῶς, πολλὰ
δὲ καὶ τοὐναντίον. εἰ δ᾽ οὕτω τοῦτ᾽ ἔχει, κίνδυνόν
φημι εἶναι φέρουσαν τοῖς παισὶ τὴν πολυμαθίαν.

ΚΛ. Πῶς οὖν καὶ τί παραινοίης ἂν τῷ νομοφύλακι ;

ΑΘ. Τοῦ πέρι λέγεις ;

ΚΛ. Τοῦ πρὸς τί παράδειγμά ποτε ἀποβλέψας
ἂν τὸ μὲν ἐῴη πάντας μανθάνειν τοὺς νέους, τὸ
C δ᾽ ἀποκωλύοι. λέγε καὶ μηδὲν ἀπόκνει λέγων.

ΑΘ. Ὦ 'γαθὲ Κλεινία, κινδυνεύω κατά γέ τινα
τρόπον εὐτυχηκέναι.

ΚΛ. Τοῦ δὴ πέρι ;

ΑΘ. Τοῦ μὴ παντάπασι παραδείγματος ἀπο-
ρεῖν. νῦν γὰρ ἀποβλέψας πρὸς τοὺς λόγους οὓς
ἐξ ἕω μέχρι δεῦρο δὴ διεληλύθαμεν ἡμεῖς, ὡς μὲν
ἐμοὶ φαινόμεθα οὐκ ἄνευ τινὸς ἐπιπνοίας θεῶν,
ἔδοξαν δ᾽ οὖν μοι παντάπασι ποιήσει τινὶ προσο-
μοίως εἰρῆσθαι. καί μοι ἴσως οὐδὲν θαυμαστὸν
D πάθος ἐπῆλθε, λόγους οἰκείους οἷον ἀθρόους ἐπι-
βλέψαντι μάλα ἡσθῆναι· τῶν γὰρ δὴ πλείστων
λόγων, οὓς ἐν ποιήμασιν ἢ χύδην οὕτως εἰρημένους
μεμάθηκα καὶ ἀκήκοα, πάντων μοι μετριώτατοί
γε εἶναι κατεφάνησαν καὶ προσήκοντες τὰ μάλιστα
ἀκούειν νέοις. τῷ δὴ νομοφύλακί τε καὶ παιδευτῇ
παράδειγμα οὐκ ἂν ἔχοιμι, ὡς οἶμαι, τούτου
βέλτιον φράζειν, ἢ ταῦτά τε διδάσκειν παρακε-
λεύεσθαι τοῖσι διδασκάλοις τοὺς παῖδας, τά τε
E τούτων ἐχόμενα καὶ ὅμοια, ἂν ἄρα που περι-
τυγχάνῃ ποιητῶν τε ποιήματα διεξιὼν καὶ γεγραμ-

perhaps,—in which everyone will agree with me,—that every poet has uttered much that is well, and much also that is ill; and this being so, I affirm that a wide range of learning involves danger to children.

CLIN. What advice then would you give the Law-warden?

ATH. About what?

CLIN. About the pattern by which he should be guided in respect of the particular subjects which he permits or forbids all the children to learn. Tell us, and without scruple.

ATH. My good Clinias, I have had, it would seem, a stroke of luck.

CLIN. How so?

ATH. In the fact that I am not wholly at a loss for a pattern. For in looking back now at the discussions which we have been pursuing from dawn up to this present hour—and that, as I fancy, not without some guidance from Heaven—it appeared to me that they were framed exactly like a poem. And it was not surprising, perhaps, that there came over me a feeling of intense delight when I gazed thus on our discourses all marshalled, as it were, in close array; for of all the many discourses which I have listened to or learnt about, whether in poems or in a loose flood of speech like ours, they struck me as being not only the most adequate, but also the most suitable for the ears of the young. No-where, I think, could I find a better pattern than this to put before the Law-warden who is educator, that he may charge the teachers to teach the children these discourses of ours, and such as resemble and accord with these; and if it should be that in his search he should light on poems of

μένα καταλογάδην ἢ καὶ ψιλῶς οὕτως ἄνευ τοῦ
γεγράφθαι λεγόμενα, ἀδελφά που τούτων τῶν
λόγων, μὴ μεθιέναι τρόπῳ μηδενί, γράφεσθαι δέ·
καὶ πρῶτον μὲν τοὺς διδασκάλους αὐτοὺς ἀναγκάζειν μανθάνειν καὶ ἐπαινεῖν, οὓς δ' ἂν μὴ ἀρέσκῃ
τῶν διδασκάλων, μὴ χρῆσθαι τούτοις συνεργοῖς,
οὓς δ' ἂν τῷ ἐπαίνῳ συμψήφους ἔχῃ, τούτοις
χρώμενον τοὺς νέους αὐτοῖς παραδιδόναι διδάσκειν
812 τε καὶ παιδεύειν· οὗτός μοι μῦθος ἐνταῦθα καὶ
οὕτω τελευτάτω, περὶ γραμματιστῶν τε εἰρημένος
ἅμα καὶ γραμμάτων.

ΚΛ. Κατὰ μὲν τὴν ὑπόθεσιν, ὦ ξένε, ἔμοιγε οὐ
φαινόμεθα ἐκτὸς πορεύεσθαι τῶν ὑποτεθέντων
λόγων· εἰ δὲ τὸ ὅλον κατορθοῦμεν ἢ μή, χαλεπὸν
ἴσως διισχυρίζεσθαι.

ΑΘ. Τότε γάρ, ὦ Κλεινία, τοῦτό γ' αὐτὸ ἔσται
καταφανέστερον, ὡς εἰκός, ὅταν, ὃ πολλάκις
εἰρήκαμεν, ἐπὶ τέλος ἀφικώμεθα πάσης τῆς δι-
εξόδου περὶ νόμων.

Β ΚΛ. Ὀρθῶς.

ΑΘ. Ἆρ' οὖν οὐ μετὰ τὸν γραμματιστὴν ὁ
κιθαριστὴς ἡμῖν προσρητέος ;

ΚΛ. Τί μήν ;

ΑΘ. Τοῖς κιθαρισταῖς μὲν τοίνυν ἡμᾶς δοκῶ
τῶν ἔμπροσθεν λόγων ἀναμνησθέντας τὸ προσῆκον
νεῖμαι τῆς τε διδασκαλίας ἅμα καὶ πάσης τῆς
περὶ τὰ τοιαῦτα παιδεύσεως.

ΚΛ. Ποίων δὴ πέρι λέγεις ;

ΑΘ. Ἔφαμεν, οἶμαι, τοὺς τοῦ Διονύσου τοὺς
ἑξηκοντούτας ᾠδοὺς διαφερόντως εὐαισθήτους δεῖν
C γεγονέναι περί τε τοὺς ῥυθμοὺς καὶ τὰς τῶν ἁρ-
μονιῶν συστάσεις, ἵνα τὴν τῶν μελῶν μίμησιν τὴν

composers, or prose-writings, or merely verbal and unwritten discourses, akin to these of ours, he must in no wise let them go, but get them written down. In the first place, he must compel the teachers themselves to learn these discourses, and to praise them, and if any of the teachers fail to approve of them, he must not employ them as colleagues; only those who agree with his praise of the discourses should he employ, and entrust to them the teaching and training of the youth. Here and herewith let me end my homily concerning writing-masters and writings.

CLIN. Judged by our original intention, Stranger, I certainly do not think that we have diverged from the line of argument we intended; but about the matter as a whole it is hard, no doubt, to be sure whether or not we are right.

ATH. That, Clinias, (as we have often said) will probably become clearer of itself,[1] when we arrive at the end of our whole exposition concerning laws.

CLIN. Very true.

ATH. After the writing-master, must we not address the lyre-master next?

CLIN. Certainly.

ATH. When assigning to the lyre-masters their proper duties in regard to the teaching and general training in these subjects, we must, as I think, bear in mind our previous declarations.[2]

CLIN. Declarations about what?

ATH. We said, I fancy, that the sixty-year-old singers of hymns to Dionysus ought to be exceptionally keen of perception regarding rhythms and harmonic compositions, in order that when dealing

---

[1] Cp. 799 D.   [2] 664 E ff., 670 A f.

εὖ καὶ τὴν κακῶς μεμιμημένην, ἐν τοῖς παθήμασιν
ὅταν ψυχὴ γίγνηται, τά τε τῆς ἀγαθῆς ὁμοιώματα
καὶ τὰ τῆς ἐναντίας ἐκλέξασθαι δυνατὸς ὢν τις τὰ
μὲν ἀποβάλλῃ, τὰ δὲ προφέρων εἰς μέσον ὑμνῇ
καὶ ἐπᾴδῃ ταῖς τῶν νέων ψυχαῖς, προκαλούμενος
ἑκάστους εἰς ἀρετῆς ἕπεσθαι κτῆσιν συνακολου-
θοῦντας διὰ τῶν μιμήσεων.

ΚΛ. Ἀληθέστατα λέγεις.

D   ΑΘ. Τούτων τοίνυν δεῖ χάριν τοῖς φθόγγοις τῆς
λύρας προσχρῆσθαι, σαφηνείας ἕνεκα τῶν χορδῶν,
τόν τε κιθαριστὴν καὶ τὸν παιδευόμενον, ἀποδιδόντας πρόσχορδα τὰ φθέγματα τοῖς φθέγμασι· τὴν
δ' ἑτεροφωνίαν καὶ ποικιλίαν τῆς λύρας, ἄλλα μὲν
μέλη τῶν χορδῶν ἱεισῶν, ἄλλα δὲ τοῦ τὴν μελῳδίαν ξυνθέντος ποιητοῦ, καὶ δὴ καὶ πυκνότητα
μάνοτητι καὶ τάχος βραδυτῆτι καὶ ὀξύτητα βαρύ-
τητι ξύμφωνον [καὶ ἀντίφωνον]¹ παρεχομένους,
E καὶ τῶν ῥυθμῶν ὡσαύτως παντοδαπὰ ποικίλματα
προσαρμόττοντας τοῖσι φθόγγοις τῆς λύρας,
πάντα οὖν τὰ τοιαῦτα μὴ προσφέρειν τοῖς μέλλουσιν ἐν τρισὶν ἔτεσι τὸ τῆς μουσικῆς χρήσιμον
ἐκλήψεσθαι διὰ τάχους. τὰ γὰρ ἐναντία ἄλληλα
ταράττοντα δυσμαθίαν παρέχει, δεῖ δὲ ὅτι μάλιστα
εὐμαθεῖς εἶναι τοὺς νέους· τὰ γὰρ ἀναγκαῖα οὐ
σμικρὰ οὐδ' ὀλίγα αὐτοῖς ἐστι προστεταγμένα
μαθήματα, δείξει δὲ αὐτὰ προϊὼν ὁ λόγος ἅμα τῷ
χρόνῳ. ἀλλὰ ταῦτα μὲν οὕτω περὶ τῆς μουσικῆς
ἡμῖν ὁ παιδευτὴς ἐπιμελείσθω· τὰ δὲ μελῶν αὐτῶν

---

¹ [καὶ ἀντίφωνον] bracketed by England.

¹ i.e. the notes of the instrument must be in accord with
those of the singer's voice. "The tune, as composed by the

with musical representations of a good kind or a
bad, by which the soul is emotionally affected, they
may be able to pick out the reproductions of the good
kind and of the bad, and having rejected the latter,
may produce the other in public, and charm the souls
of the children by singing them, and so challenge
them all to accompany them in acquiring virtue by
means of these representations.

CLIN. Very true.

ATH. So, to attain this object, both the lyre-
master and his pupil must use the notes of the lyre,
because of the distinctness of its strings, assigning
to the notes of the song notes in tune with them ; [1]
but as to divergence of sound and variety in the
notes of the harp, when the strings sound one tune
and the composer of the melody another, or when
there results a combination of low and high notes,
of slow and quick time, of sharp and grave, and all
sorts of rhythmical variations are adapted to the
notes of the lyre,—no such complications should be
employed in dealing with pupils who have to absorb
quickly, within three years, the useful elements of
music. For the jarring of opposites with one another
impedes easy learning ; and the young should above
all things learn easily, since the necessary lessons
imposed upon them are neither few nor small,—
which lessons our discourse will indicate in time as
it proceeds. So let our educator regulate these
matters in the manner stated. As regards the

poet, is supposed to have comparatively few notes, to be in
slowish time, and low down in the register ; whereas the
complicated *variation*, which he is condemning, has many
notes, is in quick time, and high up in the register."
(England.)

PLATO

αὖ καὶ ῥημάτων, οἷα τοὺς χοροδιδασκάλους καὶ ἃ
813 δεῖ διδάσκειν, καὶ ταῦτα ἡμῖν ἐν τοῖς πρόσθεν
διείρηται πάντα, ἃ δὴ καθιερωθέντα ἔφαμεν δεῖν,
ταῖς ἑορταῖς ἕκαστα ἁρμόττοντα, ἡδονὴν εὐτυχῆ
ταῖς πόλεσι παραδιδόντα ὠφελεῖν.

ΚΛ. Ἀληθῆ καὶ ταῦτα διείρηκας.

ΑΘ. Ἀληθέστατα τοίνυν. καὶ ταῦθ᾽ ἡμῖν παραλαβὼν ὁ περὶ τὴν Μοῦσαν ἄρχων αἱρεθεὶς
ἐπιμελείσθω μετὰ τύχης εὐμενοῦς, ἡμεῖς δὲ
ὀρχήσεώς τε πέρι καὶ ὅλης τῆς περὶ τὸ σῶμα
γυμναστικῆς πρὸς τοῖς ἔμπροσθεν εἰρημένοις ἀπο-
Β δῶμεν· καθάπερ μουσικῆς τὸ διδασκαλικὸν ὑπό-
λοιπον ὂν ἀπέδομεν, ὡσαύτως ποιῶμεν κατὰ[1]
γυμναστικῆς. τοὺς γὰρ παῖδάς τε καὶ τὰς παῖδας
ὀρχεῖσθαι δὴ δεῖ καὶ γυμνάζεσθαι μανθάνειν. ἦ
γάρ;

ΚΛ. Ναί.

ΑΘ. Τοῖς μὲν τοίνυν παισὶν ὀρχησταί, ταῖς δὲ
ὀρχηστρίδες ἂν εἶεν πρὸς τὸ διαπονεῖν οὐκ ἀνεπι-
τηδειότερον.

ΚΛ. Ἔστω δὴ ταύτῃ.

ΑΘ. Πάλιν δὴ τὸν τὰ πλεῖστα ἕξοντα πράγ-
C ματα καλῶμεν, τὸν τῶν παίδων ἐπιμελητήν, ὃς
τῶν τε περὶ μουσικὴν τῶν τε περὶ γυμναστικὴν
ἐπιμελούμενος οὐ πολλὴν ἕξει σχολήν.

ΚΛ. Πῶς οὖν δυνατὸς ἔσται πρεσβύτερος ὢν
τοσούτων ἐπιμελεῖσθαι;

ΑΘ. Ῥᾳδίως, ὦ φίλε. ὁ νόμος γὰρ αὐτῷ
δέδωκε καὶ δώσει προσλαμβάνειν εἰς ταύτην τὴν
ἐπιμέλειαν τῶν πολιτῶν ἀνδρῶν καὶ γυναικῶν οὓς
ἂν ἐθέλῃ, γνώσεται δὲ οὓς δεῖ, καὶ βουλήσεται μὴ

[1] κατὰ: καὶ MSS., edd.

character of the actual tunes and words which the choir-masters ought to teach, all this we have already[1] explained at length. We stated that in each case they should be adapted to a suitable festival and dedicated, and thus prove a benefit to the States, by furnishing them with felicitous enjoyment.

CLIN. This, too, you have explained truly.

ATH. Yes, most truly. These matters also let the man who is appointed our Director of Music take over and supervise, with the help of kindly fortune; and let us supplement our former statements concerning dancing and bodily gymnastics in general. Just as, in the case of music, we have supplied the regulations about tuition that were missing, so also let us now do in the case of gymnastics. Shall we not say that both girls and boys must learn both dancing and gymnastics?

CLIN. Yes.

ATH. Then for their practices it would be most proper that boys should have dancing-masters, and girls mistresses.

CLIN. I grant it.

ATH. Let us once more summon the man who will have most of these duties to perform, the Director of the Children,—who, in supervising both music and gymnastic, will have but little time to spare.

CLIN. How will he be able, at his age, to supervise so many affairs?

ATH. Quite easily. For the law has granted him, and will continue to grant him, such men or women as he wishes to take to assist him in this task of supervision: he will know himself the right persons

[1] 799 A ff., 802 A.

D πλημμελεῖν εἰς ταῦτα αἰδούμενος ἐμφρόνως καὶ
γιγνώσκων τῆς ἀρχῆς τὸ μέγεθος, λογισμῷ τε
ξυνὼν ὡς εὖ μὲν τραφέντων καὶ τρεφομένων τῶν
νέων πάντα ἡμῖν κατ᾽ ὀρθὸν πλεῖ, μὴ δέ, οὔτ᾽
εἰπεῖν ἄξιον οὔθ᾽ ἡμεῖς λέγομεν ἐπὶ καινῇ πόλει
τοὺς σφόδρα φιλομαντευτὰς σεβόμενοι. πολλὰ
μὲν οὖν ἡμῖν καὶ περὶ τούτων εἴρηται τῶν περὶ
τὰς ὀρχήσεις καὶ περὶ πᾶσαν τὴν τῶν γυμνασίων
κίνησιν· γυμνάσια γὰρ τίθεμεν καὶ τὰ περὶ τὸν
πόλεμον ἅπαντα τοῖς σώμασι διαπονήματα τοξικῆς τε καὶ πάσης ῥίψεως καὶ πελταστικῆς καὶ
E πάσης ὁπλομαχίας καὶ διεξόδων τακτικῶν καὶ
ἁπάσης πορείας στρατοπέδων καὶ στρατοπε-
δεύσεων καὶ ὅσα εἰς ἱππικὴν μαθήματα συντείνει.
πάντων γὰρ τούτων διδασκάλους τε εἶναι δεῖ
κοινούς, ἀρνυμένους μισθὸν παρὰ τῆς πόλεως,
καὶ τούτων μαθητὰς τοὺς ἐν τῇ πόλει παῖδάς τε
καὶ ἄνδρας, καὶ κόρας καὶ γυναῖκας πάντων
τούτων ἐπιστήμονας, κόρας μὲν οὔσας ἔτι πᾶσαν
τὴν ἐν ὅπλοις ὄρχησιν καὶ μάχην μεμελετη-
κυίας, γυναῖκας δὲ διεξόδων καὶ τάξεων καὶ
814 θέσεως καὶ ἀναιρέσεως ὅπλων ἡμμένας, εἰ μηδενὸς ἕνεκα <ἄλλου>,[1] ἀλλ᾽ εἴ ποτε δεήσειε πανδη-
μεὶ [πάσῃ τῇ δυνάμει][2] καταλείποντας τὴν πόλιν
ἔξω στρατεύεσθαι τοὺς φυλάξαντας παῖδάς τε καὶ
τὴν ἄλλην πόλιν, ἱκανοὺς εἶναι τό γε τοσοῦτον, ἢ
καὶ τοὐναντίον, ὅγ᾽[3] οὐδὲν ἀπώμοτον, ἔξωθεν
πολεμίους εἰσπεσόντας ῥώμῃ τινὶ μεγάλῃ καὶ βίᾳ,
βαρβάρους εἴτε Ἕλληνας, ἀνάγκην παρασχεῖν

---

[1] ⟨ἄλλου⟩ I add.
[2] [πάσῃ τῇ δυνάμει] bracketed by Burges, England.
[3] ὅγ᾽ : ὧν MSS., edd. (ὃν Badham).

86

to choose, and he will be anxious to make no blunder in these matters, recognizing the greatness of his office and wisely holding it in high respect, and holding also the rational conviction that, when the young have been, and are being, well brought up, all goes "swimmingly," but otherwise—the consequences are such as it is wrong to speak of, nor will we mention them, in dealing with a new State, out of consideration for the over-superstitious.[1] Concerning these matters also, which relate to dancing and gymnastic movements, we have already spoken at length.[2] We are establishing gymnasia and all physical exercises connected with military training,— the use of the bow and all kinds of missiles, light skirmishing and heavy-armed fighting of every description, tactical evolutions, company-marching, camp-formations, and all the details of cavalry training. In all these subjects there should be public instructors, paid by the State; and their pupils should be not only the boys and men in the State, but also the girls and women who understand all these matters—being practised in all military drill and fighting while still girls and, when grown to womanhood, taking part in evolutions and rank-forming and the piling and shouldering of arms,— and that, if for no other reason, at least for this reason, that, if ever the guards of the children and of the rest of the city should be obliged to leave the city and march out in full force, these women should be able at least to take their place; while if, on the other hand—and this is quite a possible contingency —an invading army of foreigners, fierce and strong,

[1] *i.e.* they would regard the mere mention of possible evil (esp. in connexion with anything new-born) as of ill-omen.
[2] 795 D ff.

περὶ αὐτῆς τῆς πόλεως τὴν διαμάχην γίγνεσθαι,
B πολλή που κακία πολιτείας οὕτως αἰσχρῶς τὰς
γυναῖκας εἶναι τεθραμμένας, ὡς μηδ᾽ ὥσπερ ὄρνι-
θας περὶ τέκνων μαχομένας πρὸς ὁτιοῦν τῶν
ἰσχυροτάτων θηρίων ἐθέλειν ἀποθνήσκειν τε καὶ
πάντας κινδύνους κινδυνεύειν, ἀλλ᾽ εὐθὺς πρὸς
ἱερὰ φερομένας πάντας βωμούς τε καὶ ναοὺς ἐμπιπλάναι καὶ δόξαν τοῦ τῶν ἀνθρώπων γένους κατα-
χεῖν ὡς πάντων δειλότατον φύσει θηρίων ἐστίν.

ΚΛ. Οὐ μὰ τὸν Δία, ὦ ξένε, οὐδαμῶς εὔσχημον
C γίγνοιτ᾽ ἄν, τοῦ κακοῦ χωρίς, τοῦτο ἐν πόλει ὅπου
γίγνοιτο.

ΑΘ. Οὐκοῦν τιθῶμεν τὸν νόμον τοῦτον, μέχρι
γε τοσούτου μὴ ἀμελεῖσθαι τὰ περὶ τὸν πόλεμον
γυναιξὶ δεῖν, ἐπιμελεῖσθαι δὲ πάντας τοὺς πολίτας
καὶ τὰς πολίτιδας ;

ΚΛ. Ἐγὼ γοῦν συγχωρῶ.

ΑΘ. Πάλης τοίνυν τὰ μὲν εἴπομεν, ὃ δ᾽ ἐστὶ
μέγιστον, ὡς ἐγὼ φαίην ἄν, οὐκ εἰρήκαμεν, οὐδ᾽
ἔστι ῥάδιον ἄνευ τοῦ τῷ σώματι δεικνύντα ἅμα
D καὶ τῷ λόγῳ φράζειν.   τοῦτ᾽ οὖν τότε κρινοῦμεν,
ὅταν ἔργῳ λόγος ἀκολουθήσας μηνύσῃ τι σαφὲς
τῶν τε ἄλλων ὧν εἴρηκε πέρι καὶ ὅτι τῇ πολεμικῇ
μάχῃ πασῶν κινήσεων ὄντως ἐστὶ ξυγγενὴς πολὺ
μάλισθ᾽ ἡμῖν ἡ τοιαύτη πάλη, καὶ δὴ καὶ ὅτι δεῖ
ταύτην ἐκείνης χάριν ἐπιτηδεύειν, ἀλλ᾽ οὐκ ἐκείνην
ταύτης ἕνεκα μανθάνειν.

ΚΛ. Καλῶς τοῦτό γε λέγεις.

ΑΘ. Νῦν δὴ τῆς μὲν περὶ παλαίστραν δυνάμεως

---

[1] 795 D, E.   [2] Cp. 832 E.

should force a battle round the city itself, then it would be a sore disgrace to the State if its women were so ill brought up as not even to be willing to do as do the mother-birds, which fight the strongest beasts in defence of their broods, but, instead of facing all risks, even death itself, to run straight to the temples and crowd all the shrines and holy places, and drown mankind in the disgrace of being the most craven of living creatures.

CLIN. By Heaven, Stranger, if ever this took place in a city, it would be a most unseemly thing, apart from the mischief of it.

ATH. Shall we, then, lay down this law,—that up to the point stated women must not neglect military training, but all citizens, men and women alike, must pay attention to it?

CLIN. I, for one, agree.

ATH. As regards wrestling, some points have been explained;[1] but we have not explained what is, in my opinion, the most important point, nor is it easy to express it in words without the help of a practical illustration. This point, then, we shall decide about[2] when word accompanied by deed can clearly demonstrate this fact, among the others mentioned,—that wrestling of this kind is of all motions by far the most nearly allied to military fighting; and also that it is not the latter that should be learned for the sake of the former, but, on the contrary, it is the former that should be practised for the sake of the latter.[3]

CLIN. There, at any rate, you are right.

ATH. For the present let this suffice as an

[3] Cp. 803 D.

τὸ μέχρι δεῦρ᾽ ἡμῖν εἰρήσθω· περὶ δὲ τῆς ἄλλης
E κινήσεως παντὸς τοῦ σώματος, ἧς τὸ πλεῖστον
μέρος ὄρχησίν τινά τις προσαγορεύων ὀρθῶς ἂν
φθέγγοιτο, δύο μὲν αὐτῆς εἴδη χρὴ νομίζειν εἶναι,
τὴν μὲν τῶν καλλιόνων σωμάτων ἐπὶ τὸ σεμνὸν
μιμουμένην, τὴν δὲ τῶν αἰσχιόνων ἐπὶ τὸ
φαῦλον, καὶ πάλιν τοῦ φαύλου τε δύο καὶ τοῦ
σπουδαίου δύο ἕτερα. τοῦ δὴ σπουδαίου τὴν
μὲν κατὰ πόλεμον καὶ ἐν βιαίοις ἐμπλακέντων
πόνοις σωμάτων μὲν καλῶν, ψυχῆς δ᾽ ἀνδρικῆς,
τὴν δ᾽ ἐν εὐπραγίαις τε οὔσης ψυχῆς σώφρονος ἐν
ἡδοναῖς τε ἐμμέτροις· εἰρηνικὴν ἄν τις λέγων κατὰ
φύσιν τὴν τοιαύτην ὄρχησιν λέγοι. τὴν πολε-
815 μικὴν δὴ τούτων, ἄλλην οὖσαν τῆς εἰρηνικῆς,
πυρρίχην ἄν τις ὀρθῶς προσαγορεύοι, τάς τε εὐλαβείας πασῶν πληγῶν καὶ βολῶν ἐκνεύσεσι καὶ
ὑπείξει πάσῃ καὶ ἐκπηδήσεσιν ἐν ὕψει καὶ ξὺν
ταπεινώσει μιμουμένην, καὶ τὰς ταύταις ἐναντίας,
τὰς ἐπὶ τὰ δραστικὰ φερομένας αὖ σχήματα ἔν τε
ταῖς τῶν τόξων βολαῖς καὶ ἀκοντίων καὶ πασῶν
πληγῶν μιμήματα ἐπιχειροῦσαν[1] μιμεῖσθαι. τό
τε ὀρθὸν ἐν τούτοις καὶ τὸ εὔτονον, τῶν ἀγαθῶν
σωμάτων καὶ ψυχῶν ὁπόταν γίγνηται μίμημα,
B εὐθυφερὲς ὡς τὸ πολὺ τῶν τοῦ σώματος μελῶν
γιγνόμενον, ὀρθὸν μὲν τὸ τοιοῦτον, τὸ δὲ τούτοις
τοὐναντίον οὐκ ὀρθὸν ἀποδεχόμενον. τὴν δὲ
εἰρηνικὴν ὄρχησιν τῇδ᾽ αὖ θεωρητέον ἑκάστων,
εἴτε ὀρθῶς εἴτε μὴ κατὰ φύσιν τις τῆς καλῆς

[1] ἐπιχειροῦσαν Badham : ἐπιχειρούσας MSS.

account of the functions of the wrestling-school. Motion of the whole body, other than wrestling, has for its main division what may be rightly termed dancing [1]; and we ought to consider it as consisting of two kinds,—the one representing the solemn movement of beautiful bodies, the other the ignoble movement of ugly bodies; and of these again there are two subdivisions. Of the noble kind there is, on the one hand, the motion of fighting, and that of fair bodies and brave souls engaged in violent effort; and, on the other hand, there is the motion of a temperate soul living in a state of prosperity and moderate pleasures; and this latter kind of dancing one will call, in accordance with its nature, "pacific." The warlike division, being distinct from the pacific, one may rightly term "pyrrhiché"[2]; it represents modes of eluding all kinds of blows and shots by swervings and duckings and side-leaps upward or crouching; and also the opposite kinds of motion, which lead to active postures of offence, when it strives to represent the movements involved in shooting with bows or darts, and blows of every description. In all these cases the action and the tension of the sinews are correct when there is a representation of fair bodies and souls in which most of the limbs of the body are extended straight: this kind of representation is right, but the opposite kind we pronounce to be wrong. In pacific dancing, the point we must consider in every case is whether the performer in his dances keeps

---

[1] Here a wide term, embracing all kinds of bodily gestures and posturing.

[2] The technical name for a "war-dance" ("polka") in quick time (possibly connected by P. with $\pi\hat{v}\rho$, $\pi\upsilon\rho\epsilon\tau\acute{o}s$).

PLATO

ὀρχήσεως ἀντιλαμβανόμενος ἐν χορείαις πρεπόντως εὐνόμων ἀνδρῶν διατελεῖ.

Τὴν τοίνυν ἀμφισβητουμένην ὄρχησιν δεῖ πρῶτον χωρὶς τῆς ἀναμφισβητήτου διατεμεῖν. τίς οὖν αὕτη, καὶ πῇ δεῖ χωρὶς τέμνειν ἑκατέραν ;
C ὅση μὲν βακχεία τ' ἐστὶ καὶ τῶν ταύταις ἑπομένων, αἷς [1] [Νύμφας τε καὶ] Πᾶνας καὶ Σειληνοὺς καὶ Σατύρους [ἐπονομάζοντες], ὥς φασι, μιμοῦνται κατῳνωμένους, περικαθαρμούς τε καὶ τελετάς τινας ἀποτελούντων, ξύμπαν τοῦτο τῆς ὀρχήσεως τὸ γένος οὔθ' ὡς εἰρηνικὸν οὔθ' ὡς πολεμικὸν οὔθ' ὅ τί ποτε βούλεται ῥᾴδιον ἀφορίσασθαι· διορίσασθαι μὴν μοι ταύτῃ δοκεῖ σχεδὸν ὀρθότατον
D αὐτὸ εἶναι, χωρὶς μὲν πολεμικοῦ, χωρὶς δὲ εἰρηνικοῦ θέντας εἰπεῖν ὡς οὐκ ἔστι πολιτικὸν τοῦτο τῆς ὀρχήσεως τὸ γένος, ἐνταῦθα δὲ κείμενον ἐάσαντα κεῖσθαι νῦν ἐπὶ τὸ πολεμικὸν ἅμα καὶ εἰρηνικόν, ὡς ἀναμφισβητήτως ἡμέτερον ὄν, ἐπανιέναι.

Τὸ δὲ τῆς ἀπολέμου Μούσης, ἐν ὀρχήσεσι δὲ τούς τε θεοὺς καὶ τοὺς τῶν θεῶν παῖδας τιμῶντων, ἐν μὲν ξύμπαν γίγνοιτ' ἂν γένος ἐν δόξῃ τοῦ πράττειν εὖ γιγνόμενον, τοῦτο δὲ διχῇ διαιροῖμεν
E ἄν, τὸ μὲν ἐκ πόνων τινῶν αὐτοῦ καὶ κινδύνων διαπεφευγότων εἰς ἀγαθά, μείζους ἡδονὰς ἔχον, τὸ δὲ τῶν ἔμπροσθεν ἀγαθῶν σωτηρίας οὔσης καὶ ἐπαύξης, πραοτέρας τὰς ἡδονὰς κεκτημένον ἐκείνων. ἐν δὲ δὴ τοῖς τοιούτοις που πᾶς ἄνθρωπος τὰς κινήσεις τοῦ σώματος μειζόνων μὲν τῶν ἡδονῶν οὐσῶν μείζους, ἐλαττόνων δὲ ἐλάττους κινεῖται, καὶ κοσ
92

always rightly, or improperly, to the noble kind of dancing, in the way that befits law-abiding men.

So, in the first place, we must draw a line between questionable dancing and dancing that is above question. All the dancing that is of a Bacchic kind and cultivated by those who indulge in drunken imitations of Pans, Sileni and Satyrs (as they call them), when performing certain rites of expiation and initiation,—all this class of dancing cannot easily be defined either as pacific or as warlike, or as of any one distinct kind. The most correct way of defining it seems to me to be this—to separate it off both from pacific and from warlike dancing, and to pronounce that this kind of dancing is unfitted for our citizens: and having thus disposed of it and dismissed it, we will now return to the warlike and pacific kinds which do beyond question belong to us.

That of the unwarlike Muse, in which men pay honour to the gods and the children of the gods by dances, will consist, broadly speaking, of all dancing performed under a sense of prosperity: of this we may make two subdivisions—the one being of a more joyful description, and proper to men who have escaped out of toils and perils into a state of bliss,—and the other connected rather with the preservation and increase of pre-existent blessings, and exhibiting, accordingly, joyousness of a less ardent kind. Under these conditions every man moves his body more violently when his joys are greater, less violently when they are smaller; also, he moves it less violently when he is more

---

¹ αἷς England: ἃς MSS. [Νύμφας τε καὶ] and [ἐπονομά- ζοντες] I bracket.

PLATO

μιώτερος μὲν ὢν πρός τε ἀνδρίαν μᾶλλον γεγυμ-
816 νασμένος ἐλάττους αὖ, δειλὸς δὲ καὶ ἀγύμναστος
γεγονὼς πρὸς τὸ σωφρονεῖν μείζους καὶ σφοδροτέ-
ρας παρέχεται μεταβολὰς τῆς κινήσεως· ὅλως δὲ
φθεγγόμενος, εἴτ᾽ ἐν ᾠδαῖς εἴτ᾽ ἐν λόγοις, ἡσυχίαν
οὐ πάνυ δυνατὸς τῷ σώματι παρέχεσθαι πᾶς. διὸ
μίμησις τῶν λεγομένων σχήμασι γενομένη τὴν
ὀρχηστικὴν ἐξειργάσατο τέχνην ξύμπασαν. ὁ
μὲν οὖν ἐμμελῶς ἡμῶν, ὁ δὲ πλημμελῶς ἐν τούτοις
B πᾶσι κινεῖται. πολλὰ μὲν δὴ τοίνυν ἄλλα ἡμῖν
τῶν παλαιῶν ὀνομάτων ὡς εὖ καὶ κατὰ φύσιν
κείμενα δεῖ διανοούμενον ἐπαινεῖν, τούτων δὲ ἓν
καὶ τὸ περὶ τὰς ὀρχήσεις τὰς τῶν εὖ πραττόντων,
ὄντων δὲ μετρίων αὐτῶν πρὸς τὰς ἡδονάς, ὡς
ὀρθῶς ἅμα καὶ μουσικῶς ὠνόμασεν ὅστις ποτ᾽ ἦν,
καὶ κατὰ λόγον αὐταῖς θέμενος ὄνομα ξυμπάσαις
ἐμμελείας ἐπωνόμασε, καὶ δύο δὴ τῶν ὀρχήσεων
τῶν καλῶν εἴδη κατεστήσατο, τὸ μὲν πολεμικὸν
C πυρρίχην, τὸ δὲ εἰρηνικὸν ἐμμέλειαν, ἑκατέρῳ τὸ
πρέπον τε καὶ ἁρμοττον ἐπιθεὶς ὄνομα. ἃ δὴ δεῖ
τὸν μὲν νομοθέτην ἐξηγεῖσθαι τύποις, τὸν δὲ
νομοφύλακα ζητεῖν τε καὶ ἀνερευνησάμενον, μετὰ
τῆς ἄλλης μουσικῆς τὴν ὄρχησιν συνθέντα καὶ
νείμαντα ἐπὶ πάσας ἑορτὰς τῶν θυσιῶν ἑκάστῃ τὸ
πρόσφορον, οὕτω καθιερώσαντα αὐτὰ πάντα ἐν
τάξει τοῦ λοιποῦ μὴ κινεῖν μηδὲν μήτε ὀρχήσεως
ἐχόμενον μήτε ᾠδῆς, ἐν ταῖς δ᾽ αὐταῖς ἡδοναῖς
D ὡσαύτως τὴν αὐτὴν πόλιν καὶ πολίτας διάγοντας,
ὁμοίους εἰς δύναμιν ὄντας, ζῆν εὖ τε καὶ εὐδαιμόνως.

---

[1] A decorous, stately dance ("minuet").

94

sedate and better trained in courage, but when he is cowardly and untrained .in temperance, he indulges in greater and more violent changes of motion ; and in general, no one who is using his voice, whether in song or in speech, is able to keep his body wholly at rest. Hence, when the representation of things spoken by means of gestures arose, it produced the whole art of dancing. In all these instances, one man of us moves in tune with his theme, another out of tune. Many of the names bestowed in ancient times are deserving of notice and of praise for their excellence and descriptiveness : one such is the name given to the dances of men who are in a prosperous state and indulge in pleasures of a moderate kind : how true and how musical was the name so rationally bestowed on those dances by the man (whoever he was) who first called them all "Emmeleiai," [1] and established two species of fair dances—the warlike, termed "pyrrhiché," and the pacific, termed "emmeleia"—bestowing on each its appropriate and harmonious name. These dances the lawgiver should describe in outline, and the Law-warden should search them out and, having investigated them, he should combine the dancing with the rest of the music, and assign what is proper of it to each of the sacrificial feasts, distributing it over all the feasts ; and when he has thus consecrated all these things in due order, he should thenceforth make no change in all that appertains to either dancing or singing, but this one and the same city and body of citizens should continue in one and the same way, enjoying the same pleasures and living alike in all ways possible, and so pass their lives happily and well.

Τὰ μὲν οὖν τῶν καλῶν σωμάτων καὶ γενναίων
ψυχῶν εἰς τὰς χορείας, οἵας εἴρηται δεῖν αὐτὰς
εἶναι, διαπεπέρανται· τὰ δὲ τῶν αἰσχρῶν σωμάτων
καὶ διανοημάτων καὶ τῶν ἐπὶ τὰ τοῦ γέλωτος
κωμῳδήματα τετραμμένων, κατὰ λέξιν τε καὶ ᾠδὴν
καὶ κατὰ ὄρχησιν καὶ κατὰ τὰ τούτων πάντων
μιμήματα κεκωμῳδημένα, ἀνάγκη μὲν θεάσασθαι
καὶ γνωρίζειν· ἄνευ γὰρ γελοίων τὰ σπουδαῖα καὶ
E πάντων τῶν ἐναντίων τὰ ἐναντία μαθεῖν μὲν οὐ
δυνατόν, εἰ μέλλει τις φρόνιμος ἔσεσθαι, ποιεῖν
δὲ οὐκ αὖ [1] δυνατὸν ἀμφότερα, εἴ τις ἄρα [2] μέλλει
καὶ σμικρὸν ἀρετῆς μεθέξειν, ἀλλὰ αὐτῶν ἕνεκα
τούτων καὶ μανθάνειν αὐτὰ δεῖ, τοῦ μή ποτε δι᾽
ἄγνοιαν δρᾶν ἢ λέγειν ὅσα γελοῖα μηδὲν δέον,
δούλοις δὲ τὰ τοιαῦτα καὶ ξένοις ἐμμίσθοις
προστάττειν μιμεῖσθαι, σπουδὴν δὲ περὶ αὐτὰ
εἶναι μηδέποτε μηδ᾽ ἡντινοῦν μηδέ τινα μανθάνοντα αὐτὰ γίγνεσθαι φανερὸν τῶν ἐλευθέρων,
μήτε γυναῖκα μήτε ἄνδρα, καινὸν δὲ ἀεί τι περὶ
αὐτὰ φαίνεσθαι τῶν μιμημάτων. ὅσα μὲν οὖν
περὶ γέλωτά ἐστι παίγνια, ἃ δὴ κωμῳδίαν πάντες
817 λέγομεν, οὕτω τῷ νόμῳ καὶ λόγῳ κείσθω· τῶν
δὲ σπουδαίων, ὥς φασι, τῶν περὶ τραγῳδίαν ἡμῖν
ποιητῶν, ἐάν ποτέ τινες αὐτῶν ἡμᾶς ἐλθόντες
ἐπανερωτήσωσιν οὑτωσί πως, Ὦ ξένοι, πότερον
φοιτῶμεν ὑμῖν εἰς τὴν πόλιν τε καὶ χώραν ἢ μή,
καὶ τὴν ποίησιν φέρωμέν τε καὶ ἄγωμεν, ἢ πῶς
ὑμῖν δέδοκται περὶ τὰ τοιαῦτα δρᾶν; τί οὖν ἂν
πρὸς ταῦτα ὀρθῶς ἀποκριναίμεθα τοῖς θείοις

[1] αὖ H. Richards : ἂν MSS.
[2] ἄρα : αὖ MSS., edd.

What concerns the actions of fair and noble souls in the matter of that kind of choristry which we have approved as right has now been fully discussed. The actions of ugly bodies and ugly ideas and of the men engaged in ludicrous comic-acting, in regard to both speech and dance, and the representations given by all these comedians—all this subject we must necessarily consider and estimate. For it is impossible to learn the serious without the comic, or any one of a pair of contraries without the other, if one is to be a wise man ; but to put both into practice is equally impossible, if one is to share in even a small measure of virtue ; in fact, it is precisely for this reason that one should learn them,—in order to avoid ever doing or saying anything ludicrous, through ignorance, when one ought not ; we will impose such mimicry on slaves and foreign hirelings, and no serious attention shall ever be paid to it, nor shall any free man or free woman be seen learning it, and there must always be some novel feature in their mimic shows.[1] Let such, then, be the regulations for all those laughable amusements which we all call "comedy," as laid down both by law and by argument. Now as to what are called our "serious" poets, the tragedians,—suppose that some of them were to approach us and put some such question as this,— "O Strangers, are we, or are we not, to pay visits to your city and country, and traffic in poetry ? Or what have you decided to do about this ?" What would be the right answer to make to these

---

[1] *i.e.* lest the public taste should be debased by the repeated exhibition of any one piece of vulgarity.

ἀνδράσιν; ἐμοὶ μὲν γὰρ δοκεῖ τάδε, Ὦ ἄριστοι,
B φάναι, τῶν ξένων, ἡμεῖς ἐσμὲν τραγῳδίας αὐτοὶ
ποιηταὶ κατὰ δύναμιν ὅτι καλλίστης ἅμα καὶ
ἀρίστης· πᾶσα γοῦν[1] ἡμῖν ἡ πολιτεία ξυνέστηκε
μίμησις τοῦ καλλίστου καὶ ἀρίστου βίου, ὃ δή
φαμεν ἡμεῖς γε ὄντως εἶναι τραγῳδίαν τὴν ἀλη-
θεστάτην. ποιηταὶ μὲν οὖν ὑμεῖς, ποιηταὶ δὲ
καὶ ἡμεῖς ἐσμὲν τῶν αὐτῶν, ὑμῖν ἀντίτεχνοί τε
καὶ ἀνταγωνισταὶ τοῦ καλλίστου δράματος, ὃ δὴ
νόμος ἀληθὴς μόνος ἀποτελεῖν πέφυκεν, ὡς ἡ παρ'
C ἡμῶν ἐστιν ἐλπίς. μὴ δὴ δόξητε ἡμᾶς ῥᾳδίως
γε οὕτως ὑμᾶς ποτὲ παρ' ἡμῖν ἐάσειν σκηνάς τε
πήξαντας κατ' ἀγορὰν καὶ καλλιφώνους ὑπο-
κριτὰς εἰσαγαγομένους, μεῖζον φθεγγομένους
ἡμῶν, ἐπιτρέψειν ὑμῖν δημηγορεῖν πρὸς παῖδάς
τε καὶ γυναῖκας καὶ τὸν πάντα ὄχλον, τῶν αὐτῶν
λέγοντας ἐπιτηδευμάτων πέρι μὴ τὰ αὐτὰ ἅπερ
ἡμεῖς ἀλλ' ὡς τὸ πολὺ καὶ ἐναντία τὰ πλεῖστα·
σχεδὸν γάρ τοι κἂν μαινοίμεθα τελέως ἡμεῖς τε
D καὶ ἅπασα ἡ πόλις, ἥτις οὖν ὑμῖν ἐπιτρέποι δρᾶν
τὰ νῦν λεγόμενα, πρὶν κρῖναι τὰς ἀρχὰς εἴτε
ῥητὰ καὶ ἐπιτήδεια πεποιήκατε λέγειν εἰς τὸ
μέσον εἴτε μή. νῦν οὖν, ὦ παῖδες μαλακῶν
Μουσῶν ἔκγονοι, ἐπιδείξαντες τοῖς ἄρχουσι
πρῶτον τὰς ὑμετέρας παρὰ τὰς ἡμετέρας ᾠδάς,
ἂν μὲν τὰ αὐτά γε ἢ καὶ βελτίω τὰ παρ' ὑμῶν
φαίνηται λεγόμενα, δώσομεν ὑμῖν χορόν, εἰ δὲ
μή, ὦ φίλοι, οὐκ ἄν ποτε δυναίμεθα.
E   Ταῦτ' οὖν ἔστω περὶ πᾶσαν χορείαν καὶ μάθησιν τούτων πέρι συντεταγμένα νόμοις ἔθη,

----

[1] γοῦν Bywater, England : οὖν MSS.

inspired persons regarding the matter? In my judgment, this should be the answer,[1]—" Most excellent of Strangers, we ourselves, to the best of our ability, are the authors of a tragedy at once superlatively fair and good ; at least, all our polity is framed as a representation of the fairest and best life, which is in reality, as we assert, the truest tragedy. Thus we are composers of the same things as yourselves, rivals of yours as artists and actors of the fairest drama, which, as our hope is, true law, and it alone, is by nature competent to complete. Do not imagine, then, that we will ever thus lightly allow you to set up your stage beside us in the market-place, and give permission to those imported actors of yours, with their dulcet tones and their voices louder than ours, to harangue women and children and the whole populace, and to say not the same things as we say about the same institutions, but, on the contrary, things that are, for the most part, just the opposite. In truth, both we ourselves and the whole State would be absolutely mad, were it to allow you to do as I have said, before the magistrates had decided whether or not your compositions are deserving of utterance and suited for publication. So now, ye children and offspring of Muses mild, do ye first display your chants side by side with ours before the rulers ; and if your utterances seem to be the same as ours or better, then we will grant you a chorus,[2] but if not, my friends, we can never do so."

Let such, then, be the customs ordained to go with the laws regarding all choristry and the learning

---

[1] Cp. *Rep.* 398 A, B.
[2] *i.e.* grant you leave to " stage " your play.

χωρὶς μὲν τὰ τῶν δούλων, χωρὶς δὲ τὰ τῶν δεσποτῶν, εἰ ξυνδοκεῖ.

ΚΛ. Πῶς δ' οὐ ξυνδοκεῖ νῦν γε οὕτως ;

ΑΘ. Ἔτι δὴ τοίνυν τοῖς ἐλευθέροις ἐστὶ τρία μαθήματα, λογισμοὶ μὲν καὶ τὰ περὶ ἀριθμοὺς ἓν μάθημα, μετρητικὴ δὲ μήκους καὶ ἐπιπέδου καὶ βάθους ὡς ἓν αὖ δεύτερον, τρίτον δὲ τῆς τῶν ἄστρων περιόδου πρὸς ἄλληλα ὡς πέφυκε 818 πορεύεσθαι. ταῦτα δὲ ξύμπαντα οὐχ ὡς ἀκριβείας ἐχόμενα δεῖ διαπονεῖν τοὺς πολλοὺς ἀλλά τινας ὀλίγους· οὓς δέ, προϊόντες ἐπὶ τῷ τέλει φράσομεν· οὕτω γὰρ πρέπον ἂν εἴη· τῷ πλήθει δέ, ὅσα αὐτῶν ἀναγκαῖα ὡς [1] ὀρθότατα λέγεται μὴ ἐπίστασθαι μὲν τοῖς πολλοῖς αἰσχρόν, δι' ἀκριβείας δὲ ζητεῖν πάντα οὔτε ῥᾴδιον οὔτε τὸ παράπαν δυνατόν· τὸ δὲ ἀναγκαῖον αὐτῶν οὐχ οἷόν τε ἀποβάλλειν, ἀλλ' ἔοικεν ὁ τὸν θεὸν πρῶτον Β παροιμιασάμενος εἰς ταῦτα ἀποβλέψας εἰπεῖν ὡς οὐδὲ θεὸς ἀνάγκη μή ποτε φανῇ μαχόμενος, ὅσαι θεῖαί γε, οἶμαι, τῶν [τε] ἀναγκῶν εἰσίν, ἐπεὶ τῶν γε ἀνθρωπίνων, εἰς ἃς οἱ πολλοὶ βλέποντες λέγουσι τὸ τοιοῦτον, οὗτος πάντων τῶν λόγων εὐηθέστατός ἐστι μακρῷ.

ΚΛ. Τίνες οὖν, ὦ ξένε, αἱ μὴ τοιαῦται ἀνάγκαι τῶν μαθημάτων, θεῖαι δέ ;

ΑΘ. Δοκῶ μέν, ἃς μή τις πράξας μηδὲ αὖ C μαθὼν τὸ παράπαν οὐκ ἄν ποτε γένοιτο ἀνθρώποις θεὸς οὐδὲ δαίμων οὐδὲ ἥρως, οἷος [δυνατὸς] [2] ἀνθρώπων ἐπιμέλειαν σὺν σπουδῇ

---

[1] ὡς: καί πως MSS. (ὅπως W.–Möllendorff).
[2] [δυνατὸς] bracketed by Badham.

thereof—keeping distinct those for slaves and those for masters,—if you agree.

CLIN. Of course we now agree to it.

ATH. There still remain, for the freeborn, three branches of learning : of these the first is reckoning and arithmetic ; the second is the art of measuring length and surface and solid ; the third deals with the course of the stars, and how they naturally travel in relation to one another. All these sciences should not be studied with minute accuracy by the majority of pupils, but only by a select few—and who these are we shall say when we have come near the end,—since that will be the proper place :[1] but for the bulk of the pupils, while it would be shameful for most of them not to understand all those parts of them that are most truly termed " necessary," yet it is not easy nor even at all possible for every student to go into them minutely. The necessary part of them it is impossible to reject, and probably this is what was in the mind of the original author of the proverb,[2] " Not even God will ever be seen fighting against Necessity,"—meaning by this, I suppose, all kinds of necessity that are divine, since in relation to human necessities (to which most people apply the saying when they quote it) it is of all sayings far and away the most fatuous.

CLIN. What necessities then, Stranger, belong to these sciences, that are not of this sort, but divine ?

ATH. Those, as I believe, which must be practised and learned by every god, daemon, and hero, if he is to be competent seriously to supervise man-

---

[1] Cp. 962 C, 965 A ff.   [2] Cp. 741 A.

ποιεῖσθαι. πολλοῦ δ' ἂν δεήσειεν ἄνθρωπός γε
θεῖος γενέσθαι μήτε ἓν μήτε δύο μήτε τρία μήθ'
ὅλως ἄρτια καὶ περιττὰ δυνάμενος γιγνώσκειν,
μηδὲ ἀριθμεῖν τὸ παράπαν εἰδώς, μηδὲ νύκτα καὶ
ἡμέραν διαριθμεῖσθαι δυνατὸς ὤν, σελήνης δὲ καὶ
ἡλίου καὶ τῶν ἄλλων ἄστρων περιφορᾶς ἀπείρως
D ἔχων. ταῦτ' οὖν δὴ πάντα ὡς μὲν οὐκ ἀναγκαῖά
ἐστι μαθήματα τῷ μέλλοντι σχεδὸν ὁτιοῦν τῶν
καλλίστων μαθημάτων εἴσεσθαι, πολλὴ καὶ
μωρία τοῦ διανοήματος· ποῖα δὲ ἕκαστα τούτων
καὶ πόσα καὶ πότε μαθητέον, καὶ τί μετὰ τίνος
καὶ τί χωρὶς τῶν ἄλλων, καὶ πᾶσαν τὴν τούτων
κρᾶσιν, ταῦτά ἐστιν ἃ δεῖ λαβόντα ὀρθῶς πρῶτα
ἐπὶ τἆλλα ἰόντα τούτων ἡγουμένων τῶν μαθημάτων μανθάνειν· οὕτω γὰρ ἀνάγκη φύσει κατείλη-
E φεν, ᾗ φαμὲν οὐδένα θεῶν οὔτε μάχεσθαι τὰ νῦν
οὔτε μαχεῖσθαί ποτε.

ΚΛ. Ἔοικέ γε, ὦ ξένε, νῦν οὕτω πως ῥηθέντα
ὀρθῶς εἰρῆσθαι καὶ κατὰ φύσιν ἃ λέγεις.

ΑΘ. Ἔχει μὲν γὰρ οὕτως, ὦ Κλεινία, χαλεπὸν
δὲ αὐτὰ προταξάμενον τούτῳ τῷ τρόπῳ νομο-
θετεῖν· ἀλλ' εἰς ἄλλον, εἰ δοκεῖ, χρόνον ἀκρι-
βέστερον ἂν νομοθετησαίμεθα.

ΚΛ. Δοκεῖς ἡμῖν, ὦ ξένε, φοβεῖσθαι τὸ τῆς
ἡμετέρας περὶ τῶν τοιούτων ἀπειρίας ἔθος. οὔκουν ὀρθῶς φοβεῖ· πειρῶ δὴ λέγειν μηδὲν ἀποκρυπτόμενος ἕνεκα τούτων.

819 ΑΘ. Φοβοῦμαι μὲν καὶ ταῦτα ἃ σὺ νῦν λέγεις,
μᾶλλον δ' ἔτι δέδοικα τοὺς ἡμμένους μὲν αὐτῶν

---

[1] i.e. arithmetic, geometry, and astronomy: some elementary ("necessary") knowledge of all three is indispens-
able for a thorough study of any one branch of science.

kind: a man certainly would be far from becoming godlike if he were incapable of learning the nature of one and of two, and of even and odd numbers in general, and if he knew nothing at all about counting, and could not count even day and night as distinct objects, and if he were ignorant of the circuit of the sun and moon and all the other stars. To suppose, then, that all these studies[1] are not "necessary" for a man who means to understand almost any single one of the fairest sciences, is a most foolish supposition. The first thing we must grasp correctly is this—which of these branches of study must be learnt, and how many, and at what periods, and which of them in conjunction with which, and which by themselves apart from all others, and the method of combining them; this done, and with these studies as introductory, we may proceed to the learning of the rest. For such is the natural order of procedure as determined by Necessity, against whom, as we declare, no god fights now, nor ever will fight.

CLIN. Yes, Stranger, this account of yours does seem to be in accord with nature, and true.

ATH. That is indeed the truth of the matter, Clinias; but to give legal enactment to this programme of ours is difficult. We will, if you agree, enact this more precisely on a later occasion.

CLIN. You appear to us, Stranger, to be scared by the neglect of such studies which is the habit in our countries; but you are wrong to be scared. Do not be deterred on that account, but try to proceed with your statement.

ATH. I am indeed scared about the habit you mention, but I am still more alarmed about the

τούτων τῶν μαθημάτων, κακῶς δ' ἐμμένους.
οὐδαμοῦ γὰρ δεινὸν οὐδ' ἡ σφοδρὰ [1] ἀπειρία τῶν
πάντων οὐδὲ μέγιστον κακόν, ἀλλ' ἡ πολυπειρία
καὶ πολυμαθία μετὰ κακῆς ἀγωγῆς γίγνεται πολὺ
τούτων μείζων ζημία.

ΚΛ. Ἀληθῆ λέγεις.

ΑΘ. Τοσάδε τοίνυν ἑκάστων χρὴ φάναι μανθάνειν δεῖν τοὺς ἐλευθέρους, ὅσα καὶ πάμπολυς
ἐν Αἰγύπτῳ παίδων ὄχλος ἅμα γράμμασι μαν-
B θάνει. πρῶτον μὲν γὰρ περὶ λογισμοὺς ἀτεχνῶς
παισὶν ἐξευρημένα μαθήματα μετὰ παιδιᾶς τε
καὶ ἡδονῆς μανθάνειν, μήλων τέ τινων διανομὰς [2]
καὶ στεφάνων, πλείοσιν ἅμα καὶ ἐλάττοσιν
ἁρμοττόντων ἀριθμῶν τῶν αὐτῶν, καὶ πυκτῶν καὶ
παλαιστῶν ἐφεδρείας τε καὶ συλλήξεως ἐν μέρει
καὶ ἐφεξῆς [καὶ] [3] ὡς πεφύκασι γίγνεσθαι. καὶ
δὴ καὶ παίζοντες, φιάλας ἅμα χρυσοῦ καὶ χαλκοῦ
C καὶ ἀργύρου καὶ τοιούτων τινῶν ἄλλων κεραν-
νύντες, οἱ δὲ καὶ ὅλας πως διαδιδόντες, ὅπερ
εἶπον, εἰς παιδιὰν ἐναρμόττοντες τὰς τῶν ἀναγκαίων ἀριθμῶν χρήσεις, ὠφελοῦσι τοὺς μαν-
θάνοντας εἴς τε τὰς τῶν στρατοπέδων τάξεις καὶ
ἀγωγὰς καὶ στρατείας καὶ εἰς οἰκονομίας αὖ,
καὶ πάντως χρησιμωτέρους αὐτοὺς αὑτοῖς καὶ
ἐγρηγορότας μᾶλλον τοὺς ἀνθρώπους ἀπεργά-
D ζονται. μετὰ δὲ ταῦτα ἐν ταῖς μετρήσεσιν, ὅσα
ἔχει μήκη καὶ πλάτη καὶ βάθη, περὶ ἅπαντα
ταῦτα ἐνοῦσάν τινα φύσει γελοίαν τε καὶ αἰσχρὰν

---

[1] οὐδ' ἡ σφοδρὰ Badham : οὐδὲ σφοδρὸν MSS.
[2] διανομὰς W.–Möllendorff : διανομαὶ MSS. (διανομαῖς Badham).

people who take up these very sciences for study, and do so badly.[1] Complete and absolute ignorance of them is never alarming, nor is it a very great evil; much more mischievous is a wide variety of knowledge and learning combined with bad training.

CLIN. That is true.

ATH. One ought to declare, then, that the free-born children should learn as much of these subjects as the innumerable crowd of children in Egypt[2] learn along with their letters. First, as regards counting, lessons have been invented for the merest infants to learn, by way of play and fun,—modes of dividing up apples and chaplets, so that the same totals are adjusted to larger and smaller groups, and modes of sorting out boxers and wrestlers, in byes and pairs, taking them alternately or consecutively, in their natural order. Moreover, by way of play, the teachers mix together bowls made of gold, bronze, silver and the like, and others distribute them, as I said, by groups of a single kind, adapting the rules of elementary arithmetic to play; and thus they are of service to the pupils for their future tasks of drilling, leading and marching armies, or of household management, and they render them both more helpful in every way to themselves and more alert. The next step of the teachers is to clear away, by lessons in weights and measures, a certain kind of ignorance, both absurd and disgrace-

---

[1] Cp. 886 A ff.

[2] The Egyptian priests are said to have specially drilled their scholars in arithmetic and geometry—partly with a view to their use in land-mensuration.

---

[3] [καὶ] bracketed by W.–Möllendorff.

ἄγνοιαν ἐν τοῖς ἀνθρώποις πᾶσι ταύτῃ¹ ἀπαλ-
λάττουσιν.

ΚΛ. Ποίαν δὴ καὶ τίνα λέγεις ταύτην ;

ΑΘ. Ὦ φίλε Κλεινία, παντάπασί γε μὴν καὶ
αὐτὸς ἀκούσας ὀψέ ποτε τὸ περὶ ταῦτα ἡμῶν
πάθος ἐθαύμασα, καὶ ἔδοξέ μοι τοῦτο οὐκ ἀν-
θρώπινον ἀλλὰ ὑηνῶν τινῶν εἶναι μᾶλλον θρεμμάτων, ᾐσχύνθην τε οὐχ ὑπὲρ ἐμαυτοῦ μόνον,
ἀλλὰ καὶ ὑπὲρ ἁπάντων τῶν Ἑλλήνων.

E   ΚΛ. Τοῦ πέρι ; λέγ᾽ ὅ τι καὶ φής, ὦ ξένε.

ΑΘ. Λέγω δή· μᾶλλον δὲ ἐρωτῶν σοι δείξω·
καί μοι σμικρὸν ἀπόκριναι. γιγνώσκεις που
μῆκος ;

ΚΛ. Τί μήν ;

ΑΘ. Τί δέ ; πλάτος ;

ΚΛ. Πάντως.

ΑΘ. Ἦ καὶ ταῦτα ὅτι δύ᾽ ἐστὸν καὶ τρίτον
τούτων βάθος ;

ΚΛ. Πῶς γὰρ οὔ ;

ΑΘ. Ἆρ᾽ οὖν οὐ δοκεῖ σοι ταῦτα εἶναι πάντα
μετρητὰ πρὸς ἄλληλα ;

ΚΛ. Ναί.

ΑΘ. Μῆκός τε, οἶμαι, πρὸς μῆκος, καὶ πλάτος
820 πρὸς πλάτος, καὶ βάθος ὡσαύτως δυνατὸν εἶναι
μετρεῖν φύσει.

ΚΛ. Σφόδρα γε.

ΑΘ. Εἰ δ᾽ ἔστι μήτε σφόδρα μήτ᾽ ἠρέμα δυνατὰ
ἔνια, ἀλλὰ τὰ μέν, τὰ δὲ μή, σὺ δὲ πάντα ἡγεῖ,
πῶς οἴει πρὸς ταῦτα διακεῖσθαι ;

ΚΛ. Δῆλον ὅτι φαύλως.

----

¹ ταύτῃ : ταύτης MSS., edd. (ταύτην ci. Stallb.).

ful, which is naturally inherent in all men touching
lines, surfaces and solids.

CLIN. What ignorance do you mean, and of what
kind is it?

ATH. My dear Clinias, when I was told quite
lately of our condition in regard to this matter, I
was utterly astounded myself: it seemed to me to
be the condition of guzzling swine rather than of
human beings, and I was ashamed, not only of myself, but of all the Greek world.[1]

CLIN. Why? Tell us what you mean, Stranger.

ATH. I am doing so. But I can explain it better
by putting a question. Answer me briefly: you
know what a line is?

CLIN. Yes.

ATH. And surface?

CLIN. Certainly.

ATH. And do you know that these are two things,
and that the third thing, next to these, is the solid?

CLIN. I do.

ATH. Do you not, then, believe that all these are
commensurable one with another?

CLIN. Yes.

ATH. And you believe, I suppose, that line is
really commensurable with line, surface with surface,
and solid with solid?

CLIN. Absolutely.

ATH. But supposing that some of them are
neither absolutely nor moderately commensurable,
some being commensurable and some not, whereas
you regard them all as commensurable,—what do
you think of your mental state with respect to them?

CLIN. Evidently it is a sorry state.

---

[1] Cp. *Rep.* 528 C f.

ΑΘ. Τί δ' αὖ ; μῆκός τε καὶ πλάτος πρὸς
βάθος, ἢ πλάτος τε καὶ μῆκος πρὸς ἄλληλα, ἆρ'
οὐ διανοούμεθα περὶ ταῦτα οὕτως Ἕλληνες
πάντες, ὡς δυνατά ἐστι μετρεῖσθαι πρὸς ἄλληλα
ἁμῶς γέ πως ;

B   ΚΛ. Παντάπασι μὲν οὖν.

ΑΘ. Εἰ δ' ἔστιν αὖ μηδαμῶς μηδαμῇ δυνατά,
πάντες δ', ὅπερ εἶπον, Ἕλληνες διανοούμεθα ὡς
δυνατά, μῶν οὐκ ἄξιον ὑπὲρ πάντων αἰσχυνθέντα
εἰπεῖν πρὸς αὐτούς, Ὦ βέλτιστοι τῶν Ἑλλήνων,
ἓν ἐκείνων τοῦτ' ἔστιν ὧν ἔφαμεν, αἰσχρὸν μὲν
γεγονέναι τὸ μὴ ἐπίστασθαι, τὸ δ' ἐπίστασθαι
τἀναγκαῖα οὐδὲν πάνυ καλόν ;

ΚΛ. Πῶς δ' οὔ ;

ΑΘ. Καὶ πρὸς τούτοις γε ἄλλα ἐστὶ τούτων
C ξυγγενῆ, ἐν οἷς αὖ πολλὰ ἁμαρτήματα ἐκείνων
ἀδελφὰ ἡμῖν ἐγγίγνεται τῶν ἁμαρτημάτων.

ΚΛ. Ποῖα δή ;

ΑΘ. Τὰ τῶν μετρητῶν τε καὶ ἀμέτρων πρὸς
ἄλληλα, ᾗτινι φύσει γέγονε. ταῦτα γὰρ δὴ
σκοποῦντα διαγιγνώσκειν ἀναγκαῖον ἢ παντάπασιν εἶναι φαῦλον, προβάλλοντά τε ἀλλήλοις
ἀεί, διατριβὴν τῆς πεττείας πολὺ χαριεστέραν
πρεσβυτῶν διατρίβοντα, φιλονεικεῖν ἐν ταῖς τούτων ἀξίαισι σχολαῖς.

D   ΚΛ. Ἴσως· ἔοικε γοῦν ἥ τε πεττεία καὶ ταῦτα
ἀλλήλων τὰ μαθήματα οὐ πάμπολυ κεχωρίσθαι.

ΑΘ. Ταῦτα τοίνυν ἐγὼ μέν, ὦ Κλεινία, φημὶ
τοὺς νέους δεῖν μανθάνειν· καὶ γὰρ οὔτε βλαβερὰ
οὔτε χαλεπά ἐστι, μετὰ δὲ παιδιᾶς ἅμα μανθανό-
μενα ὠφελήσει μέν, βλάψει δὲ ἡμῖν τὴν πόλιν
οὐδέν. εἰ δέ τις ἄλλως λέγει, ἀκουστέον.

108

ATH. Again, as regards the relation of line and surface to solid, or of surface and line to each other —do not all we Greeks imagine that these are somehow commensurable with one another?

CLIN. Most certainly.

ATH. But if they cannot be thus measured by any way or means, while, as I said, all we Greeks imagine that they can, are we not right in being ashamed for them all, and saying to them, " O most noble Greeks, this is one of those ' necessary ' things which we said [1] it is disgraceful not to know, although there is nothing very grand in knowing such things."

CLIN. Of course.

ATH. In addition to these there are other matters, closely related to them, in which we find many errors arising that are nearly akin to the errors mentioned.

CLIN. What are they?

ATH. Problems concerning the essential nature of the commensurable and the incommensurable. For students who are not to be absolutely worthless it is necessary to examine these and to distinguish the two kinds, and, by proposing such problems one to another, to compete in a game that is worthy of them,—for this is a much more refined pastime than draughts for old men.

CLIN. No doubt. And, after all, draughts and these studies do not seem to lie so very far apart.

ATH. I assert, then, Clinias, that these subjects must be learnt by the young; for they are, in truth, neither harmful nor hard, and when learnt by way of play they will do no damage at all to our State, but will do it good. Should anyone disagree, however, we must listen to him.

---

[1] 818 A : cp. Ar. *Pol.* 1338ᵃ 9 ff.

ΚΛ. Πῶς δ' οὔ;

ΑΘ. Ἀλλὰ μὴν ἂν οὕτω ταῦτα ἔχοντα φαίνηται,
δῆλον ὡς ἐγκρινοῦμεν αὐτά, μὴ ταύτῃ δὲ φαινόμενα
ἔχειν ἀποκριθήσεται.

Ε ΚΛ. Δῆλον· τί μήν;

ΑΘ.[1] Οὐκοῦν νῦν, ὦ ξένε, κείσθω ταῦτα ὡς
ὄντα τῶν δεόντων μαθημάτων, ἵνα μὴ διάκενα
ἡμῖν ᾖ τὰ τῶν νόμων. κείσθω μέντοι καθάπερ
ἐνέχυρα λύσιμα ἐκ τῆς ἄλλης πολιτείας, ἐὰν ἢ
τοὺς θέντας ἡμᾶς ἢ καὶ τοὺς θεμένους ὑμᾶς
μηδαμῶς φιλοφρονῆται.

ΚΛ. Δικαίαν λέγεις τὴν θέσιν.

ΑΘ. Ἄστρων δὴ τὸ μετὰ ταῦτα ὅρα τὴν
μάθησιν τοῖς νέοις, ἂν ἡμᾶς ἀρέσκῃ λεχθεῖσα ἢ
καὶ τοὐναντίον.

ΚΛ. Λέγε μόνον.

ΑΘ. Καὶ μὴν θαῦμά γε περὶ αὐτά ἐστι μέγα
καὶ οὐδαμῶς οὐδαμῇ ἀνεκτόν.

821 ΚΛ. Τὸ ποῖον δή;

ΑΘ. Τὸν μέγιστον θεὸν καὶ ὅλον τὸν κόσμον
φαμὲν οὔτε ζητεῖν δεῖν οὔτε πολυπραγμονεῖν
τὰς αἰτίας ἐρευνῶντας· οὐ γὰρ οὐδ' ὅσιον εἶναι.
τὸ δὲ ἔοικε πᾶν τούτου τοὐναντίον γιγνόμενον
ὀρθῶς ἂν γίγνεσθαι.

ΚΛ. Πῶς εἶπες;

ΑΘ. Παράδοξον μὲν τὸ λεγόμενον, καὶ οὐκ ἂν
πρεσβύταις τις οἰηθείη πρέπειν· τὸ δὲ ἐπειδάν
τίς τι καλόν τε οἰηθῇ καὶ ἀληθὲς μάθημα εἶναι
καὶ πόλει ξυμφέρον καὶ τῷ θεῷ παντάπασι
Β φίλον, οὐδενὶ δὴ τρόπῳ δυνατόν ἐστιν ἔτι μὴ
φράζειν.

---

[1] Οὐκοῦν . . . νόμων is wrongly assigned by Zur. to *Clin.*

CLIN. Of course.

ATH. Well then, if this is clearly the case, obviously we shall adopt these subjects; but if it seems clearly to be otherwise, we shall rule them out.

CLIN. Yes, obviously.

ATH. Shall we not, then, lay these down as necessary subjects of instruction, so that there may be no gap in our code of laws? Yet we ought to lay them down provisionally—like pledges capable of redemption—apart from the rest of our constitution, in case they fail to satisfy either us who enact them or you for whom they are enacted.

CLIN. Yes, that is the right way to lay them down.

ATH. Consider next whether or not we approve of the children learning astronomy.

CLIN. Just tell us your opinion.

ATH. About this there is a very strange fact—indeed, quite intolerable.

CLIN. What is that?

ATH. We commonly assert that men ought not to enquire concerning the greatest god and about the universe, nor busy themselves in searching out their causes, since it is actually impious to do so; whereas the right course, in all probability, is exactly the opposite.

CLIN. Explain yourself.

ATH. My statement sounds paradoxical, and it might be thought to be unbecoming in an old man; but the fact is that, when a man believes that a science is fair and true and beneficial to the State and altogether well-pleasing to God, he cannot possibly refrain any longer from declaring it.[1]

[1] Cp. 779 B.

PLATO

κλ. Εἰκότα λέγεις· ἀλλ' ἄστρων πέρι μάθημα τί τοιοῦτον ἀνευρήσομεν;

αθ. Ὦ ἀγαθοί, καταψευδόμεθα νῦν ὡς ἔπος εἰπεῖν Ἕλληνες πάντες μεγάλων θεῶν, Ἡλίου τε ἅμα καὶ Σελήνης.

κλ. Τὸ ποῖον δὴ ψεῦδος;

αθ. Φαμὲν αὐτὰ οὐδέποτε τὴν αὐτὴν ὁδὸν ἰέναι, καὶ ἄλλ' ἄττα ἄστρα μετὰ τούτων, ἐπονομάζοντες πλανητὰ αὐτά.

C κλ. Νὴ τὸν Δία, ὦ ξένε, ἀληθὲς τοῦτο λέγεις· ἐν γὰρ δὴ τῷ βίῳ πολλάκις ἑώρακα καὶ αὐτὸς τόν τε Ἑωσφόρον καὶ τὸν Ἕσπερον καὶ ἄλλους τινὰς οὐδέποτε ἰόντας εἰς τὸν αὐτὸν δρόμον, ἀλλὰ πάντη πλανωμένους, τὸν δὲ Ἥλιόν που καὶ Σελήνην δρῶντας ταῦτα[1] ἀεὶ πάντες ξυνεπιστάμεθα.

αθ. Ταῦτ' ἔστι τοίνυν, ὦ Μέγιλλέ τε καὶ Κλεινία, νῦν ἃ δή φημι δεῖν περὶ θεῶν τῶν κατ' οὐρανὸν τούς γε ἡμετέρους πολίτας τε καὶ τοὺς νέους τὸ μέχρι τοσούτου μαθεῖν περὶ D ἀπάντων τούτων, μέχρι τοῦ μὴ βλασφημεῖν περὶ αὐτά, εὐφημεῖν δὲ ἀεὶ θύοντάς τε καὶ ἐν εὐχαῖς εὐχομένους εὐσεβῶς.

κλ. Τοῦτο μὲν ὀρθόν, εἴ γε πρῶτον μὲν δυνατόν ἐστιν ὃ λέγεις μαθεῖν· εἶτα, εἰ μὴ λέγομέν τι περὶ αὐτῶν ὀρθῶς νῦν, μαθόντες δὲ λέξομεν, συγχωρῶ κἀγὼ τό γε τοσοῦτον καὶ τοιοῦτον ὂν μαθητέον εἶναι. ταῦτ' οὖν ὡς ἔχοντά ἐσθ' οὕτω, πειρῶ σὺ μὲν ἐξηγεῖσθαι πάντως, ἡμεῖς δὲ ξυνέπεσθαί σοι μανθάνοντες.

E αθ. Ἀλλ' ἔστι μὲν οὐ ῥάδιον ὃ λέγω μαθεῖν,

CLIN. That is reasonable; but what science of this kind shall we find on the subject of stars?

ATH. At present, my good sirs, nearly all we Greeks say what is false about those mighty deities, the Sun and Moon.

CLIN. What is the falsehood?

ATH. We assert that they, and some other stars along with them, never travel along the same path; and we call them "planets." [1]

CLIN. Yes, by Zeus, Stranger, that is true; for I, during my life, have often noticed how Phosphorus and Hesperus and other stars never travel on the same course, but "wander" all ways; but as to the Sun and Moon, we all know that they are constantly doing this.

ATH. It is precisely for this reason, Megillus and Clinias, that I now assert that our citizens and our children ought to learn so much concerning all these facts about the gods of Heaven as to enable them not to blaspheme about them, but always to speak piously both at sacrifices and when they pray reverently at prayers.

CLIN. You are right, provided that, in the first place, it is possible to learn the subject you mention; and provided also that learning will make us correct any mistakes we may be making about them now,— then I, too, agree that a subject of such importance should be learned. This being so, do you make every effort to expound the matter, and we will endeavour to follow you and learn.

ATH. Well, the matter I speak of is not an easy

[1] *i.e.* "wanderers."

---

[1] ταῦτα Paris MS.: ταῦθ' & Par. marg., Zur., *al.*

οὐδ᾽ αὖ παντάπασι χαλεπόν, οὐδέ γέ τινος
χρόνου παμπόλλου. τεκμήριον δέ· ἐγὼ τούτων
οὔτε νέος οὔτε πάλαι ἀκηκοὼς σφῶν ἂν νῦν οὐκ
ἐν πολλῷ χρόνῳ δηλῶσαι δυναίμην. καί τοι
χαλεπά γε ὄντα οὐκ ἄν ποτε οἷός τ᾽ ἦν δηλοῦν
τηλικούτοις οὖσι τηλικοῦτος.

κλ. Ἀληθῆ λέγεις. ἀλλὰ τί καὶ φὴς τοῦτο
τὸ μάθημα, ὃ θαυμαστὸν μὲν λέγεις, προσῆκον
δ᾽. αὖ μαθεῖν τοῖς νέοις, οὐ γιγνώσκειν δὲ ἡμᾶς ;
822 πειρῶ περὶ αὐτοῦ τό γε τοσοῦτον φράζειν ὡς
σαφέστατα.

αθ. Πειρατέον. οὐ γάρ ἐστι τοῦτο, ὦ ἄριστοι,
τὸ δόγμα ὀρθὸν περὶ σελήνης τε καὶ ἡλίου καὶ
τῶν ἄλλων ἄστρων, ὡς ἄρα πλανᾶταί ποτε,
πᾶν δὲ τοὐναντίον ἔχει τούτου· τὴν αὐτὴν γὰρ
αὐτῶν ὁδὸν ἕκαστον καὶ οὐ πολλὰς ἀλλὰ μίαν
ἀεὶ κύκλῳ διεξέρχεται, φαίνεται δὲ πολλὰς
φερόμενον· τὸ δὲ τάχιστον αὐτῶν ὂν βραδύτατον
οὐκ ὀρθῶς αὖ δοξάζεται, τὸ δ᾽ ἐναντίον ἐναντίως.
B ταῦτ᾽ οὖν εἰ πέφυκε μὲν οὕτως, ἡμεῖς δὲ μὴ
ταύτῃ δοξάζομεν,[1] εἰ μὲν ἐν Ὀλυμπίᾳ θεόντων
ἵππων οὕτως ἢ δολιχοδρόμων ἀνδρῶν διενοούμεθα
πέρι, καὶ προσηγορεύομεν τὸν τάχιστον μὲν ὡς
βραδύτατον, τὸν δὲ βραδύτατον ὡς τάχιστον,
ἐγκώμιά τε ποιοῦντες ᾔδομεν τὸν ἡττώμενον
νενικηκότα, οὔτε ὀρθῶς ἂν οὔτ᾽ οἶμαι προσφιλῶς
τοῖς δρομεῦσιν ἡμᾶς ἂν τὰ ἐγκώμια προσάπτειν
ἀνθρώποις οὖσι· νῦν δὲ δὴ περὶ θεοὺς τὰ αὐτὰ
C ταῦτα ἐξαμαρτανόντων ἡμῶν ἆρ᾽ οὐκ οἰόμεθα
<ὃ> γελοῖόν τε καὶ οὐκ ὀρθὸν ἐκεῖ γιγνόμενον ἦν
ἂν τότε, νῦν ἐνταυθοῖ καὶ ἐν τούτοισι γίγνεσθαι

---

[1] δοξάζομεν Ast : δόξομεν MSS.

one to learn; nor yet is it altogether difficult and demanding very prolonged study. In proof of this —although I was told of it neither in the days of my youth nor long ago, I may be able to explain it to you in a comparatively short time. Whereas, if it had been a difficult subject, I should never have been able to explain it to you at all—I at my age to you at yours.

CLIN. Very true. But what is this science which you describe as marvellous and fitting for the young to learn, and which we are ignorant about? Do try to tell us thus much, at least, about it, with all possible clearness.

ATH. I must try. The opinion, my friends, that the Sun and Moon and the rest of the stars "wander" is not correct; the truth is precisely the opposite: each of them always travels in a circle one and the same path,—not many paths, although it appears to move along many paths; and the quickest of the stars is wrongly opined to be the slowest, and vice versa.[1] If these are the real facts and we imagine otherwise,—well, suppose we held a similar notion about horses racing at Olympia, or about long-distance runners, and proclaimed the quickest to be slowest and the slowest quickest, and sang chants lauding the loser as the winner, why, then, the laudations we bestowed on the runners would be neither right nor acceptable, though they were but mortal men. But in the present case, when we commit the same error about gods, do we not think that what would have been ludicrous and wrong there and then is, here and now and in dealing with this subject, by no means ludicrous and assuredly

---

[1] Cp. *Tim.* 39 D ff.

γελοῖον μὲν οὐδαμῶς,¹ οὐ μὴν οὐδὲ θεοφιλές γε,
ψευδῆ φήμην ἡμῶν κατὰ θεῶν ὑμνούντων ;

κλ. Ἀληθέστατα, εἴπερ γε οὕτω ταῦτ᾽ ἔστιν.

αθ. Οὐκοῦν ἂν μὲν δείξωμεν οὕτω ταῦτ᾽
ἔχοντα, μαθητέα μέχρι γε τούτου τὰ τοιαῦτα
πάντα, μὴ δειχθέντων δὲ ἐατέον ; καὶ ταῦτα ἡμῖν
οὕτω ξυγκείσθω ;

D κλ. Πάνυ μὲν οὖν.

αθ. Ἤδη τοίνυν χρὴ φάναι τέλος ἔχειν τά
γε παιδείας μαθημάτων πέρι νόμιμα. περὶ δὲ
θήρας ὡσαύτως διανοηθῆναι χρή, καὶ περὶ
ἁπάντων ὁπόσα τοιαῦτα. κινδυνεύει γὰρ δὴ
νομοθέτῃ τὸ προσταττόμενον ἐπὶ μεῖζον ἰέναι²
τοῦ νόμους θέντα ἀπηλλάχθαι, ἕτερον δέ τι πρὸς
τοῖς νόμοις εἶναι μεταξύ τι νουθετήσεώς τε
E πεφυκὸς ἅμα καὶ νόμων, ὃ δὴ πολλάκις ἡμῶν
ἐμπέπτωκε τοῖς λόγοις, οἷον περὶ τὴν τῶν
σφόδρα νέων παίδων τροφήν· οὐ γὰρ ἄρρητά
φαμεν εἶναι, λέγοντές τε αὐτὰ ὡς νόμους οἴεσθαι
τιθεμένους εἶναι πολλῆς ἀνοίας γέμειν. γεγραμ-
μένων δὴ ταύτῃ τῶν νόμων τε καὶ ὅλης τῆς
πολιτείας οὐ τέλεος ὁ τοῦ διαφέροντος πολίτου
πρὸς ἀρετὴν γίγνεται ἔπαινος, ὅταν αὐτόν τις
φῇ τὸν ὑπηρετήσαντα τοῖς νόμοις ἄριστα καὶ
πειθόμενον μάλιστα, τοῦτον εἶναι τὸν ἀγαθόν·
τελεώτερον δὲ ὧδε εἰρημένον, ὡς ἄρα ὃς ἂν τοῖς
τοῦ <νομοθέτου>³ νομοθετοῦντός τε καὶ ἐπαινοῦντος καὶ ψέγοντος πειθόμενος γράμμασι
823 διεξέλθῃ τὸν βίον ἄκρατον. οὗτος ὅ τε λόγος

¹ Zur. assigns γελοῖον μὲν οὐδαμῶς to Clin. (omitting the
<δ> after οἰόμεθα).
² ἰέναι Stephens : εἶναι MSS. (ἔτι for ἐπὶ England).
³ <νομοθέτου> added in best MSS.: om. Zur., vulg.

116

not pleasing to the gods, when concerning gods we repeat a tale that is false?

CLIN. Very true, if the facts are as you say.

ATH. Then, if we demonstrate that they really are so, shall all these subjects be learnt up to the point mentioned, and, failing that demonstration, be left alone? Is that to be our agreement?

CLIN. Certainly.

ATH. We may now say that our regulations concerning subjects of education have been completed. The subject of hunting, and similar pursuits, must now be dealt with in a similar manner. The duty laid upon the lawgiver probably goes further than the bare task of enacting laws: in addition to laws, there is something else which falls naturally between advice and law—a thing which has often cropped up in the course of our discussion,[1] as, for example, in connexion with the nurture of young children: such matters, we say, should not be left unregulated, but it would be most foolish to regard those regulations as enacted laws. When, then, the laws and the whole constitution have been thus written down, our praise of the citizen who is pre-eminent for virtue will not be complete when we say that the virtuous man is he who is the best servant of the laws and the most obedient; a more complete statement will be this,—that the virtuous man is he who passes through life consistently obeying the written rules of the lawgiver, as given in his legislation, approbation and disapprobation.[2] This statement is the

---

[1] 788 A ff., 793 A ff.

[2] *i.e.* for perfect virtue there is required not only obedience to statute law, but also conformity with all the other rules of conduct laid down by the lawgiver in the less rigid form of advice ("approbation" and "disapprobation").

ὀρθότατος εἰς ἔπαινον πολίτου, τόν τε νομοθέτην
οὕτως [1] δεῖ μὴ μόνον γράφειν τοὺς νόμους, πρὸς
δὲ τοῖς νόμοις ὅσα καλὰ αὐτῷ δοκεῖ καὶ μὴ καλὰ
εἶναι νόμοις ἐμπεπλεγμένα γράφειν, τὸν δὲ ἄκρον
πολίτην μηδὲν ἧττον ταῦτα ἐμπεδοῦν ἢ τὰ ταῖς
ζημίαις ὑπὸ νόμων κατειλημμένα.

Τὸ δὲ δὴ παρὸν ἡμῖν τὰ νῦν οἷον μάρτυρα ἐπα-
B γόμενοι δηλοῖμεν [2] ἂν ὃ βουλόμεθα μᾶλλον. θήρα
γὰρ πάμπολύ τι πρᾶγμά ἐστι, περιειλημμένον
ὀνόματι νῦν σχεδὸν ἑνί. πολλὴ μὲν γὰρ ἡ τῶν
ἐνύδρων, πολλὴ δὲ ἡ τῶν πτηνῶν, πάμπολυ δὲ καὶ
τὸ περὶ τὰ πεζὰ θηρεύματα, οὐ μόνον θηρίων ἀλλὰ
καὶ τὴν τῶν ἀνθρώπων ἄξιον ἐννοεῖν θήραν, τήν
τε κατὰ πόλεμον, πολλὴ δὲ καὶ ἡ κατὰ φιλίαν
θηρεύουσα, ἡ μὲν ἔπαινον, ἡ δὲ ψόγον ἔχει· καὶ
κλωπεῖαι καὶ λῃστῶν καὶ στρατοπέδων [στρατο-
C πέδοις] [3] θῆραι. θήρας δὲ πέρι τιθέντι τῷ
νομοθέτῃ τοὺς νόμους οὔτε μὴ δηλοῦν ταῦθ'
οἷόν τε, οὔτε ἐπὶ πᾶσι τάξεις καὶ ζημίας ἐπι-
τιθέντα ἀπειλητικὰ νόμιμα τιθέναι. τί δὴ
δραστέον περὶ τὰ τοιαῦτα; τὸν μέν, τὸν νομοθέτην, ἐπαινέσαι καὶ ψέξαι χρεὼν τὰ περὶ θήρας
πρὸς τοὺς τῶν νέων πόνους τε καὶ ἐπιτηδεύματα,
τὸν δ' αὖ νέον ἀκούσαντα πείθεσθαι, καὶ μήθ'
ἡδονὴν μήτε πόνον ἐξείργειν αὐτόν, τῶν δὲ περὶ
ἕκαστα ἀπειληθέντων μετὰ ζημίας καὶ νομο-

---

[1] οὕτως W.-Möllendorff: ὄντως MSS., edd.
[2] ἐπαγόμενοι δηλοῖμεν Badham: ἐπαγόμεθα· δηλοῖ μὲν Zur.,
al. (δηλοιμεν Paris MS.).
[3] [στρατοπέδοις] I bracket.

most correct way of praising the citizen; and in this way, moreover, the lawgiver must not only write down the laws, but in addition to the laws, and combined with them, he must write down his decisions as to what things are good and what bad; and the perfect citizen must abide by these decisions no less than by the rules enforced by legal penalties.

The subject now before us we may adduce as a witness to show more clearly what we mean. Hunting is a large and complex matter, all of which is now generally embraced under this single name. Of the hunting of water-animals there are many varieties, and many of the hunting of fowls; and very many varieties also of hunts of land-animals— not of beasts only, but also, mark you, of men, both in war and often, too, in friendship, a kind of hunt that is partly approved and partly disapproved;[1] and then there are robberies and hunts carried on by pirates and by bands. When the lawgiver is making laws about hunting, he is necessarily bound to make this point clear, and to lay down minatory directions by imposing regulations and penalties for all these kinds. What then ought to be done about these matters? The lawgiver, for his part, will be right in praising or blaming hunting with an eye to the toils and pursuits of the young; and the young man will be right in listening and obeying, and in allowing neither pleasure nor toil to hinder him, and in holding in greater respect the orders that are

---

[1] Cp. *Soph.* 222 D where ἡ τῶν ἐρώντων θήρα ("the lovers' chase") is mentioned as a sub-species of θηρευτική: and in *Sympos.* 203 D the God of Love is described as "a mighty hunter" (θηρευτὴς δεινός).

D θετηθέντων τὰ μετ' ἐπαίνου ῥηθέντα μᾶλλον τιμᾶν καὶ προσταχθέντα ἀποτελεῖν.

Τούτων δὴ προρρηθέντων ἑξῆς ἂν γίγνοιτο ἔμμετρος ἔπαινος θήρας καὶ ψόγος, ἥτις μὲν βελτίους ἀποτελεῖ τὰς ψυχὰς τῶν νέων, ἐπαινοῦντος, ψέγοντος δὲ ἢ τἀναντία. λέγωμεν τοίνυν τὸ μετὰ τοῦτο ἑξῆς προσαγορεύοντες δι' εὐχῆς τοὺς νέους, Ὦ φίλοι, εἴθ' ὑμᾶς μήτε τις ἐπιθυμία μήτ' ἔρως τῆς περὶ θάλατταν θήρας ποτὲ λάβοι μηδὲ ἀγκιστρείας
E μηδ' ὅλως τῆς τῶν ἐνύδρων ζώων, μήτε ἐγρηγορόσι μήτε εὕδουσι κύρτοις ἀργὸν θήραν διαπονουμένοις. μηδ' αὖ ἄγρας ἀνθρώπων κατὰ θάλατταν λῃστείας τε ἵμερος ἐπελθὼν ὑμῖν θηρευτὰς ὠμοὺς καὶ ἀνόμους ἀποτελοῖ. κλωπείας δ' ἐν χώρᾳ καὶ πόλει μηδὲ εἰς τὸν ἔσχατον ἐπέλθοι νοῦν ἅψασθαι. μηδ' αὖ πτηνῶν θήρας αἱμύλος ἔρως
824 οὐ σφόδρα ἐλευθέριος ἐπέλθοι τινὶ νέων. πεζῶν δὴ μόνον θήρευσίς τε καὶ ἄγρα λοιπὴ τοῖς παρ' ἡμῖν ἀθληταῖς, ὧν ἡ μὲν τῶν εὐδόντων αὖ κατὰ μέρη, νυκτερεία κληθεῖσα, ἀργῶν ἀνδρῶν, οὐκ ἀξία ἐπαίνου, οὐδ' ᾗ τοι[1] διαπαύματα πόνων ἔχουσα, ἄρκυσί τε καὶ πάγαις ἀλλ' οὐ φιλοπόνου ψυχῆς νίκῃ χειρουμένων τὴν ἄγριον τῶν θηρίων ῥώμην. μόνη δὴ πᾶσι λοιπὴ καὶ ἀρίστη ἡ τῶν τετραπόδων ἵπποις καὶ κυσὶ καὶ τοῖς ἑαυτῶν θήρα σώμασιν, ὧν ἁπάντων κρατοῦσι δρόμοις
B καὶ πληγαῖς καὶ βολαῖς, αὐτόχειρες θηρεύοντες, ὅσοις ἀνδρίας τῆς θείας ἐπιμελές.

[1] ᾗ τοι: ἡ τῶν MSS. (ἧττον Burnet).

sanctioned by praise, and carrying them out, rather than those which are enacted by law under threat of penalties.

After these prefatory observations there will follow adequate praise and blame of hunting—praise of the kind which renders the souls of the young better, and blame of the kind which does the opposite. Our next step will be to address the young people with prayer—" O friends, would that you might never be seized with any desire or craving for hunting by sea, or for angling, or for ever pursuing water-animals with creels that do your lazy hunting for you, whether you sleep or wake. And may no longing for man-hunting by sea and piracy overtake you, and render you cruel and lawless hunters; and may the thought of committing robbery in country or city not so much as cross your minds. Neither may there seize upon any of the young the crafty craving for snaring birds—no very gentlemanly pursuit! Thus there is left for our athletes only the hunting and capture of land-animals. Of this branch of hunting, the kind called night-stalking, which is the job of lazy men who sleep in turn, is one that deserves no praise; nor does that kind deserve praise in which there are intervals of rest from toil, when men master the wild force of beasts by nets and traps instead of doing so by the victorious might of a toil-loving soul. Accordingly, the only kind left for all, and the best kind, is the hunting of quadrupeds with horses and dogs and the hunter's own limbs, when men hunt in person, and subdue all the creatures by means of their own running, striking and shooting—all the men, that is to say, who cultivate the courage that is divine."

PLATO

Τούτων δὴ πάντων ἔπαινος μὲν πέρι καὶ ψόγος
ὁ διειρημένος ἂν εἴη λόγος, νόμος δὲ ὅδε· τούτους
μηδεὶς τοὺς ἱεροὺς ὄντως θηρευτὰς κωλυέτω, ὅπου
καὶ ὅπῃ περ ἂν ἐθέλωσι κυνηγετεῖν· νυκτερευτὴν
δὲ ἄρκυσι καὶ πλεκταῖς πιστὸν μηδεὶς μηδέποτε
ἐάσῃ μηδαμοῦ θηρεῦσαι· τὸν ὀρνιθευτὴν δὲ ἐν
ἀργοῖς μὲν καὶ ὄρεσι μὴ κωλυέτω, ἐν ἐργασίμοις
δὲ καὶ ἱεροῖς ἀγροῖς [1] ἐξειργέτω ὁ προστυγχάνων·
C ἐνυγροθηρευτὴν δέ, πλὴν ἐν λιμέσι καὶ ἱεροῖς
ποταμοῖς τε καὶ ἔλεσι καὶ λίμναις· ἐν τοῖς
ἄλλοις δὲ ἐξέστω θηρεύειν μὴ χρώμενον ὀπῶν
ἀναθολώσει μόνον. νῦν οὖν ἤδη πάντα χρὴ
φάναι τέλος ἔχειν τά γε παιδείας πέρι νομιμα.

ΚΛ. Καλῶς ἂν λέγοις.

[1] ἀγροῖς Badham : ἀγρίοις most MSS., Zur.; al. ἀγίοις (καὶ
ἱερατικοῖς England, with one MS.).

122

Concerning the whole of this subject, the exposition we have now given will serve as the praise and blame; and the law will run thus,—"None shall hinder these truly sacred hunters from hunting wheresoever and howsoever they wish; but the night-trapper who trusts to nets and snares no one shall ever allow to hunt anywhere. The fowler no man shall hinder on fallow land or mountain; but he that finds him on tilled fields or on sacred glebes shall drive him off. The fisherman shall be allowed to hunt in all waters except havens and sacred rivers and pools and lakes, but only on condition that he makes no use of muddying juices." [1] So now, at last, we may say that all our laws about education are complete.

CLIN. You may rightly say so.

[1] *i.e.* vegetable juices which taint the water and paralyse the fish.

828 ΑΘ. Τουτων μην ἐχόμενά ἐστι τάξασθαι μὲν
καὶ νομοθετήσασθαι ἑορτὰς μετὰ τῶν ἐκ Δελφῶν
μαντειῶν, αἵτινες θυσίαι καὶ θεοῖς οἷστισιν ἄμεινον
καὶ λῷον θυούσῃ τῇ πόλει γίγνοιντ' ἄν· πότε δὲ
καὶ πόσαι τὸν ἀριθμόν, σχεδὸν ἴσως ἡμέτερον ἂν
νομοθετεῖν [ἔνιά γ']¹ αὐτῶν εἴη.

ΚΛ. Τάχ' ἂν τὸν ἀριθμόν.

ΑΘ. Τὸν ἀριθμὸν δὴ λέγωμεν πρῶτον· ἔστωσαν
B γὰρ τῶν μὲν πέντε καὶ ἑξήκοντα καὶ τριακοσίων
μηδὲν ἀπολείπουσαι, ὅπως ἂν μία γέ τις ἀρχὴ
θύῃ θεῶν ἢ δαιμόνων τινὶ ἀεὶ ὑπὲρ πόλεώς τε καὶ
αὐτῶν καὶ κτημάτων. ταῦτα δὲ ξυνελθόντες ἐξηγη-
ταὶ καὶ ἱερεῖς ἱέρειαί τε καὶ μάντεις μετὰ νομοφυλάκων ταξάντων, ἃ παραλείπειν ἀνάγκη τῷ νομοθέτῃ
καὶ δὴ καὶ αὐτοῦ τούτου χρὴ γίγνεσθαι ἐπιγνώμονας τοῦ παραλειπομένου τούτους τοὺς αὐτούς. ὁ
μὲν γὰρ δὴ νόμος ἐρεῖ δώδεκα μὲν ἑορτὰς εἶναι
τοῖς δώδεκα θεοῖς, ὧν ἂν ἡ φυλὴ ἑκάστη ἐπώνυμος
C ᾖ, θύοντας τούτων ἑκάστοις ἔμμηνα ἱερά, χορούς.
τε καὶ ἀγῶνας μουσικούς, τοὺς δὲ γυμνικοὺς κατὰ
τὸ πρέπον προσνέμοντας τοῖς θεοῖς τε αὐτοῖς ἅμα
καὶ ταῖς ὥραις ἑκάσταις, γυναικείας τε ἑορτάς,
ὅσαις χωρὶς ἀνδρῶν προσήκει καὶ ὅσαις μή, διανέμοντας. ἔτι δὲ καὶ τὸ τῶν χθονίων καὶ ὅσους αὖ

---

¹ [ἔνιά γ'] bracketed by England.

¹ Cp. 771 D ff.

BOOK VIII

ATH. Our next task is, with the help of the Delphic oracles, to arrange and ordain by law the festivals, prescribing what sacrifices, and to what deities, it will be good and right for the State to offer: the times and the number of them, however, it is, no doubt, our own business to ordain by ourselves.

CLIN. Very likely, as regards the number of them.

ATH. Then let us first state the number. There shall be not less than 365 feasts, so that some one official may always be doing sacrifice to some god or daemon on behalf of the State, the people, and their property.[1] The interpreters, the priests, the priestesses and the prophets shall assemble, and, in company with the Law-wardens, they shall ordain what the lawgiver is obliged to omit: moreover, these same persons shall determine wherein such omissions consist. For the law will state that there are twelve feasts to the twelve gods who give their names to the several tribes: to each of these they shall perform monthly sacrifices and assign choirs and musical contests, and also gymnastic contests, as is suitable both to the gods themselves and to the several seasons of the year; and they shall ordain also women's festivals, prescribing how many of these shall be for women only, and how many open also to men. Further, they must determine, in conformity with the law, the rites proper to the nether gods,

θεοὺς οὐρανίους ἐπονομαστέον καὶ τί[1] τῶν τούτοις
ἑπομένων οὐ ξυμμικτέον ἀλλὰ χωριστέον, ἐν τῷ
D τοῦ Πλούτωνος μηνὶ τῷ δωδεκάτῳ κατὰ τὸν νόμον
ἀποδιδόντας, καὶ οὐ δυσχεραντέον πολεμικοῖς
ἀνθρώποις τὸν τοιοῦτον θεόν, ἀλλὰ τιμητέον ὡς
ὄντα ἀεὶ τῷ τῶν ἀνθρώπων γένει ἄριστον· κοινωνία
γὰρ ψυχῇ καὶ σώματι διαλύσεως οὐκ ἔστιν ἢ
κρεῖττον, ὡς ἐγὼ φαίην ἂν σπουδῇ λέγων· πρὸς
τούτοις δὲ διάνοιαν χρὴ σχεῖν τοὺς διαιρήσοντας
ἱκανῶς ταῦτα τοιάνδε, ὡς ἔσθ' ἡμῖν ἡ πόλις οἵαν
οὐκ ἄν τις ἑτέραν εὕροι τῶν νῦν περὶ χρόνου
σχολῆς καὶ τῶν ἀναγκαίων ἐξουσίας, δεῖ δὲ αὐτήν,
829 καθάπερ ἕνα ἄνθρωπον, ζῆν εὖ. τοῖς δὲ εὐδαιμόνως ζῶσιν ὑπάρχειν ἀνάγκη πρῶτον τὸ μήτε
ἀδικεῖν ἄλλους μήθ' ὑφ' ἑτέρων αὐτοὺς ἀδικεῖσθαι.
τούτοιν δὲ τὸ μὲν οὐ πάνυ χαλεπόν, τοῦ δὲ μὴ
ἀδικεῖσθαι κτήσασθαι δύναμιν παγχάλεπον, καὶ
οὐκ ἔστιν αὐτὸ τελέως σχεῖν ἄλλως ἢ τελέως γενόμενον ἀγαθόν· ταὐτὸν δὴ τοῦτο ἔστι καὶ πόλει
ὑπάρχειν, γενομένῃ μὲν ἀγαθῇ βίος εἰρηνικός,
πολεμικὸς δὲ ἔξωθέν τε καὶ ἔνδοθεν, ἂν ᾖ κακή.
τούτων δὲ ταύτῃ σχεδὸν ἐχόντων οὐκ ἐν πολέμῳ
B τὸν πόλεμον ἑκάστοις γυμναστέον, ἀλλ' ἐν τῷ τῆς
εἰρήνης βίῳ. δεῖ τοίνυν πόλιν ἑκάστου μηνὸς
νοῦν κεκτημένην στρατεύεσθαι μὴ ἔλαττον μιᾶς
ἡμέρας, πλείους δέ, ὡς ἂν καὶ τοῖς ἄρχουσι
ξυνδοκῇ, μηδὲν χειμῶνας ἢ καύματα διευλαβου-
μένους, αὐτούς τε ἅμα καὶ γυναῖκας καὶ παῖδας,
ὅταν ὡς πανδημίαν ἐξάγειν δόξῃ τοῖς ἄρχουσι,

---

[1] τί W. R. Paton : τὸ MSS., edd.

---

[1] Cp. 832 C ff., 835 D, E.

and how many of the celestial gods should be invoked, and what of the rites connected with them
should not be mingled but kept apart, and put them
in the twelfth month, which is sacred to Pluto;
and this god should not be disliked by men who are
warriors, but honoured as one who is always most
good to the human race; for, as I would assert in
all seriousness, union is in no way better for soul
and body than dissolution. Moreover, if they are to
arrange these matters adequately, these persons
must believe that no other State exists which can
compare with ours in respect of the degree in which
it possesses leisure and control over the necessities
of life;[1] and believe also that it, like an individual,
ought to lead a good life. But for a good and blessed
life, the first requisite is neither to do wrong oneself
nor to suffer wrong from others. Of these, the
former is not very hard, but it is very hard to secure
immunity from suffering wrong;[2] indeed, it is impossible to gain this perfectly, except by becoming
perfectly good. So likewise a State may obtain a
life of peace if it becomes good, but if bad, a life of
war both abroad and at home. This being so, all
men must train for war not in war-time, but while
they are living in peace.[3] Therefore, a judicious
State must carry out a march, every month, for not
less than one whole day, or more (according as the
rulers decree),[4] paying no heed to cold weather or
hot: all shall join in it—men, women and children
—whenever the rulers decide to march them out

[2] Cp. 663 A, 904 E f. "Perfect goodness" helps to
secure this "immunity" because it includes the virtue of
"courage": people do not lightly provoke the brave warrior.
[3] Cp. 803 D, 814 D.   [4] Cp. 830 D.

PLATO

τοτὲ δὲ καὶ κατὰ μέρη· καί τινας ἀεὶ παιδιὰς
μηχανᾶσθαι καλὰς ἅμα θυσίαις, ὅπως ἂν γίγνων-
C ται μάχαι τινὲς ἑορταστικαί, μιμούμεναι τὰς
πολεμικὰς ὅτι μάλιστα ἐναργῶς μάχας. νικητήρια
δὲ καὶ ἀριστεῖα ἑκάστοισι τούτων δεῖ διανέμειν
ἐγκώμιά τε καὶ ψόγους ποιεῖν ἀλλήλοις, ὁποῖός
τις ἂν ἕκαστος γίγνηται κατά τε τοὺς ἀγῶνας ἐν
παντί τε αὖ τῷ βίῳ, τόν τε ἄριστον δοκοῦντα
εἶναι κοσμοῦντας καὶ τὸν μὴ ψέγοντας. ποιητὴς
δὲ ἔστω τῶν τοιούτων μὴ ἅπας, ἀλλὰ γεγονὼς
πρῶτον μὲν μὴ ἔλαττον πεντήκοντα ἐτῶν, μηδ' αὖ
τῶν ὁπόσοι ποίησιν μὲν καὶ Μοῦσαν ἱκανῶς
κεκτημένοι ἐν αὑτοῖς εἰσί, καλὸν δὲ ἔργον καὶ
D ἐπιφανὲς μηδὲν δράσαντες πώποτε· ὅσοι δὲ
ἀγαθοί τε αὐτοὶ καὶ τίμιοι ἐν τῇ πόλει, ἔργων
ὄντες δημιουργοὶ καλῶν, τὰ τῶν τοιούτων
ᾀδέσθω ποιήματα, ἐὰν καὶ μὴ μουσικὰ πεφύκῃ.
κρίσις δὲ αὐτῶν ἔστω παρά τε τῷ παιδευτῇ καὶ
τοῖς ἄλλοις νομοφύλαξι, τοῦτο ἀποδιδόντων
αὐτοῖς γέρας, παρρησίαν ἐν Μούσαις εἶναι μόνοις,
τοῖς δὲ ἄλλοις μηδεμίαν ἐξουσίαν γίγνεσθαι μηδέ
τινα τολμᾶν ᾄδειν ἀδόκιμον Μοῦσαν [μὴ κρινάν-
E των τῶν νομοφυλάκων],[1] μηδ' ἂν ἡδίων ᾖ τῶν
Θαμύρου τε καὶ Ὀρφείων ὕμνων, ἀλλ' ὅσα τε
ἱερὰ κριθέντα ποιήματα ἐδόθη τοῖς θεοῖς καὶ ὅσα
ἀγαθῶν ὄντα ἀνδρῶν ψέγοντα ἢ ἐπαινοῦντά τινας
ἐκρίθη μετρίως δρᾶν τὸ τοιοῦτον.

Τὰ αὐτὰ δὲ λέγω στρατείας τε πέρι καὶ τῆς ἐν
ποιήσεσι παρρησίας γυναιξί τε καὶ ἀνδράσιν
ὁμοίως γίγνεσθαι δεῖν. χρὴ δὲ ἀναφέρειν παραδει-

---

[1] [μὴ . . . νομοφυλάκων] bracketed by England.

en masse, and at other times they shall go in sections. Along with sacrifices, they must continually devise noble games, to serve as festival-contests, modelled as closely as possible on those of war. At each of these they must distribute prizes and awards of merit, and compose for one another speeches of praise and blame, according to the character each one exhibits not only in the contests, but in his life generally, magnifying him who is accounted most good and blaming him who is not. Such speeches not everyone shall compose; for, first, no one who is under fifty years old shall compose one, and further, no one shall do so who, though he may be fully proficient in poetry and music, has not as yet performed any noble or notable deed. But, even though they be not musical, those poems shall be sung which are composed by men [1] who are personally good and honoured in the State as performers of noble deeds. The adjudication of these shall lie with the Educator and the rest of the Law-wardens, who shall grant them the sole privilege of free speech in song; whereas to the others no permission shall be given; nor yet shall anyone venture to sing an unauthorised song— not even should it be sweeter than the hymns of Orpheus or of Thamyras,—but only such sacred poems as have won the judges' approval and have been presented to the gods, or those by good men which have been adjudged to have duly distributed praise or blame.

In regard both to military operations and to freedom of poetic speech I state that the same rules shall apply equally to both men and women. The lawgiver ought to commune with himself and

[1] Cp. 936 A.

PLATO

κνύπτα ἑαυτῷ τὸν νομοθέτην τῷ λόγῳ· Φέρε, τίνας
830 ποτὲ τρέφω τὴν πόλιν ὅλην παρασκευάσας ; ἆρ᾽
οὐκ ἀθλητὰς τῶν μεγίστων ἀγώνων, οἷς ἀνταγωνισταὶ μυρίοι ὑπάρχουσι ; Καὶ πάνυ γε, φαίη τις ἂν
ὀρθῶς λέγων. Τί δῆτα ; εἰ πύκτας ἢ παγκρατια-
στὰς ἐτρέφομεν ἤ τι τῶν τοιούτων ἕτερον ἀγωνι-
σμάτων ἀθλοῦντας, ἆρα εἰς αὐτὸν ἂν ἀπηντῶμεν
τὸν ἀγῶνα ἐν τῷ πρόσθεν χρόνῳ οὐδενὶ καθ᾽ ἡμέραν
προσμαχόμενοι ; ἢ πύκται γε ὄντες παμπόλλας ἂν
ἡμέρας ἔμπροσθεν τοῦ ἀγῶνος ἐμανθάνομέν τε ἂν
B μάχεσθαι καὶ διεπονούμεθα, μιμούμενοι πάντα
ἐκεῖνα ὁπόσοις ἐμέλλομεν εἰς τότε χρήσεσθαι περὶ
τῆς νίκης διαμαχόμενοι ; καὶ ὡς ἐγγύτατα τοῦ
ὁμοίου ἰόντες ἀντὶ ἱμάντων σφαίρας ἂν περιεδού-
μεθα, ὅπως αἱ πληγαί τε καὶ αἱ τῶν πληγῶν εὐλά-
βειαι διεμελετῶντο εἰς τὸ δυνατὸν ἱκανῶς ; εἴ τε τις
ἡμῖν συγγυμναστῶν συνέβαινεν ἀπορία πλείων, ἆρ᾽
ἂν δείσαντες τὸν τῶν ἀνοήτων γέλωτα οὐκ ἂν ἐτολ-
μῶμεν κρεμαννύντες εἴδωλον ἄψυχον γυμνάζεσθαι
πρὸς αὐτό ; καὶ ἔτι πάντων τῶν τε ἐμψύχων καὶ
C τῶν ἀψύχων ἀπορήσαντές ποτε, ἐν ἐρημίᾳ συγγυμναστῶν ἆρά γε οὐκ ἐτολμήσαμεν ἂν αὐτοὶ πρὸς
ἡμᾶς αὐτοὺς σκιαμαχεῖν ὄντως ; ἢ τί ποτε ἄλλο
τὴν τοῦ χειρονομεῖν μελέτην ἄν τις φαίη γεγονέναι ;

κλ. Σχεδόν, ὦ ξένε, οὐδὲν ἄλλο γε πλὴν τοῦτο
αὐτὸ ὃ σὺ νῦν ἔφθεγξαι.

αθ. Τί οὖν ; τὸ τῆς πόλεως ἡμῖν μάχιμον
ἢ χεῖρόν τι παρασκευασάμενον τῶν τοιούτων
ἀγωνιστῶν εἰς τὸν μέγιστον τῶν ἀγώνων ἑκάστοτε
τολμήσει παριέναι, διαμαχούμενον περὶ ψυχῆς
[τε] καὶ παίδων καὶ χρημάτων καὶ ὅλης τῆς
D πόλεως ; καὶ ταῦτα δὴ φοβηθεὶς αὐτῶν ὁ νομο-

reason thus—"Come now, what men am I to rear
up, when I have made ready the whole State? Are
they not to be competitors in the greatest of contests, wherein their antagonists will be numberless?"
"Most certainly," one would rightly reply. What
then? Suppose we had been rearing boxers or pan-
cratiasts or competitors in any similar branch of
athletics, should we have gone straight into the
contest without previously engaging in daily combat
with someone? If we were boxers, for a great many
days before the contest we should have been learning
how to fight, and working hard, practising in mimicry
all those methods we meant to employ on the day
we should be fighting for victory, and imitating the
real thing as nearly as possible: thus, we should don
padded gloves instead of proper ring-gloves, so as to
get the best possible practice in giving blows and
dodging them; and if we chanced to be very short
of training-mates, do you suppose that we should be
deterred by fear of the laughter of fools from hang-
ing up a lifeless dummy and practising on it?
Indeed, if ever we were in a desert, and without
either live or lifeless training-mates, would we not
have recourse to shadow-fighting of the most literal
kind, against ourselves? Or what else should one
call the practice of pugilistic posturing?

CLIN. There is no other name for it, Stranger, than
the one you have just given to it.

ATH. What then? Is the fighting force of our
State to venture to come forward every time to fight
for their lives, their children, their goods, and for the
whole State, after a less thorough preparation than
the competitors we have been describing? And so
is their lawgiver, through fear lest these training-

131

θέτης τὰ πρὸς ἀλλήλους γυμνάσια μὴ φαίνηταί
τισι γελοῖα, οὐκ ἄρα νομοθετήσει στρατεύεσθαι
προστάττων μάλιστα μὲν ἑκάστης ἡμέρας τά γε
σμικρὰ χωρὶς τῶν ὅπλων, χορούς τε εἰς ταῦτα
ἅμα καὶ γυμναστικὴν πᾶσαν ξυντείνων; τὰς δὲ
οἷόν τινας μείζους τε καὶ ἐνοπλίους[1] γυμνασίας
μὴ ἔλαττον ἢ κατὰ μῆνα ἕκαστον ποιεῖσθαι
E προστάξει, ἁμίλλας τε πρὸς ἀλλήλους ποιουμένους κατὰ πᾶσαν τὴν χώραν, ἐπὶ καταλήψιν
χωρίων ἁμιλλωμένους καὶ ἐνέδρας, καὶ πᾶσαν
μιμουμένους τὴν πολεμικὴν ὄντως σφαιρομαχεῖν
τε καὶ βολαῖς ὡς ἐγγύτατα τῶν ἀληθῶν χρωμένους
ὑποκινδύνοις βέλεσιν, ὅπως μὴ παντάπασιν
ἄφοβος ἡ πρὸς ἀλλήλους γίγνηται παιδιά, δείματα δὲ παρέχῃ καί τινα τρόπον δηλοῖ τόν τε
831 εὔψυχον καὶ τὸν μή, καὶ τοῖς μὲν τιμάς, τοῖς δὲ
καὶ ἀτιμίας διανέμων ὀρθῶς τὴν πόλιν ὅλην εἰς
τὸν ἀληθινὸν ἀγῶνα διὰ βίου παρασκευάζῃ χρη-
σίμην· καὶ δὴ καί τινος ἀποθανόντος οὕτως, ὡς
ἀκουσίου τοῦ φόνου γενομένου, τιθῇ τὸν ἀποκτείναντα κατὰ νόμον καθαρθέντα καθαρὸν εἶναι
χεῖρας, ἡγούμενος ἀνθρώπων μὲν τελευτησάντων
μὴ πολλῶν ἑτέρους πάλιν οὐ χείρους φύσεσθαι,
φόβου δὲ οἷον τελευτήσαντος ἐν πᾶσι τοῖς τοιούτοις βάσανον οὐχ εὑρήσειν τῶν τε ἀμεινόνων καὶ
B χειρόνων, οὐ σμικρῷ πόλει μεῖζον κακὸν ἐκείνου.

ΚΛ. Ξυμφαῖμεν ἂν ἡμεῖς γε, ὦ ξένε, τὰ τοιαῦτα
δεῖν καὶ νομοθετεῖν καὶ ἐπιτηδεύειν πόλιν ἅπασαν.

ΑΘ. Ἆρ᾽ οὖν γιγνώσκομεν ἅπαντες τὴν αἰτίαν

---

[1] ἐνοπλίους ci. Stallb., England : ἐλάττους MSS.

[1] "Sphaeromachia" was a (hand) ball contest between
opposing sides (something like our hockey or polo matches).

bouts may appear ridiculous to some, to refrain from laying down laws whereby he will ordain field-operations, of which the minor kind, without heavy arms, will take place daily, if possible,—and to this end both the choristry and all the gymnastic shall be directed,—while the others, as a major kind of gymnastics in full armour, he shall order to be held at least once a month? In this latter kind they will engage in contests with one another throughout the whole country, contending in the capturing of forts and in ambuscades and in all forms of mimic warfare; in fact, they shall do literal fighting with balls[1] and darts as nearly real as possible,—though the points of the darts shall be made less dangerous,—in order that their games of combat may not be devoid of some element of alarm, but may provide terrors and indicate to some extent who is stout-hearted and who not: to the former the lawgiver shall duly assign honours, to the latter degradation, that thus he may prepare the whole State to be serviceable throughout life in the real contest. Moreover, if a man gets killed in these sham fights, inasmuch as the murder is involuntary, he shall pronounce the slayer to be pure of hands, when he has been legally purified; for he will reflect that, when a few men die, others equally good will grow up in their place, whereas, once fear is, so to speak, dead, he will be unable to find a test to distinguish, in all such cases, the good from the bad,—and that is a far greater evil than the other for a State.

CLIN. We, at least, Stranger, would certainly agree that every State should both ordain and practise these things.

ATH. Are we all aware of the reason why such

διότι ποτὲ νῦν ἐν ταῖς πόλεσιν ἡ τοιαύτη χορεία
καὶ ἀγωνία σχεδὸν οὐδαμῇ οὐδαμῶς ἐστίν, εἰ μὴ
πάνυ τι σμικρά ; ἢ φῶμεν δι' ἀμαθίαν τῶν πολλῶν
καὶ τῶν τιθέντων αὐτοῖς τοὺς νόμους ;

ΚΛ. Τάχ' ἄν.

ΑΘ. Οὐδαμῶς, ὦ μακάριε Κλεινία· δύο δὲ χρὴ
C φάναι τούτων αἰτίας εἶναι, καὶ μάλα ἱκανάς.

ΚΛ. Ποίας ;

ΑΘ. Τὴν μέν, ὑπ' ἔρωτος πλούτου πάντα χρόνον
ἄσχολον ποιοῦντος τῶν ἄλλων ἐπιμελεῖσθαι
πλὴν τῶν ἰδίων κτημάτων, ἐξ ὧν κρεμαμένη πᾶσα
ψυχὴ πολίτου παντὸς οὐκ ἄν ποτε δύναιτο τῶν
ἄλλων ἐπιμέλειαν ἴσχειν πλὴν τοῦ καθ' ἡμέραν
κέρδους· καὶ ὅ τι μὲν πρὸς τοῦτο φέρει μάθημα ἢ
καὶ ἐπιτήδευμα, ἰδίᾳ πᾶς μανθάνειν τε καὶ ἀσκεῖν
ἑτοιμότατός ἐστι, τῶν δὲ ἄλλων καταγελᾷ.
D τοῦτο μὲν ἓν καὶ ταύτην μίαν αἰτίαν χρὴ φάναι τοῦ
μήτε τοῦτο μήτ' ἄλλο μηδὲν καλὸν κἀγαθὸν ἐθέλειν
ἐπιτήδευμα πόλιν σπουδάζειν, ἀλλὰ διὰ τὴν τοῦ
χρυσοῦ τε καὶ ἀργύρου ἀπληστίαν πᾶσαν μὲν
τέχνην καὶ μηχανὴν καλλίω τε καὶ ἀσχημονεστέ-
ραν ἐθέλειν ὑπομένειν πάντα ἄνδρα, εἰ μέλλει
πλούσιος ἔσεσθαι, καὶ πρᾶξιν πράττειν ὅσιόν τε
καὶ ἀνόσιον καὶ πάντως αἰσχράν, μηδὲν δυσχεραί-
E νοντα, ἐὰν μόνον ἔχῃ δύναμιν καθάπερ θηρίῳ τοῦ
φαγεῖν παντοδαπὰ καὶ πιεῖν ὡσαύτως καὶ ἀφροδισίων πᾶσαν πάντως παρασχεῖν πλησμονήν.

ΚΛ. Ὀρθῶς.

ΑΘ. Αὕτη μὲν τοίνυν, ἣν λέγω, μία κείσθω
διακωλύουσα αἰτία τοῦ μήτε ἄλλο καλὸν μήτε τὰ
πρὸς τὸν πόλεμον ἱκανῶς ἐᾶσαι[1] ἀσκεῖν τὰς

_____

[1] ἐᾶσαι: ἐῶσα MSS., edd. (bracketed by Hermann).

choristry and such contests do not at present exist anywhere in the States, except to a very small extent? Shall we say that this is due to the ignorance of the populace and of those who legislate for them?

CLIN.   Possibly.

ATH.   Not so, by any means, my ingenious Clinias! What we ought to say is that there are two causes, and both most weighty ones.

CLIN.   What are they?

ATH.   The first springs from a lust for wealth [1] which allows a man no leisure time for attention to anything else save his own private property; and when the soul of every citizen hangs upon this, it is incapable of attending to matters other than daily gain. Whatsoever science or pursuit leads to this, every man individually is most ready to learn and to practise; but all else he laughs to scorn. This we must assert to be one particular cause why a State is unwilling to be in earnest about this, or any other, fine and noble pursuit; and why, on the other hand, every individual, because of his greed for silver and gold, is willing to toil at every art and device, noble or ignoble, if he is likely to get rich by it,—willing, too, to perform actions both holy and unholy—nay, utterly shameful—without a scruple, provided only that he is able to sate himself to repletion, like a beast, with all manner of foods and drinks and wenchings.

CLIN.   True.

ATH.   Then let this which I describe be laid down as one cause which hinders the States from adequately practising either military operations or any other

---

[1] Cp. 705 A, 742 D.

πόλεις, ἀλλ᾽ ἐμπόρους τε καὶ ναυκλήρους καὶ
διακόνους πάντως τοὺς φύσει κοσμίους τῶν ἀνθρώπων ἀπεργαζομένη, τοὺς δὲ ἀνδρείους λῃστὰς
καὶ τοιχωρύχους καὶ ἱεροσύλους καὶ πολεμικοὺς
832 καὶ τυραννικοὺς ποιοῦσα, καὶ μάλ᾽ ἐνίοτε οὐκ
ἀφυεῖς ὄντας, δυστυχοῦντάς γε μήν.

ΚΛ. Πῶς λέγεις;

ΑΘ. Πῶς μὲν οὖν αὐτοὺς οὐ λέγοιμ᾽ ἂν τὸ
παράπαν δυστυχεῖς, οἷς γε ἀνάγκη διὰ βίου
πεινῶσι τὴν ψυχὴν ἀεὶ τὴν αὐτῶν διεξελθεῖν;

ΚΛ. Αὕτη μὲν τοίνυν μία· τὴν δὲ δὴ δευτέραν
αἰτίαν τίνα λέγεις, ὦ ξένε;

ΑΘ. Καλῶς ὑπέμνησας.

ΜΕ. [1] Αὕτη μὲν δή, φῂς σύ, μία διὰ βίου
ἄπληστος ζήτησις, παρέχουσα ἄσχολον ἕκαστον,
ἐμπόδιος γίγνεται τοῦ μὴ καλῶς ἀσκεῖν τὰ περὶ τὸν
Β πόλεμον ἑκάστους. ἔστω· τὴν δὲ δὴ δευτέραν λέγε.

ΑΘ. Μῶν οὐ λέγειν ἀλλὰ διατρίβειν δοκῶ δι᾽
ἀπορίαν;

ΜΕ. Οὔκ, ἀλλὰ οἷον μισῶν δοκεῖς ἡμῖν κολάζειν
τὸ τοιοῦτον ἦθος μᾶλλον τοῦ δέοντος τῷ παραπεπτωκότι λόγῳ.

ΑΘ. Κάλλιστα, ὦ ξένοι, ἐπεπλήξατε· καὶ τὸ
μετὰ τοῦτο ἀκούοιτ᾽ ἄν, ὡς ἔοικεν.

ΚΛ. Λέγε μόνον.

ΑΘ. Τὰς οὐ πολιτείας ἔγωγε αἰτίας εἶναί φημι
ἃς πολλάκις εἴρηκα ἐν τοῖς πρόσθεν λόγοις, δημο-
Ο κρατίαν καὶ ὀλιγαρχίαν καὶ τυραννίδα. τούτων
γὰρ δὴ πολιτεία μὲν οὐδεμία, στασιωτεῖαι δὲ

---

[1] Αὕτη κτλ. I assign this reply and the next to *Meg.* (with
Apelt and W.-Möllendorff), not to *Clin.*, as Zur. and most
edd.

noble pursuits and which turns men who are of a quiet nature [1] into traders, ship-owners, and servants, while of the bold it makes pirates, burglars, temple-robbers, fighters and despots,—and that though, in some cases, they are not ill-natured, but merely ill-fortuned.

CLIN. How so?

ATH. Well, how could I describe otherwise than as utterly unfortunate men who are compelled to go through life with hunger [2] always in their own souls?

CLIN. This, then, is one cause : what is the second cause you speak of, Stranger?

ATH. You are right in reminding me.

MEG. One cause, as you assert, is this lifelong insatiable pursuit, which wholly engrosses each man, and hinders each and all from rightly practising military operations. Be it so : now tell us the second cause.

ATH. Do you think that I am delaying to do so because I am at a loss?

MEG. No ; but we think that, owing to a sort of hatred against the character you describe, you are castigating it more severely than is required by the argument now on hand.

ATH. Your rebuke is just, Strangers ; you want, it seems, to hear what comes next.

CLIN. Only say on.

ATH. There lies a cause, as I affirm, in those non-polities which I have often mentioned [3] in our previous discourse,—namely, democracy, oligarchy, and tyranny. For none of these is a polity, but the

---

[1] Cp. 691 B, *Rep.* 410 C.
[2] *i.e.* for gold. Cp. Virgil's " auri sacra fames."
[3] 712 C ff., 713 E ff.

πᾶσαι λέγοιντ' ἂν ὀρθότατα· ἑκόντων γὰρ ἑκοῦσα
οὐδεμία, ἀλλ' ἀκόντων ἑκοῦσα ἄρχει σὺν ἀεί τινι
βίᾳ, φοβούμενος δὲ ἄρχων ἀρχόμενον οὔτε καλὸν
οὔτε πλούσιον οὔτε ἰσχυρὸν οὔτ' ἀνδρεῖον οὔτε τὸ
παράπαν πολεμικὸν ἑκὼν ἐάσει γίγνεσθαί ποτε.
ταῦτ' οὖν ἐστὶ τὰ δύο πάντων μὲν σμικροῦ
διαφερόντως αἴτια, τούτων δ' οὖν ὄντως διαφέρει.
D τὸ δὲ τῆς νῦν πολιτείας, ἣν νομοθετοῦμεν, ἃ¹
λέγομεν ἐκπέφευγεν ἀμφότερα· σχολήν τε γὰρ
ἄγει που μεγίστην, ἐλεύθεροί τε ἀπ' ἀλλήλων
εἰσί, φιλοχρήματοι δὲ ἥκιστ' ἄν, οἶμαι, γίγνοιντ'
ἂν ἐκ τούτων τῶν νόμων· ὥστ' εἰκότως ἅμα καὶ
κατὰ λόγον ἡ τοιαύτη κατάστασις πολιτείας μόνη
δέξαιτ' ἂν τῶν νῦν τὴν διαπερανθεῖσαν παιδείαν
τε ἅμα καὶ παιδιὰν πολεμικὴν ἀποτελεσθεῖσαν
ὀρθῶς τῷ λόγῳ.

ΚΛ. Καλῶς.

ΑΘ. Ἆρ' οὖν οὐ τούτοις ἐφεξῆς ἐστὶ μνησθῆναί
E ποτε περὶ ἁπάντων τῶν ἀγώνων τῶν γυμνικῶν,
ὡς ὅσα μὲν αὐτῶν πρὸς πόλεμόν ἐστιν ἀγωνίσματα
ἐπιτηδευτέον καὶ θετέον ἆθλα νικητήρια, ὅσα δὲ
μὴ χαίρειν ἐατέον; ἃ δ' ἔστιν, ἐξ ἀρχῆς ἄμεινον
ῥηθῆναί τε καὶ νομοθετηθῆναι. καὶ πρῶτον μὲν
τὰ περὶ δρόμον καὶ τάχος ὅλως ἆρ' οὐ θετέον;

ΚΛ. Θετέον.

ΑΘ. Ἔστι γοῦν πάντων πολεμικώτατον ἡ
σώματος ὀξύτης πάντως, ἡ μὲν ἀπὸ τῶν ποδῶν,
ἡ δὲ καὶ ἀπὸ τῶν χειρῶν· φυγεῖν μὲν καὶ ἑλεῖν

¹ νομοθετοῦμεν, ἃ Badham : νομοθετούμενοι MSS.

138

truest name for them all would be " faction-State " ; for none of them is a form of voluntary rule over willing subjects, but a voluntary rule over unwilling subjects accompanied always by some kind of force ; and the ruler, through fear of the subject, will never voluntarily allow him to become noble or wealthy or strong or brave or in any way warlike. These, then, are the two main causes of nearly everything, and certainly of the conditions we described. The polity, however, for which we are now legislating has escaped both these causes ; for not only does it enjoy a great amount of leisure,[1] but the citizens also are free from one another's domination, and as a consequence of these laws of ours they will be the least likely of men to be money-lovers. Hence it is both natural and logical that of all existing polities this type alone should welcome the system above described, which combines military schooling with sport, when we have rightly completed that description.

CLIN. Very good.

ATH. The next step, then, is to remind ourselves, with regard to all gymnastic contests, that all such as afford training for war should be instituted, and should have prizes assigned to them, but all that do not do so must be set aside. What these contests consist in, it will be well to have described and ordained at the beginning. First, then, should we not ordain contests in running and speed in general ?

CLIN. We should.

ATH. Most important of all things for war is, no doubt, general activity of the body, of hands as well as feet—activity of foot for flight and pursuit, and of

---

[1] Cp. 806 D, 828 D, E, etc.

833 ἡ τῶν ποδῶν, ἡ δ' ἐν ταῖς συμπλοκαῖς μάχη καὶ
σύστασις ἰσχύος καὶ ῥώμης δεομένη.

ΚΛ. Τί μήν ;

ΑΘ. Οὐ μὴν χωρίς γε ὅπλων οὐδετέρα τὴν
μεγίστην ἔχει χρείαν.

ΚΛ. Πῶς γὰρ ἄν ;

ΑΘ. Σταδιοδρόμον δὴ πρῶτον ὁ κῆρυξ ἡμῖν,
καθάπερ νῦν, ἐν τοῖς ἀγῶσι παρακαλεῖ· ὁ δὲ
εἴσεισιν ὅπλα ἔχων· ψιλῷ δὲ ἆθλα οὐ θήσομεν
ἀγωνιστῇ. πρῶτος δὲ εἴσεισιν ὁ τὸ στάδιον
ἁμιλλησόμενος σὺν τοῖς ὅπλοις, δεύτερος δὲ ὁ
B τὸν δίαυλον, καὶ τρίτος ὁ τὸν ἐφίππιον, καὶ δὴ
καὶ τέταρτος ὁ τὸν δόλιχον, καὶ πέμπτος δὲ ὃν
ἀφήσομεν πρῶτον ὡπλισμένον, ἑξήκοντα μὲν
σταδίων μῆκος πρὸς ἱερὸν Ἄρεός τι καὶ πάλιν,
βαρύτερον, ὁπλίτην ἐπονομάζοντες, λειοτέρας ὁδοῦ
διαμιλλώμενον, τὸν δὲ ἄλλον τοξότην πᾶσαν
τοξικὴν ἔχοντα στολήν, σταδίων δὲ ἑκατὸν πρὸς
Ἀπόλλωνός τε καὶ Ἀρτέμιδος ἱερὸν τὴν δι' ὀρῶν
τε καὶ παντοίας χώρας ἁμιλλώμενον. καὶ τιθέντες
C τὸν ἀγῶνα μενοῦμεν τούτους, ἕως ἂν ἔλθωσι, καὶ
τῷ νικῶντι τὰ νικητήρια δώσομεν ἑκάστων.

ΚΛ. Ὀρθῶς.

ΑΘ. Τριττὰ δὴ ταῦτα ἀθλήματα διανοηθῶμεν,
ἓν μὲν παιδικόν, ἓν δὲ ἀγενείων, ἓν δὲ ἀνδρῶν·
καὶ τοῖς μὲν τῶν ἀγενείων τὰ δύο τῶν τριῶν τοῦ
μήκους τοῦ δρόμου θήσομεν, τοῖς δὲ παισὶ τὰ
τούτων ἡμίσεα, τοξόταις τε καὶ ὁπλίταις ἁμιλ-
λωμένοις· γυναιξὶ δέ, κόραις μὲν ἀνήβοις γυμναῖς

140

hand for the stand-up fighting at close quarters which calls for sturdiness and strength.

CLIN. No doubt.

ATH. Yet, surely, neither of these is of the greatest service when it lacks weapons.

CLIN. Certainly not.

ATH. So at our contests the herald (as is now the practice) shall summon first the short-distance runner : he shall enter fully armed ; and for an unarmed competitor we shall offer no prize. First, then, there shall enter the man who, with his arms, is to run the furlong,—second, the runner of the quarter-mile,—third, the half-miler,—fourth, the runner of the three-quarters,—and fifth, that runner whom we shall despatch first, fully armed, to run a distance of four miles to a temple of Ares and back ; he shall be in heavier armour, and be called a hoplite, and he shall run over a smooth course, while his antagonist [1] shall be dressed in the full equipment of an archer, and shall run a course of twelve miles over hills and varied country to a temple of Apollo and Artemis. And having thus set up the contests, we shall await the return of these runners, and to the winner of each race we shall award the prize.

CLIN. Very right.

ATH. Let us plan these contests in three divisions —one for children, one for youths, and one for men. We shall ordain that the course for the youths' races shall be two-thirds of the full course, and that for children one-half, when they compete either as archers or as hoplites. In the case of females, we shall

[1] In this 5th race the hoplite, running the shorter course competes (on time) against the archer, running the longer course.

στάδιον καὶ δίαυλον καὶ ἐφίππιον καὶ δόλιχον,
D ἐν αὐτῷ τῷ δρόμῳ ἀμιλλωμέναις· ταῖς δὲ τρια-
καιδεκέτεσι μέχρι γάμου μενούσης κοινωνίας, μὴ
μακρότερον εἴκοσιν ἐτῶν μηδ' ἔλαττον ὀκτωκαί-
δεκα· πρεπούσῃ δὲ στολῇ ταύτας ἐσταλμένας
καταβατέον ἐπὶ τὴν ἅμιλλαν τούτων τῶν δρόμων.

Καὶ τὰ μὲν περὶ δρόμους ἀνδράσι τε καὶ γυναιξὶ
ταῦτα ἔστω· τὰ δὲ κατ' ἰσχύν, ἀντὶ μὲν πάλης
καὶ τῶν τοιούτων τὰ νῦν ὅσα βαρέα τὴν ἐν τοῖς
E ὅπλοις μάχην, ἕνα τε πρὸς ἕνα διαμαχομένους
καὶ δύο πρὸς δύο, καὶ μέχρι δέκα πρὸς δέκα
διαμιλλωμένους ἀλλήλοις. ἃ δὲ τὸν μὴ παθόντα
ἢ ποιήσαντα δεῖ νικᾶν καὶ εἰς ὁπόσα, καθάπερ
νῦν ἐν τῇ πάλῃ διενομοθετήσαντο οἱ περὶ τὴν
πάλην αὐτὴν τί τοῦ καλῶς παλαίοντος ἔργον καὶ
μὴ καλῶς, ταὐτὸν δὴ καὶ τοὺς περὶ ὁπλομαχίαν
ἄκρους παρακαλοῦντας χρὴ τούτους συννομο-
θετεῖν κελεύειν τίς νικᾶν ἄρα δίκαιος περὶ ταύτας
834 αὖ τὰς μάχας, ὅ τι μὴ παθὼν ἢ δράσας, καὶ τὸν
ἡττώμενον ὡσαύτως ἥτις διακρίνει τάξις. ταὐτὰ
δὲ καὶ περὶ τῶν θηλειῶν ἔστω νομοθετούμενα
τῶν μέχρι γάμου.

Πελταστικὴν δὲ ὅλην ἀντιστήσαντας δεῖ τῇ
τοῦ παγκρατίου μάχῃ, τόξοις καὶ πέλταις καὶ
ἀκοντίοις καὶ λίθῳ [1] [βολῇ] ἐκ χειρός τε καὶ
σφενδόνης [2] ἀμιλλωμένων, διαθεμένους αὖ περὶ
τούτων νόμους, τῷ κάλλιστα ἀποδιδόντι τὰ περὶ
ταῦτα νόμιμα τὰ γέρα καὶ τὰς νίκας διανέμειν.

Τὸ δὲ μετὰ ταῦτα ἵππων δὴ περὶ ἀγῶνος

---

[1] λίθῳ Schneider : λίθων MSS. (omitting βολῇ).
[2] σφενδόνης ci. England : σφενδόναις MSS., edd.

ordain races of a furlong, a quarter-mile, a half mile, and a three-quarters for girls under the age of puberty, who shall be stripped, and shall race on the course itself; and girls over thirteen shall continue to take part until married,[1] up to the age of twenty at most, or at least eighteen; but these, when they come forward and compete in these races, must be clad in decent apparel.

Let such, then, be the rules concerning races for men and women. As to trials of strength, instead of wrestling and the other "strong-man" events now in vogue, we shall ordain fencing in armour, both in solo-contests and in team-competitions of anything from two to ten a side. As regards the hits which a winner is to make or avoid, and how many points he must score,—just as now in the case of wrestling, those who deal with this art have fixed by law the points of good wrestling and bad, so likewise we must summon the experts in fencing under arms, and bid them help us to draw up laws by which to decide the proper winner in such fights, what he must do and what he must avoid,—and similarly the rules for determining the loser. For females also, up to the age of marriage, the same laws shall be laid down.

And in the place of the pancratium we must establish a general tourney for peltasts, who shall compete with bows, targes, javelins, and stones flung either by hand or by sling; and for these, too, we shall prescribe laws for assigning the rewards and prizes to the man who best conforms to the rules governing such contests.

After these, the next thing to ordain will be

---

[1] Cp. 785 B.

B γίγνοιτο ἑξῆς ἂν νομοθετούμενα. ἵππων δὲ ἡμῖν
χρεία μὲν οὔτε τις πολλῶν οὔτε πολλή, κατά γε
δὴ Κρήτην, ὥστε ἀναγκαῖον καὶ τὰς σπουδὰς
ἐλάττους γίγνεσθαι τάς τε ἐν τῇ τροφῇ καὶ τὰς
περὶ ἀγωνίαν αὐτῶν. ἅρματος μὲν οὖν καὶ τὸ
παράπαν οὔτε τις τροφεὺς ἡμῖν ἐστιν οὔτε τις
φιλοτιμία πρὸς ταῦτα οὐδενὶ γίγνοιτ᾽ ἂν λόγον
ἔχουσα, ὥστε τούτου μὲν ἀγωνίας, <ὃ>¹ οὐκ
ἐπιχώριον ἔσται, τιθέντας νοῦν μήτε ἔχειν μήτε
δοκεῖν κεκτῆσθαι· μονίπποις δὲ ἆθλα τιθέντες,
C πώλοις τε ἀβόλοις καὶ τελείων τε καὶ ἀβόλων
τοῖς μέσοις καὶ αὐτοῖς δὴ τοῖς τέλος ἔχουσι, κατὰ
φύσιν τῆς χώρας ἂν τὴν ἱππικὴν παιδιὰν ἀποδι-
δοῖμεν. ἔστω δὴ τούτων τε αὐτῶν κατὰ νόμον
ἅμιλλά τε καὶ φιλονεικία, φυλάρχοις τε καὶ
ἱππάρχοις δεδομένη κοινὴ κρίσις ἁπάντων τῶν
τε δρόμων αὐτῶν καὶ τῶν καταβαινόντων μεθ᾽
ὅπλων· ψιλοῖς δὲ ὅπλων οὔτ᾽ ἐν τοῖς γυμνικοῖς
οὔτ᾽ ἐνταῦθα τιθέντες ἀγωνίας ὀρθῶς ἂν νομοθε-
D τοῖμεν. τοξότης δὲ ἀφ᾽ ἵππων Κρὴς οὐκ ἄχρηστος,
οὐδ᾽ ἀκοντιστής, ὥστε ἔστω καὶ τούτων παιδιᾶς
χάριν ἔρις τε καὶ ἀγωνία. θηλείας δὲ περὶ
τούτων νόμοις μὲν καὶ ἐπιτάξεσιν οὐκ ἄξια
βιάζεσθαι τῆς κοινωνίας· ἐὰν δὲ ἐξ αὐτῶν τῶν
ἔμπροσθεν παιδευμάτων εἰς ἔθος ἰόντων ἡ φύσις
ἐνδέχηται καὶ μὴ δυσχεραίνῃ παῖδας ἢ παρθένους
κοινωνεῖν, ἐᾶν καὶ μὴ ψέγειν.

Ἀγωνία δὴ νῦν ἤδη καὶ μάθησις γυμναστικῆς,
ὅσα τε ἐν ἀγῶσι καὶ ὅσα καθ᾽ ἡμέραν ἐν διδασκά-
E λων ἐκπονούμεθα, πάντως ἤδη πέρας ἔχει· καὶ
δὴ καὶ μουσικῆς τὰ μὲν πλεῖστα ὡσαύτως δια-

horse-racing. Here, in a country like Crete, there
is not much need of horses—not in great numbers,
—so that inevitably less attention is paid either
to the rearing or the racing of horses. As to
chariots, we have no one who keeps them, nor is
anyone here likely to cherish any great ambition
respecting them, so that to establish contests for
them would run counter to native custom, and would
not only seem, but be, a foolish act. If, however,
we establish prizes for races of riding-horses—both
for young colts, and for three-year-olds, and for those
of full age—we shall be adapting the sport of horse-
racing to the character of the country. Of these
horsemen there shall be established by law a com-
petitive contest, and the phylarchs and hipparchs
shall act as public judges both of all the races and of
the armed competitors. For unarmed competitors
we should be wrong in establishing prizes, either
here or in the gymnastic sports. And for a Cretan
there is credit in being a mounted archer or javelin-
man, so we shall have contests and matches of a
sportive kind between these also. As to women,—it
is not worth while to make compulsory laws and
rules about their taking part in such sports ; but if,
as a result of earlier training which has grown into a
habit, their nature allows, and does not forbid, girls
or maidens to take part, let them do so without blame.

So now at length we have reached the end both
of competition and instruction in gymnastic, so far
as concerns our education by means of contests and
of daily teaching. Most of our account of music has
likewise been completed ; the regulations about

---

[1] ἀγωνίας my conj. (and England, independently) for
ἀγωνιστὰς of MSS. : <δ> I add, after Ast.

πεπέρανται, τὰ δὲ ῥαψῳδῶν καὶ τῶν τούτοις
ἑπομένων, καὶ ὅσαι ἐν ἑορταῖς ἅμιλλαι χορῶν
ἀναγκαῖαι γίγνεσθαι ταχθέντων τοῖς θεοῖς τε καὶ
τοῖς μετὰ θεῶν μηνῶν καὶ ἡμερῶν καὶ ἐνιαυτῶν
κοσμηθήσονται τότε, εἴτε τριετηρίδες εἴτε αὖ καὶ
835 διὰ πέμπτων ἐτῶν εἴθ᾽ ὅπῃ καὶ ὅπως ἂν ἔννοιαν
διδόντων τῶν θεῶν τάξεως πέρι διανεμηθῶσι·
τότε καὶ τοὺς μουσικῆς ἀγῶνας χρὴ προσδοκᾶν
κατὰ μέρος ἀγωνιεῖσθαι ταχθέντας ὑπό τε ἀθλο-
θετῶν καὶ τοῦ παιδευτοῦ τῶν νέων καὶ τῶν
νομοφυλάκων, εἰς κοινὸν περὶ αὐτῶν τούτων
συνελθόντων καὶ γενομένων νομοθετῶν αὐτῶν,
τοῦ τε πότε καὶ τίνες καὶ μετὰ τίνων τοὺς ἀγῶνας
ποιήσονται περὶ ἁπάντων χορῶν καὶ χορείας.
οἷα δὲ ἕκαστα αὐτῶν εἶναι δεῖ κατὰ λόγον καὶ
κατ᾽ ᾠδὰς καὶ καθ᾽ ἁρμονίας ῥυθμοῖς κραθείσας
B καὶ ὀρχήσεσι, πολλάκις εἴρηται τῷ πρώτῳ νομοθέτῃ, καθ᾽ ἃ τοὺς δευτέρους δεῖ μεταδιώκοντας
νομοθετεῖν, καὶ τοὺς ἀγῶνας πρεπόντως ἑκάστοις
θύμασιν ἐν χρόνοις προσήκουσι νείμαντας ἑορτὰς
ἀποδοῦναι τῇ πόλει ἑορτάζειν.

Ταῦτα μὲν οὖν καὶ ἄλλα τοιαῦτα οὔτε χαλεπὸν
γνῶναι τίνα τρόπον χρὴ τάξεως ἐννόμου λαγχάνειν, οὐδ᾽ αὖ μετατιθέμενα ἔνθα ἢ ἔνθα μέγα τῇ
C πόλει κέρδος ἢ ζημίαν ἂν φέροι· ἃ δὲ μὴ σμικρὸν
διαφέρει πείθειν τε χαλεπόν, θεοῦ μὲν μάλιστα
ἔργον, εἴ πως οἷόν τε ἦν ἐπιτάξεις αὐτὰς παρ᾽
ἐκείνου γίγνεσθαι, νῦν δὲ ἀνθρώπου τολμηροῦ κινδυνεύει δεῖσθαί τινος, ὃς παρρησίαν διαφερόντως
τιμῶν ἐρεῖ τὰ δοκοῦντα ἄριστ᾽ εἶναι πόλει καὶ
πολίταις, ἐν ψυχαῖς διεφθαρμέναις τὸ πρέπον καὶ

rhapsodes, however, and their retinue, and the choral contests which must accompany festivals are matters to be arranged after the gods and demigods have had their months, days and years assigned to them; then it will be seen whether they should be biennial fixtures or quadrennial, or what mode and manner of arranging them the gods may suggest. Then also, one expects, the musical contests will be held in sections, as arranged by the Masters of the Games and the Educator of the youth and the Lawwardens, meeting for this special purpose and acting in person as legislators to determine what persons, and when and with whom, are to frame the contests for all the choruses and choristry. Of what character each of these ought to be in respect of words, songs and tunes, blended with rhythm and dance, has frequently been stated [1] by the original lawgiver; the secondary lawgivers should follow him in their enactments, and they should arrange the contests at convenient times to suit the several sacrifices, and thus appoint festivals for the State to observe.

Now as to these and the like matters, it is by no means hard to perceive how they should be given legal regulation, nor indeed would a shifting of their positions cause much gain or loss to the State. But the things which do make no small difference, and of which it is hard to persuade men —these form a task especially for God (were it possible that orders should come from him): as it is, they are likely to require a bold man who, valuing candour above all else, will declare what he deems best for city and citizens, and in the midst of corrupted souls will enjoin what is fitting and

[1] In Books VI and VII.

ἑπόμενον πάσῃ τῇ πολιτείᾳ τάττων, ἐναντία λέγων
ταῖς μεγίσταισιν ἐπιθυμίαις καὶ οὐκ ἔχων βοηθὸν
ἄνθρωπον οὐδένα, λόγῳ ἑπόμενος μόνῳ μόνος.

D κλ. Τίν' αὖ νῦν, ὦ ξένε, λόγον λέγομεν; οὐ
γάρ πω μανθάνομεν.

αθ. Εἰκότως γε· ἀλλὰ δὴ πειράσομαι ἐγὼ
φράζειν ὑμῖν ἔτι σαφέστερον. ὡς γὰρ εἰς παιδείαν
ἦλθον τῷ λόγῳ, εἶδον νέους τε καὶ νέας ὁμιλοῦντας
φιλοφρόνως ἀλλήλοις. εἰσῆλθε δή με, οἷον εἰκός,
φοβηθῆναι ξυννοήσαντα τί τις χρήσεται τῇ
τοιαύτῃ πόλει ἐν ᾗ δὴ νέοι μὲν νέαι τε εὐτρεφεῖς
εἰσὶ πόνων τε σφοδρῶν καὶ ἀνελευθέρων, οἳ
E μάλιστα ὕβριν σβεννύασιν, ἀργοί, θυσίαι δὲ καὶ
ἑορταὶ καὶ χοροὶ πᾶσι μέλουσι διὰ βίου. τίνα
δή ποτε τρόπον ἐν ταύτῃ τῇ πόλει ἀφέξονται
τῶν πολλοὺς δὴ πολλὰ[1] ἐπιθυμιῶν εἰς ἔσχατα
βάλλουσῶν, ὧν ἂν ὁ λόγος προστάττῃ ἀπέχεσθαι,
νόμος ἐπιχειρῶν γίγνεσθαι; καὶ τῶν μὲν πολλῶν
οὐ θαυμαστὸν ἐπιθυμιῶν εἰ κρατοίη τὰ πρόσθεν
836 νόμιμα ταχθέντα· τὸ γὰρ μὴ πλουτεῖν τε ἐξεῖναι
ὑπερβαλλόντως ἀγαθὸν πρὸς τὸ σωφρονεῖν οὐ
σμικρόν, καὶ πᾶσα ἡ παιδεία μετρίους πρὸς τὰ
τοιαῦτ' εἴληφε νόμους, καὶ πρὸς τούτοις ἡ τῶν
ἀρχόντων ὄψις διηναγκασμένη μὴ ἀποβλέπειν
ἄλλοσε, τηρεῖν δὲ ἀεὶ τοὺς νέους. ταῦτ' οὖν
πρὸς μὲν τὰς ἄλλας ἐπιθυμίας, ὅσα γε ἀνθρώπινα,
μέτρον ἔχει· τὰ δὲ δὴ τῶν ἐρώτων παίδων τε
ἀρρένων καὶ θηλειῶν καὶ γυναικῶν ἀνδρῶν καὶ

---

[1] πολλὰ Paris MS. : καὶ πολλὰς Zur.

---

[1] 771 E ff.

in keeping with all the constitution, and gainsay the mightiest lusts, acting alone by himself with no man to help him save, as his solitary leader, Reason.

CLIN. What is it we are reasoning about now, Stranger? For we are still in the dark.

ATH. Naturally: but I will try to explain myself more clearly. When in my discourse I came to the subject of education,[1] I saw young men and maidens consorting with one another affectionately; and, naturally, a feeling of alarm came upon me, as I asked myself how one is to manage a State like this in which young men and maidens are well-nourished but exempt from those severe and menial labours which are the surest means of quenching wantonness, and where the chief occupation of everyone all through life consists in sacrifices, feasts and dances. In a State such as this, how will the young abstain from those desires which frequently plunge many into ruin,—all those desires from which reason, in its endeavour to be law,[2] enjoins abstinence? That the laws previously ordained serve to repress the majority of desires is not surprising; thus, for example, the proscription of excessive wealth is of no small benefit for promoting temperance, and the whole of our education-system contains laws useful for the same purpose; in addition to this, there is the watchful eye of the magistrates, trained to fix its gaze always on this point and to keep constant watch on the young people. These means, then, are sufficient (so far as any human means suffice) to deal with the other desires. But when we come to the amorous passions of children of both sexes and of men for women and

[2] A play on νόμος = νοῦς; cp. 836 E, 714 A.

B ἀνδρῶν γυναικῶν, ὅθεν δὴ μυρία γέγονεν ἀνθρώποις
ἰδίᾳ καὶ ὅλαις πόλεσι κακά, πῶς τις τοῦτο διευ-
λαβοῖτ᾽ ἄν, καὶ τί τεμὼν φάρμακον τούτοις
ἑκάστοις τοῦ τοιούτου κινδύνου διαφυγὴν εὑρήσει ;
πάντως οὐ ῥάδιον, ὦ Κλεινία. καὶ γὰρ οὖν πρὸς
μὲν ἄλλα οὐκ ὀλίγα ἡ Κρήτη τε ἡμῖν ὅλη καὶ
ἡ Λακεδαίμων βοήθειαν ἐπιεικῶς οὐ σμικρὰν
ξυμβάλλονται τιθεῖσι νόμους ἀλλοίους τῶν πολλῶν τρόπων, περὶ δὲ τῶν ἐρώτων, αὐτοὶ γάρ
C ἐσμεν, ἐναντιοῦνται παντάπασιν. εἰ γάρ τις
ἀκολουθῶν τῇ φύσει θήσει τὸν πρὸ τοῦ Λαΐου
νόμον, λέγων ὡς ὀρθῶς εἶχε τὸ τῶν ἀρρένων καὶ
νέων μὴ κοινωνεῖν καθάπερ θηλειῶν πρὸς μίξιν
ἀφροδισίων, μάρτυρα παραγόμενος τὴν τῶν θηρίων
φύσιν καὶ δεικνὺς πρὸς τὰ τοιαῦτα οὐχ ἁπτόμενον
ἄρρενα ἄρρενος διὰ τὸ μὴ φύσει τοῦτο εἶναι, τάχ᾽
ἂν χρῷτο ἀπιθάνῳ[1] λόγῳ καὶ ταῖς ὑμετέραις
πόλεσιν οὐδαμῶς ξυμφώνῳ.[2] πρὸς δὲ τούτοις,
ὃ διὰ παντός φαμεν δεῖν τὸν νομοθέτην διατηρεῖν,
D τοῦτο ἐν τούτοις οὐχ ὁμολογεῖ. ζητοῦμεν γὰρ
ἀεὶ δὴ τί τῶν τιθεμένων πρὸς ἀρετὴν φέρει καὶ
τί μή. φέρε δή, τοῦτο ἐὰν συγχωρῶμεν καλὸν
ἢ μηδαμῶς αἰσχρὸν νομοθετεῖσθαι τὰ νῦν, τί
μέρος ἡμῖν ξυμβάλλοιτ᾽ ἂν πρὸς ἀρετήν ; πότερον
ἐν τῇ τοῦ πεισθέντος ψυχῇ γιγνόμενον ἐμφύσεται
τὸ τῆς ἀνδρίας ἦθος, ἢ ἐν τῇ τοῦ πείσαντος τὸ
τῆς σώφρονος ἰδέας γένος ; ἢ ταῦτα μὲν οὐδεὶς
ἂν πεισθείη ποτέ, μᾶλλον δὲ ἅπαν τούτου τοὐν-

---

[1] ἀπιθάνῳ Badham : πιθανῷ MSS.
[2] ξυμφώνῳ England : ξυμφωνοῖ MSS.

---

[1] King of Thebes, father of Oedipus.

women for men,—passions which have been the cause of countless woes both to individuals and to whole States,—how is one to guard against these, or what remedy can one apply so as to find a way of escape in all such cases from a danger such as this? It is extremely difficult, Clinias. For whereas, in regard to other matters not a few, Crete generally and Lacedaemon furnish us (and rightly) with no little assistance in the framing of laws which differ from those in common use,— in regard to the passions of sex (for we are alone by ourselves) they contradict us absolutely. If we were to follow in nature's steps and enact that law which held good before the days of Laïus,[1] declaring that it is right to refrain from indulging in the same kind of intercourse with men and boys[2] as with women, and adducing as evidence thereof the nature of wild beasts, and pointing out how male does not touch male for this purpose, since it is unnatural,—in all this we would probably be using an argument neither convincing nor in any way consonant with your States. Moreover, that object which, as we affirm, the lawgiver ought always to have in view does not agree with these practices. For the enquiry we always make is this —which of the proposed laws tends toward virtue and which not. Come then, suppose we grant that this practice is now legalised, and that it is noble and in no way ignoble, how far would it promote virtue? Will it engender in the soul of him who is seduced a courageous character, or in the soul of the seducer the quality of temperance? Nobody would ever believe this; on the contrary, as all men

[2] Cp. 636 B ff., *Symp.* 181–2.

Ε ἀντίον τοῦ μὲν ταῖς ἡδοναῖς ὑπείκοντος καὶ
καρτερεῖν οὐ δυναμένου ψέξει πᾶς τὴν μαλακίαν,
τοῦ δ᾽ εἰς μίμησιν τοῦ θήλεος ἰόντος τὴν τῆς
εἰκόνος ὁμοιότητα ἆρ᾽ οὐ μέμψεται ; τίς οὖν
ἀνθρώπων τοῦτο ὂν τοιοῦτον νομοθετήσει ; σχεδὸν
οὐδείς, ἔχων γε ἐν τῷ νῷ νόμον ἀληθῆ. πῶς οὖν
φαμὲν ἀληθὲς τοῦτο εἶναι ; τὴν τῆς φιλίας τε καὶ
837 ἐπιθυμίας ἅμα καὶ τῶν λεγομένων ἐρώτων φύσιν
ἰδεῖν ἀναγκαῖον, εἰ μέλλει τις ταῦτα ὀρθῶς διανοη-
θήσεσθαι· δύο γὰρ ὄντα αὐτὰ καὶ ἐξ ἀμφοῖν
τρίτον ἄλλο εἶδος ἓν ὄνομα περιλαβὸν πᾶσαν
ἀπορίαν καὶ σκότον ἀπεργάζεται.

ΚΛ. Πῶς ;

ΑΘ. Φίλον μέν που καλοῦμεν ὅμοιον ὁμοίῳ κατ᾽
ἀρετὴν καὶ ἴσον ἴσῳ, φίλον δ᾽ αὖ καὶ τὸ δεόμενον
τοῦ πεπλουτηκότος, ἐναντίον ὂν τῷ γένει. ὅταν
δὲ ἑκάτερον γίγνηται σφοδρόν, ἔρωτα ἐπονομάζομεν.

Β ΚΛ. Ὀρθῶς.

ΑΘ. Φιλία τοίνυν ἡ μὲν ἀπὸ ἐναντίων δεινὴ
καὶ ἀγρία καὶ τὸ κοινὸν οὐ πολλάκις ἔχουσα ἐν
ἡμῖν, ἡ δ᾽ ἐκ τῶν ὁμοίων ἥμερός τε καὶ κοινὴ διὰ
βίου. μικτὴ δὲ ἐκ τούτων γενομένη πρῶτον μὲν
καταμαθεῖν οὐ ῥᾳδία, τί ποτε βούλοιτ᾽ ἂν αὑτῷ
γενέσθαι τὸν τρίτον ἔρωτά τις ἔχων τοῦτον,
ἔπειτα εἰς τοὐναντίον ὑπ᾽ ἀμφοῖν ἑλκόμενος
ἀπορεῖ, τοῦ μὲν κελεύοντος τῆς ὥρας ἅπτεσθαι,
τοῦ δὲ ἀπαγορεύοντος. ὁ μὲν γὰρ τοῦ σώματος

152

will blame the cowardice of the man who always
yields to pleasures and is never able to hold out
against them, will they not likewise reproach that
man who plays the woman's part with the resemblance he bears to his model? Is there any man,
then, who will ordain by law a practice like that?
Not one, I should say, if he has a notion of what
true law is. What then do we declare to be the
truth about this matter? It is necessary to discern
the real nature of friendship and desire and love
(so-called), if we are to determine them rightly;
for what causes the utmost confusion and obscurity
is the fact that this single term embraces these two
things, and also a third kind compounded of them
both.

CLIN. How so?

ATH. Friendship is the name we give to the
affection of like for like, in point of goodness, and of
equal for equal; and also to that of the needy for the
rich, which is of the opposite kind; and when either
of these feelings is intense we call it "love."

CLIN. True.

ATH. The friendship which occurs between opposites is terrible and fierce and seldom reciprocal
amongst men, while that based on similarity is
gentle and reciprocal throughout life. The kind
which arises from a blend of these presents
difficulties,—first, to discover what the man affected
by this third kind of love really desires to obtain,
and, in the next place, because the man himself
is at a loss, being dragged in opposite directions
by the two tendencies,—of which the one bids him
to enjoy the bloom of his beloved, while the other
forbids him. For he that is in love with the body

C ἐρῶν. καὶ τῆς ὥρας καθάπερ ὀπώρας πεινῶν ἐμ-
πλησθῆναι παρακελεύεται ἑαυτῷ, τιμὴν οὐδεμίαν
ἀπονέμων τῷ τῆς ψυχῆς ἤθει τοῦ ἐρωμένου· ὁ δὲ
πάρεργον μὲν τὴν τοῦ σώματος ἐπιθυμίαν ἔχων,
ὁρῶν δὲ μᾶλλον ἢ ἐρῶν, τῇ ψυχῇ, δὲ ὄντως [1] τῆς
ψυχῆς ἐπιτεθυμηκὼς ὕβριν ἥγηται τὴν περὶ τὸ
σῶμα τοῦ σώματος πλησμονήν, τὸ σῶφρον δὲ καὶ
ἀνδρεῖον καὶ μεγαλοπρεπὲς καὶ τὸ φρόνιμον
αἰδούμενος ἅμα καὶ σεβόμενος ἀγνεύειν ἀεὶ μεθ᾿
D ἀγνεύοντος τοῦ ἐρωμένου βούλοιτ᾿ ἄν· ὁ δὲ
μιχθεὶς ἐξ ἀμφοῖν γ᾿ [2] ἔρως οὗτός ἐσθ᾿ ὃν νῦν διεληλύθαμεν ὡς τρίτον. ὄντων δὲ τούτων τοσούτων
πότερον ἅπαντας δεῖ κωλύειν τὸν νόμον, ἀπείρ-
γοντα μὴ γίγνεσθαι ἐν ἡμῖν, ἢ δῆλον ὅτι τὸν μὲν
ἀρετῆς [τε] ὄντα καὶ τὸν νέον ἐπιθυμοῦντα ὡς
ἄριστον γίγνεσθαι βουλοίμεθ᾿ ἂν ἡμῖν ἐν τῇ
πόλει ἐνεῖναι, τοὺς δὲ δύο, εἰ δυνατὸν εἴη, κωλύοι-
μεν ἄν ; ἢ πῶς λέγομεν, ὦ φίλε Μέγιλλε ;

ΜΕ. Πάντη τοι καλῶς, ὦ ξένε, περὶ αὐτῶν
E τούτων εἴρηκας τὰ νῦν.

ΑΘ. Ἔοικά γε, ὅπερ καὶ ἐτόπαζον, τυχεῖν τῆς
σῆς, ὦ φίλε, ξυνῳδίας· τὸν δὲ νόμον ὑμῶν, ὅ τι
νοεῖ περὶ τὰ τοιαῦτα, οὐδέν με ἐξετάζειν δεῖ, δέχεσθαι δὲ τὴν τῷ λόγῳ συγχώρησιν. Κλεινίᾳ δὲ
[μετὰ ταῦτα] [3] καὶ εἰσαῦθις περὶ αὐτῶν τούτων
πειράσομαι ἐπᾴδων πείθειν. τὸ δέ μοι δεδομένον
ὑπὸ σφῷν ἴτω, καὶ διεξέλθωμεν πάντως τοὺς
νόμους.

ΜΕ. Ὀρθότατα λέγεις.

---

[1] δὲ ὄντως Badham : δεόντως MSS.
[2] γ᾿ H. Jackson, England : τρίτος MSS.
[3] [μετὰ ταῦτα] bracketed by England.

and hungering after its bloom,[1] as it were that of a ripening peach, urges himself on to take his fill of it, paying no respect to the disposition of the beloved; whereas he that counts bodily desire as but secondary, and puts longing looks in place of love,[2] with soul lusting really for soul, regards the bodily satisfaction of the body as an outrage, and, reverently worshipping temperance, courage, nobility and wisdom, will desire to live always chastely in company with the chaste object of his love. But the love which is blended of these two kinds is that which we have described just now as third. Since, then, love has so many varieties, ought the law to prohibit them all and prevent them from existing in our midst, or shall we not plainly wish that the kind of love which belongs to virtue and desires the young to be as good as possible should exist within our State, while we shall prohibit, if possible, the other two kinds? Or what is our view, my dear Megillus?

MEG. Your description of the subject, Stranger, is perfectly correct.

ATH. It seems that, as I expected, I have gained your assent; so there is no need for me to investigate your law, and its attitude towards such matters, but simply to accept your agreement to my statement. Later on I will try to charm Clinias also into agreeing with me on this subject. So let your joint admission stand at that, and let us by all means proceed with our laws.

MEG. Quite right.

---

[1] Cp. *Symp.* 183 D ff.
[2] A play on the assonance ὁρῶν = ἐρῶν.

PLATO

ΑΘ. Τέχνην δή τιν' αὖ τούτου τοῦ νόμου τῆς
838 θέσεως ἐν τῷ νῦν παρόντι τῇ μὲν ῥᾳδίαν ἔχω, τῇ
δ' αὖ τινὰ τρόπον παντάπασιν ὡς οἷόν τε χαλεπωτάτην.

ΜΕ. Πῶς δὴ λέγεις ;

ΑΘ. Ἴσμεν που καὶ τὰ νῦν τοὺς πλείστους τῶν
ἀνθρώπων, καίπερ παρανόμους ὄντας, ὡς εὖ τε
καὶ ἀκριβῶς εἴργονται τῆς τῶν καλῶν συνουσίας
οὐκ ἄκοντες, ὡς οἷόν τε δὲ μάλιστα ἑκόντες.

ΜΕ. Πότε λέγεις ;

ΑΘ. Ὅταν ἀδελφὸς ἢ ἀδελφή τῳ γένωνται
καλοί. καὶ περὶ υἱέος ἢ θυγατρὸς ὁ αὐτὸς νόμος
Β ἄγραφος ὢν ὡς οἷόν τε ἱκανώτατα φυλάττει μήτε
φανερῶς μήτε λάθρᾳ συγκαθεύδοντα ἢ πως ἄλλως
ἀσπαζόμενον ἅπτεσθαι τούτων· ἀλλ' οὐδ' ἐπιθυμία ταύτης τῆς συνουσίας τὸ παράπαν εἰσέρχεται
τοὺς πολλούς.

ΜΕ. Ἀληθῆ λέγεις.

ΑΘ. Οὐκοῦν σμικρὸν ῥῆμα κατασβέννυσι
πάσας τὰς τοιαύτας ἡδονάς ;

ΜΕ. Τὸ ποῖον δὴ λέγεις ;

ΑΘ. Τὸ ταῦτα εἶναι φάναι μηδαμῶς ὅσια,
C θεομισῆ δὲ καὶ αἰσχρῶν αἴσχιστα. τὸ δ' αἴτιον
ἆρ' οὐ τοῦτ' ἔστι, τὸ μηδένα ἄλλως λέγειν αὐτά,
ἀλλ' εὐθὺς γενόμενον ἡμῶν ἕκαστον ἀκούειν τε
λεγόντων ἀεὶ καὶ πανταχοῦ ταῦτα, ἐν γελοίοις τε
ἅμα ἐν πάσῃ τε σπουδῇ τραγικῇ λεγόμενα [1] πολλάκις, ὅταν ἢ Θυέστας ἤ τινας Οἰδίποδας εἰσάγω-
σιν, ἢ Μακαρέας τινὰς ἀδελφαῖς μιχθέντας
λαθραίως, ὀφθέντας δὲ ἑτοίμως θάνατον αὐτοῖς
ἐπιτιθέντας δίκην τῆς ἁμαρτίας ;

---

[1] λεγόμενα Orelli : λεγομένη MSS.

156

LAWS, BOOK VIII

ATH. I know of a device at present for enacting this law, which is in one way easy, but in another quite the hardest possible.

MEG. Explain your meaning.

ATH. Even at present, as we are aware, most men, however lawless they are, are effectively and strictly precluded from sexual commerce with beautiful persons,—and that not against their will, but with their own most willing consent.

MEG. On what occasions do you mean?

ATH. Whenever any man has a brother or sister who is beautiful. So too in the case of a son or daughter, the same unwritten law is most effective in guarding men from sleeping with them, either openly or secretly, or wishing to have any connexion with them,—nay, most men never so much as feel any desire for such connexion.

MEG. That is true.

ATH. Is it not, then, by a brief sentence that all such pleasures are quenched?

MEG. What sentence do you mean?

ATH. The sentence that these acts are by no means holy, but hated of God and most shamefully shameful. And does not the reason lie in this, that nobody speaks of them otherwise, but every one of us, from the day of his birth, hears this opinion expressed always and everywhere, not only in comic speech, but often also in serious tragedy—as when there is brought on to the stage a Thyestes or an Oedipus, or a Macareus having secret intercourse with a sister, and all these are seen inflicting death upon themselves willingly as a punishment for their sins?

ME. Ὀρθότατα λέγεις τό γε τοσοῦτον, ὅτι τὸ
D τῆς φήμης θαυμαστήν τινα δύναμιν εἴληχεν, ὅταν
μηδεὶς μηδαμῶς ἄλλως ἀναπνεῖν ἐπιχειρήσῃ ποτὲ
παρὰ τὸν νόμον.

ΑΘ. Οὐκοῦν ὀρθὸν τὸ νῦν δὴ ῥηθέν, ὅτι νομοθέτῃ βουλομένῳ τινὰ ἐπιθυμίαν δουλώσασθαι τῶν
διαφερόντως τοὺς ἀνθρώπους δουλουμένων ῥᾴδιον
γνῶναί γε ὅντινα τρόπον χειρώσαιτ᾿ ἄν· ὅτι καθ-
ιερώσας ταύτην τὴν φήμην παρὰ πᾶσι δούλοις
τε καὶ ἐλευθέροις καὶ παισὶ καὶ γυναιξὶ καὶ ὅλῃ
τῇ πόλει κατὰ τὰ αὐτά, οὕτω τὸ βεβαιότατον
E ἀπειργασμένος ἔσται περὶ τοῦτον τὸν νόμον.

ME. Πάνυ μὲν οὖν· ὅπως δὲ αὖ τὸ τοιοῦτον
ἐθέλοντας λέγειν πάντας δυνατὸν ἔσται ποτὲ
παρασχεῖν—

ΑΘ. Καλῶς ὑπέλαβες· αὐτὸ γὰρ τοῦτο ἦν τὸ
παρ᾿ ἐμοῦ λεχθέν, ὅτι τέχνην ἐγὼ πρὸς τοῦτον τὸν
νόμον ἔχοιμι τοῦ κατὰ φύσιν χρῆσθαι τῇ τῆς παιδογονίας συνουσίᾳ, τοῦ μὲν ἄρρενος ἀπεχομένους μὴ
κτείνοντάς τε ἐκ προνοίας τὸ τῶν ἀνθρώπων γένος,
839 μηδ᾿ εἰς πέτρας τε καὶ λίθους σπείροντας, οὗ
μήποτε φύσιν τὴν αὑτοῦ ῥιζωθὲν λήψεται γόνιμον,
ἀπεχομένους δὲ ἀρούρας θηλείας πάσης, ἐν ᾗ μὴ
βούλοιο [1] ἄν σοι φύεσθαι τὸ σπαρέν. ὁ δὴ νόμος
οὗτος διηνεκὴς μὲν γενόμενος ἅμα καὶ κρατήσας,
καθάπερ νῦν περὶ τὰς τῶν γονέων συμμίξεις κρατεῖ, ἐὰν καὶ περὶ τὰς ἄλλας νικήσῃ δικαίως, μυρία
ἀγαθὰ ἔχει. κατὰ φύσιν μὲν γὰρ πρῶτον κεῖται,
λύττης δὲ ἐρωτικῆς καὶ μανίας καὶ μοιχειῶν πασῶν
καὶ πωμάτων καὶ σιτίων εἴργεσθαι ποιεῖ τῶν

---

[1] βούλοιο some MSS., Hermann : βούλοιτ᾿ al. MSS., Zur.,
vulg.

MEG. Thus much at least you are quite right in saying—that public opinion has a surprising influence, when there is no attempt by anybody ever to breathe a word that contradicts the law.

ATH. Then is it not true, as I said just now, that when a lawgiver wishes to subdue one of those lusts which especially subdue men, it is easy for him at least to learn the method of mastering them,—that it is by consecrating this public opinion in the eyes of all alike—bond and free, women and children, and the whole State—that he will effect the firmest security for this law.

MEG. Certainly; but how it will ever be possible for him to bring it about that all are willing to say such a thing—

ATH. A very proper observation. That was precisely the reason why I stated that in reference to this law I know of a device for making a natural use of reproductive intercourse,—on the one hand, by abstaining from the male and not slaying of set purpose the human stock, nor sowing seed on rocks and stones where it can never take root and have fruitful increase; and, on the other hand, by abstaining from every female field in which you would not desire the seed to spring up. This law, when it has become permanent and prevails—if it has rightly become dominant in other cases, just as it prevails now regarding intercourse with parents,— is the cause of countless blessings. For, in the first place, it follows the dictates of nature, and it serves to keep men from sexual rage and frenzy and all kinds of fornication, and from all excess in meats

B ἀμέτρων πάντων, γυναιξί τε αὐτῶν οἰκείους εἶναι
καὶ φίλους, ἄλλα τε πάμπολλα ἀγαθὰ γίγνοιτ' ἄν,
εἰ τοῦ νόμου τις τούτου δύναιτο ἐγκρατὴς εἶναι.
τάχα δ' ἂν ἡμῖν τις παραστὰς ἀνὴρ σφοδρὸς καὶ
νέος, πολλοῦ σπέρματος μεστός, ἀκούων τιθεμένου
τοῦ νόμου λοιδορήσειεν ἂν ὡς ἀνόητα καὶ ἀδύνατα
τιθέντων νόμιμα, καὶ βοῆς πάντα ἐμπλήσειε.
πρὸς ἃ δὴ καὶ βλέψας ἐγὼ τοῦτο εἶπον τὸ ῥῆμα,
C ὥς τινα τέχνην κεκτήμην, τῇ μὲν ῥᾴστην ἁπασῶν,
τῇ δὲ χαλεπωτάτην, πρὸς τὸ τοῦτον τεθέντα ἐμμεῖναι τὸν νόμον. νοῆσαι μὲν γὰρ δὴ ῥᾷστον ὡς
δυνατόν τέ ἐστι καὶ ὅπῃ· φαμὲν γὰρ δὴ καθιερω-
θὲν τοῦτο ἱκανῶς τὸ νόμιμον πᾶσαν ψυχὴν δου-
λώσεσθαι καὶ παντάπασι μετὰ φόβου ποιήσειν
πείθεσθαι τοῖς τεθεῖσι νόμοις· ἀλλὰ γὰρ εἰς
τοῦτο προβέβηκε νῦν ὥστ' οὐδ' ἄν ποτε γενέσθαι
δοκεῖ, καθάπερ τὸ τῶν ξυσσιτίων ἐπιτήδευμα
ἀπιστεῖται, μὴ δυνατὸν εἶναι δύνασθαι διὰ βίου
D πόλιν ὅλην ζῆν πράττουσαν τοῦτο· ἐλεγχθὲν δ'
ἔργῳ καὶ γενόμενον παρ' ὑμῖν, ὅμως ἔτι τό γε
γυναικῶν οὐδὲ ἐν ταῖς ὑμετέραις πόλεσι δοκεῖ
φύσιν ἔχειν γίγνεσθαι. ταύτῃ δ' αὖ διὰ τὴν τῆς
ἀπιστίας ῥώμην εἴρηκα ἀμφότερα ταῦτα εἶναι
παγχάλεπα μεῖναι κατὰ νόμον.

ΜΕ. Ὀρθῶς γε σὺ λέγων.

ΑΘ. Ὡς δ' οὖν οὐκ ἔστιν ὑπὲρ ἄνθρωπον, οἷόν
τε δὲ γενέσθαι, βούλεσθε ὑμῖν πειραθῶ τινὰ λόγον
ἐχόμενον πιθανότητος εἰπεῖν τινός ;

ΚΛ. Πῶς γὰρ οὔ ;

---

[1] 838 B.

and drinks, and it ensures in husbands fondness for their own wives : other blessings also would ensue, in infinite number, if one could make sure of this law. Possibly, however, some young bystander, rash and of superabundant virility, on hearing of the passing of this law, would denounce us for making foolish and impossible rules, and fill all the place with his outcries ; and it was in view of this that I made the statement[1] that I knew of a device to secure the permanence of this law when passed which is at once the easiest of all devices and the hardest. For while it is very easy to perceive that this is possible, and how it is possible—since we affirm that this rule, when duly consecrated, will dominate all souls, and cause them to dread the laws enacted and yield them entire obedience,—yet it has now come to this, that men think that, even so, it is unlikely to come about,—just in the same way as, in the case of the institution of public meals, people refuse to believe that it is possible for the whole State to be able to continue this practice constantly ; and that, too, in spite of the evidence of facts and the existence of the practice in your countries; and even there, as applied to women, the practice is regarded as non-natural. Thus it was that, because of the strength of this unbelief, I said that it is most difficult to get both these matters permanently legalised.

MEG. And you were right in that.

ATH. Still, to show that it is not beyond the power of man, but possible, would you like me to try to state an argument which is not without some plausibility ?

CLIN. Certainly.

PLATO

E   ΑΘ. Πότερον οὖν τις ἀφροδισίων ῥᾶον ἂν
ἀπέχοιτο, καὶ τὸ ταχθὲν ἐθέλοι περὶ αὐτὰ μετρίως
ποιεῖν, εὖ τὸ σῶμα ἔχων καὶ μὴ ἰδιωτικῶς ἢ
φαύλως ;

  ΚΛ. Πολύ που μᾶλλον μὴ ἰδιωτικῶς.

  ΑΘ. Ἆρ᾽ οὖν οὐκ ἴσμεν τὸν Ταραντῖνον Ἴκκον
ἀκοῇ διὰ τὸν Ὀλυμπίασί τε ἀγῶνα καὶ τούς [τε]¹
840 ἄλλους, ὡς² διὰ φιλονεικίαν καὶ τέχνην καὶ τὸ
μετὰ τοῦ σωφρονεῖν ἀνδρεῖον ἐν τῇ ψυχῇ κεκτημένος, ὡς λόγος, οὔτε τινὸς πώποτε γυναικὸς
ἥψατο οὐδ᾽ αὖ παιδὸς ἐν ὅλῃ τῇ τῆς ἀσκήσεως
ἀκμῇ ; καὶ δὴ καὶ Κρίσωνα καὶ Ἀστύλον καὶ
Διόπομπον καὶ ἄλλους παμπόλλους ὁ αὐτός που
λόγος ἔχει. καίτοι τῶν γ᾽ ἐμῶν καὶ σῶν πολιτῶν,
ὦ Κλεινία, πολὺ κάκιον ἦσαν πεπαιδευμένοι τὰς
B ψυχάς, τὰ δὲ σώματα πολὺ μᾶλλον σφριγῶντες.

  ΚΛ. Ἀληθῆ ταῦτα λέγεις, ὅτι σφόδρα ὑπὸ τῶν
παλαιῶν ἐστιν εἰρημένα περὶ τούτων τῶν ἀθλητῶν
ὡς ὄντως ποτὲ γενόμενα.

  ΑΘ. Τί οὖν ; οἱ μὲν ἄρα νίκης ἕνεκα πάλης καὶ
δρόμων καὶ τῶν τοιούτων ἐτόλμησαν ἀπέχεσθαι
λεγομένου πράγματος ὑπὸ τῶν πολλῶν εὐδαίμονος, οἱ δὲ ἡμέτεροι παῖδες ἀδυνατήσουσι καρτερεῖν
πολὺ καλλίονος ἕνεκα νίκης, ἣν ἡμεῖς καλλίστην
ἐκ παίδων πρὸς αὐτοὺς λέγοντες ἐν μύθοις τε
C καὶ ἐν ῥήμασι καὶ ἐν μέλεσιν ᾄδοντες, ὡς εἰκός,
κηλήσομεν ;

  ΚΛ. Ποίας ;

  ΑΘ. Τῆς τῶν ἡδονῶν νίκης < · ἧς >³ ἐγκρατεῖς

---

¹ [τε] bracketed by Hermann.
² ὡς Heindorf : ὧν MSS.
³ ⟨ · ἧς ⟩ added by England.

ATH. Would a man be more ready to abstain from sex-indulgence, and to consent to carry out the law on this matter soberly, if he had his body not ill-trained, but in good condition, than if he had it in bad condition?

CLIN. He would be much more ready if it were not ill-trained.

ATH. Do we not know by report about Iccus[1] of Tarentum, because of his contests at Olympia and elsewhere,—how, spurred on by ambition and skill, and possessing courage combined with temperance in his soul, during all the period of his training (as the story goes) he never touched a woman, nor yet a boy? And the same story is told about Crison and Astylus and Diopompus and very many others. And yet, Clinias, these men were not only much worse educated in soul than your citizens and mine, but they also possessed much more sexual vigour of body.

CLIN. That this really happened in the case of these athletes is indeed, as you say, confidently affirmed by the ancients.

ATH. Well then, if those men had the fortitude to abstain from that which most men count bliss for the sake of victory in wrestling, running, and the like, shall our boys be unable to hold out in order to win a much nobler victory—that which is the noblest of all victories, as we shall tell them from their childhood's days, charming them into belief, we hope, by tales and sentences and songs.

CLIN. What victory?

ATH. Victory over pleasures,—which if they win,

---

[1] Cp. *Protag.* 316 D.

ὄντας ἂν ζῆν εὐδαιμόνως, ἡττωμένους δὲ τοὐναντίον ἅπαν. πρὸς δὲ τούτοις ἔτι φόβος ὁ τοῦ
μηδαμῆ μηδαμῶς ὅσιον αὐτὸ εἶναι δύναμιν ἡμῖν
οὐκ ἄρα ἕξει κρατεῖν ὧν ἄλλοι κεκρατήκασι
τούτων ὄντες χείρονες ;

κλ. Εἰκός γ᾽ οὖν.

αθ. Ἐπειδὴ τοίνυν ἐνταῦθά ἐσμεν τούτου τοῦ
D νομίμου πέρι, διὰ κάκην δὲ τὴν τῶν πολλῶν εἰς
ἀπορίαν ἐπέσομεν, φημὶ τὸ μὲν ἡμέτερον νόμιμον
ἀτεχνῶς δεῖν περὶ αὐτῶν τούτων πορεύεσθαι λέγον
ὡς οὐ δεῖ χείρους ἡμῖν εἶναι τοὺς πολίτας ὀρνίθων
καὶ ἄλλων θηρίων πολλῶν, οἳ κατὰ μεγάλας
ἀγέλας γεννηθέντες μέχρι μὲν παιδογονίας ἠίθεοι
καὶ ἀκήρατοι γάμων τε ἁγνοὶ ζῶσιν, ὅταν δ᾽ εἰς
τοῦτο ἡλικίας ἔλθωσι, συνδυασθέντες ἄρρην τὸν λοιπὸν
θηλείᾳ κατὰ χάριν καὶ θήλεια ἄρρενι τὸν λοιπὸν
E χρόνον ὁσίως καὶ δικαίως ζῶσιν, ἐμμένοντες
βεβαίως ταῖς πρώταις τῆς φιλίας ὁμολογίαις·
δεῖν δὴ θηρίων γε αὐτοὺς ἀμείνους εἶναι. ἐὰν δ᾽
οὖν ὑπὸ τῶν ἄλλων Ἑλλήνων καὶ βαρβάρων τῶν
πλείστων διαφθείρωνται, τὴν λεγομένην ἄτακτον
Ἀφροδίτην ἐν αὐτοῖς ὁρῶντές τε καὶ ἀκούοντες
μέγιστον δυναμένην, καὶ οὕτω δὴ μὴ δυνατοὶ
γίγνωνται κατακρατεῖν, δεύτερον νόμον ἐπ᾽ αὐτοῖς
μηχανᾶσθαι χρὴ τοὺς νομοφύλακας νομοθέτας
γενομένους.

841 κλ. Τίνα δὴ συμβουλεύεις αὐτοῖς τίθεσθαι
νόμον, ἐὰν ὁ νῦν τιθέμενος αὐτοὺς ἐκφύγῃ ;

αθ. Δῆλον ὅτι τὸν ἐχόμενον τούτου δεύτερον,
ὦ Κλεινία.

κλ. Τίνα λέγεις ;

αθ. Ἀγύμναστον ὅτι μάλιστα ποιεῖν τὴν τῶν

164

they will live a life of bliss, but if they lose, the very opposite. Furthermore, will not the dread that this is a thing utterly unholy give them power to master those impulses which men inferior to themselves have mastered?

CLIN. It is certainly reasonable to suppose so.

ATH. Now that we have reached this point in regard to our regulation, but have fallen into a strait because of the cowardice of the many, I maintain that our regulation on this head must go forward and proclaim that our citizens must not be worse than fowls and many other animals which are produced in large broods, and which live chaste and celibate lives without sexual intercourse until they arrive at the age for breeding; and when they reach this age they pair off, as instinct moves them, male with female and female with male; and thereafter they live in a way that is holy and just, remaining constant to their first contracts of love: surely our citizens should at least be better than these animals. If, however, they become corrupted by most of the other Hellenes or barbarians, through seeing and hearing that among them the "lawless Love" (as it is called) is of very great power, and thus become unable to overcome it, then the Law-wardens, acting as lawgivers, must devise for them a second law.

CLIN. What law do you recommend them to make if that which is now proposed slips out of their grasp?

ATH. Evidently that law which comes next to it as second.

CLIN. What is that?

ATH. One ought to put the force of pleasures as

ἡδονῶν ῥώμην, τὴν ἐπίχυσιν καὶ τροφὴν αὐτῆς
διὰ πόνων ἄλλοσε τρέποντα τοῦ σώματος. εἴη δ᾽
ἂν τοῦτο, εἰ ἀναίδεια μὴ ἐνείη τῇ τῶν ἀφροδισίων
χρήσει· σπανίῳ γὰρ αὖ τῷ τοιούτῳ δι᾽ αἰσχύνην
B χρώμενοι ἀσθενεστέραν ἂν αὐτὴν δέσποιναν
κτῷντο, ὀλιγάκις χρώμενοι. τὸ δὴ λανθάνειν
τούτων δρῶντά τι καλὸν παρ᾽ αὐτοῖς ἔστω
νόμιμον, ἔθει καὶ ἀγράφῳ νομισθὲν νόμῳ, τὸ δὲ
μὴ λανθάνειν αἰσχρόν, ἀλλ᾽ οὐ τὸ μὴ πάντως
δρᾶν. οὕτω τοῦτο αἰσχρὸν αὖ καὶ καλὸν δευτέρως
ἂν ἡμῖν ἐν νόμῳ γενόμενον κέοιτο, ὀρθότητα ἔχον
δευτέραν, καὶ τοὺς τὰς φύσεις διεφθαρμένους, οὓς
ἥττους αὑτῶν προσαγορεύομεν, ἓν γένος ὄν, περι-
C λαβόντα[1] τρία γένη βιάζοιτ᾽ ἂν μὴ παρανομεῖν.

ΚΛ. Ποῖα δή;

ΑΘ. Τό τε θεοσεβὲς ἅμα καὶ φιλότιμον καὶ
τὸ μὴ τῶν σωμάτων ἀλλὰ τῶν τρόπων τῆς
ψυχῆς ὄντων καλῶν γεγονὸς ἐν ἐπιθυμίᾳ. ταῦτα
δὴ καθάπερ ἴσως ἐν μύθῳ τὰ νῦν λεγόμεν᾽
ἐστὶν εὐχαί, πολύ γε μὴν ἄριστα, εἴπερ γίγνοιτο,
ἐν πάσαις πόλεσι γίγνοιτο ἄν. τάχα δ᾽ ἄν, εἰ
D θεὸς ἐθέλοι, κἂν δυοῖν θάτερα βιασαίμεθα περὶ
ἐρωτικῶν, ἢ μηδένα τολμᾶν μηδενὸς ἅπτεσθαι
τῶν γενναίων ἅμα καὶ ἐλευθέρων πλὴν γαμετῆς
ἑαυτοῦ γυναικός, ἄθυτα δὲ παλλακῶν σπέρματα
καὶ νόθα μὴ σπείρειν μηδὲ ἄγονα ἀρρένων
παρὰ φύσιν· ἢ τὸ μὲν τῶν ἀρρένων πάμπαν
ἀφελοίμεθ᾽ ἄν, τὸ δὲ γυναικῶν, εἴ τις συγγίγνοιτό
τινι πλὴν ταῖς μετὰ θεῶν καὶ ἱερῶν γάμων

---

[1] περιλαβόντα Stallb. : περιλαβὸν τὰ MSS.

[1] Cp. 626 E ff.

far as possible out of gear, by diverting its increase and nutriment to another part of the body by means of exercise. This would come about if indulgence in sexual intercourse were devoid of shamelessness; for if, owing to shame, people indulged in it but seldom, in consequence of this rare indulgence they would find it a less tyrannical mistress. Let them, therefore, regard privacy in such actions as honourable— sanctioned both by custom and by unwritten law; and want of privacy—yet not the entire avoidance of such actions—as dishonourable. Thus we shall have a second standard of what is honourable and shameful established by law and possessing a second degree of rectitude; and those people of depraved character, whom we describe as " self-inferior," [1] and who form a single kind, shall be hemmed in by three kinds of force and compelled to refrain from law-breaking.

CLIN. What kinds?

ATH. That of godly fear, and that of love of honour, and that which is desirous of fair forms of soul, not fair bodies. The things I now mention are, perhaps, like the visionary ideals in a story; yet in very truth, if only they were realized, they would prove a great blessing in every State. Possibly, should God so grant, we might forcibly effect one of two things in this matter of sex-relations,—either that no one should venture to touch any of the noble and freeborn save his own wedded wife, nor sow any unholy and bastard seed in fornication, nor any unnatural and barren seed in sodomy,—or else we should entirely abolish love for males, and in regard to that for women, if we enact a law that any man who has intercourse with any women save those who have been brought to his house under the sanction

Ε ἐλθούσαις εἰς τὴν οἰκίαν, ὠνηταῖς εἴτε ἄλλῳ
ὁτῳοῦν τρόπῳ κτηταῖς, μὴ λανθάνων ἄνδρας τε
καὶ γυναῖκας πάσας, τάχ᾽ ἂν ἄτιμον αὐτὸν τῶν
ἐν τῇ πόλει ἐπαίνων νομοθετοῦντες ὀρθῶς ἂν
δόξαιμεν νομοθετεῖν, ὡς ὄντως ὄντα ξενικόν. οὗτος
δὴ νόμος, εἴτε εἷς εἴτε δύο αὐτοὺς χρὴ προσαγορεύειν, κείσθω περὶ ἀφροδισίων καὶ ἁπάντων τῶν
ἐρωτικῶν, ὅσα πρὸς ἀλλήλους διὰ τὰς τοιαύτας
842 ἐπιθυμίας ὁμιλοῦντες ὀρθῶς τε καὶ οὐκ ὀρθῶς
πράττομεν.

ΜΕ. Καὶ τοίνυν, ὦ ξένε, ἐγὼ μέν τοι σφόδρα
δεχοίμην ἂν τοῦτον τὸν νόμον, ὁ δὲ δὴ Κλεινίας
αὐτὸς φραζέτω τί ποτε περὶ αὐτῶν διανοεῖται.

ΚΛ. Ἔσται ταῦτα, ὦ Μέγιλλε, ὁπόταν γε δή
μοι δόξῃ τις παραπεπτωκέναι καιρός· νῦν μὴν
ἐῶμεν τὸν ξένον ἔτι εἰς τὸ πρόσθεν προϊέναι τῶν
νόμων.

ΜΕ. Ὀρθῶς.

Β ΑΘ. Ἀλλὰ μὴν νῦν γε προϊόντες ἤδη σχεδόν
ἐσμεν ἐν τῷ κατεσκευάσθαι μὲν ξυσσίτια, ὅ φαμεν
ἄλλοθι μὲν ἂν χαλεπὸν εἶναι, ἐν Κρήτῃ δὲ οὐδεὶς
ἄλλως ἂν ὑπολάβοι δεῖν γίγνεσθαι. τὸ δὲ τίνα
τρόπον, πότερον ὡς ἐνθάδε ἢ καθάπερ ἐν Λακε-
δαίμονι, ἢ παρὰ ταῦτα ἔστι τι τρίτον εἶδος ξυσσιτίων ἀμφοῖν τούτοιν ἄμεινον ἂν ἔχον, τοῦτο οὔτ᾽
ἐξευρεῖν μοι χαλεπὸν εἶναι δοκεῖ μέγα τε ἀγαθὸν
εὑρεθὲν οὐδὲν ἀπεργάσεσθαι· καὶ γὰρ νῦν
C ἐμμελῶς ἔχειν κατεσκευασμένα.

Τούτοις δ᾽ ἐστὶν ἀκόλουθον ἡ τοῦ βίου κατα-
σκευή, τίν᾽ αὐτοῖς ἂν τρόπον ἔποιτο. βίος δὴ
ἄλλαις μὲν πόλεσι παντοδαπῶς ἂν καὶ πολλαχό-
θεν εἴη, μάλιστα δὲ ἐκ διπλασίων ἢ τούτοις· ἐκ

of Heaven and holy marriage, whether purchased or otherwise acquired, if detected in such intercourse by any man or woman, shall be disqualified from any civic commendation, as being really an alien, — probably such a law would be approved as right. So let this law—whether we ought to call it one law or two—be laid down concerning sexual commerce and love affairs in general, as regards right and wrong conduct in our mutual intercourse due to these desires.

MEG. For my own part, Stranger, I should warmly welcome this law; but Clinias must tell us himself what his view is on the matter.

CLIN. I shall do so, Megillus, when I deem the occasion suitable; but for the present let us allow the Stranger to proceed still further with his laws.

MEG. You are right.

ATH. Well, now we have arrived at this point in our progress, that common meals have been established—a thing which elsewhere, as we say, would be difficult, but in Crete no one would question its correctness. As concerns the manner of them,— whether we should adopt the Cretan fashion, or the Lacedaemonian, or whether we can find a third fashion that is better than either,—this does not seem to me a difficult problem to decide, nor indeed would its decision prove of much benefit, since these meals are now actually established in a satisfactory way.

Next to this comes the question of organising the food-supply, and how to make this fit in with the meals. In other States this supply would include all kinds of food and come from many sources, certainly from twice as many sources as it will in

γῆς γὰρ καὶ ἐκ θαλάττης τοῖς πλείστοις τῶν
Ἑλλήνων ἐστὶ κατεσκευασμένα τὰ περὶ τὴν τροφήν, τούτοις δὲ μόνον ἐκ γῆς. τῷ μὲν οὖν
νομοθέτῃ τοῦτο ῥᾷον· οὐ γὰρ μόνον ἡμίσεις αὖ
D γίγνονται νόμοι μέτριοι, πολὺ δ᾽ ἐλάττους, ἔτι δ᾽
ἐλευθέροις ἀνθρώποις μᾶλλον πρέποντες. ναυκλη-
ρικῶν μὲν γὰρ καὶ ἐμπορικῶν καὶ καπηλευτικῶν καὶ
πανδοκεύσεων καὶ τελωνικῶν καὶ μεταλλειῶν καὶ
δανεισμῶν καὶ ἐπιτόκων τόκων καὶ ἄλλων μυρίων
τοιούτων τὰ πολλὰ ἀπήλλακται χαίρειν αὐτοῖς
εἰπὼν ὁ περὶ ταύτην τὴν πόλιν νομοθέτης, γεωργοῖς δὲ καὶ νομεῦσι καὶ μελιττουργοῖς καὶ τοῖς
περὶ τὰ τοιαῦτα φυλακτηρίοις τε καὶ ἐπιστάταις
ὀργάνων νομοθετήσει, τὰ μέγιστα ἤδη νενομο-
E θετηκὼς περὶ γάμους ἅμα καὶ γενέσεις παίδων καὶ
τροφάς, ἔτι δὲ καὶ παιδείας ἀρχῶν τε καταστάσεις
ἐν τῇ πόλει. νῦν δ᾽ ἐπὶ [τοὺς]¹ τὴν τροφὴν καὶ
ὅσοι περὶ αὐτὴν ταύτην συνδιαπονοῦσιν ἀναγκαῖον νομοθετοῦντά ἐστι τρέπεσθαι.

Πρῶτον δὴ νόμοι ἔστωσαν λεγόμενοι τοὔνομα
γεωργικοί. Διὸς ὁρίου μὲν πρῶτος νόμος ὅδε
εἰρήσθω· μὴ κινείτω γῆς ὅρια μηδεὶς μήτε οἰκείου
πολίτου γείτονος μήτε ὁμοτέρμονος, ἐπ᾽ ἐσχατιᾶς
843 κεκτημένος ἄλλῳ ξένῳ γειτονῶν, νομίσας τὸ τἀκίνητα κινεῖν ἀληθῶς τοῦτο εἶναι· βουλέσθω δὲ πᾶς
πέτρον ἐπιχειρῆσαι κινεῖν τὸν μέγιστον ἄλλον
[πλὴν ὅρον]² μᾶλλον ἢ σμικρὸν λίθον ὁρίζοντα

---

¹ [τοὺς] bracketed by England.
² [πλὴν ὅρον] bracketed by Bekker, Zur.

LAWS, BOOK VIII

our State ; for most of the Greeks arrange for their
food to be derived from both land and sea, but our
people will derive it only from the land. This
makes the lawgiver's task easier ; for in this case
half the number of laws, or less, will suffice, and the
laws, too, will be better fitted for free men. For the
lawgiver of our State is rid, for the most part, of ship-
ping and merchandise and peddling and inn-keeping
and customs and mines and loans and usury, and
countless matters of a like kind ; he can say good-
bye to all such, and legislate for farmers and
shepherds and bee-keepers, and concerning the
preservation and supervision of the instruments employed in these occupations. This he will do, now
that he has already enacted the most important
laws, which deal with marriage, and with the birth
and nurture and education of the children, and with
the appointment of magistrates in the State. For
the present he must turn, in his legislating, to the
subject of food and of those whose labours contribute
to its supply.

First, then, let there be a code of laws termed
"agricultural." The first law—that of Zeus the
Boundary-god—shall be stated thus : No man shall
move boundary-marks of land, whether they be
those of a neighbour who is a native citizen or those
of a foreigner (in case he holds adjoining land on a
frontier), realising that to do this is truly to be
guilty of "moving the sacrosanct" [1]; sooner let a
man try to move the largest rock which is not a
boundary-mark than a small stone which forms a
boundary, sanctioned by Heaven, between friendly

---

[1] For the proverbial saying μὴ κινεῖν τἀκίνητα (like "Hands
off ! " or "Let sleeping dogs lie "), cp. 684 E, 913 B.

171

φιλίαν τε καὶ ἔχθραν ἔνορκον παρὰ θεῶν· τοῦ μὲν
γὰρ ὁμόφυλος Ζεὺς μάρτυς, τοῦ δὲ ξένιος, οἳ μετὰ
πολέμων τῶν ἐχθίστων ἐγείρονται· καὶ ὁ μὲν
πεισθεὶς τῷ νόμῳ ἀναίσθητος τῶν ἀπ' αὐτοῦ
κακῶν γίγνοιτ' ἄν, καταφρονήσας δὲ διτταῖς
δίκαις ἔνοχος ἔστω, μιᾷ μὲν παρὰ θεῶν καὶ
πρώτῃ, δευτέρᾳ δὲ ὑπὸ νόμου. μηδεὶς γὰρ
B ἑκὼν κινείτω γῆς ὅρια γειτόνων· ὃς δ' ἂν κινήσῃ,
μηνυέτω μὲν ὁ βουλόμενος τοῖς γεωμόροις, οἱ δὲ
εἰς τὸ δικαστήριον ἀγόντων· ἢν δέ τις ὄφλῃ τὴν
τοιαύτην δίκην, ὡς ἀνάδαστον γῆν λάθρᾳ καὶ βίᾳ
ποιοῦντος τοῦ ὀφλόντος, τιμάτω τὸ δικαστήριον ὅ
τι ἂν δέῃ πάσχειν ἢ ἀποτίνειν τὸν ἡττηθέντα.

Τὸ δὲ μετὰ τοῦτο βλάβαι πολλαὶ καὶ σμικραὶ
γειτόνων γιγνόμεναι, διὰ τὸ θαμίζειν ἔχθρας
ὄγκον μέγαν ἐντίκτουσαι, χαλεπὴν καὶ σφόδρα
C πικρὰν γειτονίαν ἀπεργάζονται. διὸ χρὴ πάντως
εὐλαβεῖσθαι γείτονα γείτονι μηδὲν ποιεῖν διάφορον, τῶν τε ἄλλων πέρι καὶ δὴ καὶ ἐπεργασίας
ξυμπάσης σφόδρα διευλαβούμενον· τὸ μὲν γὰρ
βλάπτειν οὐδὲν χαλεπόν, ἀλλ' ἀνθρώπου παντός,
τὸ δ' ἐπωφελεῖν οὐδαμῇ ἅπαντος. ὃς δ' ἂν ἐπερ-
γάζηται τὰ τοῦ γείτονος ὑπερβαίνων τοὺς ὅρους,
τὸ μὲν βλάβος ἀποτινέτω, τῆς δὲ ἀναιδείας ἅμα
D καὶ ἀνελευθερίας ἕνεκα ἰατρευόμενος διπλάσιον
τοῦ βλάβους ἄλλο ἐκτισάτω τῷ βλαφθέντι.
τούτων δὲ καὶ ἁπάντων τῶν τοιούτων ἐπιγνώμονές
τε καὶ δικασταὶ καὶ τιμηταὶ γιγνέσθων ἀγρονόμοι,
τῶν μὲν μειζόνων, καθάπερ ἐν τοῖς πρόσθεν
εἴρηται, πᾶσα ἡ τοῦ δωδεκατημορίου τάξις, τῶν

---

[1] 760 A ff. The "phrourarchs" were the (5) officers of the
(60) country police.

and hostile ground. For of the one kind Zeus the
Clansmen's god is witness, of the other Zeus the
Strangers' god; which gods, when aroused, bring
wars most deadly. He that obeys the law shall not
suffer the evils which it inflicts; but whoso despises
it shall be liable to a double penalty, the first from
the hand of Heaven, the second from the law. No
one shall voluntarily move the boundary-marks of
the land of neighbours: if any man shall move them,
whosoever wishes shall report him to the land-holders,
and they shall bring him to the law court. And if
a man be convicted,—since by such an act the convicted man is secretly and violently merging lands
in one,—the court shall estimate what the loser must
suffer or pay.

Further, many small wrongs are done against
neighbours which, owing to their frequent repetition,
engender an immense amount of enmity, and make
of neighbourhood a grievous and bitter thing.
Wherefore every neighbour must guard most carefully against doing any unfriendly act to his neighbour, and must above all things take special care
always not to encroach in the least degree on his
land; for whereas it is an easy thing and open to
anyone to do an injury, to do a benefit is by no
means open to everyone. Whosoever encroaches on
his neighbour's ground, overstepping the boundaries,
shall pay for the damage; and, by way of cure for
his shamelessness and incivility, he shall also pay
out to the injured party twice the cost of the
damage. In all such matters the land-stewards shall
act as inspectors, judges and valuers,—the whole
staff of the district, as we have said above,[1] in respect
of the more important cases, and, in respect of the

PLATO

ἐλαττόνων δὲ οἱ φρούραρχοι τούτων. καὶ ἐάν τις
βοσκήματα ἐπινέμῃ, τὰς βλάβας ὁρῶντες κρινόν-
των καὶ τιμώντων. καὶ ἐὰν ἐσμοὺς ἀλλοτρίους
σφετερίζῃ τις τῇ τῶν μελιττῶν ἡδονῇ ξυνεπόμενος,
E καὶ κατακρούων οὕτως οἰκειῶται, τινέτω τὴν
βλάβην. καὶ ἐὰν πυρεύων τὴν ὕλην μὴ διευλα-
βηθῇ τὴν[1] τοῦ γείτονος, τὴν δόξασαν ζημίαν
τοῖς ἄρχουσι ζημιούσθω. καὶ ἐὰν φυτεύων μὴ
ἀπολείπῃ τὸ μέτρον τῶν τοῦ γείτονος χωρίων,
καθάπερ εἴρηται καὶ πολλοῖς νομοθέταις ἱκανῶς,
ὧν τοῖς νόμοις χρὴ προσχρῆσθαι καὶ μὴ πάντα
ἀξιοῦν πολλὰ καὶ σμικρὰ καὶ τοῦ ἐπιτυχόντος
νομοθέτου γιγνόμενα τὸν μείζω πόλεως κοσμητὴν
844 νομοθετεῖν· ἐπεὶ καὶ τῶν ὑδάτων πέρι γεωργοῖσι
παλαιοὶ καὶ καλοὶ νόμοι κείμενοι οὐκ ἄξιοι παρ-
οχετεύειν λόγοις, ἀλλ' ὁ βουληθεὶς ἐπὶ τὸν αὐτοῦ
τόπον ἄγειν ὕδωρ ἀγέτω μέν, ἀρχόμενος ἐκ τῶν
κοινῶν ναμάτων, μὴ ὑποτέμνων πηγὰς φανερὰς
ἰδιώτου μηδενός, ᾗ δ' ἂν βούληται ἄγειν, πλὴν δι'
οἰκίας ἢ ἱερῶν τινῶν ἢ καὶ μνημάτων, ἀγέτω, μὴ
βλάπτων πλὴν αὐτῆς τῆς ὀχεταγωγίας· ἀυδρία δὲ
εἴ τισι τόποις ξύμφυτος ἐκ γῆς τὰ ἐκ Διὸς ἰόντα
B ἀποστέγει νάματα, καὶ ἐλλείπει τῶν ἀναγκαίων
πωμάτων, ὀρυττέτω μὲν ἐν τῷ αὑτοῦ χωρίῳ
μέχρι τῆς κεραμίδος γῆς, ἐὰν δ' ἐν τούτῳ τῷ
βάθει μηδαμῶς ὕδατι προστυγχάνῃ, παρὰ τῶν
γειτόνων ὑδρευέσθω μέχρι τοῦ ἀναγκαίου πώματος
ἑκάστοις τῶν οἰκετῶν· ἐὰν δὲ δι' ἀκριβείας ᾖ καὶ
τοῖς γείτοσι, τάξιν τῆς ὑδρείας ταξάμενος παρὰ

---

[1] τὴν Stephens, England : τῶν MSS.

174

less important, those of them who are " phrourarchs."
If anyone encroaches on pasture-land, these officials
shall inspect the damage, and decide and assess it.
And if any, yielding to his taste for bees, secures
for himself another man's swarm by attracting them
with the rattling of pans, he shall pay for the
damage. And if a man, in burning his own stuff,
fails to have a care for that of his neighbour, he
shall be fined in a fine fixed by the officials. So
too if a man, when planting trees, fail to leave the
due space between them and his neighbour's plot:
this has been adequately stated by many lawgivers,
whose laws we should make use of, instead of requiring the Chief Organiser of the State to legislate
about all the numerous small details which are within
the competence of any chance lawgiver. Thus, regarding water-supplies also, there are excellent old
laws laid down for farmers, which we, in our exposition, need not draw upon. Let this suffice :—
he that desires to bring water to his own land may
do so, commencing at the public cisterns, but he
must not undercut the exposed wells of any private
person : he may lead it by whatever way he wishes,
except through a house, temple or tomb, and he
must do no damage beyond the actual work of
channelling. If, in any spot, the rain-water filters
through owing to the natural dryness of the soil, and
there is a scarcity of necessary moisture, then the
owner shall dig in his own ground down to the
chalk subsoil, and if he fails to find water at this
depth, he shall procure from his neighbours just so
much as he requires for drinking purposes for all
his household ; and if his neighbours also are stinted
in their supplies, he shall apply for a ration of water

τοῖς ἀγρονόμοις, ταύτην ἡμέρας ἑκάστης κομι-
ζόμενος, οὕτω κοινωνείτω τοῖς γείτοσιν ὕδατος.
C ἐὰν δὲ ἐκ Διὸς ὕδατα γιγνόμενα, τὸν ἐπάνω
γεωργοῦντα ἢ καὶ ὁμότοιχον οἰκοῦντα τῶν ὑπο-
κάτω βλάπτῃ τις, μὴ διδοὺς ἐκροήν, ἢ τοὐναντίον
ὁ ἐπάνω μεθιεὶς εἰκῇ τὰ ῥεύματα βλάπτῃ τὸν
κάτω, καὶ περὶ ταῦτα μὴ ἐθέλωσι διὰ ταῦτα
κοινωνεῖν ἀλλήλοις, ἐν ἄστει μὲν ἀστυνόμον, ἐν
ἀγρῷ δὲ ἀγρονόμον ἐπάγων ὁ βουλόμενος ταξάσθω
τί χρὴ ποιεῖν ἑκάτερον· ὁ δὲ μὴ ἐμμένων ἐν τῇ
τάξει φθόνου θ' ἅμα καὶ δυσκόλου ψυχῆς ὑπεχέ-
D τω δίκην, καὶ ὀφλὼν διπλάσιον τὸ βλάβος ἀποτινέτω τῷ βλαφθέντι, μὴ ἐθελήσας τοῖς ἄρχουσι
πείθεσθαι.

Ὀπώρας δὲ δὴ χρὴ κοινωνίαν ποιεῖσθαι πάντας
τοιάνδε τινά. διττὰς ἡμῖν δωρεὰς ἡ θεὸς ἐχαρίσατο[1] αὕτη, τὴν μὲν παιδίαν Διονυσιάδα ἀθη-
σαύριστον, τὴν δ' εἰς ἀπόθεσιν γενομένην κατὰ
φύσιν. ἔστω δὴ περὶ ὀπώρας ὅδε νόμος ταχθείς·
ὃς ἂν ἀγροίκου ὀπώρας γεύσηται, βοτρύων εἴτε
καὶ σύκων, πρὶν ἐλθεῖν τὴν ὥραν τὴν τοῦ τρυγᾶν
E ἀρκτούρῳ ξύνδρομον, εἴτ' ἐν τοῖς αὑτοῦ χωρίοις
εἴτε καὶ ἐν ἄλλων, ἱερὰς μὲν πεντήκοντα ὀφειλέτω
τῷ Διονύσῳ δραχμάς, ἐὰν ἐκ τῶν ἑαυτοῦ δρέπῃ,
ἐὰν δ' ἐκ τῶν γειτόνων, μνᾶν, ἐὰν δ' ἐξ ἄλλων, δύο
μέρη τῆς μνᾶς. ὃς δ' ἂν τὴν γενναίαν νῦν λεγομένην σταφυλὴν ἢ τὰ γενναῖα σῦκα ἐπονομαζόμενα
ὀπωρίζειν βούληται, ἐὰν μὲν ἐκ τῶν οἰκείων

[1] ἐχαρίσατο Badham : ἔχει χάριτος MSS., edd.

176

from the land-stewards, and fetch it day by day, and so share the water with his neighbours. And if, when rain comes, any dweller on lower ground damages the farmer above him, or the adjoining dweller, by preventing its outflow,—or if, conversely, the man on higher ground damages the man below by letting out the floods carelessly,— and if, in consequence, they refuse to accommodate one another in this matter, any person who wishes shall call in a city-steward, if it is in the city, or a land-steward, if in the country, and get an order as to what each party is to do; and the man who does not abide by the order shall be liable to be charged with envy and frowardness, and if convicted he shall pay to the injured party double the damage, for refusing to obey the magistrates.

As concerns the fruit-harvest, the rule of sharing for all shall be this:—this goddess has bestowed on us two gifts, one the plaything of Dionysus which goes unstored, the other produced by nature for putting in store.[1] So let this law be enacted concerning the fruit-harvest:—whosoever shall taste of the coarse crop of grapes or figs before the season of vintage, which coincides with the rising of Arcturus, whether it be on his own land or on that of others, shall owe fifty sacred drachmae to Dionysus if he has cut them from his own trees, if from his neighbour's trees, a mina, and if from others, two-thirds of a mina. And if any man wishes to harvest "choice" grapes or "choice" figs (as they are now called), he shall gather them how and when he will if they are from

---

[1] *i.e.* (1) choice (or "dessert") fruit, for immediate use, and (2) coarse fruit, of poorer quality, for storing in bulk or making into wine.

λαμβάνῃ, ὅπως ἂν ἐθέλῃ καὶ ὁπόταν βούληται
καρπούσθω, ἐὰν δ' ἐξ ἄλλων μὴ πείσας, ἑπομένως
τῷ νόμῳ τῷ μὴ κινεῖν ὅ τι μὴ κατέθετο, ἐκείνως
845 ἀεὶ ζημιούσθω. ἐὰν δὲ δὴ δοῦλος μὴ πείσας τὸν
δεσπότην τῶν χωρίων ἅπτηταί του τῶν τοιούτων,
κατὰ ῥᾶγα βοτρύων καὶ σῦκον συκῆς ἰσαρίθμους
πληγὰς τούτοις μαστιγούσθω. μέτοικος δὲ ὠνού-
μενος τὴν γενναίαν ὀπώραν ὀπωριζέτω, ἐὰν
βούληται. ἐὰν δὲ ξένος ἐπιδημήσας ὀπώρας
ἐπιθυμῇ φαγεῖν διαπορευόμενος τὰς ὁδούς, τῆς
μὲν γενναίας ἀπτέσθω, ἐὰν βούληται, μεθ' ἑνὸς
B ἀκολούθου χωρὶς τιμῆς, ξένια δεχόμενος, τῆς δὲ
ἀγροίκου λεγομένης καὶ τῶν τοιούτων ὁ νόμος
εἰργέτω μὴ κοινωνεῖν ἡμῖν τοὺς ξένους· ἐὰν δέ τις
ἄϊστωρ ὢν αὐτὸς ἢ δοῦλος ἅψηται, τὸν μὲν δοῦλον
πληγαῖς κολάζειν, τὸν δὲ ἐλεύθερον ἀποπέμπειν
νουθετήσαντα καὶ διδάξαντα τῆς ἄλλης ὀπώρας
ἅπτεσθαι τῆς εἰς ἀπόθεσιν ἀσταφίδος οἴνου τε καὶ
ξηρῶν σύκων ἀνεπιτηδείου κεκτῆσθαι. ἀπίων δὲ
πέρι καὶ μήλων καὶ ῥοῶν καὶ πάντων τῶν τοιούτων,
C αἰσχρὸν μὲν μηδὲν ἔστω λάθρᾳ λαμβάνειν, ὁ δὲ
ληφθεὶς ἐντὸς τριάκοντα ἐτῶν γεγονὼς τυπτέσθω
καὶ ἀμυνέσθω ἄνευ τραυμάτων, δίκην δ' εἶναι
ἐλευθέρῳ τῶν τοιούτων πληγῶν μηδεμίαν· ξένῳ
δέ, καθάπερ ὀπώρας, ἐξέστω καὶ τῶν τοιούτων
μέτοχον εἶναι· ἐὰν δὲ πρεσβύτερος ὢν ἅπτηται τούτων, φαγὼν αὐτοῦ καὶ ἀποφέρων μηδέν, καθάπερ
ὁ ξένος, ταύτῃ κοινωνείτω τῶν τοιούτων ἁπάντων,
μὴ πειθόμενος δὲ τῷ νόμῳ κινδυνευέτω ἀναγώνιστος
D γίγνεσθαι περὶ ἀρετῆς, ἐὰν εἰς τότε τὰ τοιαῦτα
περὶ αὐτοῦ τοὺς τότε κριτάς τις ἀναμιμνήσκῃ.

his own trees, but if they are from another man's, and without his consent, he shall be fined every time, in pursuance of the law,[1] "thou shalt not shift what thou hast not set." And if a slave, without the consent of the master of the plots, touches any of such fruit, he shall be beaten with stripes as many as the grapes in the bunch or the figs on the fig-tree. If a resident alien buys a choice crop, he shall harvest it if he wishes. If a foreigner sojourning in the country desires to eat of the crop as he passes along the road, he, with one attendant, shall, if he wishes, take some of the choice fruit without price, as a gift of hospitality; but the law shall forbid our foreigners to share in the so-called "coarse" fruit, and the like; and should either a master or a slave touch these, in ignorance, the slave shall be punished with stripes, and the free man shall be sent off with a reproof and be instructed to touch only the other crop, which is unfitted for storing to make raisins for wine or dried figs. As to pears, apples, pomegranates, and all such fruits, it shall be no disgrace to take them privily; but the man that is caught at it, if he be under thirty years of age, shall be beaten and driven off without wounds; and for such blows a free man shall have no right to sue. A foreigner shall be allowed to share in these fruits in the same way as in the grape crop; and if a man above thirty touch them, eating on the spot and not taking any away, he shall have a share in all such fruits, like the foreigner; but if he disobeys the law, he shall be liable to be disqualified in seeking honours, in case anyone brings these facts to the notice of the judges at the time.

[1] Cp. 913 C, D.

Ὕδωρ δὲ πάντων μὲν τὸ περὶ τὰς κηπείας διαφερόντως τρόφιμον, εὐδιάφθαρτον δέ· οὔτε γὰρ γῆν
οὔτε ἥλιον οὔτε πνεύματα, τοῖς ὕδασι ξύντροφα
τῶν ἐκ γῆς ἀναβλαστανόντων, ῥάδιον φθείρειν
φαρμακεύσεσιν ἢ ἀποτροπαῖς ἢ καὶ κλοπαῖς, περὶ
δὲ τὴν ὕδατος φύσιν ἐστὶ τὰ τοιαῦτα ξύμπαντα
Ε δυνατὰ γίγνεσθαι. διὸ δὴ βοηθοῦ δεῖται νόμος.
ἔστω τοίνυν ὅδε περὶ αὐτοῦ· ἄν τις διαφθείρῃ
ἑκὼν ὕδωρ ἀλλότριον, εἴτε καὶ πηγαῖον εἴτε καὶ
συναγυρτόν, φαρμακείαις ἢ σκάμμασιν ἢ κλοπαῖς,
ὁ βλαπτόμενος δικαζέσθω πρὸς τοὺς ἀστυνόμους,
τὴν ἀξίαν τῆς βλάβης ἀπογραφόμενος· ἂν δέ τις
ὄφλῃ φαρμακείαις τισὶ βλάπτων, πρὸς τῷ τιμήματι καθηράτω τὰς πηγὰς ἢ τἀγγεῖον τοῦ ὕδατος,
ὅπῃπερ ἂν οἱ τῶν ἐξηγητῶν νόμοι ἀφηγῶν-
ται δεῖν γίγνεσθαι τὴν κάθαρσιν ἑκάστοτε καὶ
ἑκάστοις.

Περὶ δὲ ξυγκομιδῆς τῶν ὡραίων ἁπάντων,
846 ἐξέστω τῷ βουλομένῳ τὸ ἑαυτοῦ διὰ παντὸς
τόπου κομίζεσθαι, ὅπῃπερ ἂν ἢ μηδὲν μηδένα
ζημιοῖ ἢ τριπλάσιον αὐτὸς κέρδος τῆς τοῦ γείτονος ζημίας κερδαίνῃ· τούτων δὲ ἐπιγνώμονας
τοὺς ἄρχοντας γίγνεσθαι, καὶ τῶν ἄλλων ἁπάντων ὅσα τις ἂν ἑκὼν ἄκοντα βλάπτῃ βίᾳ ἢ
λάθρᾳ, αὐτὸν ἢ τῶν αὐτοῦ τι, διὰ τῶν αὐτοῦ
κτημάτων· πάντα τὰ τοιαῦτα τοῖς ἄρχουσιν
ἐπιδεικνὺς τιμωρείσθω μέχρι τριῶν μνῶν ὄντος
τοῦ βλάβους· ἐὰν δ᾽ ἔγκλημά τῳ μεῖζον ἄλλῳ
Β πρὸς ἄλλον γίγνηται, πρὸς τὰ κοινὰ δικαστήρια φέρων τὴν δίκην τιμωρείσθω τὸν ἀδικοῦντα.
ἐὰν δέ τις τῶν ἀρχόντων δοκῇ μετ᾽ ἀδίκου γνώμης

Water above all else in a garden is nourishing; but it is easy to spoil. For while soil and sun and wind, which jointly with water nourish growing plants, are not easy to spoil by means of sorcery or diverting or theft, all these things may happen to water; hence it requires the assistance of law. Let this, then, be the law concerning it :—if anyone wantonly spoil another man's water, whether in spring or in pond, by means of sorcery, digging, or theft, the injured party shall sue him before the city-stewards, recording the amount of the damage sustained; and whosoever is convicted of damaging by poisons shall, in addition to the fine, clean out the springs or the basin of the water, in whatever way the laws of the interpreters declare it right for the purification to be made on each occasion and for each plaintiff.

Touching the bringing home of all crops, whoso wills shall be permitted to fetch his own stuff through any place, provided that either he does no damage or else gains himself three times as much profit as the damage he costs his neighbour; the authority in this matter shall rest with the magistrates, as in all other cases where a man willingly injures an unwilling party either by force or secretly—whether it be the party himself he injures or some of his chattels, by means of his own chattels; in all such cases the plaintiff must report to the magistrates to get redress, where the damage is under three minas; but if a man makes a larger claim than this against another, he shall bring a suit before the public courts and punish the injurer. If any of the magistrates be thought to have given an unjust verdict in deciding the penalties, he shall

κρίνειν τὰς ζημίας, τῶν διπλασίων ὑπόδικος ἔστω
τῷ βλαφθέντι· τὰ δὲ αὖ τῶν ἀρχόντων ἀδικήματα εἰς τὰ κοινὰ δικαστήρια ἐπανάγειν τὸν
βουλόμενον <ἐν> ἑκάστῳ [1] τῶν ἐγκλημάτων.
μυρία δὲ ταῦτα ὄντα καὶ σμικρὰ νόμιμα, καθ᾽
ἃ δεῖ τὰς τιμωρίας γίγνεσθαι, λήξεών τε πέρι
C δικῶν καὶ προσκλήσεων καὶ κλητήρων, εἴτ᾽ ἐπὶ
δυεῖν εἴτ᾽ ἐφ᾽ ὁπόσων δεῖ καλεῖσθαι, καὶ πάντα
ὁπόσα τοιαῦτά ἐστιν, οὔτ᾽ ἀνομοθέτητα οἷόν τ᾽
εἶναι γέροντός τε οὐκ ἄξια νομοθέτου, νομοθε-
τούντων δ᾽ αὐτὰ οἱ νέοι πρὸς τὰ τῶν πρόσθεν
νομοθετήματα ἀπομιμούμενοι σμικρὰ πρὸς μεγάλα,
καὶ τῆς ἀναγκαίας αὐτῶν χρείας ἐμπείρως
ἴσχοντες, μέχριπερ ἂν πάντα ἱκανῶς δόξῃ κεῖ-
σθαι· τότε δὲ ἀκίνητα ποιησάμενοι ζώντων τούτοις
ἤδη χρώμενοι μέτρον [2] ἔχουσι.
D Τὸ δὲ τῶν ἄλλων δημιουργῶν ποιεῖν χρὴ κατὰ
τάδε. πρῶτον μὲν ἐπιχώριος μηδεὶς ἔστω τῶν
περὶ τὰ δημιουργικὰ τεχνήματα διαπονούντων,
μηδὲ οἰκέτης ἀνδρὸς ἐπιχωρίου· τέχνην γὰρ ἱκανὴν
πολλῆς ἀσκήσεως ἅμα καὶ μαθημάτων πολλῶν
δεομένην κέκτηται πολίτης ἀνὴρ τὸν κοινὸν τῆς
πόλεως κόσμον σῴζων καὶ κτώμενος, οὐκ ἐν
παρέργῳ δεόμενον ἐπιτηδεύειν· δύο δὲ ἐπιτηδεύματα ἢ δύο τέχνας ἀκριβῶς διαπονεῖσθαι σχεδὸν
E οὐδεμία φύσις ἱκανὴ τῶν ἀνθρωπίνων, οὐδ᾽ αὖ
τὴν μὲν αὐτὸς ἱκανῶς ἀσκεῖν, τὴν δὲ ἄλλον
ἀσκοῦντα ἐπιτροπεύειν. τοῦτ᾽ οὖν ἐν πόλει
ὑπάρχον δεῖ πρῶτον γίγνεσθαι· μηδεὶς χαλκεύων
ἅμα τεκταινέσθω, μηδ᾽ αὖ τεκταινόμενος χαλκευ-

---

[1] <ἐν> ἑκάστῳ : ἑκάστων MSS. (ἕκαστον Ast).

be liable to pay to the injured party double the amount; and whoso wishes shall bring up the wrong-doings of the magistrates before the public courts in the case of each complaint. And since there are countless petty cases for which penalties must be laid down, concerning written complaints and citations and evidence of citation,—whether the citation requires two or more witnesses,—and all matters of the like kind,—these cases cannot be left without legal regulation, but at the same time they do not deserve the attention of an aged law-giver; so the young lawgivers shall make laws for these cases, modelling their small rules on the great ones of our earlier enactments, and learning by experience how far they are necessary in practice, until it be decided that they are all adequately laid down; and then, having permanently fixed them, they shall live in the practice of them, now that they are set out in due form.

Moreover, for craftsmen we ought to make regulations in this wise. First, no resident citizen shall be numbered among those who engage in technical crafts, nor any servant of a resident. For a citizen possesses a sufficient craft, and one that needs long practice and many studies, in the keeping and conserving of the public system of the State, a task which demands his full attention: and there hardly exists a human being with sufficient capacity to carry on two pursuits or two crafts thoroughly, nor yet to practise one himself and supervise another in practising a second. So we must first of all lay down this as a fundamental rule in the State: no man who is a smith shall act as a joiner, nor shall

---

2 μέτρον Baiter; μέτριον MSS.

ὄντων ἄλλων ἐπιμελείσθω μᾶλλον ἢ τῆς αὑτοῦ
τέχνης, πρόφασιν ἔχων ὡς πολλῶν οἰκετῶν
ἐπιμελούμενος ἑαυτῷ δημιουργούντων εἰκότως
μᾶλλον ἐπιμελεῖται ἐκείνων διὰ τὸ τὴν πρόσοδον
847 ἐκεῖθεν αὑτῷ πλείω γίγνεσθαι τῆς αὑτοῦ τέχνης,
ἀλλ᾿ εἰς μίαν ἕκαστος τέχνην ἐν πόλει κεκτημένος
ἀπὸ ταύτης ἅμα καὶ τὸ ζῆν κτάσθω. τούτων δὴ
τὸν νόμον ἀστυνόμοι διαπονούμενοι σωζόντων, καὶ
τὸν μὲν ἐπιχώριον, ἐὰν εἴς τινα τέχνην ἀποκλίνῃ
μᾶλλον ἢ τὴν τῆς ἀρετῆς ἐπιμέλειαν, κολαζόντων
ὀνείδεσί τε καὶ ἀτιμίαις, μέχριπερ ἂν κατευθύ-
νωσιν εἰς τὸν αὑτοῦ δρόμον, ξένων δὲ ἄν τις ἐπιτη-
δεύῃ δύο τέχνας, δεσμοῖσί τε καὶ χρημάτων
B ζημίαις καὶ ἐκβολαῖς ἐκ τῆς πόλεως κολάζοντες
ἀναγκαζόντων ἕνα μόνον ἀλλὰ μὴ πολλοὺς εἶναι.
μισθῶν δὲ αὐτοῖς πέρι καὶ τῶν ἀναιρέσεων τῶν
ἔργων, καὶ ἐάν τις αὐτοὺς ἕτερος ἢ κεῖνοί τινα
ἄλλον ἀδικῶσι, μέχρι δραχμῶν πεντήκοντα
ἀστυνόμοι διαδικαζόντων, τὸ δὲ πλέον τούτου τὰ
κοινὰ δικαστήρια διακρινόντων κατὰ νόμον.

Τέλος δὲ ἐν τῇ πόλει μηδένα μηδὲν τελεῖν μήτε
ἐξαγομένων χρημάτων μήτ᾿ εἰσαγομένων· λιβανω-
τὸν δὲ καὶ ὅσα πρὸς [1] θεοὺς τὰ τοιαῦτ᾿ ἐστὶ ξενικὰ
C θυμιάματα, καὶ πορφύραν καὶ ὅσα βαπτὰ χρώματα, μὴ φερούσης τῆς χώρας, ἢ περί τινα ἄλλην
τέχνην δεομένην ξενικῶν τινων εἰσαγωγίμων
μηδενὸς ἀναγκαίου χάριν μήτε τις ἀγέτω, μήτε
αὖ τῶν ἐν τῇ χώρᾳ ἀναγκαίων ἐμμένειν ἐξαγέτω.
τούτων δ᾿ αὖ πάντων ἐπιγνώμονας εἶναι καὶ
ἐπιμελητὰς τῶν νομοφυλάκων, πέντε ἀφαιρεθέντων
τῶν πρεσβυτέρων, τοὺς ἑξῆς δώδεκα.

———
[1] πρὸς MSS. : περὶ Zur., vulg.

a joiner supervise others at smith-work, instead of his own craft, under the pretext that, in thus supervising many servants working for him, he naturally supervises them more carefully because he gains more profit from that source than from his own craft; but each several craftsman in the State shall have one single craft,[1] and gain from it his living. This law the city-stewards shall labour to guard, and they shall punish the resident citizen, if he turn aside to any craft rather than to the pursuit of virtue, with reproofs and degradation, until they restore him to his own proper course; and if a foreigner pursue two crafts, they shall punish him by imprisonment, money-fines, and expulsion from the State, and so compel him to act as one man and not many. And as regards wages due to craftsmen, and the cancellings of work ordered, and any injustices done to them by another, or to another by them, the city-stewards shall act as arbitrators up to a value of fifty drachmae, and in respect of larger sums the public courts shall adjudicate as the law directs.

No toll shall be paid in the State by anyone either on exported goods or on imports. Frankincense and all such foreign spices for use in religious rites, and purple and all dyes not produced in the country, and all pertaining to any other craft requiring foreign imported materials for a use that is not necessary, no one shall import; nor, on the other hand, shall he export any of the stuff which should of necessity remain in the country: and of all such matters the inspectors and supervisors shall consist of those twelve Law-wardens who remain next in order when five of the oldest are left out.

[1] Cp. *Rep.* 369 E ff., 434 A.

Περὶ δὲ ὅπλων καὶ ὅσα περὶ τὸν πόλεμον
D ἅπαντα ὄργανα, ἐάν τινος ἢ τέχνης εἰσαγωγίμου
δέῃ γίγνεσθαι ἢ φυτοῦ ἢ μεταλλευτικοῦ κτήματος
ἢ δεσμευτικοῦ ἢ ζώων τινῶν ἔνεκα τῆς τοιαύτης
χρείας, ἵππαρχοι καὶ στρατηγοὶ τούτων ἔστωσαν
κύριοι εἰσαγωγῆς τε καὶ ἐξαγωγῆς, διδούσης τε
ἅμα καὶ δεχομένης τῆς πόλεως, νόμους δὲ περὶ
τούτων νομοφύλακες τοὺς πρέποντάς τε καὶ ἱκανοὺς θήσουσι· καπηλείαν δὲ ἕνεκα χρηματισμῶν
μήτε οὖν τούτου μήτε ἄλλου μηδενὸς ἐν τῇ χώρᾳ
E ὅλῃ καὶ πόλει ἡμῖν γίγνεσθαι.

Τροφῆς δὲ καὶ διανομῆς τῶν ἐκ τῆς χώρας
ἐγγὺς τῆς τοῦ Κρητικοῦ νόμου ἔοικεν ὀρθότης ἄν
τις γιγνομένη κατὰ τρόπον γίγνεσθαι. δώδεκα
μὲν γὰρ δὴ μέρη τὰ πάντα ἐκ τῆς χώρας γιγνόμενα νέμειν χρεὼν πάντας, ᾗπερ καὶ ἀναλωτέα·
τὸ δὲ δωδέκατον μέρος ἕκαστον, οἷον πυρῶν καὶ
κριθῶν, οἷσι δὴ καὶ τὰ ἅπαντα ἀκολουθείτω τὰ
ἄλλα ὡραῖα νεμόμενα, καὶ ὅσα ζῶα ξύμπαντα
848 πράσιμ᾽ ἂν ἑκάστοις ᾖ, τριχῇ διαιρείσθω κατὰ
λόγον, ἓν μὲν μέρος τοῖς ἐλευθέροις, ἓν δὲ τοῖς
τούτων οἰκέταις, τὸ δὲ τρίτον δημιουργοῖς τε καὶ
πάντως τοῖς ξένοις, οἵ τέ τινες ἂν τῶν μετοικούν-
των ὦσι ξυνοικοῦντες, τροφῆς ἀναγκαίου δεόμενοι,
καὶ ὅσοι χρείᾳ τινὶ πόλεως ἤ τινος ἰδιωτῶν
εἰσαφικνοῦνται ἑκάστοτε· πάντων τῶν ἀναγκαίων
ἀπονεμηθὲν τρίτον μέρος ὤνιον ἐξ ἀνάγκης ἔστω
τοῦτο μόνον, τῶν δὲ δύο μερῶν μηδὲν ἐπάναγκες
ἔστω πωλεῖν. πῶς οὖν δὴ ταῦτα ὀρθότατα νέμοιτ᾽

In regard to arms and all instruments of war, if there is need to import any craft or plant or metal or rope or animal for military purposes, the hipparchs and generals shall have control of both imports and exports, when the State both gives and takes, and the Law-wardens shall enact suitable and adequate laws therefor; but no trading for the sake of gain, either in this matter or in any other, shall be carried on anywhere within the boundaries of our State and country.

Touching food-supply and the distribution of agricultural produce, a system approaching that legalised in Crete would probably prove satisfactory. The whole produce of the soil must be divided by all into twelve parts, according to the method of its consumption. And each twelfth part—of wheat and barley, for instance (and all the rest of the crops must be distributed in the same way as these, as well as all marketable animals in each district)— must be divided proportionately into three shares, of which the first shall be for the freeborn citizens, and the second for their servants; the third share shall be for craftsmen and foreigners generally, including any resident aliens who may be dwelling together and in need of necessary sustenance, and all who have come into the country at any time to transact either public or private business; and this third share of all the necessaries shall be the only one liable to compulsory sale,[1] it being forbidden to sell any portion of the other two shares compulsorily. What, then, will be the best way of making these

[1] For sales to foreigners, see below 849 A ff.: they had to buy their share of food-stuff, but the other two shares were not to be *forced* on to the market.

Β ἄν ; πρῶτον μὲν δῆλον ὅτι τῇ μὲν ἴσα, τῇ δ' οὐκ
ἴσα νέμομεν.

ΚΛ. Πῶς λέγεις ;

ΑΘ. Χείρω που καὶ βελτίω τούτων ἕκαστα
ἀνάγκη φύειν καὶ ἐκτρέφειν τὴν γῆν.

ΚΛ. Πῶς γὰρ οὔ ;

ΑΘ. Τῷ μὲν τοίνυν τοιούτῳ τῶν μερῶν τριῶν
ὄντων μηδὲν πλέον ἐχέτω μήτε τὸ τοῖς δεσπόταις
ἢ δούλοις νεμόμενον, μήτε αὖ τὸ τῶν ξένων, ἀλλὰ
τὴν τῆς ὁμοιότητος ἰσότητα ἡ νομὴ πᾶσιν ἀπο-
C διδότω τὴν αὐτήν· λαβὼν δ' ἕκαστος τῶν πολιτῶν
τὰ δύο μέρη κύριος ἔστω τῆς νομῆς δούλοις τε
καὶ ἐλευθέροις, ὁπόσ' ἂν καὶ ὁποῖα βούληται
διανέμειν· τὸ δὲ πλέον τούτων μέτροις τε καὶ
ἀριθμῷ τῇδε χρὴ διανέμεσθαι, λαβόντα τὸν
ἀριθμὸν πάντων τῶν ζῴων οἷς ἐκ τῆς γῆς δεῖ τὴν
τροφὴν γίγνεσθαι, διανέμειν.

Τὸ δὲ μετὰ τοῦτο αὐτοῖς οἰκήσεις δεῖ χωρὶς
διατεταγμένας εἶναι. τάξις δὲ ἥδε πρέπει τοῖς
τοιούτοις· δώδεκα κώμας εἶναι χρή, κατὰ μέσον
D τὸ δωδεκατημόριον ἕκαστον μίαν, ἐν τῇ κώμῃ δὲ
ἑκάστῃ πρῶτον μὲν ἱερὰ καὶ ἀγορὰν ἐξῃρῆσθαι
θεῶν τε καὶ τῶν ἑπομένων θεοῖς δαιμόνων, εἴτε
τινὲς ἔντοποι Μαγνήτων εἴτ' ἄλλων ἱδρύματα
παλαιῶν μνήμῃ διασεσωμένων εἰσί, τούτοις ἀποδιδόντας τὰς τῶν πάλαι τιμὰς ἀνθρώπων, Ἑστίας
δὲ καὶ Διὸς Ἀθηνᾶς τε καὶ ὃς ἂν ἀρχηγὸς ᾖ τῶν
ἄλλων τοῦ δωδεκάτου ἑκάστου μέρους, ἱερὰ παν-
188

divisions? It is plain, to begin with, that our division is in one way equal, in another, unequal.

CLIN. How do you mean?

ATH. Of each of these products of the soil, necessarily some parts are worse and some better.

CLIN. Of course.

ATH. In respect of this, no one of the three shares shall have an undue advantage,—neither that given to the masters, nor that of the slaves, nor that of the foreigners,—but the distribution shall assign to all the same equality of similarity. Each citizen shall take two shares and have control of the distribution of them to slaves and free men respectively, in the quantity and of the quality he desires to distribute. The surplus over and above this must be distributed by weight and number as follows,—the owner must take the number of all the animals that have to be fed on the produce of the soil, and make his distribution accordingly.

In the next place, there must be dwellings for the citizens separately arranged. A suitable arrangement for them will be this. There should be twelve villages, one in the middle of each of the twelve districts; and in each village we shall first select temples and a market-place for the gods and demigods; and if there exist any local deities of the Magnetes [1] or any shrines of other ancient gods whose memory is still preserved, we shall pay to them the same worship as did the men of old; and everywhere we shall erect temples to Hestia and Zeus and Athena, and whatever other deity is the patron of

[1] The original inhabitants of the site of Clinias's new colony (cp. 702 B, 860 E): they subsequently migrated to Magnesia in Asia Minor.

ταχοῦ ἱδρύσασθαι. πρῶτον δὲ οἰκοδομίας εἶναι
περὶ τὰ ἱερὰ ταῦτα, ὅπῃ ἂν ὁ τόπος ὑψηλότατος
Ε ᾖ, τοῖς φρουροῖς ὑποδοχὴν ὅτι μάλιστα εὐερκῆ·
τὴν δὲ ἄλλην χώραν κατασκευάζειν πᾶσαν δημιουργῶν τριακαίδεκα μέρη διελομένους, καὶ τὸ
μὲν ἐν ἄστει κατοικίζειν, διελομένους αὖ καὶ τοῦτο
εἰς τὰ δώδεκα μέρη τῆς πόλεως ἁπάσης, ἔξω τε
καὶ ἐν κύκλῳ κατανεμηθέντας, ἐν τῇ κώμῃ δὲ
ἑκάστῃ τὰ πρόσφορα γεωργοῖσι γένη τῶν δημιουργῶν συνοικίζειν. τοὺς δ' ἐπιμελητὰς εἶναι
τούτων πάντων τοὺς τῶν ἀγρονόμων ἄρχοντας,
ὅσων τε καὶ ὧντινων ὁ τόπος ἕκαστος δεῖται, καὶ
ὅπου κατοικοῦντες ἀλυπότατοί τε καὶ ὠφελι-
849 μώτατοι ἔσονται τοῖσι γεωργοῦσι. τῶν δὲ ἐν
ἄστει κατὰ τὰ αὐτὰ ἐπιμεληθῆναι [καὶ ἐπιμε-
λεῖσθαι][1] τὴν τῶν ἀστυνόμων ἀρχήν.

Τοῖς δὲ δὴ ἀγορανόμοις τὰ περὶ ἀγοράν που
δεῖ ἕκαστα μέλειν. ἡ δ' ἐπιμέλεια μετὰ τὴν τῶν
ἱερῶν ἐπίσκεψιν τῶν κατ' ἀγοράν, μή τις ἀδικῇ
τι τῆς τῶν ἀνθρώπων χρείας, τὸ δεύτερον ἂν εἴη
σωφροσύνης τε καὶ ὕβρεως ἐπισκόπους ὄντας
κολάζειν τὸν δεόμενον κολάσεως. τῶν δὲ ὠνίων,
πρῶτον μὲν τὰ περὶ τοὺς ξένους ταχθέντα πωλεῖν
Β τοῖς ἀστοῖς σκοπεῖν εἰ γίγνεται κατὰ τὸν νόμον
ἕκαστα. νόμος δ' εἷς ἔστω,[2] μηνὸς τῇ νέᾳ ὧν δεῖ
πραθῆναι τὸ μέρος τοῖς ξένοις ἐξάγειν τοὺς ἐπιτρόπους, ὅσοι τοῖς ἀστοῖς ξένοι ἢ καὶ δοῦλοι ἐπι-
τροπεύουσι, δωδεκατημόριον πρῶτον τοῦ σίτου, τὸν
δὲ ξένον εἰς πάντα τὸν μῆνα ὠνεῖσθαι σῖτον μὲν

---

[1] [καὶ ἐπιμελεῖσθαι] I bracket.
[2] δ' εἷς ἔστω : δ' ἑκάστῳ MSS. ; δὲ ἔστω Zur., vulg.

the district concerned. First, buildings shall be erected round about these temples, and wherever the ground is highest, to form a stronghold, as well fenced as possible, for the garrison; and all the rest of the land we shall provide for by dividing the craftsmen into thirteen sections, of which one shall settle in the city (and this section shall be subdivided again into twelve parts, like the whole city itself, and distributed round about it in the suburbs); and in each village we shall settle the classes of craftsmen that are serviceable to farmers. Of all these the chiefs of the land-stewards shall be the supervisors, determining how many and what craftsmen each place requires, and where they shall dwell so as to be of least trouble and greatest use to the farmers. And in like manner the board of city-stewards shall diligently supervise the craftsmen in the city.

All matters concerning the markets must be managed by the market-stewards. In addition to supervising the temples adjoining the market, to prevent any damage being done to them, they shall, secondly, supervise personal conduct, keeping an eye on temperate and outrageous behaviour, so as to punish him who needs punishment. They shall watch over commodities put up for sale, to see that the sales which citizens are directed to make to foreigners are always legally conducted. There shall be this one law—that on the first day of the month the portion of the goods which is to be sold to foreigners shall be brought out by the managers— that is, the foreigners or slaves who act as managers for the citizens; and the first commodity shall be the twelfth share of corn, and the foreigner shall

καὶ ὅσα περὶ σῖτον ἀγορᾷ τῇ πρώτῃ· δεκάτῃ δὲ
τοῦ μηνὸς τὴν τῶν ὑγρῶν οἱ μὲν πρᾶσιν, οἱ δὲ
ὠνὴν ποιείσθωσαν δι᾽ ὅλου τοῦ μηνὸς ἱκανήν·
τρίτῃ [1] δὲ εἰκάδι τῶν ζῴων ἔστω πρᾶσις, ὅσα
C πρατέα ἑκάστοις ἢ ὠνητέα αὐτοῖς δεομένοις καὶ
ὁπόσων σκευῶν ἢ χρημάτων γεωργοῖς μὲν πρᾶσις,
οἷον δερμάτων ἢ καὶ πάσης ἐσθῆτος ἢ πλοκῆς ἢ
πιλήσεως ἤ τινων ἄλλων τοιούτων, ξένοις δὲ
ἀναγκαῖον ὠνεῖσθαι παρ᾽ ἄλλων κτωμένοις. καπηλείας δὲ τούτων ἢ κριθῶν ἢ πυρῶν εἰς ἄλφιτα
νεμηθέντων, ἢ καὶ τὴν ἄλλην ξύμπασαν τροφήν,
ἀστοῖς μὲν καὶ τούτων δούλοις μήτε τις πωλείτω
D μήτε ὠνείσθω παρὰ τοιούτου μηδεὶς μηδενός, ἐν
δὲ ταῖς τῶν ξένων ξένος ἀγοραῖς πωλείτω τοῖς
δημιουργοῖς τε καὶ τούτων δούλοις, οἴνου τε μετα-
βαλλόμενος καὶ σίτου πρᾶσιν, ὃ δὴ καπηλείαν
ἐπονομάζουσιν οἱ πλεῖστοι· καὶ ζῴων διαμερισθέν-
των μάγειροι διατιθέσθων ξένοις τε καὶ δημιουργοῖς καὶ τούτων οἰκέταις. πᾶσαν δὲ ὕλην
καύσιμον ὁσημέραι ξένος ὁ βουληθεὶς ὠνείσθω
μὲν ἀθρόαν παρὰ τῶν ἐν τοῖς χωρίοις ἐπιτρόπων,
πωλείτω δὲ αὐτὸς τοῖς ξένοις, καθ᾽ ὅσον ἂν
E βούληται καὶ ὁπόταν βούληται. τῶν δὲ ἄλλων
χρημάτων πάντων καὶ σκευῶν ὁπόσων ἑκάστοισι
χρεία, πωλεῖν εἰς τὴν κοινὴν ἀγορὰν φέροντας
εἰς τὸν τόπον ἕκαστον, ἐν οἷς ἂν νομοφύλακές
τε καὶ ἀγορανόμοι μετ᾽ ἀστυνόμων τεκμηράμενοι
ἕδρας πρεπούσας ὅρους θῶνται τῶν ὠνίων· ἐν
τούτοις ἀλλάττεσθαι νόμισμά τε χρημάτων καὶ
χρήματα νομίσματος, μὴ προϊέμενον ἄλλον
ἑτέρῳ τὴν ἀλλαγήν· ὁ δὲ προέμενος ὡς πιστεύων,

[1] τρίτῃ W. R. Paton : τρίτη MSS., edd.

buy corn, and all that goes with it, at this first market. On the tenth day of the month, fluids sufficient to last through the month shall be sold by the one party and bought by the other. Thirdly, on the twentieth day, there shall be a sale of live-stock, as much as each party can buy or sell to suit their requirements, and also of all utensils or goods which the farmers have for sale, such as skins or any kind of clothing or woven stuff or felt or any such material; and these the foreigners must obtain from others by purchase. But neither these goods, nor barley or wheat ground into flour, nor any other kind of foodstuff whatsoever, may be sold by way of retail trade to the citizens or their slaves, or bought from any such retailer (but to the craftsmen and their slaves in the foreigners' market a foreigner may sell and traffic in wine and corn by way of what is generally termed " retail trade "); and the butchers shall cut up the animals and distribute the meat to the foreigners and craftsmen and their servants. Any foreigner who wishes shall buy any kind of fuel in bulk, on any day, from the managers in the districts; and he shall sell it to the foreigners in what quantity and at what time he pleases. As to all other goods and utensils that each party requires, they shall be brought for sale to the public market, each kind to its appointed place, wherever the Law-wardens and market-stewards, with the help of the city-stewards, have marked out suitable sites and set up the stalls for market-stuff: there they shall exchange coins for goods and goods for coins, and no man shall give up his share to the other without receiving its equivalent; and if any does thus give

ἐάν τε κομίσηται καὶ ἂν μή, στεργέτω ὡς
οὐκέτι δίκης οὔσης τῶν τοιούτων πέρι συναλ-
850 λάξεων. τὸ δὲ ὠνηθὲν ἢ πραθὲν ὅσῳ πλέον
ἂν ᾖ καὶ πλέονος ἢ κατὰ τὸν νόμον, ὃς εἴρηκε
πόσου προσγενομένου καὶ ἀπογενομένου δεῖ
μηδέτερα τούτων ποιεῖν, ἀναγραφήτω τότ᾽ ἤδη
παρὰ τοῖς νομοφύλαξι τὸ πλέον, ἐξαλειφέσθω δὲ
τὸ ἐναντίον. τὰ αὐτὰ δὲ καὶ περὶ μετοίκων ἔστω
τῆς ἀναγραφῆς πέρι τῆς οὐσίας. ἰέναι δὲ τὸν
βουλόμενον εἰς τὴν μετοίκησιν ἐπὶ ῥητοῖς, ὡς
οἰκήσεως οὔσης τῶν ξένων τῷ βουλομένῳ καὶ
B δυναμένῳ μετοικεῖν, τέχνην κεκτημένῳ καὶ ἐπιδη-
μοῦντι μὴ πλέον ἐτῶν εἴκοσιν, ἀφ᾽ ἧς ἂν γράψη-
ται, μετοίκιον μηδὲ σμικρὸν τελοῦντι πλὴν τοῦ
σωφρονεῖν, μηδὲ ἄλλο αὖ τέλος ἕνεκά τινος ὠνῆς
ἢ καὶ πράσεως· ὅταν δ᾽ ἐξήκωσιν οἱ χρόνοι, τὴν
αὑτοῦ λαβόντα οὐσίαν ἀπιέναι. ἐὰν δ᾽ ἐν τοῖς
ἔτεσι τούτοις αὐτῷ ξυμβῇ λόγου ἀξίῳ πρὸς εὐερ-
γεσίαν τῆς πόλεως γεγονέναι τινὰ ἱκανήν, καὶ
πιστεύῃ πείσειν βουλὴν καὶ ἐκκλησίαν ἤ τινα
C ἀναβολὴν τῆς ἐξοικήσεως ἀξιῶν αὑτῷ γίγνεσθαι
κυρίως ἢ καὶ τὸ παράπαν διὰ βίου τινὰ μονήν,
ἐπελθὼν καὶ πείσας τὴν πόλιν, ἅπερ ἂν πείσῃ,
ταῦτα αὐτῷ τέλεα γιγνέσθω. παισὶ δὲ μετοίκων,
δημιουργοῖς οὖσι καὶ γενομένοις ἐτῶν πεντεκαίδεκα, τῆς μὲν μετοικίας ἀρχέτω χρόνος ὁ μετὰ τὸ
πέμπτον καὶ δέκατον ἔτος, ἐπὶ τούτοις δὲ εἴκοσιν

----

[1] Cp. 742 C, 915 E.

it up, as it were on credit, he shall make the best of his bargain,[1] whether or not he recovers what is due to him, since in such transactions he can no longer sue. And if the purchase or sale is greater or more costly than is allowed by the law stating the limits of increase or decrease of property beyond which both of these transactions are forbidden, the amount of difference must at once (in the case of excess) be registered with the Law-wardens, and (in the case of deficiency) be cancelled. The same rule shall hold good regarding the registration of property in the case of resident aliens. Whosoever wishes shall enter on residence as an alien on fixed terms, since residence is permitted to a foreigner who is willing and able to reside, provided that he has a craft and remains in the country not more than twenty years from the date of his registration, without the payment of even a small aliens' tax, except virtuous conduct, or indeed any other tax for any buying or selling; and when his time has expired, he shall depart, taking with him his own property. And if within the period of twenty years it should happen that he has proved his merit by doing some signal service to the State, and if he believes that he can persuade the Council and Assembly to grant his request and authorize a postponement of his departure, or even an extension of his residence for life, whatever request he thus succeeds in persuading the State to grant to him shall be carried out for him in full. For the children of resident aliens, who are craftsmen and over fifteen years of age, the period of residence shall commence from the fifteenth year, and such an one, after remaining for twenty years from that date, shall depart whither

ἔτη μείνας ἴτω ὅπη αὐτῷ φίλον· μένειν δὲ ἂν
βούληται, κατὰ τὰ αὐτὰ μενέτω πείσας. ὁ δὲ
ἀπιὼν ἐξαλειψάμενος ἴτω τὰς ἀπογραφάς, αἵτινες
ἂν αὐτῷ παρὰ τοῖς ἄρχουσι γεγραμμέναι πρότερον
ὦσιν.

he pleases, or if he desires to remain, he shall gain permission in like manner, and so remain; and he that departs shall go after first cancelling the entries which were previously made by him in the register at the magistrates' office.

853   ΑΘ.   Δίκαι δὴ τὰ μετὰ ταῦτα ἀκόλουθοι ταῖς
ἔμπροσθεν πράξεσιν ἁπάσαις οὖσαι κατὰ φύσιν
γίγνοιντο ἂν τὴν τῆς διακοσμήσεως τῶν νόμων.
ὧντινων οὖν δὴ πέρι δεῖ γίγνεσθαι δίκας, τὰ μὲν
εἴρηται, τὰ κατὰ γεωργίας τε καὶ ὅσα τούτοις
εἵπετο, τὰ δὲ μέγιστα οὔτε εἴρηταί πω, καθ᾽
ἓν ἕκαστόν τε λεγόμενον [ῥηθέν],[1] ἣν δεῖ λαμβάνειν αὐτὸ τιμωρίαν καὶ τίνων ποτὲ δικαστῶν
B τυγχάνειν, μετ᾽ ἐκεῖν᾽ αὐτὰ ἑξῆς ταῦτα ῥητέον.

ΚΛ.   Ὀρθῶς.

ΑΘ.   Αἰσχρὸν μὲν δή τινα τρόπον καὶ νομοθετεῖν πάντα ὁπόσα νῦν μέλλομεν τοῦτο δρᾶν ἐν
τοιαύτῃ πόλει, ἥν φαμεν οἰκήσεσθαί τε εὖ καὶ
τεύξεσθαι πάσης ὀρθότητος πρὸς ἐπιτήδευσιν
ἀρετῆς. ἐν δὲ τῇ τοιαύτῃ τὸ καὶ ἀξιοῦν τῆς
τῶν ἄλλων μοχθηρίας τῶν μεγίστων ἐμφύεσθαί
τινα μεθέξοντα, ὥστε δεῖν νομοθετεῖν προκατα-
λαμβάνοντα καὶ ἀπειλοῦντα ἐάν τις τοιοῦτος
C γίγνηται, καὶ τούτων ἀποτροπῆς τε ἕνεκα καὶ
γενομένων κολάσεως τιθέναι ἐπ᾽ αὐτοῖς νόμους,
ὡς ἐσομένοις,[2] ὅπερ εἶπον, αἰσχρὸν μέν τινα
τρόπον· ἐπειδὴ δὲ οὐ, καθάπερ οἱ παλαιοὶ νο-
μοθέται θεῶν παισὶ νομοθετούμενοι τοῖς ἥρωσιν,
ὡς ὁ νῦν λόγος, αὐτοί τ᾽ ἐκ θεῶν ὄντες ἄλλοις
τε ἐκ τοιούτων γεγονόσιν ἐνομοθέτουν, ἀλλ᾽

---

[1] [ῥηθέν] bracketed by Ast.
[2] ἐσομένοις Steph., Hermann : ἐσομένους MSS.

BOOK IX

ATH. The method of our legislation requires that we should deal next with the judicial proceedings connected with all the transactions hitherto described. The matters which involve such proceedings have been stated [1] in part (those, namely, which concern farming and all industries dependent thereon), but we have not stated as yet the most important of such matters ; so our next step must be to state them in full, enumerating in detail what penalty must attach to each offence, and before what court it must be tried.

CLIN. True.

ATH. It is, in a sense, a shameful thing to make all those laws that we are proposing to make in a State like ours, which is, as we say, to be well managed and furnished with all that is right for the practice of virtue. In such a State, the mere supposition that any citizen will grow up to share in the worst forms of depravity practised in other States, so that one must forestall and denounce by law the appearance of any such character, and, in order to warn them off or punish them, enact laws against them, as though they were certain to appear,—this, as I have said, is in a sense shameful. But we are not now legislating, like the ancient lawgivers, for heroes and sons of gods,[2]—when, as the story goes, both the lawgivers themselves and their subjects were men of divine descent : we, on the contrary,

---

[1] 842 E ff. [2] Cp. 713 B ff.

PLATO

ἄνθρωποί τε καὶ ἀνθρώπων σπέρμασι νομοθετοῦμεν τὰ νῦν, ἀνεμέσητον δὴ φοβεῖσθαι μή τις
ἐγγίγνηται τῶν πολιτῶν ἡμῖν οἷον κερασβόλος,
D ὃς ἀτεράμων εἰς τοσοῦτον φύσει γίγνοιτ' ἂν ὥστε
μὴ τήκεσθαι, καὶ καθάπερ ἐκεῖνα τὰ σπέρματα
πυρί, νόμοις οὗτοι καίπερ οὕτως ἰσχυροῖς οὖσιν
ἄτηκτοι γίγνωνται. ὧν δὴ χάριν οὐκ ἐπίχαριν
λέγοιμ' ἂν πρῶτον νόμον ἱερῶν περὶ συλήσεως,
ἄν τις τοῦτο δρᾶν τολμᾷ. καὶ πολίτην μὲν τῶν
τεθραμμένων ὀρθῶς οὔτ' ἂν βουλοίμεθα οὔτε
ἐλπιστὸν πάνυ τι νοσῆσαί ποτε ἂν ταύτην τὴν
νόσον, οἰκέται δὲ ἂν τούτων καὶ ξένοι καὶ ξένων
δοῦλοι πολλὰ ἂν ἐπιχειρήσειαν τοιαῦτα. ὧν
ἕνεκα μὲν μάλιστα, ὅμως δὲ καὶ ξύμπασαν τὴν
854 τῆς ἀνθρωπίνης φύσεως ἀσθένειαν εὐλαβούμενος,
ἐρῶ τὸν τῶν ἱεροσυλιῶν[1] πέρι νόμον καὶ τῶν
ἄλλων πάντων τῶν τοιούτων ὅσα δυσίατα καὶ
ἀνίατα. προοίμια δὲ τούτοισι κατὰ τὸν ἔμπροσθεν
λόγον ὁμολογηθέντα προρρητέον ἅπασιν ὡς
βραχύτατα. λέγοι δή τις ἂν ἐκείνῳ διαλεγόμενος
ἅμα καὶ παραμυθούμενος, ὃν ἐπιθυμία κακὴ
παρακαλοῦσα μεθ' ἡμέραν τε καὶ ἐπεγείρουσα
νύκτωρ ἐπί τι τῶν ἱερῶν ἄγει συλήσοντα, τάδε·
B Ὦ θαυμάσιε, οὐκ ἀνθρώπινόν σε κακὸν οὐδὲ
θεῖον κινεῖ τὸ νῦν ἐπὶ τὴν ἱεροσυλίαν προτρέπον
ἰέναι, οἶστρος δέ σέ τις ἐμφυόμενος ἐκ παλαιῶν
καὶ ἀκαθάρτων τοῖς ἀνθρώποις ἀδικημάτων,
περιφερόμενος ἀλιτηριώδης, ὃν εὐλαβεῖσθαι
χρεὼν παντὶ σθένει. τίς δ' ἐστὶν εὐλάβεια μαθέ-

---

[1] ἱεροσυλιῶν Ast: ἱεροσύλων MSS.

are but mortal men legislating for the seed of men, and therefore it is permitted to us to dread lest any of our citizens should prove horny-hearted and attain to such hardness of temper as to be beyond melting; and just as those " horn-struck " [1] beans cannot be softened by boiling on the fire, so these men should be uninfluenced by laws, however powerful. So, for the sake of these gentlemen, no very gentle law shall be stated first concerning temple-robbery, in case anyone dares to commit this crime. That a rightly nurtured citizen should be infected with this disease is a thing that we should neither desire nor expect; but such attempts might often be made by their servants, and by foreigners or foreigners' slaves. Chiefly, then, on their account, and also as a precaution against the general infirmity of human nature, I will state the law about temple-robbing, and all other crimes of a like kind which are hard, if not impossible, to cure. And, in accordance with our rule as already approved,[2] we must prefix to all such laws preludes as brief as possible. By way of argument and admonition one might address in the following terms the man whom an evil desire urges by day and wakes up at night, driving him to rob some sacred object—" My good man, the evil force that now moves you and prompts you to go temple-robbing is neither of human origin nor of divine, but it is some impulse bred of old in men from ancient wrongs unexpiated, which courses round wreaking ruin; and it you must guard against with all your strength. How you must thus guard, now learn.

---

[1] *i.e.* "hard-shelled"; seeds struck by a beast's horn were vulgarly supposed to become "horny" and unfit for cooking.
[2] Cp. 718 B ff.

ὅταν σοι προσπίπτῃ τι τῶν τοιούτων δογμάτων,
ἴθι ἐπὶ τὰς ἀποδιοπομπήσεις, ἴθι ἐπὶ θεῶν
ἀποτροπαίων ἱερὰ ἱκέτης, ἴθι ἐπὶ τὰς τῶν λεγομένων ἀνδρῶν ὑμῖν ἀγαθῶν ξυνουσίας, καὶ τὰ
C μὲν ἄκουε, τὰ δὲ πειρῶ λέγειν αὐτός, ὡς δεῖ τὰ
καλὰ καὶ τὰ δίκαια πάντα ἄνδρα τιμᾷν· τὰς δὲ
τῶν κακῶν ξυνουσίας φεῦγε ἀμεταστρεπτί. καὶ
ἐὰν μέν σοι δρῶντι ταῦτα λωφᾷ τι τὸ νόσημα—
εἰ δὲ μή, καλλίω θάνατον σκεψάμενος ἀπαλ-
λάττου τοῦ βίου.

Ταῦτα ἡμῶν ἀδόντων προοίμια τοῖς πάντα
ταῦτα ἐπινοοῦσιν ὅσα ἀνόσια ἔργα καὶ πολι-
τοφθόρα, τῷ μὲν πειθομένῳ τὸν νόμον ἐᾶν σιγῇ
δεῖ, τῷ δὲ ἀπειθοῦντι μετὰ τὸ προοίμιον ᾅδειν
D μέγα, ¹Ὃς δ᾽ ἂν ἱεροσυλῶν ληφθῇ, ἐὰν μὲν ᾖ
δοῦλος ἢ ξένος, ἐν τῷ προσώπῳ καὶ ταῖς χερσὶ
γραφεὶς τὴν συμφορὰν καὶ μαστιγωθεὶς ὁπόσας
ἂν δόξῃ τοῖς δικασταῖς, ἐκτὸς τῶν ὅρων τῆς
χώρας γυμνὸς ἐκβληθήτω· τάχα γὰρ ἂν δοὺς
ταύτην τὴν δίκην γένοιτ᾽ ἂν βελτίων, σωφρονι-
σθείς. οὐ γὰρ ἐπὶ κακῷ δίκη γίγνεται οὐδεμία
γενομένη κατὰ νόμον, δυοῖν δὲ θάτερον ἀπεργάζε-
E ται σχεδόν· ἢ γὰρ βελτίονα ἢ μοχθηρότερον ἧττον
ἐξειργάσατο τὸν τὴν δίκην παρασχόντα. πολίτης
δὲ ἄν τίς ποτέ τι τοιοῦτον δρῶν ἀναφανῇ, περὶ θεοὺς
ἢ περὶ γονέας ἢ περὶ πόλιν ἠδικηκὼς τῶν μεγάλων
τινὰ καὶ ἀπορρήτων ἀδικιῶν, ὡς ἀνίατον ἤδη
τοῦτον ὄντα ὁ δικαστὴς διανοείσθω, λογιζόμενος
οἵας παιδείας τε καὶ τροφῆς ἐκ παιδὸς τυγχάνων
οὐκ ἀπέσχετο τῶν μεγίστων κακῶν. δίκη δὴ

---

¹ Cp. 871 A.   ² Cp. 862 D f., 934 A f.

When there comes upon you any such intention, betake yourself to the rites of guilt-averting, betake yourself as suppliant to the shrines of the curse-lifting deities, betake yourself to the company of the men who are reputed virtuous ; and thus learn, partly from others, partly by self-instruction, that every man is bound to honour what is noble and just ; but the company of evil men shun wholly, and turn not back. And if it be so that by thus acting your disease grows less, well ; but if not, then deem death the more noble way, and quit yourself of life."

As we chant this prelude to those who purpose all these unholy deeds, destructive of civic life, the law itself we must leave unvoiced [1] for him who obeys ; but for him who disobeys we must suffer the law, following on the prelude, to utter aloud this chant : " Whosoever is caught robbing a temple, if he be a foreigner or a slave, his curse shall be branded on his forehead and on his hands, and he shall be scourged with so many stripes as the judges decree, and he shall be cast out naked beyond the borders of the country ; for, after paying this penalty, he might perchance be disciplined into a better life. For no penalty that is legally imposed aims at evil, but it effects, as a rule, one or other of two results,—it makes the person who suffers it either better or less bad. [2] But if any citizen is ever convicted of such an act,—that is, of committing some great and infamous wrong against gods, parents, or State—the judge shall regard him as already incurable, reckoning that, in spite of all the training and nurture he has had from infancy, he has not refrained from the worst iniquity. For him

τούτῳ θάνατος ἐλάχιστον τῶν κακῶν, τοὺς δὲ
855 ἄλλους παράδειγμα ὀνήσει γενόμενος ἀκλεὴς καὶ
ὑπὲρ τοὺς τῆς χώρας ὅρους ἀφανισθείς· παισὶ δὲ
καὶ γένει, ἐὰν φύγωσι τὰ πατρῷα ἤθη, κλέος
ἔστω καὶ λόγος ἔντιμος λεγόμενος, ὡς εὖ τε καὶ
ἀνδρείως εἰς ἀγαθὸν ἐκ κακοῦ διαπεφευγότων.
δημόσια δὲ χρήματα οὐδενὸς τῶν τοιούτων τῇ
πολιτείᾳ πρέπον ἂν εἴη γίγνεσθαι, ἐν ᾗ δεῖ τοὺς
αὐτοὺς ἀεὶ καὶ ἴσους ὄντας διατελεῖν κλήρους.
ζημίας δ' ἐκτίσεις, ὅταν ἀδικεῖν ἄξια δοκῇ τις
χρημάτων, ἐκτίνειν, ἂν ᾖ τί τῳ[1] τοῦ κλήρου
κατεσκευασμένου περιττεῦον, μέχρι τοσούτου
B ζημιωθέντα, τὸ δὲ πλέον μή. τὰς δ' εἰς ταῦτα
ἀκριβείας ἐκ τῶν ἀπογραφῶν νομοφύλακες σκο-
ποῦντες τὸ σαφὲς ἐξαγγελλόντων ἀεὶ τοῖς δικασταῖς, ὅπως ἂν τῶν κλήρων ἀργὸς μηδεὶς μηδέποτε
γίγνηται δι' ἀπορίαν χρημάτων. ζημίας δὲ ἄν τις
πλέονος ἄξιος εἶναι δοκῇ, ἐὰν ἄρα μή τινες ἐθέλωσιν αὐτὸν τῶν φίλων ἐγγυᾶσθαί τε καὶ ξυνεκ-
τίνοντες ἀπελευθεροῦν, δεσμοῖς τε χρονίοις καὶ
C ἐμφανέσι καί τισι προπηλακισμοῖς κολάζειν,
ἄτιμον δὲ παντάπασι μηδένα εἶναι μηδέποτε μηδ'
ἐφ' ἑνὶ τῶν ἁμαρτημάτων, μηδ' ὑπερόριον φυγάδα·
θάνατον δὲ ἢ δεσμοὺς ἢ πληγὰς ἤ τινας ἀμόρφους
ἕδρας ἢ στάσεις ἢ παραστάσεις εἰς ἱερὰ ἐπὶ τὰ τῆς
χώρας ἔσχατα, ἢ χρημάτων καθάπερ ἔμπροσθεν
εἴπομεν ἐκτίσεις γίγνεσθαι δεῖν τὴν δίκην ταύτην,
γιγνέσθω. δικασταὶ δὲ ἔστωσαν θανάτου πέρι
νομοφύλακές τε καὶ τὸ τῶν περυσινῶν ἀρχόντων

---

[1] τί τῳ W. R. Paton, England : τι τῶν MSS.

[1] Cp. 745 A B.   [2] Cp. 865 E ff., 877 C ff.

the penalty is death, the least of evils ; and, moreover, by serving as an example, he will benefit others,
when himself disgraced and removed from sight
beyond the borders of the country ; but his children
and family, if they shun their father's ways, shall be
honoured, and honourable mention shall be made of
them, seeing that they have done well and bravely in
leaving the ways of vice for those of virtue.   That
the goods of any such criminal should be confiscated
would not be fitting in a State in which the allotments must remain always identical and equal in
number.   Whosoever is held to have done a wrong
which deserves a money-fine must pay the fine
exacted when the fine comes within the limits of the
surplus he has over when his allotment has been
equipped, but not what exceeds this : the precise
facts in such cases the Law-wardens must find out
from the registers,[1] and they must inform the judges
of the true state of each case, in order to prevent
any allotment falling out of cultivation through lack
of money.   And if any man is held to deserve a
larger fine, in case none of his friends are willing to
go bail or, by clubbing together, to pay the sum and
set him free, then we must punish him by long
imprisonment, of a public kind, and by measures of
degradation ; but no one shall be absolutely outlawed
for any single crime, even though he be banished
from the country.[2]   The punishments to be inflicted
shall be death, or imprisonment, or stripes, or seats
or stations or exposures of a degrading kind at
temples or at outermost boundaries, or money-fines of
the kind we have stated,—where such punishments
are required.   In cases where the penalty is death,
the judges shall be the Law-wardens together with

ἀριστίνδην ἀπομερισθὲν δικαστήριον· εἰσαγωγὰς
D δὲ τούτων καὶ προσκλήσεις καὶ ὅσα τοιαῦτα, καὶ
ὡς δεῖ γίγνεσθαι, τοῖς νεωτέροις νομοθέταις χρὴ
μέλειν· τὴν διαψήφισιν δὲ ἡμέτερον ἔργον νομοθετεῖν. ἔστω δὴ φανερὰ μὲν ἡ ψῆφος τιθεμένη,
πρὸ τούτου δὲ κατὰ τὸ στόμα τοῦ διώκοντός τε
καὶ φεύγοντος ὁ δικαστὴς ἑξῆς ἡμῖν ἐγγύτατα
κατὰ πρέσβιν ἱζέσθω, πάντες δ᾽ οἱ πολῖται, ὅσοιπερ
ἂν ἄγωσι σχολήν, ἐπήκοοι ἔστωσαν σπουδῇ τῶν
E τοιούτων δικῶν. λέγειν δὲ ἕνα λόγον, πρῶτον
μὲν τὸν διώκοντα, τὸν δὲ φεύγοντα δεύτερον· μετὰ
δὲ τοὺς λόγους τούτους ἄρχεσθαι μὲν τὸν γεραί-
τατον ἀνακρίνοντα, ἰόντα εἰς τὴν τῶν λεχθέντων
σκέψιν ἱκανήν, μετὰ δὲ τὸν πρεσβύτατον ἑξῆς
ἅπαντας χρὴ διεξελθεῖν ὅ τι ἂν παρ᾽ ἑκατέρου τις
τῶν ἀντιδίκων ῥηθὲν ἢ μὴ ῥηθὲν ἐπιποθῇ τινὰ
τρόπον· ὁ δὲ μηδὲν ποθῶν ἄλλῳ τὴν ἀνάκρισιν
παραδιδότω. τῶν δὲ ῥηθέντων ἐπισφραγισα-
μένους ὅσα ἂν εἶναι καίρια δοκῇ, γράμμασι σημεῖα
856 ἐπιβάλλοντας πάντων τῶν δικαστῶν, θεῖναι ἐπὶ
τὴν Ἑστίαν, καὶ πάλιν αὔριον εἰς ταὐτὸν ξυνελ-
θόντας ὡσαύτως τε ἀνακρίνοντας διεξελθεῖν τὴν
δίκην, καὶ σημεῖα ἐπιβάλλοντας αὖ τοῖς λεχθεῖσι·
καὶ τρὶς δράσαντας τοῦτο, τεκμήριά τε καὶ
μάρτυρας ἱκανῶς παραλαβόντας, ψῆφον ἱερὰν
ἕκαστον φέροντα καὶ ὑποσχόμενον πρὸς τῆς
Ἑστίας εἰς δύναμιν τὰ δίκαια καὶ ἀληθῆ κρίνειν,
οὕτω τέλος ἐπιθεῖναι τῇ τοιαύτῃ δίκῃ.

---

[1] Cp. 767 D.

LAWS, BOOK IX

the court of last year's magistrates selected by merit.¹
In respect of these cases the younger lawgivers must
attend to the indictments and summonses and all
such matters, and the procedure involved, while it is
our task to regulate by law the method of voting.
The votes shall be cast openly, and, before this takes
place, our judges shall be seated, facing the plaintiff
and defendant, in a closely-packed row in order of
seniority, and all the citizens who have leisure to do
so shall attend and listen attentively to the trials.
One speech shall be made by the plaintiff first, and
secondly one by the defendant; and after these
speeches the oldest judge shall lead off with his
survey of the case, in which he shall review in detail
the statements made; and after the oldest, each of
the other judges in turn must discuss every point
which he has noticed in which either of the litigants
has been guilty of making any kind of omission or
blunder in his statement; and he that has no such
criticism to make shall pass on the task of reviewing
to his neighbour; and when such of the statements
as the judges have pronounced relevant have been
confirmed by affixing to the documents the signatures
of all the judges, they shall lay them up at the altar
of Hestia.   On the morrow again they shall assemble
at the same place and discuss the case, and they shall
make their pronouncements in the same manner, and
shall again sign the statements.   And after doing
this thrice,—during which proceedings they shall pay
full attention to evidence and witnesses,—each of
the judges shall cast a sacred vote, promising by
Hestia to give just and true judgment to the best of
his power; and thus they shall bring to its end this
form of trial.

PLATO

B　Μετὰ δὲ τὰ περὶ θεοὺς τὰ περὶ κατάλυσιν τῆς
πολιτείας· ὃς ἂν ἄγων εἰς ἀρχὴν ἄνθρωπον δουλῶ-
ται μὲν τοὺς νόμους, ἑταιρείαις δὲ τὴν πόλιν ὑπήκοον ποιῇ, καὶ βιαίως δὴ πᾶν τοῦτο πράττων καὶ
στάσιν ἐγείρων παρανομῇ, τοῦτον δὴ διανοεῖσθαί
δεῖ πάντων πολεμιώτατον ὅλῃ τῇ πόλει. τὸν δὲ
κοινωνοῦντα μὲν τῶν τοιούτων μηδενί, τῶν μεγίστων δὲ μετέχοντα ἀρχῶν ἐν τῇ πόλει, λεληθότα
τε ταῦτα αὐτὸν ἢ μὴ λεληθότα, δειλίᾳ δ᾽ ὑπὲρ
C πατρίδος αὐτοῦ μὴ τιμωρούμενον, δεῖ δεύτερον
ἡγεῖσθαι τὸν τοιοῦτον πολίτην κάκῃ. πᾶς δὲ
ἀνὴρ οὗ καὶ σμικρὸν ὄφελος ἐνδεικνύτω ταῖς
ἀρχαῖς εἰς κρίσιν ἄγων τὸν ἐπιβουλεύοντα βιαίου
πολιτείας μεταστάσεως ἅμα καὶ παρανόμου.
δικασταὶ δὲ ἔστωσαν τούτοις οἵπερ τοῖς ἱερο-
σύλοις, καὶ πᾶσαν τὴν κρίσιν ὡσαύτως αὐτοῖς
γίγνεσθαι καθάπερ ἐκείνοις, τὴν ψῆφον δὲ θάνατον φέρειν τὴν πλήθει νικῶσαν. ἑνὶ δὲ λόγῳ,
πατρὸς ὀνείδη καὶ τιμωρίας παίδων μηδενὶ ξυν-
D ἔπεσθαι, πλὴν ἐάν τινι πατὴρ καὶ πάππος καὶ
πάππου πατὴρ ἐφεξῆς ὄφλωσι θανάτου δίκην·
τούτους δὲ ἡ πόλις ἔχοντας τὴν αὑτῶν οὐσίαν,
πλὴν ὅσον κατεσκευασμένου τοῦ κλήρου παντελῶς,
εἰς τὴν αὑτῶν ἀρχαίαν ἐκπεμπέσθω πατρίδα καὶ
πόλιν. οἷς δ᾽ ἂν τῶν πολιτῶν υἱεῖς ὄντες τυγχάνωσι πλείους ἑνός, μὴ ἔλαττον δέκα ἔτη γεγονότες, κληρῶσαι μὲν τούτων δέκα οὓς ἂν ἀποφήνῃ
πατὴρ ἢ πάππος ὁ πρὸς πατρὸς ἢ μητρός· τῶν
E δὲ λαχόντων τὰ ὀνόματα εἰς Δελφοὺς πεμφθέντων·
ὃν δ᾽ ἂν ὁ θεὸς ἀνέλῃ, κληρονόμον εἰς τὸν οἶκον
καταστῆσαι τὸν τῶν ἐκλιπόντων, τύχῃ ἀμείνονι.

LAWS, BOOK IX

Next to cases which concern religion come those which concern the dissolution of the polity. Whosoever enslaves the laws by making them subject to men, and makes the State subject to a faction, and acts illegally in doing all this by violence and in stirring up civil strife,—such a man must be deemed the worst of all enemies to the whole State. And the man who, though he takes part in none of these doings, yet fails to observe them, while he has a share in the chief offices of State, or else, though he observes them, fails to defend his country and punish them, owing to his cowardice,—a citizen of such a kind must be counted second in order of badness. Every man who is of the least worth shall inform the magistrates by prosecuting the plotter on a charge of violent and illegal revolution : they shall have the same judges as the temple-robbers had, and the whole trial shall be conducted just as it was in their case, and the death penalty shall be imposed by a majority of votes. As a summary rule, the disgrace or punishment inflicted on a father shall not descend upon his children, except in a case where not only the father, but his father and grandfather before him, have all been condemned on a capital charge : in such a case, the children, while retaining their own property, excepting only the allotment with its full equipment, shall be deported by the State to their original country and State. And from the sons of citizens who happen to have more than one son over ten years old, ten shall be chosen by lot—after application made by the father or by the paternal or maternal grandfather, —and the names thus chosen shall be sent to Delphi ; and that man whom the oracle names shall be established as the allotment-holder in the house of those departed,—be it with happier fortune !

ΚΛ. Καλῶς.

ΑΘ. Κοινὸς δ᾽ ἔτι τρίτος κείσθω[1] νόμος, περὶ
δικαστῶν τε οὓς δεῖ δικάζειν αὐτοῖς, καὶ ὁ τρόπος
τῶν δικῶν, οἷς ἂν προδόσεως αἰτίαν ἐπιφέρων τις
εἰς δικαστήριον ἄγῃ. καὶ μονῆς ὡσαύτως ἐκγόνοις
καὶ ἐξόδου τῆς πατρίδος εἷς ἔστω περὶ ταῦτα
857 νόμος οὗτος τρισί, προδότῃ καὶ ἱεροσύλῳ καὶ τῷ
τοὺς τῆς πόλεως νόμους βίᾳ ἀπολλύντι. κλέπτῃ
δέ, ἐάν τε μέγα ἐάν τε σμικρὸν κλέπτῃ τις, εἷς
αὖ νόμος κείσθω καὶ μία δίκης τιμωρία ξύμπασι·
τὸ μὲν γὰρ κλαπὲν δὴ χρεὼν διπλάσιον πρῶτον
ἐκτίνειν, ἐὰν ὄφλῃ τις τὴν τοιαύτην δίκην καὶ
ἱκανὴν ἔχῃ τὴν ἄλλην οὐσίαν ἀποτίνειν ὑπὲρ
τὸν κλῆρον, ἐὰν δὲ μή, δεδέσθαι ἕως ἂν ἐκτίσῃ
ἢ πείσῃ τὸν καταδικασάμενον. ἐὰν δέ τις ὄφλῃ
Β κλοπῆς δημοσίᾳ δίκην, πείσας τὴν πόλιν ἢ τὸ
κλέμμα ἐκτίσας διπλοῦν ἀπαλλαττέσθω τῶν
δεσμῶν.

ΚΛ. Πῶς δὴ λέγομεν, ὦ ξένε, μηδὲν διαφέρειν
τῷ κλέπτοντι, μέγα ἢ σμικρὸν ὑφελομένῳ καὶ ἐξ
ἱερῶν ἢ ὁσίων καὶ ὅσα ἄλλα ἐστὶ περὶ κλοπὴν
πᾶσαν ἀνομοιότητα ἔχοντα, οἷς δεῖ ποικίλοις
οὖσιν ἕπεσθαι τὸν νομοθέτην μηδὲν ὁμοίαις ζημίαις
ζημιοῦντα;

ΑΘ. Ἄριστ᾽, ὦ Κλεινία· σχεδόν τί με ὥσπερ
C φερόμενον ἀντικρούσας ἀνήγειρας, ἐννενοηκότα δὲ
καὶ πρότερον ὑπέμνησας ὅτι τὰ περὶ τὴν τῶν
νόμων θέσιν οὐδενὶ τρόπῳ πώποτε γέγονεν ὀρθῶς

---

[1] κείσθω : εἷς ἔστω MSS., edd. (England ci. τις for εἷς).

[1] But cp. 859 B ff., 933 E ff.

CLIN. Very good.

ATH. Moreover, a third general law shall be laid down, dealing with the judges to be employed and the manner of the trials, in cases where one man prosecutes another on a charge of treason; and concerning the offspring, likewise, whether they are to remain in their country or be expelled, this one law shall apply to the three cases of the traitor, the temple-robber, and the man who wrecks the State laws by violence. For the thief also, whether he steals a great thing or a small, one law and one legal penalty shall be enacted for all alike [1]: first, he must pay twice the value of the stolen article, if he loses his case and possesses enough property over and above his allotment wherewith to pay; but if not, he must be put in prison until either he has paid the sum or has been let off by the prosecutor. And if a man be cast in a suit for theft from the State, on obtaining pardon from the State, or after payment of double the sum stolen, he shall be let out of prison.

CLIN. How comes it, Stranger, that we are ruling that it makes no difference to the thief whether the thing he steals be great or small, and whether the place it is stolen from be holy or unhallowed, or whatever other differences may exist in the manner of a theft; whereas the lawgiver ought to suit the punishment to the crime by inflicting dissimilar penalties in these varying cases?

ATH. Well said, Clinias! You have collided with me when I was going, as it were, full steam ahead, and so have woken me up. You have reminded me of a previous reflection of mine, how that none of the attempts hitherto made at legislation have ever

διαπεπονημένα, ὥς γε ἐν τῷ νῦν παραπεπτωκότι [1]
λέγειν. πῶς δ᾽ αὖ καὶ τοῦτο λέγομεν; οὐ κακῶς
ἀπηκάσαμεν, ὅτε δούλοις ὡς ἰατρευομένοις ὑπὸ
δούλων ἀπηκάζομεν πάντας τοὺς νῦν νομοθετου-
μένους. εὖ γὰρ ἐπίστασθαι δεῖ τὸ τοιόνδε, ὡς εἰ
καταλάβοι ποτέ τις ἰατρὸς τῶν ταῖς ἐμπειρίαις
D ἄνευ λόγου τὴν ἰατρικὴν μεταχειριζομένων ἐλεύθερον ἐλευθέρῳ νοσοῦντι διαλεγόμενον ἰατρόν, καὶ
τοῦ φιλοσοφεῖν ἐγγὺς χρώμενον [μὲν] [2] τοῖς
λόγοις, ἐξ ἀρχῆς τε ἁπτόμενον τοῦ νοσήματος,
περὶ φύσεως πάσης ἐπανιόντα τῆς τῶν σωμάτων, ταχὺ καὶ σφόδρα γελάσειεν ἂν καὶ οὐκ
ἂν ἄλλους εἴποι λόγους ἢ τοὺς περὶ τὰ τοιαῦτ᾽
ἀεὶ προχείρους ὄντας τοῖς πλείστοις λεγομένοις
ἰατροῖς· φαίη γὰρ ἂν Ὦ μῶρε, οὐκ ἰατρεύεις τὸν
νοσοῦντα, ἀλλὰ σχεδὸν παιδεύεις, ὡς ἰατρὸν ἀλλ᾽
E οὐχ ὑγιῆ δεόμενον γίγνεσθαι.

ΚΛ. Οὐκοῦν λέγων τὰ τοιαῦτα ὀρθῶς ἂν
λέγοι;

ΑΘ. Τάχ᾽ ἄν, εἰ προσδιανοοῖτό γε ὡς ὅστις
περὶ νόμων οὕτω διεξέρχεται, καθάπερ ἡμεῖς τὰ
νῦν, παιδεύει τοὺς πολίτας, ἀλλ᾽ οὐ νομοθετεῖ.
ἆρ᾽ οὖν οὐ καὶ τοῦτ᾽ ἂν πρὸς τρόπου λέγειν
φαίνοιτο;

ΚΛ. Ἴσως.

ΑΘ. Εὐτυχὲς δὲ ἡμῶν τὸ παρὸν γέγονεν.

ΚΛ. Τὸ ποῖον δή;

ΑΘ. Τὸ μηδεμίαν ἀνάγκην εἶναι νομοθετεῖν,
858 ἀλλ᾽ αὐτοὺς ἐν σκέψει γενομένους περὶ πάσης
πολιτείας πειρᾶσθαι κατιδεῖν τό τε ἄριστον καὶ

---

[1] παραπεπτωκότι MSS. : παρόντι MSS. marg., Zur., vulg.
[2] [μὲν] bracketed by W.-Möllendorff.

been carried out rightly—as in fact we may infer from the instance before us. What do I mean to imply by this remark? It was no bad comparison we made [1] when we compared all existing legislation to the doctoring of slaves by slaves. For one should carefully notice this, that if any of the doctors who practise medicine by purely empirical methods, devoid of theory, were to come upon a free-born doctor conversing with a free-born patient, and using arguments, much as a philosopher would, dealing with the course of the ailment from its origin and surveying the natural constitution of the human body,—he would at once break out into a roar of laughter, and the language he would use would be none other than that which always comes ready to the tongue of most so-called "doctors": "You fool," he would say, "you are not doctoring your patient, but schooling him, so to say, as though what he wanted was to be made, not a sound man, but a doctor."

CLIN. And in saying so, would he not be right?

ATH. Possibly, provided that he should also take the view that the man who treats of laws in the way that we are now doing is schooling the citizens rather than legislating. Would he not seem to be right in saying that, too?

CLIN. Probably.

ATH. How fortunate we are in the conclusion we have now come to!

CLIN. What conclusion?

ATH. This,—that there is no need to legislate, but only to become students ourselves, and endeavour to discern in regard to every polity how the best

[1] 720 A ff.

τὸ ἀναγκαιότατον, τίνα τρόπον ἂν γιγνόμενον
γίγνοιτο. καὶ δὴ καὶ τὸ νῦν ἔξεστιν ἡμῖν, ὡς
ἔοικεν, εἰ μὲν βουλόμεθα, τὸ βέλτιστον σκοπεῖν,
εἰ δὲ βουλόμεθα, τὸ ἀναγκαιότατον περὶ νόμων.
αἱρώμεθα οὖν ὁπότερον δοκεῖ.

ΚΛ.   Γελοίαν, ὦ ξένε, προτιθέμεθα τὴν αἵρεσιν,
καὶ ἀτεχνῶς ὥσπερ κατεχομένοις νομοθέταις
B ὅμοιοι γιγνοίμεθ' ἂν ὑπὸ μεγάλης τινὸς ἀνάγκης
ἤδη νομοθετεῖν, ὡς οὐκέτ' ἐξὸν εἰς αὔριον. ἡμῖν
δ', εἰπεῖν σὺν θεῷ, ἔξεστι, καθάπερ ἢ λιθολό-
γοις ἢ καί τινος ἑτέρας ἀρχομένοις συστάσεως,
παραφορήσασθαι χύδην ἐξ ὧν ἐκλεξόμεθα τὰ
πρόσφορα τῇ μελλούσῃ γενήσεσθαι συστάσει, καὶ
δὴ καὶ κατὰ σχολὴν ἐκλέξασθαι. τιθῶμεν οὖν
ἡμᾶς νῦν εἶναι μὴ τοὺς ἐξ ἀνάγκης οἰκοδομοῦντας,
ἀλλὰ τοὺς ἐπὶ σχολῆς ἔτι τὰ μὲν παρατιθεμένους,
τὰ δὲ ξυνιστάντας, ὥστε ὀρθῶς ἔχει τὰ μὲν ἤδη
C τῶν νόμων λέγειν ὡς τιθέμενα, τὰ δ' ὡς παρατιθέ-
μενα.

ΑΘ.   Γένοιτο γοῦν ἄν, ὦ Κλεινία, κατὰ φύσιν
μᾶλλον ἡμῖν ἡ σύνοψις τῶν νόμων. ἴδωμεν γὰρ
οὖν, ὦ πρὸς θεῶν, τὸ τοιόνδε περὶ νομοθετῶν.

ΚΛ.   Τὸ ποῖον δή;

ΑΘ.   Γράμματα μέν που καὶ ἐν γράμμασι λόγοι
καὶ ἄλλων εἰσὶ πολλῶν ἐν ταῖς πόλεσι γεγραμ-
μένοι, γράμματα δὲ καὶ τὰ τοῦ νομοθέτου καὶ
λόγοι.

ΚΛ.   Πῶς γὰρ οὔ;

ΑΘ.   Πότερον οὖν τοῖς μὲν τῶν ἄλλων συγγράμ-
D μασι, ποιητῶν καὶ ὅσοι ἄνευ μέτρων καὶ μετὰ
μέτρων τὴν αὐτῶν εἰς μνήμην ξυμβουλὴν περὶ

form might come about, and how that which is the least elaborate possible. Moreover, we are now allowed, as it seems, to study, if we choose, the best form of legislation, or, if we choose, the least elaborate. So let us make our choice between these two.

CLIN. The choice we propose, Stranger, is an absurd one: we should be acting like legislators who were driven by some overpowering necessity to pass laws on the spot, because it is impossible for them to do so on the morrow. But for us (if Heaven will) it is quite possible to do as bricklayers do, or men starting on any other kind of construction,—that is, to collect material piecemeal, from which we may select what is suitable for the edifice we intend to build, and, what is more, select it at our leisure. Let us assume, then, that we are not now building under compulsion, but that we are still at leisure, and engaged partly in collecting material and partly in putting it together; so that we may rightly say that our laws are being in part already erected and in part collected.

ATH. In this way, Clinias, our survey of laws will at any rate follow nature's course more closely. Now let us consider, I adjure you, the following point about legislators.

CLIN. What point?

ATH. We have in our States not only the writings and written speeches of many other people, but also the writings and speeches of the lawgiver.

CLIN. Certainly.

ATH. Are we, then, to pay attention to the compositions of the others—poets, and all who, either with or without metre, have composed and

βίου κατέθεντο συγγράψαντες, προσέχωμεν τὸν
νοῦν, τοῖς δὲ τῶν νομοθετῶν μὴ προσέχωμεν;
ἢ πάντων μάλιστα;

ΚΛ. Πολύ γε.

ΑΘ. Ἀλλὰ δῆτα οὐ χρὴ τὸν νομοθέτην μόνον
τῶν γραφόντων περὶ καλῶν καὶ ἀγαθῶν καὶ δικαίων ξυμβουλεύειν, διδάσκοντα οἶά τέ ἐστι καὶ
ὡς ἐπιτηδευτέον αὐτὰ τοῖς μέλλουσιν εὐδαίμοσιν
ἔσεσθαι.

ΚΛ. Καὶ πῶς οὔ;

E   ΑΘ. Ἀλλὰ αἰσχρὸν δὴ μᾶλλον Ὁμήρῳ τε καὶ
Τυρταίῳ καὶ τοῖς ἄλλοις ποιηταῖς περὶ βίου τε
καὶ ἐπιτηδευμάτων κακῶς θέσθαι γράψαντας,
Λυκούργῳ δὲ ἧττον καὶ Σόλωνι καὶ ὅσοι δὴ νομο-
θέται γενόμενοι γράμματα ἔγραψαν; ἢ τό γε
ὀρθὸν πάντων δεῖ γραμμάτων τῶν ἐν ταῖς πόλεσι
τὰ περὶ τοὺς νόμους γεγραμμένα φαίνεσθαι δια-
πτυττόμενα μακρῷ κάλλιστά τε καὶ ἄριστα,
τὰ δὲ τῶν ἄλλων ἢ κατ’ ἐκεῖνα ξυνεπόμενα
859 ἢ διαφωνοῦντα αὐτοῖς εἶναι καταγέλαστα;
οὕτω διανοώμεθα περὶ νόμων δεῖν γραφῆς γίγνεσθαι ταῖς πόλεσιν, ἐν πατρός τε καὶ μητρὸς
σχήμασι φιλούντων τε καὶ νοῦν ἐχόντων φαίνεσθαι τὰ γεγραμμένα, ἢ κατὰ τύραννον καὶ
δεσπότην, τάξαντα καὶ ἀπειλήσαντα, γράψαντα
ἐν τοίχοις ἀπηλλάχθαι; σκοπῶμεν οὖν δὴ καὶ
τὰ νῦν ἡμεῖς πότερα ταύτῃ πειρώμεθα λέγειν
B διανοηθέντες περὶ νόμων, εἴτ’ οὖν δυνάμεθα εἴτε
μή, ἀλλ’ οὖν τό γε πρόθυμον παρεχόμενοι· καὶ
κατὰ ταύτην τὴν ὁδὸν ἰόντες, ἂν ἄρα τι καὶ δέῃ
πάσχειν, πάσχωμεν. ἀγαθὸν δ’ εἴη γε,[1] καὶ ἂν
θεὸς ἐθέλῃ, γίγνοιτ’ ἂν ταύτῃ.

put on record their counsels concerning life,—but to pay no attention to those of the lawgivers? Or should we not attend to them above all others?

CLIN. Yes, far above all.

ATH. But we surely do not mean that the law-giver alone of all the writers is not to give counsel about what is noble, good and just, teaching what these are, and how those who intend to be happy must practise them.

CLIN. Of course he must do so.

ATH. Well then, is it more disgraceful on the part of Homer and Tyrtaeus and the rest of the poets to lay down in their writings bad rules about life and its pursuits, and less disgraceful on the part of Lycurgus and Solon and all the legislators who have written? Or rather, is it not right that, of all the writings which exist in States, those which concern laws should be seen, when unrolled, to be by far the fairest and best, and all other writings to be either modelled on them or, if disagreeing with them, contemptible? Are we to conceive that the written laws in our States should resemble persons moved by love and wisdom, such as a father or a mother, or that they should order and threaten, like some tyrant and despot, who writes his decree on the wall, and there is an end of it? So let us now consider whether we are going to try to discuss laws with this intention—showing zeal, at any rate, whether or not we may prove successful; and if, in proceeding on this course, we must meet with mishap, so be it. Yet we pray that it may be well with us, and if God wills, it shall be well.

---

[1] γε England : τε MSS.

κλ.   Καλῶς εἴρηκας, ποιῶμέν τε ὡς λέγεις.

αθ.   Διασκεπτέον ἄρα πρῶτον, ὥσπερ ἐπεχειρή-
σαμεν, ἀκριβῶς τὸν περὶ τῶν τε ἱεροσυλούντων καὶ
κλοπῆς πάσης πέρι καὶ ἀδικημάτων ξυμπάντων·
καὶ οὐ δυσχεραντέον εἰ μεταξὺ νομοθετοῦντες τὰ
C μὲν ἔθεμεν, τῶν δ' ἔτι διασκοποῦμεν πέρι· νομο-
θέται γὰρ γιγνόμεθα, ἀλλ' οὔκ ἐσμέν πω, τάχα δὲ
ἴσως ἂν γενοίμεθα. εἰ δὴ δοκεῖ περὶ ὧν εἴρηκα,
ὡς εἴρηκα, σκοπεῖσθαι, σκοπῶμεν.

κλ.   Παντάπασι μὲν οὖν.

αθ.   Περὶ δὴ καλῶν καὶ δικαίων ξυμπάντων
πειρώμεθα κατιδεῖν τὸ τοιόνδε, ὅπῃ ποτὲ ὁμολογοῦμεν νῦν καὶ ὅπῃ διαφερόμεθα ἡμεῖς τε ἡμῖν
αὐτοῖς, οὐ δὴ φαῖμεν ἂν προθυμεῖσθαί γε, εἰ μηδὲν
D ἄλλο, διαφέρειν τῶν πλείστων, οἱ πολλοί τε αὐτοὶ
πρὸς αὑτοὺς αὖ.

κλ.   Τὰς ποίας δὲ δὴ διαφορὰς ἡμῶν ἐννοηθεὶς
λέγεις;

αθ.   Ἐγὼ πειράσομαι φράζειν. περὶ δικαιοσύνης ὅλως καὶ τῶν δικαίων ἀνθρώπων τε καὶ
πραγμάτων καὶ πράξεων πάντες πως ξυνομο-
λογοῦμεν πάντα εἶναι ταῦτα καλά, ὥστε οὐδ'
εἴ τις διϊσχυρίζοιτο [εἶναι][1] τοὺς δικαίους ἀνθρώπους, ἂν καὶ τυγχάνωσιν ὄντες αἰσχροὶ τὰ σώματα, κατ' αὐτό γε τὸ δικαιότατον ἦθος ταύτῃ
E παγκάλους εἶναι, σχεδὸν οὐδεὶς ἂν λέγων οὕτω
πλημμελῶς δόξειε λέγειν.

κλ.   Οὐκοῦν ὀρθῶς;

αθ.   Ἴσως· ἴδωμεν δὲ ὡς, εἰ πάντ' ἐστὶ καλὰ
ὅσα δικαιοσύνης ἔχεται, τῶν πάντων τοι καὶ τὰ
παθήματα ἡμῖν ἐστι σχεδὸν τοῖς ποιήμασιν ἴσα.

[1] [εἶναι] bracketed by Hermann.

218

CLIN. You are right : let us do as you say.

ATH. First of all, since we have started on it, we must examine closely the law about temple-robbers and all forms of thieving and wrong-doing ; nor should we be vexed by the fact that, although we enacted some points while legislating, there are some points still under consideration : for we are in process of becoming lawgivers, and may perhaps become so, but we are not lawgivers as yet. So if we agree to consider the matters I have mentioned in the way I have mentioned, let us so consider them.

CLIN. Most certainly.

ATH. In respect of goodness and justice as a whole, let us try to discern this,—how far we now agree with ourselves, and how far we differ (for we should certainly say that we desire, if nothing else, to differ at least from the majority of men), and how far also the majority agree or differ among themselves.

CLIN. What differences of ours have you in mind ?

ATH. I will try to explain. Concerning justice in general, and men, things, or actions that are just, we all agree that these are all beautiful, so that no one would be regarded as saying what was wrong even if he should maintain that just men, however ugly in body, are quite beautiful in respect of their very just character.

CLIN. Would not that be right ?

ATH. Perhaps ; but let us observe this,—that if all things which belong to justice are beautiful, that "all" includes for us passions[1] nearly as much as actions.

---

[1] *i.e.* " sufferings."

ΚΛ. Τί οὖν δή ;

ΑΘ. Ποίημα μέν, ὅπερ ἂν ᾖ δίκαιον, σχεδὸν ὅσονπερ ἂν τοῦ δικαίου κοινωνῇ, κατὰ τοσοῦτον καὶ τοῦ καλοῦ μετέχον ἐστίν.

ΚΛ. Τί μήν ;

ΑΘ. Οὐκοῦν καὶ πάθος ὅπερ ἂν δικαίου κοινωνῇ,
860 κατὰ τοσοῦτον γίγνεσθαι καλὸν ὁμολογούμενον, οὐκ ἂν διαφωνοῦντα παρέχοι τὸν λόγον ;

ΚΛ. Ἀληθῆ.

ΑΘ. Ἐὰν δέ γε δίκαιον μὲν ὁμολογῶμεν, αἰσχρὸν δὲ εἶναι πάθος, διαφωνήσει τό τε δίκαιον καὶ τὸ καλὸν λεχθέντων τῶν δικαίων αἰσχίστων εἶναι.

ΚΛ. Πῶς τοῦτο εἴρηκας ;

ΑΘ. Οὐδὲν χαλεπὸν ἐννοεῖν· οἱ γὰρ ὀλίγῳ πρόσθεν τεθέντες ἡμῖν νόμοι πάντων ἐναντιώτατα παραγγέλλειν δόξειαν ἂν τοῖς νῦν λεγομένοις.

ΚΛ. Ποίοις ;

Β ΑΘ. Τὸν ἱερόσυλόν που ἐτίθεμεν δικαίως ἂν ἀποθνήσκειν καὶ τὸν τῶν εὖ κειμένων νόμων πολέμιον, καὶ μέλλοντες δὴ νόμιμα τοιαῦτα τιθέναι πάμπολλα ἐπέσχομεν, ἰδόντες ὡς ταῦτά ἐστι μὲν ἄπειρα παθήματα πλήθει καὶ μεγέθεσι,[1] δικαιότατα δὲ πάντων παθημάτων καὶ ξυμπάντων αἴσχιστα. μῶν οὐχ οὕτως ἡμῖν τά τε δίκαια καὶ τὰ καλὰ τοτὲ μὲν ὡς ταὐτὰ ξύμπαντα, τοτὲ δὲ ὡς ἐναντιώτατα φανεῖται ;

ΚΛ. Κινδυνεύει.

ΑΘ. Τοῖς μὲν τοίνυν πολλοῖς οὕτω περὶ τὰ τοιαῦτα ἀσυμφώνως τὰ καλὰ καὶ τὰ δίκαια διερριμμένα προσαγορεύεται.

ΚΛ. Φαίνεται γοῦν, ὦ ξένε.

---

[1] μεγέθεσι MSS. : μεγέθει Zur., vulg.

CLIN. Well, what then?

ATH. Every just action, in so far as it shares in justice, practically in the same degree partakes of beauty.

CLIN. Yes.

ATH. It is agreed also—if our argument is to be consistent—that a passion which shares in justice, becomes, so far, beautiful.

CLIN. True.

ATH. But if we agree that a passion though just is unseemly, then justice and beauty will be at discord, when just things are called most unseemly.

CLIN. What do you mean by that?

ATH. It is not hard to grasp. The laws we enacted a short time ago might seem to enjoin what is absolutely contrary to our present statements.

CLIN. What statements?

ATH. We laid it down [1] that it is just to put to death the temple-robber and the enemy of the rightly-enacted laws; and then, when we were minded to enact a host of similar rules, we held our hand, since we perceived that such rules involve passions infinite both in number and in magnitude, and that, although they are eminently just, they are also eminently unseemly. Thus the just and the beautiful will seem to us at one moment wholly identical, at another, utterly opposed, will they not?

CLIN. I am afraid so.

ATH. Thus it is that by the multitude the beautiful and the just are flung apart, and inconsistent language is used about them.

CLIN. It certainly seems so, Stranger.

[1] 854 B ff.

ΑΘ. Τὸ τοίνυν ἡμέτερον, ὦ Κλεινία, πάλιν
ἴδωμεν, πῶς αὖ περὶ αὐτὰ ταῦτα ἔχει τῆς
συμφωνίας.

ΚΛ. Ποίας δὴ πρὸς ποῖον ; [1]

ΑΘ. Ἐν τοῖς ἔμπροσθεν λόγοις οἶμαι διαρρήδην
ἐμὲ εἰρηκέναι πως, εἰ δ' οὖν μὴ πρότερον, ἀλλὰ
νῦν ὡς λέγοντά με τίθετε——

ΚΛ. Τὸ ποῖον ;

D ΑΘ. Ὡς οἱ κακοὶ πάντες εἰς πάντα εἰσὶν
ἄκοντες κακοί. τούτου δὲ οὕτως ἔχοντος ἀνάγκη
που τούτῳ ξυνέπεσθαι τὸν ἑξῆς λόγον.

ΚΛ. Τίνα λέγεις ;

ΑΘ. Ὡς ὁ μὲν ἄδικός που κακός, ὁ δὲ κακὸς
ἄκων τοιοῦτος. ἀκουσίως δὲ ἑκούσιον οὐκ ἔχει
πράττεσθαί ποτε λόγον· ἄκων οὖν ἐκείνῳ φαίνοιτ'
ἂν ἀδικεῖν ὁ ἀδικῶν τῷ τὴν ἀδικίαν ἀκούσιον
τιθεμένῳ· καὶ δὴ καὶ νῦν ὁμολογητέον ἐμοί,
ξύμφημι γὰρ ἄκοντας ἀδικεῖν πάντας· εἰ καί
E τις φιλονεικίας ἢ φιλοτιμίας ἕνεκα ἄκοντας μὲν
ἀδίκους εἶναί φησιν, ἀδικεῖν μὴν ἑκόντας πολλούς,
ὅ γ' ἐμὸς λόγος ἐκεῖνος, ἀλλ' οὐχ οὗτος· τίνα
οὖν αὖ τρόπον ἔγωγε ξυμφωνοίην ἂν τοῖς ἐμαυτοῦ
λόγοις ; εἴ με, ὦ Κλεινία καὶ Μέγιλλε, ἐρωτῶτε,
Εἰ δὴ ταῦτα οὕτως ἔχοντά ἐστιν, ὦ ξένε, τί
συμβουλεύεις ἡμῖν περὶ τῆς νομοθεσίας τῇ τῶν

---

[1] ποῖον Ast : ποίαν MSS.

---

[1] 731 C, 734 B : cp. Ar. *Eth. N.* 1109[b] 30 ff.
[2] In what follows, the *Athenian*, adopting the Socratic dictum
that " vice is involuntary " (cp. *Tim.* 86 E ff.), applies it to the
special vice of injustice ; but here his view is found to conflict
with the popular view which distinguishes between voluntary

LAWS, BOOK IX

ATH. Then let us look again at our own view, and see how far it is consistent in this respect.

CLIN. What kind of consistency, and in respect of what, do you mean?

ATH. I believe that I expressly stated[1] in our previous discourse,—or, if I did not do it before, please assume that I now assert——

CLIN. What?

ATH. That all bad men are in all respects unwillingly bad; and, this being so, our next statement must agree therewith.

CLIN. What statement do you mean?

ATH. This,—that the unjust man is, indeed, bad, but the bad man is unwillingly bad.[2] But it is illogical to suppose that a willing deed is done unwillingly; therefore he that commits an unjust act does so unwillingly in the opinion of him who assumes that injustice is involuntary—a conclusion which I also must now allow; for I agree that all men do unjust acts unwillingly; so, since I hold this view—and do not share the opinion of those who, through contentiousness or arrogance, assert that, while there are some who are unjust against their will, yet there are also many who are unjust willingly,—how am I to prove consistent with my own statements? Suppose you two, Megillus and Clinias, put this question to me—" If this is the state of the case, Stranger, what counsel do you give us in regard to legislating for

---

and involuntary acts of injustice, and assigns to them different legal penalties. If this popular distinction is wrong, the lawgiver must either (a) simply apply the Socratic rule, and enact that all unjust acts are involuntary and deserve therefore equal penalties, or (b) draw a new distinction, which *Ath.* proceeds to do in 861 E ff. (see note *ad loc.*).

Μαγνήτων πόλει ; πότερον νομοθετεῖν ἢ μή ;
Πῶς γὰρ οὔ ; φήσω. Διοριεῖς οὖν αὐτοῖς ἀκούσιά
τε καὶ ἑκούσια ἀδικήματα, καὶ τῶν μὲν ἑκουσίων
ἁμαρτημάτων τε καὶ ἀδικημάτων μείζους τὰς ζημίας
861 θήσομεν, τῶν δ' ἐλάττους ; ἢ πάντων ἐξ ἴσης, ὡς
οὐκ ὄντων ἀδικημάτων τὸ παράπαν ἑκουσίων ;

ΚΛ. Ὀρθῶς μέντοι λέγεις, ὦ ξένε. καὶ τούτοις
δὴ τί χρησόμεθα τοῖς νῦν λεγομένοις ;

ΑΘ. Καλῶς ἤρου. πρῶτον μὲν τοίνυν αὐτοῖς
τόδε χρησώμεθα——

ΚΛ. Τὸ ποῖον ;

ΑΘ. Ἀναμνησθῶμεν ὡς ἔμπροσθεν νῦν δὴ
καλῶς ἐλέγομεν ὅτι περὶ τὰ δίκαια εἴη παμπόλλη
τις ἡμῶν ταραχή τε καὶ ἀσυμφωνία. τοῦτο δὲ
B λαβόντες πάλιν ἐρωτῶμεν ἡμᾶς αὐτούς, Ἆρ' οὖν
περὶ τὴν τούτων ἀπορίαν οὔτ' ἐξευπορήσαντες
οὔτε διορισάμενοι τί ποτ' ἐστὶ ταῦτα ἀλλήλων
διαφέροντα, ἃ δὴ κατὰ πάσας τὰς πόλεις ὑπὸ
νομοθετῶν πάντων τῶν πώποτε γενομένων ὡς
δύο εἴδη τῶν ἀδικημάτων ὄντα, τὰ μὲν ἑκούσια,
τὰ δὲ ἀκούσια, ταύτῃ καὶ νομοθετεῖται· ὁ δὲ παρ'
ἡμῶν νῦν δὴ ῥηθεὶς λόγος, ὥσπερ παρὰ θεοῦ
λεχθείς, τοσοῦτον μόνον εἰπὼν ἀπαλλάξεται, δοὺς
δὲ οὐδένα λόγον ὡς ὀρθῶς εὕρηκε κατανομοθετήσει
C τινὰ τρόπον ; Οὐκ ἔστιν, ἀλλὰ ἀνάγκη πως ταῦτα
ἔμπροσθεν τοῦ νομοθετεῖν δηλῶσαι δύο τε ὄντα
καὶ τὴν διαφορὰν ἀλλήλων,[1] ἵνα, ὅταν ἑκατέρῳ
τις τὴν δίκην ἐπιτιθῇ, πᾶς ἐπακολουθῇ τοῖς λεγο-

――――――
[1] ἀλλήλων Hermann : ἄλλην MSS.

the Magnesian State? Shall we legislate or shall
we not?" "Legislate by all means," I shall reply.
"Will you make a distinction, then, between voluntary and involuntary wrong-doings, and are we to
enact heavier penalties for the crimes and wrong-
doings that are voluntary, and lighter penalties for
the others? Or shall we enact equal penalties for
all, on the view that there is no such thing as a
voluntary act of injustice?"

CLIN. What you say, Stranger, is quite right: so
what use are we to make of our present arguments?

ATH. A very proper question! The use we shall
make of them, to begin with, is this ——

CLIN. What?

ATH. Let us recall how, a moment ago, we rightly
stated that in regard to justice we are suffering from
the greatest confusion and inconsistency. Grasping
this fact, let us again question ourselves,—"As to
our perplexity about these matters, since we have
neither got it clear nor defined the point of difference
between those two kinds of wrong-doing, voluntary
and involuntary, which are treated as legally distinct
in every State by every legislator who has ever yet
appeared,—as to this, is the statement we recently
made to stand, like a divine oracle, as a mere *ex
cathedra* statement, unsupported by any proof, and to
serve as a kind of master-enactment [1]?" That is impossible; and before we legislate we are bound first
to make it clear somehow that these wrong-doings
are two-fold, and wherein their difference consists, in
order that when we impose the penalty on either
kind, everyone may follow our rules, and be able to

---

[1] Literally, "to legislate down" (*i.e.* over-rule the popular
objection to our Socratic view).

μένοις καὶ δυνατὸς ᾖ τό τε πρεπόντως τεθὲν ἀμῇ
γέ πῃ κρῖναι καὶ τὸ μή.

ΚΛ. Καλῶς ἡμῖν φαίνει λέγειν, ὦ ξένε· δυοῖν
γὰρ θάτερον ἡμᾶς χρεών, ἢ μὴ λέγειν ὡς πάντα
ἀκούσια τὰ ἀδικήματα, ἢ τοῦτο ὡς ὀρθῶς εἴρηται
D πρῶτον διορίσαντας δηλῶσαι.

ΑΘ. Τούτοιν τοίνυν τοῖν δυοῖν τὸ μὲν οὐκ
ἀνεκτὸν ἐμοὶ πάντως που γίγνεσθαι, τό γε δὴ
μὴ λέγειν οὕτως οἰόμενον ἔχειν τἀληθές· οὐ γὰρ
ἂν νόμιμον οὐδ᾽ ὅσιον ἂν εἴη· κατὰ τίνα δὲ
τρόπον ἐστὸν δύο, εἰ μὴ τῷ τε ἀκουσίῳ καὶ τῷ
ἑκουσίῳ διαφέρετον ἑκάτερον, [ἀλλὰ]¹ ἄλλῳ τινὶ
δή ποτε πειρατέον ἀμῶς γέ πως δηλοῦν.

ΚΛ. Παντάπασι μὲν οὖν, ὦ ξένε, τοῦτό γε οὐχ
οἷόν τε ἄλλως πως ἡμᾶς διανοηθῆναι.

E ΑΘ. Ταῦτα ἔσται. φέρε δή, βλάβαι μέν, ὡς
ἔοικεν, ἀλλήλων τῶν πολιτῶν ἐν ταῖς κοινωνίαις
τε καὶ ὁμιλίαις πολλαὶ γίγνονται, καὶ τό γε
ἑκούσιόν τε καὶ ἀκούσιον ἐν αὐταῖς ἄφθονόν
ἐστιν.

ΚΛ. Πῶς γὰρ οὔ;

ΑΘ. Μὴ τοίνυν τις τὰς βλάβας πάσας ἀδικίας
τιθεὶς οὕτως οἴηται καὶ τὰ ἄδικα ἐν αὐταῖσι
ταύτῃ γίγνεσθαι διπλᾶ, τὰ μὲν ἑκούσια δή, τὰ
δ᾽ ἀκούσια· βλάβαι γὰρ ἀκούσιοι τῶν πάντων
οὔτ᾽ ἀριθμοῖς οὔτε μεγέθεσιν ἐλάττους εἰσὶ τῶν

---

¹ [ἀλλὰ] bracketed by W.-Möllendorff.

---

¹ The proper distinction to be drawn (as *Ath.* proceeds to
argue) is not that between voluntary and involuntary acts of
injustice (since there are no such voluntary acts), but that
between "injuries" (βλάβαι, "acts causing loss") and "acts
of injustice." Injustice is really a quality of the agent rather

form some judgment regarding the suitability or otherwise of our enactments.

CLIN. What you say, Stranger, appears to us to be excellent: we ought to do one of two things,—either not assert that all unjust acts are involuntary, or else make our distinctions first, then prove the correctness of that assertion.

ATH. Of these alternatives the first is to me quite intolerable—namely, not to assert what I hold to be the truth,—for that would be neither a lawful thing to do nor a pious. But as to the question how such acts are two-fold,—if the difference does not lie in that between the voluntary and the involuntary, then we must try to explain it by means of some other distinction.[1]

CLIN. Well, certainly, Stranger, about this matter there is no other plan we can possibly adopt.

ATH. It shall be done. Come now, in dealings and intercourse between citizens, injuries committed by one against another are of frequent occurrence, and they involve plenty of the voluntary as well as of the involuntary.

CLIN. To be sure!

ATH. Let no one put down all injuries as acts of injustice and then regard the unjust acts involved as two-fold in the way described, namely, that they are partly voluntary and partly involuntary (for, of the total, the involuntary injuries are not less than the voluntary either in number or in magnitude); but

---

than of the act, and (like all vice) is a form of un-reason : as the slave of un-reason, the unjust man is never a free agent. Hence the task of the lawgiver is two fold, (1) to make good the "injuries," and (2) to cure the agent of his "injustice" by restoring the power of reason ("moral sense") in his soul.

ἑκουσίων· σκοπεῖσθε δὲ εἴ τέ τι λέγω λέγων ἃ
862 μέλλω λέγειν, εἴτε καὶ μηδὲν τὸ παράπαν. οὐ
γάρ φημι ἔγωγε, ὦ Κλεινία καὶ Μέγιλλε, εἴ τίς
τινά τι πημαίνει μὴ βουλόμενος, ἀλλ᾿ ἄκων,
ἀδικεῖν μέν, ἄκοντα μήν, καὶ ταύτῃ μὲν δὴ νομοθετήσω τοῦτο ὡς ἀκούσιον ἀδίκημα νομοθετῶν,
ἀλλ᾿ οὐδὲ ἀδικίαν τὸ παράπαν θήσω τὴν τοιαύτην
βλάβην, οὔτε ἂν μείζων οὔτε ἂν ἐλάττων τῳ
γίγνηται. πολλάκις δὲ ὠφέλειαν οὐκ ὀρθὴν γενομένην, τὸν τῆς ὠφελείας αἴτιον ἀδικεῖν φήσομεν,
B ἐὰν ᾖ γ᾿ ἐμὴ νικᾷ. σχεδὸν γάρ, ὦ φίλοι, οὔτ᾿
εἴ τίς τῳ διδωσί τι τῶν ὄντων, οὔτ᾿ εἰ τοὐναντίον
ἀφαιρεῖται, δίκαιον ἁπλῶς ἢ ἄδικον χρὴ τὸ
τοιοῦτον οὕτω λέγειν, ἀλλ᾿ ἐὰν ἤθει καὶ δικαίῳ
τρόπῳ χρώμενός τις ὠφελῇ τινά τι καὶ βλάπτῃ,
τοῦτό ἐστι τῷ νομοθέτῃ θεατέον, καὶ πρὸς δύο
ταῦτα δὴ βλεπτέον, πρός τε ἀδικίαν καὶ βλάβην,
καὶ τὸ μὲν βλαβὲν ἀβλαβὲς[1] τοῖς νόμοις εἰς τὸ
δυνατὸν ποιητέον, τό τε ἀπολόμενον σώζοντα καὶ
τὸ πεσὸν ὑπό του πάλιν ἐξορθοῦντα καὶ τὸ
C θανατωθὲν ἢ τρωθὲν ὑγιές, τὸ δὲ ἀποίνοις ἐξιλα-
σθὲν τοῖς δρῶσι καὶ πάσχουσιν ἑκάστας τῶν
βλάψεων ἐκ διαφορᾶς εἰς φιλίαν πειρατέον ἀεὶ
καθιστάναι τοῖς νόμοις.

ΚΛ. Καλῶς ταῦτά γε.

ΑΘ. Τὰς τοίνυν ἀδίκους αὖ βλάβας καὶ κέρδη
ἐάν τις ἀδικῶν τινὰ κερδαίνειν ποιῇ, τούτων ὁπόσα
μὲν ἰατά, ὡς οὐσῶν ἐν ψυχῇ νόσων, ἰᾶσθαι· τὸ
δὲ τῆς ἰάσεως ἡμῖν τῆς ἀδικίας τῇδε ῥέπειν χρὴ
φάναι——

---

[1] βλαβὲν ἀβλαβὲς Badham : ἀβλαβὲς ὑγιὲς MSS. (βλαβὲν in
marg.): βλαβὲν ὑγιὲς Zur., al.

228

consider whether in saying what I am now going to say I am speaking sense or absolute nonsense. For what I assert, Megillus and Clinias, is not that, if one man harms another involuntarily and without wishing it, he acts unjustly though involuntarily, nor shall I legislate in this way, pronouncing this to be an involuntary act of injustice, but I will pronounce that such an injury is not an injustice at all, whether it be a greater injury or a less. And, if my view prevails, we shall often say that the author of a benefit wrongly done commits an injustice; for as a rule, my friends, neither when a man gives some material object to another, nor when he takes it away, ought one to term such an act absolutely just or unjust, but only when a man of just character and disposition does any benefit or injury to another,—that is what the lawgiver must look at; he must consider these two things, injustice and injury, and the injury inflicted he must make good so far as possible by legal means; he must conserve what is lost, restore what has been broken down, make whole what is wounded or dead; and when the several injuries have been atoned for by compensation, he must endeavour always by means of the laws to convert the parties who have inflicted them and those who have suffered them from a state of discord to a state of amity.

CLIN. He will be right in doing that.

ATH. As regards unjust injuries and gains, in case one man causes another to gain by acting unjustly towards him, all such cases as are curable we must cure, regarding them as diseases of the soul. And we should affirm that our cure for injustice lies in this direction——

κλ. Πῇ;

D   αθ. Ὅπως ὅ τί τις ἂν ἀδικήσῃ μέγα ἢ σμικρόν,
ὁ νόμος αὐτὸν διδάξει καὶ ἀναγκάσει τὸ παράπαν
εἰς αὖθις τὸ τοιοῦτον ἢ μηδέποτε ἑκόντα τολμῆσαι
ποιεῖν ἢ διαφερόντως ἧττον πολύ, πρὸς τῇ τῆς
βλάβης ἐκτίσει. ταῦτα εἴτε ἔργοις ἢ λόγοις, ἢ
μεθ᾽ ἡδονῶν ἢ λυπῶν, ἢ τιμῶν ἢ ἀτιμιῶν, καὶ
χρημάτων ζημίας ἢ καὶ δώρων, ἢ καὶ τὸ παράπαν
ᾧτινι τρόπῳ ποιήσει τις μισῆσαι μὲν τὴν ἀδικίαν,
στέρξαι δὲ ἢ μὴ μισεῖν τὴν τοῦ δικαίου φύσιν,
αὐτό ἐστι τοῦτο ἔργον τῶν καλλίστων νόμων.
E ὃν δ᾽ ἂν ἀνιάτως εἰς ταῦτα ἔχοντα αἴσθηται
νομοθέτης, δίκην τούτοισι καὶ νόμον θήσει τίνα;
γιγνώσκων που τοῖς τοιούτοις πᾶσιν ὡς οὔτε
αὐτοῖς ἔτι ζῆν ἄμεινον τούς τε ἄλλους ἂν διπλῇ
ὠφελοῖεν ἀπαλλαττόμενοι τοῦ βίου, παράδειγμα
μὲν τοῦ μὴ ἀδικεῖν τοῖς ἄλλοις γενόμενοι, ποι-
863 οῦντες δὲ ἀνδρῶν κακῶν ἔρημον τὴν πόλιν· οὕτω
[μὲν] δὴ τῶν τοιούτων πέρι .νομοθέτῃ κολαστὴν
τῶν ἁμαρτημάτων θάνατον ἀνάγκη νέμειν, ἄλλως
δὲ οὐδαμῶς.

κλ. Ἔοικε μέν πως λέγεσθαι τὰ παρὰ σοῦ
καὶ μάλα μετρίως, ἥδιον δ᾽ ἂν ἔτι σαφέστερον
ἀκούσαιμεν ταῦτα ῥηθέντα, τὸ τῆς ἀδικίας τε
καὶ βλάβης διάφορον καὶ τὸ τῶν ἑκουσίων καὶ
ἀκουσίων ὡς ἐν τούτοις διαπεποίκιλται.

αθ. Πειρατέον τοίνυν ὡς κελεύετε δρᾶν καὶ
B λέγειν. δῆλον γὰρ ὅτι τοσόνδε γε περὶ ψυχῆς
καὶ λέγετε πρὸς ἀλλήλους καὶ ἀκούετε, ὡς ἐν
μὲν ἐν αὐτῇ τῆς φύσεως εἴτε τι πάθος εἴτε τι

---

[1] Cp. 957 E, *Rep.* 410 A.

CLIN. What direction?

ATH. In this,—that whenever any man commits any unjust act, great or small, the law shall instruct him and absolutely compel him for the future either never willingly to dare to do such a deed, or else to do it ever so much less often, in addition to paying for the injury. To effect this, whether by action or speech, by means of pleasures and pains, honours and dishonours, money-fines and money-gifts, and in general by whatsoever means one can employ to make men hate injustice and love (or at any rate not hate) justice,—this is precisely the task of laws most noble. But for all those whom he perceives to be incurable in respect of these matters, what penalty shall the lawgiver enact, and what law? The lawgiver will realise that in all such cases not only is it better for the sinners themselves to live no longer, but also that they will prove of a double benefit to others by quitting life—since they will both serve as a warning to the rest not to act unjustly, and also rid the State of wicked men,[1]—and thus he will of necessity inflict death as the chastisement for their sins, in cases of this kind, and of this kind only.

CLIN. What you have said seems very reasonable; but we should be glad to hear a still clearer statement respecting the difference between injury and injustice, and how the distinction between the voluntary and the involuntary applies in these cases.

ATH. I must endeavour to do as you bid me, and explain the matter. No doubt in conversing with one another you say and hear said at least thus much about the soul, that one element in its nature (be it affection or part) is "passion," which is an inbred

231

μέρος ὢν ὁ θυμός, δύσερι καὶ δύσμαχον κτῆμα
ἐμπεφυκός, ἀλογίστῳ βίᾳ πολλὰ ἀνατρέπει.

κλ.   Πῶς δ' οὔ;

αθ.   Καὶ μὴν ἡδονήν γε οὐ ταὐτὸν τῷ θυμῷ
προσαγορεύομεν, ἐξ ἐναντίας δὲ αὐτῷ φαμὲν
ῥώμης δυναστεύουσαν πειθοῖ μετὰ ἀπάτης
[βιαίου]¹ πράττειν ὅ τί περ ἂν αὐτῆς ἡ βούλησις
ἐθελήσῃ.

κλ.   Καὶ μάλα.

αθ.   Τρίτον μὴν ἄγνοιαν λέγων ἄν τις τῶν
ἁμαρτημάτων αἰτίαν οὐκ ἂν ψεύδοιτο.   διχῇ μὴν
διελόμενος αὐτὸ ὁ νομοθέτης ἂν βελτίων εἴη, τὸ
μὲν ἁπλοῦν αὐτοῦ κούφων ἁμαρτημάτων αἴτιον
ἡγούμενος, τὸ δὲ διπλοῦν, ὅταν ἀμαθαίνῃ τις μὴ
μόνον ἀγνοίᾳ ξυνεχόμενος, ἀλλὰ καὶ δόξῃ σοφίας,
ὡς εἰδὼς παντελῶς περὶ ἃ μηδαμῶς οἶδε, μετὰ μὲν
ἰσχύος καὶ ῥώμης ἑπομένης μεγάλων καὶ ἀμούσων
ἁμαρτημάτων τιθεὶς αἴτια τὰ τοιαῦτα, ἀσθενείας
δὲ ἑπομένης, παίδειά τε ἁμαρτήματα καὶ πρεσβυτέρων γιγνόμενα, θήσει μὲν ἁμαρτήματα καὶ ὡς
ἁμαρτάνουσι νόμου τάξει, πραοτάτους γε μὴν
πάντων καὶ συγγνώμης πλείστης ἐχομένους.

κλ.   Εἰκότα λέγεις.

αθ.   Ἡδονῆς μὲν τοίνυν καὶ θυμοῦ λέγομεν
σχεδὸν ἅπαντες ὡς ὁ μὲν κρείττων ἡμῶν, ὁ δὲ
ἥττων ἐστί· καὶ ἔχει ταύτῃ.

κλ.   Παντάπασι μὲν οὖν.

αθ.   Ἀγνοίας δέ γε ὡς ὁ μὲν ἡμῶν κρείττων, ὁ
δὲ ἥττων, οὐκ ἠκούσαμεν πώποτε.

---

¹ [βιαίου] I bracket (οὐ βίᾳ England).

---

¹ Cp. 864 D f., 908 E ; Ar. *Eth. N.* 1110ᵇ 18 ff.

quality of a contentious and pugnacious kind, and one that overturns many things by its irrational force.

CLIN. Of course.

ATH. Moreover, we distinguish "pleasure" from passion, and we assert that its mastering power is of an opposite kind, since it effects all that its intention desires by a mixture of persuasion and deceit.

CLIN. Exactly.

ATH. Nor would it be untrue to say that the third cause of sins is ignorance.[1] This cause, however, the lawgiver would do well to subdivide into two, counting ignorance in its simple form to be the cause of minor sins, and in its double form—where the folly is due to the man being gripped not by ignorance only, but also by a conceit of wisdom,[2] as though he had full knowledge of things he knows nothing at all about,—counting this to be the cause of great and brutal sins when it is joined with strength and might, but the cause of childish and senile sins when it is joined with weakness; and these last he will count as sins and he will ordain laws, as for sinners, but laws that will be, above all others, of the most mild and merciful kind.

CLIN. That is reasonable.

ATH. And pretty well everyone speaks of one man being "superior," another "inferior," to pleasure or to passion; and they are so.

CLIN. Most certainly.

ATH. But we have never heard it said that one man is "superior," another "inferior," to ignorance.[3]

---

[2] Cp. 732 A, *Phileb.* 48 E.

[3] *i.e.* ignorance is not regarded as an active force (like passion or pleasure) capable of opposing reason and tyrannizing over the soul.

E   κλ.   Ἀληθέστατα.

ΑΘ.   Πάντα δέ γε προτρέπειν ταὐτά φαμεν εἰς
τὴν αὑτοῦ βούλησιν ἐπισπώμενον ἕκαστον εἰς
τἀναντία πολλάκις ἅμα.

κλ.   Πλειστάκις μὲν οὖν.

ΑΘ.   Νῦν δή σοι τό τε δίκαιον καὶ τὸ ἄδικον, ὅ
γε ἐγὼ λέγω, σαφῶς ἂν διορισαίμην οὐδὲν ποι-
κίλλων. τὴν γὰρ τοῦ θυμοῦ καὶ φόβου καὶ
ἡδονῆς καὶ λύπης καὶ φθόνων καὶ ἐπιθυμιῶν ἐν
ψυχῇ τυραννίδα, ἐάν τέ τι βλάπτῃ καὶ ἐὰν μή,
πάντως ἀδικίαν προσαγορεύω, τὴν δὲ τοῦ ἀρίστου
864 δόξαν, ὅπῃπερ ἂν ἐφέσθαι τούτου [1] ἡγήσωνται
πόλις εἴτε ἰδιῶταί τινες, ἐὰν αὕτη κρατοῦσα ἐν
ψυχῇ διακοσμῇ πάντα ἄνδρα, κἂν σφάλληταί τι,
δίκαιον μὲν πᾶν εἶναι φατέον τὸ ταύτῃ πραχθὲν
καὶ τὸ τῆς τοιαύτης ἀρχῆς γιγνόμενον ὑπήκοον
ἑκάστων καὶ ἐπὶ τὸν ἅπαντα ἀνθρώπων βίον
ἄριστον, δοξάζεσθαι δὲ ὑπὸ πολλῶν ἀκούσιον
ἀδικίαν εἶναι τὴν τοιαύτην βλάβην. ἡμῖν δὲ οὐκ
B ἔστι τὰ νῦν ὀνομάτων πέρι δύσερις λόγος, ἀλλ'
ἐπειδὴ τῶν ἁμαρτανομένων τρία εἴδη δεδήλωται
γιγνόμενα, ταῦτα εἰς μνήμην πρῶτον ἔτι μᾶλλον
ἀναληπτέον. λύπης μὲν οὖν, ἣν θυμὸν καὶ φόβον
ἐπονομάζομεν, ἓν εἶδος ἡμῖν ἐστίν.

κλ.   Πάνυ μὲν οὖν.

ΑΘ.   Ἡδονῆς δ' αὖ καὶ ἐπιθυμιῶν δεύτερον,
ἐλπίδων δὲ καὶ δόξης τῆς ⟨μὴ⟩ [2] ἀληθοῦς περὶ
τὸ ⟨τοῦ⟩ ἀρίστου ἐφέσθαι [3] τρίτον ἕτερον. τούτου
δὲ αὖ τοῦ τρίτου διχῇ τμηθέντος πέντε εἴδη γέγο-

---

[1] ἐφέσθαι τούτου : ἔσεσθαι τούτων MSS.
[2] ⟨μὴ⟩ added by Ritter (ἀμαθοῦς for ἀληθοῦς England).

CLIN. Quite true.

ATH. And we assert that all these things urge each man often to go counter to the actual bent of his own inclination.

CLIN. Very frequently.

ATH. Now I will define for you, clearly and without complication, my notion of justice and injustice. The domination of passion and fear and pleasure and pain and envies and desires in the soul, whether they do any injury or not, I term generally "injustice"; but the belief in the highest good—in whatsoever way either States or individuals think they can attain to it,—if this prevails in their souls and regulates every man, even if some damage be done, we must assert that everything thus done is just, and that in each man the part subject to this governance is also just, and best for the whole life of mankind, although most men suppose that such damage is an involuntary injustice. But we are not now concerned with a verbal dispute. Since, however, it has been shown that there are three kinds of sinning, we must first of all recall these still more clearly to mind. Of these, one kind, as we know, is painful; and that we term passion and fear.[1]

CLIN. Quite so.

ATH. The second kind consists of pleasure and desires; the third, which is a distinct kind, consists of hopes and untrue belief regarding the attainment of the highest good. And when this last kind is subdivided into three,[2] five classes are made, as we

---

[1] Cp. *Phileb.* 40 D, E.   [2] Cp. 863 C, D.

---

[3] τὸ ⟨τοῦ⟩ ἀρίστου ἐφέσθαι : τὸ ἄριστον ἔφεσις MSS., edd. (ἄφεσις ci. Grou, ὕφεσις H. Jackson).

νεν, ὡς νῦν φαμέν· οἷς νόμους διαφέροντας
C ἀλλήλων πέντε εἴδεσι θετέον ἐν δυοῖν γένεσιν.

ΚΛ. Τίσι τούτοις ;

ΑΘ. Τὸ μὲν διὰ βιαίων καὶ ξυμφανῶν [1] πράξεων
πραττόμενον ἑκάστοτε, τὸ δὲ μετὰ σκότους καὶ
ἀπάτης λαθραίως γιγνόμενον, ἔστι δ' ὅτε καὶ δι'
ἀμφοῖν τούτοιν πραχθέν· ᾧ δὴ καὶ νόμοι τρα-
χύτατοι γίγνοιντο ἄν, εἰ τὸ προσῆκον μέρος ἔχοιεν.

ΚΛ. Εἰκὸς γοῦν.

ΑΘ. Ἴωμεν δὴ τὰ μετὰ ταῦτα ἐκεῖσε ὁπόθεν
ἐξέβημεν δεῦρο, περαίνοντες τὴν θέσιν τῶν νόμων.
D ἦν δὲ ἡμῖν κείμενα περί τε τῶν συλώντων, οἶμαι,
τοὺς θεοὺς καὶ τὰ περὶ τῶν προδοτῶν, ἔτι δὲ τῶν
τοὺς νόμους διαφθειρόντων ἐπὶ καταλύσει τῆς
παρούσης πολιτείας. τούτων δή τις ἂν ἴσως
πράξειέ τι μανείς, ἢ νόσοις ἢ γήρᾳ ὑπερμέτρῳ
ξυνεχόμενος ἢ παιδίᾳ χρώμενος, οὐδέν πω τῶν
τοιούτων διαφέρων· ὧν ἂν γίγνηταί τι φανερὸν
τοῖς ἐκλεχθεῖσιν ἑκάστοτε δικασταῖς ἀναφέροντος
τοῦ δράσαντος ἢ τοῦ σκηπτομένου ὑπὲρ τοῦ
ποιήσαντος, κριθῇ δὲ οὕτω διατεθεὶς παρανομῆσαι,
E τὴν μὲν βλάβην ἣν ἄν τινα καταβλάψῃ πάντως
ἁπλῆν ἀποτινέτω, τῶν δὲ ἄλλων δικαιωμάτων
ἀφείσθω, πλὴν ἂν ἄρα τινὰ ἀποκτείνας μὴ καθαρὸς ᾖ τὰς χεῖρας φόνου· οὕτω δ' εἰς ἄλλην χώραν
καὶ τόπον ἀπελθὼν οἰκείτω τὸν ἐνιαυτὸν ἐκδημῶν,
πρότερον δὲ ἐλθὼν τοῦ χρόνου ὃν ὁ νόμος ὥρισεν,
ἢ καὶ πάσης ἐπιβὰς τῆς οἰκείας χώρας, ἐν δημοσίῳ

---

[1] ξυμφανῶν Faehse : ξυμφώνων MSS. : ἀξυμφώνων Zur.

now assert ; and for these five classes we must enact distinct laws, of two main types.

CLIN.   What are they ?

ATH.   The one concerns acts done on each occasion by violent and open means, the other acts done privily under cover of darkness and deceit, or sometimes acts done in both these ways,—and for acts of this last kind the laws will be most severe, if they are to prove adequate.

CLIN.   Naturally.

ATH.   Let us revert next to that point from which we digressed,[1] and proceed with our enactment of the laws. We had, I believe, laid down the laws dealing with those who plunder the gods and with traitors, and also with those who wreck the laws with intent to overthrow the existing constitution. An act of this kind a man might commit when mad, or when suffering from some disease or from excessive senility, or in a state of childishness, whereby he is no better than a madman. If any case of this kind is ever brought to the notice of the selected judges, either on the information of the doer of the act or on that of him who is pleading for the doer, and if it be judged that he was in this state of madness when he broke the law, then he shall certainly pay for the damage he has done, but only the exact sum, and he shall be acquitted of the other charges, unless it be that he has killed a man and has not purged his hands from blood : in this case he shall depart into another country and place, and dwell there as an exile for a year ; and should he return within the time fixed by the law or set foot at all within his own country, he shall be put in the public gaol by

---

[1] *i.e.* 857 B.

δεσμῷ δεθεὶς ὑπὸ τῶν νομοφυλάκων δύο ἐνιαυ-
865 τοὺς οὕτως ἀπαλλαττέσθω τῶν δεσμῶν.

Φθόνος οὐδείς,[1] καθάπερ ἠρξάμεθα, [πει-
ρώμεθα][2] διὰ τέλους παντὸς εἴδους πέρι φόνου
θεῖναι τοὺς νόμους, καὶ πρῶτον μὲν τὰ βίαια
καὶ ἀκούσια λέγωμεν. εἴ τις ἐν ἀγῶνι καὶ
ἄθλοις δημοσίοις ἄκων, εἴτε παραχρῆμα εἴτε
καὶ ἐν ὑστέροις χρόνοις ἐκ τῶν πληγῶν, ἀπέκτεινέ τινα φίλιον, ἢ κατὰ πόλεμον ὡσαύτως ἢ
κατὰ μελέτην τὴν πρὸς πόλεμον, ποιουμένων
B ἄσκησιν τῶν ἀκοντίων[3] ψιλοῖς σώμασιν ἢ μετά
τινων ὅπλων ἀπομιμουμένων τὴν πολεμικὴν
πρᾶξιν, καθαρθεὶς κατὰ τὸν ἐκ Δελφῶν κομι-
σθέντα περὶ τούτων νόμον ἔστω καθαρός. ἰατρῶν
δὲ πέρι πάντων, ἂν ὁ θεραπευόμενος ὑπ' αὐτῶν
ἀκόντων τελευτᾷ, καθαρὸς ἔστω κατὰ νόμον.

Ἐὰν δὲ αὐτόχειρ μέν, ἄκων δὲ ἀποκτείνῃ τις
ἕτερος ἕτερον, εἴτε τῷ ἑαυτοῦ σώματι ψιλῷ εἴτε
ὀργάνῳ ἢ βέλει ἢ πώματος ἢ σίτου δόσει ἢ πυρὸς
ἢ χειμῶνος προσβολῇ ἢ στερήσει πνεύματος,
αὐτὸς τῷ ἑαυτοῦ σώματι ἢ δι' ἑτέρων σωμάτων,
C πάντως ἔστω μὲν ὡς αὐτόχειρ, δίκας δὲ τινέτω
τὰς τοιάσδε· ἐὰν μὲν δοῦλον κτείνῃ, νομίζων τὸν
ἑαυτοῦ διειργάσθαι τὸν τοῦ τελευτήσαντος δεσπότην ἀβλαβῆ παρεχέτω καὶ ἀζήμιον, ἢ δίκην
εἰς τὴν ἀξίαν τοῦ τελευτήσαντος ὑπεχέτω διπλῆν·
τῆς δὲ ἀξίας οἱ δικασταὶ διάγνωσιν ποιείσθωσαν·
καθαρμοῖς δὲ χρήσασθαι μείζοσί τε καὶ πλείοσι τῶν

---

[1] Φθόνος οὐδείς, : φθόνου δὴ MSS. : φόνου δὴ Zur., vulg.

the Law-wardens for the space of two years, and not
let out of gaol until after that time.

We need not hesitate to enact laws about every
class of murder on similar lines, now that we have
made a beginning. First we shall deal with the
cases that are violent and involuntary. If a man
has killed a friend in a contest or in public games
—whether his death has been immediate or as the
after-effect of wounds,—or similarly if he has killed
him in war or in some action of training for war,
either when practising javelin-work without armour
or when engaged in some warlike manœuvre in
heavy armour,—then, when he has been purified as
the Delphic rule on this matter directs, he shall be
accounted pure. So too with respect to all doctors,
if the patient dies against the will of his doctor, the
doctor shall be accounted legally pure.

And if one man kills another of his own act, but
involuntarily,—whether it be with his own unarmed
body, or by a tool or a weapon, or by a dose of drink
or of solid food, or by application of fire or of cold, or
by deprivation of air, and whether he does it himself
with his own body or by means of other bodies,—in
all cases it shall be accounted to be his own personal
act, and he shall pay the following penalties. If
he kill a slave, he shall secure the master against
damage and loss, reckoning as if it were a slave of
his own that had been destroyed, or else he shall be
liable to a penalty of double the value of the dead
man,—and the judges shall make an assessment of
his value,—and he must also employ means of
purification greater and more numerous than those

---

[2] [πειρώμεθα] I bracket, as wanting in best MSS.

[3] ἀκοντίων : ἀρχόντων MSS. (Burnet brackets τῶν ἀρχόντων).

D περὶ τὰ ἆθλα ἀποκτεινάντων· τούτων δ' ἐξηγητὰς
εἶναι κυρίους οὓς ἂν ὁ θεὸς ἀνέλῃ· ἐὰν δὲ αὐτοῦ
δοῦλον, καθηράμενος ἀπαλλαττέσθω τοῦ φόνου
κατὰ νόμον. ἐὰν δέ τις ἐλεύθερον ἄκων ἀποκτείνῃ,
τοὺς μὲν καθαρμοὺς τοὺς αὐτοὺς καθαρθήτω τῷ
τὸν δοῦλον ἀποκτείναντι, παλαιὸν δέ τινα τῶν
ἀρχαίων μύθων λεγόμενον μὴ ἀτιμαζέτω. λέγεται
δὲ ὡς ὁ θανατωθεὶς ἄρα βιαίως, ἐν ἐλευθέρῳ
φρονήματι βεβιωκώς, θυμοῦταί τε τῷ δράσαντι
E νεοθνὴς ὤν, καὶ φόβου καὶ δείματος ἅμα διὰ τὴν
βίαιον πάθην αὐτὸς πεπληρωμένος, ὁρῶν τε τὸν
ἑαυτοῦ φονέα ἐν τοῖς ἤθεσι τοῖς τῆς ἑαυτοῦ συνη-
θείας ἀναστρεφόμενον δειμαίνει, καὶ ταραττόμενος
αὐτὸς ταράττει κατὰ δύναμιν πᾶσαν τὸν δράσαντα,
μνήμην ξύμμαχον ἔχων, αὐτόν τε καὶ τὰς πράξεις
αὐτοῦ. διὸ δὴ χρεών ἐστιν ἄρα ὑπεξελθεῖν τῷ
παθόντι τὸν δράσαντα τὰς ὥρας πάσας τοῦ
ἐνιαυτοῦ καὶ ἐρημῶσαι πάντας τοὺς οἰκείους
τόπους ξυμπάσης τῆς πατρίδος· ἐὰν δὲ ξένος ὁ
τελευτήσας ᾖ, καὶ τῆς τοῦ ξένου χώρας εἰργέσθω
866 τοὺς αὐτοὺς χρόνους. τούτῳ δὴ τῷ νόμῳ ἐὰν μὲν
ἑκὼν πείθηταί τις, ὁ τοῦ τελευτήσαντος γένει
ἐγγύτατα, ἐπίσκοπος ὢν τούτων πάντων γενομένων, ἐχέτω συγγνώμην τε καὶ ἄγων πρὸς αὐτὸν
εἰρήνην μέτριος ἂν εἴη πάντως· ἐὰν δέ τις ἀπειθῇ
καὶ πρῶτον μὲν ἀκάθαρτος ὢν εἰς τὰ ἱερὰ τολμᾷ
πορεύεσθαι καὶ θύειν, ἔτι δὲ τοὺς χρόνους μὴ
B ἐθέλῃ πληροῦν ἀποξενούμενος τοὺς εἰρημένους, ὁ
τοῦ τελευτήσαντος γένει ἐγγύτατα ἐπεξίτω μὲν

employed by persons who kill a man at games, and those interpreters [1] whom the oracle names shall be in charge of these rites; but if it be a slave of his own that he has killed, he shall be set free after the legal purification. And if anyone kill a free man involuntarily, he shall undergo the same purifications as the man that has killed a slave; and there is an ancient tale, told of old, to which he must not fail to pay regard. The tale is this,—that the man slain by violence, who has lived in a free and proud spirit, is wroth with his slayer when newly slain, and being filled also with dread and horror on account of his own violent end, when he sees his murderer going about in the very haunts which he himself had frequented, he is horror-stricken; and being disquieted himself, he takes conscience as his ally, and with all his might disquiets his slayer— both the man himself and his doings. Wherefore it is right for the slayer to retire before his victim for a full year, in all its seasons, and to vacate all the spots he owned in all parts of his native land; and if the dead man be a Stranger, he shall be barred also from the Stranger's country for the same period. If a man willingly obeys this law, he that is nearest of kin to the dead man, having the supervision of the performance of all these rules, shall pardon him and live at peace with him, and in doing so he will be acting with perfect propriety; but if a man disobeys, and dares, in the first place, to approach the altars and to do sacrifice while still unpurified, and if he refuses, further, to fulfil the times appointed in exile, then the next of kin to the dead man shall

---

[1] Cp. 759 C.

PLATO

φόνου τῷ κτείναντι, διπλᾶ δὲ πάντα ἔστω τὰ
τιμωρήματα τῷ ὀφλόντι. ἐὰν δ' ὁ προσήκων
ἐγγύτατα μὴ ἐπεξίῃ τῷ παθήματι, τὸ μίασμα ὡς
εἰς αὐτὸν περιεληλυθὸς τοῦ παθόντος προστρεπο-
μένου τὴν πάθην, ὁ βουλόμενος ἐπεξελθὼν τούτῳ
δίκην πέντε ἔτη ἀποσχέσθαι τῆς αὑτοῦ πατρίδος
ἀναγκαζέτω κατὰ νόμον.

Ἐὰν δὲ ξένος ἄκων ξένον κτείνῃ τῶν ἐν τῇ πόλει,
ἐπεξίτω μὲν ὁ βουλόμενος ἐπὶ τοῖς αὐτοῖς νόμοις,
C μέτοικος δὲ ὢν ἀπενιαυτησάτω, ξένος δὲ ἂν ᾖ
παντάπασι, πρὸς τῷ καθαρμῷ, ἐάν τε ξένον ἐάν
τε μέτοικον ἐάν τε ἀστὸν κτείνῃ, τὸν βίον ἅπαντα
τῆς χώρας τῆς τῶν νόμων τῶνδε κυρίας εἰργέσθω·
ἐὰν δ' ἔλθῃ παρανόμως, οἱ νομοφύλακες θανάτῳ
ζημιούντων αὐτόν, καὶ ἐὰν ἔχῃ οὐσίαν τινά, τῷ
D τοῦ παθόντος ἐγγύτατα γένει παραδιδόντων. ἐὰν
δὲ ἄκων ἔλθῃ, ἂν μὲν κατὰ θάλατταν ἐκπίπτῃ
πρὸς τὴν χώραν, σκηνησάμενος ἐν θαλάττῃ τέγγων
τοὺς πόδας πλοῦν ἐπιφυλαττέτω, κατὰ γῆν δὲ
ἂν βίᾳ ὑπό τινων ἀχθῇ, ἡ πρώτη προστυχοῦσα
ἀρχὴ τῶν ἐν τῇ πόλει λύσασα εἰς τὴν ὑπερορίαν
ἐκπεμπέτω ἄσυλον.

Ἐὰν δ' ἄρα τις αὐτόχειρ μὲν κτείνῃ ἐλεύθερον,
θυμῷ δὲ ᾖ τὸ πεπραγμένον ἐκπραχθέν, διχῇ δεῖ
πρῶτον τὸ τοιοῦτον διαλαβεῖν. θυμῷ γὰρ δὴ
πέπρακται καὶ τοῖς ὅσοι ἂν ἐξαίφνης μὲν καὶ
E ἀπροβουλεύτως τοῦ ἀποκτεῖναι πληγαῖς ἤ τινι
τοιούτῳ διαφθείρωσί τινα παραχρῆμα τῆς ὁρμῆς

prosecute the slayer for murder, and in case of conviction all the penalties shall be doubled. And should the nearest relative fail to prosecute for the crime, it shall be as though the pollution had passed on to him, through the victim claiming atonement for his fate ; and whoso pleases shall bring a charge against him, and compel him by law to quit his country for five years.

And if a Stranger involuntarily kills a Stranger who is resident in the State, whoso pleases shall prosecute him under the same laws ; and if he be a resident alien, he shall be exiled for a year, while if he be altogether a Stranger—whether the man slain be a Stranger or resident alien or citizen—in addition to the purifications imposed, he shall be barred for all his life from the country which ordains these laws ; and if he transgresses the law, and comes back to it, the Law-wardens shall punish him with death ; and if he has any property, they shall hand it over to the next of kin of the victim. And should he come back unwillingly, in case he be shipwrecked off the coast of the country, he shall camp with his feet in the sea, and watch for a ship to take him off; or in case he be brought in by people forcibly by land, the first magistrate of the State that meets with him shall loose him, and send him out over the border unharmed.

If a person with his own hand kills a free man, and the deed be done in passion, in a case of this kind we must begin by making a distinction between two varieties of the crime. For murder is committed in passion by those who, on a sudden and without intent to kill, destroy a man by blows or some such means in an immediate attack, when the

PLATO

γενομένης, μεταμέλειά τε εὐθὺς τοῦ πεπραγμένου
γίγνηται, θυμῷ δὲ καὶ ὅσοι προπηλακισθέντες
λόγοις ἢ καὶ ἀτίμοις ἔργοις, μεταδιώκοντες τὴν
τιμωρίαν, ὕστερον ἀποκτείνωσί τινα βουληθέντες
κτεῖναι, καὶ τὸ πεπραγμένον αὐτοῖς ἀμεταμέλητον
γίγνηται. διττοὺς μὲν δὴ τοὺς φόνους, ὡς ἔοικε,
867 θετέον, καὶ σχεδὸν ἀμφοτέρους θυμῷ γεγονότας,
μεταξὺ δέ που τοῦ τε ἑκουσίου καὶ ἀκουσίου
δικαιότατ᾿ ἂν λεγομένους. οὐ μὴν ἀλλ᾿ εἰκών
ἐσθ᾿ ἑκάτερος· ὁ μὲν τὸν θυμὸν φυλάττων καὶ οὐκ
ἐκ τοῦ παραχρῆμα ἐξαίφνης ἀλλὰ μετὰ ἐπιβουλῆς
ὕστερον χρόνῳ τιμωρούμενος ἑκουσίῳ ἔοικεν, ὁ δὲ
ἀταμιεύτως ταῖς ὀργαῖς καὶ ἐκ τοῦ παραχρῆμα
εὐθὺς χρώμενος ἀπροβουλεύτως ὅμοιος μὲν ἀκουσίῳ, ἔστι δὲ οὐδ᾿ οὗτος αὖ παντάπασιν ἀκούσιος,
Β ἀλλ᾿ εἰκὼν ἀκουσίου. διὸ χαλεποὶ διορίζειν οἱ τῷ
θυμῷ πραχθέντες φόνοι, πότερον ἑκουσίους αὐτοὺς
ἢ τινας ὡς ἀκουσίους νομοθετητέον. βέλτιστον
μὴν καὶ ἀληθέστατον εἰς εἰκόνα μὲν ἄμφω θεῖναι,
τεμεῖν δὲ αὐτὼ χωρὶς τῇ ἐπιβουλῇ καὶ ἀπροβουλίᾳ,
καὶ τοῖς μὲν μετ᾿ ἐπιβουλῆς τε καὶ ὀργῇ κτείνασι
τὰς τιμωρίας χαλεπωτέρας, τοῖς δὲ ἀπροβουλεύτως τε καὶ ἐξαίφνης πραοτέρας νομοθετεῖν· τὸ
γὰρ ἐοικὸς μείζονι κακῷ μειζόνως, τὸ δ᾿ ἐλάττονι
C τιμωρητέον ἐλαττόνως. ποιητέον δὴ καὶ τοῖς
ἡμετέροις νόμοις οὕτως.

ΚΛ. Παντάπασι μὲν οὖν.

ΑΘ. Πάλιν ἐπανελθόντες τοίνυν λέγωμεν Ἄν
ἄρα τις αὐτόχειρ μὲν κτείνῃ ἐλεύθερον, τὸ δὲ
244

deed is at once followed by repentance; and it is also a case of murder done in passion whenever men who are insulted by shameful words or actions seek for vengeance, and end by killing a man with deliberate intent to kill, and feel no repentance for the deed. We must lay it down, as it seems, that these murders are of two kinds, both as a rule done in passion, and most properly described as lying midway between the voluntary and the involuntary. None the less, each of these kinds tends to resemble one or other of these contraries; for the man who retains his passion and takes vengeance, not suddenly on the spur of the moment, but after lapse of time, and with deliberate intent, resembles the voluntary murderer; whereas the man who does not nurse his rage, but gives way to it at once on the spur of the moment and without deliberate intent, has a likeness to the involuntary murderer; yet neither is he wholly involuntary, but bears a resemblance thereto. Thus murders done in passion are difficult to define, —whether one should treat them in law as voluntary or involuntary. The best and truest way is to class them both as resemblances, and to distinguish them by the mark of deliberate intent or lack of intent, and to impose more severe penalties on those who slay with intent and in anger, and milder penalties on those who do so without intent and on a sudden. For that which resembles a greater evil must be more heavily punished, that which resembles a lesser evil more lightly. So our laws also must do likewise.

CLIN. They must, most certainly.

ATH. Returning, then, to our task, let us make this pronouncement :—If a man with his own hand

πεπραγμένον ἀπροβουλεύτως ὀργῇ τινὶ γένηται
πραχθέν, τὰ μὲν ἄλλα, καθάπερ ἄνευ θυμοῦ
κτείναντι προσῆκέ τῳ πάσχειν, πασχέτω, δύο δ'
ἐξ ἀνάγκης ἔτη φευγέτω κολάζων τὸν αὑτοῦ θυ-
D μόν. ὁ δὲ θυμῷ μέν, μετ' ἐπιβουλῆς δὲ κτείνας,
τὰ μὲν ἄλλα κατὰ τὸν πρόσθεν αὖ, τρία δὲ ἔτη,
καθάπερ ἅτερος ἔφευγε τὰ δύο, φευγέτω, μεγέθει
θυμοῦ πλείω τιμωρηθεὶς χρόνον. καθόδου δὲ
πέρι τούτοις ὧδ' ἔστω. χαλεπὸν μὲν ἀκριβῶς
νομοθετεῖν· ἔστι γὰρ ὅτε τούτοιν ὁ τῷ νόμῳ
ταχθεὶς χαλεπώτερος ἡμερώτερος ἄν, ὁ δὲ ἡμερώτερος χαλεπώτερος ἂν εἴη, καὶ τὰ περὶ τὸν
φόνον ἀγριωτέρως ἂν πράξειεν, ὁ δὲ ἡμερωτέρως·
ὡς δὲ τὸ πολὺ κατὰ τὰ νῦν εἰρημένα ξυμβαίνει
E γιγνόμενα· τούτων οὖν πάντων ἐπιγνώμονας
εἶναι χρὴ νομοφύλακας, ἐπειδὰν δὲ ὁ χρόνος
ἔλθῃ τῆς φυγῆς ἑκατέρῳ, πέμπειν αὐτῶν δικαστὰς
δώδεκα ἐπὶ τοὺς ὅρους τῆς χώρας, ἐσκεμμένους ἐν
τῷ χρόνῳ τούτῳ τὰς τῶν φυγόντων πράξεις ἔτι
σαφέστερον, καὶ τῆς αἰδοῦς τε πέρι καὶ κατα-
δοχῆς τούτων δικαστὰς γίγνεσθαι· τοὺς δὲ αὖ
τοῖς δικασθεῖσιν ὑπὸ τῶν τοιούτων ἀρχόντων
868 ἐμμένειν. ἐὰν δ' αὖθίς ποτε κατελθὼν ὁπότερος
αὐτοῖν ἡττηθεὶς ὀργῇ πράξῃ ταὐτὸν τοῦτο, φυγὼν
μηκέτι κατέλθῃ, κατελθὼν δὲ κατὰ τὴν τοῦ ξένου
ἄφιξιν, ταύτῃ πασχέτω. δοῦλον δὲ ὁ κτείνας
ἑαυτοῦ μὲν καθηράσθω, ἐὰν δὲ ἀλλότριον θυμῷ,

---

[1] Cp. 855 C.

slay a free man, and the deed be done in rage without deliberate intent, he shall suffer such other penalties as it is proper to the man to suffer who has slain without passion, and he shall be compelled to go into exile for two years, thereby chastising his own passion. And he that slays in passion and with deliberate intent shall be treated in other respects like the former, but shall be exiled for three years— instead of two, like the other,—receiving a longer period of punishment because of the greatness of his passion. As regards the return home, in such cases it shall be on this wise. (It is a difficult matter to legislate for with exactness; for sometimes the more dangerous of the two murderers in the eye of the law might prove the more gentle and the gentler the more dangerous, and the latter might have committed the murder more savagely, the former more gently; though as a rule matters turn out in the way we have stated: so, regarding all these regulations the Law-wardens must act as supervisors). When the period of exile in each case has elapsed, they must send twelve of their number to the borders of the country to act as judges—they having made during the interval a still closer investigation into the actions of the exiles; and these men shall serve also as judges in regard to the matter of giving them pardon and admitting them back; and the exiles must abide by the verdicts of these magistrates. And if either of them, after his return, again yields to rage and commits the same act, he shall be exiled, and never again return; and if he returns, he shall suffer the same fate as the returned Stranger.[1] He that slays a slave of his own shall purify himself; and if he kill another man's slave in rage, he shall

διπλῇ τὸ βλάβος ἐκτισάτω τῷ κεκτημένῳ. ὅστις
δ' ἂν τῶν ἀποκτεινάντων πάντων μὴ πείθηται τῷ
νόμῳ, ἀλλ' ἀκάθαρτος ὢν ἀγοράν τε καὶ ἆθλα καὶ
τὰ ἄλλα ἱερὰ μιαίνῃ, ὁ βουλόμενος τόν τε ἐπι-
B τρέποντα τῶν προσηκόντων τῷ τελευτήσαντι καὶ
τὸν ἀποκτείναντα εἰς δίκην καταστήσας τὴν
διπλασίαν χρημάτων τε καὶ τῶν ἄλλων πράξεων
ἀναγκαζέτω πράττειν τε καὶ ἐκτίνειν, τὸ δὲ ἔκτισ-
μα αὐτὸς αὑτῷ κομιζέσθω κατὰ τὸν νόμον. ἐὰν
δέ τις θυμῷ δοῦλος δεσπότην αὐτοῦ κτείνῃ, τοὺς
προσήκοντας τοῦ τελευτήσαντος χρωμένους τῷ
κτείναντι χρείαν ἣν ἂν ἐθέλωσι, πλὴν μηδαμῇ
C μηδαμῶς ζωγροῦντας, καθαροὺς εἶναι. ἐὰν δὲ
ἄλλον τις δοῦλος ἐλεύθερον ἀποκτείνῃ θυμῷ,
παραδιδόντων οἱ δεσπόται τὸν δοῦλον τοῖς προσήκουσι τοῦ τελευτήσαντος, οἱ δὲ ἐξ ἀνάγκης μὲν
θανατωσάντων τὸν δράσαντα, τρόπῳ δὲ ᾧ ἂν
ἐθέλωσιν.

Ἐὰν δέ, ὃ γίγνεται μέν, ὀλιγάκις δέ, διὰ θυμὸν
πατὴρ ἢ μήτηρ υἱὸν ἢ θυγατέρα πληγαῖς ἤ τινι
τρόπῳ βιαίῳ κτείνῃ, καθάρσεις μὲν τὰς αὐτὰς
τοῖς ἄλλοις καθαίρεσθαι[1] καὶ ἐνιαυτοὺς τρεῖς
D ἀπενιαυτεῖν, κατελθόντων δὲ τῶν κτεινάντων
ἀπαλλάττεσθαι γυναῖκά τε ἀπ' ἀνδρὸς καὶ τὸν
ἄνδρα ἀπὸ γυναικός, καὶ μή ποτ' ἔτι κοινῇ παιδο-
ποιήσασθαι μηδὲ ξυνέστιον ὧν ἔκγονον ἢ ἀδελφὸν
ἀπεστέρηκε γίγνεσθαί ποτε μηδὲ κοινωνὸν ἱερῶν·
ὁ δὲ ἀσεβῶν τε περὶ ταῦτα καὶ ἀπειθῶν ὑπόδικος
ἀσεβείας γιγνέσθω τῷ ἐθέλοντι. γυναῖκα δὲ
γαμετὴν ἐὰν ἀνὴρ δι' ὀργὴν κτείνῃ τινά τις, ἢ γυνὴ
ἑαυτῆς ἄνδρα ταὐτὸν τοῦτο ὡσαύτως ἐργάσηται,

---

[1] καθαίρεσθαι Euseb., Hermann : καθαιρέσθω MSS.

pay to the owner twice the damage. And if anyone of all these types of slayers disobeys the law and, being unpurified, defiles the market and the games and other sacred assemblies, whoso pleases shall prosecute both that member of the dead man's kindred who permits this and the slayer himself, and shall compel the one of them to exact, and the other to pay, double the amount of the money-fines and of the other exactions[1]; and the sum so paid he shall keep for himself as the law directs. If a slave kills his own master in rage, the kindred of the dead man shall treat the slayer how they please,—save that they must not in any wise let him live,—and shall be held guiltless. And if a slave kill a free man (other than his master) in rage, his masters shall hand over the slave to the kindred of the dead man, and they shall be compelled to put the criminal to death, doing so in whatever manner they choose.

If in a fit of rage a father or mother slays a son or daughter by means of blows or some kind of violence,—an occurrence which, though rare, does sometimes happen,—the slayer must make the same purifications as the other slayers, and be exiled for three years; and when the slayers have returned, the wife must be separated from the husband and the husband from the wife, and they must never again have a child, nor shall they ever share a home with those whom the slayer has robbed of child or brother, nor shall they take part in their worship; he that is disobedient and impious concerning this matter shall be liable to an action for impiety at the hands of whoso pleases. And if a husband in a fit of rage kills his wedded wife, or if a wife in like manner

---

[1] Such as the costs of the purification-rites.

Ε καθαίρεσθαι μὲν τοὺς αὐτοὺς καθαρμούς, τριετεῖς
δὲ ἀπενιαυτήσεις διατελεῖν. κατελθὼν δὲ ὅ τι
τοιοῦτον δράσας τοῖς αὐτοῦ παισὶν ἱερῶν μὴ
κοινωνείτω μηδὲ ὁμοτράπεζος γιγνέσθω ποτέ·
ἀπειθῶν δὲ ὁ γεννήτωρ ἢ ὁ γεννηθεὶς ἀσεβείας αὖ
ὑπόδικος γιγνέσθω τῷ ἐθέλοντι. καὶ ἐὰν ἀδελφὸς
ἀδελφὸν ἢ ἀδελφὴν ἢ ἀδελφὴ ἀδελφὸν ἢ ἀδελφὴν
θυμῷ κτείνῃ, τὰ μὲν τῶν καθαρμῶν καὶ ἀπενιαυ-
τήσεων ὡσαύτως, καθάπερ εἴρηται τοῖς γονεῦσι καὶ
τοῖς ἐκγόνοις, εἰρήσθω δεῖν γίγνεσθαι καὶ τούτοις
ὧν ἀδελφούς τε ἀδελφῶν καὶ γονέας ἐστέρηκε
παίδων, τούτοις δὲ ξυνέστιος αὐτὸς [1] μηδέποτε γιγ-
869 νέσθω μηδὲ κοινωνὸς ἱερῶν· ἐὰν δέ τις ἀπειθῇ, τῷ
τῆς περὶ ταῦτα ἀσεβείας εἰρημένῳ νόμῳ ὑπόδικος
ὀρθῶς ἂν γίγνοιτο μετὰ δίκης.

Ἐὰν δ' ἄρα τις εἰς τοσοῦτον ἀκρατὴς θυμοῦ
γίγνηται πρὸς τοὺς γεννήσαντας, ὥστε μανίαις
ὀργῆς τῶν γεννητόρων τολμῆσαι κτεῖναί τινα, ἐὰν
μὲν ὁ τελευτήσας πρὶν τελευτῆσαι τὸν δράσαντα
φόνου ἀφιῇ ἑκών, καθάπερ οἱ τὸν ἀκούσιον φόνον
ἐξεργασάμενοι καθαρθεὶς καὶ τἆλλα ὅσαπερ ἐκεῖ-
Β νοι πράξας καθαρὸς ἔστω, ἐὰν δὲ μὴ ἀφῇ, πολλοῖς
ἔνοχος ἔστω νόμοις ὁ δράσας τι τοιοῦτον· καὶ γὰρ
αἰκίας δίκαις ταῖς ἐσχάταις ἔνοχος ἂν γίγνοιτο
καὶ ἀσεβείας ὡσαύτως καὶ ἱεροσυλίας, τὴν τοῦ
γεννήτου ψυχὴν συλήσας, ὥστ' εἴπερ οἷόν τ' ἦν τὸ
πολλάκις ἀποθνήσκειν τὸν αὐτόν, καὶ τὸν πατρο-
φόνον ἢ μητροκτόνον ἐξεργασάμενον θυμῷ τοῦτο
δικαιότατον θανάτων πολλῶν ἦν τυγχάνειν. ᾧ
γὰρ μόνῳ οὐδ' ἀμυνομένῳ θάνατον [μέλλοντι ὑπὸ

[1] αὐτὸς: αὐτοῖς MSS., edd. (αὖ ci. England).

kills her husband, they must undergo the same purifications, and remain exiled for three years. And when one who has committed such a crime returns, he shall never take part in worship with his children, nor sit at table with them ; and if either the parent or the child disobeys, he shall be liable to a charge of impiety at the hands of whoso pleases. And if in rage a brother kill a brother or a sister, or a sister kill a brother or a sister, it shall be declared that they must undergo the same purifications and banishment as have been ordained for parents and children,—namely, that the homicide shall never share in the house or in the worship of those brothers or parents whom he has robbed of brothers or of children ; and if anyone disobeys, he will rightly and justly be liable to the law laid down concerning such cases of impiety.

If any man gets into such an uncontrollable rage with his parents as actually to dare to kill a parent in the madness of his rage, then, in case the dead person before dying voluntarily acquits the culprit of murder, he shall be held pure, after he has purified himself in the same manner as those who have committed an involuntary murder, and done as they in all other respects ; but in case the dead person does not so acquit him, then he that has done such a deed is liable to a number of laws : for outrage he will be liable to most heavy penalties, and likewise for impiety and temple-robbing, since he has robbed his parent of life ; so that if " to die a hundred deaths " were possible for any one man, that a parricide or a matricide, who did the deed in rage, should undergo a hundred deaths would be a fate most just. Since every law will forbid

τῶν γονέων τελευτήσεσθαι],[1] παρέξει νόμος οὐδεὶς
C κτεῖναι τὸν πατέρα ἢ μητέρα, τοὺς εἰς φῶς τὴν
ἐκείνου φύσιν ἀγαγόντας, ἀλλ᾽ ὑπομείναντα τὰ
πάντα πάσχειν πρίν τι δρᾶν τοιοῦτον νομοθετήσει, πῶς τούτῳ δίκης γε ἄλλως προσῆκον
τυγχάνειν ἂν γίγνοιτο ἐν νόμῳ; κείσθω δὴ τῷ
πατέρα ἢ μητέρα ἀποκτείναντι θυμῷ θάνατος ἡ
ζημία.

Ἀδελφὸς δ᾽ ἐὰν ἀδελφὸν κτείνῃ ἐν στάσεσι
μάχης γενομένης ἤ τινι τρόπῳ τοιούτῳ, ἀμυνόμε-
D νος ἄρχοντα χειρῶν πρότερον, καθάπερ πολέμιον
ἀποκτείνας ἔστω καθαρός· καὶ ἐὰν πολίτης πολίτην ὡσαύτως ἢ ξένος ξένον· ἐὰν δὲ ἀστὸς ξένον
ἢ ξένος ἀστὸν ἀμυνόμενος κτείνῃ, κατὰ ταὐτὰ
ἔστω τοῦ καθαρὸς εἶναι. καὶ ἐὰν δοῦλος δοῦλον,
ὡσαύτως· ἐὰν δὲ αὖ δοῦλος ἐλεύθερον ἀμυνόμενος
ἀποκτείνῃ, καθάπερ ὁ κτείνας πατέρα, τοῖς αὐτοῖς
ἔνοχος ἔστω νόμοις. ὃ δὲ περὶ τῆς ἀφέσεως
εἴρηται φόνου πατρί, ταὐτὸν τοῦτο ἔστω περὶ
E ἁπάσης τῶν τοιούτων ἀφέσεως, ἐὰν ὁστισοῦν
ὁτῳοῦν ἀφιῇ τοῦτο ἑκών, ὡς ἀκουσίου γεγονότος
τοῦ φόνου οἵ τε καθαρμοὶ γιγνέσθωσαν τῷ
δράσαντι καὶ ἐνιαυτὸς εἰς ἔστω τῆς ἐκδημίας ἐν
νόμῳ.

Καὶ τὰ μὲν δὴ βίαιά τε καὶ ἀκούσια καὶ κατὰ
τὸν θυμὸν γιγνόμενα περὶ φόνους μετρίως εἰρήσθω·
τὰ δὲ περὶ τὰ ἑκούσια καὶ κατ᾽ ἀδικίαν πᾶσαν
γιγνόμενα τούτων πέρι καὶ <ἐξ>[2] ἐπιβουλῆς δι᾽
ἥττας ἡδονῶν τε καὶ ἐπιθυμιῶν καὶ φθόνων, ταῦτα
μετ᾽ ἐκεῖνα ἡμῖν λεκτέον.

---

[1] [μέλλοντι . . . τελευτήσεσθαι] bracketed by England.
[2] <ἐξ> I add.

the man to kill father or mother, the very authors of his existence, even for the sake of saving his own life, and will ordain that he must suffer and endure everything rather than commit such an act,— in what other way than this can such a man be fittingly dealt with by law, and receive his due reward? Be it enacted, therefore, that for the man who in rage slays father or mother the penalty is death.

If a brother kill a brother in fight during a civil war, or in any such way, acting in self-defence against the other, who first started the brawl, he shall be counted as one who has slain an enemy, and be held guiltless; so too, when a citizen has killed a citizen in like manner, or a Stranger a Stranger. And if a citizen kill a Stranger in self-defence, or a Stranger a citizen, he shall be accounted pure in the same way. So likewise, if a slave kill a slave; but if a slave kill a free man in self-defence, he shall be liable to the same laws as he that kills a father. And what has been said about remission of the charge in the case of the murder of a father shall hold equally good in all such cases—if any man voluntarily acquit any culprit of this charge, the purifications for the culprit shall be made as though the murder were involuntary, and one year of exile shall be imposed by law.

Let us take this as an adequate statement respecting murder-cases that involve violence, and are involuntary and done in passion. Next to these we must state the regulations regarding such acts when voluntary and involving iniquity of all kinds and premeditated,—acts caused by yielding to pleasure or lust or envy.

ΚΛ. Ὀρθῶς λέγεις.

ΑΘ. Πάλιν δὴ πρῶτον περὶ τῶν τοιούτων
870 εἰς δύναμιν εἴπωμεν ὁπόσα ἂν εἴη. τὸ μὲν δὴ
μέγιστον ἐπιθυμία κρατοῦσα ψυχῆς ἐξηγριωμένης
ὑπὸ πόθων. τοῦτο δ' ἐστὶ μάλιστα ἐνταῦθα οὗ
πλεῖστός τε καὶ ἰσχυρότατος ἵμερος ὢν τυγχάνει
τοῖς πολλοῖς, ἡ τῶν χρημάτων τῆς ἀπλήστου
καὶ ἀπείρου κτήσεως ἔρωτας μυρίους ἐντίκτουσα
δύναμις διὰ φύσιν τε καὶ ἀπαιδευσίαν τὴν κακήν.
τῆς δὲ ἀπαιδευσίας ἦν τὸ κακῶς ἐπαινεῖσθαι
πλοῦτον αἰτία φήμη[1] πρὸς τῶν Ἑλλήνων τε
καὶ βαρβάρων· πρῶτον γὰρ τῶν ἀγαθῶν αὐτὸ
B προκρίνοντες τρίτον ὂν τούς τ' ἐπιγιγνομένους
λωβῶνται καὶ ἑαυτούς. τὸ γὰρ ἀληθὲς λέγεσθαι
περὶ τοῦ πλούτου κατὰ πόλεις πάσας, πάντων
κάλλιστον καὶ ἄριστον, ὡς ἕνεκα σώματός ἐστι,
καὶ σῶμα ψυχῆς ἕνεκα· ἀγαθῶν μὲν οὖν ὄντων ὧν
ἕνεκα ὁ πλοῦτος εἶναι πέφυκε, τρίτον ἂν εἴη μετὰ
σώματος ἀρετὴν καὶ ψυχῆς. διδάσκαλος οὖν ἂν
ὁ λόγος οὗτος γίγνοιτο ὡς οὐ χρὴ πλουτεῖν ζητεῖν
τὸν εὐδαίμονα ἐσόμενον, ἀλλὰ δικαίως πλουτεῖν
C καὶ σωφρόνως· καὶ φόνοι οὕτως οὐκ ἂν γίγνοιντο
ἐν πόλεσι φόνοις δεόμενοι καθαίρεσθαι. νῦν δέ,
ὅπερ ἀρχόμενοι τούτων εἴπομεν, ἓν μὲν τοῦτ'
ἔστι καὶ μέγιστον ὃ ποιεῖ φόνου ἑκουσίου τὰς
μεγίστας δίκας· δεύτερον δὲ φιλοτίμου ψυχῆς
ἕξις, φθόνους ἐντίκτουσα, χαλεποὺς ξυνοίκους

---

[1] ἦν τὸ . . . φήμη: ἡ τοῦ . . . φήμῃ MSS., edd.

---

[1] Cp. 697 B, 831 C ; Ar. *Pol.* 1323ᵃ 25 ff.; *Eth. N.* 1098ᵇ
13 ff.

LAWS, BOOK IX

CLIN. You are right.

ATH. First, let us once more state, as best we can, how many these causes are likely to be. The greatest is lust, which masters a soul that is made savage by desires; and it occurs especially in connexion with that object for which the most frequent and intense craving afflicts the bulk of men,—the power which wealth possesses over them, owing to the badness of their nature and lack of culture, to breed in them countless lustings after its insatiable and endless acquisition. And of this lack of culture the cause is to be found in the ill-praising of wealth in the common talk of both Greeks and barbarians; for by exalting it as the first of "goods,"[1] when it should come but third, they ruin both posterity and themselves. The noblest and best course of all in all States is that the truth should be stated about wealth,—namely, that it exists for the sake of the body, and the body for the sake of the soul; so that, while the objects for which it really exists are "goods," yet wealth itself will come third, after goodness of body and of soul. So this law will serve as an instructor, to teach that the man who intends to be happy must seek not to be wealthy, but to be justly and temperately wealthy; and if this were so, no murders that needed purging by murders would occur in States. But, as things now stand, this love of riches is—as we said[2] when we began this subject—one cause, and a very great cause, which produces the most serious of trials for wilful murder. A second cause is the temper of the ambitious soul, which breeds envies that are

---

[2] 831 C ; cp. Ar. *Pol.* 1271ᵃ 17.

μάλιστα μὲν αὐτῷ τῷ κεκτημένῳ τὸν φθόνον,
δευτέροις δὲ τοῖς ἀρίστοις τῶν ἐν τῇ πόλει.
τρίτον δὲ οἱ δειλοὶ καὶ ἄδικοι φόβοι πολλοὺς
D δὴ φόνους εἰσὶν ἐξειργασμένοι, ὅταν ᾖ τῳ πραττό-
μένα ἢ πεπραγμένα ἃ μηδένα βούλονταί σφισι
ξυνειδέναι γιγνόμενα ἢ γεγονότα· τοὺς οὖν τούτων
μηνυτὰς ἀναιροῦσι θανάτοις, ὅταν ἄλλῳ μηδενὶ
δύνωνται τρόπῳ.

Τούτων δὴ πάντων πέρι προοίμια μὲν εἰρημένα ταῦτ᾽ ἔστω, καὶ πρὸς τούτοις, ὃν καὶ
πολλοὶ λόγον τῶν ἐν ταῖς τελεταῖς περὶ τὰ
τοιαῦτα ἐσπουδακότων ἀκούοντες σφόδρα πεί-
θονται, τὸ τῶν τοιούτων τίσιν ἐν ᾍδου γίγνεσθαι
καὶ πάλιν ἀφικομένοις δεῦρο ἀναγκαῖον εἶναι τὴν
E κατὰ φύσιν δίκην ἐκτῖσαι, τὴν τοῦ παθόντος
ἅπερ αὐτὸς ἔδρασεν, ὑπ᾽ ἄλλου τοιαύτῃ μοίρᾳ
τελευτῆσαι τὸν τότε βίον. πειθομένῳ μὲν δὴ
καὶ πάντως φοβουμένῳ ἐξ αὐτοῦ τοῦ προοιμίου
τὴν τοιαύτην δίκην οὐδὲν δεῖ τὸν ἐπὶ τούτῳ νόμον
871 ὑμνεῖν, ἀπειθοῦντι δὲ νόμος ὅδε εἰρήσθω τῇ
γραφῇ· Ὃς ἂν ἐκ προνοίας τε καὶ ἀδίκως
ὁντιναοῦν τῶν ἐμφυλίων αὐτόχειρ κτείνῃ, πρῶτον
μὲν τῶν νομίμων εἰργέσθω, μήτε ἱερὰ μήτε
ἀγορὰν μήτε λιμένας μήτε ἄλλον κοινὸν ξύλλογον
μηδένα μιαίνων, ἐάν τέ τις ἀπαγορεύῃ τῷ δράσαντι ταῦτα ἀνθρώπων καὶ ἐὰν μή· ὁ γὰρ νόμος
ἀπαγορεύει, καὶ ἀπαγορεύων ὑπὲρ πάσης τῆς
πόλεως ἀεὶ φαίνεταί τε καὶ φανεῖται. ὁ δὲ μὴ ἐπ-

---

[1] Cp. 722 D: whereas the law coerces, its "prelude"
seeks to persuade.

[2] This implies the (Pythagorean) doctrine of re-incar-
nation: cp. 904 C, *Rep.* 614 E ff., *Tim.* 90 E ff.

dangerous associates for the man that feels the
envy, in the first place, and dangerous also for the
best citizens in the State. Thirdly, fears bred of
cowardice and iniquity have wrought many murders,
—in cases where men do or have done things concerning which they desire that no one should share
their secret; consequently, if there are any who
might expose their secret, they remove them by
death, whenever they can do so by no other
means.

Concerning all these matters, the preludes mentioned shall be pronounced, and, in addition to
them, that story which is believed by many when
they hear it from the lips of those who seriously
relate such things at their mystic rites,—that
vengeance for such acts is exacted in Hades,[1] and
that those who return again to this earth[2] are
bound to pay the natural penalty,—each culprit the
same, that is, which he inflicted on his victim,—and
that their life on earth must end in their meeting
a like fate at the hands of another. To him who
obeys, and fully dreads such a penalty, there is
no need to add to the prelude by reciting the law
on the subject; but to the disobedient this is the
law which shall be stated in the written code:—
Whosoever of deliberate intent and unjustly slays
with his own hand any of the tribesmen shall,
in the first place, be debarred from the lawful
assemblies, and shall not defile either temples or
market or harbours or any other place of meeting,
whether or not any person warns off the doer of
such deeds—for he is warned off by the law, which
is, and always will continue, warning him thus
publicly, on behalf of the whole State; and the

B ἐξιὼν δέον ἢ μὴ προαγορεύων εἴργεσθαι τῶν ἐντὸς
ἀνεψιότητος, πρὸς ἀνδρῶν τε καὶ γυναικῶν προσήκων τῷ τελευτήσαντι, πρῶτον μὲν τὸ μίασμα εἰς
αὑτὸν καὶ τὴν τῶν θεῶν ἔχθραν δέχοιτο, ὡς ἡ
τοῦ νόμου ἀρὰ τὴν φήμης[1] προτρέπεται, τὸ δὲ
δεύτερον ὑπόδικος τῷ ἐθέλοντι τιμωρεῖν ὑπὲρ τοῦ
τελευτήσαντος γιγνέσθω. ὁ δὲ ἐθέλων τιμωρεῖν,
τῶν τε ἐπὶ τούτοις λουτρῶν φυλακῆς πέρι καὶ
ὅσων ἂν ἑτέρων ὁ θεὸς περὶ ταῦτα νόμιμα
C παραδῷ, πάντα ἀποτελῶν καὶ τὴν πρόρρησιν
προαγορεύων, ἴτω ἀναγκάζων τὸν δράσαντα ὑπέχειν τὴν τῆς δίκης πρᾶξιν κατὰ νόμον. ταῦτα δὲ
ὅτι μὲν γίγνεσθαι χρεών ἐστι διά τινων ἐπευχῶν
καὶ θυσιῶν θεοῖς τισίν, οἷς τῶν τοιούτων μέλει,
φόνους μὴ γίγνεσθαι κατὰ πόλεις, ῥᾴδιον ἀποφαίνεσθαι νομοθέτῃ· τίνες δ' εἰσὶν οἱ θεοὶ καὶ τίς
[ὁ][2] τρόπος τῶν τοιούτων δικῶν τῆς εἰσαγωγῆς
ὀρθότατα πρὸς τὸ θεῖον ἂν γιγνόμενος εἴη, νομοφύλακες μετ' ἐξηγητῶν καὶ μάντεων καὶ τοῦ θεοῦ
D νομοθετησάμενοι τὰς δίκας εἰσαγόντων ταύτας.
δικαστὰς δὲ αὐτῶν εἶναι τοὺς αὐτοὺς οὕσπερ τοῖς
τὰ ἱερὰ συλῶσι διαδικάζειν ἐρρήθη κυρίως. ὁ
δὲ ὀφλὼν θανάτῳ ζημιούσθω καὶ μὴ ἐν τῇ τοῦ
παθόντος χώρᾳ θαπτέσθω, ἀναιδείας ἕνεκα πρὸς
τῷ ἀσεβεῖν. φυγὼν δὲ καὶ μὴ 'θελήσας κρίσιν
ὑποσχεῖν φευγέτω ἀειφυγίαν· ἐὰν δέ τις ἐπιβῇ

---

[1] φήμης : φήμην MSS., edd.
[2] [ὁ] bracketed by England.

---

[1] Cp. 877 C, D.   [2] 855 C ff.

man who fails to prosecute him when he ought, or fails to warn him of the fact that he is thus debarred, if he be of kin to the dead man on either the male or female side, and not further removed than a cousin,[1] shall, first, receive upon himself the defilement and the wrath of the gods, since the curse of the law brings also upon him that of the divine voice, and, secondly, he shall be liable to the action of whosoever pleases to punish him on behalf of the dead man. And he that wishes to punish him shall duly perform all that concerns the observance of the purifications proper therefor, and whatsoever else the god prescribes as lawful in these cases, and he shall recite the pronouncement of warning; and thus he shall go and compel the culprit to submit to the execution of the penalty according to law. That it is necessary that these proceedings should be accompanied by certain invocations and sacrifices to those gods whose concern it is that murders should not occur in States, it is easy for the lawgiver to demonstrate: who these gods are, and what method for bringing such prosecutions would be the most correct in point of ritual,—this the Law-wardens, in conjunction with the interpreters and seers and with the god, shall ordain; and so they shall bring these prosecutions. And the judges in these cases shall be the same persons who form—as we described[2]—the final court of trial for robbers of temples. He that is convicted shall be punished by death, and he shall not be buried in the land of the victim, because of the shamelessness as well as impiety of his act. If the culprit flees and refuses to come up for judgment, he shall be exiled with an unending exile; and if any such

τούτων τῆς τοῦ φονευθέντος χώρας, ὁ προστυχὼν
πρῶτος τῶν οἰκείων τοῦ ἀποθανόντος ἢ καὶ τῶν
Ε πολιτῶν ἀνατὶ κτεινέτω ἢ δήσας τοῖς ἄρχουσι
τῶν τὴν δίκην κρινάντων κτεῖναι παραδότω. ὁ
δὲ ἐπισκηπτόμενος ἅμα καὶ κατεγγυάτω τὸν ᾧ
ἂν ἐπισκήπτηται· ὁ δὲ παρεχέτω τρεῖς[1] ἐγγυητὰς ἀξιόχρεως, οὓς ἂν ἡ τῶν περὶ ταῦτα δικαστῶν
ἀρχὴ κρίνῃ, [τρεῖς ἐγγυητὰς ἀξιόχρεως][2] παρέξειν
ἐγγυωμένους εἰς δίκην· ἐὰν δὲ ἢ μὴ ἐθέλῃ ἢ
ἀδυνατῇ τις καθιστάναι, τὴν ἀρχὴν παραλα-
βοῦσαν δήσασαν φυλάττειν καὶ παρέχειν εἰς
872 τὴν κρίσιν τῆς δίκης. ἐὰν δὲ αὐτόχειρ μὲν μή,
βουλεύσῃ δὲ θάνατόν τις ἄλλος ἑτέρῳ καὶ τῇ
βουλήσει τε καὶ ἐπιβουλεύσει ἀποκτείνας αἴτιος
ὢν καὶ μὴ καθαρὸς τὴν ψυχὴν τοῦ φόνου ἐν
πόλει ἐνοικῇ, γιγνέσθων καὶ τούτῳ κατὰ ταὐτὰ
αἱ κρίσεις τούτων πέρι, πλὴν τῆς ἐγγύης, τῷ δὲ
ὀφλόντι ταφῆς τῆς οἰκείας ἐξέστω τυχεῖν, τὰ δὲ
ἄλλα κατὰ ταὐτὰ ὡσαύτως τῷ πρόσθεν ῥηθέντι
περὶ αὐτὸν γιγνέσθω· τὰ αὐτὰ δὲ ἔστω ταῦτα
ξένοισί τε πρὸς ξένους καὶ ἀστοῖσι καὶ ξένοις
Β πρὸς ἀλλήλους, δούλοις τε αὖ πρὸς δούλους, τῆς
τε αὐτοχειρίας πέρι καὶ ἐπιβουλεύσεως, πλὴν τῆς
ἐγγύης· ταύτην δέ, καθάπερ εἴρηται τοὺς αὐτόχειρας κατεγγυᾶσθαι, τὸν [δὲ][3] προαγορεύοντα
τὸν φόνον ἅμα κατεγγυᾶν καὶ τούτους. ἐὰν δὲ
δοῦλος ἐλεύθερον ἑκών, εἴτε αὐτόχειρ εἴτε βου-
λεύσας, ἀποκτείνῃ καὶ ὄφλῃ τὴν δίκην, ὁ τῆς

---

[1] τρεῖς: τοὺς MSS., edd.
[2] [τρεῖς ἐγγυητὰς ἀξιόχρεως] I bracket (Hermann brackets
the previous τοὺς ἐγγυητὰς ἀξιόχρεως).

person sets foot in the country of the murdered man, he of the dead man's relatives or of the citizens that first meets with him shall slay him with impunity, or else bind him and hand him over to those magistrates who have judged the case, to be slain. The prosecutor, in a murder-charge, must at once demand bail from the defendant; and the latter shall provide three substantial securities—as approved by the court of the judges in such cases—, who guarantee to produce him at the trial; and if a man be unwilling or unable to provide these sureties, the court must take, bind and keep him, and produce him at the trial of the case. If a man does not slay another with his own hand, but plots death for him, and after killing him by design and plotting resides in the State, being responsible for the murder and not innocent or pure of heart in respect of it,—in his case the prosecutions on this charge shall proceed in the same way, except in the matter of bail. And the person convicted shall be allowed to have burial at home; but all else shall be carried out in his case in the same way as in the case last described. And these same regulations shall govern all cases where Strangers are at law with Strangers, or citizens and Strangers at law with each other, or slaves with slaves, in respect both of actual murder and of plotting to murder, except as regards bail; and as to this, just as it has been said that the actual murderers must be secured by guarantors, so these persons too must provide security to the person who proclaims the murder. If a slave wilfully slay a free man, either by his own hand or by plotting, and be convicted at the trial, the public executioner

---

³ [δὲ] bracketed by England.

πόλεως κοινὸς δήμιος ἄγων πρὸς τὸ μνῆμα τοῦ
ἀποθανόντος, ὅθεν ἂν ὁρᾷ τὸν τύμβον, μαστι-
C γώσας ὁπόσας ἂν ὁ ἑλὼν προστάττῃ, ἐάνπερ
βίῳ παιόμενος ὁ φονεύς, θανατωσάτω. ἐὰν δέ
τις δοῦλον κτείνῃ μηδὲν ἀδικοῦντα, φόβῳ δὲ μὴ
μηνυτὴς αἰσχρῶν ἔργων καὶ κακῶν αὐτοῦ γίγνηται, ἤ τινος ἕνεκα ἄλλου τοιούτου, καθάπερ ἂν
εἰ πολίτην κτείνας ὑπεῖχε φόνου δίκας, ὡσαύτως
καὶ τοῦ τοιούτου δούλου κατὰ τὰ αὐτὰ ἀποθανόντος οὕτως ὑπεχέτω.

    Ἐὰν δὲ δὴ γίγνηται ἐφ' οἷσι καὶ νομοθετεῖν
δεινὸν καὶ οὐδαμῶς προσφιλές, μὴ νομοθετεῖν
δὲ ἀδύνατον, ξυγγενῶν αὐτόχειρας φόνους ἢ
D δι' ἐπιβουλεύσεως γενομένους, ἑκουσίους τε καὶ
ἀδίκους πάντως, οἳ τὰ μὲν πολλὰ ἐν κακῶς
οἰκούσαις καὶ τρεφομέναις γίγνονται πόλεσι,
γένοιντο δ' ἄν πού τι καὶ ἐν ᾗ μή ποτέ τις ἂν
προσδοκήσειε χώρᾳ, λέγειν μὲν δὴ χρεὼν αὖ
πάλιν τὸν ἔμπροσθε σμικρῷ ῥηθέντα λόγον, ἂν
ἄρα τις ἀκούων ἡμῶν οἷος ἀποσχέσθαι γένηται
μᾶλλον ἑκὼν διὰ τὰ τοιαῦτα φόνων τῶν πάντῃ
ἀνοσιωτάτων. ὁ γὰρ δὴ μῦθος ἢ λόγος, ἢ ὅ τι
E χρὴ προσαγορεύειν αὐτόν, ἐκ παλαιῶν ἱερέων
εἴρηται σαφῶς, ὡς ἡ τῶν ξυγγενῶν αἱμάτων
τιμωρὸς δίκη ἐπίσκοπος νόμῳ χρῆται τῷ νῦν δὴ
λεχθέντι καὶ ἔταξεν ἄρα δράσαντί τι τοιοῦτον
παθεῖν ταῦτα ἀναγκαίως ἅπερ ἔδρασεν· εἰ πατέρα
ἀπέκτεινέ ποτέ τις, αὐτὸν τοῦτο ὑπὸ τέκνων
τολμῆσαι βίᾳ πάσχοντα ἔν τισι χρόνοις, καὶ[1]

---

[1] καὶ: κἂν MSS.

of the State shall drag him in the direction of the
tomb of the dead man to a spot from which he
can see the tomb, and there scourge him with as
many stripes as the prosecutor shall prescribe ; and
if the murderer be still alive after the beating, he
shall put him to death. And if a man kill a slave
when he is doing no wrong, actuated by fear lest
the slave should expose his own foul and evil deeds,
or for any other such reason, just as he would have
been liable to a charge of murder for slaying a
citizen, so likewise he shall be liable in the same
way for the death of such a slave.

Should cases occur of a kind for which it is a formid-
able and most unwelcome task to legislate, and yet
impossible not to legislate,—such as murders of kinsfolk, either by a man's own hand or by plotting, which
are wholly wilful and wicked,—crimes that occur for
the most part in States with bad organisation and
nurture, but may occur at times even in a country
where one would not expect them,—we must again
recite the story we uttered [1] a moment ago, if
haply anyone, on hearing us, may become more
strongly disposed in consequence voluntarily to
abstain from murders of the most impious kind.
The myth or story (or whatever one should call it)
has been clearly stated, as derived from ancient
priests, to the effect that Justice, the avenger of
kindred blood, acting as overseer, employs the law
just mentioned, and has ordained that the doer of
such a deed must of necessity suffer the same as
he has done ; if ever a man has slain his father,
he must endure to suffer the same violent fate at
his own children's hands in days to come ; or if he

[1] 870 D, E.

εἰ μητέρα, γενέσθαι τε αὐτὸν θηλείας μετασχόντα
φύσεως ἀναγκαῖον γενόμενόν τε ὑπὸ τῶν γεννη-
θέντων λιπεῖν τὸν βίον ἐν χρόνοις ὑστέροις· τοῦ
γὰρ κοινοῦ μιανθέντος αἵματος οὐκ εἶναι κάθαρσιν
ἄλλην, οὐδὲ ἔκπλυτον ἐθέλειν γίγνεσθαι τὸ μι-
873 ανθὲν πρὶν φόνον φόνῳ ὁμοίῳ ὅμοιον ἡ δράσασα
ψυχὴ τίσῃ καὶ πάσης τῆς ξυγγενείας τὸν θυμὸν
ἀφιλασαμένη κοιμίσῃ. ταῦτα δὴ παρὰ θεῶν μέν
τινα φοβούμενον τὰς τιμωρίας εἴργεσθαι χρὴ τὰς
τοιαύτας· εἰ δέ τινας οὕτως ἀθλία ξυμφορὰ
καταλάβοι, ὥστε πατρὸς ἢ μητρὸς ἢ ἀδελφῶν
ἢ τέκνων ἐκ προνοίας ἑκουσίως ψυχὴν τολμῆσαι ἀποστερεῖν σώματος, ὁ παρὰ τοῦ θνητοῦ
νομοθέτου νόμος ὧδε περὶ τῶν τοιούτων νομοθετεῖ,
B προρρήσεις μὲν τὰς περὶ τῶν νομίμων εἴργεσθαι
καὶ ἐγγύας τὰς αὐτὰς εἶναι, καθάπερ ἐρρήθη
τοῖς ἔμπροσθεν, ἐὰν δέ τις ὄφλῃ φόνου τοιούτου
τούτων κτείνας τινά, οἱ μὲν τῶν δικαστῶν ὑπηρέ-
ται καὶ ἄρχοντες ἀποκτείναντες εἰς τεταγμένην
τρίοδον ἔξω τῆς πόλεως ἐκβαλλόντων γυμνόν, αἱ
δὲ ἀρχαὶ πᾶσαι ὑπὲρ ὅλης τῆς πόλεως, λίθον
ἕκαστος φέρων, ἐπὶ τὴν κεφαλὴν τοῦ νεκροῦ
βάλλων ἀφοσιούτω τὴν πόλιν ὅλην, μετὰ δὲ
τοῦτο εἰς τὰ τῆς χώρας ὅρια φέροντες ἐκβαλ-
C λόντων τῷ νόμῳ ἄταφον. τὸν δὲ δὴ πάντων
οἰκειότατον καὶ λεγόμενον φίλτατον ὃς ἂν ἀποκτείνῃ, τί χρὴ πάσχειν ; λέγω δὲ ὃς ἂν ἑαυτὸν
κτείνῃ, τὴν τῆς εἱμαρμένης βίᾳ ἀποστερῶν μοῖραν,
μήτε πόλεως ταξάσης δίκῃ, μήτε περιωδύνῳ
264

has slain his mother, he must of necessity come to birth-sharing in the female nature, and when thus born be removed from life by the hands of his offspring in afterdays; for of the pollution of common blood there is no other purification, nor does the stain of pollution admit of being washed off before the soul which committed the act pays back murder for murder, like for like, and thus by propitiation lays to rest the wrath of all the kindred. Wherefore, in dread of such vengeances from Heaven a man should refrain himself; if, however, any should be overtaken by a disaster so lamentable that they have the audacity deliberately and of free will to reave soul from body for father, mother, brethren or children, in such cases the ordinance of the law of the mortal lawgiver stands thus:—The warnings of exclusion from customary places, and the sureties, are the same as those prescribed for former cases; and if any man be convicted of such a murder, and of having slain any of the persons named, the officers of the judges and magistrates shall kill him and cast him out naked at an appointed cross-roads outside the city; and all the magistrates, acting on behalf of the whole State, shall take each a stone and cast it on the head of the corpse, and thus make atonement for the whole State; and after this they shall carry the corpse to the borders of the land and cast it out unburied, according to law.

Now he that slays the person who is, as men say, nearest and dearest of all,—what penalty should he suffer? I mean the man that slays himself,—violently robbing himself of his Fate-given share of life, when this is not legally ordered by the State, and when he is not compelled to it by the occurrence of some intoler-

ἀφύκτῳ προσπεσούσῃ τύχῃ ἀναγκασθείς, μηδὲ
αἰσχύνης τινὸς ἀπόρου καὶ ἀβίου μεταλαχών,
ἀργίᾳ δὲ καὶ ἀνανδρίας δειλίᾳ ἑαυτῷ δίκην ἄδικον
ἐπιθῇ. τούτῳ δὴ τὰ μὲν ἄλλα θεὸς οἶδεν ἃ χρὴ
D νόμιμα γίγνεσθαι περὶ καθαρμούς τε καὶ ταφάς,
ὧν ἐξηγητάς τε ἅμα καὶ τοὺς περὶ ταῦτα νόμους
ἐπανερομένους χρὴ τοὺς ἐγγύτατα γένει ποιεῖν
αὐτοῖσι κατὰ τὰ προσταττόμενα· τάφους δ᾽ εἶναι
τοῖς οὕτω φθαρεῖσι πρῶτον μὲν κατὰ μόνας μηδὲ
μεθ᾽ ἑνὸς ξυντάφου, εἶτα ἐν τοῖς τῶν δώδεκα ὁρί-
οισι μερῶν τῶν ὅσα ἀργὰ καὶ ἀνώνυμα, θάπτειν
ἀκλεεῖς αὐτούς, μήτε στήλαις μήτε ὀνόμασι δη-
λοῦντας τοὺς τάφους.

Ἐὰν δ᾽ ἄρα ὑποζύγιον ἢ ζῶον ἄλλο τι φονεύσῃ
E τινά, πλὴν τῶν ὅσα ἐν ἀγῶνι τῶν δημοσίᾳ τιθεμένων
ἀθλεύοντά τι τοιοῦτον δράσῃ, ἐπεξίτωσαν μὲν οἱ
προσήκοντες τοῦ φόνου τῷ κτείναντι, διαδικαζόντων
δὲ τῶν ἀγρονόμων οἷσιν ἂν καὶ ὁπόσοις προστάξῃ ὁ
προσήκων, τὸ δὲ ὀφλὸν ἔξω τῶν ὅρων τῆς χώρας
ἀποκτείναντας διορίσαι. ἐὰν δὲ ἄψυχόν τι ψυχῆς
ἄνθρωπον στερήσῃ, πλὴν ὅσα κεραυνὸς ἤ τι παρὰ
θεοῦ τοιοῦτον βέλος ἰόν, τῶν δὲ ἄλλων ὅσα τινὸς
προσπεσόντος, ἢ αὐτὸ ἐμπεσὸν κτείνῃ τινά, δικαστὴν μὲν αὐτῷ καθιζέτω τῶν γειτόνων τὸν
874 ἐγγύτατα ὁ προσήκων γένει, ἀφοσιούμενος ὑπὲρ
αὑτοῦ τε καὶ ὑπὲρ τῆς συγγενείας ὅλης, τὸ δὲ
ὀφλὸν ἐξορίζειν, καθάπερ ἐρρήθη τὸ τῶν ζῴων
γένος. ἐὰν δὲ τεθνεὼς μὲν αὖ τις φανῇ, ἄδηλος
δὲ ὁ κτείνας ᾖ καὶ μὴ ἀμελῶς ζητοῦσιν ἀνεύρετος

able and inevitable misfortune, nor by falling into some disgrace that is beyond remedy or endurance,—but merely inflicting upon himself this iniquitous penalty owing to sloth and unmanly cowardice. In this case, the rest of the matters—concerning the rules about rites of purification and of burial—come within the cognizance of the god, and regarding these the next of kin must seek information from the interpreters and the laws dealing with these matters, and act in accordance with their instructions : but for those thus destroyed the tombs shall be, first, in an isolated position with not even one adjacent, and, secondly, they shall be buried in those borders of the twelve districts which are barren and nameless, without note, and with neither headstone nor name to indicate the tombs.

If a mule or any other animal murder anyone,— except when they do it when taking part in a public competition,—the relatives shall prosecute the slayer for murder, and so many of the land-stewards as are appointed by the relatives shall decide the case, and the convicted beast they shall kill and cast out beyond the borders of the country. If a lifeless thing rob a man of life—except it be lightning or some bolt from heaven,—if it be anything else than these which kills someone, either through his falling against it or its falling upon him, then the relative shall set the nearest neighbour to pass judgment on it, thus making atonement on behalf of himself and all his kindred, and the thing convicted they shall cast beyond the borders, as was stated in respect of animals.

If anyone be found evidently dead, and if his slayer be unknown and undiscoverable after

γίγνηται, τὰς μὲν προρρήσεις τὰς αὐτὰς γίγνεσθαι
καθάπερ τοῖς ἄλλοις, προαγορεύειν δὲ τὸν φόνον
Β τῷ δράσαντι καὶ ἐπιδικασάμενον ἐν ἀγορᾷ κηρῦξαι
τῷ κτείναντι τὸν καὶ τὸν καὶ ὠφληκότι φόνου
μὴ ἐπιβαίνειν ἱερῶν μηδὲ ὅλης χώρας τῆς τοῦ
παθόντος, ὡς, ἂν φανῇ καὶ γνωσθῇ, ἀποθανού-
μενον καὶ ἔξω τῆς τοῦ παθόντος χώρας ἐκβλη-
θησόμενον ἄταφον. οὗτος δὴ νόμος εἷς ἡμῖν ἔστω
κυρίως περὶ φόνου κείμενος.

Καὶ τὰ μὲν περὶ τὰ τοιαῦτα μέχρι τούτων οὕτως·
ὧν δὲ ὁ κτείνας ἐφ᾽ οἷς τε ὀρθῶς ἂν καθαρὸς εἴη, τάδ᾽
ἔστω. νύκτωρ φῶρα εἰς οἰκίαν εἰσιόντα ἐπὶ κλοπῇ
χρημάτων ἐὰν ἑλὼν κτείνῃ τις, καθαρὸς ἔστω·
Ϲ καὶ ἐὰν λωποδύτην ἀμυνόμενος ἀποκτείνῃ, καθαρὸς ἔστω· καὶ ἐὰν ἐλευθέραν γυναῖκα βιάζηταί
τις ἢ παῖδα περὶ τὰ ἀφροδίσια, νηποινὶ τεθνάτω
ὑπό τε τοῦ ὑβρισθέντος βίᾳ καὶ ὑπὸ πατρὸς ἢ
ἀδελφῶν ἢ υἱέων. ἐάν τε ἀνὴρ ἐπιτύχῃ γαμετῇ
γυναικὶ βιαζομένῃ, κτείνας τὸν βιαζόμενον ἔστω
καθαρὸς ἐν τῷ νόμῳ. καὶ ἐάν τις πατρὶ βοηθῶν
θάνατον, μηδὲν ἀνόσιον δρῶντι, κτείνῃ τινά, ἢ
μητρὶ ἢ τέκνοις ἢ ἀδελφοῖς ἢ ξυγγεννήτορι
D τέκνων, πάντως καθαρὸς ἔστω.

Τὰ μὲν τοίνυν περὶ τροφήν τε ζώσης ψυχῆς
καὶ παιδείαν, ὧν αὐτῇ τυχούσῃ μὲν βιωτόν,
ἀτυχησάσῃ δὲ τοὐναντίον, καὶ περὶ θανάτων τῶν
βιαίων ἃς δεῖ τιμωρίας γίγνεσθαι, νενομοθετήσθω·
τὰ δὲ περὶ τὴν τῶν σωμάτων τροφὴν μὲν καὶ
268

careful search, then the warnings shall be the same as in the other cases, including the warning of death to the doer of the deed, and the prosecutor, when he has proved his claim, shall give public warning in the market-place to the slayer of So-and-so, convicted of murder, not to set foot in holy places nor anywhere in the country of the victim, since, if he appears and is known, he shall be put to death and be cast out from the country of the victim without burial. So let this stand as one section of our code of law dealing with murder.

Thus far we have dealt with crimes of the kind described ; in what follows we shall describe the cases and the circumstances under which the slayer will rightly be pronounced guiltless. If a man catch and slay a thief who is entering his house by night to steal goods, he shall be guiltless ; and if a man in self-defence slay a footpad, he shall be guiltless. The man who forcibly violates a free woman or boy shall be slain with impunity by the person thus violently outraged, or by his father or brother or sons. And should a man discover his wedded wife being violated, if he kills the violator he shall be guiltless before the law. And if a man slay anyone when warding off death from his father (when he is doing no wrong), or from his mother or children or brethren, or from the mother of his own children, he shall be wholly guiltless.

Thus let it be laid down by law respecting the nurture and training of living souls,—which when gained make life livable, but when missed, unlivable, —and respecting the punishments which ought to be imposed in cases of violent death. The regulations regarding the nurture and training of the body

269

παιδείαν εἴρηται, τὸ δ᾽ ἐχόμενον τούτων, αἱ βίαιοι
πράξεις ὑπ᾽ ἀλλήλων ἀκούσιοί τε καὶ ἑκούσιοι
γιγνόμεναι διοριστέον εἰς δύναμιν αἵ τέ εἰσι καὶ
E ὅσαι, καὶ ὧν ἂν τυγχάνουσαι τιμωρήσεων τὸ
πρόσφορον ἔχοιεν ἂν ἕκασται· ταῦτα μετ᾽ ἐκεῖνα,
ὡς ἔοικεν, ὀρθῶς ἂν νομοθετοῖτο.

Τραύματα δὴ καὶ πηρώσεις ἐκ τραυμάτων τά γε
δεύτερα μετὰ θανάτους καὶ ὁ φαυλότατος ἂν τάξειε
τῶν ἐπὶ νόμων τρεπομένων <τάξιν>.¹ τὰ δὴ τραύματα, καθάπερ οἱ φόνοι διῄρηντο, διαιρετέον, τὰ μὲν
ἀκούσια, τὰ δὲ θυμῷ, τὰ δὲ φόβῳ, τὰ δὲ ὁπόσα ἐκ
προνοίας ἑκούσια ξυμβαίνει γιγνόμενα. προρρητέον δή τι περὶ πάντων τῶν τοιούτων τοιόνδε, ὡς
ἄρα νόμους ἀνθρώποις ἀναγκαῖον τίθεσθαι καὶ
ζῆν κατὰ νόμους, ἢ μηδὲν διαφέρειν τῶν πάντῃ
875 ἀγριωτάτων θηρίων. ἡ δὲ αἰτία τούτων ἥδε, ὅτι
φύσις ἀνθρώπων οὐδενὸς ἱκανὴ φύεται ὥστε
γνῶναί τε τὰ συμφέροντα ἀνθρώποις εἰς πολιτείαν καὶ γνοῦσα τὸ βέλτιστον ἀεὶ δύνασθαί τε
καὶ ἐθέλειν πράττειν. γνῶναι μὲν γὰρ πρῶτον·
χαλεπὸν ὅτι πολιτικῇ καὶ ἀληθεῖ τέχνῃ οὐ τὸ
ἴδιον ἀλλὰ τὸ κοινὸν ἀνάγκη μέλειν—τὸ μὲν γὰρ
κοινὸν ξυνδεῖ, τὸ δὲ ἴδιον διασπᾷ τὰς πόλεις—καὶ
ὅτι ξυμφέρει τῷ κοινῷ τε καὶ ἰδίῳ, τοῖν ἀμφοῖν,
ἢν τὸ κοινὸν τιθῆται καλῶς μᾶλλον ἢ τὸ ἴδιον·
B δεύτερον δέ, ἐὰν ἄρα καὶ τὸ γνῶναί τις ὅτι ταῦτα
οὕτω πέφυκε λάβῃ ἱκανῶς ἐν τέχνῃ, μετὰ δὲ
τοῦτο ἀνυπεύθυνός τε καὶ αὐτοκράτωρ ἄρξῃ
πόλεως, οὐκ ἄν ποτε δύναιτο ἐμμεῖναι τούτῳ τῷ
δόγματι καὶ διαβιῶναι τὸ μὲν κοινὸν ἡγούμενον

¹ νόμων . . . ⟨τάξιν⟩ : νόμων MSS. : νόμον Zur., vulg.
(Winckelmann adds τάξιν before τρεπομένων).

have been stated[1]: but what comes next, namely, violent actions, both voluntary and involuntary, done by one against another,—these we must define as clearly as we can, stating their character and number and what punishment each duly deserves: such enactments, as it seems, will rightly follow on the foregoing.

Next in order after cases of death even the least competent of those who essay legislation would place cases of wounds and maiming. Wounds, just like murders, must be classed under several heads,— the involuntary, those done in passion, those done in fear, and all those that are voluntary and deliberate. Concerning all such cases we must make a prefatory pronouncement to this effect :—It is really necessary for men to make themselves laws and to live according to laws, or else to differ not at all from the most savage of beasts. The reason thereof is this,—that no man's nature is naturally able both to perceive what is of benefit to the civic life of men and, perceiving it, to be alike able and willing to practise what is best. For, in the first place, it is difficult to perceive that a true civic art necessarily cares for the public, not the private, interest,—for the public interest bind States together, whereas the private interest rends them asunder,—and to perceive also that it benefits both public and private interests alike when the public interest, rather than the private, is well enacted. And, secondly, even if a man fully grasps the truth of this as a principle of art, should he afterwards get control of the State and become an irresponsible autocrat, he would never prove able to abide by this view and to continue always fostering

[1] 813 D ff.

τρέφων ἐν τῇ πόλει, τὸ δὲ ἴδιον ἑπόμενον τῷ
κοινῷ, ἀλλ' ἐπὶ πλεονεξίαν καὶ ἰδιοπραγίαν ἡ
θνητὴ φύσις αὐτὸν ὁρμήσει ἀεί, φεύγουσα μὲν
C ἀλόγως τὴν λύπην, διώκουσα δὲ τὴν ἡδονήν, τοῦ
δὲ δικαιοτέρου τε καὶ ἀμείνονος ἐπίπροσθεν ἄμφω
τούτω προστήσεται, καὶ σκότος ἀπεργαζομένη ἐν
αὑτῇ πάντων κακῶν ἐμπλήσει πρὸς τὸ τέλος
αὑτήν τε καὶ τὴν πόλιν ὅλην· ἐπεὶ ταῦτα εἴ ποτέ
τις ἀνθρώπων φύσει ἱκανός, θείᾳ μοίρᾳ γεννηθείς,
παραλαβεῖν δυνατὸς εἴη, νόμων οὐδὲν ἂν δέοιτο
τῶν ἀρξόντων ἑαυτοῦ· ἐπιστήμης γὰρ οὔτε νόμος
οὔτε τάξις οὐδεμία κρείττων, οὐδὲ θέμις ἐστὶ νοῦν
οὐδενὸς ὑπήκοον οὐδὲ δοῦλον ἀλλὰ πάντων
D ἄρχοντα εἶναι, ἐάνπερ ἀληθινὸς ἐλεύθερός τε
ὄντως ᾖ κατὰ φύσιν. νῦν δέ—οὐ γάρ ἐστιν
οὐδαμοῦ οὐδαμῶς, ἀλλ' ἢ κατὰ βραχύ· διὸ δὴ τὸ
δεύτερον αἱρετέον, τάξιν τε καὶ νόμον, ἃ δὴ τὸ
μὲν ὡς ἐπὶ τὸ πολὺ ὁρᾷ καὶ βλέπει, τὸ δ' ἐπὶ πᾶν
ἀδυνατεῖ. ταῦτα δὴ τῶνδε εἵνεκα εἴρηται· νῦν
ἡμεῖς τάξομεν τί χρὴ τὸν τρώσαντα ἤ τι βλάψαν-
τα ἕτερον ἄλλον παθεῖν ἢ ἀποτίνειν. πρόχειρον
δὴ παντὶ περὶ παντὸς ὑπολαβεῖν ὀρθῶς, Τὸν τί
E τρώσαντα ἢ τίνα ἢ πῶς ἢ πότε λέγεις; μυρία
γὰρ ἕκαστά ἐστι τούτων καὶ πάμπολυ διαφέροντα
ἀλλήλων. ταῦτ' οὖν δὴ δικαστηρίοις ἐπιτρέπειν
κρίνειν πάντα ἢ μηδὲν ἀδύνατον. ἐν μὲν γὰρ
κατὰ πάντων ἀναγκαῖον ἐπιτρέπειν κρῖναι, τὸ

---

[1] Cp. *Protag.* 352 B f. ; Ar. *Eth. N.* 1145b 24 ff.

the public interest in the State as the object of first
importance, to which the private interest is but
secondary ; rather, his mortal nature will always
urge him on to grasping and self-interested action,
irrationally avoiding pain and pursuing pleasure ;
both these objects it will prefer above justice and
goodness, and by causing darkness within itself it
will fill to the uttermost both itself and the whole
State with all manner of evils. Yet if ever there
should arise a man competent by nature and by a
birthright of divine grace to assume such an office,
he would have no need of rulers over him ; for no
law or ordinance is mightier than Knowledge,[1] nor is it
right for Reason to be subject or in thrall to anything,
but to be lord of all things, if it is really true to its
name and free in its inner nature. But at present
such a nature exists nowhere at all, except in small
degree ; wherefore we must choose what is second
best, namely, ordinance and law, which see and
discern the general principle, but are unable to see
every instance in detail.

This declaration has been made for the sake
of what follows : now we shall ordain what the
man who has wounded, or in some way injured,
another must suffer or pay. And here, of course,
it is open to anyone, in regard to any case, to
interrupt us, and quite properly, with the question
—" What wounds has the man you speak of inflicted,
and on whom, and how and when ? For cases of
wounding are countless in their variety, and they
differ vastly from one another." So it is impossible
for us either to commit all these cases to the law
courts for trial, or to commit none of them. Yet in
regard to them all there is one point that we must
of necessity commit for decision,—the question of

273

PLATO

πότερον ἐγένετο ἢ οὐκ ἐγένετο ἕκαστον τούτων·
876 τὸ δὲ μηδὲν ἐπιτρέπειν αὖ περὶ τοῦ τί δεῖ ζημιοῦσθαι καὶ πάσχειν τί χρεὼν τὸν ἀδικήσαντα τούτων τι, ἀλλ' αὐτὸν περὶ πάντων νομοθετῆσαι
σμικρῶν καὶ μεγάλων, σχεδὸν ἀδύνατον.

ΚΛ. Τίς οὖν ὁ μετὰ τοῦτον λόγος ;

ΑΘ. Ὅδε, ὅτι τὰ μὲν ἐπιτρεπτέον δικαστηρίοις,
τὰ δὲ οὐκ ἐπιτρεπτέον, ἀλλ' αὐτῷ νομοθετητέον.

ΚΛ. Ποῖα δὴ νομοθετητέον τε καὶ ποῖα ἀποδο-
τέον κρίνειν τοῖς δικαστηρίοις ;

ΑΘ. Τάδε δὴ μετὰ ταῦτα ὀρθότατ' ἂν εἰπεῖν
B εἴη, ὡς ἐν πόλει ἐν ᾗ δικαστήρια φαῦλα καὶ
ἄφωνα κλέπτοντα τὰς αὐτῶν δόξας κρύβδην τὰς
κρίσεις διαδικάζει, καὶ ὃ τούτου δεινότερον, ὅταν
μηδὲ σιγῶντα ἀλλὰ θορύβου μεστά, καθάπερ
θέατρα, ἐπαινοῦντά τε βοῇ καὶ ψέγοντα τῶν
ῥητόρων ἑκάτερον ἐν μέρει κρίνῃ, χαλεπὸν τότε
πάθος ὅλῃ τῇ πόλει γίγνεσθαι φιλεῖ. τοῖς οὖν
δὴ τοιούτοις δικαστηρίοις νομοθετεῖν ὑπό τινος
ἀνάγκης ληφθέντα οὐκ εὐτυχὲς μέν, ὅμως δὲ ἐξ
ἀνάγκης εἰλημμένον ὅτι περὶ σμικρότατα ἐπιτρε-
C πτέον αὐτοῖς τάττειν τὰς ζημίας, τὰ δὲ πλεῖστα
αὐτὸν νομοθετεῖν διαρρήδην, ἄν τις ἄρα τοιαύτῃ
πολιτείᾳ νομοθετῇ ποτέ. ἐν ᾗ δὲ ἂν πόλει δικαστήρια εἰς δύναμιν ὀρθῶς καθεστῶτα ᾖ τραφέντων τε εὖ τῶν μελλόντων δικάζειν δοκιμασθέντων
τε διὰ πάσης ἀκριβείας, ἐνταῦθα ὀρθὸν καὶ ἔχον
εὖ καὶ καλῶς τὰ πολλὰ ἐπιτρέπειν κρίνειν τοῖς
τοιούτοις δικασταῖς τῶν ὀφλόντων πέρι, τί χρὴ
274

LAWS, BOOK IX

fact, whether or not each of the alleged acts took place ; and it is practically impossible for the lawgiver to refuse in all cases to commit to the courts the question regarding the proper penalty or fine to be inflicted on the culprit, and himself to pass laws respecting all such cases, great and small.

CLIN. What, then, is to be our next statement?

ATH. This,—that some matters are to be committed to the courts, while others are not to be so committed, but enacted by the lawgiver.

CLIN. What are the matters to be enacted, and what are to be handed over to the law courts for decision?

ATH. It will be best to make the following statement next,—that in a State where the courts are poor and dumb and decide their cases privily, secreting their own opinions, or (and this is a still more dangerous practice) when they make their decisions not silently but filled with tumult, like theatres, roaring out praise or blame of each speaker in turn, —then the whole State, as a rule, is faced with a difficult situation. To be compelled by some necessity to legislate for law courts of this kind is no happy task ; but when one is so compelled, one must commit to them the right of fixing penalties only in a very few cases, dealing oneself with most cases by express legislation—if indeed one ever legislates at all for a State of that description. On the other hand, in a State where the courts have the best possible constitution, and the prospective judges are well-trained and tested most strictly, there it is right, and most fitting and proper, that we should commit to such judges for decision most of the questions regarding what penalties convicted criminals should

πάσχειν αὐτοὺς ἢ ἀποτίνειν. ἡμῖν δὴ τὰ νῦν
D ἀνεμέσητον τὸ μὴ νομοθετεῖν αὐτοῖς τὰ μέγιστα
καὶ πλεῖστα, ἃ καὶ φαυλοτέρως ἂν πεπαιδευμένοι δικασταὶ δύναιντο κατιδεῖν καὶ προσάπτειν
ἑκάστῳ τῶν ἁμαρτημάτων τὴν ἀξίαν τοῦ πάθους
τε καὶ πράξεως· ἐπειδὴ δὲ οἷς ἡμεῖς νομοθετοῦμεν,
οὐχ ἥκιστα ἐμμελεῖς αὐτοὺς οἰόμεθ᾽ ἂν τῶν
τοιούτων γίγνεσθαι κριτάς, ἐπιτρεπτέον δὴ τὰ
πλεῖστα. οὐ μὴν ἀλλ᾽ ὅπερ πολλάκις εἴπομέν
τε καὶ ἐδράσαμεν ἐν τῇ τῶν ἔμπροσθεν νομο-
E θετήσει νόμων, τὸ περιγραφήν τε καὶ τοὺς τύπους
τῶν τιμωριῶν εἰπόντας δοῦναι τὰ παραδείγματα
τοῖσι δικασταῖς τοῦ μήποτε βαίνειν ἔξω τῆς
δίκης, τότε τε ἦν ὀρθότατα ἔχον καὶ δὴ καὶ νῦν
τοῦτ᾽ αὐτὸ ποιητέον, ἐπανελθόντας ἤδη πάλιν
ἐπὶ τοὺς νόμους.

Ἡ δὴ γραφὴ περὶ τραύματος ὧδε ἡμῖν κείσθω.
ἐάν τις διανοηθεὶς τῇ βουλήσει κτεῖναί τινα
φίλιον, πλὴν ὧν ὁ νόμος ἐφίησι, τρώσῃ μέν,
ἀποκτεῖναι δὲ ἀδυνατήσῃ, τὸν διανοηθέντα τε
877 καὶ τρώσαντα οὕτως οὐκ ἄξιον ἐλεεῖν, οὐδὲ
αἰδούμενον ἄλλως ἢ καθάπερ ἀποκτείναντα
ὑπέχειν τὴν δίκην φόνου ἀναγκάζειν· τὴν δὲ οὐ
παντάπασι κακὴν τύχην αὐτοῦ σεβόμενον καὶ
τὸν δαίμονα, ὃς αὐτὸν καὶ τὸν τρωθέντα ἐλεήσας
ἀπότροπος αὐτοῖς ἐγένετο μὴ τῷ μὲν ἀνίατον
ἕλκος γενέσθαι, τῷ δὲ ἐπάρατον τύχην καὶ
ξυμφοράν, τούτῳ δὴ χάριν τῷ δαίμονι διδόντα
καὶ μὴ ἐναντιούμενον τὸν μὲν θάνατον ἀφελεῖν
τοῦ τρώσαντος, μετάστασιν δὲ εἴς τινα [1] γείτονα

---

[1] εἴς τινα H. Richards : εἰς τὴν MSS., edd.

---

[1] Cp. 770 B, 846 B, C.

suffer or pay. On the present occasion we may well be pardoned if we refrain from ordaining for them by law the points that are most important and most numerous, which even ill-educated judges could discern, and could assign to each offence the penalty merited by the wrong as suffered and committed; and seeing that the people for whom we are legislating are themselves likely, as we suppose, to become not the least capable of judges of such matters, we must commit most of them to them. None the less, that course which we frequently adopted [1] when laying down our former laws, both by word and action—when we stated an outline and typical cases of punishments, and gave the judges examples, so as to prevent their ever overstepping the bounds of justice,—that course was a perfectly right one then, and now also we ought to adopt it, when we return again at last to the task of legislation.

So let our written law concerning wounding run thus:—If any man purposing of intent to kill a friendly person—save such as the law sends him against,— wounds him, but is unable to kill him, he that has thus purposed and dealt the wound does not deserve to be pitied; rather he is to be regarded exactly as a slayer, and must be compelled to submit to trial for murder; yet out of respect for his escape from sheer ill-fortune and for his Genius [2]—who in pity alike for him and for the wounded man saved the wound of the one from proving fatal and the fortune and crime of the other from proving accursed,—in gratitude to this Genius, and in compliance therewith, the wounder shall be relieved of the death-penalty, but

---

[2] For "daemon" in this sense of "tutelary Genius" or "Guardian-angel," cp. 732 C, *Rep.* 619 D, E.

B πόλιν αὐτῷ γίγνεσθαι διὰ βίου, καρπούμενον
ἅπασαν τὴν αὐτοῦ κτῆσιν. βλάβος δέ, εἰ κατέ-
βλαψε τὸν τρωθέντα, ἐκτίνειν τῷ βλαφθέντι·
τιμᾶν δὲ τὸ δικαστήριον ὅπερ ἂν τὴν δίκην κρίνῃ·
κρίνειν δὲ οἵπερ ἂν τοῦ φόνου ἐδίκασαν, εἰ ἐτε-
λεύτησεν ἐκ τῆς πληγῆς τοῦ τραύματος.

Γονέας δ' ἂν παῖς ἢ δοῦλος δεσπότην ὡσαύτως ἐκ
προνοίας τρώσῃ, θάνατον εἶναι τὴν ζημίαν. καὶ ἐὰν
ἀδελφὸς ἀδελφὸν ἢ ἀδελφὴν ἢ ἀδελφὴ ἀδελφὸν ἢ
C ἀδελφὴν ὡσαύτως τρώσῃ, καὶ ὄφλῃ τραύματος
ἐκ προνοίας, θάνατον εἶναι τὴν ζημίαν. γυνὴ δὲ
ἄνδρα ἑαυτῆς ἐξ ἐπιβουλῆς τοῦ ἀποκτεῖναι
τρώσασα, ἢ ἀνὴρ τὴν ἑαυτοῦ γυναῖκα, φευγέτω
ἀειφυγίαν· τὴν δὲ κτῆσιν, ἐὰν μὲν υἱεῖς ἢ θυγα-
τέρες αὐτοῖς ὦσι παῖδες ἔτι, τοὺς ἐπιτρόπους
ἐπιτροπεύειν καὶ ὡς ὀρφανῶν τῶν παίδων ἐπιμελεῖσθαι, ἐὰν δὲ ἄνδρες ἤδη,[1] ἐπάναγκες ἔστω
τρέφεσθαι τὸν φεύγοντα ὑπὸ τῶν ἐκγόνων, τὴν
δὲ οὐσίαν [ἐὰν] αὐτοὺς κεκτῆσθαι. ἄπαις δὲ
ὅστις ἂν τοιαύταις ξυμφοραῖς περιπέσῃ, τοὺς
D συγγενεῖς συνελθόντας μέχρι ἀνεψιῶν παίδων
τοῦ πεφευγότος ἀμφοτέρωθεν, πρός τε ἀνδρῶν
καὶ πρὸς γυναικῶν, κληρονόμον εἰς τὸν οἶκον
τοῦτον τῇ πόλει τετταρακοντακαιπεντακισχιλιοσ-
τὸν καταστῆσαι βουλευομένους μετὰ νομοφυλάκων καὶ ἱερέων, διανοηθέντας τρόπῳ καὶ λόγῳ
τοιῷδε, ὡς οὐδεὶς οἶκος τῶν τετταράκοντα καὶ
πεντακισχιλίων τοῦ ἐνοικοῦντός ἐστιν οὐδὲ ξύμπαντος τοῦ γένους οὕτως ὡς τῆς πόλεως δημόσιός
E τε καὶ ἴδιος. δεῖ δὴ τήν γε πόλιν τοὺς αὐτῆς
οἴκους ὡς ὁσιωτάτους τε καὶ εὐτυχεστάτους
κεκτῆσθαι κατὰ δύναμιν. ὅταν οὖν τις ἅμα

shall be deported for life to a neighbouring State, enjoying the fruits of all his own possessions. If he has done damage to the wounded man, he shall pay for it in full to him that is damaged ; and the damage shall be assessed by the court which decides the case, which court shall consist of those who would have tried the culprit for murder if the man had died of the wound he received.

If in like manner, deliberately, a son wound his parents or a slave his master, death shall be the penalty ; and if a brother wound in like manner a brother or sister, or a sister wound a brother or sister, and be convicted of wounding deliberately, death shall be the penalty. A wife that has wounded her husband, or a husband his wife, with intent to kill, shall be exiled for life : if they have sons or daughters who are still children, the guardians shall administer their property, and shall take charge of the children as orphans ; but if they be already grown men, the offspring shall be compelled to support their exiled parent, and they shall possess his property. If any person overtaken by such a disaster be childless, the kinsfolk on both sides, both male and female, as far as cousins' children, shall meet together and appoint an heir for the house in question—the 5040th in the State,— taking counsel with the Law-wardens and priests ; and they shall bear in mind this principle, that no house of the 5040 belongs as much, either by private or public right, to the occupier or to the whole of his kindred as it belongs to the State ; and the State must needs keep its own houses as holy and happy as possible. Therefore, whenever any house is at once

---

[1] ἄνδρες ἤδη, Jernstedt, England : ἄνδρες, μὴ MSS.

δυστυχήσῃ [1] καὶ ἀσεβηθῇ τῶν οἴκων, ὥστε τὸν
κεκτημένον ἐν αὐτῷ παῖδας μὲν μὴ καταλιπεῖν,
ἤίθεον δὲ ἢ καὶ γεγαμηκότα ἄπαιδα τελευτῆσαι
φόνου ὀφλόντα ἑκουσίου ἤ τινος ἁμαρτήματος
ἄλλου τῶν περὶ θεοὺς ἢ πολίτας, ὧν ἂν θάνατος
ἐν τῷ νόμῳ ζημία διαρρήδην ᾖ κειμένη, ἢ καὶ ἐν
ἀειφυγίᾳ τις φεύγῃ τῶν ἀνδρῶν ἄπαις, τοῦτον
πρῶτον μὲν καθήρασθαι καὶ ἀποδιοπομπήσασθαι
τὸν οἶκον χρεὼν ἔστω κατὰ νόμον, ἔπειτα συνελ-
878 θόντας, καθάπερ εἴπομεν νῦν δή, τοὺς οἰκείους ἅμα
νομοφύλαξι σκέψασθαι γένος ὅ τί περ ἂν ᾖ τῶν
ἐν τῇ πόλει εὐδοκιμώτατον πρὸς ἀρετὴν καὶ ἅμα
εὐτυχές, ἐν ᾧ ἂν παῖδες γεγονότες ὦσι πλείους·
ὅθεν ἕνα τῷ τοῦ τελευτήσαντος πατρὶ καὶ τοῖς
ἄνω τοῦ γένους υἱὸν ὡς ἐκείνων εἰσποιοῦντας,
φήμης ἕνεκα ἐπονομάζοντας, γεννήτορά τε αὐτοῖς
καὶ ἑστιοῦχον καὶ θεραπευτὴν ὁσίων τε καὶ ἱερῶν
ἐπ' ἀμείνοσι τύχαις γίγνεσθαι τοῦ πατρός· τούτῳ
B τῷ τρόπῳ ἐπευξαμένους αὐτὸν κληρονόμον καταστῆσαι κατὰ νόμον, τὸν δ' ἐξαμαρτόντα ἀνώνυ-
μον ἐᾶν καὶ ἄπαιδα καὶ ἄμοιρον κεῖσθαι, ὁπόταν
αὐτὸν καταλάβωσιν αἱ τοιαῦται ξυμφοραί.

Ἔστι δὲ οὐ πάντων, ὡς ἔοικε, τῶν ὄντων ὅρος
ὅρῳ προσμιγνύς, ἀλλ' οἷς ἐστὶ μεθόριον, τοῦτο ἐν
μέσῳ ὅρων προτεῖνον [2] ἑκατέρῳ προσβάλλον
γίγνοιτ' ἂν ἀμφοῖν μεταξύ. καὶ δὴ καὶ τῶν
ἀκουσίων τε καὶ ἑκουσίων τὸ θυμῷ γιγνόμενον

---

[1] δυστυχήσῃ H. Richards : δυστυχηθῇ MSS.
[2] προτεῖνον : πρότερον MSS., edd.

unhappy and unholy, in that the owner thereof
leaves no children, but—being either unmarried or,
though married, childless—dies, after having been
convicted of wilful murder or of some other offence
against gods or citizens for which death is the
penalty expressly laid down in the law; or else if
any man who is without male issue be exiled for life;
—then they shall be in duty bound, in the first
place, to make purifications and expiations for this
house, and, in the next place, the relatives, as we
said just now, must meet together and in consultation with the Law-wardens consider what family
there is in the State which is pre-eminent for goodness, and prosperous withal, and containing several
children. Then from the family selected they shall
adopt one child on behalf of the dead man's father
and ancestors to be a son of theirs, and they shall
name him after one of them, for the sake of the
omen—with a prayer that in this wise he may prove
to them a begetter of offspring, a hearth-master and
a minister in holy and sacred things, and be blest
with happier fortune than his (official) father; him
they shall thus establish legally as lot-holder, and
the offender they shall suffer to lie nameless and
childless and portionless, whenever such calamities
overtake him.

It is not the fact, as it would seem, that in the case
of all objects boundary is contiguous with boundary;
but where there is a neutral strip, which lies
between the two boundaries, impinging on each, it
will be midway between both. And that is precisely the description we gave [1] of the passionate
action as one which lies midway between in-

[1] 867 A.

ἔφαμεν εἶναι τοιοῦτον. τραυμάτων οὖν ἔστω τῶν[1]
ὀργῇ γενομένων· ἐὰν ὄφλῃ τις, πρῶτον μὲν τίνειν
C τοῦ βλάβους τὴν διπλασίαν, ἂν τὸ τραῦμα
ἰάσιμον ἀποβῇ, τῶν δὲ ἀνιάτων τὴν τετραπλασίαν. ἐὰν δὲ ἰάσιμον μέν, αἰσχύνην δὲ μεγάλην
τινὰ προσβάλλῃ τῷ τρωθέντι καὶ ἐπονείδιστον,
τὴν τριπλασίαν[2] ἐκτίνειν. ὅσα δέ τις τρώσας
τινὰ μὴ μόνον βλάπτῃ τὸν παθόντα, ἀλλὰ καὶ
τὴν πόλιν, ποιήσας ἀδύνατον τῇ πατρίδι πρὸς
πολεμίους βοηθεῖν, τοῦτον δὲ μετὰ τῶν ἄλλων
ζημιῶν ἐκτίνειν καὶ τῇ πόλει τὴν βλάβην· πρὸς
γὰρ ταῖς αὑτοῦ στρατείαις καὶ ὑπὲρ τοῦ ἀδυνα-
τοῦντος στρατευέσθω καὶ τὰς ὑπὲρ ἐκείνου πολε-
D μικὰς ταττέσθω τάξεις, ἢ μὴ δρῶν ταῦτα ὑπόδικος
τῷ ἐθέλοντι τῆς ἀστρατείας γιγνέσθω κατὰ νόμον.
τὴν δὲ δὴ τῆς βλάβης ἀξίαν, εἴτε διπλῆν εἴτε
τριπλῆν εἴτε καὶ τετραπλασίαν, οἱ καταψηφισά-
μενοι δικασταὶ ταττόντων. ἐὰν δὲ ὁμόγονος
ὁμόγονον τὸν αὐτὸν τρόπον τούτῳ τρώσῃ, τοὺς
γεννήτας καὶ τοὺς συγγενεῖς, μέχρι ἀνεψιῶν
παίδων πρὸς γυναικῶν καὶ ἀνδρῶν, γυναῖκάς τε
E καὶ ἄνδρας συνελθόντας, κρίναντας παραδιδόναι
τιμᾶν τοῖς γεννήσασι κατὰ φύσιν· ἐὰν δὲ ἀμφισ-
βητήσιμος ἡ τίμησις γίγνηται, τοὺς πρὸς ἀνδρῶν
εἶναι τιμῶντας κυρίους· ἐὰν δὲ ἀδυνατῶσιν αὐτοί,
τοῖς νομοφύλαξι τελευτῶντας ἐπιτρέπειν. ἐκγόνοις δὲ πρὸς γονέας εἶναι τῶν τοιούτων τραυμάτων δικαστὰς μὲν τοὺς ὑπὲρ ἑξήκοντα ἔτη

---

[1] ἔστω τῶν MSS.: ἐνεστώτων Zur. vulg.
[2] τριπλασίαν Sydenham, Orelli : τετραπλασίαν MSS.

LAWS, BOOK IX

voluntary and voluntary actions. So let the law
stand thus respecting woundings committed in
anger :—If a person be convicted, in the first place
he shall pay double the damage, in case the wound
prove to be curable, but four times the damage in
case of incurable wounds. And if the wound be
curable, but cause great shame and disgrace to the
wounded party, the culprit shall pay three times the
damage. And if ever a person, in wounding anyone,
do damage to the State as well as to the victim, by
rendering him incapable of helping his country
against its enemies, such a person, in addition to the
rest of the damages, shall pay also for the damage
done to the State : in addition to his own military
service, he shall do service also as a substitute for the
incapacitated man, and carry out his military duties
in his place, or, if he fails to do so, he shall by law be
liable to prosecution for shirking military service, at
the hands of anyone who pleases. The due proportion of the damage payable—whether two, three, or
four times the actual amount—shall be fixed by the
judges who have voted on the case. If a kinsman
wound a kinsman in the same way as the person just
mentioned, the members of his tribe and kin, both
males and females, as far as cousins' children on both
the male and female side, shall meet together and,
after coming to a decision, shall hand over the case
to the natural parents for assessment of the damage ;
and if the assessment be disputed, the kindred on
the male side shall be authorized to make a binding
assessment ; and if they prove unable to do so, they
shall refer the matter finally to the Law-wardens.
When woundings of this kind are inflicted by children
on parents, the judges shall be, of necessity, men

283

γεγονότας ἐπάναγκες, οἷς ἂν παῖδες μὴ ποιητοὶ
ἀληθινοὶ δὲ ὦσιν· ἂν δέ τις ὄφλῃ, τιμᾶν εἰ
τεθνάναι χρὴ τὸν τοιοῦτον εἴτε τι μεῖζον ἕτερον
τούτου πάσχειν ἢ καὶ μὴ πολλῷ σμικρότερον·
καὶ τῶν ξυγγενῶν τοῦ δράσαντος μηδένα δικάζειν,
879 μηδ' ἐὰν γεγονὼς ᾖ τὸν χρόνον ὅσον ὁ νόμος
εἴρηκε. δοῦλος δ' ἐάν τις ἐλεύθερον ὀργῇ τρώσῃ,
παραδότω τὸν δοῦλον ὁ κεκτημένος τῷ τρωθέντι
χρῆσθαι ὅ τι ἂν ἐθέλῃ· ἐὰν δὲ μὴ παραδιδῷ,
αὐτὸς τὴν βλάβην ἐξιάσθω. ἐὰν δὲ ἐκ συνθήκης
αἰτιᾶται τοῦ δούλου καὶ τοῦ τρωθέντος μηχανὴν
εἶναί τις τὸ γεγονός, ἀμφισβητησάτω· ἐὰν δὲ μὴ
ἕλῃ, τριπλασίαν ἐκτισάτω τὴν βλάβην, ἑλὼν δὲ
ἀνδραποδισμοῦ ὑπόδικον ἐχέτω τὸν τεχνάζοντα
B μετὰ τοῦ δούλου. ὃς δ' ἂν ἄκων ἄλλος ἄλλον
τρώσῃ, τὸ βλάβος ἁπλοῦν ἀποτινέτω· τύχης γὰρ
νομοθέτης οὐδεὶς ἱκανὸς ἄρχειν· δικασταὶ δὲ
ὄντων οἵπερ τοῖς ἐκγόνοις πρὸς τοὺς γεννήτορας
ἐρρήθησαν, καὶ τιμώντων τὴν ἀξίαν τῆς βλάβης.

Βίαια μὲν δὴ πάνθ' ἡμῖν τὰ προειρημένα πάθη,
βίαιον δὲ καὶ τὸ τῆς αἰκίας πᾶν γένος. ὧδε οὖν
χρὴ περὶ τῶν τοιούτων πάντα ἄνδρα καὶ παῖδα
καὶ γυναῖκα ἀεὶ διανοεῖσθαι, τὸ πρεσβύτερον ὡς
οὐ σμικρῷ τοῦ νεωτέρου ἐστὶ πρεσβευόμενον ἔν τε
θεοῖσι καὶ ἐν ἀνθρώποις τοῖς μέλλουσι σώζεσθαι
C καὶ εὐδαιμονεῖν. αἰκίαν οὖν περὶ πρεσβύτερον
ἐν πόλει γενομένην ὑπὸ νεωτέρου ἰδεῖν αἰσχρὸν
284

over sixty years of age who have genuine, and not merely adopted, children of their own; and if a person be convicted, they shall assess the penalty—whether such a person ought to be put to death, or ought to suffer some other punishment still more severe, or possibly a little less severe: but none of the relatives of the culprit shall act as a judge, not even if he be of the full age stated in the law. If a slave wound a free man in rage, his owner shall hand over the slave to the wounded man to be dealt with just as he pleases; and if he do not hand over the slave, he shall himself make good the damage to the full. And if any man alleges that the deed was a trick concocted by the slave in collusion with the wounded party, he shall dispute the case: if he fail to win it, he shall pay three times the damage, but if he win, he shall hold liable for kidnapping the man who contrived the trick in collusion with the slave. Whoever wounds another involuntarily shall pay a single equivalent for the damage (since no law-giver is able to control fortune), and the judges shall be those designated to act in cases of the wounding of parents by children; and they shall assess the due proportion of damage payable.

All the cases we have now dealt with are of suffering due to violence, and the whole class of cases of " outrage " involve violence. Regarding such cases, the view that should be held by everyone,—man, woman and child,—is this, that the older is greatly more revered than the younger, both among the gods and among those men who propose to keep safe and happy. An outrage perpetrated by a younger against an older person is a shameful thing to see happening in a State, and a thing hateful to God:

καὶ θεομισές· ἔοικε δὲ νέῳ παντὶ ὑπὸ γέροντος
πληγέντι ῥᾳθύμως ὀργὴν ὑποφέρειν, αὐτῷ τιθε-
μένῳ τιμὴν ταύτην εἰς γῆρας. ὧδε οὖν ἔστω·
πᾶς ἡμῖν αἰδείσθω τὸν ἑαυτοῦ πρεσβύτερον ἔργῳ
τε καὶ ἔπει· τὸν δὲ προέχοντα εἴκοσιν ἡλικίας
ἔτεσιν, ἄρρενα ἢ θῆλυν, νομίζων ὡς πατέρα ἢ
μητέρα διευλαβείσθω, καὶ πάσης τῆς δυνατῆς
D ἡλικίας αὐτὸν φιτῦσαι καὶ τεκεῖν ἀπέχοιτο ἀεὶ θεῶν
γενεθλίων χάριν· ὡς δ' αὕτως καὶ ξένου ἀπείρ-
γοιτο, εἴτε πάλαι ἐνοικοῦντος εἴτε νεήλυδος
ἀφιγμένου· μήτε γὰρ ὑπάρχων μήτε ἀμυνόμενος
τὸ παράπαν τολμάτω πληγαῖς τὸν τοιοῦτον
νουθετεῖν. ξένον δὲ ἂν ἀσελγαίνοντα καὶ θρασυνό-
μενον, ἑαυτὸν τύπτοντα, οἴηται δεῖν κολασθῆναι,
λαβὼν πρὸς τὴν ἀρχὴν τῶν ἀστυνόμων ἀπαγέτω,
τοῦ τύπτειν δὲ εἰργέσθω, ἵνα πόρρω γίγνηται τοῦ
E τὸν ἐπιχώριον ἂν τολμῆσαί ποτε πατάξαι. οἱ δ'
ἀστυνόμοι παραλαβόντες τε καὶ ἀνακρίναντες,
τὸν ξενικὸν αὖ θεὸν εὐλαβούμενοι, ἐὰν ἄρα
ἀδίκως δοκῇ ὁ ξένος τὸν ἐπιχώριον τύπτειν, τῇ
μάστιγι τὸν ξένον, ὅσας ἂν αὐτὸς πατάξῃ, τοσαύ-
τας δόντες τῆς θρασυξενίας παυόντων· ἐὰν δὲ μὴ
ἀδικῇ, ἀπειλήσαντές τε καὶ ὀνειδίσαντες τῷ ἀπα-
γαγόντι μεθιέντων ἄμφω. ἧλιξ δὲ ἥλικα <ἢ> [1]
καὶ τὸν ἄπαιδα προέχοντα ἡλικίᾳ ἑαυτοῦ ἐὰν
880 τύπτῃ, γέρων τε γέροντα, καὶ ἐὰν νέος νέον,
ἀμυνέσθω κατὰ φύσιν ἄνευ βέλους ψιλαῖς ταῖς

---

[1] <ἢ> added by Ast, Burges.

---

[1] For the respect due to Strangers as a *religious* duty, cp.
729 E ff.

when a young man is beaten by an old man, it is meet that, in every case, he should quietly endure his anger, and thus store up honour for the time of his own old age. Therefore let the law stand thus :— Everyone shall reverence his elder both by deed and word ; whosoever, man or woman, exceeds himself in age by twenty years he shall regard as a father or a mother, and he shall keep his hands off that person, and he shall ever refrain himself, for the sake of the gods of birth, from all the generation of those who are potentially his own bearers and begetters. So likewise he shall keep his hands off a Stranger, be he long resident or newly arrived ; neither as aggressor nor in self-defence shall he venture at all to chastise such an one with blows. If he deems that a Stranger has shown outrageous audacity in beating him and needs correction, he shall seize the man and take him before the bench of the city-stewards (but refrain from beating him), so that he may flee the thought of ever daring to strike a native. And the city-stewards shall take over the Stranger and examine him—with due respect for the God of Strangers ; [1] and if he really appears to have beaten the native unjustly, they shall give the Stranger as many strokes of the scourge as he himself inflicted, and make him cease from his foreign frowardness ; but if he has not acted unjustly, they shall threaten and reprove the man who arrested him, and dismiss them both. If a man of a certain age beat a man of his own age, or one above his own age who is childless, —whether it be a case of an old man beating an old man, or of a young man beating a young man, —the man attacked shall defend himself with bare hands, as nature dictates, and without a weapon.

χερσίν. ὁ δὲ ὑπὲρ τετταράκοντα γεγονὼς ἔτη ἐὰν
τολμᾷ τῷ μάχεσθαι εἴτε ἄρχων εἴτε ἀμυνόμενος,
ἄγροικος καὶ ἀνελεύθερος ἂν λεγόμενος ἀνδραπο-
δώδης τε, δίκης ἂν ἐπονειδίστου τυγχάνων τὸ
πρέπον ἔχοι. καὶ ἐὰν μέν τις τοιούτοις παραμυ-
θίοις εὐπειθὴς γίγνηται, εὐήνιος ἂν εἴη· ὁ δὲ
δυσπειθὴς καὶ μηδὲν προοιμίου φροντίζων δέχοιτ'
B ἂν τὸν τοιόνδε ἑτοίμως νόμον· ἐάν τις τύπτῃ τὸν
πρεσβύτερον εἴκοσιν ἔτεσιν ἢ πλείοσιν ἑαυτοῦ,
πρῶτον μὲν ὁ προστυγχάνων, ἐὰν μὴ ἧλιξ μηδὲ
νεώτερος ᾖ [τῶν μαχομένων],[1] διειργέτω ἢ κακὸς
ἔστω κατὰ νόμον· ἐὰν δὲ ἐν τῇ τοῦ πληγέντος
ἡλικίᾳ ἢ ἔτι νεώτερος, ἀμυνέτω ὡς ἀδελφῷ ἢ πατρὶ
ἢ ἔτι ἀνωτέρω τῷ ἀδικουμένῳ· πρὸς δ' ἔτι δίκην
ὑπεχέτω τῆς αἰκίας ὁ τὸν πρεσβύτερον, ὡς εἴρηται, τολμήσας τύπτειν, καὶ ἐὰν ὄφλῃ τὴν δίκην,
C δεδέσθω μηδὲν ἐνιαυτοῦ σμικρότερον· ἐὰν δὲ οἱ
δικασταὶ τιμήσωσι πλείονος, ἔστω κύριος ὁ τιμη-
θεὶς αὐτῷ χρόνος. ἐὰν δὲ ξένος ἢ τῶν μετοίκων
τις τύπτῃ τὸν πρεσβύτερον εἴκοσιν ἔτεσιν ἢ
πλείοσιν ἑαυτοῦ, περὶ μὲν τῶν παραγενομένων
τῆς βοηθείας ὁ αὐτὸς νόμος ἐχέτω τὴν αὐτὴν
δύναμιν, ὁ δὲ τὴν τοιαύτην δίκην ἡττηθείς, ξένος
μὲν ὢν καὶ μὴ ξύνοικος, δύο ἔτη δεδεμένος ἐκτινέτω
ταύτην αὐτὴν τὴν δίκην, ὁ δὲ μέτοικός τε ὢν καὶ
ἀπειθῶν τοῖς νόμοις τρία ἔτη δεδέσθω, ἐὰν μὴ τὸ
δικαστήριον πλείονος αὐτῷ χρόνου τιμήσῃ τὴν
D δίκην. ζημιούσθω δὲ καὶ ὁ παραγενόμενος ὁτῳοῦν
τούτων καὶ μὴ βοηθήσας κατὰ νόμον, ὁ μὲν μεγίστου τιμήματος ὢν μνᾷ, δευτέρου δὲ ὢν πεντήκοντα

---

[1] [τῶν μαχομένων] I bracket.

But if a man over forty ventures to fight, whether as aggressor or in self-defence, he shall be called a knave and a boor, and if he finds himself incurring a degrading sentence, he will be getting his deserts. Any man who lends a ready ear to such exhortations will prove easy to manage ; but he that is intractable and pays no regard to the prelude will hearken readily to a law to this effect :—If anyone beats a person who is twenty or more years older than himself, in the first place, whoever comes upon them, if he be neither of equal age nor younger, shall try to separate them, or else be held to be a coward in the eyes of the law ; and if he be of a like age with the man assaulted or still younger, he shall defend him who is wronged as he would a brother or a father or a still older progenitor. Further, he that dares to strike the older man in the way described shall be liable also to an action for outrage, and if he be convicted, he shall be imprisoned for not less than a year ; and if the judges assess the penalty at a longer period, the period so assessed shall be binding on him. And if a Stranger or a resident alien beat a man older than himself by twenty or more years, the same law regarding help from bystanders shall be equally binding ; and he that is cast in a suit of this kind, if he be a non-resident Stranger, shall be imprisoned for two years and fulfil this sentence ; and he that is a resident alien and disobeys the laws shall be imprisoned for three years, unless the court assess his penalty at a longer period. And the man who is a bystander in any of these cases of assault, and who fails to give help as the law prescribes, shall be penalised—by a fine of a mina, if he be a man of the highest property-class ; of fifty drachmae, if he be of the second class ; of thirty

289

δραχμαῖς, τρίτου δὲ τριάκοντα, εἴκοσι δὲ τοῦ
τετάρτου. δικαστήριον δὲ γιγνέσθω τοῖς τοιού-
τοισι στρατηγοὶ καὶ ταξίαρχοι φύλαρχοί τε καὶ
ἵππαρχοι.

Νόμοι δέ, ὡς ἔοικεν, οἱ μὲν τῶν χρηστῶν
Ε ἀνθρώπων ἕνεκα γίγνονται, διδαχῆς χάριν τοῦ
τίνα τρόπον ὁμιλοῦντες ἀλλήλοις ἂν φιλοφρόνως οἰκοῖεν, οἱ δὲ τῶν τὴν παιδείαν διαφυγόντων,
ἀτεράμονι χρωμένων τινὶ φύσει καὶ μηδὲν τεγ-
χθέντων, ὥστε μὴ οὐκ ἐπὶ πᾶσαν ἰέναι κάκην.
οὗτοι τοὺς μέλλοντας λόγους ῥηθήσεσθαι πεποι-
ηκότες ἂν εἶεν· οἷς δὴ τοὺς νόμους ἐξ ἀνάγκης
ὁ νομοθέτης ἂν νομοθετοῖ, βουλόμενος αὐτῶν
μηδέποτε χρείαν γίγνεσθαι. πατρὸς γὰρ ἢ μητρὸς
ἢ τούτων ἔτι προγόνων ὅστις τολμήσει ἅψασθαί
ποτε βιαζόμενος αἰκίᾳ τινί, μήτε τῶν ἄνω δείσας
θεῶν μῆνιν μήτε τῶν ὑπὸ γῆς τιμωρῶν [1] λεγομένων,
881 ἀλλὰ ὡς εἰδὼς ἃ μηδαμῶς οἶδε, καταφρονῶν τῶν
παλαιῶν καὶ ὑπὸ πάντων εἰρημένων παρανομεῖ,
τούτῳ δεῖ τινὸς ἀποτροπῆς ἐσχάτης. θάνατος
μὲν οὖν οὐκ ἔστιν ἔσχατον, οἱ δὲ ἐν Ἅιδου
τούτοισι λεγόμενοι πόνοι ἔτι τε τούτου [2] εἰσὶ
μᾶλλον ἐν ἐσχάτοις, καὶ ἀληθέστατα λέγοντες
οὐδὲν ἀνύτουσι ταῖς τοιαύταις ψυχαῖς ἀποτροπῆς·
οὐ γὰρ ἂν ἐγίγνοντό ποτε μητραλοῖαί τε καὶ τῶν
Β ἄλλων γεννητόρων ἀνόσιοι πληγῶν τόλμαι. δεῖ
δὴ τὰς ἐνθάδε κολάσεις περὶ τὰ τοιαῦτα τούτοισι

---

[1] τιμωρῶν Winckelmann : τιμωριῶν MSS.

drachmae, if of the third ; and of twenty drachmae, if of the fourth class.   And the court for such cases shall consist of the generals, taxiarchs, phylarchs, and hipparchs.

Laws, it would seem, are made partly for the sake of good men, to afford them instruction as to what manner of intercourse will best secure for them friendly association one with another, and partly also for the sake of those who have shunned education, and who, being of a stubborn nature, have had no softening treatment [1] to prevent their taking to all manner of wickedness.   It is because of these men that the laws which follow have to be stated,—laws which the lawgiver must enact of necessity, on their account, although wishing that the need for them may never arise.   Whosoever shall dare to lay hands on father or mother, or their progenitors, and to use outrageous violence, fearing neither the wrath of the gods above nor that of the Avengers (as they are called) of the underworld, but scorning the ancient and worldwide traditions (thinking he knows what he knows not at all), and shall thus transgress the law,—for such a man there is needed some most severe deterrent.   Death is not a most severe penalty ; and the punishments we are told of in Hades for such offences, although more severe than death and described most truly, yet fail to prove any deterrent to souls such as these,—else we should never find cases of matricide and of impiously audacious assaults upon other progenitors.   Consequently, the punishments inflicted upon these men here in their lifetime

[1] Cp. 853 D.

---

[2] τούτου my conj. (so too Burges) : τούτων MSS., edd.

τὰς ἐν τῷ ζῆν μηδὲν τῶν ἐν "Αιδου λείπεσθαι
κατὰ δύναμιν. ἔστω δὴ λεγόμενον τὸ μετὰ τοῦτο
τῇδε· ὃς ἂν τολμήσῃ πατέρα ἢ μητέρα ἢ τούτων
πατέρας ἢ μητέρας τύπτειν μὴ μανίαις ἐχόμενος,
πρῶτον μὲν ὁ προστυγχάνων καθάπερ ἐν τοῖς
ἔμπροσθεν βοηθείτω, καὶ ὁ μὲν μέτοικος [ἢ]¹ ξένος
εἰς προεδρίαν τῶν ἀγώνων καλείσθω βοηθῶν,
μὴ βοηθήσας δὲ ἀειφυγίαν ἐκ τῆς χώρας
C φευγέτω· ὁ δὲ μὴ μέτοικος βοηθῶν μὲν ἔπαινον
ἐχέτω, μὴ βοηθῶν δὲ ψόγον· δοῦλος δὲ βοηθήσας
μὲν ἐλεύθερος γιγνέσθω, μὴ βοηθήσας δὲ πληγὰς
ἑκατὸν τῇ μάστιγι τυπτέσθω, ἐν ἀγορᾷ μὲν ἂν
γίγνηται τὸ γιγνόμενον, ὑπ' ἀγορανόμων, ἐὰν δ'
ἐκτὸς ἀγορᾶς ἐν ἄστει, τῶν ἀστυνόμων κολάζειν
τὸν ἐπιδημοῦντα, ἐὰν δὲ κατ' ἀγροὺς τῆς χώρας
που, τοὺς τῶν ἀγρονόμων ἄρχοντας. ἐὰν δ' ἐπιχώριος ὁ παρατυγχάνων ᾖ τις, ἐάν τε παῖς ἐάν τε
ἀνὴρ ἐάν τ' οὖν γυνή, ἀμυνέτω πᾶς τὸν ἀνόσιον
D ἐπονομάζων· ὁ δὲ μὴ ἀμύνων ἀρᾷ ἐνεχέσθω Διὸς
ὁμογνίου καὶ πατρῴου κατὰ νόμον. ἐὰν δέ τις
ὄφλῃ δίκην αἰκίας γονέων, πρῶτον μὲν φευγέτω
ἀειφυγίαν ἐξ ἄστεος εἰς τὴν ἄλλην χώραν καὶ
πάντων ἱερῶν εἰργέσθω· μὴ δὲ εἰργόμενον κολαζόντων αὐτὸν ἀγρονόμοι πληγαῖς καὶ πάντως ὡς ἂν
ἐθέλωσι· κατελθὼν δὲ θανάτῳ ζημιούσθω. ἐὰν
δέ τις τῷ τοιούτῳ ὅσοι ἐλεύθεροι συμφάγῃ ἢ
συμπίῃ ἤ τινα τοιαύτην ἄλλην κοινωνίαν κοινω-

¹ [ἢ] bracketed by England.

for crimes of this kind must, so far as possible, fall in no way short of the punishments in Hades. So the next pronouncement shall run thus :—Whosoever shall dare to beat his father or mother, or their fathers or mothers, if he be not afflicted with madness,—in the first place, the bystander shall give help, as in the former cases, and the resident Stranger who helps shall be invited to a first-row seat at the public games, but he who fails to help shall be banished from the country for life ; and the non-resident Stranger shall receive praise if he helps, and blame if he does not help ; and the slave who helps shall be made free, but if he fails to help he shall be beaten with 100 stripes of a scourge by the market-stewards, if the assault occur in the market, and if it occur in the city, but outside the market-place, the punishment shall be inflicted by the city-steward in residence, and if it occur in any country district, by the officers of the country-stewards. And the bystander who is a native—whether man, woman, or boy—shall in every case drive off the attacker, crying out against his impiety ; and he that fails to drive him off shall be liable by law to the curse of Zeus, guardian-god of kinship and parentage. And if a man be convicted on a charge of outrageous assault upon parents, in the first place he shall be banished for life from the city to other parts of the country, and he shall keep away from all sacred places ; and if he fails to keep away, the country-stewards shall punish him with stripes, and in any other way they choose, and if he returns again he shall be punished with death. And if any free man voluntarily eat or drink or hold any similar intercourse with such an one, or even give him merely a greet-

E νήσῃ, ἢ καὶ μόνον ἐντυγχάνων που προσάπτηται
ἐκών, μήτε εἰς ἱερὸν ἔλθῃ μηδὲν μήτ᾽ εἰς ἀγορὰν
μήτ᾽ εἰς πόλιν ὅλως πρότερον ἢ καθήρηται,
νομίζων κεκοινωνηκέναι ἀλιτηριώδους τύχης· ἐὰν
δὲ ἀπειθῶν νόμῳ ἱερὰ καὶ πόλιν μιαίνῃ παρανόμως, ὃς ἂν τῶν ἀρχόντων αἰσθόμενος μὴ
ἐπάγῃ δίκην τῷ τοιούτῳ, ἐν εὐθύναις ἔστω τῶν
κατηγορημάτων τῶν μεγίστων ἐν τοῦτο[1] αὐτῷ.
882 ἐὰν δὲ αὖ δοῦλος τύπτῃ τὸν ἐλεύθερον, εἴτ᾽ οὖν
ξένον εἴτε ἀστόν, βοηθείτω μὲν ὁ προστυγχάνων
ἢ κατὰ τὸ τίμημα τὴν εἰρημένην ζημίαν ἀποτινέτω,
συνδήσαντες δὲ οἱ προστυγχάνοντες μετὰ τοῦ
B πληγέντος παραδόντων τῷ ἀδικουμένῳ· ὁ δὲ παρα-
λαβών, δήσας ἐν πέδαις καὶ μαστιγώσας ὁπόσας
ἂν ἐθέλῃ, μηδὲν βλάπτων τὸν δεσπότην, παραδότω ἐκείνῳ κεκτῆσθαι κατὰ νόμον. ὁ δὲ νόμος
ἔστω· Ὃς ἂν ἐλεύθερον δοῦλος ὢν τύπτῃ μὴ τῶν
ἀρχόντων κελευόντων, παραλαβὼν ὁ κεκτημένος
παρὰ τοῦ πληγέντος δεδεμένον αὐτὸν μὴ λύσῃ
πρὶν ἂν ὁ δοῦλος πείσῃ τὸν πληγέντα ἄξιος εἶναι
C τοῦ λελυμένος ζῆν. τὰ αὐτὰ δὲ γυναικί τε ἔστω
πρὸς ἀλλήλας περὶ πάντων τῶν τοιούτων νόμιμα,
καὶ πρὸς ἄνδρας γυναιξὶ καὶ ἀνδράσι πρὸς
γυναῖκας.

---

[1] ἐν τοῦτο Bekker: ἐν τούτῳ MSS., Zur.

ing when he meets him, he shall not enter any holy place or the market or any part of the city until he be purified, but he shall regard himself as having incurred a share of contagious guilt; and should he disobey the law and illegally defile sacred things and the State, any magistrate who notices his case and fails to bring him up for trial shall have to face this omission as one of the heaviest charges against him at his audit. If it be a slave that strikes the free man—stranger or citizen—the bystander shall help, failing which he shall pay the penalty as fixed according to his assessment;[1] and the bystanders together with the person assaulted shall bind the slave, and hand him over to the injured person, and he shall take charge of him and bind him in fetters, and give him as many stripes with the scourge as he pleases, provided that he does not spoil his value to the damage of his master, to whose ownership he shall hand him over according to law. The law shall stand thus :—Whosoever, being a slave, beats a free man without order of the magistrates,—him his owner shall take over in bonds from the person assaulted, and he shall not loose him until the slave have convinced the person assaulted that he deserves to live loosed from bonds. The same laws shall hold good for all such cases when both parties are women, or when the plaintiff is a woman and the defendant a man, or the plaintiff a man and the defendant a woman.

[1] Cp. 880 D.

I

884 ΑΘ. Μετὰ δὲ τὰς αἰκίας περὶ παντὸς ἐν
εἰρήσθω τοιόνδε τι νόμιμον βιαίων πέρι· τῶν
ἀλλοτρίων μηδένα μηδὲν φέρειν μηδὲ ἄγειν, μηδ᾽
αὖ χρῆσθαι μηδενὶ τῶν τοῦ πέλας, ἐὰν μὴ πείσῃ
τὸν κεκτημένον· ἐκ γὰρ δὴ τοῦ τοιούτου πάντα
ἠρτημένα τὰ εἰρημένα κακὰ γέγονε καί ἐστι καὶ
ἔσται. μέγιστα δὲ δὴ τῶν λοιπῶν αἱ τῶν νέων
ἀκολασίαι τε καὶ ὕβρεις· εἰς μέγιστα δέ, ὅταν
εἰς ἱερὰ γίγνωνται, καὶ διαφερόντως αὖ μεγάλα,
ὅταν εἰς δημόσια καὶ ἅγια ἢ κατὰ μέρη κοινὰ
φυλετῶν ἤ τινων ἄλλων τοιούτων κεκοινωνηκότων·
εἰς ἱερὰ δὲ ἴδια καὶ τάφους δεύτερα καὶ δευτέρως.
885 εἰς δὲ γονέας τρίτα, χωρὶς τῶν ἔμπροσθεν εἰρημένων ὅταν ὑβρίζῃ τις. τέταρτον δὲ γένος ὕβρεως,
ὅταν ἀφροντιστῶν τις τῶν ἀρχόντων ἄγῃ ἢ φέρῃ
ἢ χρῆταί τινι τῶν ἐκείνων μὴ πείσας αὐτούς·
πέμπτον δὲ τὸ πολιτικὸν ἂν εἴη ἑκάστου τῶν
πολιτῶν ὑβρισθὲν δίκην ἐπικαλούμενον. οἷς δὴ
δοτέον εἰς κοινὸν νόμον ἑκάστοις. ἱεροσυλία μὲν
γὰρ εἴρηται ξυλλήβδην, βίαιός τε καὶ λάθρα ἐὰν
B γίγνηται, τί χρὴ πάσχειν· ὅσα δὲ λόγῳ καὶ

---

[1] Cp. 868 C ff., 877 B ff., 930 E ff.
[2] Cp. 941 D, E.
[3] Cp. 854 B ff.

PLATO

BOOK X

ATH. Next after cases of outrage we shall state
for cases of violence one universally inclusive principle of law, to this effect:—No one shall carry or
drive off anything which belongs to others, nor shall
he use any of his neighbour's goods unless he has
gained the consent of the owner; for from such
action proceed all the evils above mentioned—past,
present and to come. Of the rest, the most grave
are the licentious and outrageous acts of the young;
and outrages offend most gravely when they are
directed against sacred things, and they are especially
grave when they are directed against objects which
are public as well as holy, or partially public, as
being shared in by the members of a tribe or other
similar community. Second, and second in point of
gravity, come offences against sacred objects and
tombs that are private; and third, offences against
parents, when a person commits the outrage otherwise than in the cases already described.[1] A fourth [2]
kind of outrage is when a man, in defiance of the
magistrates, drives or carries off or uses any of their
things without their own consent; and a fifth kind
will be an outrage against the civic right of an
individual private citizen which calls for judicial
vindication. To all these severally one all-embrac-
ing law must be assigned. As to temple-robbing,[3]
whether done by open violence or secretly, it has
been already stated summarily what the punishment
should be; and in respect of all the outrages, whether

PLATO

ὅσα ἔργῳ περὶ θεοὺς ὑβρίζει τις λέγων ἢ πράττων, τὸ παραμύθιον ὑποθεμένῳ ῥητέον ἃ δεῖ πάσχειν. ἔστω δὴ τόδε· θεοὺς ἡγούμενος εἶναι κατὰ νόμους οὐδεὶς πώποτε οὔτε ἔργον ἀσεβὲς εἰργάσατο ἑκὼν οὔτε λόγον ἀφῆκεν ἄνομον, ἀλλὰ ἕν δή τι τῶν τριῶν πάσχων, ἢ τοῦτο ὅπερ εἶπον οὐχ ἡγούμενος, ἢ τὸ δεύτερον ὄντας οὐ φροντίζειν ἀνθρώπων, ἢ τρίτον εὐπαραμυθήτους εἶναι θυσίαις τε καὶ εὐχαῖς παραγομένους.

C   ΚΛ. Τί οὖν δὴ δρῶμεν ἂν ἢ καὶ λέγοιμεν πρὸς αὐτούς;

ΑΘ. ᾿Ω 'γαθέ, ἐπακούσωμεν αὐτῶν πρῶτον ἃ τῷ καταφρονεῖν ἡμῶν προσπαίζοντας αὐτοὺς λέγειν μαντεύομαι.

ΚΛ. Ποῖα δή;

ΑΘ. Ταῦτα τάχ' ἂν ἐρεσχηλοῦντες εἴποιεν, ᾿Ω ξένε ᾿Αθηναῖε καὶ Λακεδαιμόνιε καὶ Κνώσιε, ἀληθῆ λέγετε. ἡμῶν γὰρ οἱ μὲν τὸ παράπαν θεοὺς οὐδαμῶς νομίζομεν,[1] οἱ δὲ [μηδὲν ἡμῶν φροντίζειν, οἱ δὲ εὐχαῖς παράγεσθαι,] οἵους ὑμεῖς λέγετε. ἀξιοῦμεν δή, καθάπερ ὑμεῖς ἠξιώκατε

D   περὶ νόμων, πρὶν ἀπειλεῖν ἡμῖν σκληρῶς ὑμᾶς πρότερον ἐπιχειρεῖν πείθειν καὶ διδάσκειν ὡς εἰσὶ θεοί, τεκμήρια λέγοντας ἱκανά, καὶ ὅτι βελτίους ἢ παρὰ τὸ δίκαιον ὑπό τινων δώρων παρατρέπεσθαι κηλούμενοι. νῦν μὲν γὰρ ταῦτα ἀκούοντές τε καὶ τοιαῦθ' ἕτερα τῶν λεγομένων ἀρίστων εἶναι ποιητῶν τε καὶ ῥητόρων καὶ μάντεων καὶ ἱερέων καὶ ἄλλων μυριάκις [2] μυρίων οὐκ ἐπὶ τὸ μὴ δρᾶν τὰ ἄδικα τρεπόμεθα οἱ

---

[1] νομίζομεν MSS.: νομίζουσιν Zur., vulg.
[2] μυριάκις MSS.: πολλάκις Zur., vulg.

298

of word or deed, which a man commits, either by
tongue or hand, against the gods, we must state the
punishment he should suffer, after we have first
delivered the admonition. It shall be as follows :—
No one who believes, as the laws prescribe, in the
existence of the gods has ever yet done an impious
deed voluntarily, or uttered a lawless word : he that
acts so is in one or other of these three conditions of
mind—either he does not believe in what I have
said ; or, secondly, he believes that the gods exist,
but have no care for men ; or, thirdly, he believes
that they are easy to win over when bribed by
offerings and prayers.[1]

CLIN. What, then, shall we do or say to such
people ?

ATH. Let us listen first, my good sir, to what they,
as I imagine, say mockingly, in their contempt for
us.

CLIN. What is it ?

ATH. In derision they would probably say this :
" O Strangers of Athens, Lacedaemon and Crete,
what you say is true. Some of us do not believe in
gods at all ; others of us believe in gods of the kinds
you mention. So we claim now, as you claimed in
the matter of laws, that before threatening us harshly,
you should first try to convince and teach us, by
producing adequate proofs, that gods exist, and that
they are too good to be wheedled by gifts and turned
aside from justice. For as it is, this and such as this is
the account of them we hear from those who are reputed
the best of poets, orators, seers, priests, and thousands
upon thousands of others ; and consequently most of
us, instead of seeking to avoid wrong-doing, do the

[1] Cp. *Rep.* 364 B ff.

πλεῖστοι, δράσαντες δ' ἐξακεῖσθαι πειρώμεθα.
Ε παρὰ δὲ δὴ νομοθετῶν φασκόντων εἶναι μὴ
ἀγρίων ἀλλὰ ἡμέρων, ἀξιοῦμεν πειθοῖ πρῶτον
χρῆσθαι πρὸς ἡμᾶς, εἰ μὴ πολλῷ βελτίω τῶν
ἄλλων λέγοντας περὶ θεῶν ὡς εἰσίν, ἀλλ' οὖν
βελτίω γε πρὸς ἀλήθειαν· καὶ τάχα πειθοίμεθ'
ἂν ἴσως ὑμῖν. ἀλλ' ἐπιχειρεῖτε, εἴ τι μέτριον
λέγομεν, εἰπεῖν ἃ προκαλούμεθα.

ΚΛ. Οὐκοῦν, ὦ ξένε, δοκεῖ ῥᾴδιον εἶναι ἀληθεύον-
886 τας λέγειν ὡς εἰσὶ θεοί;

ΑΘ. Πῶς;

ΚΛ. Πρῶτον μὲν γῆ καὶ ἥλιος ἄστρα τε τὰ
ξύμπαντα καὶ τὰ τῶν ὡρῶν διακεκοσμημένα
καλῶς οὕτως, ἐνιαυτοῖς τε καὶ μησὶ διειλημμένα·
καὶ ὅτι πάντες Ἕλληνές τε καὶ βάρβαροι
νομίζουσιν εἶναι θεούς.

ΑΘ. Φοβοῦμαί γε, ὦ μακάριε, τοὺς μοχθηρούς,
οὐ γὰρ δή ποτε εἴποιμ' ἂν ὥς γε αἰδοῦμαι, μή
πως ἡμῶν καταφρονήσωσιν. ὑμεῖς μὲν γὰρ οὐκ
ἴστε αὐτῶν πέρι τὴν τῆς διαφθορᾶς[1] αἰτίαν, ἀλλ'
ἡγεῖσθε ἀκρατείᾳ[2] μόνον ἡδονῶν τε καὶ ἐπιθυ-
Β μιῶν ἐπὶ τὸν ἀσεβῆ βίον ὁρμᾶσθαι τὰς ψυχὰς
αὐτῶν.

ΚΛ. Τὸ δὲ τί πρὸς τούτοις αἴτιον ἄν, ὦ ξένε,
εἴη;

ΑΘ. Σχεδὸν ὃ παντάπασιν ὑμεῖς ἔξω ζῶντες
οὐκ ἂν εἰδείητε, ἀλλὰ ὑμᾶς ἂν λανθάνοι.

ΚΛ. Τί δὴ τοῦτο φράζεις τὰ νῦν;

ΑΘ. Ἀμαθία τις μάλα χαλεπὴ δοκοῦσα εἶναι
μεγίστη φρόνησις.

---

[1] διαφθορᾶς Cornarius : διαφορᾶς MSS.
[2] ἀκρατείᾳ MSS. : δι' ἀκρασίαν Zur.

wrong and then try to make it good. Now from law-givers like you, who assert that you are gentle rather than severe, we claim that you should deal with us first by way of persuasion; and if what you say about the existence of the gods is superior to the arguments of others in point of truth, even though it be but little superior in eloquence, then probably you would succeed in convincing us. Try then, if you think this reasonable, to meet our challenge."

CLIN. Surely it seems easy, Stranger, to assert with truth that gods exist?

ATH. How so?

CLIN. First, there is the evidence of the earth, the sun, the stars, and all the universe, and the beautiful ordering of the seasons, marked out by years and months; and then there is the further fact that all Greeks and barbarians believe in the existence of gods.

ATH. My dear sir, these bad men cause me alarm —for I will never call it " awe "—lest haply they scoff at us. For the cause of the corruption in their case is one you are not aware of; since you imagine that it is solely by their incontinence in regard to pleasures and desires that their souls are impelled to that impious life of theirs.

CLIN. What other cause can there be, Stranger, besides this?

ATH. One which you, who live elsewhere, could hardly have any knowledge of or notice at all.

CLIN. What is this cause you are now speaking of?

ATH. A very grievous unwisdom which is reputed to be the height of wisdom.

κλ. Πῶς λέγεις;

αθ. Εἰσὶν ἡμῖν ἐν γράμμασι λόγοι κείμενοι, οἳ
παρ' ὑμῖν οὐκ εἰσὶ δι' ἀρετὴν πολιτείας, ὡς ἐγὼ
C μανθάνω, οἱ μὲν ἔν τισι μέτροις, οἱ δὲ καὶ ἄνευ
μέτρων, λέγοντες περὶ θεῶν, οἱ μὲν παλαιότατοι,
ὡς γέγονεν ἡ πρώτη φύσις οὐρανοῦ τῶν τε ἄλλων,
προϊόντες δὲ τῆς ἀρχῆς οὐ πολὺ θεογονίαν δι-
εξέρχονται, γενόμενοί τε ὡς πρὸς ἀλλήλους ὡμί-
λησαν. ἃ τοῖς ἀκούουσιν εἰ μὲν εἰς ἄλλο τι
καλῶς ἢ μὴ καλῶς ἔχει, οὐ ῥᾴδιον ἐπιτιμᾶν
παλαιοῖς οὖσιν, εἰς μέντοι γονέων τε θεραπείας
καὶ τιμὰς οὐκ ἂν ἔγωγέ ποτε ἐπαινῶν εἴποιμι
οὔτε ὡς ὠφέλιμα οὔτε ὡς τὸ παράπαν ὄντως
D εἴρηται. τὰ μὲν οὖν δὴ τῶν ἀρχαίων πέρι μεθεί-
σθω καὶ χαιρέτω, καὶ ὅπῃ θεοῖσι φίλον λεγέσθω
ταύτῃ· τὰ δὲ τῶν νέων ἡμῖν καὶ σοφῶν αἰτιαθήτω
ὅπῃ κακῶν αἴτια. τόδε οὖν οἱ τῶν τοιούτων
ἐξεργάζονται λόγοι. ἐμοῦ γὰρ καὶ σοῦ, ὅταν
τεκμήρια λέγωμεν ὡς εἰσὶ θεοί, ταῦτα αὐτὰ
προφέροντες, ἥλιόν τε καὶ σελήνην καὶ ἄστρα
καὶ γῆν ὡς θεοὺς καὶ θεῖα ὄντα, ὑπὸ τῶν σοφῶν
τούτων ἀναπεπεισμένοι ἂν λέγοιεν ὡς γῆν τε
E καὶ λίθους ὄντα αὐτὰ καὶ οὐδὲν τῶν ἀνθρωπείων
πραγμάτων φροντίζειν δυνάμενα, λόγοισι δὲ ταῦτα
εὖ πως εἰς τὸ πιθανὸν περιπεπεμμένα.

κλ. Χαλεπόν γε λόγον, ὦ ξένε, εἰρηκὼς τυγ-
χάνεις, εἴ γε εἷς ἦν μόνον· νῦν δὲ ὅτε πάμπολλοι
τυγχάνουσιν, ἔτι χαλεπώτερον ἂν εἴη.

---

[1] By Hesiod, Pherecydes, etc.
[2] Materialists such as Democritus.

CLIN. What do you mean?

ATH. We at Athens have accounts[1] preserved in writing (though, I am told, such do not exist in your country, owing to the excellence of your polity), some of them being in a kind of metre, others without metre, telling about the gods: the oldest of these accounts relate how the first substance of Heaven and all else came into being, and shortly after the beginning they go on to give a detailed theogony, and to tell how, after they were born, the gods associated with one another. These accounts, whether good or bad for the hearers in other respects, it is hard for us to censure because of their antiquity; but as regards the tendance and respect due to parents, I certainly would never praise them or say that they are either helpful or wholly true accounts. Such ancient accounts, however, we may pass over and dismiss: let them be told in the way best pleasing to the gods. It is rather the novel views of our modern scientists[2] that we must hold responsible as the cause of mischief. For the result of the arguments of such people is this,—that when you and I try to prove the existence of the gods by pointing to these very objects—sun, moon, stars, and earth—as instances of deity and divinity, people who have been converted by these scientists will assert that these things are simply earth and stone, incapable of paying any heed to human affairs, and that these beliefs of ours are speciously tricked out with arguments to make them plausible.

CLIN. The assertion you mention, Stranger, is indeed a dangerous one, even if it stood alone; but now that such assertions are legion, the danger is still greater.

ΑΘ. Τί οὖν δή; τί λέγομεν; τί χρὴ δρᾶν
ἡμᾶς; πότερον ἀπολογησώμεθα οἷον κατηγο-
ρήσαντός τινος ἐν ἀσεβέσιν ἀνθρώποις ἡμῶν,
887 [φεύγουσι περὶ τῆς νομοθεσίας, λέγουσιν] [1] ὡς
δεινὰ ἐργαζόμεθα νομοθετοῦντες ὡς ὄντων θεῶν;
ἢ χαίρειν ἐάσαντες ἐπὶ τοὺς νόμους τρεπώμεθα
πάλιν, μὴ καὶ τὸ προοίμιον ἡμῖν μακρότερον
γίγνηται τῶν νόμων; οὐ γάρ τι βραχὺς ὁ λόγος
ἐκταθεὶς ἂν γίγνοιτο, εἰ τοῖσιν ἐπιθυμοῦσιν
ἀσεβεῖν τὰ μὲν ἀποδείξαιμεν μετρίως τοῖς λόγοις,
ὧν ἔφραζον δεῖν πέρι λέγειν, τῶν δὲ εἰς φόβον
τρέψαιμεν, τὰ δὲ δυσχεραίνειν ποιήσαντες, ὅσα
πρέπει μετὰ ταῦτα ἤδη νομοθετοῖμεν.

Β ΚΛ. Ἀλλ', ὦ ξένε, πολλάκις μὲν ὥς γε ἐν
ὀλίγῳ χρόνῳ τοῦτ' αὐτὸ εἰρήκαμεν, ὡς οὐδὲν ἐν
τῷ παρόντι δεῖ προτιμᾶν βραχυλογίαν μᾶλλον ἢ
μῆκος· οὐδεὶς γὰρ ἡμᾶς, τὸ λεγόμενον, ἐπείγων
διώκει· γελοῖον δὴ καὶ φαῦλον τὸ πρὸ τῶν βελτίσ-
των τὰ βραχύτερα αἱρουμένους φαίνεσθαι. διαφέρει δ' οὐ σμικρὸν ἀμῶς γέ πως πιθανότητά
τινα τοὺς λόγους ἡμῶν ἔχειν, ὡς θεοί τ' εἰσὶ καὶ
ἀγαθοί, δίκην τιμῶντες διαφερόντως ἀνθρώπων·
C σχεδὸν γὰρ τοῦτο ἡμῖν ὑπὲρ ἁπάντων τῶν νόμων
κάλλιστόν τε καὶ ἄριστον προοίμιον ἂν εἴη.
μηδὲν οὖν δυσχεράναντες μηδὲ ἐπειχθέντες, ἥντινά
ποτε ἔχομεν δύναμιν εἰς πειθὼ τῶν τοιούτων

_____

[1] [φεύγουσι . . . λέγουσιν] I bracket.

ATH. What then? What shall we say? What must we do? Are we to make our defence as it were before a court of impious men, where someone had accused us of doing something dreadful by assuming in our legislation the existence of gods? Or shall we rather dismiss the whole subject and revert again to our laws, lest our prelude prove actually more lengthy than the laws? For indeed our discourse would be extended in no small degree if we were to furnish those men who desire to be impious with an adequate demonstration by means of argument concerning those subjects which ought, as they claimed, to be discussed, and so to convert them to fear of the gods, and then finally, when we had caused them to shrink from irreligion, to proceed to enact the appropriate laws.

CLIN. Still, Stranger, we have frequently (considering the shortness of the time) made [1] this very statement,—that we have no need on the present occasion to prefer brevity of speech to lengthiness (for, as the saying goes, "no one is chasing on our heels"); and to show ourselves choosing the briefest in preference to the best would be mean and ridiculous. And it is of the highest importance that our arguments, showing that the gods exist and that they are good and honour justice more than do men, should by all means possess some degree of persuasiveness; for such a prelude is the best we could have in defence, as one may say, of all our laws. So without any repugnance or undue haste, and with all the capacity we have for endowing such arguments with

---

[1] Cp. 701 C, D; 858 A ff.: all this discussion is supposed to have taken place on one and the same day,—hence the ref. to "shortness of time."

λόγων, μηδὲν ἀποθέμενοι διεξέλθωμεν εἰς τὸ
δυνατὸν ἱκανῶς.

ΑΘ. Εὐχήν μοι δοκεῖ παρακαλεῖν ὁ λεγόμενος
ὑπὸ σοῦ νῦν λόγος, ἐπειδὴ προθύμως συντείνεις·
μέλλειν δὲ οὐκέτι ἐγχωρεῖ λέγειν. φέρε δή, πῶς
ἄν τις μὴ θυμῷ λέγοι περὶ θεῶν ὡς εἰσίν; ἀνάγκη
γὰρ δὴ χαλεπῶς φέρειν καὶ μισεῖν ἐκείνους οἳ
D τούτων ἡμῖν αἴτιοι τῶν λόγων γεγένηνται καὶ
γίγνονται νῦν, οὐ πειθόμενοι τοῖς μύθοις, οὓς ἐκ
νέων παίδων ἔτι ἐν γάλαξι τρεφόμενοι τροφῶν
τε ἤκουον καὶ μητέρων, οἷον ἐν ἐπῳδαῖς μετά τε
παιδιᾶς καὶ μετὰ σπουδῆς λεγομένων, καὶ μετὰ
θυσιῶν ἐν εὐχαῖς αὐτοὺς ἀκούοντές τε, καὶ ὄψεις
ὁρῶντες ἑπομένας αὐτοῖς ἃς ἥδιστα ὅ γε νέος ὁρᾷ
τε καὶ ἀκούει πραττομένας θυόντων, ἐν σπουδῇ
<τε>[1] τῇ μεγίστῃ τοὺς αὑτῶν γονέας ὑπὲρ
αὑτῶν τε καὶ ἐκείνων ἐσπουδακότας, <καὶ>[2]
ὡς ὅτι μάλιστα οὖσι θεοῖς εὐχαῖς προσδιαλεγο-
μένους καὶ ἱκετείαις, ἀνατέλλοντός τε ἡλίου καὶ
E σελήνης καὶ πρὸς δυσμὰς ἰόντων προκυλίσεις
ἅμα καὶ προσκυνήσεις ἀκούοντές τε καὶ ὁρῶντες
Ἑλλήνων τε καὶ βαρβάρων πάντων ἐν συμφοραῖς
παντοίαις ἐχομένων καὶ ἐν εὐπραγίαις, οὐχ ὡς
οὐκ ὄντων, ἀλλ' ὡς ὅτι μάλιστα ὄντων καὶ οὐδαμῇ
ὑποψίαν ἐνδιδόντων ὡς οὐκ εἰσὶ θεοί,—τούτων
δὴ πάντων ὅσοι καταφρονήσαντες οὐδὲ ἐξ ἑνὸς
ἱκανοῦ λόγου, ὡς φαῖεν ἂν ὅσοι καὶ σμικρὸν νοῦ
κέκτηνται, νῦν ἀναγκάζουσιν ἡμᾶς λέγειν ἃ
888 λέγομεν, πῶς τούτους ἄν τις ἐν πραέσι λόγοις

---

[1] <τε> added by W. R. Paton, England.
[2] <καὶ> added by Ast, England.

persuasiveness, let us expound them as fully as we can, and without any reservation.

ATH. This speech of yours seems to me to call for a prefatory prayer, seeing that you are so eager and ready; nor is it possible any longer to defer our statement. Come, then; how is one to argue on behalf of the existence of the gods without passion? For we needs must be vexed and indignant with the men who have been, and now are, responsible for laying on us this burden of argument, through their disbelief in those stories which they used to hear, while infants and sucklings, from the lips of their nurses and mothers—stories chanted to them, as it were, in lullabies, whether in jest or in earnest; and the same stories they heard repeated also in prayers at sacrifices, and they saw spectacles which illustrated them, of the kind which the young delight to see and hear when performed at sacrifices; and their own parents they saw showing the utmost zeal on behalf of themselves and their children in addressing the gods in prayers and supplications, as though they most certainly existed; and at the rising and setting of the sun and moon they heard and saw the prostrations and devotions of all the Greeks and barbarians, under all conditions of adversity and prosperity, directed to these luminaries, not as though they were not gods, but as though they most certainly were gods beyond the shadow of a doubt—all this evidence is contemned by these people, and that for no sufficient reason, as everyone endowed with a grain of sense would affirm; and so they are now forcing us to enter on our present argument. How, I ask, can one possibly use mild terms in admonishing such men, and at the same

δύναιτο νουθετῶν ἅμα διδάσκειν περὶ θεῶν πρῶτον ὡς εἰσί ; τολμητέον δέ· οὐ γὰρ ἅμα γε δεῖ
μανῆναι τοὺς μὲν ὑπὸ λαιμαργίας ἡδονῆς ἡμῶν,
τοὺς δ᾽ ὑπὸ τοῦ θυμοῦσθαι τοῖς τοιούτοις.

Ἴτω δὴ πρόρρησις τοιάδε τις ἄθυμος τοῖς οὕτω
τὴν διάνοιαν διεφθαρμένοις, καὶ λέγωμεν πράως,
σβέσαντες τὸν θυμόν, ὡς ἑνὶ διαλεγόμενοι τῶν
τοιούτων, Ὦ παῖ, νέος εἶ· προϊὼν δέ σε ὁ χρόνος
B ποιήσει πολλὰ ὧν νῦν δοξάζεις μεταβαλόντα ἐπὶ
τἀναντία τίθεσθαι. περίμεινον οὖν εἰς τότε
κριτὴς περὶ τῶν μεγίστων γίγνεσθαι· μέγιστον
δὲ ὃ νῦν οὐδὲν ἡγεῖ σύ, τὸ περὶ τοὺς θεοὺς ὀρθῶς
διανοηθέντα ζῆν καλῶς ἢ μή. πρῶτον δὲ περὶ
αὐτῶν ἕν τι μέγα σοι μηνύων οὐκ ἄν ποτε φανείην
ψευδής, τὸ τοιόνδε· οὐ σὺ μόνος οὐδὲ οἱ σοὶ
φίλοι πρῶτοι καὶ πρῶτον ταύτην δόξαν περὶ
θεῶν ἔσχετε, γίγνονται δὲ ἀεὶ πλείους ἢ ἐλάττους
ταύτην τὴν νόσον ἔχοντες. τόδε τοίνυν σοι παρα-
γεγονὼς αὐτῶν πολλοῖσι φράζοιμ᾽ ἄν, τὸ μηδένα
C πώποτε λαβόντα ἐκ νέου ταύτην τὴν δόξαν περὶ
θεῶν, ὡς οὐκ εἰσί, διατελέσαι πρὸς γῆρας μείν-
αντα ἐν ταύτῃ τῇ διανοήσει· τὰ δύο μέντοι πάθη
περὶ θεοὺς μεῖναι, πολλοῖσι μὲν οὔ, μεῖναι δὲ
οὖν τισί, τὸ τοὺς θεοὺς εἶναι μέν, φροντίζειν δὲ
οὐδὲν τῶν ἀνθρωπίνων, καὶ τὸ μετὰ τοῦτο, ὡς
φροντίζουσι μέν, εὐπαραμύθητοι δ᾽ εἰσὶ θύμασι
καὶ εὐχαῖς. τὸ δὴ σαφὲς ἂν γενόμενόν σοι περὶ
308

time teach them, to begin with, that the gods do exist? Yet one must bravely attempt the task; for it would never do for both parties to be enraged at once,—the one owing to greed for pleasure, the other with indignation at men like them.

So let our prefatory address to the men thus corrupted in mind be dispassionate in tone, and, quenching our passion, let us speak mildly, as though we were conversing with one particular person of the kind described, in the following terms: "My child, you are still young, and time as it advances will cause you to reverse many of the opinions you now hold: so wait till then before pronouncing judgment on matters of most grave importance; and of these the gravest of all—though at present you regard it as naught—is the question of holding a right view about the gods and so living well, or the opposite. Now in the first place, I should be saying what is irrefutably true if I pointed out to you this signal fact, that neither you by yourself nor yet your friends are the first and foremost to adopt this opinion about the gods; rather is it true that people who suffer from this disease are always springing up, in greater or less numbers. But I, who have met with many of these people, would declare this to you, that not a single man who from his youth has adopted this opinion, that the gods have no existence, has ever yet continued till old age constant in the same view; but the other two false notions about the gods do remain—not, indeed, with many, but still with some,—the notion, namely, that the gods exist, but pay no heed to human affairs, and the other notion that they do pay heed, but are easily won over by prayers and offerings. For a doctrine about them

αὐτῶν κατὰ δύναμιν δόγμα, ἂν ἐμοὶ πείθῃ, περι-
μενεῖς ἀνασκοπῶν εἴτε οὕτως εἴτε ἄλλως ἔχει,
D πυνθανόμενος παρά τε τῶν ἄλλων καὶ δὴ καὶ
μάλιστα καὶ παρὰ τοῦ νομοθέτου. ἐν δὲ δὴ
τούτῳ τῷ χρόνῳ μὴ τολμήσῃς περὶ θεοὺς μηδὲν
ἀσεβῆσαι. πειρατέον γὰρ τῷ τοὺς νόμους σοι
τιθέντι νῦν καὶ εἰς αὖθις διδάσκειν περὶ αὐτῶν
τούτων ὡς ἔχει.

ΚΛ. Κάλλισθ᾽ ἡμῖν, ὦ ξένε, μέχρι γε τοῦ νῦν
εἴρηται.

ΑΘ. Παντάπασι μὲν οὖν, ὦ Μέγιλλέ τε καὶ
Κλεινία· λελήθαμεν δ᾽ ἡμᾶς αὐτοὺς εἰς θαυμαστὸν λόγον ἐμπεπτωκότες.

ΚΛ. Τὸν ποῖον δὴ λέγεις;
E ΑΘ. Τὸν παρὰ πολλοῖς δοξαζόμενον εἶναι
σοφώτατον ἁπάντων λόγων.

ΚΛ. Φράζ᾽ ἔτι σαφέστερον.

ΑΘ. Λέγουσί πού τινες ὡς πάντα ἐστὶ τὰ
πράγματα γιγνόμενα καὶ γενόμενα καὶ γενησό-
μενα τὰ μὲν φύσει, τὰ δὲ τύχῃ, τὰ δὲ διὰ
τέχνην.

ΚΛ. Οὐκοῦν καλῶς;

ΑΘ. Εἰκός γέ τοί που σοφοὺς ἄνδρας ὀρθῶς
λέγειν. ἑπόμενοί γε μὴν αὐτοῖς σκεψώμεθα τοὺς
889 ἐκεῖθεν, τί ποτε καὶ τυγχάνουσι διανοούμενοι.

ΚΛ. Πάντως.

ΑΘ. Ἔοικε, φασί, τὰ μὲν μέγιστα αὐτῶν καὶ
κάλλιστα ἀπεργάζεσθαι φύσιν καὶ τύχην, τὰ δὲ
σμικρότερα τέχνην, ἣν δὴ παρὰ φύσεως λαμβά-
νουσαν τὴν τῶν μεγάλων καὶ πρώτων γένεσιν
ἔργων πλάττειν καὶ τεκταίνεσθαι πάντα τὰ σμικρότερα, ἃ δὴ τεχνικὰ πάντες προσαγορεύομεν.

310

that is to prove the truest you can possibly form
you will, if you take my advice, wait, considering
the while whether the truth stands thus or otherwise, and making enquiries not only from all other
men, but especially from the lawgiver; and in the
meantime do not dare to be guilty of any impiety
in respect of the gods. For it must be the endeavour of him who is legislating for you both now
and hereafter to instruct you in the truth of these
matters.

CLIN. Our statement thus far, Stranger, is most
excellent.

ATH. Very true, O Megillus and Clinias; but we
have plunged unawares into a wondrous argument.

CLIN. What is it you mean?

ATH. That which most people account to be the
most scientific of all arguments.

CLIN. Explain more clearly.

ATH. It is stated by some that all things which
are coming into existence, or have or will come into
existence, do so partly by nature, partly by art, and
partly owing to chance.

CLIN. Is it not a right statement?

ATH. It is likely, to be sure, that what men of
science say is true. Anyhow, let us follow them up,
and consider what it is that the people in their camp
really intend.

CLIN. By all means let us do so.

ATH. It is evident, they assert, that the greatest
and most beautiful things are the work of nature
and of chance, and the lesser things that of art,—
for art receives from nature the great and primary
products as existing, and itself moulds and shapes all
the smaller ones, which we commonly call "artificial."

ΚΛ. Πῶς λέγεις ;

B   ΑΘ. Ὧδ' ἔτι σαφέστερον ἐρῶ. πῦρ καὶ ὕδωρ
καὶ γῆν καὶ ἀέρα φύσει πάντα εἶναι καὶ τύχῃ
φασί, τέχνῃ δὲ οὐδὲν τούτων· καὶ τὰ μετὰ ταῦτα
αὖ σώματα, γῆς τε καὶ ἡλίου καὶ σελήνης ἄστρων τε πέρι, διὰ τούτων γεγονέναι παντελῶς
ὄντων ἀψύχων· τύχῃ δὲ φερόμενα τῇ τῆς δυνάμεως ἕκαστα ἑκάστων, ᾗ ξυμπέπτωκεν ἁρμόττοντα
οἰκείως πως, θερμὰ ψυχροῖς ἢ ξηρὰ πρὸς ὑγρὰ
C   καὶ μαλακὰ πρὸς σκληρά, καὶ πάντα ὁπόσα τῇ
τῶν ἐναντίων κράσει κατὰ τύχην ἐξ ἀνάγκης
συνεκεράσθη, ταύτῃ καὶ κατὰ ταῦτα οὕτω γεγεννηκέναι τόν τε οὐρανὸν ὅλον καὶ πάντα ὁπόσα
κατ' οὐρανόν, καὶ ζῷα αὖ καὶ φυτὰ ξύμπαντα,
ὡρῶν πασῶν ἐκ τούτων γενομένων, οὐ διὰ νοῦν,
φασίν, οὐδὲ διά τινα θεὸν οὐδὲ διὰ τέχνην, ἀλλὰ
ὃ λέγομεν, φύσει καὶ τύχῃ. τέχνην δὲ ὕστερον
ἐκ τούτων ὑστέραν γενομένην, αὐτὴν θνητὴν ἐκ
θνητῶν, ὕστερα γεγεννηκέναι παιδιάς τινας ἀλη-
D   θείας οὐ σφόδρα μετεχούσας, ἀλλὰ εἴδωλ' ἄττα
ξυγγενῆ ἑαυτῶν, οἷ' ἡ γραφικὴ γεννᾷ καὶ μουσικὴ
καὶ ὅσαι ταύταις εἰσὶ συνέριθοι τέχναι. αἳ δέ
τι καὶ σπουδαῖον ἄρα γεννῶσι τῶν τεχνῶν, εἶναι
ταύτας ὁπόσαι τῇ φύσει ἐκοίνωσαν τὴν αὑτῶν
δύναμιν, οἷον αὖ ἰατρικὴ καὶ γεωργικὴ καὶ γυμ-
ναστική. καὶ δὴ καὶ τὴν πολιτικὴν σμικρόν τι
μέρος εἶναί φασι κοινωνοῦσαν[1] φύσει, τέχνῃ δὲ
τὸ πολύ· οὕτω δὲ καὶ τὴν νομοθεσίαν πᾶσαν οὐ
E   φύσει, τέχνῃ δέ, ἧς οὐκ ἀληθεῖς εἶναι τὰς θέσεις.

[1] κοινωνοῦσαν : κοινωνοῦν MSS. (τῆς πολιτικῆς H. Richards,
England).

CLIN. How do you mean?

ATH. I will explain it more clearly. Fire and water and earth and air, they say, all exist by nature and chance, and none of them by art; and by means of these, which are wholly inanimate, the bodies which come next—those, namely, of the earth, sun, moon and stars—have been brought into existence. It is by chance all these elements move, by the interplay of their respective forces, and according as they meet together and combine fittingly,—hot with cold, dry with moist, soft with hard, and all such necessary mixtures as result from the chance combination of these opposites,—in this way and by these means they have brought into being the whole Heaven and all that is in the Heaven, and all animals, too, and plants—after that all the seasons had arisen from these elements; and all this, as they assert, not owing to reason, nor to any god or art, but owing, as we have said, to nature and chance.[1] As a later product of these, art comes later; and it, being mortal itself and of mortal birth, begets later playthings which share but little in truth, being images of a sort akin to the arts themselves—images such as painting begets, and music, and the arts which accompany these. Those arts which really produce something serious are such as share their effect with nature,—like medicine, agriculture, and gymnastic. Politics too, as they say, shares to a small extent in nature, but mostly in art; and in like manner all legislation which is based on untrue assumptions is due, not to nature, but to art.

[1] This is a summary of the doctrines of the Atomists (Leucippus and Democritus) who denied the creative agency of Reason. Similar views were taught, later, by Epicurus and Lucretius.

ΚΛ. Πῶς λέγεις ;

ΑΘ. Θεούς, ὦ μακάριε, εἶναι πρῶτόν φασιν
οὗτοι τέχνῃ, οὐ φύσει ἀλλά τισι νόμοις, καὶ τούτους ἄλλους ἄλλῃ, ὅπῃ ἕκαστοι ἑαυτοῖσι[1] συν-
ωμολόγησαν νομοθετούμενοι· καὶ δὴ καὶ τὰ καλὰ
φύσει μὲν ἄλλα εἶναι, νόμῳ δὲ ἕτερα· τὰ δὲ δὴ
δίκαια οὐδ' εἶναι τὸ παράπαν φύσει, ἀλλ'
ἀμφισβητοῦντας διατελεῖν ἀλλήλοις καὶ μετα-
τιθεμένους ἀεὶ ταῦτα· ἃ δ' ἂν μετάθωνται καὶ
890 ὅταν, τότε κύρια ἕκαστα εἶναι, γιγνόμενα τέχνῃ
καὶ τοῖς νόμοις, ἀλλ' οὐ δή τινι φύσει. ταῦτ'
ἐστίν, ὦ φίλοι, ἅπαντα ἀνδρῶν σοφῶν παρὰ νέοις
ἀνθρώποις, ἰδιωτῶν τε καὶ ποιητῶν, φασκόντων
εἶναι τὸ δικαιότατον ὅ τί τις ἂν νικᾷ βιαζόμενος,
ὅθεν ἀσέβειαί τε ἀνθρώποις ἐμπίπτουσι νέοις,
ὡς οὐκ ὄντων θεῶν οἵους ὁ νόμος προστάττει
διανοεῖσθαι δεῖν, στάσεις τε διὰ ταῦτα, ἑλκόντων
πρὸς τὸν κατὰ φύσιν ὀρθὸν βίον, ὅς ἐστι τῇ
ἀληθείᾳ κρατοῦντα ζῆν τῶν ἄλλων καὶ μὴ
δουλεύοντα ἑτέροισι κατὰ νόμον.

Β ΚΛ. Οἷον διελήλυθας, ὦ ξένε, λόγον καὶ ὅσην
λώβην ἀνθρώπων νέων δημοσίᾳ πόλεσί τε καὶ
ἰδίοις οἴκοις.

ΑΘ. Ἀληθῆ μέντοι λέγεις, ὦ Κλεινία. τί οὖν

---

[1] ἑαυτοῖσι MSS. : ἑκάστοις Zur.

---

[1] A view ascribed to Critias.
[2] Cp. Ar. *Eth. N.* 1094ᵇ 14 ff.
[3] This antithesis between "Nature" (φύσις) and "Convention" (νόμος) was a familiar one in ethical and political
discussion from the time of the Sophists. The supremacy of
"Nature," as an ethical principle, was maintained (it is said)

CLIN. What do you mean?

ATH. The first statement, my dear sir, which these people make about the gods is that they exist by art and not by nature,—by certain legal conventions[1] which differ from place to place, according as each tribe agreed when forming their laws. They assert, moreover, that there is one class of things beautiful by nature, and another class beautiful by convention[2]; while as to things just, they do not exist at all by nature, but men are constantly in dispute about them and continually altering them, and whatever alteration they make at any time is at that time authoritative, though it owes its existence to art and the laws, and not in any way to nature. All these, my friends, are views which young people imbibe from men of science, both prose-writers and poets, who maintain that the height of justice is to succeed by force; whence it comes that the young people are afflicted with a plague of impiety, as though the gods were not such as the law commands us to conceive them; and, because of this, factions also arise, when these teachers attract them towards the life that is right "according to nature," which consists in being master over the rest in reality, instead of being a slave to others according to legal convention.[3]

CLIN. What a horrible statement you have described, Stranger! And what widespread corruption of the young in private families as well as publicly in the States!

ATH. That is indeed true, Clinias. What, then,

by Hippius and Prodicus; that of "Convention," by Protagoras and Gorgias: Plato goes behind both to the higher principle of Reason (νοῦς), cp. *Introd.* p. xiv.

οἴει χρῆναι δρᾶν τὸν νομοθέτην οὕτω τούτων
πάλαι παρεσκευασμένων; ἢ μόνον ἀπειλεῖν
στάντα ἐν τῇ πόλει ξύμπασι τοῖς ἀνθρώποις,
ὡς εἰ μὴ φήσουσιν εἶναι θεοὺς καὶ διανοηθήσονται
δοξάζοντες τοιούτους οἵους φησὶν ὁ νόμος· καὶ
περὶ καλῶν καὶ δικαίων καὶ περὶ ἀπάντων τῶν
C μεγίστων ὁ αὐτὸς λόγος, ὅσα δὴ [1] πρὸς ἀρετὴν
τείνει καὶ κακίαν, ὡς δεῖ ταῦτα οὕτω πράττειν
διανοουμένους ὅπηπερ ἂν ὁ νομοθέτης ὑφηγήσηται
γράφων· ὃς δ' ἂν μὴ παρέχηται ἑαυτὸν τοῖς
νόμοις εὐπειθῆ, τὸν μὲν δεῖν τεθνάναι, τὸν δέ
τινα πληγαῖς καὶ δεσμοῖς, τὸν δὲ ἀτιμίαις, ἄλλους
δὲ πενίαις κολάζεσθαι καὶ φυγαῖς· πειθὼ δὲ τοῖς
ἀνθρώποις, ἅμα τιθέντα αὐτοῖς τοὺς νόμους,
μηδεμίαν ἐθέλειν [2] τοῖς λόγοις προσάπτοντα εἰς
δύναμιν ἡμεροῦν;

D ΚΛ. Μηδαμῶς, ὦ ξένε, ἀλλ' εἴπερ τυγχάνει
γε οὖσα καὶ σμικρὰ πειθώ τις περὶ τὰ τοιαῦτα,
δεῖ μηδαμῇ κάμνειν τόν γε ἄξιον καὶ σμικροῦ
νομοθέτην, ἀλλὰ πᾶσαν, τὸ λεγόμενον, φωνὴν
ἱέντα τῷ παλαιῷ [νόμῳ] [3] ἐπίκουρον γίγνεσθαι
λόγῳ, ὡς εἰσὶ θεοὶ καὶ ὅσα νῦν δὴ διῆλθες σύ,
καὶ δὴ καὶ νόμῳ αὐτῷ βοηθῆσαι καὶ τέχνῃ, ὡς
ἐστὸν φύσει ἢ φύσεως οὐχ ἥττονι,[4] εἴπερ νοῦ
γέ ἐστι γεννήματα κατὰ λόγον ὀρθόν, ὡς [5] σύ
τε λέγειν μοι φαίνει καὶ ἐγώ σοι πιστεύω τὰ νῦν.

ΑΘ. Ὦ προθυμότατε Κλεινία, τί δ'; οὐ χαλεπά

---

[1] δὴ Apelt : δὲ MSS. : τε Zur., vulg.
[2] ἐθέλειν : ἔχειν MSS., edd. (susp. England).
[3] [νόμῳ] bracketed by Winckelmann, England.
[4] ἥττονι Hermann : ἥττον MSS.
[5] ὡς Stallbaum : ὃν MSS.

do you think the lawgiver ought to do, seeing that these people have been armed in this way for a long time past? Should he merely stand up in the city and threaten all the people that unless they affirm that the gods exist and conceive them in their minds to be such as the law maintains;[1] and so likewise with regard to the beautiful and the just and all the greatest things, as many as relate to virtue and vice, that they must regard and perform these in the way prescribed by the lawgiver in his writings; and that whosoever fails to show himself obedient to the laws must either be put to death or else be punished, in one case by stripes and imprisonment, in another by degradation, in others by poverty and exile? But as to persuasion, should the lawgiver, while enacting the people's laws, refuse to blend any persuasion with his statements, and thus tame them so far as possible?

CLIN. Certainly not, Stranger; on the contrary, if persuasion can be applied in such matters in even the smallest degree, no lawgiver who is of the slightest account must ever grow weary, but must (as they say) "leave no stone unturned"[2] to reinforce the ancient saying that gods exist, and all else that you recounted just now; and law itself he must also defend and art, as things which exist by nature or by a cause not inferior to nature, since according to right reason they are the offspring of mind, even as you are now, as I think, asserting; and I agree with you.

ATH. What now, my most ardent Clinias? Are

---

[1] Cp. 634 D, E; 859 B, *al.*
[2] Literally, "utter every voice" (leave nothing unsaid).

Ε τέ ἐστι ξυνακολουθεῖν λόγοις οὕτως εἰς πλήθη
λεγόμενα, μήκη τε αὖ κέκτηται διωλύγια ;

ΚΛ. Τί δαί, ὦ ξένε ; περὶ μέθης μὲν καὶ
μουσικῆς οὕτω μακρὰ λέγοντας ἡμᾶς αὐτοὺς
περιεμείναμεν, περὶ θεῶν δὲ καὶ τῶν τοιούτων
οὐχ ὑπομενοῦμεν ; καὶ μὴν καὶ νομοθεσίᾳ γέ
ἐστί που τῇ μετὰ φρονήσεως μεγίστη βοήθεια,
891 διότι τὰ περὶ νόμους προστάγματα ἐν γράμμασι
τεθέντα, ὡς δώσοντα εἰς πάντα χρόνον ἔλεγχον,
πάντως ἠρεμεῖ, ὥστε οὔτ᾽ εἰ χαλεπὰ κατ᾽ ἀρχὰς
ἀκούειν ἐστὶ φοβητέον, ἅ γ᾽ ἔσται καὶ τῷ
δυσμαθεῖ πολλάκις ἐπανιόντι σκοπεῖν, οὔτε εἰ
μακρά, ὠφέλιμα δέ· διὰ ταῦτα λόγον οὐδαμῇ
ἔχει οὐδὲ ὅσιον ἔμοιγε εἶναι φαίνεται τὸ μὴ οὐ
βοηθεῖν τούτοις τοῖς λόγοις πάντα ἄνδρα κατὰ
δύναμιν.

ΜΕ. Ἄριστα, ὦ ξένε, δοκεῖ μοι λέγειν Κλεινίας.

Β ΑΘ. Καὶ μάλα γε, ὦ Μέγιλλε· ποιητέον τε ὡς
λέγει. καὶ γὰρ εἰ μὴ κατεσπαρμένοι ἦσαν οἱ
τοιοῦτοι λόγοι ἐν τοῖς πᾶσιν ὡς ἔπος εἰπεῖν
ἀνθρώποις, οὐδὲν ἂν ἔδει τῶν ἐπαμυνούντων
λόγων ὡς εἰσὶ θεοί· νῦν δὲ ἀνάγκη. νόμοις οὖν
διαφθειρομένοις τοῖς μεγίστοις ὑπὸ κακῶν ἀνθρώπων τίνα καὶ μᾶλλον προσήκει βοηθεῖν ἢ νομοθέτην ;

ΜΕ. Οὐκ ἔστιν.

ΑΘ. Ἀλλὰ δὴ λέγε μοι πάλιν, Κλεινία, καὶ
C σύ· κοινωνὸν γὰρ δεῖ σε εἶναι τῶν λόγων·

---

[1] In Books I and II.
[2] Cp. 811 D.

not statements thus made to the masses difficult for us to keep up with in argument, and do they not also involve us in arguments portentously long?

CLIN. Well now, Stranger, if we had patience with ourselves when we discoursed at such length on the subjects of drinking and music,[1] shall we not exercise patience in dealing with the gods and similar subjects? Moreover, such a discourse is of the greatest help for intelligent legislation, since legal ordinances when put in writing remain wholly unchanged, as though ready to submit to examination for all time, so that one need have no fear even if they are hard to listen to at first, seeing that even the veriest dullard can come back frequently to examine them, nor yet if they are lengthy, provided that they are beneficial. Consequently, in my opinion, it could not possibly be either reasonable or pious for any man to refrain from lending his aid to such arguments to the best of his power.[2]

MEG. What Clinias says, Stranger, is, I think, most excellent.

ATH. Most certainly it is, Megillus; and we must do as he says. For if the assertions mentioned had not been sown broadcast well-nigh over the whole world of men, there would have been no need of counter-arguments to defend the existence of the gods; but as it is, they are necessary. For when the greatest laws are being destroyed by wicked men, who is more bound to come to their rescue than the lawgiver?

MEG. No one.

ATH. Come now, Clinias, do you also answer me again, for you too must take a hand in the argument) : it appears that the person who makes

319

κινδυνεύει γὰρ ὁ λέγων ταῦτα πῦρ καὶ ὕδωρ
καὶ γῆν καὶ ἀέρα πρῶτα ἡγεῖσθαι τῶν πάντων
εἶναι, καὶ τὴν φύσιν ὀνομάζειν ταῦτα αὐτά,
ψυχὴν δὲ ἐκ τούτων ὕστερον. ἔοικε δὲ οὐ
κινδυνεύειν, ἀλλὰ ὄντως σημαίνειν ταῦτα ἡμῖν
τῷ λόγῳ.

κλ. Πάνυ μὲν οὖν.

αθ. Ἆρ᾽ οὖν πρὸς Διὸς οἷον πηγήν τινα
ἀνοήτου δόξης ἀνευρήκαμεν ἀνθρώπων ὁπόσοι
πώποτε τῶν περὶ φύσεως ἐφήψαντο ζητημάτων ;
σκόπει πάντα λόγον ἐξετάζων· οὐ γὰρ δὴ
D σμικρόν γε τὸ διαφέρον, εἰ φανεῖεν οἱ λόγων
ἁπτόμενοι ἀσεβῶν ἄλλοις τε ἐξάρχοντες μηδὲ
εὖ τοῖς λόγοις ἀλλ᾽ ἐξημαρτημένως χρώμενοι.
δοκεῖ τοίνυν μοι ταῦτα οὕτως ἔχειν.

κλ. Εὖ λέγεις· ἀλλ᾽ ὅπῃ, πειρῶ φράζειν.

αθ. Ἔοικε τοίνυν ἀηθεστέρων ἁπτέον εἶναι
λόγων.

κλ. Οὐκ ὀκνητέον, ὦ ξένε. μανθάνω γὰρ ὡς
νομοθεσίας ἐκτὸς οἰήσει βαίνειν, ἐὰν τῶν τοιούτων
ἁπτώμεθα λόγων. εἰ δὲ ἔστι μηδαμῇ ἑτέρως
συμφωνῆσαι τοῖς νῦν κατὰ νόμον λεγομένοις
E [θεοῖς] [1] ὡς ὀρθῶς ἔχουσιν ἢ ταύτῃ, λεκτέον, ὦ
θαυμάσιε, καὶ ταύτῃ.

αθ. Λέγοιμ᾽ ἄν, ὡς ἔοικεν, ἤδη σχεδὸν οὐκ
εἰωθότα λόγον τινὰ τόνδε. ὃ πρῶτον γενέσεως
καὶ φθορᾶς αἴτιον ἁπάντων, τοῦτο οὐ πρῶτον
ἀλλὰ ὕστερον ἀπεφήναντο εἶναι γεγονὸς οἱ τὴν

---

[1] [θεοῖς] bracketed by Stallbaum, Zur.

these statements holds fire, water, earth and air to be the first of all things, and that it is precisely to these things that he gives the name of "nature," while soul he asserts to be a later product therefrom. Probably, indeed, he does not merely "appear" to do this, but actually makes it clear to us in his account.

CLIN. Certainly.

ATH. Can it be then, in Heaven's name, that now we have discovered, as it were, a very fountain-head of irrational opinion in all the men who have ever yet handled physical investigations? Consider, and examine each statement. For it is a matter of no small importance if it can be shown that those who handle impious arguments, and lead others after them, employ their arguments not only ill, but erroneously. And this seems to me to be the state of affairs.

CLIN. Well said; but try to explain wherein the error lies.

ATH. We shall probably have to handle rather an unusual argument.

CLIN. We must not shrink, Stranger. You think, I perceive, that we shall be traversing alien ground, outside legislation, if we handle such arguments. But if there is no other way in which it is possible for us to speak in concert with the truth, as now legally declared, except this way, then in this way, my good sir, we must speak.

ATH. It appears, then, that I may at once proceed with an argument that is somewhat unusual; it is this. That which is the first cause of becoming and perishing in all things, this is declared by the arguments which have produced the soul of the impious

τῶν ἀσεβῶν ψυχὴν ἀπεργασάμενοι λόγοι, ὃ δὲ
ὕστερον πρότερον, ὅθεν ἡμαρτήκασι περὶ θεῶν
τῆς ὄντως οὐσίας.

892 ΚΛ. Οὔπω μανθάνω.

ΑΘ. Ψυχήν, ὦ ἑταῖρε, ἠγνοηκέναι κινδυνεύουσι
μὲν ὀλίγου ξύμπαντες οἷόν τε ὂν τυγχάνει καὶ
δύναμιν ἣν ἔχει, τῶν τε ἄλλων αὐτῆς πέρι καὶ
δὴ καὶ γενέσεως, ὡς ἐν πρώτοις ἐστὶ σωμάτων
ἔμπροσθεν πάντων γενομένη, καὶ μεταβολῆς τε
αὐτῶν καὶ μετακοσμήσεως ἁπάσης ἄρχει παντὸς
μᾶλλον. εἰ δέ ἐστι ταῦτα οὕτως, ἆρ' οὐκ ἐξ
ἀνάγκης τὰ ψυχῆς συγγενῆ πρότερα ἂν εἴη
γεγονότα τῶν σώματι προσηκόντων, οὔσης γ'
B αὐτῆς[1] πρεσβυτέρας ἢ σώματος ;

ΚΛ. Ἀνάγκη.

ΑΘ. Δόξα δὴ καὶ ἐπιμέλεια καὶ νοῦς καὶ τέχνη
καὶ νόμος σκληρῶν καὶ μαλακῶν καὶ βαρέων καὶ
κούφων πρότερα ἂν εἴη· καὶ δὴ καὶ τὰ μεγάλα
καὶ πρῶτα ἔργα καὶ πράξεις τέχνης ἂν γίγνοιτο,
ὄντα ἐν πρώτοις, τὰ δὲ φύσει καὶ φύσις, ἣν οὐκ
ὀρθῶς ἐπονομάζουσιν αὐτὸ τοῦτο, ὕστερα καὶ
ἀρχόμενα ἂν ἐκ τέχνης εἴη καὶ νοῦ.

C ΚΛ. Πῶς οὐκ ὀρθῶς ;

ΑΘ. Φύσιν βούλονται λέγειν γένεσιν τὴν περὶ
τὰ πρῶτα. εἰ δὲ φανήσεται ψυχὴ πρῶτον, οὐ
πῦρ οὐδὲ ἀήρ, ψυχὴ δ' ἐν πρώτοις γεγενημένη,
σχεδὸν ὀρθότατα λέγοιτ' ἂν εἶναι διαφερόντως
φύσει. ταῦτ' ἔσθ' οὕτως ἔχοντα, ἂν ψυχήν τις
ἐπιδείξῃ πρεσβυτέραν οὖσαν σώματος, ἄλλως δὲ
οὐδαμῶς.

---

[1] γ' αὐτῆς Burnet (after Euseb.): ταύτης MSS.

322

to be not first, but generated later, and that which is the later to be the earlier; and because of this they have fallen into error regarding the real nature of divine existence.

CLIN. I do not yet understand.

ATH. As regards the soul, my comrade, nearly all men appear to be ignorant of its real nature and its potency, and ignorant not only of other facts about it, but of its origin especially,—how that it is one of the first existences, and prior to all bodies, and that it more than anything else is what governs all the changes and modifications of bodies. And if this is really the state of the case, must not things which are akin to soul be necessarily prior in origin to things which belong to body, seeing that soul is older than body?[1]

CLIN. Necessarily.

ATH. Then opinion and reflection and thought and art and law will be prior to things hard and soft and heavy and light; and further, the works and actions that are great and primary will be those of art, while those that are natural, and nature itself,—which they wrongly call by this name—will be secondary, and will derive their origin from art and reason.

CLIN. How are they wrong?

ATH. By "nature" they intend to indicate production of things primary; but if soul shall be shown to have been produced first (not fire or air), but soul first and foremost,—it would most truly be described as a superlatively "natural" existence. Such is the state of the case, provided that one can prove that soul is older than body, but not otherwise.

[1] Cp. *Tim.* 34 D.

κλ. Ἀληθέστατα λέγεις.

ΑΘ. Οὐκοῦν τὰ μετὰ ταῦτα ἐπ᾽ αὐτὸ δὴ τοῦτο
στελλώμεθα;

D κλ. Τί μήν;

ΑΘ. Φυλάττωμεν δὴ παντάπασιν ἀπατηλὸν
λόγον, μή πη πρεσβύτας ἡμᾶς ὄντας νεοπρεπὴς
ὢν παραπείσῃ καὶ διαφυγὼν καταγελάστους
ποιήσῃ, καὶ δόξωμεν μείζονα ἐπιβαλλόμενοι καὶ
τῶν σμικρῶν ἀποτυχεῖν. σκοπεῖτε οὖν· εἰ καθάπερ ποταμὸν ἡμᾶς ἔδει τρεῖς ὄντας διαβαίνειν
ῥέοντα σφόδρα, νεώτατος δ᾽ ἐγὼ τυγχάνων ἡμῶν
καὶ πολλῶν ἔμπειρος ῥευμάτων εἶπον ὅτι πρῶτον
E ἐμὲ χρῆναι πειραθῆναι κατ᾽ ἐμαυτόν, καταλι-
πόντα ὑμᾶς ἐν ἀσφαλεῖ, σκέψασθαι εἰ διαβατός
ἐστι πρεσβυτέροις οὖσι καὶ ὑμῖν, ἢ πῶς ἔχει,
καὶ φανέντος μὲν ταύτῃ καλεῖν ὑμᾶς τότε καὶ
συνδιαβιβάζειν ἐμπειρίᾳ, εἰ δὲ ἄβατος ἦν ὡς
ὑμῖν, ἐν ἐμοὶ τὸν κίνδυνον γεγονέναι, μετρίως ἂν
ἐδόκουν λέγειν. καὶ δὴ καὶ νῦν ὁ μέλλων ἐστὶ
λόγος σφοδρότερος καὶ σχεδὸν ἴσως ἄβατος ὡς
τῇ σφῷν ῥώμῃ· μὴ δὴ σκοτοδινίαν ἴλιγγόν τε
ὑμῖν ἐμποιήσῃ παραφερόμενός τε καὶ ἐρωτῶν
893 ἀήθεις ὄντας ἀποκρίσεων, εἶτ᾽ ἀσχημοσύνην ἀπρέ-
πειάν τε ἐντέκῃ ἀηδῆ, δοκεῖ δή μοι χρῆναι ποιεῖν
οὑτωσὶ τὰ νῦν ἐμέ, ἀνερωτᾶν πρῶτον ἐμαυτὸν
ἀκουόντων ὑμῶν ἐν ἀσφαλεῖ, καὶ μετὰ ταῦτα
ἀποκρίνασθαι πάλιν ἐμέ, καὶ τὸν λόγον ἅπαντα
οὕτω διεξελθεῖν, μέχριπερ ἂν ψυχῆς πέρι δια-
περάνηται καὶ δείξῃ πρότερον ὂν ψυχὴν σώματος.

---

[1] Cp. 886 B.
[2] Cp. 896 B, C.

CLIN. Most true.

ATH. Shall we then, in the next place, address ourselves to the task of proving this?

CLIN. Certainly.

ATH. Let us guard against a wholly deceitful argument, lest haply it seduce us who are old with its specious youthfulness, and then elude us and make us a laughing-stock, and so we get the reputation of missing even little things while aiming at big things. Consider then. Suppose that we three had to cross a river that was in violent flood, and that I, being the youngest of the party and having often had experience of currents, were to suggest that the proper course is for me to make an attempt first by myself—leaving you two in safety—to see whether it is possible for you older men also to cross, or how the matter stands, and then, if the river proved to be clearly fordable, I were to call you, and, by my experience, help you across, while if it proved impassable for such as you, in that case the risk should be wholly mine,—such a suggestion on my part would have sounded reasonable. So too in the present instance; the argument now in front of us is too violent, and probably impassable, for such strength as you possess; so, lest it make you faint and dizzy as it rushes past and poses you with questions you are unused to answering,[1] and thus causes an unpleasing lack of shapeliness and seemliness, I think that I ought now to act in the way described—question myself first, while you remain listening in safety, and then return answer to myself, and in this way proceed through the whole argument until it has discussed in full the subject of soul, and demonstrated that soul is prior to body.[2]

ΚΛ. Ἄριστ᾽, ὦ ξένε, δοκεῖς ἡμῖν εἰρηκέναι,
ποίει τε ὡς λέγεις.

Β ΑΘ. Ἄγε δή, θεὸν εἴποτε παρακλητέον ἡμῖν,
νῦν ἔστω τοῦτο οὕτω γενόμενον· ἐπί γε ἀπόδειξιν
ὡς εἰσὶ τὴν αὐτῶν σπουδῇ πάσῃ παρακεκλήσθων·
ἐχόμενοι δὲ ὥς τινος ἀσφαλοῦς πείσματος ἐπεισ-
βαίνωμεν εἰς τὸν νῦν λόγον. καί μοι ἐλεγχομένῳ
περὶ τὰ τοιαῦτα ἐρωτήσεσι τοιαῖσδε ἀσφαλέστατα
ἀποκρίνεσθαι φαίνεται κατὰ τάδε· Ὦ ξένε,
ὁπόταν φῇ τις, ἆρα ἕστηκε μὲν πάντα, κινεῖται
δὲ οὐδέν; ἢ τούτῳ πᾶν τοὐναντίον; ἢ τὰ μὲν
C αὐτῶν κινεῖται, τὰ δὲ μένει; Τὰ μὲν κινεῖταί
που, φήσω, τὰ δὲ μένει. Μῶν οὖν οὐκ ἐν χώρᾳ
τινὶ τά τε ἑστῶτα ἕστηκε καὶ τὰ κινούμενα
κινεῖται; Πῶς γὰρ οὔ; Καὶ τὰ μέν γε ἐν μιᾷ
ἕδρᾳ που τοῦτο ἂν δρῴη, τὰ δὲ ἐν πλείοσι. Τὰ
τὴν τῶν ἑστώτων ἐν μέσῳ λαμβάνοντα δύναμιν
λέγεις, φήσομεν, ἐν ἑνὶ κινεῖσθαι, καθάπερ ἡ τῶν
ἑστάναι λεγομένων κύκλων στρέφεται περιφορά;
Ναί. μανθάνομεν δέ γε ὡς ἐν ταύτῃ τῇ περιφορᾷ
τὸν μέγιστον καὶ τὸν σμικρότατον κύκλον ἅμα
περιάγουσα ἡ τοιαύτη κίνησις ἀνὰ λόγον ἑαυτὴν
D διανέμει σμικροῖς τε καὶ μείζοσιν, ἐλάττων τε
οὖσα καὶ πλείων κατὰ λόγον. διὸ δὴ τῶν θαυ-
μαστῶν ἁπάντων πηγὴ γέγονεν, ἅμα μεγάλοις
καὶ σμικροῖς κύκλοις βραδυτῆτάς τε καὶ τάχη
ὁμολογούμενα πορεύουσα, ἀδύνατον ὡς ἄν τις
ἐλπίσειε γίγνεσθαι πάθος. Ἀληθέστατα λέγεις.
Τὰ δέ γε κινούμενα ἐν πολλοῖς φαίνει μοι λέγειν
ὅσα φορᾷ κινεῖται μεταβαίνοντα εἰς ἕτερον ἀεὶ

---

[1] Cp. *Soph.* 255 ff. ; *Tim.* 57 ff.

CLIN. Your suggestion, Stranger, we think excellent; so do as you suggest.

ATH. Come then,—if ever we ought to invoke God's aid, now is the time it ought to be done. Let the gods be invoked with all zeal to aid in the demonstration of their own existence. And let us hold fast, so to speak, to a safe cable as we embark on the present discussion. And it is safest, as it seems to me, to adopt the following method of reply when questions such as this are put on these subjects; for instance, when a man asks me—" Do all things stand still, Stranger, and nothing move? Or is the exact opposite the truth? Or do some things move and some remain at rest?" My answer will be, " Some things move, others remain at rest."[1] " Then do not the standing things stand, and the moving things move, in a certain place?" " Of course." " And some will do this in one location, and others in several." " You mean," we will say, " that those which have the quality of being at rest at the centre move in one location, as when the circumference of circles that are said to stand still revolves?" " Yes. And we perceive that motion of this kind, which simultaneously turns in this revolution both the largest circle and the smallest, distributes itself to small and great proportionally, altering in proportion its own quantity; whereby it functions as the source of all such marvels as result from its supplying great and small circles simultaneously with harmonizing rates of slow and fast speeds—a condition of things that one might suppose to be impossible." " Quite true." " And by things moving in several places you seem to me to mean all things that move by locomotion, con-

τόπον, καὶ τοτὲ μέν ἐστιν ὅτε βάσιν ἑνὸς κεκτη-
Ε μένα τινὸς κέντρου, τοτὲ δὲ πλείονα τῷ περι-
κυλινδεῖσθαι. προστυγχάνοντα δ' ἑκάστοτε
ἑκάστοις, τοῖς ἑστῶσι μὲν διασχίζεται, τοῖς δ'
ἄλλοις ἐξ ἐναντίας ἀπαντῶσι καὶ φερομένοις εἰς
ἓν γιγνόμενα μέσα τε καὶ μεταξὺ τῶν τοιούτων
συγκρίνεται. Λέγω γὰρ οὖν ταῦτα οὕτως ἔχοντα
ὡς σὺ λέγεις. Καὶ μὴν καὶ συγκρινόμενα μὲν
αὐξάνεται, διακρινόμενα δὲ φθίνει τότε ὅταν ἡ
καθεστηκυῖα ἑκάστων ἕξις διαμένῃ· μὴ μενούσης
δὲ αὐτῆς δι' ἀμφότερα ἀπόλλυται. γίγνεται δὴ
894 πάντων γένεσις, ἡνίκ' ἂν τί πάθος ᾖ; δῆλον ὡς
ὁπόταν ἀρχὴ λαβοῦσα αὔξην εἰς τὴν δευτέραν
ἔλθῃ μετάβασιν καὶ ἀπὸ ταύτης εἰς τὴν πλησίον,
καὶ μέχρι τριῶν ἐλθοῦσα αἴσθησιν σχῇ τοῖς
αἰσθανομένοις. μεταβάλλον μὲν οὖν οὕτω καὶ
μετακινούμενον γίγνεται πᾶν· ἔστι δὲ ὄντως ὄν,
ὁπόταν μένῃ· μεταβαλὸν δὲ εἰς ἄλλην ἕξιν
διέφθαρται παντελῶς. ἆρ' οὖν κινήσεις πάσας
εἰρήκαμεν ὡς ἐν εἴδεσι λαβεῖν μετ' ἀριθμοῦ, πλήν
Β γε, ὦ φίλοι, δυοῖν;

ΚΛ. Ποίαιν δή;

ΑΘ. Σχεδόν, ὦ 'γαθέ, ἐκείναιν, ὧν ἔνεκα πᾶσα
ἡμῖν ἐστὶν ἡ σκέψις τὰ νῦν.

---

[1] i.e. with a forward *gliding* motion, as opposed to *rolling*
forward (like a car wheel).

[2] i.e. as solid, liquid, or gaseous substance.

[3] This account of the derivation of the sense-world from
the "starting-principle" (ἀρχή) is obscure. It is generally
interpreted as a "geometrical allegory," the stages of de-
velopment being from point to line, from line to surface,
from surface to solid,—this last only being perceptible by
the senses (cp. Ar. *de An.* 404ᵇ 18 ff.).

[4] The 8 kinds of motion here indicated are—(1) circular

tinually passing from one spot to another, and sometimes resting on one axis[1] and sometimes, by revolving, on several axes. And whenever one such object meets another, if the other is at rest, the moving object is split up; but if they collide with others moving to meet them from an opposite direction, they form a combination which is midway between the two." "Yes, I affirm that these things are so, just as you describe." "Further, things increase when combined and decrease when separated in all cases where the regular constitution[2] of each persists; but if this does not remain, then both these conditions cause them to perish. And what is the condition which must occur in everything to bring about generation? Obviously whenever a starting-principle receiving increase comes to the second change, and from this to the next, and on coming to the third admits of perception by percipients.[3] Everything comes into being by this process of change and alteration; and a thing is really existent whenever it remains fixed, but when it changes into another constitution it is utterly destroyed." Have we now, my friends, mentioned all the forms of motion, capable of numerical classification,[4] save only two?

CLIN. What two?

ATH. Those, my good sir, for the sake of which, one may say, the whole of our present enquiry was undertaken.

motion round a fixed centre; (2) locomotion (gliding or rolling); (3) combination; (4) separation; (5) increase; (6) decrease; (7) becoming; (8) perishing. The remaining two kinds (as described below) are—(9) other-affecting motion (or secondary causation); and (10) self-and-other-affecting motion (or primary causation).

PLATO

ΚΛ. Λέγε σαφέστερον.

ΑΘ. Ψυχῆς ἦν ἕνεκά που;

ΚΛ. Πάνυ μὲν οὖν.

ΑΘ. Ἔστω τοίνυν ἡ μὲν ἕτερα δυναμένη κινεῖν κίνησις, ἑαυτὴν δὲ ἀδυνατοῦσα, ἀεὶ μία τις, ἡ δὲ ἑαυτήν τ᾽ ἀεὶ καὶ ἕτερα δυναμένη κατά τε συγκρίσεις ἔν τε διακρίσεσιν αὔξαις τε καὶ τῷ ἐναντίῳ καὶ γενέσεσι καὶ φθοραῖς ἄλλη μία τις
C αὖ τῶν πασῶν κινήσεων.

ΚΛ. Ἔστω γὰρ οὖν.

ΑΘ. Οὐκοῦν τὴν μὲν ἕτερον ἀεὶ κινοῦσαν καὶ μεταβαλλομένην ὑφ᾽ ἑτέρου θήσομεν ἐνάτην αὖ, τὴν δὲ ἑαυτὴν κινοῦσαν καὶ ἕτερα, ἐναρμόττουσαν πᾶσι μὲν ποιήμασι, πᾶσι δὲ παθήμασι, καλουμένην τε[1] ὄντως τῶν ὄντων πάντων μεταβολὴν καὶ κίνησιν, ταύτην δὴ[2] δεκάτην σχεδὸν ἐροῦμεν.

D ΚΛ. Παντάπασι μὲν οὖν.

ΑΘ. Τῶν δὴ δέκα μάλιστα ἡμῖν κινήσεων τίν᾽ ἂν προκρίναιμεν ὀρθότατα πασῶν ἐρρωμενεστάτην τε εἶναι καὶ πρακτικὴν διαφερόντως;

ΚΛ. Μυρίῳ ἀνάγκη που φάναι διαφέρειν τὴν αὐτὴν αὑτὴν δυναμένην κινεῖν, τὰς δὲ ἄλλας πάσας ὑστέρας.

ΑΘ. Εὖ λέγεις. ἆρ᾽ οὖν ἡμῖν τῶν νῦν οὐκ ὀρθῶς ῥηθέντων μεταθετέον ἓν ἢ καὶ δύο;

ΚΛ. Ποῖα φῄς;

ΑΘ. Τὸ τῆς δεκάτης ῥηθὲν σχεδὸν οὐκ ὀρθῶς εἴρηται.

ΚΛ. Πῇ;

ΑΘ. Πρῶτον γενέσει τ᾽ ἐστὶ καὶ ῥώμῃ κατὰ

---

[1] τε England : δὲ MSS.
[2] δὴ : δὲ MSS. (bracketed by England)

CLIN. Explain more clearly.

ATH. It was undertaken, was it not, for the sake of soul?

CLIN. Certainly.

ATH. As one of the two let us count that motion which is always able to move other things, but unable to move itself; and that motion which always is able to move both itself and other things,—by way of combination and separation, of increase and decrease, of generation and corruption,—let us count as another separate unit in the total number of motions.

CLIN. Be it so.

ATH. Thus we shall reckon as ninth on the list that motion which always moves another object and is moved by another; while that motion which moves both itself and another, and which is harmoniously adapted to all forms of action and passion, and is termed the real change and motion of all that really exists,—it, I presume, we shall call the tenth.

CLIN. Most certainly.

ATH. Of our total of ten motions, which shall we most correctly adjudge to be the most powerful of all and excelling in effectiveness?

CLIN. We are bound to affirm that the motion which is able to move itself excels infinitely, and that all the rest come after it.

ATH. Well said. Must we, then, alter one or two of the wrong statements we have now made?

CLIN. Which do you mean?

ATH. Our statement about the tenth seems wrong.

CLIN. How?

ATH. Logically it is first in point of origin and

λόγον· τὸ δὲ μετὰ τοῦτο ἔχομεν τούτου δεύτερον,
Ε ἄρτι ῥηθὲν ἀτόπως ἔνατον.

ΚΛ. Πῶς λέγεις ;

ΑΘ. Ὧδε. ὅταν ἕτερον ἄλλο ἡμῖν μεταβάλῃ
καὶ τοῦτο ἄλλο ἕτερον ἀεί, τῶν τοιούτων ἆρα
ἔσται ποτέ τι πρῶτον μεταβάλλον ; καὶ πῶς, ὅ
γ' ἂν¹ ὑπ' ἄλλου κινῆται, τοῦτ' ἔσται ποτὲ τῶν
ἀλλοιούντων πρῶτον ; ἀδύνατον γάρ. ἀλλ' ὅταν
ἄρα αὐτὸ αὑτὸ κινῆσαν ἕτερον ἀλλοιώσῃ, τὸ δ'
ἕτερον ἄλλο, καὶ οὕτω δὴ χίλια ἐπὶ μυρίοις γίγ-
895 νηται τὰ κινηθέντα, μῶν ἀρχή τις αὐτῶν ἔσται
τῆς κινήσεως ἁπάσης ἄλλη πλὴν ἡ τῆς αὐτῆς
αὑτὴν κινησάσης μεταβολή ;

ΚΛ. Κάλλιστα εἶπες, συγχωρητέα τε τούτοις.

ΑΘ. Ἔτι δὴ καὶ τῇδε εἴπωμεν, καὶ ἀποκρινώμεθα πάλιν ἡμῖν αὐτοῖσιν. εἰ σταίη πως τὰ
πάντα ὁμοῦ γενόμενα, καθάπερ οἱ πλεῖστοι τῶν
τοιούτων τολμῶσι λέγειν, τίν' ἄρα ἐν αὐτοῖς
ἀνάγκη πρώτην κίνησιν γενέσθαι τῶν εἰρημένων ;
τὴν² <αὑτὴν>³ αὑτὴν δή που κινοῦσαν· ὑπ'
ἄλλου γὰρ οὐ μήποτε ἔμπροσθεν μεταπέσῃ,
Β μηδεμιᾶς γε ἐν αὐτοῖς οὔσης ἔμπροσθεν μεταπτώσεως. ἀρχὴν ἄρα κινήσεων πασῶν καὶ
πρώτην ἔν τε ἑστῶσι γενομένην καὶ ἐν κινουμένοις
οὖσαν τὴν αὐτὴν κινοῦσαν φήσομεν ἀναγκαίως
εἶναι πρεσβυτάτην καὶ κρατίστην μεταβολὴν
πασῶν, τὴν δὲ ἀλλοιουμένην ὑφ' ἑτέρου, κινοῦσάν
τε⁴ ἕτερα δευτέραν.

¹ ὅ γ' ἂν Apelt, England : ὅταν MSS.
² τὴν . . . μεταπτώσεως is assigned to Clin. by Zur. and
most edd. I follow Hermann and Burnet.
³ <αὑτὴν> added by Euseb., Burnet.
⁴ τε Ast : δὲ MSS.

power ; and the next one is second to it, although we absurdly called it ninth a moment ago.

CLIN. What do you mean ?

ATH. This : when we find one thing changing another, and this in turn another, and so on,—of these things shall we ever find one that is the prime cause of change ? How will a thing that is moved by another ever be itself the first of the things that cause change ? It is impossible. But when a thing that has moved itself changes another thing, and that other a third, and the motion thus spreads progressively through thousands upon thousands of things, will the primary source of all their motions be anything else than the movement of that which has moved itself ?

CLIN. Excellently put, and we must assent to your argument.

ATH. Further, let us question and answer ourselves thus :—Supposing that the Whole of things were to unite and stand still,—as most of these thinkers[1] venture to maintain,—which of the motions mentioned would necessarily arise in it first ? That motion, of course, which is self-moving ; for it will never be shifted beforehand by another thing, since no shifting force exists in things beforehand. Therefore we shall assert that inasmuch as the self-moving motion is the starting-point of all motions and the first to arise in things at rest and to exist in things in motion, it is of necessity the most ancient and potent change of all, while the motion which is altered by another thing and itself moves others comes second.

---

[1] *E.g.* Anaxagoras, who taught, originally, "all things were together (ὁμοῦ) ;" and the Eleatic School (Parmenides, etc.) asserted that the Real World (τὸ ὄν) is One and motionless ; cp, *Theaet.* 180 E.

ΚΛ.   Ἀληθέστατα λέγεις.

ΑΘ.   Ὁπότε δὴ τοίνυν ἐνταῦθά ἐσμεν τοῦ λόγου,
C τόδε ἀποκρινώμεθα.

ΚΛ.   Τὸ ποῖον ;

ΑΘ.   Ἐὰν ἴδωμέν που ταύτην γενομένην ἔν τῳ [1]
γηΐνῳ ἢ ἐνύδρῳ ἢ πυροειδεῖ, κεχωρισμένῳ ἢ καὶ
ξυμμιγεῖ, τί ποτε φήσομεν ἐν τῷ τοιούτῳ πάθος
εἶναι ;

ΚΛ.   Μῶν ἄρα με ἐρωτᾷς εἰ ζῆν αὐτὸ προσ-
ερούμεν ὅταν αὐτὸ αὑτὸ κινῇ ;

ΑΘ.   Ναί.

ΚΛ.   Ζῆν· πῶς γὰρ οὔ ;

ΑΘ.   Τί δαί ; ὁπόταν ψυχὴν ἔν τισιν ὁρῶμεν,
μῶν ἄλλο ἢ ταὐτὸν τούτῳ ; ζῆν ὁμολογητέον ;

ΚΛ.   Οὐκ ἄλλο.

D ΑΘ.   Ἔχε δὴ πρὸς Διός· ἆρ’ οὐκ ἂν ἐθέλοις
περὶ ἕκαστον τρία νοεῖν ;

ΚΛ.   Πῶς λέγεις ;

ΑΘ.   Ἓν μὲν τὴν οὐσίαν, ἓν δὲ τῆς οὐσίας τὸν
λόγον, ἓν δὲ τὸ ὄνομα. καὶ δὴ καὶ ἐρωτήσεις εἶναι
περὶ τὸ ὂν ἅπαν δύο.

ΚΛ.   Πῶς δύο ;

ΑΘ.   Τοτὲ μὲν ἡμῶν ἕκαστον τοὔνομα προτεινόμενον αὐτὸ τὸν λόγον ἀπαιτεῖν, τοτὲ δὲ τὸν
λόγον αὐτὸν προτεινόμενον ἐρωτᾶν αὖ τοὔνομα.

ΚΛ.[2]   Ἆρά γε τὸ τοιόνδε αὖ βουλόμεθα νῦν
λέγειν ;

ΑΘ.   Τὸ ποῖον ;

---

[1] τῳ England : τῷ MSS.
[2] I follow Schneider and England in the assignment of the
next eight lines (Zur., al., give only Τὸ ποῖον ; and Ναί to
Clin.).

CLIN. Most true.

ATH. Now that we have come to this point in our discourse, here is a question we may answer.

CLIN. What is it?

ATH. If we should see that this motion had arisen in a thing of earth or water or fire, whether separate or in combination, what condition should we say exists in such a thing?

CLIN. What you ask me is, whether we are to speak of a thing as "alive" when it moves itself?

ATH. Yes.

CLIN. It is alive, to be sure.

ATH. Well then, when we see soul in things, must we not equally agree that they are alive?

CLIN. We must.

ATH. Now stop a moment, in Heaven's name! Would you not desire to observe three points about every object?

CLIN. What do you mean?

ATH. One point is the substance, one the definition of the substance, and one the name;[1] and, moreover, about everything that exists there are two questions to be asked.

CLIN. How two?

ATH. At one time each of us, propounding the name by itself, demands the definition; at another, propounding the definition by itself, he demands the name.

CLIN. Is it something of this kind we mean now to convey?

ATH. Of what kind?

---

[1] Cp *Epist.* 7, 342 A, B.

Ε ΚΛ. Ἔστι που δίχα διαιρούμενον ἐν ἄλλοις τε
καὶ ἐν ἀριθμῷ. τούτῳ δὴ τῷ κατ᾽ ἀριθμὸν ὄνομα
μὲν ἄρτιον, λόγος δὲ ἀριθμὸς διαιρούμενος εἰς
ἴσα δύο μέρη.

ΑΘ. Ναί. τὸ τοιοῦτον φράζω. μῶν οὖν οὐ
ταὐτὸν ἑκατέρως προσαγορεύομεν, ἄν τε τὸν λόγον
ἐρωτώμενοι τοὔνομα ἀποδιδῶμεν, ἄν τε τοὔνομα
τὸν λόγον, ἄρτιον ὀνόματι καὶ λόγῳ, δίχα διαιρούμενον ἀριθμόν, προσαγορεύοντες ταὐτὸν ὄν;

ΚΛ. Παντάπασι μὲν οὖν.

ΑΘ. Ὧι δὴ ψυχὴ τοὔνομα, τίς τούτου λόγος;
896 ἔχομεν ἄλλον πλὴν τὸν νῦν δὴ ῥηθέντα, τὴν δυναμένην αὐτὴν αὑτὴν κινεῖν κίνησιν;

ΚΛ. Τὸ ἑαυτὸ κινεῖν φῂς λόγον ἔχειν τὴν
αὐτὴν οὐσίαν ἥνπερ τοὔνομα ὃ δὴ πάντες ψυχὴν
προσαγορεύομεν;

ΑΘ. Φημί γε. εἰ δ᾽ ἐστὶ τοῦτο οὕτως ἔχον, ἆρα
ἔτι ποθοῦμεν μὴ ἱκανῶς δεδεῖχθαι ψυχὴν ταὐτὸν
ὂν καὶ τὴν πρώτην γένεσιν καὶ κίνησιν τῶν τε
ὄντων καὶ γεγονότων καὶ ἐσομένων καὶ πάντων αὖ
Β τῶν ἐναντίων τούτοις, ἐπειδή γε ἀνεφάνη μεταβολῆς τε καὶ κινήσεως ἁπάσης αἰτία ἅπασιν;

ΚΛ. Οὔκ, ἀλλὰ ἱκανώτατα δέδεικται ψυχὴ
τῶν πάντων πρεσβυτάτη, γενομένη γε ἀρχὴ
κινήσεως.

ΑΘ. Ἆρ᾽ οὖν οὐχ ἡ δι᾽ ἕτερ... ἐν ἄλλῳ γιγνομένη κίνησις, αὐτὸ δὲ ἐν αὑτῷ μηδέποτε παρέχουσ...
κινεῖσθαι μηδέν, δευτέρα τε καὶ ὁπόσων ἀριθμῶν

CLIN. We have instances of a thing divisible into two halves, both in arithmetic and elsewhere; in arithmetic the name of this is "the even," and the definition is "a number divisible into two equal parts."

ATH. Yes, that is what I mean. So in either case it is the same object, is it not, which we describe, whether, when asked for the definition, we reply by giving the name, or, when asked for the name, we give the definition,—describing one and the same object by the name "even," and by the definition "a number divisible into two halves"?

CLIN. Most certainly.

ATH. What is the definition of that object which has for its name "soul"? Can we give it any other definition than that stated just now—"the motion able to move itself"?

CLIN. Do you assert that "self-movement" is the definition of that very same substance which has "soul" as the name we universally apply to it?

ATH. That is what I assert. And if this be really so, do we still complain that it has not been sufficiently proved that soul is identical with the prime origin and motion of what is, has been, and shall be, and of all that is opposite to these, seeing that it has been plainly shown to be the cause of all change and motion in all things?

CLIN. We make no such complaint; on the contrary, it has been proved most sufficiently that soul is of all things the oldest, since it is the first principle of motion.

ATH. Then is not that motion which, when it arises in one object, is caused by another, and which never supplies self-motion to anything, second in

βούλοιτο ἄν τις ἀριθμεῖν αὐτὴν πολλοστήν,
τοσούτων, σώματος οὖσα ὄντως ἀψύχου μεταβολή ;

ΚΛ.   Ὀρθῶς.

ΑΘ.   Ὀρθῶς ἄρα καὶ κυρίως ἀληθέστατά τε καὶ
C τελεώτατα εἰρηκότες ἂν εἶμεν ψυχὴν μὲν προτέραν
γεγονέναι σώματος ἡμῖν, σῶμα δὲ δεύτερόν τε καὶ
ὕστερον ψυχῆς ἀρχούσης ἀρχόμενον κατὰ φύσιν.

ΚΛ.   Ἀληθέστατα μὲν οὖν.

ΑΘ.   Μεμνήμεθά γε μὴν ὁμολογήσαντες ἐν τοῖς
πρόσθεν ὡς, εἰ ψυχὴ φανείη πρεσβυτέρα σώματος
οὖσα, καὶ τὰ ψυχῆς τῶν τοῦ σώματος ἔσοιτο πρεσ-
βύτερα.

ΚΛ.   Πάνυ μὲν οὖν.

D   ΑΘ.   Τρόποι δὲ καὶ ἤθη καὶ βουλήσεις καὶ
λογισμοὶ καὶ δόξαι ἀληθεῖς ἐπιμέλειαί τε καὶ
μνῆμαι πρότερα μήκους σωμάτων καὶ πλάτους
καὶ βάθους καὶ ῥώμης εἴη γεγονότα ἄν, εἴπερ
καὶ ψυχὴ σώματος.

ΚΛ.   Ἀνάγκη.

ΑΘ.   Ἆρ᾿ οὖν τὸ μετὰ τοῦτο ὁμολογεῖν ἀναγκαῖον τῶν τε ἀγαθῶν αἰτίαν εἶναι ψυχὴν καὶ τῶν
κακῶν καὶ καλῶν καὶ αἰσχρῶν δικαίων τε καὶ
ἀδίκων καὶ πάντων τῶν ἐναντίων, εἴπερ τῶν
πάντων γε αὐτὴν θήσομεν αἰτίαν ;

ΚΛ.   Πῶς γὰρ οὔ ;

ΑΘ.   Ψυχὴν δὴ διοικοῦσαν καὶ ἐνοικοῦσαν ἐν
E ἅπασι τοῖς πάντη κινουμένοις μῶν οὐ καὶ τὸν
οὐρανὸν ἀνάγκη διοικεῖν φάναι ;

ΚΛ.   Τί μήν ;

ΑΘ.   Μίαν ἢ πλείους ; Πλείους· ἐγὼ ὑπὲρ
σφῷν ἀποκρινοῦμαι. δυοῖν μέν γέ που ἔλαττον

338

order—or indeed as far down the list as one cares to put it,—it being the change of a really soulless body?

CLIN. True.

ATH. Truly and finally, then, it would be a most veracious and complete statement to say that we find soul to be prior to body, and body secondary and posterior, soul governing and body being governed according to the ordinance of nature.

CLIN. Yes, most veracious.

ATH. We recollect, of course, that we previously agreed [1] that if soul could be shown to be older than body, then the things of soul also will be older than those of body.

CLIN. Certainly we do.

ATH. Moods and dispositions and wishes and calculations and true opinions and considerations and memories will be prior to bodily length, breadth, depth and strength, if soul is prior to body.

CLIN. Necessarily.

ATH. Must we then necessarily agree, in the next place, that soul is the cause of things good and bad, fair and foul, just and unjust, and all the opposites, if we are to assume it to be the cause of all things?

CLIN. Of course we must.

ATH. And as soul thus controls and indwells in all things everywhere that are moved, must we not necessarily affirm that it controls Heaven also?

CLIN. Yes.

ATH. One soul, is it, or several? I will answer for you—"several." Anyhow, let us assume not

---

[1] 892 A, B.

μηδὲν τιθῶμεν, τῆς τε εὐεργέτιδος καὶ τῆς τἀναντία δυναμένης ἐξεργάζεσθαι.

ΚΛ. Σφόδρα ὀρθῶς εἴρηκας.

ΑΘ. Εἶεν. ἄγει μὲν δὴ ψυχὴ πάντα τὰ κατ᾽
οὐρανὸν καὶ γῆν καὶ θάλατταν ταῖς αὑτῆς κινή-
897 σεσιν, αἷς ὀνόματά ἐστι βούλεσθαι, σκοπεῖσθαι,
ἐπιμελεῖσθαι, βουλεύεσθαι, δοξάζειν ὀρθῶς, ἐψευσ-
μένως, χαίρουσαν, λυπουμένην, θαρροῦσαν, φο-
βουμένην, μισοῦσαν, στέργουσαν καὶ πάσαις ὅσαι
τούτων ξυγγενεῖς ἢ πρωτουργοὶ κινήσεις τὰς δευ-
τερουργοὺς αὖ παραλαμβάνουσαι κινήσεις σωμάτων ἄγουσι πάντα εἰς αὔξησιν καὶ φθίσιν καὶ
διάκρισιν καὶ σύγκρισιν· καὶ τούτοις ἑπομένας
θερμότητας, ψύξεις, βαρύτητας, κουφότητας,
Β σκληρὸν καὶ μαλακόν, λευκὸν καὶ μέλαν, αὐστηρὸν
καὶ γλυκὺ καὶ πᾶσιν οἷς ψυχὴ χρωμένη, νοῦν μὲν
προσλαβοῦσα ἀεί, οἷον ὀρθῶς θεός,[1] ὀρθὰ καὶ
εὐδαίμονα παιδαγωγεῖ πάντα, ἀνοίᾳ δὲ ξυγγενο-
μένη πάντα αὖ τἀναντία τούτοις ἀπεργάζεται.
τιθῶμεν ταῦτα οὕτως ἔχειν, ἢ ἔτι διστάζομεν εἰ
ἑτέρως πως ἔχει ;

ΚΛ. Οὐδαμῶς.

ΑΘ. Πότερον οὖν δὴ ψυχῆς γένος ἐγκρατὲς
οὐρανοῦ καὶ γῆς καὶ πάσης τῆς περιόδου γεγονέναι φῶμεν ; τὸ φρόνιμον καὶ ἀρετῆς πλῆρες, ἢ τὸ
C μηδέτερα κεκτημένον ; βούλεσθε οὖν πρὸς ταῦτα
ὧδε ἀποκρινώμεθα ;

ΚΛ. Πῶς ;

ΑΘ. Εἰ μέν, ὦ θαυμάσιε, φῶμεν, ἡ ξύμπασα

---

[1] οἷον ὀρθῶς θεός: θεὸν (al. θεῖον) ὀρθῶς θεοῖς (marg. θεὸς οὖσα)
MSS. : θεὸν θεὸς οὖσα Zur. (θεῖον ὀρθῶς θέουσα Winck., Herm. :
θεῖον ὀρθῶς θεὸς ὥς Stallb.).

less than two—the beneficent soul and that which
is capable of effecting results of the opposite kind.

CLIN. You are perfectly right.

ATH. Very well, then. Soul drives all things in
Heaven and earth and sea by its own motions,
of which the names are wish, reflection, forethought,
counsel, opinion true and false, joy, grief, confidence,
fear, hate, love, and all the motions that are akin to
these or are prime-working motions; these, when
they take over the secondary motions of bodies,
drive them all to increase and decrease and separation and combination,[1] and, supervening on these,
to heat and cold, heaviness and lightness, hardness
and softness, whiteness and blackness, bitterness
and sweetness, and all those qualities which soul
employs, both when it governs all things rightly and
happily as a true goddess, in conjunction with reason,
and when, in converse with unreason, it produces
results which are in all respects the opposite. Shall
we postulate that this is so, or do we still suspect
that it may possibly be otherwise?

CLIN. By no means.

ATH. Which kind of soul, then, shall we say is in
control of Heaven and earth and the whole circle?
That which is wise and full of goodness, or that which
has neither quality? To this shall we make reply as
follows?

CLIN. How?

ATH. If, my good sir, we are to assert that the

---

[1] Cp. 894 B, C.

οὐρανοῦ ὁδὸς ἅμα καὶ φορὰ καὶ τῶν ἐν αὐτῷ ὄντων
ἁπάντων νοῦ κινήσει καὶ περιφορᾷ καὶ λογισμοῖς
ὁμοίαν φύσιν ἔχει καὶ ξυγγενῶς ἔρχεται, δῆλον
ὡς τὴν ἀρίστην ψυχὴν φατέον ἐπιμελεῖσθαι τοῦ
κόσμου παντὸς καὶ ἄγειν αὐτὸν τὴν τοιαύτην ὁδὸν
ἐκείνην.

κλ. Ὀρθῶς.

D   αθ. Εἰ δὲ μανικῶς τε καὶ ἀτάκτως ἔρχεται, τὴν
κακήν.

κλ. Καὶ ταῦτα ὀρθῶς.

αθ. Τίνα οὖν δὴ νοῦ κίνησις φύσιν ἔχει; τοῦτο
ἤδη χαλεπόν, ὦ φίλοι, ἐρώτημα ἀποκρινόμενον
εἰπεῖν ἐμφρόνως. διὸ δὴ καὶ ἐμὲ τῆς ἀποκρίσεως
ὑμῖν δίκαιον τὰ νῦν προσλαμβάνειν.

κλ. Εὖ λέγεις.

αθ. Μὴ τοίνυν ἐξ ἐναντίας οἷον εἰς ἥλιον
ἀποβλέποντες, νύκτα ἐν μεσημβρίᾳ ἐπαγόμενοι,
ποιησώμεθα τὴν ἀπόκρισιν, ὡς νοῦν ποτὲ θνητοῖς
ὄμμασιν ὀψόμενοί τε καὶ γνωσόμενοι ἱκανῶς·
E πρὸς δὲ εἰκόνα τοῦ ἐρωτωμένου βλέποντας ἀσφα-
λέστερον ὁρᾶν.

κλ. Πῶς λέγεις;

αθ. Ἧι προσέοικε κινήσει νοῦς τῶν δέκα
ἐκείνων κινήσεων τὴν εἰκόνα λάβωμεν· ἣν συνανα-
μνησθεὶς ὑμῖν ἐγὼ κοινῇ τὴν ἀπόκρισιν ποιήσομαι.

κλ. Κάλλιστα ἂν λέγοις.

αθ. Μεμνήμεθα τοίνυν τό γε τοσοῦτον τῶν
τότε ἔτι, ὅτι τῶν πάντων τὰ μὲν κινεῖσθαι, τὰ δὲ
μένειν ἔθεμεν;

---

[1] i.e. the uniform revolution of a sphere in the same spot
and on its own axis: cp. 898 A; Tim. 34 A, B; 90 C, D.

whole course and motion of Heaven and of all it contains have a motion like to the motion and revolution and reckonings of reason,[1] and proceed in a kindred manner, then clearly we must assert that the best soul regulates the whole cosmos and drives it on its course, which is of the kind described.

CLIN. You are right.

ATH. But the bad soul, if it proceeds in a mad and disorderly way.

CLIN. That also is right.

ATH. Then what is the nature of the motion of reason? Here, my friends, we come to a question that is difficult to answer wisely; consequently, it is fitting that you should now call me in to assist you with the answer.

CLIN. Very good.

ATH. In making our answer let us not bring on night, as it were, at midday, by looking right in the eye of the sun,[2] as though with mortal eyes we could ever behold reason and know it fully; the safer way to behold the object with which our question is concerned is by looking at an image of it.

CLIN. How do you mean?

ATH. Let us take as an image that one of the ten motions which reason resembles; reminding ourselves of which [3] I, along with you, will make answer.

CLIN. You will probably speak admirably.

ATH. Do we still recollect thus much about the things then described, that we assumed that, of the total, some were in motion, others at rest?

[2] Cp. *Rep.* 516 A ff.
[3] Cp. 893 B ff.; the motion to which reason is likened is the first of the ten.

ΚΛ. Ναί.

ΑΘ. Τῶν δ᾽ αὖ κινουμένων τὰ μὲν ἐν ἑνὶ τόπῳ
898 κινεῖσθαι, τὰ δ᾽ ἐν πλείοσι φερόμενα.

ΚΛ. Ἔστι ταῦτα.

ΑΘ. Τούτοιν δὴ τοῖν κινήσεοιν τὴν ἐν ἑνὶ φερομένην ἀεὶ περί γέ τι μέσον ἀνάγκη [1] κινεῖσθαι τῶν
ἐντόρνων οὖσαν μίμημά τι κύκλων, εἶναί τε αὐτὴν
τῇ τοῦ νοῦ περιόδῳ πάντως ὡς δυνατὸν οἰκειοτάτην
τε καὶ ὁμοίαν.

ΚΛ. Πῶς λέγεις ;

ΑΘ. Τὸ κατὰ ταὐτὰ δή που καὶ ὡσαύτως καὶ
ἐν τῷ αὐτῷ καὶ περὶ τὰ αὐτὰ καὶ πρὸς τὰ αὐτὰ
καὶ <καθ᾽> [2] ἕνα λόγον καὶ τάξιν μίαν ἄμφω
κινεῖσθαι λέγοντες νοῦν τήν τε ἐν ἑνὶ φερομένην
Β κίνησιν, σφαίρας ἐντόρνου ἀπεικασμένα φοραῖς,
οὐκ ἄν ποτε φανεῖμεν φαῦλοι δημιουργοὶ λόγῳ
καλῶν εἰκόνων.

ΚΛ. Ὀρθότατα λέγεις.

ΑΘ. Οὐκοῦν αὖ ἥ γε μηδέποτε ὡσαύτως μηδὲ
κατὰ τὰ αὐτὰ μηδὲ ἐν ταὐτῷ μηδὲ περὶ ταὐτὰ
μηδὲ πρὸς ταὐτὰ μηδ᾽ ἐν ἑνὶ φερομένη μηδ᾽ ἐν
C κόσμῳ μηδ᾽ ἐν τάξει μηδὲ ἔν τινι λόγῳ κίνησις
ἀνοίας ἂν ἁπάσης εἴη ξυγγενής ;

ΚΛ. Εἴη γὰρ ἂν ἀληθέστατα.

ΑΘ. Νῦν δὴ χαλεπὸν οὐδὲν ἔτι διαρρήδην
εἰπεῖν ὡς, ἐπειδὴ ψυχὴ μέν ἐστιν ἡ περιάγουσα
ἡμῖν πάντα, τήνδε [3] οὐρανοῦ περιφορὰν ἐξ ἀνάγκης περιάγειν φατέον ἐπιμελουμένην καὶ κοσμοῦσαν ἤτοι τὴν ἀρίστην ψυχὴν ἢ τὴν ἐναντίαν.

---

[1] ἀνάγκη : ἀνάγκῃ MSS., edd.
[2] <καθ᾽> added by Ast.
[3] τήνδε Apelt : τὴν δὲ MSS., edd.

CLIN. Yes.

ATH. And further, that, of those in motion, some move in one place, others move in several places?

CLIN. That is so.

ATH. And that, of these two motions, the motion which moves in one place must necessarily move always round some centre, being a copy of the turned wheels; and that this has the nearest possible kinship and similarity to the revolution of reason?[1]

CLIN. How do you mean?

ATH. If we described them both as moving regularly and uniformly in the same spot, round the same things and in relation to the same things, according to one rule and system—reason, namely, and the motion that spins in one place (likened to the spinning of a turned globe),—we should never be in danger of being deemed unskilful in the construction of fair images by speech.

CLIN. Most true.

ATH. On the other hand, will not the motion that is never uniform or regular or in the same place or around or in relation to the same things, not moving in one spot nor in any order or system or rule—will not this motion be akin to absolute unreason?

CLIN. It will, in very truth.

ATH. So now there is no longer any difficulty in stating expressly that, inasmuch as soul is what we find driving everything round, we must affirm that this circumference of Heaven is of necessity driven round under the care and ordering of either the best soul or its opposite.

[1] Cp. *Tim.* 33 B, 34 A ; *Rep.* 436 B ff.

ΚΛ. Ὦ ξένε, ἀλλὰ ἔκ γε τῶν νῦν εἰρημένων οὐδ᾽ ὅσιον ἄλλως λέγειν ἢ πᾶσαν ἀρετὴν ἔχουσαν ψυχὴν μίαν ἢ πλείους περιάγειν αὐτά.

ΑΘ. Κάλλιστα, ὦ Κλεινία, ὑπήκουσας τοῖς D λόγοις.   τόδε δὲ προσυπάκουσον ἔτι.

ΚΛ. Τὸ ποῖον ;

ΑΘ. Ἥλιον καὶ σελήνην καὶ τὰ ἄλλα ἄστρα, εἴπερ ψυχὴ περιάγει πάντα, ἆρ᾽ οὐ καὶ ἐν ἕκαστον ;

ΚΛ. Τί μήν ;

ΑΘ. Περὶ ἑνὸς δὴ ποιησώμεθα λόγους, οἳ καὶ ἐπὶ πάντα ἡμῖν ἄστρα ἁρμόττοντες φανοῦνται.

ΚΛ. Τίνος ;

ΑΘ. Ἡλίου πᾶς ἄνθρωπος σῶμα μὲν ὁρᾷ, ψυχὴν δὲ οὐδείς· οὐδὲ γὰρ ἄλλου σώματος οὐδενὸς οὔτε ζῶντος οὔτε ἀποθνήσκοντος τῶν ζῴων, ἀλλὰ ἐλπὶς πολλὴ τὸ παράπαν τὸ γένος ἡμῖν E τοῦτο ἀναίσθητον πάσαις ταῖς τοῦ σώματος αἰσθήσεσι περιπεφυκέναι, νοητὸν δ᾽ εἶναι νῷ μόνῳ <ᾧ> [1] δὴ καὶ διανοήματι λάβωμεν αὐτοῦ πέρι τὸ τοιόνδε.

ΚΛ. Ποῖον ;

ΑΘ. Ἥλιον εἰ περιάγει ψυχή, τριῶν αὐτὴν ἓν λέγοντες δρᾶν σχεδὸν οὐκ ἀποτευξόμεθα.

ΚΛ. Τίνων ;

ΑΘ. Ὡς ἢ ἐνοῦσα ἐντὸς τῷ περιφερεῖ τούτῳ φαινομένῳ σώματι πάντη διακομίζει τὸ τοιοῦτον, καθάπερ ἡμᾶς ἡ παρ᾽ ἡμῖν ψυχὴ πάντη περιφέρει· ἢ ποθεν ἔξωθεν σῶμα αὑτῇ πορισαμένη πυρὸς ἢ

---

[1] <ᾧ> I add : Zur. adds μόνῳ.

[1] *i.e.* envelopes the body and its sense-organs (like circumambient air).

CLIN. But, Stranger, judging by what has now been said, it is actually impious to make any other assertion than that these things are driven round by one or more souls endowed with all goodness.

ATH. You have attended to our argument admirably, Clinias. Now attend to this further point.

CLIN. What is that?

ATH. If soul drives round the sum total of sun, moon and all other stars, does it not also drive each single one of them?

CLIN. Certainly.

ATH. Then let us construct an argument about one of these stars which will evidently apply equally to them all.

CLIN. About which one?

ATH. The sun's body is seen by everyone, its soul by no one. And the same is true of the soul of any other body, whether alive or dead, of living beings. There is, however, a strong suspicion that this class of object, which is wholly imperceptible to sense, has grown round all the senses of the body,[1] and is an object of reason alone. Therefore by reason and rational thought let us grasp this fact about it,—

CLIN. What fact?

ATH. If soul drives round the sun, we shall be tolerably sure to be right in saying that it does one of three things.

CLIN. What things?

ATH. That either it exists everywhere inside of this apparent globular body and directs it, such as it is, just as the soul in us moves us about in all ways; or, having procured itself a body of fire or

τινὸς ἀέρος, ὡς λόγος ἐστί τινων, ὠθεῖ βίᾳ σώματι
899 σῶμα· ἢ τρίτον αὐτὴ ψιλὴ σώματος οὖσα, ἔχουσα
δὲ δυνάμεις ἄλλας τινὰς ὑπερβαλλούσας, θαύματι
ποδηγεῖ.

κλ.[1] Ναί· τοῦτο μὲν ἀνάγκη, τούτων ἕν γέ τι
δρῶσαν ψυχὴν πάντα διάγειν.

αθ. Αὐτοῦ δῆτα μεῖνον.[2] ταύτην τὴν ψυχήν,
εἴτε ἐν ἅρμασιν ἐνοῦσα ἡμῖν ἡλίου[3] ἄγει φῶς τοῖς
ἅπασιν εἴτ' ἔξωθεν εἴθ' ὅπως εἴθ' ὅπῃ, θεὸν ἡγεῖσθαι χρεὼν πάντα ἄνδρα. ἢ πῶς ;

B κλ. Ναί, τόν γέ που μὴ ἐπὶ τὸ ἔσχατον
ἀφιγμένον ἀνοίας.

αθ. Ἄστρων δὲ δὴ πέρι πάντων καὶ σελήνης
ἐνιαυτῶν τε καὶ μηνῶν καὶ πασῶν ὡρῶν πέρι
τίνα ἄλλον λόγον ἐροῦμεν ἢ τὸν αὐτὸν τοῦτον, ὡς
ἐπειδὴ ψυχὴ μὲν ἢ ψυχαὶ πάντων τούτων αἴτιαι
ἐφάνησαν, ἀγαθαὶ δὲ πᾶσαν ἀρετήν, θεοὺς αὐτὰς
εἶναι φήσομεν, εἴτε ἐν σώμασιν ἐνοῦσαι, ζῷα ὄντα,
κοσμοῦσι πάντα οὐρανὸν εἴτε ὅπῃ τε καὶ ὅπως ;
ἔσθ'· ὅστις ταῦτα ὁμολογῶν ὑπομενεῖ μὴ θεῶν
εἶναι πλήρη πάντα ;

C κλ. Οὐκ ἔστιν οὕτως, ὦ ξένε, παραφρονῶν
οὐδείς.

αθ. Τῷ μὲν τοίνυν μὴ νομίζοντι θεοὺς ἐν τῷ
πρόσθεν χρόνῳ, ὦ Μέγιλλέ τε καὶ Κλεινία,
εἰπόντες ὅρους ἀπαλλαττώμεθα.

---

[1] After Ficinus and Hermann I give Ναί . . . διάγειν to
Clin. ; Zur., *al.*, give only Ναί.
[2] δῆτα μεῖνον.: δὴ ἄμεινον MSS. (Apelt also ci. μεῖνον :
Schneider and England bracket αὐτοῦ δὴ ἄμεινον and add δὴ
after ταύτην).
[3] ἐνοῦσα . . . ἡλίου : ἔχουσα . . . ἥλιον MSS., edd.

LAWS, BOOK X

air (as some argue), it in the form of body pushes forcibly on the body from outside ; or, thirdly, being itself void of body, but endowed with other surpassingly marvellous potencies, it conducts the body.

CLIN. Yes, it must necessarily be the case that soul acts in one of these ways when it propels all things.

ATH. Here, I pray you, pause. This soul,—whether it is by riding in the car of the sun,[1] or from outside, or otherwise, that it brings light to us all—every man is bound to regard as a god. Is not that so?

CLIN. Yes ; everyone at least who has not reached the uttermost verge of folly.

ATH. Concerning all the stars and the moon, and concerning the years and months and all seasons, what other account shall we give than this very same,—namely, that, inasmuch as it has been shown that they are all caused by one or more souls, which are good also with all goodness, we shall declare these souls to be gods, whether it be that they order the whole heaven by residing in bodies, as living creatures, or whatever the mode and method ? Is there any man that agrees with this view who will stand hearing it denied that " all things are full of gods " ? [2]

CLIN. There is not a man, Stranger, so wrong-headed as that.

ATH. Let us, then, lay down limiting conditions for the man who up till now disbelieves in gods, O Megillus and Clinias, and so be quit of him.

[1] Cp. *Tim.* 41 D, E, where the Creator is said to apportion a soul to each star, in which it rides "as though in a chariot."
[2] A dictum of Thales: Ar. *de An.* 411a 7 ff.

κλ.   Τίνας ;

αθ.   Ἢ διδάσκειν ἡμᾶς ὡς οὐκ ὀρθῶς λέγομεν
τιθέμενοι ψυχὴν γένεσιν ἀπάντων εἶναι πρώτην καὶ
τἆλλα ὁπόσα τούτῳ ξυνεπόμενα εἴπομεν, ἢ μὴ
δυνάμενον βέλτιον λέγειν ἡμῶν ἡμῖν πείθεσθαι
καὶ ζῆν θεοὺς ἡγούμενον εἰς τὸν ἐπίλοιπον βίον.
D ὁρῶμεν οὖν εἴτε ἱκανῶς ἤδη τοῖς οὐχ ἡγουμένοις
θεοὺς εἰρήκαμεν ὡς εἰσὶ θεοί, εἴτε ἐπιδεῶς.

κλ.   Ἥκιστά γε, ὦ ξένε, πάντων ἐπιδεῶς.

αθ.   Τούτοις μὲν τοίνυν ἡμῖν τὸ λόγων τέλος
ἐχέτω· τὸν δὲ ἡγούμενον μὲν θεοὺς εἶναι, μὴ
φροντίζειν δὲ αὐτοὺς τῶν ἀνθρωπίνων πραγμάτων,
παραμυθητέον. Ὦ ἄριστε δή, φῶμεν, ὅτι μὲν
ἡγεῖ θεούς, συγγένειά τις ἴσως σε θεία πρὸς τὸ
ξύμφυτον ἄγει τιμᾶν καὶ νομίζειν εἶναι· κακῶν δὲ
E ἀνθρώπων καὶ ἀδίκων τύχαι ἰδίᾳ καὶ δημοσίᾳ,
ἀληθείᾳ μὲν οὐκ εὐδαίμονες, δόξαις δὲ εὐδαιμονι-
ζόμεναι σφόδρα ἀλλ᾽ οὐκ ἐμμελῶς, ἄγουσί σε πρὸς
ἀσέβειαν, ἔν τε Μούσαις οὐκ ὀρθῶς ὑμνούμεναι
ἅμα καὶ ἐν παντοίοις λόγοις. ἢ καὶ πρὸς τέλος
ἴσως [ἀνοσίους]¹ ἀνθρώπους ὁρῶν ἐλθόντας
γήραος,² παῖδας παίδων καταλιπόντας ἐν τιμαῖς
900 ταῖς μεγίσταις, ταράττει <ὅταν>³ τὸ νῦν ἐν ἅπασι
τούτοις [ἰδὼν] ἢ δι᾽ ἀκοῆς αἰσθόμενος ἢ καὶ παντάπασιν αὐτὸς αὐτόπτης προστύχῃς⁴ πολλῶν
ἀσεβημάτων καὶ δεινῶν γενομένων τισὶ δι᾽ αὐτὰ
ταῦτα ἐκ σμικρῶν εἰς τυραννίδας τε καὶ τὰ μέγιστα
ἀφικομένοις·⁵ τότε διὰ πάντα τὰ τοιαῦτα δῆλος

¹ [ἀνοσίους] omitted in best MSS.
² γήραος : γηραιούς MSS., edd.
³ <ὅταν> added by Euseb.
⁴ προστύχῃς : προστυχὴς MSS. : προστυχὼν Zur., vulg.
⁵ ἀφικομένοις Ritter : ἀφικομένους MSS., edd.

CLIN.   What conditions?

ATH.   That either he must teach us that we are
wrong in laying down that soul is of all things the
first production, together with all the consequential
statements we made,—or, if he is unable to improve
on our account, he must believe us, and for the rest
of his life live in veneration of the gods.   Let us,
then, consider whether our argument for the
existence of the gods addressed to those who
disbelieve in them has been stated adequately or
defectively.

CLIN.   Anything rather than defectively, Stranger.

ATH.   Then let our argument have an end, in so
far as it is addressed to these men.   But the man
who holds that gods exist, but pay no regard to
human affairs,—him we must admonish.   "My good
sir," let us say, "the fact that you believe in gods is
due probably to a divine kinship drawing you to
what is of like nature, to honour it and recognise its
existence ; but the fortunes of evil and unjust men,
both private and public,—which, though not really
happy, are excessively and improperly lauded as
happy by public opinion,—drive you to impiety by
the wrong way in which they are celebrated, not
only in poetry, but in tales of every kind.   Or
again, when you see men attaining the goal of old
age, and leaving behind them children's children in
the highest offices, very likely you are disturbed,
when amongst the number of these you discover—
whether from hearsay or from your own personal
observation—some who have been guilty of many
dreadful impieties, and who, just because of these,
have risen from a small position to royalty and the
highest rank ; then the consequence of all this

εἰ μέμφεσθαι μὲν θεοὺς ὡς αἰτίους ὄντας τῶν
τοιούτων διὰ ξυγγένειαν οὐκ ἂν ἐθέλων· ἀγόμενος
δὲ ὑπό τινος ἀλογίας ἅμα καὶ οὐ δυνάμενος
B δυσχεραίνειν θεοὺς εἰς τοῦτο νῦν τὸ πάθος ἐλήλυ-
θας ὥστ᾽ εἶναι μὲν δοκεῖν αὐτούς, τῶν δὲ ἀνθρωπίνων καταφρονεῖν καὶ ἀμελεῖν πραγμάτων. ἵνα
οὖν μὴ ἐπὶ μεῖζον ἔλθῃ σοι πάθος πρὸς ἀσέβειαν τὸ
νῦν παρὸν δόγμα, ἀλλ᾽, ἐάν πως <οἷόν τε>,[1] οἷον
ἀποδιοπομπήσασθαι λόγοις αὐτὸ προσιὸν γενώ-
μεθα δυνατοί, πειρώμεθα, συνάψαντες τὸν ἑξῆς
λόγον ᾧ πρὸς τὸν τὸ παράπαν οὐχ ἡγούμενον θεοὺς
ἐξ ἀρχῆς διεπερανάμεθα, τούτῳ τὰ νῦν προσχρή-
C σασθαι. σὺ δ᾽, ὦ Κλεινία τε καὶ Μέγιλλε, ὑπὲρ
τοῦ νέου καθάπερ ἐν τοῖς ἔμπροσθεν ἀποκρινόμενοι
διαδέχεσθε· ἂν δέ τι δύσκολον ἐμπίπτῃ τοῖς
λόγοις, ἐγὼ σφῷ ὥσπερ νῦν δὴ δεξάμενος διαβιβῶ
τὸν ποταμόν.

ΚΛ. Ὀρθῶς λέγεις· καὶ σύ τε οὕτω ταῦτα
δρᾶ ποιήσομέν τε ἡμεῖς εἰς τὸ δυνατὸν ἃ
λέγεις.

ΑΘ. Ἀλλ᾽ οὐδὲν τάχ᾽ ἂν ἴσως εἴη χαλεπὸν
ἐνδείξασθαι τούτῳ[2] γε, ὡς ἐπιμελεῖς σμικρῶν εἰσὶ
θεοὶ οὐχ ἧττον ἢ τῶν μεγέθει διαφερόντων. ἤκουε
D γάρ που καὶ παρῆν τοῖς νῦν δὴ λεγομένοις, ὡς
ἀγαθοί γε ὄντες πᾶσαν ἀρετὴν τὴν τῶν πάντων
ἐπιμέλειαν οἰκειοτάτην αὐτῶν οὖσαν κέκτηνται.

ΚΛ. Καὶ σφόδρα γε ἐπήκουεν.

ΑΘ. Τὸ μετὰ τοῦτο τοίνυν κοινῇ συνεξεταζόντων,
τίνα λέγοντες ἀρετὴν αὐτῶν ὁμολογοῦμεν αὐτοὺς

---

[1] <οἷόν τε> I add (ἐναντίως for ἐάν πως, Apelt).
[2] τούτῳ England : τοῦτό MSS.

clearly is that, since on the one hand you are unwilling to hold the gods responsible for such things
because of your kinship to them, and since on the
other hand you are driven by lack of logic and
inability to repudiate the gods, you have come to
your present morbid state of mind, in which you
opine that the gods exist, but scorn and neglect
human affairs. In order, therefore, that your present
opinion may not grow to a greater height of morbid
impiety, but that we may succeed in repelling the
onset of its pollution (if haply we are able) by
argument, let us endeavour to attach our next
argument to that which we set forth in full to him
who utterly disbelieves in gods, and thereby to
employ the latter as well." And do you, Clinias
and Megillus, take the part of the young man in
answering, as you did before; and should anything
untoward occur in the course of the argument, I will
make answer for you, as I did just now, and convey
you across the stream.[1]

CLIN. A good suggestion! We will do our best
to carry it out; and do you do likewise.

ATH. Well, there will probably be no difficulty in
proving to this man that the gods care for small
things no less than for things superlatively great.
For, of course, he was present at our recent argument,
and heard that the gods, being good with all goodness, possess such care of the whole as is most proper
to themselves.

CLIN. Most certainly he heard that.

ATH. Let us join next in enquiring what is that
goodness of theirs in respect of which we agree that

---

[1] Cp. 892 D, E.

PLATO

ἀγαθοὺς εἶναι. φέρε, τὸ σωφρονεῖν νοῦν τε
κεκτῆσθαί φαμεν ἀρετῆς, τὰ δ' ἐναντία κακίας ;

ΚΛ. Φαμέν.

ΑΘ. Τί δαί ; ἀρετῆς μὲν ἀνδρίαν εἶναι, δειλίαν
δὲ κακίας ;

ΚΛ. Πάνυ μὲν οὖν.

Ε ΑΘ. Καὶ τὰ μὲν αἰσχρὰ τούτων, τὰ δὲ καλὰ
φήσομεν ;

ΚΛ. Ἀνάγκη.

ΑΘ. Καὶ τῶν μὲν προσήκειν ἡμῖν, εἴπερ, ὁπόσα
φλαῦρα, θεοῖς δὲ οὔτε μέγα οὔτε σμικρὸν τῶν
τοιούτων μετὸν ἐροῦμεν ;

ΚΛ. Καὶ ταῦθ' οὕτως ὁμολογοῖ πᾶς ἄν.

ΑΘ. Τί δαί ; ἀμέλειάν τε καὶ ἀργίαν καὶ τρυφὴν
εἰς ἀρετὴν ψυχῆς θήσομεν ; ἢ πῶς λέγεις ;

ΚΛ. Καὶ πῶς ;

ΑΘ. Ἀλλ' εἰς τοὐναντίον ;

ΚΛ. Ναί.

901 ΑΘ. Τἀναντία ἄρα τούτοις εἰς τοὐναντίον.

ΚΛ. Τοὐναντίον.

ΑΘ. Τί οὖν δή ; τρυφῶν καὶ ἀμελὴς ἀργός τε,
ὃν ὁ ποιητὴς κηφῆσι κοθούροισι μάλιστα εἴκελον
ἔφασκεν εἶναι, γίγνοιτ' ἂν [ὁ]¹ τοιοῦτος πᾶς
ἡμῖν ;

ΚΛ. Ὀρθότατά γε εἰπών.

ΑΘ. Οὐκοῦν τόν γε θεὸν οὐ ῥητέον ἔχειν ἦθος
τοιοῦτον ὅ γέ τοι αὐτὸς μισεῖ· τῷ τέ τι τοιοῦτον
φθέγγεσθαι πειρωμένῳ οὐκ ἐπιτρεπτέον.

ΚΛ. Οὐ μὲν δή· πῶς γὰρ ἄν ;

ΑΘ. Ὧι δὴ προσήκει μὲν πράττειν καὶ ἐπιμε-

¹ [ὁ] bracketed by Burnet.

354

they are good.   Come now, do we say that prudence and the possession of reason are parts of goodness, and the opposites of these of badness?

CLIN.   We do say so.

ATH.   And further, that courage is part of goodness, and cowardice of badness?

CLIN.   Certainly.

ATH.   And shall we say that some of these are foul, others fair?

CLIN.   Necessarily.

ATH.   And shall we say that all such as are mean belong to us, if to anyone, whereas the gods have no share in any such things, great or small?

CLIN.   To this, too, everyone would assent.

ATH.   Well then, shall we reckon neglect, idleness and indolence as goodness of soul?   Or how say you?

CLIN.   How could we?

ATH.   As the opposite, then?

CLIN.   Yes.

ATH.   And the opposites of these as of the opposite quality of soul?

CLIN.   Of the opposite quality.

ATH.   What then?   He who is indolent, careless and idle will be in our eyes what the poet described [1] —" a man most like to sting-less drones "?

CLIN.   A most true description.

ATH.   That God has such a character we must certainly deny, seeing that he hates it; nor must we allow anyone to attempt to say so.

CLIN.   We could not possibly allow that.

ATH.   When a person whose duty it is especially

---

[1] Hesiod *Op. D.* 303 f. : τῷ δὲ θεοὶ νεμεσῶσι καὶ ἀνέρες ὅς κεν ἀεργὸς | ζώῃ, κηφήνεσσι κοθούροις εἴκελος ὁρμήν.

B λεῖσθαι διαφερόντως τινός, ὁ δὲ τούτου γε νοῦς
τῶν μὲν μεγάλων ἐπιμελεῖται, τῶν σμικρῶν δὲ
ἀμελεῖ, κατὰ τίνα ἐπαινοῦντες τὸν τοιοῦτον λόγον
οὐκ ἂν παντάπασι πλημμελοῖμεν; σκοπῶμεν δὲ
ὧδε. ἆρ᾽ οὐ κατὰ δύο εἴδη τὸ τοιοῦτον πράττει ὁ
πράττων, εἴτε θεὸς εἴτ᾽ ἄνθρωπος;

ΚΛ. Ποίω δὴ λέγομεν;

ΑΘ. Ἡ διαφέρον οὐδὲν οἰόμενος εἶναι τῷ ὅλῳ
C ἀμελουμένων τῶν σμικρῶν, ἢ ῥαθυμίᾳ καὶ τρυφῇ,
εἰ διαφέρειν,¹ ὁ δὲ ἀμελεῖ. ἢ ἔστιν ἄλλως πως
γιγνομένη ἀμέλεια; οὐ γάρ που ὅταν γε ἀδύνατον
ᾖ τῶν ἀπάντων ἐπιμελεῖσθαι, τότε ἀμέλεια ἔσται
τῶν σμικρῶν ἢ μεγάλων μὴ ἐπιμελουμένῳ, ὧν ἂν
δυνάμει θεὸς ἢ φαῦλός τις ὢν ἐλλιπὴς καὶ μὴ
δυνατὸς ἐπιμελεῖσθαι γίγνηται.

ΚΛ. Πῶς γὰρ ἄν;

ΑΘ. Νῦν δὴ δύ᾽ ὄντες τρισὶν ἡμῖν οὖσιν ἀπο-
κρινάσθωσαν οἱ θεοὺς μὲν ἀμφότεροι ὁμολογοῦν-
τες εἶναι, παραιτητοὺς δὲ ἅτερος, ὁ δὲ ἀμελεῖς τῶν
D σμικρῶν. πρῶτον μὲν θεοὺς ἀμφότεροί φατε
γιγνώσκειν καὶ ὁρᾶν καὶ ἀκούειν πάντα, λαθεῖν
δὲ αὐτοὺς οὐδὲν δυνατὸν εἶναι τῶν ὁπόσων
εἰσὶν [αἱ]² αἰσθήσεις τε καὶ ἐπιστῆμαι. ταύτῃ
λέγετε ἔχειν ταῦτα, ἢ πῶς;

ΚΛ. Οὕτως.

ΑΘ. Τί δαί; δύνασθαι πάντα ὁπόσων αὖ
δύναμίς ἐστι θνητοῖς τε καὶ ἀθανάτοις;

ΚΛ. Πῶς γὰρ οὐ συγχωρήσονται καὶ ταῦτα
οὕτως ἔχειν;

---

¹ διαφέρειν: διαφέρει MSS., edd.
² [αἱ] om. Euseb.: bracketed by Hermann.

to act and care for some object has a mind that cares
for great things, but neglects small things, on what
principle could we praise such a person without the
utmost impropriety? Let us consider the matter in
this way: the action of him who acts thus, be he
god or man, takes one of two forms, does it not?

CLIN. What forms?

ATH. Either because he thinks that neglect of
the small things makes no difference to the whole,
or else, owing to laziness and indolence, he neglects
them, though he thinks they do make a difference.
Or is there any other way in which neglect occurs?
For when it is impossible to care for all things, it
will not in that case be neglect of great things or
small when a person—be he god or common man—
fails to care for things which he lacks the power and
capacity to care for.

CLIN. Of course not.

ATH. Now to us three let these two men make
answer, of whom both agree that gods exist, but the
one asserts that they can be bribed, and the other
that they neglect the small. First, you both
assert that the gods know and hear and see all
things,[1] and that nothing of all that is apprehended
by senses or sciences can escape their notice; do you
assert that this is so, or what?

CLIN. That is what we assert.[2]

ATH. And further, that they can do all that can
be done by mortal or immortal?

CLIN. They will, of course, admit that this also is
the case.

[1] Cp. 641 E.
[2] Here, and in what follows, Clinias is answering on behalf
of the two misbelievers.

E   ΑΘ.   Καὶ μὴν ἀγαθούς γε καὶ ἀρίστους ὡμολο-
γήκαμεν αὐτοὺς εἶναι πέντε ὄντες.

     ΚΛ.   Σφόδρα γε.

     ΑΘ.   Ἆρ᾽ οὖν οὐ ῥᾳθυμίᾳ μὲν καὶ τρυφῇ ἀδύνα-
τον αὐτοὺς ὁμολογεῖν πράττειν ὁτιοῦν τὸ παράπαν,
ὄντας γε οἵους λέγομεν ; δειλίας γὰρ ἔκγονος ἔν
γε ἡμῖν ἀργία, ῥᾳθυμία δὲ ἀργίας καὶ τρυφῆς.

     ΚΛ.   Ἀληθέστατα λέγεις.

     ΑΘ.   Ἀργίᾳ μὲν δὴ καὶ ῥᾳθυμίᾳ οὐδεὶς ἀμελεῖ
θεῶν· οὐ γὰρ μέτεστιν αὐτῷ που δειλίας.

     ΚΛ.   Ὀρθότατα λέγεις.

902   ΑΘ.   Οὐκοῦν τὸ λοιπόν, εἴπερ ἀμελοῦσι τῶν
σμικρῶν καὶ ὀλίγων τῶν περὶ τὸ πᾶν, ἢ γιγνώσ-
κοντες ὡς τὸ παράπαν οὐδενὸς τῶν τοιούτων
ἐπιμελεῖσθαι δεῖ, δρῷεν ἂν τοῦτο, ἢ τί τὸ λοιπὸν
πλὴν τῷ γιγνώσκειν τοὐναντίον ;

     ΚΛ.   Οὐδέν.

     ΑΘ.   Πότερον οὖν, ὦ ἄριστε καὶ βέλτιστε, θῶμέν
σε λέγοντα, ὡς ἀγνοοῦντάς τε καὶ δέον ἐπιμελεῖσθαι δι᾽ ἄγνοιαν ἀμελοῦντας, ἢ γιγνώσκοντας ὅτι
δεῖ, καθάπερ οἱ φαυλότατοι τῶν ἀνθρώπων λέγονται ποιεῖν, εἰδότες ἄλλα εἶναι βελτίω πράττειν ὧν
δὴ πράττουσι διά τινας ἥττας ἡδονῶν ἢ λυπῶν
B οὐ ποιεῖν ;

     ΚΛ.   Πῶς γὰρ ἄν ;

     ΑΘ.   Οὐκοῦν δὴ τά γε ἀνθρώπινα πράγματα
τῆς τε ἐμψύχου μετέχει φύσεως ἅμα, καὶ θεοσε-
βέστατον αὐτό ἐστι πάντων ζώων ἄνθρωπος ;

     ΚΛ.   Ἔοικε γοῦν.

358

ATH. And it is undeniable that all five of us agreed that the gods are good, yea, exceeding good.

CLIN. Most certainly.

ATH. Being, then, such as we agree, is it not impossible to allow that they do anything at all in a lazy and indolent way? For certainly amongst us mortals idleness is the child of cowardice, and laziness of idleness and indolence.

CLIN. Very true.

ATH. None, then, of the gods is neglectful owing to idleness and laziness, seeing that none has any part in cowardice.

CLIN. You are very right.

ATH. Further, if they do neglect the small and scant things of the All, they will do so either because they know that there is no need at all to care for any such things or—well, what other alternative is there except the opposite of knowing?

CLIN. There is none.

ATH. Shall we then assume, my worthy and excellent sir, that you assert that the gods are ignorant, and that it is through ignorance that they are neglectful when they ought to be showing care,—or that they know indeed what is needful, yet act as the worst of men are said to do, who, though they know that other things are better to do than what they are doing, yet do them not, owing to their being somehow defeated by pleasures or pains?

CLIN. Impossible.

ATH. Do not human affairs share in animate nature, and is not man himself, too, the most god-fearing of all living creatures?

CLIN. That is certainly probable.

ΑΘ. Θεῶν γε μὴν κτήματά φαμεν εἶναι πάντα ὁπόσα θνητὰ ζῷα, ὧνπερ καὶ τὸν οὐρανὸν ὅλον.

ΚΛ. Πῶς γὰρ οὔ;

ΑΘ. Ἤδη τοίνυν σμικρὰ ἢ μεγάλα τις φάτω
C ταῦτα εἶναι τοῖς θεοῖς· οὐδετέρως γὰρ τοῖς κεκτημένοις ἡμᾶς ἀμελεῖν ἂν εἴη προσῆκον, ἐπιμελεστάτοις γε οὖσι καὶ ἀρίστοις. σκοπῶμεν γὰρ δὴ καὶ τόδε ἔτι πρὸς τούτοις.

ΚΛ. Τὸ ποῖον;

ΑΘ. Τὸ περί τε αἰσθήσεως καὶ δυνάμεως, ἆρ' οὐκ ἐναντίως ἀλλήλοιν πρὸς ῥαστώνην καὶ χαλεπότητά ἐστον πεφυκότε;

ΚΛ. Πῶς λέγεις;

ΑΘ. Ὁρᾶν μέν που καὶ ἀκούειν τὰ σμικρὰ χαλεπώτερον ἢ τὰ μεγάλα, φέρειν δὲ αὖ καὶ κρατεῖν καὶ ἐπιμελεῖσθαι τῶν σμικρῶν καὶ ὀλίγων παντὶ ῥᾷον ἢ τῶν ἐναντίων.

D ΚΛ. Καὶ πολύ γε.

ΑΘ. Ἰατρῷ δὲ προστεταγμένον ὅλον τι θεραπεύειν βουλομένῳ καὶ δυναμένῳ, τῶν μὲν μεγάλων ἐπιμελουμένῳ, τῶν μορίων δὲ καὶ σμικρῶν ἀμελοῦντι, ἕξει ποτὲ καλῶς αὐτῷ τὸ πᾶν;

ΚΛ. Οὐδαμῶς.

ΑΘ. Οὐ μὴν οὐδὲ κυβερνήταις οὐδὲ στρατηγοῖς οὐδ' οἰκονόμοις οὐδ' αὖ τισι πολιτικοῖς οὐδ' ἄλλῳ τῶν τοιούτων οὐδενὶ χωρὶς τῶν ὀλίγων καὶ
E σμικρῶν πολλὰ ἢ μεγάλα· οὐδὲ γὰρ ἄνευ σμικρῶν τοὺς μεγάλους φασὶν οἱ λιθολόγοι λίθους εὖ κεῖσθαι.

ΚΛ. Πῶς γὰρ ἄν;

ΑΘ. Μὴ τοίνυν τόν γε θεὸν ἀξιώσωμέν ποτε θνητῶν δημιουργῶν φαυλότερον, οἳ τὰ προσ-

ATH. We affirm that all mortal creatures are possessions of the gods, to whom belongs also the whole heaven.

CLIN. Of course.

ATH. That being so, it matters not whether a man says that these things are small or great in the eyes of the gods; for in neither case would it behove those who are our owners to be neglectful, seeing that they are most careful and most good. For let us notice this further fact——

CLIN. What is it?

ATH. In regard to perception and power,—are not these two naturally opposed in respect of ease and difficulty?

CLIN. How do you mean?

ATH. It is more difficult to see and hear small things than great; but everyone finds it more easy to move, control and care for things small and few than their opposites.

CLIN. Much more.

ATH. When a physician is charged with the curing of a whole body, if, while he is willing and able to care for the large parts, he neglects the small parts and members, will he ever find the whole in good condition?

CLIN. Certainly not.

ATH. No more will pilots or generals or house-managers, nor yet statesmen or any other such persons, find that the many and great thrive apart from the few and small; for even masons say that big stones are not well laid without little stones.

CLIN. They cannot be.

ATH. Let us never suppose that God is inferior to mortal craftsmen who, the better they are, the more

ἥκοντα αὐτοῖς ἔργα, ὅσῳπερ ἂν ἀμείνους ὦσι,
τόσῳ ἀκριβέστερα καὶ τελεώτερα μιᾷ τέχνῃ
σμικρὰ καὶ μεγάλα ἀπεργάζονται· τὸν δὲ θεόν,
ὄντα τε σοφώτατον βουλόμενόν τ' ἐπιμελεῖσθαι
903 καὶ δυνάμενον, ὧν μὲν ῥᾷον ἦν ἐπιμεληθῆναι
σμικρῶν ὄντων μηδαμῇ ἐπιμελεῖσθαι καθάπερ
ἀργὸν ἢ δειλόν τινα διὰ πόνους ῥᾳθυμοῦντα, τῶν
δὲ μεγάλων.

ΚΛ. Μηδαμῶς δόξαν τοιαύτην περὶ θεῶν, ὦ
ξένε, ἀποδεχώμεθα· οὐδαμῇ γὰρ οὔτε ὅσιον οὔτ'
ἀληθὲς τὸ διανόημα διανοοίμεθ' ἄν.

ΑΘ. Δοκοῦμεν δέ μοι νῦν ἤδη καὶ μάλα
μετρίως διειλέχθαι τῷ φιλαιτίῳ τῆς ἀμελείας πέρι
θεῶν.

ΚΛ. Ναί.

ΑΘ. Τῷ γε βιάζεσθαι τοῖς λόγοις ὁμολογεῖν
B αὐτὸν μὴ λέγειν ὀρθῶς. ἐπῳδῶν γε μὴν προσ-
δεῖσθαί μοι δοκεῖ μύθων ἔτι τινῶν.

ΚΛ. Ποίων, ὦ 'γαθέ;

ΑΘ. Πείθωμεν τὸν νεανίαν τοῖς λόγοις ὡς τῷ
τοῦ παντὸς ἐπιμελουμένῳ πρὸς τὴν σωτηρίαν
καὶ ἀρετὴν τοῦ ὅλου πάντ' ἐστὶ συντεταγμένα,
ὧν καὶ τὸ μέρος εἰς δύναμιν ἕκαστον τὸ προσῆκον
πάσχει καὶ ποιεῖ. τούτοις δ' εἰσὶν ἄρχοντες
προστεταγμένοι ἑκάστοις ἐπὶ τὸ σμικρότατον
ἀεὶ πάθης καὶ πράξεως, εἰς μερισμὸν τὸν ἔσχα-
C τον <τὸ>[1] τέλος ἀπειργασμένοι· ὧν ἓν καὶ τὸ
σόν, ὦ σχέτλιε, μόριον εἰς τὸ πᾶν ξυντείνει
βλέπον ἀεί, καίπερ πάνσμικρον ὄν. σὲ δὲ
λέληθε περὶ τοῦτο αὐτὸ ὡς γένεσις ἕνεκα ἐκείνου
γίγνεται πᾶσα, ὅπως ᾖ ἡ τῷ τοῦ παντὸς βίῳ
ὑπάρχουσα εὐδαίμων οὐσία, οὐχ ἕνεκα σοῦ

accurately and perfectly do they execute their proper tasks, small and great, by one single art,—or that God, who is most wise, and both willing and able to care, cares not at all for the small things which are the easier to care for—like one who shirks the labour because he is idle and cowardly,—but only for the great.

CLIN. By no means let us accept such an opinion of the gods, Stranger : that would be to adopt a view that is neither pious nor true at all.

ATH. And now, as I think, we have argued quite sufficiently with him who loves to censure the gods for neglect.

CLIN. Yes.

ATH. And it was by forcing him by our arguments to acknowledge that what he says is wrong. But still he needs also, as it seems to me, some words of counsel to act as a charm upon him.

CLIN. What kind of words, my good sir ?

ATH. Let us persuade the young man by our discourse that all things are ordered systematically by Him who cares for the World-all with a view to the preservation and excellence of the Whole, whereof also each part, so far as it can, does and suffers what is proper to it. To each of these parts, down to the smallest fraction, rulers of their action and passion are appointed to bring about fulfilment even to the uttermost fraction ; whereof thy portion also, O perverse man, is one, and tends therefore always in its striving towards the All, tiny though it be. But thou failest to perceive that all partial generation is for the sake of the Whole, in order that for the life of the World-all blissful existence may be secured,—

---

[1] <τὸ> added by Stephens.

γιγνομένη, σὺ δὲ ἕνεκα ἐκείνου. πᾶς γὰρ ἰατρὸς
καὶ πᾶς ἔντεχνος δημιουργὸς παντὸς μὲν ἕνεκα
πάντα ἐργάζεται, πρὸς τὸ κοινῇ ξυντείνων βέλτιστον, μέρος μὴν ἕνεκα ὅλου καὶ οὐχ ὅλον μέρους
D ἕνεκα ἀπεργάζεται. σὺ δὲ ἀγανακτεῖς ἀγνοῶν
ὅπῃ τὸ περὶ σὲ ἄριστον τῷ παντὶ ξυμβαίνει καὶ
σοὶ κατὰ δύναμιν τὴν τῆς κοινῆς γενέσεως. ἐπεὶ
δὲ ἀεὶ ψυχὴ συντεταγμένη σώματι τοτὲ μὲν
ἄλλῳ, τοτὲ δὲ ἄλλῳ, μεταβάλλει παντοίας
μεταβολὰς δι' ἑαυτὴν ἢ δι' ἑτέραν ψυχήν, οὐδὲν
ἄλλο ἔργον τῷ πεττευτῇ λείπεται πλὴν μετα-
τιθέναι τὸ μὲν ἄμεινον γιγνόμενον ἦθος εἰς βελτίω
τόπον, χεῖρον δὲ εἰς τὸν χείρονα, κατὰ τὸ πρέπον
αὐτῶν ἕκαστον, ἵνα τῆς προσηκούσης μοίρας
λαγχάνῃ.

E ΚΛ. Πῇ λέγεις;

ΑΘ. Ἧιπερ ἂν ἔχοι λόγον ῥᾳστώνη ἐπιμελείας
θεοῖς τῶν πάντων, ταύτῃ μοι δοκῶ φράζειν· εἰ
μὴ[1] γὰρ πρὸς τὸ ὅλον ἀεὶ βλέπων πλάττοι τις
μετασχηματίζων τὰ πάντα, οἷον ἐκ πυρὸς ὕδωρ
[ἔμψυχον],[2] καὶ μὴ ξύμπολλα ἐξ ἑνὸς ἢ ἐκ
904 πολλῶν ἕν, πρώτης ἢ δευτέρας ἢ καὶ τρίτης
γενέσεως μετειληφότα πλήθεσιν ἄπειρ'[3] ἂν εἴη
[τὰ] τῆς μετατιθεμένης κοσμήσεως· νῦν δ' ἐστὶ
θαυμαστὴ ῥᾳστώνη τῷ τοῦ παντὸς ἐπιμελουμένῳ.

ΚΛ. Πῶς αὖ λέγεις;

ΑΘ. Ὧδε. ἐπειδὴ κατεῖδεν ἡμῶν ὁ βασιλεὺς
ἐμψύχους οὔσας τὰς πράξεις ἁπάσας καὶ πολλὴν

---

[1] μὴ Apelt : μὲν MSS.
[2] [ἔμψυχον] I bracket (ἔμψυχρον Stallb.).
[3] ἄπειρ' MSS.: ἄπορ' MS. marg., Zur.; MSS. om. τὰ (vulg. om. τῆς).

it not being generated for thy sake, but thou for its
sake. For every physician and every trained craftsman works always for the sake of a Whole, and
strives after what is best in general, and he produces
a part for the sake of a whole, and not a whole for
the sake of a part ; but thou art vexed, because thou
knowest not how what is best in thy case for the
All turns out best for thyself also, in accordance
with the power of your common origin. And inasmuch as soul, being conjoined now with one body,
now with another, is always undergoing all kinds of
changes either of itself or owing to another soul,
there is left for the draughts-player no further
task,—save only to shift the character that grows
better to a superior place, and the worse to a worse,
according to what best suits each of them, so that
to each may be allotted its appropriate destiny.

CLIN. In what way do you mean ?

ATH. The way I am describing is, I believe, that
in which supervision of all things is most easy for
the gods. For if one were to shape all things, without a constant view to the Whole, by transforming
them (as, for instance, fire into water), instead of
merely converting one into many or many into one,
then when things had shared in a first, or second, or
even third generation,[1] they would be countless in
number in such a system of transformations ; but as
things are, the task before the Supervisor of the
All is wondrous easy.

CLIN. How do you mean ?

ATH. Thus :—Since our King saw that all actions
involve soul, and contain much good and much evil,

---

[1] This seems to refer to three stages of the soul's incarnation ; see p. 367, n. 2.

μὲν ἀρετὴν ἐν αὐταῖς οὖσαν, πολλὴν δὲ κακίαν,
ἀνώλεθρον δὲ ὂν γενόμενον, ἀλλ᾽ οὐκ αἰώνιον,
ψυχὴν καὶ σῶμα, καθάπερ οἱ κατὰ νόμον ὄντες
θεοί—γένεσις γὰρ οὐκ ἄν ποτε ἦν ζώων ἀπολο-
B μένου τούτοιν θατέρου—καὶ τὸ μὲν ὠφελεῖν ἀεὶ
πεφυκός, ὅσον ἀγαθὸν ψυχῆς, διενοήθη, τὸ δὲ
κακὸν βλάπτειν· ταῦτα πάντα ξυνιδὼν ἐμηχανή-
σατο ποῦ κείμενον ἕκαστον τῶν μερῶν νικῶσαν
ἀρετήν, ἡττωμένην δὲ κακίαν, ἐν τῷ παντὶ
παρέχοι μάλιστ᾽ ἂν καὶ ῥᾷστα καὶ ἄριστα.
μεμηχάνηται δὴ πρὸς πᾶν τοῦτο τὸ ποῖόν τι
γιγνόμενον ἀεὶ ποίαν ἕδραν δεῖ μεταλάμβανον
οἰκίζεσθαι καὶ τίνας ποτὲ τόπους. τῆς δὲ γενέσεως τοῦ ποίου τινὸς ἀφῆκε ταῖς βουλήσεσιν
C ἑκάστων ἡμῶν τὰς αἰτίας. ὅπῃ γὰρ ἂν ἐπιθυμῇ
καὶ ὁποῖός τις ὢν τὴν ψυχήν, ταύτῃ σχεδὸν
ἑκάστοτε καὶ τοιοῦτος γίγνεται ἅπας ἡμῶν ὡς
τὸ πολύ.

ΚΛ. Τὸ γοῦν εἰκός.

ΑΘ. Μεταβάλλει μὲν τοίνυν πάνθ᾽ ὅσα μέτοχά
ἐστι ψυχῆς, ἐν ἑαυτοῖς κεκτημένα τὴν τῆς μεταβολῆς αἰτίαν· μεταβάλλοντα δὲ φέρεται κατὰ
τὴν τῆς εἱμαρμένης τάξιν καὶ νόμον. σμικρότερα
μὲν τῶν ἠθῶν μεταβάλλοντα ἐλάττω κατὰ τὸ
τῆς χώρας ἐπίπεδον μεταπορεύεται, πλείω δὲ καὶ
D ἀδικώτερα μεταπεσόντα εἰς βάθος τά τε κάτω
λεγόμενα τῶν τόπων, ὅσα Ἅιδην τε καὶ τὰ
τούτων ἐχόμενα τῶν ὀνομάτων ἐπονομάζοντες
σφόδρα φοβοῦνται καὶ ὀνειροπολοῦσι ζῶντες δια-
λυθέντες τε τῶν σωμάτων. μείζω δὲ δὴ ψυχὴ

---

[1] Cp. Tim. 37 C ff.

and that body and soul are, when generated, indestructible but not eternal,[1] as are the gods ordained by law (for if either soul or body had been destroyed, there would never have been generation of living creatures), and since He perceived that all soul that is good naturally tends always to benefit, but the bad to injure,—observing all this, He designed a location for each of the parts, wherein it might secure the victory of goodness in the Whole and the defeat of evil most completely, easily, and well. For this purpose He has designed the rule which prescribes what kind of character should be set to dwell in what kind of position and in what regions; [2] but the causes of the generation of any special kind he left to the wills of each one of us men.[3] For according to the trend of our desires and the nature of our souls, each one of us generally becomes of a corresponding character.

CLIN. That is certainly probable.

ATH. All things that share in soul change, since they possess within themselves the cause of change, and in changing they move according to the law and order of destiny; the smaller the change of character, the less is the movement over surface in space, but when the change is great and towards great iniquity, then they move towards the deep and the so-called lower regions, regarding which—under the names of Hades and the like—men are haunted by most fearful imaginings, both when alive and when disparted from their bodies. And whenever the soul gets a

[2] Cp. *Tim.* 42 B ff. where it is said that the soul of the good man returns at death to its native star, while that of the bad takes the form of a woman in its second, and that of a beast in its third incarnation.

[3] Cp. *Rep.* 617 E.

κακίας ἢ ἀρετῆς ὁπόταν μεταλάβῃ διὰ τὴν αὑτῆς
βούλησίν τε καὶ ὁμιλίαν γενομένην ἰσχυράν,
ὁπόταν μὲν ἀρετῇ θείᾳ προσμίξασα γίγνηται
διαφερόντως τοιαύτη, διαφέροντα καὶ μετέβαλε
τόπον, ἁγίαν ὁδὸν[1] μετακομισθεῖσα εἰς ἀμείνω
Ε τινὰ τόπον ἕτερον· ὅταν δὲ τἀναντία, ἐπὶ τἀναντία
μεθιδρύσασα τὸν αὑτῆς βίον.

αὕτη τοι δίκη ἐστὶ θεῶν οἳ Ὄλυμπον ἔχουσιν,
ὦ παῖ καὶ νεανίσκε ἀμελεῖσθαι δοκῶν ὑπὸ θεῶν·
κακίω μὲν γιγνόμενον πρὸς τὰς κακίους ψυχάς,
ἀμείνω δὲ πρὸς τὰς ἀμείνους, πορευόμενον ἔν τε
ζωῇ καὶ ἐν πᾶσι θανάτοις πάσχειν τε ἃ προσῆκον
δρᾶν ἐστὶ τοῖς προσφέρεσι τοὺς προσφερεῖς καὶ
905 ποιεῖν.[2] ταύτης τῆς δίκης οὔτε σὺ μή ποτε οὔτε
εἰ ἄλλος ἀτυχὴς γενόμενος ἐπεύξηται περιγεν-
έσθαι θεῶν· ἣν πασῶν δικῶν διαφερόντως
ἔταξάν τε οἱ τάξαντες χρεών τε ἐξευλαβεῖσθαι
τὸ παράπαν. οὐ γὰρ ἀμεληθήσει ποτὲ ὑπ' αὐτῆς·
οὐχ οὕτω σμικρὸς ὢν δύσει κατὰ τὸ τῆς γῆς
βάθος, οὐδ' ὑψηλὸς γενόμενος εἰς τὸν οὐρανὸν
ἀναπτήσει, τίσεις δὲ αὐτῶν τὴν προσήκουσαν
τιμωρίαν εἴτ' ἐνθάδε μένων εἴτε καὶ ἐν Ἅιδου
Β διαπορευθεὶς εἴτε καὶ τούτων εἰς ἀγριώτερον ἔτι
διακομισθεὶς τόπον. ὁ αὐτὸς δὲ λόγος σοι καὶ
περὶ ἐκείνων ἂν εἴη, τῶν οὓς σὺ κατιδὼν ἐκ
σμικρῶν μεγάλους γεγονότας ἀνοσιουργήσαντας
ἤ τι τοιοῦτον πράξαντας ᾠήθης ἐξ ἀθλίων εὐ-

[1] ἁγίαν ὁδὸν Badham : ἅγιον ὅλον MSS., edd.(ἄλλον Winck.).
[2] καὶ ποιεῖν placed by Zur., vulg.; after πάσχειν τε, but by
MSS. after προσφερεῖς (so Hermann).

[1] Odyss. XIX. 43.

specially large share of either virtue or vice, owing to the force of its own will and the influence of its intercourse growing strong, then, if it is in union with divine virtue, it becomes thereby eminently virtuous, and moves to an eminent region, being transported by a holy road to another and a better region ; whereas, if the opposite is the case, it changes to the opposite the location of its life's abode. "This is the just decree of the gods who inhabit Olympus," [1] O thou child and stripling who thinkest thou art neglected by the gods,—the decree that as thou becomest worse, thou goest to the company of the worse souls, and as thou becomest better, to the better souls ; and that, alike in life and in every shape of death, thou both doest and sufferest what it is befitting that like should do towards like.[2] From this decree of Heaven neither wilt thou nor any other luckless wight ever boast that he has escaped ; for this decree is one which the gods who have enjoined it have enjoined above all others, and meet it is that it should be most strictly observed. For by it thou wilt not ever be neglected, neither if thou shouldest dive, in thy very littleness, into the depths of the earth below, nor if thou shouldest soar up to the height of Heaven above ; but thou shalt pay to the gods thy due penalty, whether thou remainest here on earth, or hast passed away to Hades, or art transported to a region yet more fearsome. And the same rule, let me tell thee, will apply also to those whom thou sawest growing to great estate from small after doing acts of impiety or other such evil,—concerning whom thou didst deem that they had risen from misery to happiness, and

[2] Cp. 728 B f., 837 A.

δαίμονας γεγονέναι, κᾷτα ὡς ἐν κατόπτροις αὐτῶν
ταῖς πράξεσιν ἡγήσω καθεωρακέναι τὴν πάντων
ἀμέλειαν θεῶν, οὐκ εἰδὼς αὐτῶν τὴν συντέλειαν,
C ὅπη ποτὲ τῷ παντὶ ξυμβάλλεται. γιγνώσκειν
δὲ αὐτήν, ὦ πάντων ἀνδρειότατε, πῶς οὐ δεῖν
δοκεῖς; ἥν τις μὴ γιγνώσκων οὐδ' ἂν τύπον ἴδοι
ποτέ, οὐδὲ λόγον[1] ξυμβάλλεσθαι περὶ βίου δυνατὸς ἂν γένοιτο εἰς εὐδαιμονίαν τε καὶ δυσδαίμονα
τύχην. ταῦτα εἰ μέν σε πείθει Κλεινίας ὅδε
καὶ ξύμπασα ἡμῶν ἥδε ἡ γερουσία, περὶ θεῶν
ὡς οὐκ οἶσθα ὅ τι λέγεις, καλῶς ἄν σοι ὁ θεὸς
αὐτὸς ξυλλαμβάνοι· εἰ δ' ἐπιδεὴς ἔτι λόγου τινὸς
ἂν εἴης, λεγόντων ἡμῶν πρὸς τὸν τρίτον ἐπάκουε,
D εἰ νοῦν καὶ ὁπωσοῦν ἔχεις. ὅτι μὲν γὰρ θεοί
τ' εἰσὶ καὶ ἀνθρώπων ἐπιμελοῦνται, ἔγωγε οὐ
παντάπασι φαύλως ἂν φαίην ἡμῖν ἀποδεδεῖχθαι·
τὸ δὲ παραιτητοὺς αὖ θεοὺς[2] εἶναι τοῖσιν
ἀδικοῦσι, δεχομένους δῶρα, οὔτε τινὶ συγχω-
ρητέον παντί τ' αὖ κατὰ δύναμιν τρόπῳ ἐλεγ-
κτέον.

ΚΛ. Κάλλιστ' εἶπες, ποιῶμέν τε ὡς λέγεις.

ΑΘ. Φέρε δὴ πρὸς θεῶν αὐτῶν, τίνα τρόπον
παραιτητοὶ γίγνοιντ' ἂν ἡμῖν, εἰ γίγνοιντο αὖ;
E καὶ τίνες ἢ ποῖοί τινες ὄντες; ἄρχοντας μὲν
ἀναγκαῖόν που γίγνεσθαι τούς γε διοικήσοντας
τὸν ἅπαντα ἐνδελεχῶς οὐρανόν.

ΚΛ. Οὕτως.

ΑΘ. Ἀλλ' ἄρα τίσι προσφερεῖς τῶν ἀρχόντων;
ἢ τίνες τούτοις, ὧν δυνατὸν ἡμῖν ἀπεικάζουσι
τυγχάνειν μείζοσιν ἐλάττονας; πότερον ἡνίοχοι

---

[1] οὐδὲ λόγον MSS.: οὐδ' ἂν λόγους al. MSS., Zur.
[2] αὖ θεοὺς MSS.: αὐτοὺς Stobaeus, Zur.

didst imagine, therefore, that in their actions, as in mirrors, thou didst behold the entire neglect of the gods, not knowing of their joint contribution and how it contributes to the All. And surely, O most courageous of men, thou canst not but suppose that this is a thing thou must needs learn. For if a man learns not this, he can never see even an outline of the truth, nor will he be able to contribute an account of life as regards its happiness or its unhappy fortune. If Clinias here and all our gathering of elders succeed in convincing thee of this fact, that thou knowest not what thou sayest about the gods, then God Himself of His grace will aid thee ; but shouldest thou still be in need of further argument, give ear to us while we argue with the third unbeliever, if thou hast sense at all. For we have proved, as I would maintain, by fairly sufficient argument that the gods exist and care for men ; the next contention, that the gods can be won over by wrongdoers,[1] on the receipt of bribes, is one that no one should admit, and we must try to refute it by every means in our power.

CLIN. Admirably spoken : let us do as you say.

ATH. Come now, in the name of these gods themselves I ask—in what way would they come to be seduced by us, if seduced they were ? Being what in their essence and character ? Necessarily they must be rulers, if they are to be in continual control of the whole heaven.

CLIN. True.

ATH. But to which kind of rulers are they like ? Or which are like to them, of those rulers whom we can fairly compare with them, as small with great ?

---

[1] Cp. Hom. *Il.* IX. 497 ff., τοὺς (θεοὺς) . . . λοιβῇ τε κνίσῃ τε παρατρωπῶσ᾽ ἄνθρωποι κτλ.

τινες ἂν εἶεν τοιοῦτοι ζευγῶν ἁμιλλωμένων
ἢ πλοίων κυβερνῆται ; τάχα δὲ κἂν ἀπεικα-
σθεῖεν στρατοπέδων ἄρχουσί τισιν. εἴη δ' ἂν καὶ
νόσων πόλεμον εὐλαβουμένοις ἰατροῖς ἐοικέναι
906 περὶ σώματα, ἢ γεωργοῖς περὶ φυτῶν γένεσιν
εἰωθυίας ὥρας χαλεπὰς διὰ φόβων προσδεχο-
μένοις, ἢ καὶ ποιμνίων ἐπιστάταις. ἐπειδὴ γὰρ
συγκεχωρήκαμεν ἡμῖν αὐτοῖς εἶναι μὲν τὸν οὐρανὸν πολλῶν μεστὸν ἀγαθῶν, εἶναι δὲ καὶ τῶν
ἐναντίων, πλειόνων δὲ τῶν μή, μάχη δή, φαμέν,
ἀθάνατός ἐστιν ἡ τοιαύτη καὶ φυλακῆς θαυ-
μαστῆς δεομένη, ξύμμαχοι δὲ ἡμῖν θεοί τε ἅμα
καὶ δαίμονες, ἡμεῖς δ' αὖ κτήματα θεῶν καὶ
δαιμόνων· φθείρει δὲ ἡμᾶς ἀδικία καὶ ὕβρις μετὰ
B ἀφροσύνης, σώζει δὲ δικαιοσύνη καὶ σωφροσύνη
μετὰ φρονήσεως, ἐν ταῖς τῶν θεῶν ἐμψύχοις
οἰκοῦσαι δυνάμεσι, βραχὺ δέ τι καὶ τῇδε ἄν τις
τῶν τοιούτων ἐνοικοῦν ἡμῖν σαφὲς ἴδοι. ψυχαὶ
δή τινες ἐπὶ γῆς οἰκοῦσαι καὶ ἄδικον λῆμμα
κεκτημέναι, δῆλον ὅτι θηριώδεις πρὸς τὰς τῶν
φυλάκων ψυχὰς ἄρα κυνῶν ἢ τὰς τῶν νομέων
ἢ πρὸς τὰς τῶν παντάπασιν ἀκροτάτων δεσποτῶν προσπίπτουσαι πείθουσι θωπείαις λόγων,
C καὶ ἐν εὐκταίαις τισὶν ἐπῳδαῖς, ὡς αἱ φῆμαί φασιν
αἱ τῶν κακῶν, ἐξεῖναι πλεονεκτοῦσι σφίσιν ἐν
ἀνθρώποις πάσχειν μηδὲν χαλεπόν. φαμὲν δ'
εἶναί που τὸ νῦν ὀνομαζόμενον ἁμάρτημα τὴν
πλεονεξίαν ἐν μὲν σαρκίνοις σώμασι νόσημα

---

[1] Cp. 904 A ff., 896 C ff., *Rep.* 379 C.
[2] Cp. *Phaedo* 62 B.

Would drivers of rival teams resemble them, or pilots of ships? Or perhaps they might be likened to rulers of armies; or possibly they might be compared to physicians watching over a war against bodily disease, or to farmers fearfully awaiting seasons of wonted difficulty for the generation of plants, or else to masters of flocks. For seeing that we have agreed [1] among ourselves that the heaven is full of many things that are good, and of the opposite kind also, and that those not good are the more numerous, such a battle, we affirm, is undying, and needs a wondrous watchfulness,—the gods and daemons being our allies, and we the possession [2] of the gods and daemons; and what destroys us is iniquity and insolence combined with folly, what saves us, justice and temperance combined with wisdom, which dwell in the animate powers of the gods, and of which some small trace may be clearly seen here also residing in us. But there are certain souls that dwell on earth and have acquired unjust gain which, being plainly bestial, beseech the souls of the guardians—whether they be watch-dogs or herdsmen or the most exalted of masters—trying to convince them by fawning words and prayerful incantations that (as the tales of evil men relate) they can profiteer among men on earth without any severe penalty: but we assert that the sin now mentioned, of profiteering or "over-gaining," is what is called in the case of fleshly bodies "disease," [3] in

---

[3] Cp. *Rep.* 609, *Symp.* 188 A ff., where the theory is stated that health depends upon the "harmony," or equal balance, of the constituent elements of the body ("heat" and "cold," "moisture" and "dryness,"); when any of these (opposite) elements is in excess ($\pi\lambda\epsilon o\nu\epsilon\kappa\tau\epsilon\hat{\iota}$), disease sets in. So, too, in the "body politic," the excess of due measure by any element, or member, is injustice.

καλούμενον, ἐν δὲ ὥραις ἐτῶν καὶ ἐνιαυτοῖς
λοιμόν, ἐν δὲ πόλεσι καὶ πολιτείαις τοῦτο αὐτό,
ῥήματι [1] μετεσχηματισμένον, ἀδικίαν.

ΚΛ. Παντάπασι μὲν οὖν.

ΑΘ. Τοῦτον δὴ τὸν λόγον ἀναγκαῖον λέγειν
τὸν λέγοντα ὡς εἰσὶ συγγνώμονες ἀεὶ θεοὶ τοῖς
D τῶν ἀνθρώπων ἀδίκοις καὶ ἀδικοῦσιν, ἂν αὐτοῖς
τῶν ἀδικημάτων τις ἀπονέμῃ, καθάπερ <εἰ> [2]
κυσὶ λύκοι τῶν ἁρπασμάτων σμικρὰ ἀπονέμοιεν,
οἱ δὲ ἡμερούμενοι τοῖς δώροις συγχωροῖεν τὰ
ποίμνια διαρπάζειν. ἆρ᾽ οὐχ οὗτος ὁ λόγος ὁ
τῶν φασκόντων παραιτητοὺς εἶναι θεούς ;

ΚΛ. Οὗτος μὲν οὖν.

ΑΘ. Τίσιν οὖν δὴ τῶν προρρηθέντων ἀπει-
κάζων ὁμοίους φύλακας εἶναι θεοὺς οὐκ ἂν καταγέλαστος γίγνοιτο ἀνθρώπων ὁστισοῦν ; πότερον
E κυβερνήταις, λοιβῇ τε οἴνου κνίσῃ τε παρατρεπο-
μένοις αὐτοῖς, ἀνατρέπουσι δὲ ναῦς τε καὶ ναύτας ;

ΚΛ. Μηδαμῶς.

ΑΘ. ᾽Αλλ᾽ οὔ τι μὴν ἡνιόχοισί γε ἐν ἀμίλλῃ
συντεταγμένοις, πεισθεῖσιν ὑπὸ δωρεᾶς ἑτέροισι
τὴν νίκην ζεύγεσι προδοῦναι.

ΚΛ. Δεινὴν γὰρ εἰκόνα λέγοις ἂν λέγων τὸν
λόγον τοῦτον.

ΑΘ. Οὐ μὴν οὐδὲ στρατηγοῖς γε οὐδ᾽ ἰατροῖς
οὐδὲ γεωργοῖς οὐδὲ νομεῦσιν, οὐ μὴν οὐδέ τισι
κυσὶ κεκηλημένοις ὑπὸ λύκων.

ΚΛ. Εὐφήμει· πῶς γὰρ ἄν ;

907 ΑΘ. ᾽Αλλ᾽ οὐ πάντων φυλάκων εἰσὶ μέγιστοι
καὶ περὶ τὰ μέγιστα ἡμῖν οἱ πάντες θεοί ;

[1] αὐτό, ῥήματι MSS., Burnet : αὖ τὸ ῥῆμα MSS. marg., Zur.
[2] <εἰ> added by Hermann.

that of seasons and years " pestilence," and in that of States and polities, by a verbal change, this same sin is called " injustice."

CLIN. Certainly.

ATH. Such must necessarily be the account of the matter given by the man who says that the gods are always merciful to unjust men and those who act unjustly, provided that one gives them a share of one's unjust gains ; it is just as if wolves were to give small bits of their prey to watch-dogs, and they being mollified by the gifts were to allow them to go ravening among the flocks. Is not this the account given by the man who asserts that the gods are open to bribes ?

CLIN. It is.

ATH. To which of the guardians aforementioned might a man liken the gods without incurring ridicule ? Is it to pilots, who, when warped themselves by wine's " flow and flavour," [1] overturn both ships and sailors ?

CLIN. By no means.

ATH. And surely not to drivers ranged up for a race and seduced by a gift to lose it in favour of other teams ?

CLIN. If that was the account you gave of them, it would indeed be a horrible comparison.

ATH. Nor, surely, to generals or physicians or farmers or herdsmen ; nor yet to dogs charmed by wolves ?

CLIN. Hush ! That is quite impossible.

ATH. Are not all gods the greatest of all guardians, and over the greatest things ?

----

[1] *Il.* IX. 500 (quoted above, p. 371, n. 1).

κλ. Πολύ γε.

αθ. Τοὺς δὴ κάλλιστά τε πράγματα φυλάττοντας διαφέροντάς τε αὐτοὺς φυλακῆς[1] πρὸς ἀρετὴν κυνῶν χείρους καὶ ἀνθρώπων μέσων εἶναι φήσομεν, οἳ τὸ δίκαιον οὐκ ἄν ποτε προδοῖεν ἕνεκα δώρων παρὰ ἀδίκων ἀνδρῶν ἀνοσίως διδομένων ;

Β κλ. Οὐδαμῶς· οὔτε ἀνεκτὸς ὁ λόγος, τῶν τε περὶ πᾶσαν ἀσέβειαν ὄντων κινδυνεύει πᾶς ὁ ταύτης τῆς δόξης ἀντεχόμενος πάντων ἂν τῶν ἀσεβῶν κεκρίσθαι δικαιότατα κάκιστός τε εἶναι καὶ ἀσεβέστατος.

αθ. Τὰ μὲν δὴ προτεθέντα τρία, θεοί τε ὡς εἰσὶ καὶ ὡς ἐπιμελεῖς καὶ παρὰ τὸ δίκαιον ὡς παντάπασιν ἀπαραίτητοι, φῶμεν ἱκανῶς ἀποδεδεῖχθαί που ;

κλ. Πῶς γὰρ οὔ ; καὶ σύμψηφοί γε τούτοις τοῖς λόγοις ἐσμέν.

αθ. Καὶ μὴν εἴρηταί γέ πως σφοδρότερον διὰ C φιλονικίαν τῶν κακῶν ἀνθρώπων. τούτου γε μὴν ἕνεκα, ὦ φίλε Κλεινία, πεφιλονίκηνται, μή ποτε λόγοις ἡγῶνται κρατοῦντες ἐξουσίαν εἶναι σφίσιν ἃ βούλονται πράττειν οἱ κακοί, ἃ δὴ καὶ ὅσα καὶ οἷα περὶ θεοὺς διανοοῦνται. προθυμία μὲν δὴ διὰ ταῦτα νεωτέρως εἰπεῖν ἡμῖν γέγονεν· εἰ δέ τι καὶ βραχὺ προὔργου πεποιήκαμεν εἰς τὸ πείθειν πη τοὺς ἄνδρας ἑαυτοὺς μὲν μισῆσαι, τὰ δ' ἐναντία πως ἤθη στέρξαι, καλῶς ἡμῖν D εἰρημένον ἂν εἴη τὸ προοίμιον ἀσεβείας πέρι νόμων.

κλ. Ἀλλὰ ἐλπίς· εἰ δὲ μή, τό γε τοῦ λόγου γένος οὐκ αἰτιάσονται[2] τὸν νομοθέτην.

[1] φυλακῆς : φυλακῇ MSS., edd.
[2] αἰτιάσονται ; αἰτιάσεται MSS., edd.

CLIN. Yes, by far.

ATH. Shall we say that those who watch over the fairest things, and who are themselves eminently good at keeping watch, are inferior to dogs and ordinary men, who would never betray justice for the sake of gifts impiously offered by unjust men?

CLIN. By no means; it is an intolerable thing to say, and whoever embraces such an opinion would most justly be adjudged the worst and most impious of all the impious men who practise impiety in all its forms.

ATH. May we now say that we have fully proved our three propositions,—namely, that the gods exist, and that they are careful, and that they are wholly incapable of being seduced to transgress justice?

CLIN. Certainly we may; and in these statements you have our support.

ATH. And truly they have been made in somewhat vehement terms, in our desire for victory over those wicked men; and our desire for victory was due to our fear lest haply, if they gained the mastery in argument, they should suppose they had gained the right to act as they chose—those men who wickedly hold all those false notions about the gods. On this account we have been zealous to speak with special vigour; and if we have produced any good effect, however small, in the way of persuading the men to hate themselves and to feel some love for an opposite kind of character, then our prelude to the laws respecting impiety will not have been spoken amiss.

CLIN. Well, there is hope; and if not, at any rate no fault will be found with the lawgiver in respect of the nature of the argument.

ΑΘ. Μετὰ τὸ προοίμιον τοίνυν λόγος οἷος ἂν
τῶν νόμων ἑρμηνεὺς ὀρθῶς γίγνοιτο ἡμῖν, προαγορεύων ἐξίστασθαι πᾶσι τοῖς ἀσεβέσι τρόπων
τῶν αὑτῶν εἰς τοὺς εὐσεβεῖς. τοῖς δὲ μὴ πειθομένοις ἀσεβείας ὅδε ἔστω πέρι νόμος· Ἐάν τις
ἀσεβῇ λόγοις εἴτ᾽ ἔργοις, ὁ παρατυγχάνων
E ἀμυνέτω σημαίνων πρὸς ἄρχοντας, τῶν δὲ ἀρχόντων οἱ πρῶτοι πυθόμενοι πρὸς τὸ περὶ τούτων
ἀποδεδειγμένον κρίνειν δικαστήριον εἰσαγαγόντων
κατὰ τοὺς νόμους· ἐὰν δέ τις ἀκούσασα ἀρχὴ μὴ
δρᾷ ταῦτα, αὐτὴ ἀσεβείας ὑπόδικος γιγνέσθω τῷ
ἐθέλοντι τιμωρεῖν ὑπὲρ τῶν νόμων. ἐὰν δέ τις
ὄφλῃ, τιμάτω τὸ δικαστήριον ἐν[1] ἑκάστῳ τῶν
908 καθ᾽ ἓν ἀσεβούντων τίμημα. δεσμὸς μὲν οὖν ὑπαρχέτω πᾶσι· δεσμωτηρίων δὲ ὄντων ἐν τῇ πόλει
τριῶν, ἑνὸς μὲν κοινοῦ τοῖς πλείστοις περὶ ἀγοράν,
σωτηρίας ἕνεκα τοῖς πολλοῖς τῶν σωμάτων, ἑνὸς
δὲ περὶ τὸν τῶν νύκτωρ συλλεγομένων ξύλλογον,
σωφρονιστήριον ἐπονομαζόμενον, ἑνὸς δὲ αὖ κατὰ
μέσην τὴν χώραν, ὅπηπερ ἂν ἔρημός τε καὶ ὡς
ὅτι μάλιστα ἀγριώτατος ᾖ τόπος, τιμωρίας ἔχων
ἐπωνυμίαν φήμην τινά. περὶ ἀσέβειαν δὲ ὄντων
B αἰτίαις μὲν τρισίν, αἷσπερ καὶ διήλθομεν, δύο δὲ
ἐξ ἑκάστης τῆς τοιαύτης αἰτίας γενομένων, ἐξ ἂν
γίγνοιντο, ἃ καὶ διακρίσεως ἄξια γένη τῶν περὶ τὰ
θεῖα ἐξαμαρτανόντων, οὐκ ἴσης οὐδ᾽ ὁμοίας δίκης
δεόμενα. ᾧ γὰρ ἂν μὴ νομίζοντι θεοὺς εἶναι τὸ
παράπαν ἦθος φύσει προσγένηται δίκαιον, μι-
σοῦντές τε γίγνονται τοὺς κακούς, καὶ τῷ δυσχε-

---

[1] ἐν Schneider, Hermann : ἐν MSS.

[1] Cp. 767 C, D, 855 C.

ATH. After the prelude it will be proper for us to have a statement of a kind suitable to serve as the laws' interpreter, forewarning all the impious to quit their ways for those of piety. For those who disobey, this shall be the law concerning impiety :—If anyone commits impiety either by word or deed, he that meets with him shall defend the law by informing the magistrates, and the first magistrates who hear of it shall bring the man up before the court [1] appointed to decide such cases as the laws direct; and if any magistrate on hearing of the matter fail to do this, he himself shall be liable to a charge of impiety at the hands of him who wishes to punish him on behalf of the laws. And if a man be convicted, the court shall assess one penalty for each separate act of impiety. Imprisonment shall be imposed in every case ; and since there are three prisons in the State (namely, one public prison near the market for most cases, to secure the persons of the average criminals ; a second, situated near the assembly-room of the officials who hold nightly assemblies,[2] and named the " reformatory " ; and a third, situated in the middle of the country, in the wildest and loneliest spot possible, and named after " retribution " [3]), and since men are involved in impiety from the three causes which we have described, and from each such cause two forms of impiety result—consequently those who sin in respect of religion fall into six classes which require to be distinguished, as needing penalties that are neither equal nor similar. For while those who, though they utterly disbelieve in the existence of the gods, possess by nature a just character, both hate the evil and, because of their

[2] Cp. 909 A, 961 A ff.   [3] Cp. 704 B.

ραίνειν τὴν ἀδικίαν οὔτε τὰς τοιαύτας πράξεις
προσίενται πράττειν τούς τε μὴ δικαίους τῶν
C ἀνθρώπων φεύγουσι καὶ τοὺς δικαίους στέργουσιν.
οἷς δ' ἂν πρὸς τῇ δόξῃ τῇ θεῶν ἔρημα εἶναι
πάντα ἀκράτειαί τε ἡδονῶν καὶ λυπῶν προσ-
πέσωσι, μνῆμαί τε ἰσχυραὶ καὶ μαθήσεις ὀξεῖαι
παρῶσι, τὸ μὲν μὴ νομίζειν θεοὺς ἀμφοῖν ἂν
ἐνυπάρχοι κοινὸν πάθος, τῇ δὲ τῶν ἄλλων ἀνθρώπων λώβῃ τὸ μὲν ἐλάττω, τὸ δὲ πλείω κακὰ
ἐργάζοιτ' ἄν. ὁ μὲν γὰρ λόγῳ τε ἂν περὶ θεοὺς
παρρησίας εἴη μεστὸς καὶ περὶ θυσίας τε καὶ
D ὅρκους, καὶ ὡς τῶν ἄλλων καταγελῶν τάχ' ἂν
ἑτέρους τοιούτους ἀπεργάζοιτο, δίκης μὴ τυγ-
χάνων· ὁ δὲ δὴ δοξάζων μὲν καθάπερ ἅτερος,
εὐφυὴς δὲ ἐπικαλούμενος, δόλου δὴ καὶ ἐνέδρας
πλήρης, ἐξ ὧν μάντεις τε κατασκευάζονται πολλοὶ
καὶ περὶ πᾶσαν τὴν μαγγανείαν γεγενημένοι,[1]
γίγνονται δὲ ἐξ αὐτῶν ἔστιν ὅτε καὶ τύραννοι καὶ
δημηγόροι καὶ στρατηγοί, καὶ τελεταῖς δὲ ἰδίαις
ἐπιβεβουλευκότες, σοφιστῶν τε ἐπικαλουμένων
μηχαναί. τούτων δὴ πολλὰ μὲν εἴδη γένοιτ' ἄν·
E τὰ δὲ νόμων ἄξια θέσεως δύο, ὧν τὸ μὲν εἰρωνικὸν
οὐχ ἑνὸς οὐδὲ δυοῖν ἄξια θανάτοιν ἁμάρτανον, τὸ δὲ
νουθετήσεως ἅμα καὶ δεσμῶν δεόμενον. ὡσαύτως
δὲ καὶ τὸ θεοὺς νομίζον ἀμελεῖν δύ' ἕτερα γεννᾷ
καὶ τὸ παραιτητοὺς ἄλλα δύο. τούτων δὴ ταύτῃ
διεστηκότων τοὺς μὲν ὑπ' ἀνοίας ἄνευ κάκης ὀργῆς
τε καὶ ἤθους γεγενημένους εἰς τὸ σωφρονιστήριον

---

[1] γεγενημένοι : κεκινημένοι MSS.

[1] i.e. "hypocritical," hiding impiety under a cloak of
religion.

380

dislike of injustice, are incapable of being induced to commit unjust actions, and flee from unjust men and love the just, on the other hand, those who, besides holding that the world is empty of gods, are afflicted by incontinence in respect of pleasures and pains, and possess also powerful memories and sharp wits—though both these classes share alike in the disease of atheism, yet in respect of the amount of ruin they bring on other people, the latter class would work more and the former less of evil. For whereas the one class will be quite frank in its language about the gods and about sacrifices and oaths, and by ridiculing other people will probably convert others to its views, unless it meets with punishment, the other class, while holding the same opinions as the former, yet being specially " gifted by nature " and being full of craft and guile, is the class out of which are manufactured many diviners and experts in all manner of jugglery ; and from it, too, there spring sometimes tyrants and demagogues and generals, and those who plot by means of peculiar mystic rites of their own, and the devices of those who are called " sophists." Of these there may be many kinds ; but those which call for legislation are two, of which the " ironic "[1] kind commits sins that deserve not one death only or two, while the other kind requires both admonition and imprisonment. Likewise also the belief that the gods are neglectful breeds two other kinds of impiety ; and the belief in their being open to bribes, other two. These kinds being thus distinguished, those criminals who suffer from folly,[2] being devoid of evil disposition and character, shall be placed by the judge according to

[2] Cp. 863 B, C.

ὁ δικαστὴς τιθέμενος νόμῳ τιθέσθω μηδὲν ἔλαττον
ἐτῶν πέντε. ἐν τούτῳ δὲ τῷ χρόνῳ μηδεὶς τῶν
909 πολιτῶν αὐτοῖς ἄλλος συγγιγνέσθω πλὴν οἱ τοῦ
νυκτερινοῦ ξυλλόγου κοινωνοῦντες, ἐπὶ νουθετήσει τε καὶ τῇ τῆς ψυχῆς σωτηρίᾳ ὁμιλοῦντες·
ὅταν δ' ὁ χρόνος αὐτοῖς ἐξέλθῃ τῶν δεσμῶν, ἐὰν
μὲν δοκῇ τις σωφρονεῖν αὐτῶν, οἰκείτω μετὰ τῶν
σωφρόνων, ἐὰν δὲ μή, ὀφείλῃ δ' αὖθις τὴν τοιαύτην δίκην, θανάτῳ ζημιούσθω. ὅσοι δ' ἂν
θηριώδεις γένωνται πρὸς τῷ θεοὺς [μὴ]¹ νομίζειν
B ἢ ἀμελεῖς ἢ παραιτητοὺς εἶναι, καταφρονοῦντες
δὲ τῶν ἀνθρώπων ψυχαγωγῶσι μὲν πολλοὺς τῶν
ζώντων, τοὺς δὲ τεθνεῶτας φάσκοντες ψυχα-
γωγεῖν καὶ θεοὺς ὑπισχνούμενοι πείθειν, ὡς
θυσίαις τε καὶ εὐχαῖς καὶ ἐπῳδαῖς γοητεύοντες,
ἰδιώτας τε καὶ ὅλας οἰκίας καὶ πόλεις χρημάτων
χάριν ἐπιχειρῶσι κατ' ἄκρας ἐξαιρεῖν, τούτων δὲ
ὃς ἂν ὀφλὼν εἶναι δόξῃ, τιμάτω τὸ δικαστήριον
αὐτῷ κατὰ νόμον δεδέσθαι μὲν ἐν τῷ τῶν μεσο-
C γείων δεσμωτηρίῳ, προσιέναι δὲ αὐτῷ μηδένα
ἐλεύθερον μηδέποτε, τακτὴν δὲ ὑπὸ τῶν νομοφυλάκων αὐτοὺς τροφὴν παρὰ τῶν οἰκετῶν
λαμβάνειν. ἀποθανόντα δὲ ἔξω τῶν ὁρίων ἐκ-
βάλλειν ἄταφον· ἐὰν δέ τις ἐλεύθερος συνθάπτῃ,
δίκας ἀσεβείας τῷ ἐθέλοντι λαγχάνειν ὑπεχέτω.
παῖδας δὲ ἂν μὲν καταλίπῃ τῇ πόλει ἱκανούς,
οἱ τῶν ὀρφανῶν ἐπιμελούμενοι καὶ τούτων, ὡς
D ὄντων ὀρφανῶν, ἐπιμελείσθων μηδὲν χεῖρον τῶν
ἄλλων ἀπὸ τῆς ἡμέρας ἧς ἂν ὁ πατὴρ αὐτῶν
ὄφλῃ τὴν δίκην.

¹ [μὴ] bracketed by Stallb., Hermann.

law in the reformatory for a period of not less than five years, during which time no other of the citizens shall hold intercourse with them, save only those who take part in the nocturnal assembly,[1] and they shall company with them to minister to their souls' salvation by admonition; and when the period of their incarceration has expired, if any of them seems to be reformed, he shall dwell with those who are reformed, but if not, and if he be convicted again on a like charge, he shall be punished by death. But as to all those who have become like ravening beasts, and who, besides holding that the gods are negligent or open to bribes, despise men, charming the souls of many of the living, and claiming that they charm the souls of the dead, and promising to persuade the gods by bewitching them, as it were, with sacrifices, prayers and incantations,[2] and who try thus to wreck utterly not only individuals, but whole families and States for the sake of money, —if any of these men be pronounced guilty, the court shall order him to be imprisoned according to law in the mid-country gaol, and shall order that no free man shall approach such criminals at any time, and that they shall receive from the servants a ration of food as fixed by the Law-wardens. And he that dies shall be cast outside the borders without burial; and if any free man assist in burying him, he shall be liable to a charge of impiety at the hands of anyone who chooses to prosecute. And if the dead man leaves children fit for citizenship, the guardians of orphans shall take them also under their charge from the day of their father's conviction, just as much as any other orphans.

[1] Cp. 908 A.   [2] Cp. 933 A, *Rep.* 364 B ff.

PLATO

Κοινὸν δ᾽ ἐπὶ τούτοις πᾶσι νόμον κεῖσθαι
χρεών, ὃς ἐλάττω τε εἰς θεοὺς αὐτῶν τοὺς πολλοὺς ἔργῳ καὶ λόγῳ πλημμελεῖν ἂν ποιοῖ, καὶ
δὴ καὶ ἀνοήτους ἧττον γίγνεσθαι, διὰ τὸ μὴ
ἐξεῖναι θεοπολεῖν παρὰ νόμον. ἔστω γὰρ νόμος
ὅδε τοῖς ξύμπασι κείμενος ἁπλῶς· Ἱερὰ μηδὲ εἷς
ἐν ἰδίαις οἰκίαις ἐκτήσθω. θύειν δ᾽ ὅταν ἐπὶ νοῦν ἴῃ
E τινί, πρὸς τὰ δημόσια ἴτω θύσων, καὶ τοῖς ἱερεῦσί
τε καὶ ἱερείαις ἐγχειριζέτω τὰ θύματα, οἷς ἁγνεία
τούτων ἐπιμελής· συνευξάσθω δὲ αὐτός τε καὶ
ὃν ἂν ἐθέλῃ μετ᾽ αὐτοῦ ξυνεύχεσθαι. ταῦτα δὲ
γιγνόμενα τῶν τοιῶνδε χάριν ἔστω· ἱερὰ καὶ
θεοὺς οὐ ῥᾴδιον ἱδρύεσθαι, μεγάλης δὲ διανοίας
τινὸς ὀρθῶς δρᾶν τὸ τοιοῦτον, ἔθος τε γυναιξί τε
δὴ διαφερόντως πάσαις καὶ τοῖς ἀσθενοῦσι πάντῃ
καὶ κινδυνεύουσι καὶ ἀποροῦσιν, ὅπῃ τις ἂν
ἀπορῇ, καὶ τοὐναντίον ὅταν εὐπορίας τινὸς λά-
βωνται, καθιεροῦν τε τὸ παρὸν ἀεὶ καὶ θυσίας
910 εὔχεσθαι καὶ ἱδρύσεις ὑπισχνεῖσθαι θεοῖς καὶ
δαίμοσι καὶ παισὶ θεῶν, ἔν τε φάσμασιν ἐγρηγορότας διὰ φόβους καὶ ἐν ὀνείροις, ὡς δ᾽ αὕτως
ὄψεις πολλὰς ἀπομνημονεύοντας, ἑκάσταισί τε αὐτῶν ἄκη ποιουμένους, βωμοὺς καὶ ἱερὰ πάσας μὲν
οἰκίας, πάσας δὲ κώμας ἔν τε καθαροῖς ἱδρυομένους
ἐμπιπλάναι καὶ ὅπῃ τις ἔτυχε τῶν τοιούτων. ὧν
ἕνεκα χρὴ πάντων ποιεῖν κατὰ τὸν νῦν λεγόμενον
νόμον· πρὸς τούτοις δὲ ἕνεκα τῶν ἀσεβούντων,
B ἵνα μὴ καὶ ταῦτα κλέπτοντες ταῖς πράξεσιν, ἱερά
384

For all these offenders one general law must be laid down, such as will cause the majority of them not only to offend less against the gods by word and deed, but also to become less foolish, through being forbidden to trade in religion illegally. To deal comprehensively with all such cases the following law shall be enacted :—No one shall possess a shrine in his own house : when anyone is moved in spirit to do sacrifice, he shall go to the public places to sacrifice, and he shall hand over his oblations to the priests and priestesses to whom belongs the consecration thereof ; and he himself, together with any associates he may choose, shall join in the prayers. This procedure shall be observed for the following reasons :—It is no easy task to found temples and gods, and to do this rightly needs much deliberation ; yet it is customary for all women especially, and for sick folk everywhere, and those in peril or in distress (whatever the nature of the distress), and conversely for those who have had a slice of good fortune, to dedicate whatever happens to be at hand at the moment, and to vow sacrifices and promise the founding of shrines to gods and demi-gods and children of gods ; and through terrors caused by waking visions or by dreams, and in like manner as they recall many visions and try to provide remedies for each of them, they are wont to found altars and shrines, and to fill with them every house and every village, and open places too, and every spot which was the scene of such experiences. For all these reasons their action should be governed by the law now stated ; and a further reason is this —to prevent impious men from acting fraudulently in regard to these matters also, by setting up shrines and

τε καὶ βωμοὺς ἐν ἰδίαις οἰκίαις ἱδρυόμενοι, λάθρᾳ
τοὺς θεοὺς ἵλεως οἰόμενοι ποιεῖν θυσίαις τε καὶ
εὐχαῖς, εἰς ἄπειρον τὴν ἀδικίαν αὐξάνοντες αὑτοῖς
τε ἐγκλήματα πρὸς θεῶν ποιῶνται καὶ τοῖς ἐπι-
τρέπουσιν, οὖσιν αὐτῶν βελτίοσι, καὶ πᾶσα οὕτως
ἡ πόλις ἀπολαύῃ τῶν ἀσεβῶν τρόπον τινὰ δικαίως. τὸν μὲν δὴ νομοθέτην ὁ θεὸς οὐ μέμψεται·
κείσθω γὰρ νόμος οὗτος· Μὴ κεκτῆσθαι θεῶν ἐν
C ἰδίαις οἰκίαις ἱερά· τὸν δὲ φανέντα κεκτημένον
ἕτερα καὶ ὀργιάζοντα πλὴν τὰ δημόσια, ἐὰν μὲν
ἄδικον μηδὲν τῶν μεγάλων καὶ ἀνοσίων εἰργασ-
μένος ἀνὴρ ἢ καὶ γυνὴ κεκτηταί τις, ὁ μὲν αἰσθα-
νόμενος εἰσαγγελλέτω τοῖς νομοφύλαξιν, οἱ δὲ
προστατόντων εἰς τὰ δημόσια ἀποφέρειν ἱερὰ
τὰ ἴδια, μὴ πείθοντες δὲ ζημιούντων, ἕως ἂν
D ἀπενεχθῇ· ἐὰν δέ τις ἀσεβήσας μὴ παιδίων ἀλλ'
ἀνδρῶν ἀσέβημα ἀνοσίων γένηται φανερός εἴτε
ἐν ἰδίοις ἱδρυσάμενος εἴτ᾽ ἐν δημοσίοις θύσας ἱερὰ
θεοῖς οἱστισινοῦν, ὡς οὐ καθαρὸς ὢν θύων, θανάτῳ
ζημιούσθω. τὸ δὲ παίδειον ἢ μὴ κρίναντες οἱ νομοφύλακες, εἰς τὸ δικαστήριον οὕτως εἰσαγαγόντες
τὴν τῆς ἀσεβείας δίκην τούτοις ἐπιτελούντων.

altars in private houses, thinking to propitiate the gods privily by sacrifices and vows, and thus increasing infinitely their own iniquity, whereby they make both themselves and those better men who allow them guilty in the eyes of the gods, so that the whole State reaps the consequences of their impiety in some degree—and deserves to reap them. The lawgiver himself, however, will not be blamed by the god; for this shall be the law laid down:— Shrines of the gods no one must possess in a private house; and if anyone is proved to possess and worship at any shrine other than the public shrines —be the possessor man or woman,—and if he is guilty of no serious act of impiety, he that notices the fact shall inform the Law-wardens, and they shall give orders for the private shrines to be removed to the public temples, and if the owner disobeys the order, they shall punish him until he removes them. And if anyone be proved to have committed an impious act, such as is not the venial offence of children, but the serious irreligion of grown men, whether by setting up a shrine on private ground, or on public ground, by doing sacrifice to any gods whatsoever, for sacrificing in a state of impurity he shall be punished with death. And the Law-wardens shall judge what is a childish or venial offence and what not, and then shall bring the offenders before the court, and shall impose upon them the due penalty for their impiety.

913   ΑΘ.   Τὸ δὴ μετὰ ταῦτ' εἴη ξυμβόλαια ἂν πρὸς
ἀλλήλους ἡμῖν δεόμενα προσηκούσης τάξεως.
ἁπλοῦν δέ γ' ἐστί που τό γε τοιοῦτον· Μήτε οὖν
τις τῶν ἐμῶν χρημάτων ἅπτοιτο εἰς δύναμιν, μηδ'
αὖ κινήσειε μηδὲ τὸ βραχύτατον ἐμὲ μηδαμῇ
μηδαμῶς πείθων· κατὰ ταὐτὰ δὲ ταῦτα καὶ περὶ
τὰ τῶν ἄλλων ἐγὼ δρῴην, νοῦν ἔχων ἔμφρονα.
θησαυρὸν δὴ λέγωμεν πρῶτον τῶν τοιούτων· ὃν
τις αὑτῷ καὶ τοῖς αὑτοῦ κειμήλιον ἔθετο, μὴ τῶν
ἐμῶν ὢν πατέρων, μήθ' εὑρεῖν ποτε θεοῖς εὐξαίμην
B μήθ' εὑρὼν κινήσαιμι, μηδ' αὖ τοῖς λεγομένοις
μάντεσιν ἀνακοινώσαιμι τοῖς ἁμῶς γέ πώς μοι
ξυμβουλεύσουσιν[1] ἀνελεῖν τὴν γῆ παρακαταθήκην. οὐ γάρ ποτε τοσοῦτον εἰς χρημάτων
ὠφεληθείην ἂν κτῆσιν ἀνελών, ὅσον εἰς ὄγκον
πρὸς ἀρετὴν ψυχῆς καὶ τὸ δίκαιον ἐπιδιδοίην ἂν
μὴ ἀνελόμενος, κτῆμα ἀντὶ κτήματος ἄμεινον ἐν
ἀμείνονι κτησάμενος, δίκην ἐν τῇ ψυχῇ πλούτου
προτιμήσας ἐν οὐσίᾳ κεκτῆσθαι πρότερον· ἐπὶ
πολλοῖς γὰρ δὴ λεγόμενον εὖ τὸ μὴ κινεῖν τὰ
ἀκίνητα καὶ περὶ τούτου λέγοιτ' ἂν ὡς ἑνὸς
C ἐκείνων ὄντος.   πείθεσθαι δὲ χρὴ καὶ τοῖς περὶ
ταῦτα λεγομένοις μύθοις, ὡς εἰς παίδων γενεὰν
οὐ ξύμφορα τὰ τοιαῦτα. ὃς δ' ἂν παίδων τε
ἀκηδὴς γένηται καὶ τοῦ θέντος τὸν νόμον ἀμελή-

---

[1] ξυμβουλεύσουσιν Stephens : ξυμβουλεύουσιν MSS.

BOOK XI

ATH. In the next place our business transactions one with another will require proper regulation. The following will serve for a comprehensive rule :—— So far as possible, no one shall touch my goods nor move them in the slightest degree, if he has in no wise at all got my consent; and I must act in like manner regarding the goods of all other men, keeping a prudent mind. As the first of such things let us mention treasure : that which a man has laid by in store for himself and his family (he not being one of my parents), I must never pray to the gods to find, nor, if I do find it, may I move it, nor may I ever tell of it to the soothsayers (so-called), who are certain to counsel me to take up what is laid down in the ground. For never should I gain so much pecuniary profit by its removal, as I should win increase in virtue of soul and in justice by not removing it; and by preferring to gain justice in my soul rather than money in my purse, I should be winning a greater in place of a lesser gain, and that too in a better part of me. The rule,[1] "Thou shalt not move the immovable," is rightly applicable to many cases; and the case before us is one of them. And men ought also to believe the stories told about these matters,—how that such conduct is injurious to the getting of children. But if any man proves to be both regardless of children and neglectful of

[1] Cp. 684 E, 843 A.

σας, ἃ μήτε αὐτὸς κατέθετο μήτε αὖ πατέρων
τις πατήρ, μὴ πείσας τὸν θέμενον ἀνέληται,
κάλλιστον νόμων διαφθείρων καὶ ἁπλούστατον,
καὶ οὐδαμῇ ἀγεννοῦς ἀνδρὸς νομοθέτημα, ὃς
D εἶπεν, ἃ μὴ κατέθου, μὴ ἀνέλῃ,—τούτοιν τοῖν
δυοῖν νομοθέταιν καταφρονήσαντα καὶ ἀνελόμενον
οὔ τι σμικρόν, ὃ μὴ κατέθετο αὐτός, πλῆθος δ'
ἔστιν ὅτε θησαυροῦ παμμέγεθες, τί χρὴ πάσχειν ;
ὑπὸ μὲν δὴ θεῶν, ὁ θεὸς οἶδεν· ὁ δὲ κατιδὼν
πρῶτος ἀγγελλέτω, ἐὰν μὲν ἐν ἄστει γίγνηται τὸ
τοιοῦτον, τοῖς ἀστυνόμοις, ἐὰν δὲ τῆς πόλεως ἐν
914 ἀγορᾷ που, τοῖσιν ἀγορανόμοις, ἐὰν δὲ τῆς ἄλλης
χώρας, ἀγρονόμοις τε καὶ τοῖς τούτων ἄρχουσι
δηλωσάτω. δηλωθέντων δὲ ἡ πόλις εἰς Δελφοὺς
πεμπέτω· ὅ τι δ' ἂν ὁ θεὸς ἀναιρῇ περί τε τῶν
χρημάτων καὶ τοῦ κινήσαντος, τοῦτο ἡ πόλις
ὑπηρετοῦσα ταῖς μαντείαις δράτω τοῦ θεοῦ. καὶ
ἐὰν μὲν ἐλεύθερος ὁ μηνύσας ᾖ, δόξαν ἀρετῆς
κεκτήσθω, μὴ μηνύσας δέ, κακίας· δοῦλος δ' ἐὰν
ᾖ, μηνύσας μὲν ἐλεύθερος ὑπὸ τῆς πόλεως ὀρθῶς
γίγνοιτ' ἂν ἀποδιδούσης τῷ δεσπότῃ τὴν τιμήν,
μὴ μηνύων δὲ θανάτῳ ζημιούσθω.

B   Τούτῳ δ' ἑπόμενον ἑξῆς ἂν γίγνοιτο τὸ περὶ
σμικρὰ καὶ μεγάλα ταὐτὸν τοῦτο νόμιμον ξυνακολουθεῖν. ἄν τις τῶν αὑτοῦ τι καταλίπῃ που ἑκὼν
εἴτ' ἄκων, ὁ προστυγχάνων ἐάτω κεῖσθαι νομίζων
φυλάττειν ἐνοδίαν δαίμονα τὰ τοιαῦτα ὑπὸ τοῦ
νόμου τῇ θεῷ καθιερωμένα. ἂν δὲ παρὰ ταῦτά

---

[1] Solon.   [2] Cp. 759 Cf., 772 D.
[3] Hecate (= Artemis).

the legislator, and, without the consent of the depositor, takes up a treasure which neither he himself nor any of his forefathers has deposited, and thus breaks a law most fair, and that most comprehensive ordinance of the noble man [1] who said, "Take not up what you laid not down,"—the man who despises these two lawgivers and takes up what he has not laid down himself, it being no small thing but sometimes a vast quantity of treasure,—what penalty should such a man suffer? God knows what, at the hands of gods; but the man that first notices an act of this kind shall report it, if it occur in the city, to the city-stewards, or if in a public market, to the market-stewards; and if it occur in the country outside, he shall declare it to the rural stewards and their officers. And when such declarations are made, the State shall send to Delphi; [2] and whatever the god pronounces concerning the goods and him that moved them, that the State shall execute, acting as agent on behalf of the oracles of the god. And if the informer be a free man, he shall win a reputation for virtue, but for vice if he fail to inform; and if he be a slave, as a reward for informing it will be right that he should be set free, by the State offering his price to his master, whereas he shall be punished by death if he fail to give information.

Following on this there should come next a similar rule about matters great and small, to reinforce it. If a man, whether willingly or unwillingly, leaves any of his goods behind, he that happens on them shall let them lie, believing that the Goddess of the Wayside [3] guards them, as things dedicated to her divinity by the law. Should

PLATO

τις ἀπειθῶν ἀναιρούμενος οἴκαδε φέρῃ, ἂν μὲν
σμικρᾶς τιμῆς ἄξιον ὢν δοῦλος, ὑπὸ τοῦ προστυγ-
χάνοντος μὴ ἔλαττον τριακονταέτους πολλὰς
C πληγὰς μαστιγούσθω· ἐὰν δέ τις ἐλεύθερος, πρὸς
τῷ ἀνελεύθερος εἶναι δοκεῖν καὶ ἀκοινώνητος
νόμων δεκαπλάσιον τῆς τιμῆς τοῦ κινηθέντος
ἀποτινέτω τῷ καταλιπόντι. ἐὰν δέ τις ἐπαιτιᾶ-
ται τῶν αὑτοῦ χρημάτων ἔχειν τινὰ πλέον ἢ καὶ
σμικρότερον, ὁ δὲ ὁμολογῇ μὲν ἔχειν, μὴ τὸ
ἐκείνου δέ, ἂν μὲν ἀπογεγραμμένον ᾖ παρὰ τοῖς
ἄρχουσι τὸ κτῆμα κατὰ νόμον, τὸν ἔχοντα
καλείσθω πρὸς τὴν ἀρχήν, ὁ δὲ καθιστάτω. γενομένου δὲ ἐμφανοῦς, ἐὰν ἐν τοῖς γράμμασιν
ἀπογεγραμμένον φαίνηται ποτέρου τῶν ἀμφισ-
D βητούντων, ἔχων οὗτος ἀπίτω· ἐὰν δέ τινος ἄλλου
τῶν μὴ παρόντων, ὁπότερος ἂν παράσχῃ τὸν
ἐγγυητὴν ἀξιόχρεων, ὑπὲρ τοῦ ἀπόντος, ὡς
παραδώσων ἐκείνῳ, κατὰ τὴν ἐκείνου ἀφαίρεσιν
ἀφαιρείσθω. ἐὰν δὲ παρὰ τοῖς ἄρχουσι τὸ ἀμφισ-
βητούμενον μὴ ἀπογεγραμμένον ᾖ, κείσθω μὲν
μέχρι δίκης παρὰ τρισὶ τῶν ἀρχόντων τοῖς
πρεσβυτάτοις· ἐὰν δὲ τὸ μεσεγγυωθὲν θρέμμα
ᾖ, τὸν νικηθέντα περὶ αὐτοῦ δίκῃ τὴν τροφὴν
ἐκτίνειν τοῖς ἄρχουσι· τὴν δὲ κρίσιν διαδικάζειν
ἐντὸς τριῶν ἡμερῶν τοὺς ἄρχοντας.
E   Ἀγέτω τὸν ἑαυτοῦ δοῦλον ὁ βουλόμενος, ἐὰν ἔμ-
φρων ᾖ, χρησόμενος ὅ τι ἂν ἐθέλῃ τῶν ὁπόσα ὅσια·

---

[1] Cp. 745 A, B.

anyone transgress this rule and disobediently take up such things and carry them home, he being a slave and the article of small value, then the man who meets with him, being over thirty years old, shall scourge him with many stripes; but if he be a free man, he shall not only be accounted illiberal and a rebel against the laws, but he shall in addition pay back ten times the value of the article moved to the man who left it behind. And if one man charges another with possessing any of his goods, be it great or small, and the man so charged allows that he has the article, but denies that it is the other man's,—then, if the article in question has been registered [1] with the magistrates according to law, the plaintiff shall summon the man who possesses it before the magistrate, and he shall produce it in court. And the article being thus exhibited, if it be clearly recorded in the records to which of the disputants it belongs, he shall take it and depart; but should it belong to another third party, not then present, whichever of the two claimants produces a sufficient guarantor shall take it away on behalf of the absent party, in pursuance of his right of removal, to hand it over to him. But if the article in dispute be not registered with the magistrates, it shall be kept in charge of the three senior magistrates up to the time of the trial; and if the article in pledge be a beast, the man that loses the case concerning it shall pay the magistrates for its keep; and the magistrates shall decide the case within three days.

Any person—provided that he be in his senses —may lay hands, if he wishes, on his own slave, to employ him for any lawful purpose; and on be-

ἀγέτω δὲ καὶ ὑπὲρ ἄλλου τῶν οἰκείων ἢ φίλων
τὸν ἀφεστῶτα ἐπὶ σωτηρίᾳ. ἐὰν δέ τις ἀφαιρῆταί
τινα εἰς ἐλευθερίαν ὡς δοῦλον ἀγόμενον, μεθιέτω
μὲν ὁ ἄγων, ὁ δὲ ἀφαιρούμενος ἐγγυητὰς τρεῖς
ἀξιόχρεως καταστήσας οὕτως ἀφαιρείσθω κατὰ
ταῦτα, ἄλλως δὲ μή. ἐὰν δὲ παρὰ ταῦτά τις
915 ἀφαιρῆται, τῶν βιαίων ἔνοχος ἔστω καὶ ἁλοὺς
τὴν διπλασίαν τοῦ ἐπιγραφέντος βλάβους τῷ
ἀφαιρεθέντι τινέτω. ἀγέτω δὲ καὶ τὸν ἀπελεύ-
θερον, ἐάν τις μὴ θεραπεύῃ τοὺς ἀπελευθερώσαν-
τας ἢ μὴ ἱκανῶς. θεραπεία δὲ φοιτᾶν τρὶς τοῦ
μηνὸς τὸν ἀπελευθερωθέντα πρὸς τὴν τοῦ ἀπελευθερώσαντος ἑστίαν, ἐπαγγελλόμενον ὅ τι χρὴ
δρᾶν τῶν δικαίων καὶ ἅμα δυνατῶν, καὶ περὶ γάμου
ποιεῖν ὅ τί περ ἂν ξυνδοκῇ τῷ γενομένῳ δεσπότῃ·
πλουτεῖν δὲ τοῦ ἀπελευθερώσαντος μὴ ἐξεῖναι
B μᾶλλον· τὸ δὲ πλέον γιγνέσθω τοῦ δεσπότου. μὴ
πλείω δὲ εἴκοσιν ἐτῶν μένειν τὸν ἀφεθέντα, ἀλλὰ
καθάπερ καὶ τοὺς ἄλλους ξένους ἀπιέναι λαβόντα
τὴν αὑτοῦ πᾶσαν οὐσίαν, ἐὰν μὴ πείσῃ τούς τε
ἄρχοντας καὶ τὸν ἀπελευθερώσαντα. ἐὰν δὲ τῷ
ἀπελευθερωθέντι ἢ καὶ τῶν ἄλλων τῳ ξένων
οὐσία πλείων γίγνηται τοῦ τρίτου μεγέθει τιμήματος, ᾗ ἂν τοῦτο ἡμέρᾳ γένηται, τριάκοντα
ἡμερῶν ἀπὸ ταύτης τῆς ἡμέρας λαβὼν ἀπίτω τὰ
C ἑαυτοῦ, καὶ μηδεμία τῆς μονῆς παραίτησις ἔτι
τούτῳ παρ' ἀρχόντων γιγνέσθω. ἐὰν δέ τις
ἀπειθῶν τούτοις εἰσαχθεὶς εἰς δικαστήριον ὄφλῃ,
θανάτῳ τε ζημιούσθω καὶ τὰ χρήματα αὐτοῦ

---

[1] Cp. 850 B.
[2] Cp. 744 C, E, 756 D.

half of another man (one of his relatives or friends)
he may lay hands on the runaway slave, to secure
his safe keeping. And if a man tries to remove to
freedom anyone who is being carried off as a slave,
the man who is carrying him off shall let him go,
and he that is removing him shall do so on the
production of three substantial sureties, but not
otherwise; and if anyone removes a slave contrary
to these conditions, he shall be liable for assault,
and if convicted he shall pay double his registered
value to the man deprived. And a man may arrest
also a freedman, if in any case he fails to attend, or
to attend sufficiently, on those who have freed him;
and such tendance shall consist in the coming of
the freedman three times a month to the home of
the man that freed him, and there undertaking to
do those duties which are both just and feasible, and
in regard to marriage also to act as may seem good
also to his former master. The freedman shall not
be permitted to be more wealthy than the man who
freed him; and, if he is, the excess shall be made
over to his master. He that is let go free shall not
remain in the country more than twenty years, but
shall depart, like all other foreigners,[1] taking with
him all the property he owns,—unless he gains the
consent of the magistrates and also of the man who
freed him. And if a freedman, or any other foreigner,
acquire property exceeding in amount the third
valuation,[2] within thirty days from the day on which
he acquires this excess he shall take his own property
and depart, and he shall have no further right to
request from the magistrates permission to remain;
and if he disobeys these rules and is summoned
before the court and convicted, he shall be punished

PLATO

γιγνέσθω δημόσια. δίκαι δ᾽ ἔστωσαν τούτων
ἐν ταῖς φυλετικαῖσι δίκαις, ἐὰν μὴ πρότερον ἐν
γείτοσιν ἢ ἐν αἱρετοῖσι δικασταῖς ἀπαλλάττωνται
πρὸς ἀλλήλους τῶν ἐγκλημάτων.

Ἐὰν δὲ ὡς αὑτοῦ ἐφάπτηται ζώου καὶ ὁτουοῦν ἢ
D τινος ἑτέρου τῶν αὑτοῦ χρημάτων, ἀναγέτω μὲν ὁ
ἔχων εἰς πρατῆρα ἢ τὸν δόντα ἀξιόχρεών τε καὶ
ἔνδικον ἤ τινι τρόπῳ παραδόντα ἄλλῳ κυρίως, εἰς
μὲν πολίτην ἢ καὶ μέτοικον τῶν ἐν τῇ πόλει ἡμερῶν
τριάκοντα, εἰς δὲ ξενικὴν παράδοσιν πέντε μηνῶν,
ἧς μέσος ὁ μὴν ἐν ᾧ τρέπεται θερινὸς ἥλιος εἰς τὰ
χειμερινά. ὅσα δὲ διά τινος ὠνῆς ἢ καὶ πράσεως
ἀλλάττεταί τις ἕτερος ἄλλῳ, διδόντα ἐν χώρᾳ τῇ
τεταγμένῃ ἑκάστοις κατ᾽ ἀγορὰν καὶ δεχόμενον
ἐν τῷ παραχρῆμα τιμήν, οὕτως ἀλλάττεσθαι,
ἄλλοθι δὲ μηδαμοῦ, μηδ᾽ ἐπὶ ἀναβολῇ πρᾶσιν
E μηδὲ ὠνὴν ποιεῖσθαι μηδενός. ἐὰν δὲ ἄλλως ἢ
ἐν ἄλλοις τόποις ὁτιοῦν ἀνθ᾽ ὁτουοῦν διαμείβηται
ἕτερος ἄλλῳ, πιστεύων πρὸς ὃν ἂν ἀλλάττηται,
ποιείτω ταῦτα ὡς οὐκ οὐσῶν δικῶν κατὰ νόμον
περὶ τῶν μὴ πραθέντων κατὰ τὰ νῦν λεγόμενα.
ἐράνων δὲ πέρι, τὸν βουλόμενον ἐρανίζειν φίλον
παρὰ φίλοις· ἐὰν δέ τις διαφορὰ γίγνηται περὶ
τῆς ἐρανίσεως, οὕτω πράττειν ὡς δικῶν μηδενὶ
περὶ τούτων μηδαμῶς ἐσομένων. ὃς δ᾽ ἂν ἀποδόμενος τιμήν του λάβῃ μὴ ἐλάττω δραχμῶν
πεντήκοντα, παραμενέτω κατὰ πόλιν ἐξ ἀνάγκης

¹ Cp. 952 E.   ² Cp. 849 E.
³ Cp. *Rep.* 556 B.

by death, and his goods shall be confiscated. Such cases shall be tried before the tribal courts, unless the parties first get a settlement of their charges against one another before neighbours or chosen jurors.

If anyone claims as his own the beast of any other man, or any other of his chattels, the man who holds it shall refer the matter to the person who, as being its substantial and lawful owner, sold it or gave it, or made it over to him in some other valid way; and this he shall do within thirty days, if the reference be made to a citizen or metic in the city, or, in the case of a foreign delivery, within five months, of which the middle month shall be that which includes the summer solstice.[1] And when one man makes an exchange with another by an act of buying or selling, the exchange shall be made by a transfer of the article in the place appointed therefor in the market, and nowhere else, and by payment of the price on the spot, and no purchase or sale shall be made on credit;[2] and if anyone makes an exchange with another otherwise or in other places, trusting the man with whom he is dealing, he shall do so on the understanding that there are no suits by law touching things not sold according to the rules now prescribed.[3] As regards club-collections,[4] whoso wishes may collect as a friend among friends; but if any dispute arises concerning the collection, they must act on the understanding that in regard to these matters no legal actions are possible. If any man receives for the sale of any article a price of not less than fifty drachmae, he shall be com-

[4] *i.e.* of subscriptions due from members of a (dining) club, or of money raised as a loan to a member in time of need.

δέκα ἡμέρας, ὁ δὲ πριάμενος ἴστω τὴν οἰκίαν τὴν
916 τοῦ ἀποδομένου, τῶν περὶ τὰ τοιαῦτα ἐγκλημάτων
εἰωθότων γίγνεσθαι χάριν καὶ τῶν ἀναγωγῶν
τῶν κατὰ νόμους εἵνεκα. ἡ δὲ κατὰ νόμους
ἀναγωγὴ καὶ μὴ τῇδε ἔστω· ἐάν τις ἀνδράποδον
ἀποδῶται κάμνον φθόῃ ἢ λιθῶν ἢ στραγγουριῶν
ἢ τῇ καλουμένῃ ἱερᾷ νόσῳ ¹ ἢ καὶ ἑτέρῳ τινὶ ἀδήλῳ
τοῖς πολλοῖς νοσήματι μακρῷ καὶ δυσιάτῳ κατὰ
τὸ σῶμα ἢ κατὰ τὴν διάνοιαν, ἐὰν μὲν ἰατρῷ τις
ἢ γυμναστῇ, μὴ ἀναγωγῆς ἔστω τούτῳ πρὸς τὸν
τοιοῦτον τυγχάνειν, μηδ' ἐὰν τἀληθές τις προει-
B πὼν ἀποδῶταί τῳ· ἐὰν δέ τις ἰδιώτῃ τι τῶν
τοιούτων ἀποδῶται δημιουργός, ὁ πριάμενος ἐντὸς
ἐκμήνου ἀναγέτω, πλὴν τῆς ἱερᾶς· ταύτης δ' ἐντὸς
ἐνιαυτοῦ τὴν ἀναγωγὴν ἐξέστω ποιεῖσθαι τῆς
νόσου. διαδικαζέσθω δὲ ἔν τισι τῶν ἰατρῶν, οὓς
ἂν κοινῇ προβαλόμενοι ἕλωνται· τὸν δὲ ὀφλόντα
τὴν δίκην διπλάσιον ἀποτίνειν τῆς τιμῆς ἧς ἂν
C ἀποδῶται. ἐὰν δὲ ἰδιώτῃ τις ἰδιώτης, ἀναγωγὴν
μὲν εἶναι, καθάπερ καὶ τοῖς πρόσθεν ἐρρήθη, καὶ
τὴν διαδικασίαν, ὁ δὲ ὀφλὼν τὴν τιμὴν ἁπλῆν
ἀποτινέτω. ἐὰν δὲ ἀνδροφόνον ἀποδῶταί τίς τινι
εἰδότι μὲν εἰδώς, μὴ τυγχανέτω ἀναγωγῆς τοῦ
τοιούτου τῆς πράσεως, μὴ δὲ εἰδότι τὴν μὲν
ἀναγωγὴν εἶναι τότε ὅταν τις αἴσθηται τῶν
πριαμένων, ἐν πέντε δὲ τῶν νομοφυλάκων τοῖς
νεωτάτοις εἶναι τὴν κρίσιν, εἰδὼς δὲ ἂν κριθῇ, τάς
τε οἰκίας τοῦ πριαμένου καθηράτω κατὰ τὸν τῶν

---

¹ *i.e.* epilepsy.

pelled to remain in the city for ten days, and the seller's residence shall be made known to the buyer, because of the charges which are commonly brought in connexion with such transactions, and because of the acts of restitution permitted by law. Such legal restitution, or non-restitution, shall be on this wise :— If a man sell a slave who is suffering from phthisis or stone or strangury or the "sacred disease" [1] (as it is called), or from any other complaint, mental or physical, which most men would fail to notice, although it be prolonged and hard to cure,—in case the purchaser be a doctor or a trainer, it shall not be possible for him to gain restitution for such a case, nor yet if the seller warned the purchaser of the facts. But if any professional person sell any such slave to a lay person, the buyer shall claim restitution within six months, saving only in the case of epilepsy, for which disease he shall be permitted to claim within twelve months. The action shall be tried before a bench of doctors nominated and chosen by both the parties ; and the party that loses his case shall pay double the selling price of the slave. If a lay person sells to a lay person, there shall be the same right of restitution and trial as in the cases just mentioned ; but the losing party shall pay the selling price only. If a man wittingly sells a murderer, if the buyer is aware of the fact, he shall have no claim to restitution for the purchase of such an one ; but if the buyer be ignorant, he shall have right of restitution as soon as the fact is perceived, and the trial shall take place before a court of the five youngest Law-wardens, and if it be decided that the seller acted wittingly, he shall purify the houses of the buyer as ordained by the

ἐξηγητῶν νόμον, τῆς τιμῆς τε ἀποδότω τῷ πρια-
μένῳ τριπλάσιον.

D Ὁ δὲ ἀλλαττόμενος ἢ νόμισμα ἀντὶ νομίσματος
ἢ καὶ τῶν ἄλλων ζώων ὁτιοῦν ἢ καὶ μὴ ζώων
ἀκίβδηλον πᾶν διδότω καὶ δεχέσθω τῷ νόμῳ
ξυνεπόμενος· προοίμιον δέ, καθάπερ ἄλλων
νόμων, δεξώμεθα καὶ περὶ ὅλης ταύτης τῆς κάκης.
κιβδηλείαν δὲ χρὴ πάντα ἄνδρα διανοηθῆναι
καὶ ψεῦδος καὶ ἀπάτην ὡς ἔν τι γένος ὄν,
τοῦτο ᾧ τὴν φήμην ἐπιφέρειν εἰώθασιν οἱ πολλοί, κακῶς λέγοντες, ὡς ἐν καιρῷ γιγνόμενον
ἑκάστοτε τὸ τοιοῦτον πολλάκις ἂν ὀρθῶς ἔχοι·
E τὸν καιρὸν δὲ καὶ ὅπου καὶ ὁπότε ἀτάκτως
καὶ ἀορίστως ἐῶντες τῇ λέξει ταύτῃ πολλὰ
ζημιοῦνταί τε καὶ ζημιοῦσιν ἑτέρους. νομοθέτῃ
δὲ οὐκ ἐγχωρεῖ τοῦτο ἀόριστον ἐᾶν, ἀλλ᾽ ἢ μείζους
ἢ ἐλάττους ὅρους ἀεὶ δεῖ διασαφεῖν, καὶ δὴ καὶ
νῦν ὡρίσθω· Ψεῦδος μηδεὶς μηδὲν μηδ᾽ ἀπάτην
μηδέ τι κίβδηλον, γένος ἐπικαλούμενος θεῶν, μήτε
λόγῳ μήτε ἔργῳ πράξειεν, ὁ μὴ θεομισέστατος
917 ἔσεσθαι μέλλων. οὗτος δ᾽ ἐστὶν ὃς ἂν ὅρκους
ὀμνὺς ψευδεῖς μηδὲν φροντίζῃ θεῶν, δεύτερος δὲ
ὃς ἂν ἐναντίον τῶν κρειττόνων αὑτοῦ ψεύδηται.
κρείττους δὲ οἱ ἀμείνους τῶν χειρόνων πρεσβῦταί
τε ὡς ἐπὶ τὸ πᾶν εἰπεῖν τῶν νέων, διὸ καὶ γονεῖς
κρείττους ἐκγόνων καὶ ἄνδρες δὴ γυναικῶν καὶ
παίδων ἄρχοντές τε ἀρχομένων. οὓς αἰδεῖσθαι
πᾶσι πάντας πρέπον ἂν εἴη ἐν ἄλλῃ τε ἀρχῇ
πάσῃ καὶ ἐν ταῖς πολιτικαῖς δὴ μάλιστα ἀρχαῖς·

interpreters,[1] and he shall pay three times the selling price to the buyer.

He that exchanges for money either money or anything else, living or not living, shall give and receive every such article unadulterated, conforming to the law; and touching all knavery of this sort, as in the case of other laws, let us hearken to a prelude. Adulteration should be regarded by every man as coming under the same head as falsehood and fraud—a class of actions concerning which the mob are wont to say, wrongly, that any such action will generally be right if it be done opportunely: but the proper "opportunity," the when and the where, they leave unprescribed and undefined, so that by this saying they often bring loss both to themselves and to others. But it is not fitting for the lawgiver to leave this matter undefined; he must always declare clearly the limitations, great or small, and this shall now be done:—No man, calling the gods to witness, shall commit, either by word or deed, any falsehood, fraud or adulteration, if he does not mean to be most hateful to the gods; and such an one is he who without regard of the gods swears oaths falsely, and he also who lies in the presence of his superiors. Now the better are the superiors of the worse, and the older in general of the younger; wherefore also parents are superior to their offspring, men to women and children, rulers to ruled.[2]   And it will be proper for all to revere all these classes of superiors, whether they be in other positions of authority or in offices of State above all; and to enforce this is just the

---

[1] The officials in charge of (Delphic) religious rites; cp. 759 C, 828 B.

[2] Cp. 690 A ff.

ὅθεν [οὖν] ὁ νῦν παρὼν ἡμῖν λόγος ἐλήλυθε. πᾶς
B γὰρ τῶν κατ' ἀγορὰν ὁ κιβδηλεύων τι ψεύδεται
καὶ ἀπατᾷ καὶ τοὺς θεοὺς παρακαλῶν ἐπόμνυσιν
ἐν τοῖς τῶν ἀγορανόμων νόμοισί τε καὶ φυλακτηρίοις, οὔτε ἀνθρώπους αἰδούμενος οὔτε θεοὺς
σεβόμενος. πάντως μὲν δὴ καλὸν ἐπιτήδευμα
θεῶν ὀνόματα μὴ χραίνειν ῥᾳδίως, ἔχοντα ὡς
ἔχουσιν ἡμῶν ἑκάστοτε τὰ πολλὰ οἱ πλεῖστοι
καθαρότητός τε καὶ ἁγνείας τὰ περὶ τοὺς θεούς.
εἰ δ' οὖν μὴ πείθοιτο, ὅδε νόμος· Ὁ πωλῶν ὁτιοῦν
ἐν ἀγορᾷ μηδέποτε δύο εἴπῃ τιμὰς ὧν ἂν πωλῇ,
C ἁπλῆν δὲ εἰπών, ἂν μὴ τυγχάνῃ ταύτης, ἀποφέρων
ὀρθῶς ἂν ἀποφέροι πάλιν, καὶ ταύτης τῆς ἡμέρας
μὴ τιμήσῃ πλέονος μηδὲ ἐλάττονος· ἔπαινος δὲ
ὅρκος τε περὶ παντὸς τοῦ πωλουμένου ἀπέστω.
ἐὰν δέ τις ἀπειθῇ τούτοις, ὁ παρατυγχάνων τῶν
ἀστῶν μὴ ἔλαττον ἢ τριάκοντα γεγονὼς ἔτη
κολάζων μὲν τὸν ὀμνύντα ἀνατὶ τυπτέτω, ἀφροντιστῶν δὲ καὶ ἀπειθῶν ἔνοχος ἔστω ψόγῳ προδο-
σίας τῶν νόμων. τὸν δὲ δὴ κίβδηλόν τι πωλοῦντα
D καὶ μὴ δυνάμενον τοῖς νῦν πείθεσθαι λόγοις ὁ
προστυγχάνων τῶν γιγνωσκόντων, δυνατὸς ὢν
ἐξελέγχειν, ἐναντίον ἐλέγξας τῶν ἀρχόντων, ὁ μὲν
δοῦλος φερέσθω τὸ κιβδηλευθὲν καὶ ὁ μέτοικος, ὁ
δὲ πολίτης μὴ ἐλέγχων μὲν ὡς ἀποστερῶν τοὺς
θεοὺς κακὸς ἀγορευέσθω, ἐλέγξας δὲ ἀναθέτω τοῖς
τὴν ἀγορὰν ἔχουσι θεοῖς. ὁ δὲ δὴ φανερὸς γενόμενός
τι πωλῶν τοιοῦτον πρὸς τῷ στερηθῆναι τοῦ
κιβδηλευθέντος, ὁπόσης ἂν τιμῆς ἀξιώσῃ τὸ πωλού-

purpose of our present discourse. For everyone who adulterates any market commodity, lies and deceives and, calling Heaven to witness, takes an oath in front of the laws and cautions of the market-stewards, neither regarding men nor revering gods. Certainly it is a good practice to refrain from sullying lightly divine names, and to behave with such purity and holiness as most of us generally exhibit in matters of religion; if however this rule is disobeyed, the law runs thus:—He that sells any article in the market shall never name two prices for what he is selling; he shall name one price only, and if he fails to get this, he will be entitled to take the article away; but he shall not put any other price, greater or less, upon it on that day; and there shall be no puffing or taking of oaths about anything put up for sale. If any man disobeys these rules, any townsman who is present, not being under thirty years of age, shall punish with a beating the seller who swears, and he shall do so with impunity; but if he is disobedient and neglects to do so, he shall be liable to reprobation for betraying the laws. And if a man is selling an adulterated article, and is incapable of obeying our present rules, any person who is present and aware of the fact and able to expose him shall take for himself the adulterated article, if he expose him before a magistrate, he being himself a slave or a metic,—but if he be a citizen, he shall be declared to be wicked, as a robber of the gods, if he fail to expose the guilty man; while if he does expose him, he shall offer the article to the gods who preside over the market. He that is found out in selling any such article, in addition to being deprived of the adulterated article, shall be beaten in the market-

μενον, κατὰ δραχμὴν ἑκάστην τῇ μάστιγι τυπτέ-
E σθω πληγὰς ὑπὸ κήρυκος ἐν τῇ ἀγορᾷ κηρύξαντος
ὧν ἕνεκα μέλλει τύπτεσθαι. τὰ δὲ κιβδηλεύματά
τε καὶ κακουργίας τῶν πωλούντων οἵ τε ἀγορανόμοι καὶ οἱ νομοφύλακες πυθόμενοι τῶν ἐμπείρων
περὶ ἕκαστα, ἀναγραψάντων ἅ τε χρὴ ποιεῖν τὸν
πωλοῦντα καὶ ἃ μή, καὶ πρόσθε τοῦ ἀγορανομίου
θέντων ἐν στήλῃ γράψαντες νόμους εἶναι τοῖς
918 περὶ τὴν τῆς ἀγορᾶς χρείαν μηνυτὰς σαφεῖς. τὰ
δὲ περὶ τῶν ἀστυνόμων ἐν τοῖς πρόσθεν ἱκανῶς
εἴρηται. ἐὰν δέ τι προσδεῖν δοκῇ, νομοφύλαξιν
ἐπανακοινώσαντες καὶ γράψαντες τὸ δοκοῦν
ἐλλιπεῖν[1] εἰς ἀστυνόμιον θέντων ἐν στήλῃ τά τε
πρῶτα καὶ τὰ δεύτερα τεθέντα αὐτοῖσι τῆς ἀρχῆς
νόμιμα.

Κιβδήλοις δ' ἐπιτηδεύμασιν ἕπεται κατὰ
πόδα καπηλείας ἐπιτηδεύματα. ταύτης δὲ πέρι
ξυμπάσης συμβουλὴν πρῶτον δόντες καὶ λόγον
B ἐπ' αὐτῇ νόμον ὕστερον ἐπιθώμεθα. καπηλεία
γὰρ κατὰ πόλιν πᾶσα γέγονεν οὐ βλάβης ἕνεκα
τό γε κατὰ φύσιν, πᾶν δὲ τοὐναντίον· πῶς γὰρ
οὐκ εὐεργέτης πᾶς ὃς ἂν οὐσίαν χρημάτων
ὡντινωνοῦν ἀσύμμετρον οὖσαν καὶ ἀνώμαλον
ὁμαλήν τε καὶ σύμμετρον ἀπεργάζηται; τοῦτο
ἡμῖν χρὴ φάναι καὶ τὴν τοῦ νομίσματος ἀπεργάζεσθαι δύναμιν, καὶ τὸν ἔμπορον ἐπὶ τούτῳ
τετάχθαι δεῖ λέγειν. καὶ μισθωτὸς καὶ παν-
δοκεὺς καὶ ἄλλα, τὰ μὲν εὐσχημονέστερα, τὰ δὲ
C ἀσχημονέστερα γιγνόμενα, τοῦτό γε πάντα δύ-
ναται, πᾶσιν ἐπικουρίαν ταῖς χρείαις ἐξευπορεῖν

---

[1] ἐλλιπεῖν Hermann : ἐκλιπεῖν MSS.

place with stripes—one stripe for every drachma in the price he asks for the article—after that the herald has first proclaimed the crimes for which the seller is to be beaten. Touching acts of fraud and wrongful acts done by sellers, the market-stewards and the Law-wardens, after making enquiry from experts in each trade, shall write out rules as to what the seller ought to do or avoid doing, and shall post them up on a pillar in front of the stewards' office, to serve as written laws and clear instructors for those engaged in business in the market. The duties of the city-stewards have been fully stated already;[1] in case any addition seems to be required, they shall inform the Law-wardens, and write out what seems to be wanting; and they shall post up on the pillar at the city-stewards' office both the primary and the secondary regulations pertaining to their office.

Following close upon practices of adulteration follow practices of retail trading; concerning which, as a whole, we shall first offer counsel and argument, and then impose on it a law. The natural purpose for which all retail trading comes into existence in a State is not loss, but precisely the opposite; for how can any man be anything but a benefactor if he renders even and symmetrical the distribution of any kind of goods which before was unsymmetrical and uneven? And this is, we must say, the effect produced by the power of money, and we must declare that the merchant is ordained for this purpose. And the hireling and the innkeeper and the rest—some more and some less respectable trades,—all have this function, namely, to provide all men with full satisfaction of their needs and with even-

[1] Cp. 759 A ff., 849 E f., 881 C.

καὶ ὁμαλότητα ταῖς οὐσίαις. τί ποτε δὴ τὸ μὴ
καλὸν αὐτὸ μηδ᾿ εὔσχημον δοκεῖν εἶναι, καὶ τί
τὸ διαβεβληκὸς τυγχάνει, ἴδωμεν, ἵν᾿ εἰ μὴ καὶ
τὸ ὅλον, ἀλλ᾿ οὖν μέρη γε ἐξιασώμεθα νόμῳ.
πρᾶγμ᾿ ἔσθ᾿, ὡς ἔοικεν, οὐ φαῦλον, οὐδὲ σμικρᾶς
δεόμενον ἀρετῆς.

ΚΛ. Πῶς λέγεις;

ΑΘ. Ὦ φίλε Κλεινία, σμικρὸν γένος ἀνθρώπων
καὶ φύσει ὀλίγον καὶ ἄκρᾳ τροφῇ τεθραμμένον,
ὅταν εἰς χρείας τε καὶ ἐπιθυμίας τινῶν ἐμπίπτῃ,
D καρτερεῖν πρὸς τὸ μέτριον δυνατόν ἐστι, καὶ ὅταν
ἐξῇ χρήματα λαβεῖν πολλά, νήφει καὶ πρότερον
αἱρεῖται τοῦ πολλοῦ τὸ τοῦ μέτρου ἐχόμενον·
τὰ δὲ τῶν ἀνθρώπων πλήθη πᾶν τοὐναντίον ἔχει
τούτοις, δεόμενά τε ἀμέτρως δεῖται καὶ ἐξὸν
κερδαίνειν τὰ μέτρια ἀπλήστως αἱρεῖται κερδαί-
νειν· διὸ πάντα τὰ περὶ τὴν καπηλείαν καὶ
ἐμπορίαν καὶ πανδοκείαν γένη διαβέβληταί τε καὶ
ἐν αἰσχροῖς γέγονεν ὀνείδεσιν. ἐπεὶ εἴ τις, ὃ μή
ποτε γένοιτο οὐδ᾿ ἔσται, προσαναγκάσειε—γε-
E λοῖον μὲν εἰπεῖν, ὅμως δὲ εἰρήσεται—πανδοκεῦσαι
τοὺς πανταχῇ ἀρίστους ἄνδρας ἐπί τινα χρόνον
ἢ καπηλεύειν ἤ τι τῶν τοιούτων πράττειν, ἢ καὶ
γυναῖκας ἔκ τινος ἀνάγκης εἱμαρμένης τοῦ τοιούτου μετασχεῖν τρόπου, γνοίημεν ἂν ὡς φίλον καὶ
ἀγαπητόν ἐστιν ἕκαστον τούτων καί, εἰ κατὰ
λόγον ἀδιάφθορον γίγνοιτο, ἐν μητρὸς ἂν καὶ
919 τροφοῦ σχήματι τιμῷτο τὰ τοιαῦτα πάντα. νῦν
δὲ ὁπόταν εἰς ἐρήμους τις καπηλείας ἕνεκα τόπους

---

[1] *i.e.* by equalizing the distribution of goods throughout
the community. Cp. Ar. *Pol.* 1257ᵃ 14 ff.

ness in their properties.[1] Let us see then wherein trade is reputed to be a thing not noble nor even respectable, and what has caused it to be disparaged, in order that we may remedy by law parts of it at least, if not the whole. This is an undertaking, it would seem, of no slight importance, and one that calls for no little virtue.

CLIN. How do you mean?

ATH. My dear Clinias, small is the class of men —rare by nature and trained, too, with a superlative training—who, when they fall into divers needs and lusts, are able to stand out firmly for moderation, and who, when they have the power of taking much wealth, are sober, and choose what is of due measure rather than what is large. The disposition of the mass of mankind is exactly the opposite of this; when they desire, they desire without limit, and when they can make moderate gains, they prefer to gain insatiably; and it is because of this that all the classes concerned with retail trade, commerce, and inn-keeping are disparaged and subjected to violent abuse. Now if anyone were to do what never will be done (Heaven forbid!)—but I shall make the supposition, ridiculous though it is—namely, compel the best men everywhere for a certain period to keep inns or to peddle or to carry on any such trade,—or even to compel women by some necessity of fate to take part in such a mode of life,—then we should learn how that each of these callings is friendly and desirable; and if all these callings were carried on according to a rule free from corruption, they would be honoured with the honour which one pays to a mother or a nurse. But as things are now, whenever a man has planted his house, with a view to

καὶ πανταχόσε μήκη ἔχοντας ὁδῶν ἱδρυσάμενος
οἰκήσεις, ἐν ἀπορίᾳ γιγνομένους καταλύσεσιν
ἀγαπηταῖς δεχόμενος, ἢ ὑπὸ χειμώνων ἀγρίων
βίᾳ ἐλαυννομένοις [1] εὐδιεινὴν γαλήνην παρασχὼν
ἢ πνίγεσιν ἀναψυχήν, τὰ μετὰ ταῦτα οὐχ ὡς ἑταί-
ρους δεξάμενος φιλικὰ παράσχῃ ξένια ἑπόμενα
ταῖς ὑποδοχαῖς, ὡς δ' ἐχθροὺς αἰχμαλώτους κεχει-
ρωμένους ἀπολυτρώσῃ τῶν μακροτάτων καὶ ἀδίκων
B καὶ ἀκαθάρτων λύτρων, ταῦτά ἐστι καὶ τὰ τοιαῦτα ἐν ξύμπασι τοῖς τοιούτοις [ὀρθῶς] [2] ἁμαρ-
τανόμενα τὰς διαβολὰς τῇ τῆς ἀπορίας ἐπι-
κουρήσει παρεσκευακότα. τούτων οὖν χρὴ φάρμακον ἀεὶ τέμνειν τὸν νομοθέτην. ὀρθὸν μὲν δὴ
πάλαι τε εἰρημένον ὡς πρὸς δύο μάχεσθαι καὶ
ἐναντία χαλεπόν, καθάπερ ἐν ταῖς νόσοις πολλοῖς
τε ἄλλοισι· καὶ δὴ καὶ νῦν ἡ τούτων καὶ περὶ
ταὐτά ἐστι πρὸς δύο μάχη, πενίαν καὶ πλοῦτον,
τὸν μὲν ψυχὴν διεφθαρκότα τρυφῇ τῶν ἀν-
C θρώπων, τὴν δὲ λύπαις προτετραμμένην εἰς
ἀναισχυντίαν αὐτήν. τίς οὖν δὴ τῆς νόσου
ταύτης ἀρωγὴ γίγνοιτ' ἂν ἐν νοῦν ἐχούσῃ πόλει;
πρῶτον μὲν ὅ τι σμικροτάτῳ χρῆσθαι κατὰ
δύναμιν τῷ τῶν καπήλων γένει, ἔπειτα τούτοις
τῶν ἀνθρώπων προστάττειν ὧν διαφθειρομένων
οὐκ ἂν γίγνοιτο μεγάλη λύμη τῇ πόλει, τρίτον
δὲ αὐτοῖς τοῖς μετασχοῦσι τούτων τῶν ἐπιτηδευμάτων εὑρεῖν μηχανὴν ὅπως ἤθη μὴ ἀνέδην
D ἀναισχυντίας τε καὶ ἀνελευθέρου ψυχῆς μέτοχα
συμβήσεται γίγνεσθαι ῥᾳδίως. μετὰ δὴ τὰ νῦν
εἰρημένα περὶ ταῦτα νόμος ἀγαθῇ τύχῃ τοιόσδε

[1] ἐλαυνομένοις Stephens, Ast: ἐλαυνομένους MSS.

retail trade, in a desert place and with all the roads
from it lengthy, if in this welcome lodging he
receives travellers in distress, providing tranquillity
and calm to those buffeted by fierce storms or restful
coolness after torrid heat,—the next thing is that,
instead of treating them as comrades and providing
friendly gifts as well as entertainment, he holds them
to ransom, as if they were captive foemen in his hands,
demanding very high sums of unjust and unclean
ransom-money; it is criminal practices such as this,
in the case of all these trades, that afford grounds of
complaint against this way of succouring distress.
For these evils, then, the lawgiver must in each case
provide a medicine. It is an old and true saying that
it is hard to fight against the attack of two foes [1]
from opposite quarters, as in the case of diseases and
many other things; and indeed our present fight in
this matter is against two foes, poverty and plenty,[2]
of which the one corrupts the soul of men with
luxury, while the other by means of pain plunges
it into shamelessness. What remedy, then, is to be
found for this disease in a State gifted with understanding? The first is to employ the trading class
as little as possible; the second, to assign to that
class those men whose corruption would prove no
great loss to the State; the third, to find a means
whereby the dispositions of those engaged in these
callings may not quite so easily become infected by
shamelessness and meanness of soul. After the
declarations now made, let our law on these matters

---

[1] Cp. *Phaedo* 89 C: πρὸς δύο λέγεται οὐδ' ὁ Ἡρακλῆς οἷός τε
εἶναι.
[2] Cp. 679 B, 705 B.

---

[2] [ὀρθῶς] bracketed by Wagner: αἰσχρῶς Zur., vulg.

ἡμῖν γιγνέσθω· Μαγνήτων, οὓς ὁ θεὸς ἀνορθῶν
πάλιν κατοικίζει, γεωμόροι ὅσοι τῶν τετταράκοντα καὶ πεντακισχιλίων ἑστιῶν εἰσί, μήτε
κάπηλος ἑκὼν μηδ' ἄκων μηδεὶς γιγνέσθω μήτ'
ἔμπορος μήτε διακονίαν μηδ' ἥντινα κεκτημένος
ἰδιώταις τοῖς μὴ ἐξ ἴσου ἑαυτῷ, πλὴν πατρὶ καὶ
E μητρὶ καὶ τοῖς ἔτι τούτων εἰς τὸ ἄνω γένεσι
καὶ πᾶσι τοῖς αὑτοῦ πρεσβυτέροις ὅσοι ἐλεύθεροι ἐλευθέρως. τὸ δ' ἐλευθερικὸν καὶ ἀνελεύθερον ἀκριβῶς μὲν οὐ ῥᾴδιον νομοθετεῖν, κρινέσθω γε μὴν ὑπὸ τῶν τὰ ἀριστεῖα εἰληφότων
τῷ ἐκείνων μίσει τε καὶ ἀσπασμῷ. ὃς δ' ἂν
καπηλείας τῆς ἀνελευθέρου τέχνῃ τινὶ μετάσχῃ,
γραφέσθω μὲν αὐτὸν γένους αἰσχύνης ὁ βουλόμενος πρὸς τοὺς ἀρετῇ πρώτους κεκριμένους, ἐὰν
δὲ δόξῃ ἀναξίῳ ἐπιτηδεύματι καταρρυπαίνειν τὴν
αὑτοῦ πατρῴαν ἑστίαν, δεθεὶς ἐνιαυτὸν ἀπο-
920 σχέσθω τοῦ τοιούτου, καὶ ἐὰν αὖθις, ἔτη δύο, καὶ
ἐφ' ἑκάστης ἁλώσεως τοὺς δεσμοὺς μὴ παυέσθω
διπλασιάζων τοῦ ἔμπροσθεν χρόνου.[1] δεύτερος
μὴν νόμος· Μέτοικον εἶναι χρεὼν ἢ ξένον ὃς ἂν
μέλλῃ καπηλεύσειν. τὸ δὲ τρίτον καὶ τρίτος·
Ὅπως ὡς ἄριστος ἢ καὶ κακὸς ὡς ἥκιστα ὁ τοιοῦτος
ἡμῖν ᾖ ξύνοικος ἐν τῇ πόλει, τοὺς νομοφύλακας
χρὴ νοῆσαι φύλακας εἶναι μὴ μόνον ἐκείνων οὓς
φυλάττειν ῥᾴδιον μὴ παρανόμους καὶ κακοὺς
γίγνεσθαι, ὅσοι γενέσει καὶ τροφαῖς εὖ πεπαί-

[1] τοῦ . . . χρόνου Ast : τὸν . . . χρόνον MSS. (bracketed
by England)

---

[1] Cp. 702 B ff., 848 C ff.
[2] Literally "free men,"—the Greek word connoting
generosity, culture and dignity, like our "gentle."

(Heaven prosper it!) run in this wise:—Amongst
the Magnesians,[1] whom the god is restoring and
founding afresh, none of all the landholders who
belong to the 5040 houses shall, either willingly or
unwillingly, become a retail trader or a merchant, or
engage in any menial service for private persons who
do not make an equal return to himself, save only
for his father and mother and those of a still earlier
generation, and all that are elder than himself, they
being gentlemen[2] and his a gentleman's service.
What is becoming, what unbecoming a gentleman it
is not easy to fix by law; it shall, however, be
decided by those persons who have achieved public
distinction[3] for their aversion to the one and their
devotion to the other. If any citizen in any craft
engages in ungentlemanly peddling, whoso will shall
indict him for shaming his family before a bench of
those adjudged to be the first in virtue, and if it
be held that he is sullying his paternal hearth by an
unworthy calling, he shall be imprisoned for a year
and so restrained therefrom; if he repeats the
offence, he shall get two years' imprisonment, and
for each subsequent conviction the period of imprisonment shall go on being doubled. Now comes
a second law:—Whosoever intends to engage in
retail trade must be a resident alien or a foreigner.
And thirdly, this third law:—In order that such an
one may be as good as possible, or as little as
possible bad, he being a resident in our State, the
Law-wardens must bear in mind that they are
guardians not only of those who, being well-trained
both by birth and nurture, are easy to guard from
lawless and evil ways, but also of those who are

[3] Cp. 914 A, 922 A ff.

PLATO

B δευνται, τοὺς δὲ μὴ τοιούτους ἐπιτηδεύματά τε
ἐπιτηδεύοντας ἃ ῥοπὴν [1] ἔχει τινὰ ἰσχυρὰν πρὸς
τὸ προτρέπειν κακοὺς γίγνεσθαι, φυλακτέον
μᾶλλον· ταύτῃ δὴ τὰ περὶ τὴν καπηλείαν πολλὴν
οὖσαν καὶ πολλὰ ἐπιτηδεύματα τοιαῦτα κεκτημένην, ὅσαπερ ἂν αὐτῶν λειφθῇ δόξαντα ἐκ
πολλῆς ἀνάγκης ἐν τῇ πόλει δεῖν εἶναι, συνελθεῖν
αὖ χρεὼν περὶ ταῦτα τοὺς νομοφύλακας μετὰ τῶν
ἐμπείρων ἑκάστης καπηλείας, καθάπερ ἔμπροσθεν
C ἐπετάξαμεν τῆς κιβδηλείας πέρι, ξυγγενοῦς τούτῳ
πράγματος, συνελθόντας δὲ ἰδεῖν λῆμμά τε καὶ
ἀνάλωμα τί ποτε τῷ καπήλῳ κέρδος ποιεῖ τὸ
μέτριον, γράψαντας δὲ θεῖναι τὸ γιγνόμενον
ἀνάλωμα καὶ λῆμμα καὶ φυλάττειν, τὰ μὲν
ἀγορανόμους, τὰ δὲ ἀστυνόμους, τὰ δὲ ἀγρονόμους.
καὶ σχεδὸν οὕτως ἂν καπηλεία τὰ μὲν ὠφελοίη
ἑκάστους, σμικρότατα δὲ ἂν βλάπτοι τοὺς ἐν
ταῖς πόλεσι χρωμένους.

D "Οσα τις ἂν ὁμολογῶν ξυνθέσθαι μὴ ποιῇ
κατὰ τὰς ὁμολογίας, πλὴν ὧν ἂν νόμοι ἀπείργωσιν
ἢ ψήφισμα, ἤ τινος ὑπὸ ἀδίκου βιασθεὶς ἀνάγκης ὁμολογήσῃ, καὶ ἐὰν ὑπὸ τύχης ἀπροσδοκήτου
τις ἄκων κωλυθῇ, δίκας εἶναι τῶν ἄλλων ἀτελοῦς
ὁμολογίας ἐν ταῖς φυλετικαῖσι δίκαις, ἐὰν ἐν διαι-
τηταῖς ἢ γείτοσιν ἔμπροσθεν μὴ δύνωνται διαλ-
λάττεσθαι. Ἡφαίστου καὶ Ἀθηνᾶς ἱερὸν τὸ τῶν
δημιουργῶν γένος, οἳ τὸν βίον ἡμῖν ξυγκατε-
E σκευάκασι τέχναις, "Αρεος δ' αὖ καὶ Ἀθηνᾶς οἱ

---

[1] ἃ ῥοπὴν Hermann : ἀποτροπὴν MSS. : ἃ τροπὴν Zur.

---

[1] Cp. 917 E.

412

otherwise, and who follow pursuits which greatly tend to urge them on the road to vice; and these they must guard the more. Accordingly, with respect to retail trading, which is a multifarious occupation, embracing many callings of a similar nature,—with respect (I mean) to so many branches of it as are allowed to exist, as being deemed absolutely necessary to the State,—concerning these the procedure shall be the same as that previously prescribed in the case of the kindred matter of adulteration[1]: the Law-wardens must meet in consultation with experts in every branch of retail trade, and at their meetings they must consider what standard of profits and expenses produces a moderate gain for the trader, and the standard of profits and expenses thus arrived at they must prescribe in writing; and this they must insist on—the market-stewards, the city-stewards, and the rural stewards, each in their own sphere. So possibly, by this means, retail trade would be of benefit to all classes, and would do but little damage to those in the States who practise it.

Touching agreements, whenever a man undertakes and fails to fulfil his agreement—unless it be such as is forbidden by the laws or by a decree, or one made under forcible and unjust compulsion, or when the man is involuntarily prevented from fulfilling it owing to some unforeseen accident,—in all other cases of unfulfilled agreements, actions may be brought before the tribal courts, if the parties are unable to come to a previous settlement before arbitrators or neighbours. Sacred to Hephaestus and Athena is the class of craftsmen who have furnished our life with the arts, and to Ares and

τὰ τῶν δημιουργῶν σώζοντες τέχναισιν ἑτέραις
ἀμυντηρίοις ἔργα· δικαίως δὲ καὶ τὸ τούτων γένος
ἱερόν ἐστι τούτων τῶν θεῶν. οὗτοι δὴ πάντες
χώραν καὶ δῆμον θεραπεύοντες διατελοῦσιν, οἱ
μὲν ἄρχοντες τῶν κατὰ πόλεμον ἀγώνων, οἱ δὲ
ὀργάνων τε καὶ ἔργων ἀποτελοῦντες γένεσιν
ἔμμισθον· οἷς δὴ περὶ τὰ τοιαῦτα οὐ πρέπον ἂν
εἴη ψεύδεσθαι, θεοὺς προγόνους αὐτῶν αἰδου-
921 μένους. ἂν δή τις δημιουργῶν εἰς χρόνον εἰρημένον ἔργον μὴ ἀποτελέσῃ διὰ κάκην, μηδὲν τὸν
βιοδότην θεὸν ἐπαιδεσθείς, ἡγούμενος ὡς οἰκεῖον
συγγνώμονα εἶναι θεόν, οὐδὲν τῷ νῷ βλέπων,
πρῶτον μὲν δίκην τῷ θεῷ ὑφέξει, δεύτερον δὲ
ἑπόμενος αὐτῷ νόμος κείσθω· Τὴν τιμὴν τῶν
ἔργων ὀφειλέτω ὧν ἂν τὸν ἐκδόντα ψεύσηται καὶ
πάλιν ἐξ ἀρχῆς ἐν τῷ ῥηθέντι χρόνῳ προῖκα
ἐξεργαζέσθω. καὶ ἀναιρουμένῳ δ᾽ ἔργον ξυμβου-
B λευτὴς νόμος ἅπερ τῷ πωλοῦντι ξυνεβούλευε μὴ
πλέονος τιμᾶν διαπειρώμενον ἀλλ᾽ ὡς ἁπλούσ-
τατα τῆς ἀξίας, ταὐτὸν δὴ προστάττει καὶ τῷ
ἀναιρουμένῳ· γιγνώσκει γὰρ ὅ γε δημιουργὸς τὴν
ἀξίαν. ἐν ἐλευθέρων οὖν πόλεσιν οὐ δή ποτε
χρὴ τέχνῃ, σαφεῖ τε καὶ ἀψευδεῖ φύσει πράγματι,
διαπειρᾶσθαι τῶν ἰδιωτῶν τεχνάζοντα αὐτὸν τὸν
δημιουργόν· δίκας δὲ εἶναι τούτων τῷ ἀδικουμένῳ
πρὸς τὸν ἀδικοῦντα. ἐὰν δέ τις ἐκδοὺς αὖ δη-
C μιουργῷ μὴ ἀποδῷ τοὺς μισθοὺς ὀρθῶς κατὰ τὴν
ἔννομον ὁμολογίαν γενομένην, Δία δὲ πολιοῦχον
καὶ Ἀθηνᾶν κοινωνοὺς πολιτείας ἀτιμάζων, βραχὺ

414

Athena belong those who safeguard the products of
these craftsmen by other defensive arts ; rightly is
this class also sacred to these deities. These all
continually serve both the country and the people :
the one class are leaders in the contests of war, the
others produce for pay instruments and works ; and
it would be unseemly for these men to lie concerning
their crafts, because of their reverence for their
divine ancestors. If any craftsman fail to execute
his work within the time named, owing to baseness
—he not revering the god who gives him his livelihood, but deeming him (in his blindness of mind)
to be merciful because of his kinship,—he shall, in
the first place, pay a penalty to the god, and,
secondly, there shall be a law enacted to suit his
case :—He shall owe the price of the works regarding which he has lied to the person who gave him
the order, and within the stated time he shall
execute them all over again gratis. And as it coun-
selled the seller, so the law counsels the contractor
who undertakes a work not to give in too high an
estimate for it, but to estimate it simply at its real
worth ; this same charge the law gives, I say, to the
contractor, for he as a craftsman certainly knows
what its worth is. In States composed of gentlemen it is wrong for a craftsman to try by his art
(which is essentially truthful and sincere) to impose
artfully upon lay persons ; and in such cases the
wronged shall be entitled to prosecute the wrong-
doer. If, on the other hand, a man who has given
an order to a craftsman fails to pay him his wage
duly according to the legal agreement, and sets at
naught Zeus, the Patron of the State, and Athena,
who are partners in the constitution,—thereby dis-

κέρδος ἀγαπῶν, λύῃ μεγάλας κοινωνίας, νόμος ὁ
βοηθῶν ἔστω τῷ τῆς πόλεως ξυνδέσμῳ μετὰ
θεῶν· Ὃς γὰρ ἂν προαμειψάμενος ἔργον μισθοὺς
μὴ ἀποδιδῷ ἐν χρόνοις τοῖς ὁμολογηθεῖσι, διπλοῦν
πραττέσθω· ἐὰν δὲ ἐνιαυτὸς ἐξέλθῃ, τῶν ἄλλων
D ἀτόκων ὄντων χρημάτων, ὁπόσα δανεισμῷ ξυμ-
βάλλει τις, οὗτος τῇ δραχμῇ ἑκάστου μηνὸς
ἐπωβελίαν κατατιθέτω· δίκας δὲ εἶναι τούτων
ἐν τοῖς κατὰ φυλὰς δικαστηρίοις.

Ὡς δὲ ἐν παρέργῳ περὶ τῶν κατὰ πόλεμον
δημιουργῶν ὄντων σωτηρίας, στρατηγῶν τε καὶ
ὅσοι περὶ ταῦτα τεχνικοί, δίκαιον εἰπεῖν, ὅτι τὸ
παράπαν ἐμνήσθημεν δημιουργῶν· ὃς[1] τούτοις αὖ,
καθάπερ ἐκείνοις, οἷον ἑτέροις οὖσι δημιουργοῖς, ἐάν
τις ἄρα καὶ τούτων ἀνελόμενος δημόσιον ἔργον εἴθ'
E ἑκὼν εἴτε προσταχθὲν καλῶς ἐξεργάσηται, τὰς
τιμάς, οἳ δὴ μισθοὶ πολεμικοῖς ἀνδράσιν εἰσίν,
ἀποδιδῷ δικαίως, ὁ νόμος αὐτὸν ἐπαινῶν οὔποτε
καμεῖται· ἐὰν δὲ προαμειψάμενος ἔργον τι τῶν
κατὰ πόλεμον καλῶν ἔργων μὴ ἀποδιδῷ, μέμψεται. νόμος οὖν οὗτος ἐπαίνῳ περὶ τούτων ἡμῖν
μεμιγμένος κείσθω, ξυμβουλευτικός, οὐ βιαστικός,
922 τῷ πλήθει τῶν πολιτῶν, τιμᾶν τοὺς ἀγαθοὺς
ἄνδρας, ὅσοι σωτῆρές εἰσι τῆς πόλεώς εἰσι ξυμπάσης
εἴτε ἀνδρείαις εἴτε πολεμικαῖς μηχαναῖς, δευτέ-
ρους· πρώτοις γὰρ τὸ μέγιστον γέρας δεδόσθω

---

[1] ὃς Schneider : ὡς MSS.

---

[1] *i.e.* bear no interest. Cp. 742 C ; *Rep.* 556 A ; Ar. *Pol.*
1258b 5 ff.

solving great partnerships through love of a little gain,—then, with the help of the gods, this law shall lend aid to the bonds that unite the State :—Whosoever has previously received the work ordered and fails to pay the price within the period agreed shall be bound to pay double the price; and if a year have elapsed, although all other monies on loan are barren,[1] this man shall pay as interest one obol on each drachma for every month [2] of arrears; and actions for these cases shall take place before the tribal courts.

And now that we have made mention of craftsmen in general, it is right to allude in passing to those whose craft is military security,—that is to say, military commanders and all experts in such matters. As to the former craftsmen, so to these men, as craftsmen of another sort,—whenever any of them, either voluntarily or under orders, undertakes any public work and executes it well,—whosoever shall duly pay to these men those honours which are the soldier's wages, him the law will never weary of lauding; but if he has previously received some noble work of a military kind and fails to pay for it, the law will blame him. So, touching this matter, let there be laid down this law, coupled with laudation,—a law which counsels rather than compels the mass of citizens to honour as second in merit those brave men who, either by bold deeds or by military devices, are protectors of the State ; for first in merit come those on whom the greatest reward must be bestowed— namely, those who have proved themselves able pre-

[2] As a drachma = 6 obols, the interest would amount to 200 p. c. per annum.

τοῖς τὰ τῶν ἀγαθῶν νομοθετῶν γράμματα τιμᾷν
διαφερόντως δυνηθεῖσιν.

Τὰ μὲν δὴ μέγιστα τῶν ξυμβολαίων, ὅσα πρὸς
ἀλλήλους ἄνθρωποι ξυμβάλλουσι, πλήν γε ὀρφαν-
ικῶν καὶ τῆς τῶν ἐπιτρόπων ἐπιμελείας τῶν
ὀρφανῶν, σχεδὸν ἡμῖν διατέτακται· ταῦτα δὲ δὴ
μετὰ τὰ νῦν εἰρημένα ἀναγκαῖον ἀμῶς γέ πως
B τάξασθαι. τούτων δὲ ἀρχαὶ πάντων αἵ τε τῶν
τελευτᾷν μελλόντων ἐπιθυμίαι τῆς διαθέσεως
αἵ τε τῶν μηδὲν τὸ παράπαν διαθεμένων τύχαι.
ἀναγκαῖον δὲ εἶπον, ὦ Κλεινία, βλέψας αὐτῶν
πέρι πρός τε τὸ δύσκολον καὶ χαλεπόν   οὐδὲ γὰρ
ἄτακτον δυνατόν ἐστ᾽ αὐτὸ ἐᾶν· πολλὰ γὰρ ἕκαστοι καὶ διάφορα ἀλλήλων καὶ ἐναντία τιθεῖντ᾽ ἂν
τοῖς τε νόμοις καὶ τοῖς τῶν ζώντων ἤθεσι καὶ τοῖς
αὐτῶν τοῖς ἔμπροσθεν, πρὶν διατίθεσθαι μέλλειν,
C εἴ τις ἐξουσίαν δώσει ἁπλῶς οὕτω κυρίαν εἶναι
διαθήκην ἣν ἄν τις διαθῆται ὁπωσοῦν ἔχων πρὸς
τῷ τοῦ βίου τέλει. ἀνοήτως γὰρ δὴ καὶ διατεθρυμ-
μένως τινὰ τρόπον ἔχομεν οἱ πλεῖστοι, ὅταν ἤδη
μέλλειν ἡγώμεθα τελευτᾷν.

ΚΛ.   Πῶς τοῦτο, ὦ ξένε, λέγεις ;

ΑΘ.   Χαλεπόν ἐστ᾽, ὦ Κλεινία, μέλλων ἄνθρωπος τελευτήσειν, καὶ μεστὸν λόγου τοῖς νομοθέταις
εὖ μάλα φοβεροῦ καὶ δυσχεροῦς.

ΚΛ.   Πῇ ;

ΑΘ.   Ζητῶν εἶναι κύριος ἁπάντων εἴωθε μετ᾽
D ὀργῆς λέγειν.

ΚΛ.   Ποῖα δή ;

ΑΘ.   Δεινόν γε, ὦ θεοί, φησίν, εἰ τὰ ἐμὰ ἐμοὶ

---

[1] Cp. 919 D, E.

eminently to honour the written code of the good lawgivers.[1]

We have now made regulations for most of the more important business dealings between man and man, excepting those regarding orphans and the care of orphans by their guardians; so, after those now dealt with, these matters must necessarily receive some kind of regulation. All these have their starting-points either in the desire of those at the point of death to devise their property, or in the accidental cases of those who die without making a testament; and it was in view of the complex and difficult nature of these cases, Clinias, that I made use of the word "necessarily." And it is, indeed, impossible to leave them without regulation; for individuals might set down many wishes both at variance with one another and contrary to the laws as well as to the dispositions of the living, and also to their own former dispositions in the days before they proposed making a will, if any will that a man makes were to be granted absolute and unconditional validity, no matter what his state of mind at the end of his life. For most of us are more or less in a dull and enfeebled state of mind, when we imagine that we are nearly at the point of death.

CLIN. What do you mean by this, Stranger?

ATH. A man at the point of death, Clinias, is a difficult subject, and overflowing with speech that is most alarming and vexatious to a lawgiver.

CLIN. How so?

ATH. Since he claims to be lord of all he has, he is wont to speak angrily.

CLIN. What will he say?

ATH. "Good heavens!" he cries, "what a mon-

PLATO

μηδαμῶς ἐξέσται δοῦναί τε ὅτῳ ἂν ἐθέλω καὶ μή,
καὶ τῷ μὲν πλείω, τῷ δ' ἐλάττονα τῶν ὁπόσοι
περὶ ἐμὲ φαῦλοι καὶ ὅσοι ἀγαθοὶ γεγόνασι φανερῶς, βασανισθέντες ἱκανῶς ἐν νόσοις, οἱ δ' ἐν γήρᾳ
καὶ ἄλλαις παντοίαισι τύχαις.

ΚΛ. Οὐκοῦν, ὦ ξένε, καλῶς δοκοῦσί σοι
λέγειν ;

E   ΑΘ. Μαλθακοὶ ἔμοιγ', ὦ Κλεινία, δοκοῦσιν οἱ
πάλαι νομοθετοῦντες γεγονέναι καὶ ἐπὶ σμικρὸν
τῶν ἀνθρωπίνων πραγμάτων βλέποντές τε καὶ
διανοούμενοι νομοθετεῖν.

ΚΛ. Πῶς λέγεις ;

ΑΘ. Τὸν λόγον τοῦτον, ὦ 'γαθέ, φοβούμενοι,
τὸν νόμον ἐτίθεσαν τόνδε, ἐξεῖναι τὰ ἑαυτοῦ
διατίθεσθαι ἁπλῶς ὅπως ἄν τις ἐθέλῃ τὸ παράπαν,
923 ἐγὼ δὲ καὶ σὺ τοῖς ἐν τῇ σῇ πόλει μέλλουσι
τελευτᾶν ἀποκρινούμεθα ἐμμελέστερον.

ΚΛ. Πῶς ;

ΑΘ. Ὦ φίλοι, φήσομεν, καὶ ἀτεχνῶς ἐφήμεροι,
χαλεπὸν ὑμῖν ἐστι γιγνώσκειν τὰ ὑμέτερ' αὐτῶν
χρήματα καὶ πρός γε ὑμᾶς αὐτούς, ὥσπερ καὶ τὸ
τῆς Πυθίας γράμμα φράζει, τὰ νῦν. ἔγωγ' οὖν
νομοθέτης ὢν οὔθ' ὑμᾶς ὑμῶν αὐτῶν εἶναι τίθημι
οὔτε τὴν οὐσίαν ταύτην, ξύμπαντος δὲ τοῦ γένους
ὑμῶν τοῦ τε ἔμπροσθεν καὶ τοῦ ἔπειτα ἐσομένου,
καὶ ἔτι μᾶλλον τῆς πόλεως εἶναι τό τε γένος πᾶν
B   καὶ τὴν οὐσίαν. καὶ οὕτω τούτων ἐχόντων οὐκ,
ἐάν τις ὑμᾶς θωπείαις ὑποδραμὼν ἐν νόσοις ἢ
γήρᾳ σαλεύοντας παρὰ τὸ βέλτιστον διατίθεσθαι
420

strous shame it is, if I am not to be allowed at all to give, or not give, my own things to whomsoever I will—and more to one, less to another, according as they have proved themselves good to me or bad, when fully tested in times of sickness, or else in old age and in other happenings of every kind."

CLIN. And do you not think, Stranger, that what they say is right?

ATH. What I think, Clinias, is this—that the old lawgivers were cowardly, and gave laws with a short view and a slight consideration of human affairs.

CLIN. How do you mean?

ATH. It was through fear, my dear sir, of that angry speech that they made the law allowing a man unconditionally to dispose by will of his goods exactly how he pleases. But you and I will make a more suitable answer to those in your State who are at the point of death.

CLIN. In what way?

ATH. O friends, we will say, for you, who are literally but creatures of a day, it is hard at present to know your own possessions and, as the Pythian oracle declares,[1] your own selves, to boot. So I, as lawgiver, make this ruling—that both you yourself and this your property are not your own, but belong to the whole of your race, both past and future, and that still more truly does all your race and its property belong to the State; and this being so, I will not willingly consent if anyone persuades you to make a will contrary to what is best, by fawning on you and helping you when afflicted by disease or age; rather will I legislate

[1] Alluding to the dictum, "Know thyself"; cp. *Protag.* 343 B.

πείθῃ, ξυγχωρήσομαι ἑκών, ὅ τι δὲ τῇ πόλει τε
ἄριστον πάσῃ καὶ γένει, πρὸς πᾶν τοῦτο βλέπων
νομοθετήσω, τὸ ἑνὸς ἑκάστου κατατιθεὶς ἐν
μοίραις ἐλάττοσι δικαίως. ὑμεῖς δὲ ἡμῖν ἵλεῴ τε
καὶ εὐμενεῖς ὄντες πορεύοισθε ᾗπερ κατὰ φύσιν
νῦν πορεύεσθε τὴν ἀνθρωπίνην· ἡμῖν δὲ περὶ τῶν
C ἄλλων τῶν ὑμετέρων μελήσει, κηδομένοις ὅτι
μάλιστα εἰς δύναμιν οὐ τῶν μέν, τῶν δὲ οὔ.
ταῦτα μὲν οὖν παραμύθιά τε καὶ προοίμια τῶν τε
ζώντων, ὦ Κλεινία, καὶ τῶν τελευτώντων ἔστω,
νόμος δὲ ὅδε·

Ὃς ἂν διαθήκην γράφῃ τὰ αὑτοῦ διατιθέμενος, παίδων ὢν πατήρ, πρῶτον μὲν τῶν
υἱέων κληρονόμον ὃν ἂν ἀξιώσῃ γίγνεσθαι γραφέτω, τῶν δὲ ἄλλων παίδων ὃν ἂν μὲν ἑτέρῳ
ποιεῖσθαι διδῷ δεχομένῳ, γραφέσθω τοῦτο αὐτό.
ἐὰν δὲ περιγίγνηταί τις τῶν υἱέων αὐτῷ μὴ ἐπί
D τινι κλήρῳ πεποιημένος, ὃν κατὰ νόμον ἐλπὶς εἰς
ἀποικίαν ἐκπεμφθήσεσθαι, τούτῳ τῶν ἄλλων χρημάτων ἐξέστω τῷ πατρὶ διδόναι ὅσα ἂν ἐθέλῃ,
πλὴν τοῦ πατρῴου κλήρου καὶ τῆς περὶ τὸν
κλῆρον κατασκευῆς πάσης· καὶ ἐὰν πλείους ὦσι,
πρὸς μέρος ὁ πατὴρ ὅπῃ ἂν ἐθέλῃ νεμέτω τὰ
περιόντα τοῦ κλήρου. ὅτῳ δ' ἂν τῶν υἱέων ὑπάρχων οἶκος ᾖ, μὴ νέμειν τούτῳ τῶν χρημάτων,
θυγατρί τε ὡσαύτως ᾗ μὲν ἂν ἐγγεγυημένος ὡς
E ἀνὴρ ἐσόμενος ᾖ, μὴ νέμειν· ᾗ δ' ἂν μή, νέμειν.
ἐὰν δέ τῳ τῶν υἱέων ἢ καὶ τῶν θυγατέρων φανῇ
κλῆρος ἐπιχώριος τῆς διαθήκης γενόμενος ὕστερον,
τῷ κληρονόμῳ τοῦ τὴν διαθήκην διαθεμένου κατα-

---

[1] *i.e.* one of the 5040 allotments, cp. 737 C ff.

with a general view to what is best for your whole
race and State, justly accounting of minor importance the interest of the individual. May it be that
you will feel kindly disposed and at peace with us
as you journey towards that bourne whither, by the
natural law of our human life, you now are travelling: the rest of your affairs shall be our care, and
we will watch over them all, without exception, to
the best of our power. This shall serve, Clinias,
alike for consolation and for prelude for both the
living and the dying, and the law shall run as
follows :—

Whosoever writes a will disposing of his property, if he be the father of children, he shall
first write down the name of whichever of his sons
he deems worthy to be his heir, and if he offers any
one of his other children to another man to be
adopted by him, this also he shall write down; and
if he has any son besides that is not adopted for any
lot,[1] of whom he has hopes that he will be sent out
by law to a colony, to him the father shall be
allowed to give so much of his other property as he
wishes, saving only the ancestral lot and all the
equipment of that lot; and if there be several more
sons, the father shall divide among them the surplus,
over and above the lot, in whatever way he chooses.
And if a son already possesses a house, he shall not
assign him goods, and so likewise in the case of a
daughter, if she is betrothed to a husband, he shall
not assign goods, but if not so betrothed, he shall
assign. And if, after the will is made, it is discovered that one of the sons or daughters owns a lot
in the district, then that person shall resign his
legacy in favour of the heir of him that made the

λειπέτω. ἐὰν δὲ ἄρρενας μὲν μὴ λείπῃ, θηλείας
δὲ ὁ διατιθέμενος, ἄνδρα μὲν τῶν θυγατέρων ᾗτινι
ἂν ἐθέλῃ, υἱὸν δὲ αὑτῷ καταλειπέτω, γράψας
κληρονόμον. ἐὰν δὲ υἱός τῳ τελευτήσῃ παῖς ὤν,
πρὶν εἰς ἄνδρας δυνατὸς εἶναι τελεῖν, εἴτε γεννητὸς
ὢν εἴτε ποιητός, γραφέτω καὶ περὶ τῆς τοιαύτης
924 τύχης ὁ τὴν διαθήκην γράφων τίνα χρὴ παῖδα
αὑτῷ δεύτερον ἐπὶ τύχαις ἀμείνοσι γίγνεσθαι.
ἐὰν δέ τις ἄπαις ὢν τὸ παράπαν διαθήκην γράφῃ,
τὸ τῆς ἐπικτήτου δεκατημόριον ἐξελόμενος, ἐὰν
ἐθέλῃ τῳ δωρεῖσθαι, δωρείσθω· τὰ δὲ ἄλλα
παραδιδοὺς πάντα τῷ ποιηθέντι ἄμεμπτος ἵλεων
υἱὸν αὐτὸν ποιείσθω ξὺν νόμῳ.

Ὧι δ' ἂν ἐπιτρόπων οἱ παῖδες δέωνται, ἐὰν
μὲν διαθέμενος τελευτᾷ καὶ γράψας ἐπιτρόπους τοῖς παισὶν ἑκόντας τε καὶ ὁμολογοῦντας
B ἐπιτροπεύσειν οὑστινασοῦν καὶ ὁπόσους ἂν ἐθέλῃ,
κατὰ ταῦτα τὰ γραφέντα ἡ τῶν ἐπιτρόπων
αἵρεσις γιγνέσθω κυρία· ἐὰν δὲ ἢ τὸ παράπαν
μὴ διαθέμενος τελευτήσῃ τις ἢ τῆς τῶν ἐπιτρόπων αἱρέσεως ἐλλιπής, ἐπιτρόπους εἶναι τοὺς
ἐγγύτατα γένει πρὸς πατρὸς καὶ μητρὸς κυρίους,
δύο μὲν πρὸς πατρός, δύο δὲ πρὸς μητρός, ἕνα
δὲ ἐκ τῶν τοῦ τελευτήσαντος φίλων· τούτους
δ' οἱ νομοφύλακες καθιστάντων τῷ δεομένῳ τῶν
C ὀρφανῶν. καὶ πάσης τῆς ἐπιτροπῆς καὶ τῶν
ὀρφανῶν πεντεκαίδεκα τῶν νομοφυλάκων οἱ πρεσβύτατοι πάντων ἐπιμελείσθων ἀεὶ κατὰ πρέσβιν
καὶ κατὰ τρεῖς διελόμενοι σφᾶς αὑτούς, κατ'
ἐνιαυτὸν τρεῖς καὶ κατ' ἐνιαυτὸν ἄλλον ἕτεροι

will. If the testator leave no male children, but
females, he shall bequeath to whichever daughter he
chooses a husband, and to himself a son, and write
him down as his heir;[1] and if a man has a son,
whether his own or adopted, who dies in childhood
before reaching man's estate, in this case also, when
making his will, he shall state in writing who is to
be his son's successor, and with happier luck. If
any testator be wholly childless, he shall take out a
tenth part of his surplus property and shall give it to
any person, if he so chooses; but all the rest he
shall hand over to his adopted heir, and him he shall
make his son with mutual good-will and the blessing
of the law.

When a man's children need guardians, if he
die after making a will and naming what persons
and how many he desires to act as guardians to
his children, and if they are willing and consent to
act, then the choice of guardians in this document
shall be final; but if a man dies either wholly
intestate or having omitted from his will the choice
of guardians, then the nearest of kin on both the
father's and the mother's side, two from each side,
together with one of the friends of the deceased,
shall act as official guardians, and these the Law-
wardens shall appoint in the case of each orphan
that requires them. All that appertains to guardianship and the orphans shall be supervised by fifteen
of the Law-wardens, who shall be the eldest of the
whole body, and shall divide themselves into threes
according to seniority, three acting one year and
another three a second year, until five yearly periods

---

[1] *i.e.* he shall select a citizen to become his heir by
marrying one of his daughters.

τρεῖς, ἕως ἂν αἱ πέντε περίοδοι γίγνωνται κύκλῳ·
καὶ τοῦτο ἐκλιπέτω μηδέποτε κατὰ δύναμιν.

Ὃς δ' ἂν μηδὲν τὸ παράπαν διαθέμενος ἀποθάνῃ,
παῖδας μὲν καταλιπὼν δεομένους ἐπιτροπῆς, τῶν
αὐτῶν νόμων τούτων ἡ χρεία τῶν παίδων αὐτοῦ
D μετεχέτω· θηλείας δὲ ἂν καταλίπῃ τις ἀπροσδο-
κήτῳ τύχῃ χρησάμενος, συγγνώμην τῷ τιθέντι τὸν
νόμον ἐχέτω, ἐὰν τῶν τριῶν αὐτοῦ πρὸς τὰ δύο
ἐπισκοπῶν τὴν ἔκδοσιν τῶν θυγατέρων ποιῆται,
πρός τε τὴν τοῦ γένους ἀγχιστείαν καὶ τὴν τοῦ
κλήρου σωτηρίαν, τὸ δὲ τρίτον, ὅπερ ἂν πατὴρ
διασκέψαιτο, ἐξ ἁπάντων τῶν πολιτῶν βλέπων
εἰς ἤθη τε καὶ τρόπους τὸν ἐπιτήδειον αὑτῷ μὲν
υἱόν, νυμφίον δ' εἶναι τῇ θυγατρί, τοῦτο δὲ παρα-
E λείπῃ διὰ τὴν ἀδύνατον σκέψιν. νόμος τοίνυν εἰς
δύναμιν ὅδε περὶ τῶν τοιούτων κείσθω· Ἐὰν ὁ
μὴ διαθέμενος θυγατέρας λίπῃ, τοῦ ἀποθανόντος
ἀδελφὸς ὁμοπάτωρ ἢ ἄκληρος ὁμομήτριος ἐχέτω
τὴν θυγατέρα καὶ τὸν κλῆρον τοῦ τελευτήσαντος.
ἐὰν δὲ μὴ ᾖ ἀδελφός, ἀδελφοῦ δὲ παῖς, ὡσαύτως,
ἐὰν ἐν ἡλικίᾳ πρὸς ἀλλήλους ὦσιν· ἐὰν δὲ μηδὲ
εἷς τούτων, ἀδελφῆς δὲ παῖς ᾖ, κατὰ ταὐτά·
τέταρτος δὲ πατρὸς ἀδελφός, πέμπτος δὲ τούτου
παῖς, ἕκτος δὲ ἀδελφῆς πατρὸς ἔκγονος. ὡσαύτως
δὲ τὸ γένος ἀεὶ πορευέσθω κατ' ἀγχιστείαν, ἐάν τις
925 παῖδας θηλείας καταλίπῃ, δι' ἀδελφῶν τε καὶ
ἀδελφιδῶν ἐπανιόν, ἔμπροσθε μὲν τῶν ἀρρένων,
ὕστερον δὲ θηλειῶν ἑνὶ γένει.

Τὴν δὲ τοῦ τῶν γάμων χρόνου συμμετρίαν τε καὶ

---

[1] i.e. in marriage: the "lot" is to pass on always to the
next of kin, cf. 925 D, E.

have passed in rotation; and this process shall go on, so far as possible, without a break.

And if any man die wholly intestate, leaving children that require guardianship, his unfriended children shall share in these same laws. And if a man meets with some unforeseen mischance and leaves daughters, he shall pardon the lawgiver if he regulates the betrothal of the daughters with an eye to two points out of three—namely, nearness of kinship and the security of the lot—and omits the third point, which a father would take into consideration,—namely, the selecting out of all the citizens of a person suited by character and conduct to be a son to himself and a spouse for his daughter,—if, I say, the lawgiver passes this over owing to the impossibility of taking it into consideration. Accordingly, the law that we shall enact, as the best in our power touching such matters, will be this:—If a man dies intestate and leaves daughters, that brother who is born of the same father or of the same mother and who is without a lot shall take the daughter [1] and the lot of the deceased; failing a brother, if there be a brother's son, the procedure shall be the same, provided that the parties be of an age suited the one to the other; failing one of these, the same rule shall hold for a sister's son; then, fourthly, for a father's brother; and, fifthly, for his son; and, sixthly, for the son of a father's sister. In like manner, if a man leaves female children, the right of kinship shall proceed always by degrees of consanguinity, going up through brothers and brother's children, first the males, and secondly the females in one line.

The suitability or otherwise of the time of

ἀμετρίαν ὁ δικαστὴς σκοπῶν κρινέτω, γυμνοὺς μὲν
τοὺς ἄρρενας, γυμνὰς δὲ ὀμφαλοῦ μέχρι θεώμενος
τὰς θηλείας· ἐὰν δὲ τοῖς οἰκείοις ἀπορία ξυγγενῶν
ᾖ, μέχρι μὲν ἀδελφοῦ υἱιδῶν, μέχρι δὲ πάππου
παίδων ὡσαύτως, τῶν ἄλλων ὅντιν' ἂν ἡ παῖς
μετ' ἐπιτρόπων αἱρῆται τῶν πολιτῶν ἑκούσιον
B ἑκουσία, κληρονόμος γιγνέσθω τοῦ τελευτήσαντος
καὶ τῆς θυγατρὸς νυμφίος. ἔστι¹ δὲ πολλὰ πολλῶν <ἐμποδὼν>² καὶ πλείων ἀπορία τῶν τοιούτων
γίγνοιτ' ἂν ἔστιν ὅτε ἐν αὐτῇ τῇ πόλει· ἂν οὖν δή
τις ἀπορουμένη τῶν αὐτόθεν ὁρᾷ τινὰ εἰς ἀποικίαν
ἀπεσταλμένον, ᾗ δὲ κατὰ νοῦν αὐτῇ κληρονόμον
ἐκεῖνον γίγνεσθαι τῶν τοῦ πατρός, ἐὰν μὲν ξυγγενὴς ᾖ, κατὰ τὴν τάξιν τοῦ νόμου ἐπὶ τὸν κλῆρον
πορευέσθω, ἐὰν δὲ ἐκτὸς γένους, τῶν ἐν τῇ πόλει
C ὄντων ἔξω τῆς συγγενείας, κύριος ἔστω κατὰ τὴν
τῶν ἐπιτρόπων καὶ τῆς παιδὸς τοῦ τελευτήσαντος
αἵρεσιν γῆμαι καὶ τὸν κλῆρον ἐπανελθὼν οἴκαδε
λαβεῖν τοῦ μὴ διαθεμένου.

Ἄπαις δὲ ἀρρένων τε καὶ θηλειῶν τὸ παράπαν ὃς ἂν μὴ διαθέμενος τελευτᾷ, τὰ μὲν
ἄλλα περὶ τοῦ τοιούτου κατὰ τὸν ἔμπροσθεν
ἐχέτω νόμον, θήλεια δὲ καὶ ἄρρην, οἷον ξύν-
νομοι, ἴτωσαν ἐκ τοῦ γένους εἰς τὸν ἐξηρημω-
μένον ἑκάστοτε οἶκον, ὧν ὁ κλῆρος γιγνέσθω
D κυρίως, ἀδελφὴ μὲν πρῶτον, ἀδελφοῦ δὲ θυγάτηρ
δευτέρα, τρίτη δὲ ἔκγονος ἀδελφῆς, τετάρτη δὲ
πατρὸς ἀδελφή, καὶ πέμπτη πατρὸς ἀδελφοῦ παῖς,
ἕκτη δὲ ἀδελφῆς πατρὸς ἂν εἴη παῖς· συνοικίζειν
δὲ ταύτας ἐκείνοις κατ' ἀγχιστείαν καὶ θέμιν, ὡς

¹ ἔστι Apelt : ἔτι MSS., edd.
² <ἐμποδὼν> I add (πολλὴ for πολλὰ Ast).

428

marriage the judge shall decide by inspection, viewing the males naked and the females naked down to the navel. And if there be in the family a lack of kinsmen as far as brother's grandchildren, and likewise as far as grandfather's children, whomsoever of the other citizens the girl, aided by her guardians, shall choose, that man (if both he and the girl are willing) shall become the heir of the deceased and the spouse of his daughter. But obstacles often occur, and there might be times when there was an unusual dearth of such men in the city itself: so if any girl, being at a loss to find a spouse on the spot, sees one that has emigrated to a colony and desires that he should become heir to her father's property, if so be that he is related, he shall proceed to the lot, according to the ordinance of the law; but if he be outside the kin, and there be no one of near kin in the State, then by the choice of the guardians and of the daughter of the deceased he shall be entitled to marry and to take the lot of the intestate man on his return home.

Whosoever dies intestate, being without any issue, male or female, in his case all other matters shall be governed by the previous law; and a man and woman from the family shall in each such instance go into the deserted house as joint assignees, and their claim to the lot shall be made valid; and the female claims to inheritance shall come in this order —first, a sister; second, a brother's daughter; third, a sister's daughter; fourth, a father's sister; fifth, a father's brother's daughter; sixth, a father's sister's daughter; and these shall share the home with the male kinsmen according to the degree of relationship

ἔμπροσθεν ἐνομοθετήσαμεν. μὴ δὴ λανθανέτω τὸ
τῶν τοιούτων νόμων ἡμᾶς βάρος, ὡς χαλεπῶς
ἔστιν ὅτε προστάττει τῷ τοῦ τελευτήσαντος κατὰ
γένος οἰκείῳ γαμεῖν τὴν ξυγγενῆ, μὴ δοκεῖ δὲ
σκοπεῖν ἃ μυρία ἐν ἀνθρώποις ἐμπόδια γίγνεται
Ε τοῖς τοιούτοις ἐπιτάγμασι τοῦ μήτινα ἐθέλειν
πείθεσθαι, πρότερον δὲ οὕστινας ὁτιοῦν ἂν βουλη-
θῆναι παθεῖν, ὁπόταν ἢ σωμάτων νοσήματα καὶ
πηρώσεις ἢ διανοίας ἔν τισι τῶν ἐπιταττομένων
γαμεῖν ἢ γαμεῖσθαι γίγνηται. τούτων δὴ μηδὲν
φροντίζειν τάχ᾽ ἂν ὁ νομοθέτης δόξειέ τισιν, οὐκ
ὀρθῶς δοκοῦν. ἔστω τοίνυν εἰρημένον ὑπέρ τε
νομοθέτου καὶ ὑπὲρ νομοθετουμένου σχεδὸν οἷον
κοινὸν προοίμιον, συγγνώμην μὲν τῷ νομοθέτῃ
τοὺς ἐπιταττομένους δεόμενον ἔχειν, ὅτι τῶν κοινῶν ἐπιμελούμενος οὐκ ἄν ποτε δύναιτο διοικεῖν
ἅμα καὶ τὰς ἰδίας ἑκάστῳ γιγνομένας ξυμφοράς,
926 ξυγγνώμην δ᾽ αὖ καὶ τοῖς νομοθετουμένοις, ὡς τὰ
τοῦ νομοθετοῦντος εἰκότως ἐνίοτε οὐ δύνανται
προστάγματα τελεῖν, ἃ μὴ γιγνώσκων προστάττει.

ΚΛ. Τί δή τις οὖν, ὦ ξένε, δρῶν πρὸς τὰ τοιαῦτα
ἐμμετρότατος ἂν εἴη;

ΑΘ. Διαιτητάς, ὦ Κλεινία, τοῖς τοιούτοις
νόμοις καὶ νομοθετουμένοις ἀναγκαῖον αἱρεῖσθαι.

ΚΛ. Πῶς λέγεις;

ΑΘ. Ἔστιν ὅτε πλουσίου πατρὸς ἀδελφιδοῦς
τὴν τοῦ θείου θυγατέρα ἑκὼν οὐκ ἂν ἐθέλοι λαμ-
Β βάνειν, τρυφῶν καὶ ἐπὶ μείζοσι γάμοις τὴν διάνοιαν
ἐπέχων· ἔστι δ᾽ ὅτε καὶ ξυμφορὰν τὴν μεγίστην
430

and right, as we previously enacted. Now we must not fail to notice how burdensome such a law may prove, in that sometimes it harshly orders the next of kin to the deceased to marry his kinswoman, and that it appears to overlook the thousands of impediments which in human life prevent men from being willing to obey such orders and cause them to prefer any other alternative, however painful, in cases where either of the parties ordered to marry is suffering from diseases or defects of mind or body. Some might suppose that the lawgiver is paying no heed to these considerations, but they would be wrong. On behalf, therefore, of the lawgiver as well as of him to whom the law applies let a kind of general prelude be uttered, requesting those to whom the order is given to pardon the lawgiver because it is impossible for him, in his care for the public interests, to control also the private misfortunes which befall individuals, and requesting pardon also for the subjects of the law, inasmuch as they are naturally unable at times to carry out ordinances of the lawgiver laid down by him in ignorance.

CLIN. As regards this, Stranger, what would be the most rational course of action to adopt ?

ATH. It is necessary, Clinias, that for laws of this kind, and those whom they affect, arbitrators should be chosen.

CLIN. How do you mean ?

ATH. It might happen that a nephew, who has a rich father, would be loth to take to wife his uncle's daughter, giving himself airs and being minded to make a grander match. Or again, when what the lawgiver enjoins would be a fearful calamity, a man

τοῦ νομοθέτου προστάττοντος ἀπειθεῖν ἀναγ-
κάζοιτ' ἂν τῷ νόμῳ, μαινόμενα κηδεύματα ἀναγ-
κάζοντος λαμβάνειν ἢ δεινὰς ἄλλας σωμάτων ἢ
ψυχῶν ξυμφοράς, ἃς ἀβίωτον ζῆν κεκτημένῳ. ὁ
δὴ νῦν λόγος ἡμῖν περὶ τούτων ὅδε νόμος κείσθω·
Ἐάν τινες ἄρα περὶ διαθήκης ἐγκαλῶσι τοῖς κει-
μένοις νόμοις, περί τε ἄλλων ὡντινωνοῦν καὶ δὴ
C καὶ περὶ γάμων, ἦ μὴν παρόντα καὶ ζῶντα αὐτὸν
τὸν νομοθέτην μήποτ' ἂν ἀναγκάσαι πράττειν
οὕτω, μηδὲ γῆμαι μηδὲ γήμασθαι, τοὺς νῦν ἀναγ-
καζομένους ἑκάτερα δρᾶν, ὁ δέ τις τῶν οἰκείων ἤ
τις ἐπίτροπος φῇ, διαιτητὰς φάναι καὶ πατέρας
τοὺς πεντεκαίδεκα τῶν νομοφυλάκων καταλιπεῖν
τοῖς ὀρφανοῖς καὶ ὀρφαναῖς τὸν νομοθέτην· πρὸς
D οὓς ἐπανιόντες διαδικαζέσθων οἱ περί τινος τῶν
τοιούτων ἀμφισβητοῦντες, κύρια τελοῦντες τὰ
τούτων δόγματα. ἂν δέ τῳ μείζων δύναμις ἐπανα-
τίθεσθαι δοκῇ τοῖς νομοφύλαξιν, εἰς τὸ τῶν
ἐκκρίτων δικαστῶν δικαστήριον εἰσάγων αὐτοὺς
διαδικαζέσθω περὶ τῶν ἀμφισβητουμένων· τῷ δὲ
ἡττηθέντι παρὰ τοῦ νομοθέτου ψόγος καὶ ὄνειδος
κείσθω, πολλῶν χρημάτων νοῦν κεκτημένῳ ζημία
βαρυτέρα.

Νῦν δὴ τοῖς ὀρφανοῖς παισὶ γένεσις οἷον δευτέρα τις γίγνοιτ' ἄν. μετὰ μὲν οὖν τὴν πρώτην
E ἑκάστοις εἴρηνται τροφαὶ καὶ παιδεύσεις· μετὰ
δὲ τὴν δευτέραν, ἔρημον πατέρων γενομένην,

---

[1] Cp. 775 D ff., 855 C.
[2] *i.e.* be "born again" as children of the State, with the
Law-wardens as their new official parents, as explained
below.

might be compelled to disobey the law—for instance, when the law would force him to enter into an alliance with madness or some other dire affliction of body or soul, such as makes life intolerable for the person so allied. This statement of ours shall now be laid down as a law in the following terms :— If any man have a complaint against the ordained laws concerning testaments in respect of any detail, and especially of those relating to marriage ; and if he affirms on oath that of a truth the lawgiver himself, were he alive and present, would never have compelled the parties to act as they are now being compelled to act in respect of marrying and giving in marriage ; and if, on the other hand, some relative or guardian supports the compulsion of the law ; what we declare is that the lawgiver has left us the fifteen Law-wardens to act for the orphans, male and female, as both arbitrators and parents, and to these all who dispute about any such matters shall go for judgment, and their verdict shall be carried out as final. If, however, anyone maintains that this is to confer too much power on the Law-wardens, he shall summon his opponents before the court of select judges [1] and secure a decision regarding the points in dispute. On him that is defeated there shall be imposed by the lawgiver censure and disgrace,—a penalty heavier than a large fine in the eyes of a man of right mind.

Accordingly, orphan children will undergo a kind of second birth.[2] How in each case they should be reared and trained after their first birth we have already described ; [3] and now we must contrive some means whereby, after their

[3] In Books II. and VII.

μηχανᾶσθαι δεῖ τίνα τρόπον ἡ τῆς ὀρφανίας τύχη
τοῖς γενομένοις ὀρφανοῖς ὡς ἥκιστα ἔλεον ἕξει τῆς
συμφορᾶς. πρῶτον μὲν δεῖ[1] νομοθετεῖν αὐτοῖς
τοὺς νομοφύλακας ἀντὶ γεννητόρων πατέρας οὐ
χείρους, καὶ δὴ καὶ <τρεῖς>[2] καθ' ἕκαστον ἐνιαυτὸν ὡς οἰκείων ἐπιμελεῖσθαι προστάττομεν, ἐμμελῆ
τούτοις τε αὐτοῖς περὶ τροφῆς ὀρφανῶν προοι-
μιασάμενοι καὶ τοῖς ἐπιτρόποις. εἰς τινα γὰρ οὖν
μοι καιρὸν φαινόμεθα τοὺς ἔμπροσθεν λόγους
927 διεξελθεῖν, ὡς ἄρα αἱ τῶν τελευτησάντων ψυχαὶ
δύναμιν ἔχουσί τινα τελευτήσασαι, ᾗ τῶν κατ'
ἀνθρώπους πραγμάτων ἐπιμελοῦνται. ταῦτα δὲ
ἀληθεῖς μέν, μακροὶ δ' εἰσὶ περιέχοντες λόγοι.
πιστεύειν δὲ ταῖς ἄλλαις φήμαις χρεὼν περὶ τὰ
τοιαῦτα, οὕτω πολλαῖσι καὶ σφόδρα παλαιαῖς
οὔσαις· πιστεύειν δ' αὖ καὶ τοῖς νομοθετοῦσι ταῦθ'
οὕτως ἔχειν, ἄνπερ μὴ παντάπασιν ἄφρονες
φαίνωνται. ταύτῃ δὲ εἰ ταῦτ' ἐστὶ κατὰ φύσιν,
πρῶτον μὲν τοὺς ἄνω θεοὺς φοβείσθων, οἳ τῶν
B ὀρφανῶν τῆς ἐρημίας αἰσθήσεις ἔχουσιν, εἶτα τὰς
τῶν κεκμηκότων ψυχάς, αἷς ἐστιν ἐν τῇ φύσει
τῶν αὐτῶν ἐκγόνων κήδεσθαι διαφερόντως καὶ
τιμῶσί τε αὐτοὺς εὐμενεῖς εἶναι καὶ ἀτιμάζουσι
δυσμενεῖς, ἔτι δὲ τὰς τῶν ζώντων μέν, ἐν γήρᾳ δὲ
ὄντων καὶ ἐν μεγίσταις τιμαῖς, ὅτι οὗπερ[3] πόλις
εὐνομοῦσα εὐδαιμονεῖ, τούτους οἱ παῖδες παίδων
φιλοστοργοῦντες ζῶσι μεθ' ἡδονῆς· καὶ τὰ περὶ
C ταῦτα ὀξὺ μὲν ἀκούουσι, βλέπουσί τε ὀξύ, τοῖς
τε περὶ αὐτὰ δικαίοις εὐμενεῖς εἰσί, νεμεσῶσί

---

[1] δεῖ: δὴ MSS.: δή φαμεν (MS. marg.) Zur., vulg.
[2] <τρεῖς> added by Susemihl, Ritter.
[3] ὅτι οὗπερ: ὅπουπερ MSS. (ὅπου γὰρ Hermann).

second birth in which they are destitute of parents, their orphan condition may be as free as possible from piteous misery for those who have become orphans. In the first place, to act in the room of their begetters, as parents of no inferior kind, we must legally appoint the Law-wardens; and we charge three of these, year by year,[1] to care for the orphans as their own, having already given both to these men and to the guardians a suitable prelude of directions concerning the nurture of orphans. Opportune, indeed, as I think, was the account we previously gave[2] of how the souls of the dead have a certain power of caring for human affairs after death. The tales which contain this doctrine are true, though long; and while it is right to believe the other traditions about such matters, which are so numerous and exceeding old, we must also believe those who lay it down by law that these are facts, unless it is plain that they are utter fools. So if this is really the state of the case, the guardians shall fear, first, the gods above who pay regard to the solitude of orphans; and, secondly, the souls of the dead, whose natural instinct it is to care especially for their own offspring, and to be kindly disposed to those who respect them and hostile to those who disrespect them; and, thirdly, they shall fear the souls of the living who are old and who are held in most high esteem; since where the State flourishes under good laws, their children's children revere the aged with affection and live in happiness. These old people are keen of eye and keen of ear to mark such matters, and while they are gracious towards those who deal justly therein, they are very wroth

[1] Cp. 924 C.   [2] 865 E ff.

τε μάλιστα αὖ τοῖς εἰς ὀρφανὰ καὶ ἔρημα ὑβρί-
ζουσι, παρακαταθήκην εἶναι μεγίστην ἡγούμενοι
καὶ ἱερωτάτην. οἷς ἐπίτροπον καὶ ἄρχοντα πᾶσι
δεῖ τὸν νοῦν, ᾧ καὶ βραχὺς ἐνείη, προσέχοντα, καὶ
εὐλαβούμενον περὶ τροφήν τε καὶ παιδείαν
ὀρφανῶν, ὡς ἔρανον εἰσφέροντα ἑαυτῷ τε καὶ τοῖς
αὑτοῦ, κατὰ δύναμιν πάντως πᾶσαν εὐεργετεῖν. ὁ
μὲν δὴ πεισθεὶς τῷ πρὸ τοῦ νόμου μύθῳ καὶ
D μηδὲν εἰς ὀρφανὸν ὑβρίσας οὐκ εἴσεται ἐναργῶς
τὴν περὶ τὰ τοιαῦτα ὀργὴν νομοθέτου, ὁ δὲ ἀπειθὴς καί τινα πατρὸς ἢ μητρὸς ἔρημον ἀδικῶν
διπλῆν τινέτω πᾶσαν τὴν βλάβην ἢ περὶ τὸν
ἀμφιθαλῆ γενόμενος κακός.

Τὴν δὲ ἄλλην νομοθεσίαν ἐπιτρόποισί τε
περὶ ὀρφανοὺς ἄρχουσί τε περὶ τὴν ἐπιμέλειαν
τῶν ἐπιτρόπων, εἰ μὲν μὴ¹ παράδειγμά² τε
τροφῆς παίδων ἐλευθέρων ἐκέκτηντο αὐτοὶ τρέ-
φοντες τοὺς αὑτῶν καὶ τῶν οἰκείων χρημάτων
E ἐπιμελούμενοι, ἔτι δὲ νόμους περὶ αὐτῶν τούτων μετρίως διειρημένους εἶχον, εἶχέ τινα λόγον
ἂν ἐπιτροπικούς τινας νόμους, ὡς ὄντας ἰδίᾳ
διαφέροντας πολύ, τιθέναι, ποικίλλοντας ἐπιτηδεύμασιν ἰδίοις τὸν τῶν ὀρφανῶν βίον παρὰ
τὸν τῶν μή· νῦν δὲ εἰς μὲν τὰ τοιαῦτα ξύμπαντα οὐ πολὺ διαφέρον ἡ παρ᾽ ἡμῖν ὀρφανία
κέκτηται τῆς πατρονομικῆς, τιμαῖς δὲ καὶ ἀτιμίαις
ἅμα καὶ ἐπιμελείαισιν οὐδαμῶς ἐξισοῦσθαι φιλεῖ.

¹ μὴ Baiter : δὴ MSS.
² παράδειγμά MSS. : παραδείγματά Zur.

with those who despitefully entreat orphans and
waifs, regarding these as a trust most solemn and
sacred. To all these authorities the guardian
and official if he has a spark of sense—must pay
attention; he must show as much care regarding
the nurture and training of the orphans as if he
were contributing to his own support and that of
his own children, and he must do them good in
every way to the utmost of his power. He, then,
that obeys the tale prefixed to the law and in no wise
misuses the orphan will have no direct experience
of the anger of the lawgiver against such offences;
but the disobedient and he that wrongs any who
has lost father or mother shall in every case pay a
penalty double of that due from the man who
offends against a child with both parents living.

As regards further legal directions either to
guardians concerning orphans or to magistrates concerning the supervision of the guardians,—if they did
not already possess a pattern of the way to nurture
free children in the way they themselves nurture
their own children and supervise their household
goods, and if they did not also possess laws regulating
these same affairs in detail, then it would have been
reasonable enough to lay down laws concerning
guardianship, as a peculiar and distinct branch of
law, marking out with special regulations of its own
the life of the orphan as contrasted with the non-
orphan; but, as the matter stands, the condition
of orphanhood in all these respects does not differ
greatly with us from the condition of parental
control, although as a rule in respect of public
estimation and of the care bestowed on the children
they are on quite a different level. Consequently,

928 διὸ δὴ περὶ τοῦτο αὐτὸ τὴν ὀρφανῶν πέρι νομοθεσίαν παραμυθούμενός τε καὶ ἀπειλῶν ὁ νόμος
ἐσπούδακεν. ἔτι δ᾽ ἀπειλή τις ἂν τοιάδε εἴη
μάλα ἔγκαιρος· Ὃς ἂν θῆλυν εἴτε ἄρρενα ἐπιτρο-
πεύῃ, καὶ ὃς ἂν ἐπιτρόπου φύλαξ τῶν νομοφυλάκων καταστὰς ἐπιμελῆται, μὴ χεῖρον ἀγαπάτω
τῶν αὑτοῦ τέκνων τὸν τῆς ὀρφανικῆς μετειληφότα
τύχης, μηδὲ τῶν οἰκείων τῶν τοῦ τρεφομένου
χεῖρον χρημάτων ἐπιμελείσθω, βέλτιον δὲ ἢ τῶν
αὑτοῦ κατὰ προθυμίαν.

B Ἕνα δὲ τοῦτον νόμον ἔχων ὀρφανῶν πέρι
πᾶς ἐπιτροπευέτω· ἐὰν δὲ ἄλλως τις περὶ τὰ
τοιαῦτα πράττῃ παρὰ τὸν νόμον τόνδε, ὁ μὲν
ἄρχων ζημιούτω τὸν ἐπίτροπον, ὁ δὲ ἐπίτροπος
τὸν ἄρχοντα εἰς τὸ τῶν ἐκκρίτων δικαστήριον
εἰσάγων ζημιούτω τῷ δόξαντι τιμήματι τῷ
δικαστηρίῳ διπλῇ. ἐὰν δ᾽ ἐπίτροπος ἀμελεῖν
ἢ κακουργεῖν δοκῇ τοῖς οἰκείοις ἢ καὶ τῶν
ἄλλων τινὶ πολιτῶν, εἰς ταὐτὸν ἀγέτω δικα-
C στήριον· ὅ τι δ᾽ ἂν ὄφλῃ, τετραπλασίαν μὲν
τούτου τίνειν, γιγνέσθω δὲ τὸ μὲν ἥμισυ τοῦ
παιδός, τὸ δ᾽ ἥμισυ τοῦ καταδικασαμένου τὴν
δίκην. ἅμα δ᾽ ἂν ἡβήσῃ τις τῶν ὀρφανῶν, ἐὰν
ἡγῆται κακῶς ἐπιτροπευθῆναι, μέχρι πέντε ἐτῶν
ἐξηκούσης τῆς ἐπιτροπῆς ἔστω δίκην λαχεῖν
ἐπιτροπίας· ἐὰν δέ τις ὄφλῃ τῶν ἐπιτρόπων,
τιμᾶν τὸ δικαστήριον ὅ τι χρὴ παθεῖν ἢ ἀποτίνειν,
ἐὰν δὲ δὴ τῶν ἀρχόντων, ἀμελείᾳ μὲν δόξας
κακῶσαι τὸν ὀρφανόν, ὅ τι χρὴ τίνειν αὐτὸν τῷ
D παιδί, τιμάτω τὸ δικαστήριον, ἐὰν δὲ ἀδικίᾳ, πρὸς

in its regulations concerning orphans the law has emphasized this very point both by admonition and by threat. A threat, moreover, of the following kind will be extremely opportune:—Whosoever is guardian of a male or female child, and whosoever of the Law-wardens is appointed supervisor of a guardian, shall show as much affection for the child whom Fate has made an orphan as for his own children, and he shall zealously care for the goods of his nursling as much as for his own goods—or rather, more.

Every guardian shall observe this one law in the discharge of his office; and if any act in such matters contrary to this law, the magistrate shall punish him if he be a guardian, and, if he be a magistrate, the guardian shall summon him before the court of the select judges, and fine him double the penalty adjudged by the court. And if a guardian be held by the child's relatives, or by any other citizen, to be guilty of neglecting or mal-treating his ward, they shall bring him before the same court, and he shall pay four times the damages assessed, and of this amount one half shall go to the child, the other half to the successful prosecutor. When an orphan has reached full age, if he thinks that he has been badly cared for, he shall be allowed to bring an action concerning the guardianship within a period of five years after the date of its expiration; and if the guardian lose his case, the court shall assess the amount of his penalty or fine; and if it be a magistrate that is held to have injured the orphan by neglect, the court shall assess what sum he shall pay to the child, but if the injury be due to unjust dealing, in addition to the fine he shall

τῷ τιμήματι τῆς ἀρχῆς τῶν νομοφυλάκων ἀφ-
ιστάσθω, τὸ δὲ κοινὸν τῆς πόλεως ἕτερον νομοφύλακα ἀντὶ τούτου καθιστάτω τῇ χώρᾳ καὶ τῇ
πόλει.

Διαφοραὶ πατέρων τε πρὸς αὑτῶν παῖδας
γίγνονται καὶ παίδων πρὸς γεννητὰς μείζους ἢ
χρεών, ἐν αἷς οἵ τε πατέρες ἡγοῖντ᾽ ἂν δεῖν τὸν νομοθέτην νομοθετεῖν ἐξεῖναί σφισιν ἐὰν βούλωνται τὸν
υἱὸν ὑπὸ κήρυκος ἐναντίον ἁπάντων ἀπειπεῖν υἱὸν
E κατὰ νόμον μηκέτ᾽ εἶναι, υἱεῖς τ᾽ αὖ σφίσι πατέρας
ὑπὸ νόσων ἢ γήρως διατιθεμένους αἰσχρῶς ἐξεῖναι
παρανοίας γράφεσθαι. ταῦτα δὲ ὄντως ἐν παγ-
κάκων ἤθεσιν ἀνθρώπων γίγνεσθαι φιλεῖ, ἐπεὶ
ἡμίσεών γε ὄντων τῶν κακῶν, οἷον μὴ κακοῦ μὲν
πατρός, υἱέος δέ, ἢ τοὐναντίον, οὐ γίγνονται ξυμ-
φοραὶ τηλικαύτης ἔχθρας ἔκγονοι. ἐν μὲν οὖν
ἄλλῃ πολιτείᾳ παῖς ἀποκεκηρυγμένος οὐκ ἂν ἐξ
ἀνάγκης ἄπολις εἴη, ταύτης δέ, ἧς οἵδε οἱ νόμοι
ἔσονται, ἀναγκαίως ἔχει εἰς ἄλλην χώραν ἐξοικίζε-
929 σθαι τὸν ἀπάτορα· πρὸς γὰρ τοῖς τετταράκοντα
καὶ πεντακισχιλίοις οἴκοις οὐκ ἔστιν ἕνα προσγε-
νέσθαι. διὸ δὴ δεῖ τὸν ταῦτα πεισόμενον ἐν δίκῃ
μὴ ὑπὸ ἑνὸς πατρός, ὑπὸ δὲ τοῦ γένους ἀπορρη-
θῆναι παντός. ποιεῖν δὲ χρὴ τῶν τοιούτων πέρι
κατὰ νόμον τοιόνδε τινά· Ὃν ἂν θυμὸς ἐπίῃ
μηδαμῶς εὐτυχής, εἴτ᾽ οὖν ἐν δίκῃ εἴτε καὶ μή,
ὃν ἔτεκέ τε καὶ ἐξεθρέψατο, τοῦτον ἐπιθυμεῖν
ἀπαλλάξαι τῆς αὑτοῦ ξυγγενείας, μὴ φαύλως
B οὕτως ἐξέστω μηδ᾽ εὐθὺς τοῦτο δρᾶν, πρῶτον δὲ
συλλεξάτω τοὺς αὑτοῦ ξυγγενεῖς μέχρι ἀνεψιῶν

be removed from his office of Law-warden, and the public authority of the State shall appoint another in his place to act as Law-warden for the country and the State.

Between fathers and their children, and children and their fathers, there arise differences greater than is right, in the course of which fathers, on the one hand, are liable to suppose that the law-giver should give them legal permission to proclaim publicly by herald, if they so wish, that their sons have legally ceased to be their sons; while the sons, on the other hand, claim permission to indict their fathers for insanity when they are in a shameful condition owing to illness or old age. These results are wont to occur among men who are wholly evil of character, since where only half of them are evil —the son being evil and the father not, or *vice versa*—such enmity does not issue in calamitous consequences. Now, whereas under another polity a son when disinherited would not necessarily cease to be a citizen, it is necessary in our State (of which these are to be the laws) that the fatherless man should emigrate to another State, since it is impossible that a single household should be added to our 5040; consequently it is necessary that the person upon whom this punishment is to be inflicted legally should be disinherited, not by his father only, but by the whole family. Such cases should be dealt with according to a law such as this :—If any man is urged by a most unhappy impulse of anger to desire, rightly or wrongly, to expel from his own kindred one whom he has begotten and reared, he shall not be permitted to do this informally and immediately, but he shall, first of all, assemble his own kinsfolk

καὶ τοὺς τοῦ υἱέος ὡσαύτως τοὺς πρὸς μητρός,
κατηγορείτω δὲ ἐν τούτοις, διδάσκων ὡς ἄξιος
ἅπασιν ἐκ τοῦ γένους ἐκκεκηρῦχθαι, δότω δὲ καὶ
τῷ υἱεῖ λόγους τοὺς ἴσους, ὡς οὐκ ἄξιός ἐστι
τούτων οὐδὲν πάσχειν· καὶ ἐὰν μὲν πείθῃ ὁ
πατὴρ καὶ συμψήφους λάβῃ πάντων τῶν ξυγγενῶν ὑπὲρ ἥμισυ, πλὴν πατρὸς διαψηφιζομένων[1]
καὶ μητρὸς καὶ τοῦ φεύγοντος, τῶν γε[2] ἄλλων
C ὁπόσοιπερ ἂν ὦσι γυναικῶν εἴτε ἀνδρῶν τέλειοι,
ταύτῃ μὲν καὶ κατὰ ταῦτα ἐξέστω τῷ πατρὶ τὸν
υἱὸν ἀποκηρύττειν, ἄλλως δὲ μηδαμῶς. τὸν δ᾽
ἀποκηρυχθέντα ἐάν τις τῶν πολιτῶν υἱὸν βούληται θέσθαι, μηδεὶς νόμος ἀπειργέτω ποιεῖσθαι· τὰ
γὰρ τῶν νέων ἤθη πολλὰς μεταβολὰς ἐν τῷ βίῳ
μεταβάλλειν ἑκάστοτε πέφυκεν· ἀποκηρυχθέντα
δὲ ἄν τις δέκα ἐτῶν μὴ ἐπιθυμήσῃ θετὸν υἱὸν
D ποιήσασθαι, τοὺς τῶν ἐπιγόνων ἐπιμελητὰς τῶν
εἰς τὴν ἀποικίαν ἐπιμελεῖσθαι καὶ τούτων, ὅπως
ἂν μετάσχωσι τῆς αὐτῆς ἀποικίας ἐμμελῶς. ἐὰν
δέ τίς τινα νόσος ἢ γῆρας ἢ καὶ τρόπων χαλεπότης
ἢ καὶ ξύμπαντα ταῦτα ἔκφρονα ἀπεργάζηται
διαφερόντως τῶν πολλῶν, καὶ λανθάνῃ τοὺς
ἄλλους πλὴν τῶν συνδιαιτωμένων, οἰκοφθορῇ δὲ
ὡς ὢν τῶν αὐτοῦ κύριος, ὁ δὲ υἱὸς ἀπορῇ καὶ
ὀκνῇ τὴν τῆς παρανοίας γράφεσθαι δίκην, νόμος
E αὐτῷ κείσθω πρῶτον μὲν πρὸς τοὺς πρεσβυτάτους
τῶν νομοφυλάκων ἐλθόντα διηγήσασθαι τὴν τοῦ
πατρὸς ξυμφοράν, οἱ δὲ κατιδόντες ἱκανῶς ξυμ-
βουλευόντων ἐάν τε δέῃ γράφεσθαι καὶ ἐὰν μὴ

---

[1] διαψηφιζομένων Baiter : διαψηφιζομένου MSS.
[2] γε Hermann : τε MSS. ; δὲ Ast, Zur.

as far as cousins and likewise his son's kinsfolk on
the mother's side, and in the presence of these he
shall accuse his son, showing how he deserves at the
hands of all to be expelled from the family, and he
shall grant to the son an equal length of time for
arguing that he does not deserve to suffer any such
treatment ; and if the father convinces them and
gains the votes of more than half the family (votes
being given by all the other adults of both sexes,
save only the father, the mother, and the son who is
defendant), in this way and on these conditions, but
not otherwise, the father shall be permitted to
disinherit his son. And as regards the man disinherited, if any citizen desires to adopt him as his son,
no law shall prevent him from doing so, (for the
characters of the young naturally undergo many
changes during their life) ; but if within ten years no
one offers to adopt the disinherited man, then the
controllers of the surplus children designed for
emigration shall take control of these persons also,
in order that they may be duly included in the same
scheme of emigration. And if a man becomes
unusually demented owing to illness or old age or
crabbedness, or a combination of these complaints,
but his condition remains unnoticed by all except
those who are living with him, and if he regards
himself as master of his own property and wastes his
goods, while his son feels at a loss and scruples to
indict him for insanity,—in such a case a law shall
be enacted on behalf of the son whereby he shall, in
the first instance, go to the eldest of the Law-
wardens and report to them his father's condition,
and they, after full enquiry, shall advise whether or
not he ought to bring an indictment ; and if they

τὴν γραφήν, ἐὰν δὲ ξυμβουλεύσωσι, γιγνέσθωσαν
τῷ γραφομένῳ μάρτυρες ἅμα καὶ ξύνδικοι. ὁ δὲ
ὀφλὼν τοῦ λοιποῦ χρόνου ἄκυρος ἔστω τῶν αὑτοῦ
καὶ τὸ σμικρότατον διατίθεσθαι, καθάπερ παῖς
δὲ οἰκείτω τὸν ἐπίλοιπον βίον.

Ἐὰν δὲ ἀνὴρ καὶ γυνὴ μηδαμῇ ξυμφέρωνται
τρόπων δυστυχίᾳ χρώμενοι, δέκα μὲν ἄνδρας τῶν
νομοφυλάκων ἐπιμελεῖσθαι τῶν τοιούτων ἀεὶ χρεὼν
930 τοὺς μέσους, δέκα δὲ τῶν περὶ γάμους γυναικῶν
ὡσαύτως· καὶ ἐὰν μὲν δὴ ξυναλλάττειν δύνωνται,
ταῦτ᾽ ἔστω κύρια, ἐὰν δ᾽ αἱ ψυχαὶ κυμαίνωσι μειζόνως αὐτῶν, ζητεῖν κατὰ δύναμιν οἵτινες ἑκατέρῳ
ξυνοικήσουσιν. εἰκὸς δὲ εἶναι τοὺς τοιούτους μὴ
πραέσιν ἤθεσι κεχρημένους·[1] βαθύτερα δὴ τούτοις
καὶ πραότερα τρόπων ἤθη ξύννομα πειρᾶσθαι
προσαρμόττειν. καὶ ὅσοι μὲν ἂν ἄπαιδες αὐτῶν
ἢ ὀλιγόπαιδες ὄντες διαφέρωνται, καὶ παίδων
Β ἕνεκα τὴν συνοίκησιν ποιεῖσθαι· ὅσοι δ᾽ ἂν
ἱκανῶν ὄντων παίδων, τῆς συγκαταγηράσεως
ἕνεκα καὶ ἐπιμελείας ἀλλήλων τὴν διάζευξίν τε
καὶ σύζευξιν ποιεῖσθαι χρεών. ἐὰν δὲ τελευτᾷ
γυνὴ καταλείπουσα παῖδας θηλείας τε καὶ ἄρρενας, συμβουλευτικὸς ἂν εἴη νόμος ὁ τιθέμενος,
οὐκ ἀναγκαστικός, τρέφειν τοὺς ὄντας παῖδας μὴ
μητρυιὰν ἐπαγόμενον· μὴ δὲ ὄντων ἐξ ἀνάγκης
γαμεῖν, μέχριπερ ἂν ἱκανοὺς γεννήσῃ παῖδας τῷ
C τε οἴκῳ καὶ τῇ πόλει. ἢν δὲ ὁ ἀνὴρ ἀποθάνῃ
παῖδας ἱκανοὺς λιπών, ἡ μήτηρ τῶν παίδων

---

[1] κεχρημένους MSS. : κεκραμένους MSS. marg., Zur.

---

[1] Cp. 784 A ff., 794 B.

advise him to bring an indictment, they shall act
for him, when he brings it, both as witnesses and
advocates; and the father that is convicted shall
thenceforward have no power to administer even the
smallest tittle of his property, and shall be counted
as a child in the house for the rest of his life.

If a man and his wife, being of unhappy dispositions, in no wise agree together, it is right
that they should be under the constant control
of ten members of the Board of Law-wardens,
of middle age, together with ten of the women
in charge of marriage.[1] If these officials are able
to bring about a reconciliation, this arrangement
shall hold good; but if their passions rage too high
for harmony, the officials shall, so far as possible,
seek out other suitable unions for each of them.
And since it is probable that such persons are not of
a gentle disposition, they must endeavour to yoke
with them dispositions that are more gentle and
sedate.[2] If those who quarrel are childless, or have
but few children, they must form unions with a view
to children; but if they have children enough, then
the object both of the separation and of the new
union should be to obtain companionship and mutual
assistance in old age. If a man's wife dies, leaving
both male and female children, there shall be a law,
advisory rather than compulsory, directing the
husband to rear the children without introducing a
step-mother; but if there be no children, the
widower must of necessity marry, until he has
begotten children sufficient alike for his household
and the State. And if the husband dies, leaving
sufficient children, the mother of the children shall

[2] Cp. 773 C.

αὑτοῦ μένουσα τρεφέτω· νεωτέρα δ᾽ ἂν δοκῇ τοῦ
δέοντος εἶναι πρὸς τὸ ζῆν ἂν¹ ὑγιαίνουσα ἄνανδρος, οἱ προσήκοντες πρὸς τὰς τῶν γάμων ἐπι-
μελουμένας γυναῖκας κοινούμενοι τὸ δοκοῦν αὑτοῖς
τε καὶ ἐκείναις περὶ τῶν τοιούτων ποιούντων·
ἐὰν δὲ ἐνδεεῖς τέκνων ὦσι, καὶ παίδων ἕνεκα·
D παίδων δὲ ἱκανότης ἀκριβὴς ἄρρην καὶ θήλεια
ἔστω τῷ νόμῳ. ὅταν δὲ ὁμολογῆται μὲν τὸ
γενόμενον εἶναι τῶν ποιουμένων ἔκγονον, δέηται
δὲ κρίσεως τίνι τὸ γεννηθὲν ἕπεσθαι χρεών, δούλη
μὲν ἐὰν συμμίξῃ δούλῳ ἢ ἐλευθέρῳ ἢ ἀπελευθέρῳ,
πάντως τοῦ δεσπότου ἔστω τῆς δούλης τὸ γεν-
νώμενον· ἐὰν δέ τις ἐλευθέρα δούλῳ συγγίγνηται,
τοῦ δεσπότου ἔστω τὸ γιγνόμενον [τοῦ δούλου]·²
ἐὰν δ᾽ ἐξ αὑτοῦ δούλης ἢ ἐκ δούλου ἑαυτῆς, καὶ
περιφανὲς τοῦτ᾽ ᾖ, τὸ μὲν τῆς γυναικὸς αἱ γυναῖκες
E εἰς ἄλλην χώραν ἐκπεμπόντων σὺν τῷ πατρί, τὸ
δὲ τοῦ ἀνδρὸς οἱ νομοφύλακες σὺν τῇ γεννησάσῃ.

Γονέων δὲ ἀμελεῖν οὔτε θεὸς οὔτε ἄνθρωπος νοῦν
ἔχων ξύμβουλός ποτε γένοιτ᾽ ἂν οὐδεὶς οὐδενί.
φρονῆσαι δὲ χρὴ περὶ θεῶν θεραπείας τοιόνδε
προοίμιον ἂν γενόμενον, εἰς τὰς τῶν γεννησάντων
τιμάς τε καὶ ἀτιμίας ὀρθῶς συντεταγμένον· Νόμοι
931 περὶ θεοὺς ἀρχαῖοι κεῖνται παρὰ πᾶσι διχῇ. τοὺς
μὲν γὰρ τῶν θεῶν ὁρῶντες σαφῶς τιμῶμεν, τῶν δ᾽
εἰκόνας ἀγάλματα ἱδρυσάμενοι, οὓς ἡμῖν ἀγάλ-
λουσι καίπερ ἀψύχους ὄντας ἐκείνους ἡγούμεθα

¹ ἂν H. Richards : αὖ MSS., edd.
² [τοῦ δούλου] wanting in best MSS., bracketed by England.

¹ The object of this rule dealing with irregular connexions
between free citizens and slaves is to prevent any of slave
descent acquiring rights of property in the State.

remain there and rear them; but if it be deemed
that she is unduly young to be able to live healthfully
without a husband, the relatives shall report the case
to the women in charge of marriage, and shall take
such action as may seem good to them and to themselves; and if there be a lack of children, they shall
also act with a view to the supply of children;
and the number which constitutes a bare sufficiency
of children shall be fixed by the law at one of each
sex. Whenever, in spite of agreement as to who a
child's parents are, a decision is required as to which
parent the child should follow, the rule is this:[1] in
all cases where a slave-woman has been mated with
a slave or with a free man or a freedman, the child
shall belong to the slave-woman's master; but if a
free woman mates with a slave, the issue shall belong
to the slave's master; and if the child be a master's
by his own slave-woman, or a mistress's by her own
slave, and the facts of the case are quite clear, then
the women officials shall send away the woman's child,
together with its father, to another country, and the
Law-wardens shall send away the man's child,
together with its mother.

Neglect of parents is a thing that no god nor
any right-minded man would ever recommend to
anyone; and one ought to recognize how fitly
a prelude of the following kind, dealing with
worship paid to the gods, would apply to the
honours and dishonours paid to parents:—The
ancient laws of all men concerning the gods are
two-fold: some of the gods whom we honour we see
clearly,[2] but of others we set up statues as images,
and we believe that when we worship these, lifeless

[2] *i.e.* stars; cp. 821 B.

τοὺς ἐμψύχους θεοὺς πολλὴν διὰ ταῦτ᾽ εὔνοιαν
καὶ χάριν ἔχειν. πατὴρ οὖν ὅτῳ καὶ μήτηρ ἢ
τούτων πατέρες ἢ μητέρες ἐν οἰκίᾳ κεῖνται κει-
μήλιοι ἀπειρηκότες γήρᾳ, μηδεὶς διανοηθήτω ποτὲ
ἄγαλμα αὑτῷ, τοιοῦτον ἐφέστιον ἵδρυμα [ἐν οἰκίᾳ]¹
ἔχων, μᾶλλον κύριον ἔσεσθαι, ἐὰν δὴ κατὰ τρόπον
γε ὀρθῶς αὐτὸ θεραπεύῃ ὁ κεκτημένος.

B   ΚΛ. Τίνα δὴ τὴν ὀρθότητα εἶναι φράζεις ;

ΑΘ. Ἐγὼ ἐρῶ· καὶ γὰρ οὖν ἄξιον, ὦ φίλοι,
ἀκούειν τά γε δὴ τοιαῦτα.

ΚΛ. Λέγε μόνον.

ΑΘ. Οἰδίπους, φαμέν, ἀτιμασθεὶς ἐπεύξατο
τοῖς αὑτοῦ τέκνοις ἃ δὴ καὶ πᾶς ὑμνεῖ τέλεα καὶ
ἐπήκοα γενέσθαι παρὰ θεῶν, Ἀμύντορά τε Φοίνικι
τῷ ἑαυτοῦ ἐπαράσασθαι παιδὶ θυμωθέντα καὶ
Ἱππολύτῳ Θησέα καὶ ἑτέρους ἄλλοις μυρίους
μυρίοις, ὧν γέγονε σαφὲς ἐπηκόους εἶναι γονεῦσι
C πρὸς τέκνα θεούς· ἀραῖος γὰρ γονεὺς ἐκγόνοις ὡς
οὐδεὶς ἕτερος ἄλλοις, δικαιότατα. μὴ δή τις
ἀτιμαζομένῳ μὲν διαφερόντως πατρὶ πρὸς παίδων
καὶ μητρὶ θεὸν ἐπήκοον εὐχαῖς ἡγείσθω γίγνεσθαι
κατὰ φύσιν· τιμωμένῳ δὲ ἄρα καὶ περιχαρεῖ
σφόδρα γενομένῳ, καὶ διὰ τὰ τοιαῦτα εὐχαῖς
λιπαρῶς εἰς ἀγαθὰ τοῖς παισὶ παρακαλοῦντος
θεούς, οὐκ ἄρα τὰ τοιαῦτα ἀκούειν ἐξ ἴσου καὶ
νέμειν ἡμῖν αὐτοὺς ἡγησόμεθα ; ἀλλ᾽ οὐκ ἄν ποτε
δίκαιοι νομεῖς εἶεν ἀγαθῶν, ὃ δή φαμεν ἥκιστα
D θεοῖς εἶναι πρέπον.

¹ [ἐν οἰκίᾳ] bracketed by Cobet, England.

---

¹ Cp. Aesch. Sept. c. Theb. 709 ff.; Soph. O. C. 1432 ff.
² Cp. Hom. Il. IX. 446 ff. : Phoenix, to avenge his neglected
mother, seduced his father's mistress.

though they be, the living gods beyond feel great good-will towards us and gratitude. So if any man has a father or a mother, or one of their fathers or mothers, in his house laid up bed-ridden with age, let him never suppose that, while he has such a figure as this upon his hearth, any statue could be more potent, if so be that its owner tends it duly and rightly.

CLIN. And what do you say is the right way?

ATH. I will tell you : for in truth, my friends, matters of this sort deserve a hearing.

CLIN. Say on.

ATH. Oedipus, when he was dishonoured (so our story runs), invoked upon his children curses [1] which, as all men allege, were granted by Heaven and fulfilled ; and we tell how Amyntor in his wrath cursed his son Phoenix,[2] and Theseus cursed Hippolytus,[3] and countless other parents cursed countless other sons, which curses of parents upon sons it is clearly proved that the gods grant ; for a parent's curse laid upon his children is more potent than any other man's curse against any other, and most justly so. Let no man suppose, then, that when a father or a mother is dishonoured by the children, in that case it is natural for God to hearken especially to their prayers, whereas when the parent is honoured and is highly pleased and earnestly prays the gods, in consequence, to bless his children—are we not to suppose that they hearken equally to prayers of this kind, and grant them to us ? For if not, they could never be just dispensers of blessings ; and that, as we assert, would be most unbecoming in gods.

---

[3] Cp. 687 E, Eur. *Hipp.* 884 ff.: Hippolytus was falsely charged with dishonouring his step-mother, Phaedra.

κλ. Πολύ γε.

αθ. Οὐκοῦν διανοηθῶμεν ὃ σμικρῷ πρότερον
εἴπομεν, ὡς οὐδὲν πρὸς θεῶν τιμιώτερον ἄγαλμ᾽
ἂν κτησαίμεθα πατρὸς καὶ προπάτορος παρει-
μένων γήρᾳ καὶ μητέρων τὴν αὐτὴν δύναμιν
ἐχουσῶν, οὓς ὅταν ἀγάλλῃ τις τιμαῖς, γέγηθεν ὁ
θεός· οὐ γὰρ ἂν ἐπήκοος ἦν αὐτῶν. θαυμαστὸν
γὰρ δή που τὸ προγόνων ἵδρυμα ἡμῖν ἐστί,
Ε διαφερόντως τῶν ἀψύχων· τὰ μὲν γὰρ θεραπευό-
μενα ὑφ᾽ ἡμῶν, ὅσα ἔμψυχα, ξυνεύχεται ἑκάστοτε, καὶ ἀτιμαζόμενα τἀναντία, τὰ δ᾽ οὐδέτερα,
ὥστε ἂν ὀρθῶς τις χρῆται πατρὶ καὶ προπάτορι
καὶ πᾶσι τοῖς τοιούτοις, πάντων πρὸς θεοφιλῆ
μοῖραν κυριώτατα ἀγαλμάτων ἂν κεκτῇτο.

κλ. Κάλλιστ᾽ εἶπες.

αθ. Πᾶς δὴ νοῦν ἔχων φοβεῖται καὶ τιμᾷ
γονέων εὐχάς, εἰδὼς πολλοῖς καὶ πολλάκις ἐπι-
τελεῖς γενομένας. τούτων οὖν οὕτω φύσει δια-
τεταγμένων τοῖς μὲν ἀγαθοῖς ἕρμαιον πρόγονοι
932 γηραιοί, ζῶντες μέχρι τῶν ἐσχάτων τοῦ βίου, καὶ
ἀπιόντες [νέοι][1] σφόδρα ποθεινοί, τοῖς δὲ κακοῖς
εὖ μάλα φοβεροί. πᾶς δὴ τιμάτω πάσαις τιμαῖς
ταῖς ἐννόμοις τοὺς αὑτοῦ γεννήτορας τοῖς νῦν
πεισθεὶς λόγοις· εἰ δ᾽ οὖν τινὰ κατέχοι φήμη
κωφὸν[2] τῶν τοιούτων προοιμίων, νόμος ὅδε ἐπὶ
τούτοις ὀρθῶς κείμενος ἂν εἴη· Ἐάν τις ἐν τῇδε
τῇ πόλει γονέων ἀμελέστερον ἔχῃ τοῦ δέοντος,

---

[1] [νέοι] bracketed by W.-Möllendorff : ἀπόντες νέοις
Winckelmann, Zur.

[2] κωφὸν England : κωφὴ MSS.

CLIN. Most, indeed.

ATH. Let us maintain, then,—as we said a moment ago—that in the eyes of the gods we can possess no image more worthy of honour than a father or forefather laid up with old age, or a mother in the same condition; whom when a man worships with gifts of honour, God is well pleased, for otherwise He would not grant their prayers. For the shrine which is an ancestor is marvellous in our eyes, far beyond that which is a lifeless thing; for while those which are alive pray for us when tended by us and pray against us when dishonoured, the lifeless images do neither; so that if a man rightly treats his father and forefather and all such ancestors, he will possess images potent above all others to win for him a heaven-blest lot.[1]

CLIN. Most excellent!

ATH. Every right-minded man fears and respects the prayers of parents, knowing that many times and in many cases they have proved effective. And since this is the ordinance of nature, to good men aged forefathers are a heavenly treasure while they live, up to the very last hours of life, and when they depart they are sorely regretted; but to the bad they are truly fearsome. Therefore let every man, in obedience to these counsels, honour his own parents with all the due legal honours. If, however, "report convicts"[2] any of deafness to such preludes, the following law will be enacted rightly to deal with them :—If any person in this State be unduly neglectful of his parents,[3] and fail to consider them

[2] Alluding to Pindar's phrase (*Ol.* 7. 18) ὁ δ' ὄλβιος ὃν φᾶμαι κατέχοντ' ἀγαθαί. Cp. Eur. *Hipp.* 1466.
[3] Cp. 717 D, 881 D.

451

PLATO

B καὶ μὴ τῶν υἱέων καὶ πάντων τῶν ἐκγόνων αὐτοῦ καὶ ἑαυτοῦ μειζόνως εἰς ἅπαντα ἐπιτρέπων καὶ ἀποπληρῶν ἢ τὰς βουλήσεις, ἐξαγγελλέτω μὲν ὁ πάσχων τι τοιοῦτον, εἴτε αὐτὸς εἴτε τινὰ πέμπων, πρὸς τρεῖς μὲν τῶν νομοφυλάκων τοὺς πρεσβυτάτους, τρεῖς δ' αὖ τῶν περὶ γάμους γυναικῶν ἐπιμελουμένων· οἱ δ' ἐπιμελείσθωσαν, κολάζοντες τοὺς ἀδικοῦντας νέους μὲν ὄντας ἔτι πληγαῖς καὶ δεσμοῖς, μέχριπερ ἂν ἐτῶν ἄνδρες

C μὲν τυγχάνωσιν ὄντες τριάκοντα, γυναῖκες δὲ δέκα πλείοσιν ἔτεσι κολαζέσθωσαν ταῖς αὐταῖς κολάσεσιν. ἐὰν δὲ πόρρωτέρω τούτων τῶν ἐτῶν ὄντες τῶν αὐτῶν ἀμελειῶν περὶ γονέας μὴ ἀφιστῶνται, κακῶσι δέ τινάς τινες, εἰς δικαστήριον εἰσαγόντων αὐτοὺς εἰς ἕνα καὶ ἑκατὸν[1] τῶν πολιτῶν, οἵτινες ἂν ὦσι πρεσβύτατοι ἁπάντων· ἂν δέ τις ὄφλῃ, τιμάτω τὸ δικαστήριον ὅ τι χρὴ τίνειν ἢ πάσχειν, ἀπόρρητον μηδὲν ποιούμενοι ὅσων δυνατὸς ἄνθρωπος πάσχειν ἢ τίνειν.

D ἐὰν δέ τις ἀδυνατῇ κακούμενος φράζειν, ὁ πυθόμενος τῶν ἐλευθέρων ἐξαγγελλέτω τοῖς ἄρχουσιν ἢ κακὸς ἔστω καὶ ὑπόδικος τῷ ἐθέλοντι βλάβης. ἐὰν δὲ δοῦλος μηνύσῃ, ἐλεύθερος ἔστω, καὶ ἐὰν μὲν τῶν κακούντων ἢ κακουμένων δοῦλος, ὑπὸ τῆς ἀρχῆς ἀφείσθω, ἐὰν δέ τινος ἄλλου τῶν πολιτῶν, τὸ δημόσιον ὑπὲρ αὐτοῦ τιμὴν τῷ κεκτημένῳ καταβαλλέτω· τοῖς ἄρχουσι δὲ ἐπιμελὲς ἔστω μή τις ἀδικῇ τὸν τοιοῦτον τιμωρούμενος τῆς μηνύσεως ἕνεκα.

E Ὅσα τις ἄλλος ἄλλον πημαίνει φαρμάκοις, τὰ μὲν θανάσιμα αὐτῶν διείρηται, τῶν δ' ἄλλων

---

[1] ἑκατὸν Bekker, most edd. : ἕκαστον MSS., Zur.

in all things more than his sons or any of his offspring, or even himself, and to fulfil their wishes, let the parent who suffers any such neglect report it, either in person or by a messenger, to the three eldest Law-wardens, and to three of the women in charge of marriage ; and these shall take the matter in hand, and shall punish the wrongdoers with stripes and imprisonment if they are still young—up to the age of thirty if they are men, while if they are women they shall suffer similar punishment up to the age of forty. And if, when they have passed these limits of age, they do not desist from the same acts of neglect towards their parents, but in some cases maltreat them, they shall be summoned before a court of 101 citizens, who shall be the oldest citizens of all ; and if a man be convicted, the court shall assess what his fine or punishment must be, regarding no penalty as excluded which man can suffer or pay. If any parent when maltreated is unable to report the fact, that free man who hears of it shall inform the magistrate, failing which he shall be esteemed base, and shall be liable to an action for damage at the hands of anyone who chooses. If a slave gives information he shall be set free : he shall be set free by the Board of Magistrates if he be a slave of either the injured party or the injurers ; but if he belong to any other citizen, the State Treasury shall pay his owner a price for him ; and the magistrates shall take care that no one does injury to such a man in revenge for his giving information.

We have already [1] dealt fully with cases where one man injures another by poisons so that death is the

---

[1] 869 E ff.

περὶ βλάψεων, εἴτε τις ἄρα πώμασιν ἢ καὶ
βρώμασιν ἢ ἀλείμμασιν ἑκὼν ἐκ προνοίας
πημαίνει, τούτων οὐδέν πω διερρήθη. διτταὶ
γὰρ δὴ φαρμακεῖαι κατὰ τὸ τῶν ἀνθρώπων
οὖσαι γένος ἐπίσχουσι τὴν διάρρησιν. ἢν μὲν
933 γὰρ τὰ νῦν διαρρήδην εἴπομεν, σώμασι σώματα
κακουργοῦσά ἐστι κατὰ φύσιν· ἄλλη δὲ ἢ
μαγγανείαις τέ τισι καὶ ἐπῳδαῖς καὶ καταδέσεσι
λεγομέναις πείθει τοὺς μὲν τολμῶντας βλάπτειν
αὐτούς, ὡς <ὄντως>[1] δύνανται τὸ τοιοῦτον, τοὺς
δ' ὡς παντὸς μᾶλλον ὑπὸ τούτων δυναμένων
γοητεύειν βλάπτονται. ταῦτ' οὖν καὶ περὶ τὰ
τοιαῦτα ξύμπαντα οὔτε ῥᾴδιον ὅπως ποτὲ πέφυκε
γιγνώσκειν, οὔτ' εἴ τις γνοίη, πείθειν εὐπετὲς
ἑτέρους. ταῖς δὲ ψυχαῖς τῶν ἀνθρώπων δυσω-
B πουμέναις πρὸς ἀλλήλους περὶ τὰ τοιαῦτα οὐκ
ἄξιον ἐπιχειρεῖν [πείθειν][2], ἄν ποτε ἄρα ἴδωσί που
κήρινα μιμήματα πεπλασμένα, εἴτ' ἐπὶ θύραις εἴτ'
ἐπὶ τριόδοις εἴτ' ἐπὶ μνήμασι γονέων αὐτῶν τινές,
ὀλιγωρεῖν πάντων τῶν τοιούτων διακελεύεσθαι
μὴ σαφὲς ἔχουσι δόγμα περὶ αὐτῶν. διαλα-
βόντας δὲ διχῇ τὸν τῆς φαρμακείας πέρι νόμον,
ὁποτέρως ἄν τις ἐπιχειρῇ φαρμάττειν, πρῶτον
μὲν δεῖσθαι καὶ παραινεῖν καὶ συμβουλεύειν μὴ
C δεῖν ἐπιχειρεῖν τοιοῦτο δρᾶν μηδὲ καθάπερ παῖδας
τοὺς πολλοὺς τῶν ἀνθρώπων δειματοῦντας[3]
φοβεῖν, μηδ' αὖ τὸν νομοθέτην τε καὶ τὸν δικαστὴν ἀναγκάζειν ἐξιᾶσθαι τῶν ἀνθρώπων τοὺς
τοιούτους φόβους, ὡς πρῶτον μὲν τὸν ἐπιχει-

---

[1] ⟨ὄντως⟩ I add.
[2] [πείθειν] I bracket (κἄν for ἄν Schramm).
[3] δειματοῦντας England : δειμαίνοντας MSS.

result; but we have not as yet dealt fully with any
of the minor cases in which wilful and deliberate
injury is caused by means of potions, foods, and
unguents. A division in our treatment of poisoning
cases is required by the fact that, following the
nature of mankind, they are of two distinct types.
The type that we have now expressly mentioned is
that in which injury is done to bodies by bodies
according to nature's laws. Distinct from this is
the type which, by means of sorceries and incantations and spells (as they are called), not only convinces those who attempt to cause injury that they
really can do so, but convinces also their victims
that they certainly are being injured by those who
possess the power of bewitchment. In respect of
all such matters it is neither easy to perceive what
is the real truth, nor, if one does perceive it, is it
easy to convince others. And it is futile to approach
the souls of men who view one another with dark
suspicion if they happen to see images of moulded
wax at doorways, or at points where three ways
meet, or it may be at the tomb of some ancestor,
to bid them make light of all such portents, when
we ourselves hold no clear opinion concerning them.
Consequently, we shall divide the law about poisoning under two heads, according to the modes in
which the attempt is made;[2] and, as a preliminary,
we shall entreat, exhort, and advise that no one
must attempt to commit such an act, or to frighten
the mass of men, like children, with bogeys, and so
compel the legislator and the judge to cure men of
such fears, inasmuch as, first, the man who attempts

---

[1] *i.e.* attacking body or mind.

455

ροῦντα φαρμάττειν οὐκ εἰδότα τί δρᾷ, τά τε κατὰ
σώματα, ἐὰν μὴ τυγχάνῃ ἐπιστήμων ὢν ἰατρικῆς,
τά τε αὖ περὶ τὰ μαγγανεύματα, ἐὰν μὴ μάντις
ἢ τερατοσκόπος ὢν τυγχάνῃ. λεγέσθω δὴ λόγος
D ὅδε νόμος περὶ φαρμακείας· Ὃς ἂν φαρμακεύῃ
τινὰ ἐπὶ βλάβῃ μὴ θανασίμῳ μήτε αὑτοῦ μήτε
ἀνθρώπων τῶν ἐκείνου, βοσκημάτων δὲ ἢ σμηνῶν,
εἴτ᾽ <ἐπ᾽>[1] ἄλλῃ βλάβῃ εἴτ᾽ οὖν θανασίμῳ, ἐὰν μὲν
ἰατρὸς ὢν τυγχάνῃ καὶ ὄφλῃ δίκην φαρμάκων,
θανάτῳ ζημιούσθω, ἐὰν δὲ ἰδιώτης, ὅ τι χρὴ
παθεῖν ἢ ἀποτίνειν, τιμάτω περὶ αὐτοῦ τὸ δικαστήριον. ἐὰν δὲ καταδέσεσιν ἢ ἐπαγωγαῖς ἤ
τισιν ἐπῳδαῖς ἢ τῶν τοιούτων [φαρμακειῶν] ᾧ-
E τινιοῦν[2] δόξῃ ὅμοιος εἶναι βλάπτοντι, ἐὰν μὲν
μάντις ὢν ἢ τερατοσκόπος, τεθνάτω, ἐὰν δ᾽ ἄνευ
μαντικῆς, ὃ ἄν τις[3] φαρμακείας ὄφλῃ, ταὐτὸν καὶ
τούτῳ γιγνέσθω· περὶ γὰρ αὖ καὶ τούτου τιμάτω
τὸ δικαστήριον ὅ τι ἂν αὐτοῖς δεῖν αὐτὸν δόξῃ
πάσχειν ἢ ἀποτίνειν.

Ὅσα τις ἂν ἕτερος ἄλλον πημήνῃ κλέπτων
ἢ βιαζόμενος, ἂν μὲν μείζω, μείζονα τὴν ἔκτισιν
τῷ πημανθέντι τινέτω, ἐλάττω δὲ ζημιώσας
σμικροτέραν, παρὰ πάντα δὲ τοσαύτην ἡλίκα
ἂν ἑκάστοτε ζημιώσῃ τίς τινα, μέχριπερ ἂν
ἰάσηται τὸ βλαβέν. δίκην δὲ ἕκαστος [πρὸς][4]
ἑκάστῳ τῷ κακουργήματι σωφρονιστύος ἕνεκα
934 ξυνεπομένην προσεκτισάτω, ὁ μὲν ἀνοίᾳ κακουρ-
γήσας ἀλλοτρίᾳ, πειθοῖ διὰ νεότητα ἤ τι τοιοῦτον
χρησάμενος, ἐλαφροτέραν, ὁ δὲ διὰ οἰκείαν

[1] ⟨ἐπ᾽⟩ I add.
[2] [φαρμακειῶν] ᾧτινιοῦν Hermann : φαρμακειῶν ὠντινωνοῦν
MSS.

456

poisoning knows not what he is doing either in regard to bodies (unless he be a medical expert) or in respect of sorceries (unless he be a prophet or diviner). So this statement shall stand as the law about poisoning :—Whosoever shall poison any person so as to cause an injury not fatal either to the person himself or to his employes, or so as to cause an injury fatal or not fatal to his flocks or to his hives,—if the agent be a doctor, and if he be convicted of poisoning, he shall be punished by death ; but if he be a lay person, the court shall assess in his case what he shall suffer or pay. And if it be held that a man is acting like an injurer by the use of spells, incantations, or any such mode of poisoning, if he be a prophet or diviner, he shall be put to death ; but if he be ignorant of the prophetic art, he shall be dealt with in the same way as a layman convicted of poisoning,—that is to say, the court shall assess in his case also what shall seem to them right for him to suffer or pay.

In all cases where one man causes damage to another by acts of robbery[1] or violence, if the damage be great, he shall pay a large sum as compensation to the damaged party, and a small sum if the damage be small ; and as a general rule, every man shall in every case pay a sum equal to the damage done, until the loss is made good ; and, in addition to this, every man shall pay the penalty which is attached to his crime by way of corrective. The penalty shall be lighter in the case of one who

[1] Cp. 857 A ff.

---

[3] ὃ ἄν τις Hermann : ὧν τῆς MSS.
[4] [πρὸs] bracketed by Stephens (πρὸs ἑκάστῳ by England).

ἄνοιαν ἢ δι᾽ ἀκράτειαν ἡδονῶν ἢ λυπῶν, ἐν
φόβοις δειλοῖς¹ ἤ τισιν ἐπιθυμίαις ἢ φθόνοις
ἢ θυμοῖς δυσιάτοις γιγνόμενος, βαρυτέραν, οὐχ
ἕνεκα τοῦ κακουργῆσαι διδοὺς τὴν δίκην, οὐ γὰρ
τὸ γεγονὸς ἀγένητον ἔσται ποτέ, τοῦ δ᾽ εἰς τὸν
αὖθις ἕνεκα χρόνον ἢ τὸ παράπαν μισῆσαι τὴν
ἀδικίαν αὐτόν τε καὶ τοὺς ἰδόντας αὐτὸν δικαι-
B ούμενον, ἢ λωφῆσαι μέρη πολλὰ τῆς τοιαύτης
ξυμφορᾶς. ὧν δὴ πάντων ἕνεκα χρὴ καὶ πρὸς
πάντα τὰ τοιαῦτα βλέποντας τοὺς νόμους τοξότου
μὴ κακοῦ στοχάζεσθαι δίκην τοῦ τε μεγέθους τῆς
κολάσεως ἑκάστων ἕνεκα καὶ παντελῶς τῆς ἀξίας.
ταὐτὸν δ᾽ ἔργον δρῶντα ξυνυπηρετεῖν δεῖ τῷ
νομοθέτῃ τὸν δικαστήν, ὅταν αὐτῷ τις νόμος
ἐπιτρέπῃ τιμᾶν ὅ τι χρὴ πάσχειν τὸν κρινόμενον
C ἢ ἀποτίνειν· τὸν δέ, καθάπερ ζωγράφον, ὑπογρά-
φειν ἔργα ἑπόμενα τῇ γραφῇ. ὃ δὴ καὶ νῦν, ὦ
Μέγιλλε καὶ Κλεινία, ποιητέον ἡμῖν ὅτι κάλλιστα
καὶ ἄριστα· τῶν κλοπαίων τε καὶ βιαίων πάντων
τὰς ζημίας λεγομένας οἵας δεῖ γίγνεσθαι, λεκτέον,
ὅπως ἂν ἡμῖν παρείκωσι θεοὶ καὶ θεῶν παῖδες
νομοθετεῖν.

Μαινόμενος δὲ ἄν τις ᾖ, μὴ φανερὸς ἔστω
κατὰ πόλιν· οἱ προσήκοντες δ᾽ ἑκάστων κατὰ τὰς
οἰκίας φυλαττόντων αὐτούς, ὅτῳ ἂν ἐπίστωνται
D τρόπῳ, ἢ ζημίαν ἐκτινόντων, ὁ μὲν τοῦ μεγίστου
τιμήματος ἑκατὸν δραχμάς, ἐάν τ᾽ οὖν δοῦλον ἐάν
τ᾽ οὖν καὶ ἐλεύθερον περιορᾷ, δευτέρου δὲ τιμήματος

---

¹ δειλοῖς Winckelmann : δειλίας (al. δεινῶς) MSS.

---

¹ Cp. 862 D ff.

has done wrong owing to another's folly—the wrong-doer being over-persuaded because of his youth or for some such reason; and it shall be heavier when the man has done wrong owing to his own folly, because of his incontinence in respect of pleasures and pains and the overpowering influence of craven fears or of incurable desires, envies and rages. And he shall pay the penalty, not because of the wrong-doing,—for what is done can never be undone,—but in order that for the future both he himself and those who behold his punishment may either utterly loathe his sin or at least renounce [1] to a great extent such lamentable conduct. For all these reasons and with a view to all these objects, the law, like a good archer, must aim in each case at the amount of the punishment, and above all at its fitting amount; and the judge must assist the lawgiver in carrying out this same task, whenever the law entrusts to him the assessment of what the defendant is to suffer or pay, while the lawgiver, like a draughtsman, must give a sketch in outline of cases which illustrate the rules of the written code. And that, O Megillus and Clinias, is the task which we must now execute as fairly and well as we can: we must state what penalties should be ordained for all cases of robbery and violence, in so far as the gods and sons of gods may suffer us to ordain them by law.

If any be a madman, he shall not appear openly in the city; the relatives of such persons shall keep them indoors, employing whatever means they know of, or else they shall pay a penalty; a person belonging to the highest property-class shall pay a hundred drachmae, whether the man he is neglecting be a free man or a slave,—one belonging to the second

τέτταρα μέρη τῆς μνᾶς τῶν πέντε, τρία δ᾽ ὁ
τρίτος, καὶ δύο ὁ τέταρτος. μαίνονται μὲν οὖν
πολλοὶ πολλοὺς τρόπους, οὓς μὲν νῦν εἴπομεν,
ὑπὸ νόσων, εἰσὶ δὲ οἳ διὰ θυμοῦ κακὴν φύσιν
ἅμα καὶ τροφὴν γενομένην· οἳ δὴ σμικρᾶς ἔχθρας
γενομένης πολλὴν φωνὴν ἱέντες κακῶς ἀλλήλους
Ε βλασφημοῦντες λέγουσιν, οὐ πρέπον ἐν εὐνόμῳ
πόλει γίγνεσθαι τοιοῦτον οὐδὲν οὐδαμῇ οὐδαμῶς,
εἷς δὴ περὶ κακηγορίας ἔστω νόμος περὶ πάντας
ὅδε· Μηδένα κακηγορείτω μηδείς· ὁ δὲ ἀμφισβη-
τῶν ἔν τισι λόγοις ἄλλος ἄλλῳ διδασκέτω καὶ
μανθανέτω τόν τε ἀμφισβητοῦντα καὶ τοὺς
παρόντας ἀπεχόμενος πάντως τοῦ κακηγορεῖν.
ἐκ γὰρ τοῦ κατεύχεσθαί τε ἀλλήλοις ἐπαρωμένους
καὶ δι᾽ αἰσχρῶν ὀνομάτων ἐπιφέρειν γυναικείους
935 ἑαυτοῖς φήμας, πρῶτον μὲν ἐκ λόγων, κούφου
πράγματος, ἔργῳ μίση τε καὶ ἔχθραι βαρύταται
γίγνονται· πράγματι γὰρ ἀχαρίστῳ, θυμῷ, χαρι-
ζόμενος ὁ λέγων, ἐμπιπλὰς ὀργὴν κακῶν ἑστια-
μάτων, ὅσον ὑπὸ παιδείας ἡμερώθη ποτέ, πάλιν
ἐξαγριῶν τῆς ψυχῆς τὸ τοιοῦτον, θηριούμενος ἐν
δυσκολίᾳ ζῶν γίγνεται, πικρὰν τοῦ θυμοῦ χάριν
ἀποδεχόμενος. μετεκβαίνειν δὲ αὖ πως εἰώθασι
πάντες θαμὰ ἐν τοῖς τοιούτοις εἰς τό τι γελοῖον
Β περὶ τοῦ ἐναντίου φθέγγεσθαι· ὅ τις ἐθιζόμενος
οὐδεὶς πώποτε ὃς οὐ τοῦ σπουδαίου τρόπου ἤτοι
τὸ παράπαν διήμαρτεν ἢ μεγαλονοίας ἀπώλεσε
μέρη πολλά. ὧν δὴ χάριν ἐν μὲν ἱερῷ τὸ παράπαν μηδεὶς τοιοῦτον φθέγξηται μηδέποτε μηδὲν
μηδ᾽ ἔν τισι δημοτελέσι θυσίαις, μηδ᾽ αὖ ἐν
ἄθλοις μηδ᾽ ἐν ἀγορᾷ μηδ᾽ ἐν δικαστηρίῳ μηδ᾽ ἐν

class shall pay four-fifths of a mina—one of the third class, three-fifths,—and one of the fourth class, two-fifths. There are many and various forms of madness : in the cases now mentioned it is caused by disease, but cases also occur where it is due to the natural growth and fostering of an evil temper, by which men in the course of a trifling quarrel abuse one another slanderously with loud cries—a thing which is unseemly and totally out of place in a well-regulated State. Concerning abuse there shall be this one law to cover all cases:—No one shall abuse anyone. If one is disputing with another in argument, he shall either speak or listen, and he shall wholly refrain from abusing either the disputant or the bystanders. For from those light things, words, there spring in deed things most heavy to bear, even hatreds and feuds, when men begin by cursing one another and foully abusing one another in the manner of fish-wives; and the man who utters such words is gratifying a thing most ungracious and sating his passion with foul foods, and by thus brutalizing afresh that part of his soul which once was humanized by education, he makes a wild beast of himself through his rancorous life, and wins only gall for gratitude from his passion. In such disputes all men are commonly wont to proceed to indulge in ridicule of their opponent; but everyone who has ever yet indulged in this practice has either failed to achieve a virtuous disposition, or else has lost in great measure his former high-mindedness. No man, therefore, shall ever in any wise utter such words in any holy place or at any public sacrifice or public games, or in the market or the court or any public assembly; in every such

ξυλλόγῳ κοινῷ μηδενί· κολαζέτω δὲ ὁ τούτων
ἄρχων ἕκαστος [1] [ἀνατί],[2] ἢ μηδέποτ᾽ ἀριστείων
C πέρι φιλονεικήσῃ, νόμων ὡς οὐ κηδόμενος οὐδὲ
ποιῶν τὰ προσταχθέντα ὑπὸ τοῦ νομοθέτου. ἐὰν
δέ τις ἐν ἄλλοις τόποις λοιδορίας ἄρχων ἢ ἀμυνόμενος ὁστισοῦν μὴ ἀπέχηται τῶν τοιούτων
λόγων, ὁ προστυγχάνων πρεσβύτερος ὢν τῷ
νόμῳ ἀμυνέτω, πληγαῖς ἐξείργων τοὺς θυμῷ
ἑταίρῳ [3] κακῷ φιλοφρονουμένους, ἢ ἐνεχέσθω τῇ
τεταγμένῃ ζημίᾳ.

Λέγομεν δὴ τὰ νῦν ὡς ὁ λοιδορίαις συμπλεκό-
μενος ἄνευ τοῦ γελοῖα ζητεῖν λέγειν οὐ δυνατός
ἐστι χρῆσθαι, καὶ τοῦτο λοιδοροῦμεν, ὁπόταν
D θυμῷ γιγνόμενον ᾖ. τί δὲ δή; τὴν τῶν κωμῳδῶν
προθυμίαν τοῦ γελοῖα εἰς τοὺς ἀνθρώπους λέγειν
ἢ παραδεχώμεθα, ἐὰν ἄνευ θυμοῦ τὸ τοιοῦτον ἡμῖν
τοὺς πολίτας ἐπιχειρῶσι κωμῳδοῦντες λέγειν, ἢ
διαλάβωμεν δίχα τῷ παίζειν καὶ μή, καὶ παίζοντι
μὲν ἐξέστω τινὶ περί του λέγειν γελοῖον ἄνευ θυμοῦ,
E συντεταμένῳ δὲ καὶ μετὰ θυμοῦ, καθάπερ εἴπομεν,
μὴ ἐξέστω μηδενί; τοῦτο μὲν οὖν οὐδαμῶς ἀνα-
θετέον, ᾧ δ᾽ ἐξέστω καὶ μή, τοῦτο νομοθετησώμεθα·
ποιητῇ δὴ κωμῳδίας ἤ τινος ἰάμβων ἢ Μουσῶν
μελῳδίας μὴ ἐξέστω μήτε λόγῳ μήτε εἰκόνι μήτε
θυμῷ μήτε ἄνευ θυμοῦ μηδαμῶς μηδένα τῶν πολιτῶν κωμῳδεῖν· ἐὰν δέ τις ἀπειθῇ, τοὺς ἀθλοθέτας
936 ἐξείργειν ἐκ τῆς χώρας τὸ παράπαν αὐθημερόν, ἢ

---

[1] ἕκαστος MSS. : ἕκαστον Zur., vulg.
[2] [ἀνατί] wanting in best MSS. (added in marg.), and
bracketed by England.
[3] ἑταίρῳ England : ἑτέρῳ MSS.

---

[1] Cp. Rep. 394 ff., 606 ff.   [2] Cp. Phileb. 49 E ff.

case the magistrate concerned shall punish the offender; or, if he fail to do so, he shall be disqualified for any public distinction because of his neglect of the laws and his failure to execute the injunctions of the lawgiver. And if in other places a man abstains not from such language—whether he be the aggressor or acting in self-defence—whosoever meets with him, if he be an older man, shall vindicate the law by driving off with stripes the men who pamper passion, that evil comrade; or, if he fail to do so, he shall be liable to the appointed penalty.

We are now asserting that a man who is gripped by the habit of abuse cannot avoid trying to indulge in ridicule; and this is a thing we abuse when it is uttered in passion. What then? Are we to countenance the readiness to ridicule people which is shown by comic writers,[1] provided that in their comedies they employ this sort of language about the citizens without any show of passion? Or shall we divide ridicule under the two heads of jest and earnest, and allow anyone to ridicule any other in jest and without passion,[2] but forbid anyone (as we have already said) to do so in real earnest and with passion? We must by no means go back on what we said; but we must determine by law who is to be granted this permission, and who refused. A composer of a comedy or of any iambic or lyric song shall be strictly forbidden to ridicule any of the citizens either by word or by mimicry,[3] whether with or without passion; and if anyone disobeys, the Presidents of the Games shall on the same day banish him wholly from the country, failing which

[3] Cp. Ar. *Eth. N.* 1128ᵃ 20 ff. ; *Pol.* 1336ᵇ 2ff.

ζημιοῦσθαι μναῖς τρισὶν ἱεραῖς τοῦ θεοῦ οὗ ἂν
ὁ ἀγὼν ᾖ. οἷς δ᾽ εἴρηται πρότερον ἐξουσίαν εἶναι
[περὶ τοῦ][1] ποιεῖν εἰς ἀλλήλους, τούτοις ἄνευ
θυμοῦ μὲν μετὰ παιδιᾶς ἐξέστω, σπουδῇ δὲ ἅμα
καὶ θυμουμένοισι μὴ ἐξέστω. τούτου δὴ διά-
γνωσις ἐπιτετράφθω τῷ τῆς παιδεύσεως ὅλης
ἐπιμελητῇ τῶν νέων, καὶ ὃ μὲν ἂν οὗτος ἐγκρίνῃ,
προφέρειν εἰς τὸ μέσον ἐξέστω τῷ ποιήσαντι, ὃ
δ᾽ ἂν ἀποκρίνῃ, μήτε αὐτὸς ἐπιδεικνύσθω μηδενὶ
μήτε ἄλλον δοῦλον μηδὲ[2] ἐλεύθερόν ποτε φανῇ
B διδάξας, ἢ κακὸς εἶναι δοξαζέσθω καὶ ἀπειθὴς
τοῖς νόμοις.

Οἰκτρὸς δ᾽ οὐχ ὁ πεινῶν ἤ τι τοιοῦτο πάσχων,
ἀλλ᾽ ὁ σωφρονῶν ἤ τινα ἀρετὴν ἢ μέρος ἔχων
ταύτης, ἄν τινα ξυμφορὰν πρὸς τούτοις κεκτῆται.
διὸ θαυμαστὸν ἂν γένοιτο εἴ τις ὢν τοιοῦτος
ἀμεληθείη τὸ παράπαν, ὥστ᾽ εἰς πτωχείαν τὴν
ἐσχάτην ἐλθεῖν, δοῦλος ἢ καὶ ἐλεύθερος, ἐν
οἰκουμένῃ καὶ μετρίως πολιτείᾳ τε καὶ πόλει.
διὸ τῷ νομοθέτῃ θεῖναι νόμον ἀσφαλὲς τοιούτοις
C τοιόνδε τινά· Πτωχὸς μηδεὶς ἡμῖν ἐν τῇ πόλει
γιγνέσθω· τοιοῦτον δ᾽ ἄν τις ἐπιχειρῇ δρᾶν,
εὐχαῖς βίον ἀνηνύτοις ξυλλεγόμενος, ἐκ μὲν
ἀγορᾶς ἀγορανόμοι ἐξειργόντων αὐτόν, ἐκ δὲ τοῦ
ἄστεος ἡ τῶν ἀστυνόμων ἀρχή, ἀγρονόμοι δὲ ἐκ
τῆς ἄλλης χώρας εἰς τὴν ὑπερορίαν ἐκπεμπόντων,
ὅπως ἡ χώρα τοῦ τοιούτου ζῴου καθαρὰ γίγνηται
τὸ παράπαν.

---

[1] [περὶ τοῦ] bracketed by Ast (περί του Burnet).
[2] μηδὲ Bekker : μήτε MSS.

---

[1] Cp. 816 E, 829 C, D.

they shall be fined three minas, dedicated to the god whose festival is being held. Those to whom permission has been given, as we previously said,[1] to write songs about one another shall be allowed to ridicule others in jest and without passion; but they shall not be allowed to do so with passion and in earnest. The task of making this distinction shall be entrusted to the minister in charge of the general education of the young: whatever he shall approve, the composer shall be allowed to produce in public, but whatever he shall disapprove, the composer shall be forbidden either personally to exhibit to anyone or to be found teaching to any other person, free man or slave; and if he does so, he shall be held to be a base man and disobedient to the laws.

The man who suffers from hunger or the like is not the man who deserves pity, but he who, while possessing temperance or virtue of some sort, or a share thereof, gains in addition evil fortune; wherefore it would be a strange thing indeed if, in a polity and State that is even moderately well organised, a man of this kind (be he slave or free man) should be so entirely neglected as to come to utter beggary. Wherefore the lawgiver will be safe in enacting for such cases some such law as this:—There shall be no beggar in our State; and if anyone attempts to beg, and to collect a livelihood by ceaseless prayers, the market-stewards shall expel him from the market, and the Board of city-stewards from the city, and from any other district he shall be driven across the border by the country-stewards, to the end that the land may be wholly purged of such a creature.

Δοῦλος δ' ἂν ἢ δούλη βλάψῃ τῶν ἀλλοτρίων
D καὶ ὁτιοῦν μὴ ξυναιτίου τοῦ βλαβέντος αὐτοῦ
γενομένου κατ' ἀπειρίαν ἤ τιν' ἑτέραν χρείαν μὴ
σώφρονα, ὁ τοῦ βλάψαντος δεσπότης ἢ τὴν
βλάβην ἐξιάσθω μὴ ἐνδεῶς ἢ τὸν βλάψαντ' αὐτὸν
παραδότω· ἐὰν δ' ἐπαιτιώμενος ὁ δεσπότης κοινῇ
τοῦ βλάψαντος τέχνῃ καὶ τοῦ βλαβέντος ἐπ'
ἀποστερήσει φῇ τοῦ δούλου γεγονέναι τὴν αἰτίαν,
διαδικαζέσθω μὲν κακοτεχνιῶν τῷ φάσκοντι
βλαβῆναι, καὶ ἐὰν ἕλῃ, διπλασίαν τῆς ἀξίας τοῦ
δούλου κομιζέσθω ἧς ἂν τιμήσῃ τὸ δικαστήριον,
E ἐὰν δὲ ἡττηθῇ, τήν τε βλάβην ἐξιάσθω καὶ τὸν
δοῦλον παραδότω. καὶ ἐὰν ὑποζύγιον ἢ ἵππος ἢ
κύων ἤ τι τῶν ἄλλων θρεμμάτων σίνηταί τι τῶν
πέλας, κατὰ ταὐτὰ ἐκτίνειν τὴν βλάβην.

Ἐάν τις ἑκὼν μὴ 'θέλῃ μαρτυρεῖν, προκαλεῖσθαι[1] τὸν δεόμενον, ὁ δὲ προκληθεὶς ἀπαντάτω
πρὸς τὴν δίκην, καὶ ἐὰν μὲν εἰδῇ καὶ ἐθέλῃ μαρτυρεῖν, μαρτυρείτω, ἐὰν δὲ εἰδέναι μὴ φῇ, τοὺς τρεῖς
θεοὺς Δία καὶ Ἀπόλλωνα καὶ Θέμιν ἀπομόσας ἦ
937 μὴν μὴ εἰδέναι ἀπαλλαττέσθω τῆς δίκης. ὁ δ'
εἰς μαρτυρίαν κληθείς, μὴ ἀπαντῶν δὲ τῷ καλεσα-
μένῳ, τῆς βλάβης ὑπόδικος ἔστω κατὰ νόμον.
ἐὰν δέ τίς τινα δικάζοντα ἀναστήσηται μάρτυρα,
μαρτυρήσας μὴ διαψηφιζέσθω περὶ ταύτης τῆς
δίκης. γυναικὶ δ' ἐξέστω ἐλευθέρᾳ μαρτυρεῖν καὶ
συνηγορεῖν, ἐὰν ὑπὲρ τετταράκοντα ἔτη ἦ γεγονυῖα,

---

[1] προκαλεῖσθαι Cobet : προσκαλεῖσθαι MSS.

If a slave, male or female, do any injury to another man's goods, when the injured man himself has had no share in causing the injury through his own clumsy or careless handling, then the master of him that has done the injury shall fully make good the damage, or else shall hand over the person of the injurer : but if the master brings a charge affirming that the claim is made in order to rob him of his slave by a privy agreement between the injurer and the injured party, then he shall prosecute the man who claims that he has been injured on the charge of conspiracy ; and if he wins his case, he shall receive double the price at which the court shall assess the slave, but if he loses he shall not only make good the damage, but he shall also hand over the slave. And if it be a mule or horse or dog or any other animal that causes damage to any property belonging to a neighbour, its master shall in like manner pay compensation.

If anyone is unwilling to act as witness, the man who requires his evidence shall summon him, and the man so summoned shall attend the trial, and if he knows the facts and is willing to give evidence, he shall give it ; but in case he denies knowledge, he shall take an oath by the three gods, Zeus, Apollo, and Themis, that of a truth he has no knowledge, and this done, he shall be dismissed from the suit. And if a man summoned as witness does not attend with his summoner, he shall be legally liable to be sued for damages. And if one of the judges be summoned as a witness, he shall not vote at the trial after giving evidence. A free woman, if she be over forty years old, shall be allowed to give evidence and to support a plea, and if she have no husband,

καὶ δίκην λαγχάνειν, ἐὰν ἄνανδρος ἦ· ζῶντος δὲ
B ἀνδρὸς ἐξέστω μαρτυρῆσαι μόνον. δούλη δὲ καὶ
δούλῳ καὶ παιδὶ φόνου μόνον ἐξέστω μαρτυρεῖν
καὶ συνηγορεῖν, ἐὰν ἐγγυητὴν ἀξιόχρεων ἦ μὴν
μενεῖν καταστήσῃ μέχρι δίκης, ἐὰν ἐπισκηφθῇ τὰ
ψευδῆ μαρτυρῆσαι. ἐπισκήπτεσθαι δὲ τῶν ἀντιδίκων ἑκάτερον ὅλῃ τῇ μαρτυρίᾳ καὶ μέρει, ἐὰν τὰ
ψευδῆ φῇ τινὰ μεμαρτυρηκέναι, πρὶν τὴν δίκην
διακεκρίσθαι· τὰς δ' ἐπισκήψεις τὰς ἀρχὰς
φυλάττειν κατασεσημασμένας ὑπ' ἀμφοῖν, καὶ
παρέχειν εἰς τὴν τῶν ψευδομαρτυριῶν διάκρισιν.
C ἐὰν δέ τις ἁλῷ δὶς ψευδομαρτυρῶν, τοῦτον μηκέτι
νόμος ἀναγκαζέτω μηδεὶς μαρτυρεῖν, ἐὰν δὲ τρίς,
μηκέτ' ἐξέστω τούτῳ μαρτυρεῖν· ἐὰν δὲ τολμήσῃ
μαρτυρῆσαι τρὶς ἑαλωκώς, ἐνδεικνύτω μὲν πρὸς τὴν
ἀρχὴν ὁ βουλόμενος αὐτόν, ἡ δ' ἀρχὴ δικαστηρίῳ
παραδότω, ἐὰν δὲ ὄφλῃ, θανάτῳ ζημιούσθω. ὁπόσων δ' ἂν μαρτυρίαι ἁλῶσι δίκῃ ψευδῆ δοξάντων
μαρτυρεῖν καὶ τὴν νίκην τῷ ἑλόντι πεποιηκέναι,
ἐὰν τῶν τοιούτων ὑπὲρ ἥμισυ μαρτυριῶν καταδι-
D κασθῶσί τινες, τὴν κατὰ ταύτας ἁλοῦσαν δίκην
ἀνάδικον γίγνεσθαι, ἀμφισβήτησιν δ' εἶναι καὶ
διαδικασίαν εἴτε κατὰ ταύτας εἴτε μὴ ἡ δίκη ἐκρίθη,
ὁποτέρως δ' ἂν κριθῇ, ταύτῃ γιγνέσθω τὸ τέλος
τῶν ἔμπροσθεν δικῶν.

Πολλῶν δὲ ὄντων καὶ καλῶν ἐν τῷ τῶν ἀνθρώπων
βίῳ τοῖς πλείστοις αὐτῶν οἷον κῆρες ἐπιπεφύκασιν,
468

she shall be allowed to bring an action; but if she have a husband alive, she shall only be allowed to give evidence. A male or female slave and a child shall be allowed to give evidence and support a plea in murder cases only, provided that they furnish a substantial security that, if their evidence be denounced as false, they will remain until the trial. Either of the opposing parties in a suit may denounce all or part of the evidence, provided that he claims that false witness has been given before the action is finally decided; and the magistrates shall keep the denunciations, when they have been sealed by both parties, and shall produce them at the trial for false witness. If any person be twice convicted of false witness, no law shall compel him any longer to bear witness, and if thrice, he shall not be allowed to bear witness any longer; and if, after three convictions, a man dare to bear witness, whoso wishes shall report him to the magistrates, and they shall hand him over to the court, and if he be found guilty, he shall be punished with death. In the case of all those whose evidence is condemned at the trial,—they being adjudged to have given false witness and thus to have caused the victory of the winner,—if more than the half of their evidence be condemned, the action that was lost because of them shall be annulled, and there shall be a disputation and a trial as to whether the action was or was not decided on the evidence in question; and by the verdict then given, whichever way it goes, the result of the previous actions shall be finally determined.

Although there are many fair things in human life, yet to most of them there clings a kind of

PLATO

αἱ καταμιαίνουσί τε καὶ καταρρυπαίνουσιν αὐτά.

E καὶ δὴ καὶ δίκη ἐν ἀνθρώποις πῶς οὐ καλόν, ὃ
πάντα ἡμέρωκε τὰ ἀνθρώπινα; καλοῦ δὲ ὄντος
τούτου πῶς οὐ καὶ τὸ ξυνδικεῖν ἡμῖν γίγνοιτ' ἂν
καλόν; ταῦτα οὖν τοιαῦτα ὄντα διαβάλλει τις
κακὴ καλὸν ὄνομα προστησαμένη τέχνη,[1] ἣ
πρῶτον μὲν δή φησιν εἶναί τινα δικῶν μηχανήν,
εἶναι δ' αὖ τὴν τῷ[2] τε δικάσασθαι καὶ ξυνδικεῖν
ἄλλῳ νικᾶν δυναμένην, ἄν τ' οὖν δίκαια ἄν τε μὴ
938 τὰ περὶ τὴν δίκην ἑκάστην ᾖ πεπραγμένα· δωρεὰν
δ' αὐτῆς εἶναι τῆς τέχνης καὶ τῶν λόγων τῶν ἐκ
τῆς τέχνης, ἂν ἀντιδωρῆταί τις χρήματα. ταύτην
οὖν ἐν τῇ παρ' ἡμῖν πόλει, εἴτ' οὖν τέχνη εἴτε
ἄτεχνός ἐστί τις ἐμπειρία καὶ τριβή, μάλιστα μὲν
δὴ χρεών ἐστι μὴ φῦναι· δεομένου δὲ τοῦ νομοθέτου
πείθεσθαι καὶ μὴ ἐναντία δίκῃ φθέγγεσθαι, πρὸς
ἄλλην δὲ ἀπαλλάττεσθαι χώραν, πειθομένοις
μὲν σιγῇ, ἀπειθοῦσι δὲ φωνῇ νόμου ἥδε· Ἄν τις
B δοκῇ πειρᾶσθαι τὴν τῶν δικαίων δύναμιν ἐν
ταῖς τῶν δικαστῶν ψυχαῖς ἐπὶ τἀναντία τρέπειν
καὶ παρὰ καιρὸν πολυδικεῖν [τῶν τοιούτων][3] ἢ
καὶ ξυνδικεῖν, γραφέσθω μὲν ὁ βουλόμενος αὐτὸν
κακοδικίας ἢ καὶ ξυνδικίας κακῆς, κρινέσθω δὲ ἐν
τῷ τῶν ἐκλεκτῶν δικαστηρίῳ, ὀφλόντος δὲ τιμάτω
τὸ δικαστήριον εἴτε φιλοχρηματίᾳ δοκεῖ δρᾶν τὸ
τοιοῦτον εἴτε φιλονεικίᾳ, καὶ ἐὰν μὲν φιλονεικίᾳ,
τιμᾶν αὐτῷ τὸ δικαστήριον ὅσου χρὴ χρόνου τὸν
τοιοῦτον μηδενὶ λαχεῖν δίκην μηδὲ ξυνδικῆσαι,
ἐὰν δὲ φιλοχρηματίᾳ, τὸν μὲν ξένον ἀπιόντα ἐκ

[1] τέχνη Hermann : τέχνην MSS.
[2] αὖ τὴν τῷ : αὐτὴν τῷ Cornarius, Zur. : αὕτη τοῦ MSS.
[3] [τῶν τοιούτων] bracketed by Stephens, Stallbaum.

470

canker which poisons and corrupts them. None would deny that justice between men is a fair thing, and that it has civilized all human affairs. And if justice be fair, how can we deny that pleading is also a fair thing? But these fair things are in disrepute owing to a kind of foul art, which, cloaking itself under a fair name,[1] claims, first, that there exists a device for dealing with lawsuits, and further, that it is the one which is able, by pleading and helping another to plead, to win the victory, whether the pleas concerned be just or unjust; and it also asserts that both this art itself and the arguments which proceed from it are a gift offered to any man who gives money in exchange. This art—whether it be really an art or merely an artless trick got by habit and practice[2]—must never, if possible, arise in our State; and when the lawgiver demands compliance and no contradiction of justice, or the removal of such artists to another country,—if they comply, the law for its part shall keep silence, but if they fail to comply, its pronouncement shall be this :—If anyone be held to be trying to reverse the force of just pleas in the minds of the judges, or to be multiplying suits unduly or aiding others to do so, whoso wishes shall indict him for perverse procedure or aiding in perverse procedure, and he shall be tried before the court of select judges; and if he be convicted, the court shall determine whether he seems to be acting from avarice or from ambition ; and if from the latter, the court shall determine for how long a period such an one shall be precluded from bringing an action against anyone, or aiding anyone to do so ; while if avarice be his motive, if he be an alien he

---

[1] *i.e.* " Rhetoric."   [2] Cp. *Gorg.* 463 B.

C τῆς χώρας μήποτε πάλιν ἐλθεῖν, ἢ θανάτῳ
ζημιοῦσθαι, τὸν ἀστὸν δὲ τεθνάναι φιλοχρημο-
σύνης ἕνεκα τῆς ἐκ παντὸς τρόπου παρ' αὑτῷ
τιμωμένης· καὶ ἐάν τις φιλονεικίᾳ κριθῇ δὶς τὸ
τοιοῦτον δρᾶν, τεθνάτω.

shall be sent out of the country and forbidden to return on pain of death, but if he be a citizen he shall be put to death because of his unscrupulous devotion to the pursuit of gain. And anyone who has twice been pronounced guilty of committing such an act from ambition shall be put to death.

941 ΑΘ. Ἐὰν ὡς πρεσβευτής τις ἢ κῆρυξ καταψευ-
δόμενος τῆς πόλεως παραπρεσβεύηται πρός τινα
πόλιν, ἢ πεμπόμενος μὴ τὰς οὔσας πρεσβείας
ἐφ' αἷς πέμπεται ἀπαγγέλλῃ, ἢ πάλιν αὖ παρὰ
τῶν πολεμίων ἢ καὶ φίλων μὴ τὰ παρ' ἐκείνων
ὀρθῶς ἀποπρεσβεύσας γένηται φανερὸς ἢ κηρυ-
κεύσας, γραφαὶ κατὰ τούτων ἔστων ὡς Ἑρμοῦ
καὶ Διὸς ἀγγελίας καὶ ἐπιτάξεις παρὰ νόμον
ἀσεβησάντων, τίμημα δὲ ὅ τι χρὴ πάσχειν ἢ
Β ἀποτίνειν, ἐὰν ὄφλῃ.

Κλοπὴ μὲν χρημάτων ἀνελεύθερον, ἁρπαγὴ δὲ
ἀναίσχυντον· τῶν Διὸς δὲ υἱέων οὐδεὶς οὔτε δόλοις
οὔτε βίᾳ χαίρων ἐπιτετήδευκε τούτοιν οὐδέτερον.
μηδεὶς οὖν ὑπὸ ποιητῶν μηδ' ἄλλως ὑπό τινων
μυθολόγων πλημμελῶν περὶ τὰ τοιαῦτα ἐξαπα-
τώμενος ἀναπειθέσθω, καὶ κλέπτων ἢ βιαζόμενος
οἰέσθω μηδὲν αἰσχρὸν ποιεῖν ἀλλ' ἅπερ αὐτοὶ
θεοὶ δρῶσιν· οὔτε γὰρ ἀληθὲς οὔτ' εἰκός, ἀλλ'
ὅστις δρᾷ τοιοῦτον παρανόμως, οὔτε θεὸς οὔτε
C παῖς ἐστί ποτε θεῶν· ταῦτα δὲ νομοθέτῃ μᾶλλον
προσήκει γιγνώσκειν ἢ ποιηταῖς ξύμπασιν. ὁ
μὲν οὖν πεισθεὶς ἡμῶν τῷ λόγῳ εὐτυχεῖ τε καὶ
εἰς χρόνον ἅπαντα εὐτυχοίη, ὁ δ' ἀπιστήσας τὸ
μετὰ ταῦτα τοιῷδέ τινι ἐνεχέσθω [1] νόμῳ· Ἐάν

[1] ἐνεχέσθω Ast: μαχέσθω MSS.

---

[1] Son, and herald, of Zeus, and a master of speech (and of
lies).

BOOK XII

ATH. IF anyone, while acting as ambassador or herald, conveys false messages from his State to another State, or fails to deliver the actual message he was sent to deliver, or is proved to have brought back, as ambassador or herald, either from a friendly or hostile nation, their reply in a false form,—against all such there shall be laid an indictment for breaking the law by sinning against the sacred messages and injunctions of Hermes [1] and Zeus, and an assessment shall be made of the penalty they shall suffer or pay, if convicted.

Theft of property is uncivilized, open robbery is shameless: neither of these has any of the sons of Zeus practised, through delight in fraud or force. Let no man, therefore, be deluded concerning this or persuaded either by poets or by any perverse myth-mongers into the belief that, when he thieves or forcibly robs, he is doing nothing shameful, but just what the gods themselves do.[2] That is both unlikely and untrue; and whoever acts thus unlawfully is neither a god at all nor a child of gods; and this the lawgiver, as it behoves him, knows better than the whole tribe of poets. He, therefore, that hearkens to our speech is blessed, and deserves blessing for all time; but he that hearkens not shall, in the next place, be holden by this law :—If anyone

---

[2] Cp. *Rep.* 378 ff., 388 ff. Hermes is specially in mind, as notorious for his thefts and frauds ; cp. Hom. *Il.* 5. 390 ; 24. 395, etc.

τίς τι κλέπτῃ δημόσιον μέγα ἢ καὶ σμικρόν, τῆς
αὐτῆς δίκης δεῖ. σμικρόν τε γὰρ ὁ κλέπτων
ἔρωτι μὲν ταὐτῷ, δυνάμει δὲ ἐλάττονι κέκλοφεν·
ὅ τε τὸ μεῖζον κινῶν οὐ καταθέμενος ὅλον ἀδικεῖ·
D δίκης οὖν οὐδέτερον οὐδετέρου ἐλάττονος ἕνεκα
μεγέθους τοῦ κλέμματος ὁ νόμος ἀξιοῖ ζημιοῦν,
ἀλλὰ τῷ τὸν μὲν ἴσως ἂν ἰάσιμον ἔτ᾽ εἶναι, τὸν
δ᾽ ἀνίατον. ξένον μὲν δὴ τῶν δημοσίων ἢ δοῦλον
ἄν τίς τι κλέπτοντα ἐν δικαστηρίῳ ἕλῃ, ὡς ἰασίμῳ
ἐκ τῶν εἰκότων ὄντι, τί χρὴ παθεῖν ἢ τίνα ζημίαν
942 ἀποτίνειν αὐτόν, ἡ κρίσις γιγνέσθω· τὸν δὲ ἀστὸν
καὶ τεθραμμένον ὡς ἔσται τεθραμμένος, ἂν πατρίδα
συλῶν ἢ βιαζόμενος ἁλίσκηται, ἐάν τ᾽ ἐπ᾽ αὐτο-
φώρῳ ἐάν τε μή, σχεδὸν ὡς ἀνίατον ὄντα θανάτῳ
ζημιοῦν.

Στρατειῶν δὲ ἕνεκα πολλὴ μὲν ξυμβουλή,
πολλοὶ δὲ νόμοι γίγνονται κατὰ τρόπον, μέγιστον
δὲ τὸ μηδέποτε ἄναρχον μηδένα εἶναι, μήτ᾽ ἄρρενα
μήτε θήλειαν, μηδέ τινος ἔθει ψυχὴν εἰθίσθαι
μήτε σπουδάζοντος μήτ᾽ ἐν παιδιαῖς αὐτὸν ἐφ᾽
ἑαυτοῦ τι κατὰ μόνας δρᾶν, ἀλλ᾽ ἔν τε πολέμῳ
B παντὶ καὶ ἐν εἰρήνῃ πάσῃ πρὸς τὸν ἄρχοντα ἀεὶ
βλέποντα καὶ ξυνεπόμενον ζῆν, καὶ τὰ βραχύταθ᾽
ὑπ᾽ ἐκείνου κυβερνώμενον, οἷον ἑστάναι θ᾽ ὅταν
ἐπιτάττῃ τις καὶ πορεύεσθαι καὶ γυμνάζεσθαι
καὶ λοῦσθαι καὶ σιτεῖσθαι καὶ ἐγείρεσθαι νύκτωρ
εἴς τε φυλακὰς καὶ παραγγέλσεις, καὶ ἐν αὐτοῖς
τοῖς κινδύνοις μήτε τινὰ διώκειν μήθ᾽ ὑποχωρεῖν
ἄλλῳ ἄνευ τῆς τῶν ἀρχόντων δηλώσεως, ἑνί τε

---

[1] But cp. 857 A, B.

steals any piece of public property, he shall receive the same punishment, be it great or small. For he that steals a small thing steals with equal greed, though with less power, while he that takes a large thing which he has not deposited does wrong to the full; wherefore the law deems it right not to inflict a less penalty on the one offender than on the other on the ground that his theft is smaller, but rather because the one is possibly still curable, the other incurable. So if anyone convict in a court of law either a resident alien or a slave of stealing any piece of public property, in his case, since he is probably curable, the court shall decide what punishment he shall suffer or what fine he shall pay. But in the case of a citizen, who has been reared in the way he is to be reared,—if he be convicted of plundering or doing violence to his fatherland, whether he has been caught in the act or not, he shall be punished by death,[1] as being practically incurable.

Military organization is the subject of much consultation and of many appropriate laws. The main principle is this—that nobody, male or female, should ever be left without control, nor should anyone, whether at work or in play, grow habituated in mind to acting alone and on his own initiative, but he should live always, both in war and peace, with his eyes fixed constantly on his commander and following his lead; and he should be guided by him even in the smallest detail of his actions—for example, to stand at the word of command, and to march, and to exercise, to wash and eat, to wake up at night for sentry-duty and despatch-carrying, and in moments of danger to wait for the commander's

C λόγῳ τὸ χωρίς τι τῶν ἄλλων πράττειν διδάξαι
τὴν ψυχὴν ἔθεσι μήτε γιγνώσκειν μήτ' ἐπίστασθαι
τὸ παράπαν, ἀλλ' ἀθρόον ἀεὶ καὶ ἅμα καὶ κοινὸν
τὸν βίον ὅτι μάλιστα πᾶσι πάντων γίγνεσθαι·
τούτου γὰρ οὔτ' ἔστιν οὔτε ποτὲ μὴ γένηται
κρεῖττον οὔτε ἄμεινον οὔτε τεχνικώτερον εἰς
σωτηρίαν τὴν κατὰ πόλεμον καὶ νίκην. τοῦτο
καὶ ἐν εἰρήνῃ μελετητέον εὐθὺς ἐκ τῶν παίδων,
ἄρχειν τε ἄλλων ἄρχεσθαί θ' ὑφ' ἑτέρων· τὴν
D δ' ἀναρχίαν ἐξαιρετέον ἐκ παντὸς τοῦ βίου
ἁπάντων τῶν ἀνθρώπων τε καὶ τῶν ὑπ' ἀνθρώποις
θηρίων· καὶ δὴ καὶ χορείας πάσας εἰς τὰς ἀριστείας
τὰς κατὰ πόλεμον βλέποντας [1] χορεύειν, καὶ ὅλην
εὐκολίαν τε καὶ εὐχέρειαν ἐπιτηδεύειν τῶν αὐτῶν
εἴνεκα, καρτερήσεις τε αὖ σιτίων τε καὶ ποτῶν
καὶ χειμώνων καὶ τῶν ἐναντίων καὶ κοίτης
σκληρᾶς, καὶ τό γε μέγιστον, τὴν τῆς κεφαλῆς
καὶ ποδῶν δύναμιν μὴ διαφθείρειν τῇ τῶν ἀλλοτρίων σκεπασμάτων περικαλυφῇ, τὴν τῶν οἰκείων
E ἀπολλύντας πίλων τε καὶ ὑποδημάτων γένεσιν
καὶ φύσιν· ταῦτα γὰρ ἀκρωτήρια ὄντα σωζόμενά
τε ἔχει μεγίστην <τὴν> [2] δύναμιν παντὸς τοῦ
σώματος καὶ τοὐναντίον ἐναντίως, καὶ τὸ μὲν
ὑπηρετικώτατον ἅπαντι τῷ σώματι, τὸ δὲ ἀρχι-
κώτατον, ἔχον τὰς κυρίας ἁπάσας αἰσθήσεις
αὐτοῦ φύσει.

943 Ἔπαινον μὲν δὴ τοῦτον ἀκούειν τὸν νέον
χρῆναι δοκεῖ [3] πολεμικοῦ περὶ βίου, νόμους δ'
αὖ τούσδε· Στρατεύεσθαι τὸν καταλεγέντα

---

[1] βλέποντας W. R. Paton : βλεπούσας MSS., edd.
[2] <τὴν> added by England.
[3] χρῆναι δοκεῖ : χρῆν δοκεῖν MSS., edd.

signal before either pursuing or retreating before an enemy; and, in a word, he must instruct his soul by habituation to avoid all thought or idea of doing anything at all apart from the rest of his company, so that the life of all shall be lived *en masse* and in common; for there is not, nor ever will be, any rule superior to this or better and more effective in ensuring safety and victory in war. This task of ruling, and being ruled by, others must be practised in peace from earliest childhood;[1] but anarchy must be utterly removed from the lives of all mankind, and of the beasts also that are subject to man. Moreover, with a view to excellence in war, they shall dance all kinds of dances,[2] and with the same object they shall cultivate in general suppleness and dexterity, and endurance also in the matter of foods and drinks and cold and heat and hard beds; and, what is most important, they shall accustom themselves not to spoil the natural powers of head and feet by wrapping them in coverings of alien material, and thereby ruining the production and growth of their own natural hair and soles. For when these extremities are conserved, they keep at its highest the power of the whole body, but they effect the opposite when spoiled; and of these two extremities, the one is the chief minister of the whole body, and the other the chief master, inasmuch as, by the ordinance of nature, it contains all the leading senses of the body.

Such is the laudation of the military life to which, as we hold, the youth ought to hearken, and its laws are these :—He that is enrolled or put on some rota

[1] Cp. 803 C, D; Soph. *Antig.* 668 ff.
[2] Cp. 795 D ff., 829 B, C.

ἢ τὸν ἐν μέρει τινὶ τεταγμένον. ἐὰν δέ
τις ἐκλείπῃ τινὶ κάκῃ μὴ στρατηγῶν ἀφέντων,
γραφὰς ἀστρατείας εἶναι πρὸς τοὺς πολεμικοὺς
ἄρχοντας, ὅταν ἔλθωσιν ἀπὸ στρατοπέδου, δικάζειν δὲ τοὺς στρατεύσαντας ἑκάστους χωρὶς
ὁπλίτας τε καὶ ἱππέας καὶ τἆλλα ἐμπολέμια
B ἕκαστα ὡσαύτως, καὶ εἰσάγειν ὁπλίτας μὲν εἰς
τοὺς ὁπλίτας, ἱππέας δὲ εἰς τοὺς ἱππέας καὶ
τοὺς ἄλλους δὲ κατὰ ταὐτὰ εἰς τοὺς αὐτῶν ξυν-
νόμους· ἐὰν δέ τις ὄφλῃ, ὑπάρχειν μὲν αὐτῷ
μήποτε τῆς ὅλης ἀριστείας ἀγωνιστῇ γενέσθαι
μηδὲ ἀστρατείας ἄλλον γράψασθαί ποτε μηδὲ
κατηγόρῳ τούτων πέρι γενέσθαι, πρὸς τούτοις
δ᾽ ἔτι προστιμᾶν αὐτῷ τὸ δικαστήριον ὅ τι χρὴ
παθεῖν ἢ ἀποτίνειν. μετὰ δὲ ταῦτα ἐκδικασθεισῶν
τῶν τῆς ἀστρατείας δικῶν πάλιν ἑκάστων τούτων
ἄρχοντας ποιῆσαι ξύλλογον, ἀριστείων δὲ πέρι
κρίνεσθαι τὸν βουλόμενον ἐν τοῖς αὐτῶν ἔθνεσι,
C μὴ περὶ προτέρου πολέμου μηδὲν παρεχόμενον
μήτε τεκμήριον μήτε μαρτύρων πιστώσεις λόγων,
αὐτῆς δὲ περὶ τῆς στρατείας τῆς τότε γενομένης
αὐτοῖς. στέφανον δὲ τὸ νικητήριον ἑκάστοις εἶναι
θαλλοῦ· τοῦτον δὲ εἰς τὰ τῶν πολεμικῶν θεῶν
ἱερά, ὧν ἄν τις βούληται, γράψαντα ἀναθεῖναι
μαρτύριον εἰς τὴν τῶν ἀριστείων κρίσιν παντὸς
D τοῦ βίου καὶ τὴν τῶν δευτέρων καὶ τρίτων. ἐὰν
δὲ στρατεύσηται μέν τις, μὴ ἀπαγαγόντων δὲ
τῶν ἀρχόντων οἴκαδε προαπέλθῃ τοῦ χρόνου,
λειποταξίου τούτων εἶναι γραφὰς ἐν τοῖς αὐτοῖς
οἷσπερ τῆς ἀστρατείας, ὀφλοῦσί τε τιμωρίαι

must perform military service. If anyone, through cowardice, fail to present himself without leave from the commanders, he shall be indicted for desertion before the military officers when they return from camp, and each class of those who have served shall sit by themselves as judges—that is, hoplites, cavalry, and each of the other branches,—and they shall summon hoplites before the hoplites, cavalrymen before the cavalry, and all others in like manner before soldiers of their own class; and any man that is convicted shall be debarred from ever competing for any distinction and from ever prosecuting another for shirking service, or acting as accuser in connection with such charges; and, in addition to this, what he ought to suffer or pay shall be determined by the court. Next, when the suits for shirking service have been fully decided, the officers shall again hold a review of each class of soldiers, and he who wishes shall be tried before a court of his own colleagues on his claim for an award of merit; but any proof or verbal testimony which the claimant produces must have reference, not to any previous war, but solely to that campaign in which they have just been engaged. The prize for each class shall be a wreath of olive leaves; and this the recipient shall hang up, along with an inscription, in whatever temple of the war-gods he chooses, to serve throughout his life as a proof that he has won the first, second or third prize, as the case may be. If a man goes on military service, but returns home without leave from the officers, he shall be liable to be indicted for desertion before the same court which deals with cases of shirking service, and the same penalties which have been already prescribed shall

481

ἐπέστωσαν αἵπερ καὶ πρόσθεν ἐτέθησαν. χρὴ
μὲν δὴ πᾶσαν ἐπιφέροντα δίκην ἀνδρὶ πάντ᾽
ἄνδρα φοβεῖσθαι τὸ μήτε ἐπενεγκεῖν ψευδῆ τιμωρίαν, μήτ᾽ οὖν ἑκόντα μήτ᾽ ἄκοντα κατὰ δύναμιν·
E παρθένος γὰρ Αἰδοῦς[1] Δίκη λέγεταί τε καὶ ὄντως
εἴρηται, ψεῦδος δὲ αἰδοῖ καὶ δίκῃ νεμεσητὸν κατὰ
φύσιν. τῶν τε οὖν ἄλλων εὐλαβεῖσθαι δεῖ πέρι
πλημμελεῖν εἰς δίκην, διαφερόντως δὲ καὶ τῆς τῶν
κατὰ πόλεμον ὅπλων ἀποβολῆς, μὴ διαμαρτών
τις ἄρα τῶν ἀναγκαίων ἀποβολῶν, ὡς αἰσχρὰς
αὐτὰς εἰς ὄνειδος τιθείς, ἀναξίῳ ἀναξίας ἐπάγῃ
δίκας. ῥᾴδιον μὲν οὖν οὐδαμῶς διορίσαι τούτων
944 θάτερον, ὅμως δὲ χρὴ τὸν νόμον ἁμῶς γέ πως
ὁρίζειν πειρᾶσθαι κατὰ μέρη. μύθῳ δὴ προσχρώ-
μενοι ἅμ᾽ εἴπωμεν, εἰ κομισθεὶς ἐπὶ σκηνὴν ἄνευ
τῶν ὅπλων Πάτροκλος ἔμπνους[2] ἐγένεθ᾽, οἷον δὴ
μυρίοις συνέπεσε, τὰ δὲ πρότερα ἐκεῖνα ὅπλα, ἃ
Πηλεῖ φησὶν ὁ ποιητὴς παρὰ θεῶν προῖκα ἐν τοῖς
γάμοις ἐπιδοθῆναι Θέτιδι, ταῦτα δὲ Ἕκτωρ εἶχεν,
ἐξῆν ἂν τῶν τότε ὅσοι κακοὶ ὀνειδίζειν ὅπλων
ἀποβολὴν τῷ τοῦ Μενοιτίου. ἔτι δὲ ὁπόσοι κατὰ
B κρημνῶν ῥιφέντες ἀπώλεσαν ὅπλα, ἢ κατὰ θάλατταν, ἢ χειμάρρων[3] ἐν τόποις ὑποδεξαμένης αὐτοὺς
ἐξαίφνης πολλῆς ῥύσεως ὕδατος· ἢ μυρί᾽ ἂν ἔχοι
τις τοιαῦτα παραμυθούμενος ἐπᾴδειν, εὐδιάβολον
κακὸν καλλύνων. τεμεῖν δὴ χρεὼν κατὰ δύναμιν

---

[1] αἰδοῦς MSS. : αἰδοίη Steph., Zur.
[2] ἔμπνους MSS. : ἔκπνους MS. marg., Zur.
[3] χειμάρρων Madvig, Apelt : χειμώνων MSS., edd. (κόποις
for τόποις Stallb., al.)

---

[1] Cp. Hesiod, Op. D. 192 ff., 254 ff., ἡ δέ τε παρθένος ἐστὶ
Δίκη . . . κυδρή τ᾽ αἰδοίη τε θεοῖς κτλ.

be imposed upon him, if he is convicted. Every man, when bringing an action against another, ought rightly to dread bringing upon him, whether intentionally or unintentionally, a wrongful punishment (for Justice is, and has been truly named,[1] the daughter of Reverence, and falsehood and wrong are naturally detested by Reverence and Justice); and he should beware also of trespassing against Justice in any matter, and especially in respect of loss of arms in battle, lest by mistakenly abusing such losses as shameful, when they are really unavoidable, he may bring undeserved charges against an undeserving man. It is by no means easy to draw distinctions between such cases; but none the less the law ought to try by some means to distinguish case from case. In illustration we may cite the story of Patroclus:[2] suppose that he had been brought to his tent without his arms and had recovered—as has happened in the case of thousands,—while the arms he had had (which, as the poet relates, had been given to Peleus by the gods, as a dowry with Thetis) were in the hands of Hector,—then all the base men of those days would have been free to abuse Menoetios' son for loss of arms. Moreover, there are instances of men losing their arms through being flung down from cliffs, or on the sea, or in ravines, when overwhelmed by a sudden great rush of water, or from other mishaps, countless in number, which one could mention by way of consolation, and thereby justify an evil which lends itself to calumny. It is right, therefore, to separate, as best one can,

[2] Cp. Hom. *Il.* xvi., xvii. 125 ff., xviii. 84 ff. Patroclus (son of Menoetios) was wearing the arms of Achilles (son of Peleus) when slain by Hector.

τὸ μεῖζον καὶ τὸ δυσχερέστερον κακὸν ἀπὸ τοῦ
ἐναντίου. σχεδὸν οὖν ἐν τοῖς ὀνείδεσιν ἔχει τινὰ
τομὴν ἡ τούτων τῶν ὀνομάτων ἐπιφορά· ῥίψασπις
μὲν γὰρ οὐκ ἐν πᾶσιν ὀνομάζοιτ᾽ ἂν δικαίως, ἀπο-
C βολεὺς δὲ ὅπλων. οὐχ ὁμοίως γὰρ ὅ τε ἀφαιρεθεὶς
μετ᾽ εἰκυίας βίας γίγνοιτ᾽ ἂν ῥίψασπις ὅ τε ἀφεὶς
ἑκών, διαφέρει δὲ ὅλον που καὶ τὸ πᾶν. ὧδ᾽ οὖν
δὴ λεγέσθω νόμῳ· Ἐὰν καταλαμβανόμενός τις
ὑπὸ πολεμίων καὶ ἔχων ὅπλα μὴ ἀναστρέφῃ καὶ
ἀμύνηται, ἀφῇ δὲ ἑκὼν ἢ ῥίψῃ, ζωὴν αἰσχρὰν
ἀρνύμενος μετὰ τάχους μᾶλλον ἢ μετ᾽ ἀνδρίας
καλὸν καὶ εὐδαίμονα θάνατον, τοιαύτης μὲν ὅπλων
ἀποβολῆς ἔστω δίκη ῥιφθέντων, τῆς δὲ εἰρημένης
ἔμπροσθεν ὁ δικάζων [μὴ]¹ ἀμελείτω σκοπεῖν·
D τὸν γὰρ κακὸν ἀεὶ δεῖ κολάζειν, ἵν᾽ ἀμείνων ᾖ, οὐ
τὸν δυστυχῆ· οὐδὲν γὰρ πλέον. ζημία δὴ τῷ τὴν
τοιαύτην ἀμυντηρίων ὅπλων εἰς τοὐναντίον ἀφέντι
δύναμιν τίς ἄρα γίγνοιτ᾽ ἂν πρόσφορος; οὐ γὰρ
δυνατὸν ἀνθρώπῳ δρᾶν τοὐναντίον <ἢ> ὥς² ποτε
θεόν φασι δρᾶσαι, Καινέα τὸν Θετταλὸν ἐκ
γυναικὸς μεταβαλόντα εἰς ἀνδρὸς φύσιν· ἦν γὰρ
ἂν ἀνδρὶ ῥιψάσπιδι τρόπον τινὰ πρέπουσα πασῶν
E μάλιστα ἡ ᾽κείνῃ τῇ γενέσει ἐναντία γένεσις, εἰς
γυναῖκα ἐξ ἀνδρὸς μεταβαλοῦσα, τιμωρία τούτῳ
γενομένη. νῦν δ᾽ ὅ τι τούτων ἐγγύτατα φιλοψυχίας
ἕνεκα, ἵνα τὸν ἐπίλοιπον βίον μὴ κινδυνεύῃ, ζῇ
δὲ ὡς πλεῖστον χρόνον [ὢν] κακῷ³ ὀνείδει ξυνεχό-

¹ [μὴ] bracketed by Herm. : om. by Zur., vulg.
² <ἢ> added by H. Richards : ὢν for ὥς Ast, Zur.
³ [ὢν] κακῷ Hermann : ὢν κακὸς (or κακῶς) MSS

¹ Cp. Ovid, *Met.* 8. 305 ff., 12. 189 ff.   *Tim.* 90 E.

the greater and more serious evil from its opposite. As a rule, indeed, the employment of the names in question by way of abuse admits of a distinction; for the term "shield-flinger" would not properly be applied in all cases, but rather the term "arms-dropper." For the man who by a fair amount of violence is stripped of his arms will not be as much of a "shield-flinger" as the man who has voluntarily thrown them away—rather there is a vast difference between the two cases. So let the pronouncement of the law be this:—If a man is overtaken by his enemies and, having arms, instead of turning and defending himself, voluntarily drops his arms or flings them away, thereby gaining for himself a life that is shameful by speed of foot, rather than by bravery a noble and blessed death,—concerning the arms flung away in a loss of this sort a trial shall be held, but the judge shall pass over in his enquiry a case of the kind previously described. For the bad man one must always punish, in order to better him, but not the luckless man; for that profits not. What, then, would be a proper penalty for the man who has thrown away for naught such powerful weapons of defence? A god, it is said, once changed Kaineus the Thessalian [1] from woman's shape to man's; but it is beyond human power to do the opposite of this; otherwise, the converse transformation—changing him from a man into a woman—would be, perhaps, the most appropriate of all penalties for a "shield-flinger." As it is, to get the nearest possible approach to this, because of the man's love of life at any price, and to secure that for the rest of his life he may run no risk, but may live saddled with this disgrace as long as possible,—the law dealing

μενος, ἔστω νόμος ὅδε ἐπὶ τούτοις· Ἀνὴρ ὃς ἂν
ὄφλῃ δίκην ὡς αἰσχρῶς ἀποβαλὼν ὅπλα πολε-
μικά, τούτῳ μήτ᾽ οὖν τις στρατηγὸς μήτ᾽ ἄλλος
ποτὲ τῶν κατὰ πόλεμον ἀρχόντων ὡς ἀνδρὶ
945 στρατιώτῃ χρήσηται μηδ᾽ εἰς τάξιν κατατάξῃ
μηδ᾽ ἡντινοῦν· εἰ δὲ μή, κατευθύνειν αὐτοῦ τὸν
εὔθυνον, ἂν μὲν ᾖ τοῦ μεγίστου τιμήματος ὁ
τάξας τὸν κακόν, χιλίας, ἂν δὲ τοῦ δευτέρου,
πέντε μνᾶς, ἂν δὲ τοῦ τρίτου, τρεῖς μνᾶς, ἂν δὲ
τοῦ τετάρτου, μνᾶν. ὁ δὲ ὀφλὼν τὴν δίκην πρὸς
τῷ ἀφεῖσθαι τῶν ἀνδρείων κινδύνων κατὰ φύσιν
τὴν αὑτοῦ προσαποτισάτω μισθόν, χιλίας μέν,
ἂν τοῦ μεγίστου τιμήματος ᾖ, πέντε δέ, τοῦ δευτέ-
B ρου, τρεῖς δέ, ἂν τοῦ τρίτου, μνᾶν δὲ ὡσαύτως
καθάπερ οἱ πρόσθεν, τοῦ τετάρτου μέρους.

Εὐθύνων δὴ πέρι τίς ἡμῖν λόγος ἂν εἴη πρέπων
ἀρχόντων γενομένων τῶν μὲν κατὰ τύχην κλήρου
καὶ ἐπ᾽ ἐνιαυτόν, τῶν δ᾽ εἰς πλείονα ἔτη καὶ ἐκ
προκρίτων; τῶν δὴ τοιούτων εὐθυντὴς τίς ἱκανός,
ἄν τίς τί πῃ σκολιὸν αὐτῶν καμφθεὶς ὑπὸ βάρους
μὲν πράξῃ, τῆς δ᾽ αὑτοῦ δυνάμεως ἐνδείᾳ πρὸς
C τὴν τῆς ἀρχῆς ἀξίαν; ῥᾴδιον μὲν οὐδαμῶς εὑρεῖν
τῶν ἀρχόντων ἄρχοντα ὑπερβάλλοντα πρὸς
ἀρετήν, ὅμως δὲ πειρατέον εὐθυντάς τινας ἀνευ-
ρίσκειν θείους. ἔχει γὰρ οὖν οὕτω. πολλοὶ
καιροὶ πολιτείας λύσεώς εἰσι, καθάπερ νεὼς [ἢ
ζώου][1] τινός, οὓς ἐντόνους τε καὶ ὑποζώματα
καὶ νεύρων ἐπιτόνους, μίαν οὖσαν φύσιν διεσπαρ-

---

[1] [ἢ ζώου] I bracket (ἢ πλοίου ci. Stallb.).

---

[1] *i.e.* persons appointed to audit the accounts and
scrutinize the conduct of public officials at the expiry of

with such cases shall be this :—If any man be convicted on a charge of shamefully throwing away his
military weapons, no general or other military officer
shall ever employ him as a soldier or post him to any
rank ; otherwise, the examiner shall fine the officer
who posts the coward 1000 drachmae, if he be of
the highest property-class,—if of the second class,
five minas,—if of the third, three minas,—if of the
fourth, one mina. And the soldier who is convicted
of the charge, in addition to being debarred, as his
own nature requires, from manly risks, shall also pay
back his wage—1000 drachmae, if he be of the
highest class,—if of the second, five minas,—if of
the third, three,—and if of the fourth, one mina,
just as in the previous cases.

Respecting examiners,[1] what would be a proper
statement for us to make, seeing that some of the
magistrates are appointed by the hazard of the lot
and for a year, while others are appointed for
several years and chosen out of a number of selected
persons ? Of such, who will be a competent examiner,
in the event of any one of them acting at all crookedly
through being burdened by the weight of his office
and his own inability to support it worthily ? It is
by no means easy to find an officer of officers, who
surpasses them in excellence, but still one must try
to find some examiners of a divine quality. In fact,
the case stands thus :—The dissolution of a polity,
like that of a ship's frame, depends upon many
critical factors : these (in the case of a ship) though
one in nature are separated into many parts, and we

their term of office. Note the play on the literal sense of
εὐθυντής, "straightener" (of "crooked" actions).

μένην πολλαχοῦ πολλοῖς ὀνόμασι προσαγορεύο-
μεν· εἷς δὲ οὗτος οὐ σμικρότατος καιρὸς τοῦ
σῴζεσθαί τε καὶ διαλυθεῖσαν οἴχεσθαι πολιτείαν.
D ἂν μὲν γὰρ οἱ τοὺς ἄρχοντας ἐξευθύνοντες
βελτίους ὦσιν ἐκείνων, καὶ τοῦτ᾽ ἐν δίκῃ
ἀμέμπτῳ τε καὶ ἀμέμπτως [ᾖ],[1] ἡ πᾶσα οὕτω
θάλλει τε καὶ εὐδαιμονεῖ χώρα καὶ πόλις· ἐὰν
δ᾽ ἄλλως τὰ περὶ τὰς εὐθύνας τῶν ἀρχόντων
γίγνηται, τότε λυθείσης τῆς τὰ πάντα πολιτευ-
μάτων ξυνεχούσης εἰς ἓν δίκης ταύτῃ πᾶσα ἀρχὴ
διεσπάσθη χωρὶς ἑτέρα ἀπ᾽ ἄλλης, καὶ οὐκ εἰς
ταὐτὸν ἔτι νεύουσαι, πολλὰς ἐκ μιᾶς τὴν πόλιν
ποιοῦσαι, στάσεων ἐμπλήσασαι ταχὺ διώλεσαν.
E διὸ δὴ δεῖ πάντως τοὺς εὐθύνους θαυμαστοὺς
πᾶσαν ἀρετὴν εἶναι.

Τεκταινώμεθα δή τινα τρόπον αὐτῶν τοιάνδε
γένεσιν. κατ᾽ ἐνιαυτὸν ἕκαστον μετὰ τροπὰς
ἡλίου τὰς ἐκ θέρους εἰς χειμῶνα ξυνιέναι χρεὼν
πᾶσαν τὴν πόλιν εἰς Ἡλίου κοινὸν καὶ Ἀπόλλωνος
τέμενος, τῷ θεῷ ἀποφανουμένους ἄνδρας αὑτῶν
946 τρεῖς, ὃν ἂν ἕκαστος αὐτῶν ἡγῆται πάντῃ ἄριστον
εἶναι πλὴν αὑτοῦ, μὴ ἔλαττον πεντήκοντα γεγονότα
ἐτῶν. τῶν δὲ προκριθέντων οὓς ἂν πλεῖστοι
ἐνέγκωσι, τούτους ἐκλέξαι μέχρι τῶν ἡμίσεων, ἐὰν
ἄρτιοι γίγνωνται· περιττοὶ δὲ ἐὰν ὦσιν, ἕνα
ἀφελεῖν, ᾧ ἂν ἐλάχισται γένωνται, καταλιπεῖν δὲ
τοὺς ἡμίσεις αὐτῶν πλήθει τῶν ψήφων ἀποκρί-
ναντας· ἐὰν δέ τισιν ἴσαι γίγνωνται καὶ τὸν ἥμι-

---

[1] [ᾖ] wanting in MSS. : added in MS. marg., Zur.

---

[1] Cp. *Rep.* 422 E.
[2] Cp. 767 C, D.

call them by many names—such as stays, under-girders, bracing-ropes. For the preservation, or dissolution and disappearance, of a polity the office of examiner is such a critical factor, and that of the gravest kind. For if those who act as examiners of the magistrates are better men than they, and if they act blamelessly with blameless justice, then the whole of the State and country flourishes and is happy ; but if the examination of the magistrates is carried out otherwise, then the bond of justice which binds all political elements into one is dissolved, and in consequence every office is torn apart from every other, and they no longer tend all to the same end ; and thus out of one State they make many,[1] and by filling it with civil strife they speedily bring it to ruin. Wherefore it is most necessary that the examiners should be men of admirably complete virtue.

Let us contrive to bring them into being in some such way as this :—Every year, after the summer solstice,[2] the whole State must assemble at the common precincts of Helios and Apollo, there to present before the god the names of three out of their own number,—each citizen proposing that man, not less than fifty years old, whom (with the exception of himself) he regards as in all respects the best. Of those so nominated they shall choose out those who have gained most votes—half of the total number nominated, if that number be even, but if it be an odd number, they shall reject the one who has least votes and retain the even half, marking them off according to the number of the votes received ; and if several have an equal number of votes, thus causing the upper half-section to be too large, they shall

σὺν ἀριθμὸν πλείω ποιῶσιν, ἀφελεῖν τὸ πλέον
B ἀποκρίναντας νεότητι, τοὺς δ' ἄλλους ἐγκρίναντας
φέρειν αὖθις, μέχριπερ ἂν τρεῖς λειφθῶσιν ἄνισοι·
ἐὰν δὲ ἢ πᾶσιν ἢ τοῖν δυοῖν ἴσαι γίγνωνται, τῇ
ἀγαθῇ μοίρᾳ καὶ τύχῃ ἐπιτρέψαντας, κλήρῳ
διελόντας τὸν νικῶντα καὶ δεύτερον καὶ τρίτον
στεφανῶσαι θαλλῷ, καὶ τὰ ἀριστεῖα ἀποδόντας
πᾶσιν ἀνειπεῖν ὅτι Μαγνήτων ἡ κατὰ θεὸν πάλιν
τυχοῦσα σωτηρίας πόλις, ἀποφήνασα αὑτῆς
Ἡλίῳ ἄνδρας τοὺς ἀρίστους τρεῖς, ἀκροθίνιον
C Ἀπόλλωνι κατὰ τὸν παλαιὸν νόμον ἀνατίθησι
κοινὸν καὶ Ἡλίῳ, ὅσονπερ ἂν ἕπωνται χρόνον
τῇ κρίσει. τοιούτους [1] δὲ πρώτῳ μὲν ἐνιαυτῷ
δώδεκα εὐθύνους ἀποδεῖξαι, μέχριπερ ἂν ἑκάστῳ
πέντε καὶ ἑβδομήκοντα ἔτη ξυμβῇ γενόμενα· τὸ
λοιπὸν δὲ τρεῖς ἀεὶ προσγιγνέσθων κατ' ἐνιαυτόν.
οὗτοι δὲ τὰς ἀρχὰς πάσας [κατὰ] [2] δώδεκα μέρη
διελόμενοι πάσαις βασάνοις χρώμενοι ἐλευθέραις
ἐλεγχόντων· οἰκούντων δέ, ὅσον ἂν εὐθύνωσι
χρόνον, ἐν τῷ τοῦ Ἀπόλλωνός τε καὶ Ἡλίου
D τεμένει, ἐν ᾧπερ ἐκρίθησαν· καὶ τὰ μὲν ἴδια
ἕκαστος, τὰ δὲ καὶ κοινῇ μετ' ἀλλήλων κρίναντες
τοὺς ἄρξαντας τῇ πόλει, ἀποφηνάντων εἰς τὴν
ἀγορὰν γράμματα καταθέντες περὶ ἑκάστης
ἀρχῆς ὅ τι χρὴ παθεῖν ἢ ἀποτίνειν κατὰ τὴν
τῶν εὐθύνων γνώμην. ἥτις δ' ἂν τῶν ἀρχῶν μὴ
ὁμολογῇ κεκρίσθαι δικαίως, εἰς τοὺς ἐκλεκτοὺς
δικαστὰς εἰσαγέτω τοὺς εὐθύνους, καὶ ἐὰν μὲν

---

[1] τοιούτους England : τούτους MSS.
[2] [κατὰ] wanting in MSS. : added by MS. marg., Zur.

[1] Cp. 855 C, 926 D.

remove the excess by rejecting those that are youngest; the rest being retained on the list, they shall vote again on these, and they shall continue the same process until three be left with an unequal number of votes. If, however, all of these, or two of them, have equal votes, they shall commit the matter to good luck and chance, and distinguish by lot between the first, the second, and the third, and crown them with olive-wreaths; and when they have thus awarded the distinctions, they shall make this public proclamation:—The State of the Magnetes,—which, by God's grace, has again won salvation,—has presented to Helios the three best of its own men, and now it dedicates them, according to the ancient law, as a joint offering to Apollo and Helios of its choicest first fruits, for so long a time as they pursue their judicial task. Twelve such examiners shall be appointed in the first year, until each of them has come to the age of seventy-five; and thereafter three shall be added annually. And they, after dividing all the public offices into twelve sections, shall employ all tests, of a gentlemanly kind, in investigating them. So long as they are serving as examiners, they shall reside within the precincts of Apollo and Helios, where they were chosen. When they have judged—either each one singly or in consultation with one another—the State officials, they shall publish, by means of records placed in the market, a statement concerning what each official should suffer or pay according to the decision of the examiners. If any official claims that he has not been judged justly, he shall summon the examiners before the select judges;[1] and if he be acquitted in respect of the examiners' charges,

ἀποφύγῃ τις τὰς εὐθύνας, αὐτῶν τῶν εὐθύνων
Ε κατηγορείτω, ἐὰν ἐθέλῃ· ἐὰν δὲ ἁλῷ, ἐὰν μὲν ᾖ
τῷ θανάτῳ τετιμημένον ὑπὸ τῶν εὐθύνων, ὥσπερ
ἀνάγκη, ἁπλῶς θνῃσκέτω, τῶν δ' ἄλλων τιμημά-
των ὧν ἂν δυνατὸν ᾖ διπλῆν τῖσαι, διπλασίαν
τινέτω.

Τὰς δ' εὐθύνας αὐτῶν τούτων ἀκούειν χρὴ
τίνες ἔσονται καὶ τίνα τρόπον. ζῶσι μὲν οὖν
τούτοις τοῖς παρὰ πάσης τῆς πόλεως ἀριστείων
947 ἠξιωμένοις προεδρίαι τ' ἐν ταῖς πανηγύρεσι
πάσαις ἔστωσαν, ἔτι δὲ τῶν εἰς τοὺς Ἕλληνας
κοινῇ θυσιῶν καὶ θεωριῶν καὶ ὅσων ἂν ἑτέρων
κοινωνῶσιν ἱερῶν, ἐκ τούτων τοὺς ἄρχοντας τῆς
θεωρίας ἑκάστης ἐκπέμπειν, καὶ τούτους μόνους
δάφνης στεφάνῳ τῶν ἐν τῇ πόλει κεκοσμημένους
εἶναι,¹ καὶ ἱερέας μὲν πάντας τοῦ Ἀπόλλωνός
τε καὶ Ἡλίου, ἀρχιέρεων δὲ ἕνα κατ' ἐνιαυτὸν
τὸν πρῶτον κριθέντα τῶν γενομένων ἐκείνῳ τῷ
ἐνιαυτῷ ἱερέων, καὶ τοὔνομα ἀναγράφειν τού-
Β του κατ' ἐνιαυτόν, ὅπως ἂν γίγνηται μέτρον
ἀριθμοῦ τοῦ χρόνου, ἕως ἂν ἡ πόλις οἰκῆται.
τελευτήσασι δὲ προθέσεις τε καὶ ἐκφορὰς καὶ
θήκας διαφόρους εἶναι τῶν ἄλλων πολιτῶν,
λευκὴν μὲν τὴν στολὴν ἔχειν πᾶσαν, θρήνων δὲ
καὶ ὀδυρμῶν χωρὶς γίγνεσθαι, κορῶν δὲ χορὸν
πεντεκαίδεκα καὶ ἀρρένων ἕτερον περισταμένους
τῇ κλίνῃ ἑκατέρους οἷον ὕμνον πεποιημένον
ἔπαινον εἰς τοὺς ἱερέας ἐν μέρει ἑκατέρους ᾄδειν,
εὐδαιμονίζοντας ᾠδῇ διὰ πάσης τῆς ἡμέρας·
C ἕωθεν δ' εἰς τὴν θήκην φέρειν αὐτὴν μὲν τὴν
κλίνην ἑκατὸν τῶν νέων τῶν ἐν τοῖς γυμνασίοις,

¹ εἶναι MSS. : ἰέναι MS. marg., Zur.

he shall, if he wishes, prosecute the examiners themselves; but if he be convicted, in case the penalty imposed on him by the examiners be death, he shall simply be put to death (one death only being possible), but in the case of other penalties which admit of being doubled, he shall pay a double penalty.

As regards the examinations of these examiners themselves, it is right for us to hear what they are to be, and how they are to be conducted. During their lifetime these men, who have been deemed worthy of the highest distinction by the whole State, shall have the front seats at every festival; and from their number, too, shall be chosen the heads of every sacred mission sent out to take part in any public sacrifices, congresses or other such sacred assemblies of the Hellenes; and these alone of all the citizens shall be adorned with a crown of laurel; and they all shall be priests of Apollo and Helios, and every year that one of them who has been adjudged first of those appointed in that year shall be the high-priest, and his name they shall inscribe at the head of the year, that it may serve as a measure of the date, so long as the State remains. When they die, their laying-out, funeral and interment shall be different from that of other citizens: nothing but white raiment shall be used at it, and there shall be no dirges or lamentations; a choir of girls and another of boys shall stand round the bier, and they shall chant alternately a laudation for the priests in the form of a hymn in verse, glorifying them with their hymnody all the day long; and at the next dawn the bier itself shall be borne to the tomb by a hundred of the young men who attend the gymnasia,

οὓς ἂν οἱ προσήκοντες τοῦ τελευτήσαντος ἐπιό-
ψωνται, πρώτους δὲ προϊέναι τοὺς ἠϊθέους τὴν
πολεμικὴν σκευὴν ἐνδεδυκότας ἑκάστους, σὺν
τοῖς ἵπποισι μὲν ἱππέας, σὺν δὲ ὅπλοις ὁπλίτας,
D καὶ τοὺς ἄλλους ὡσαύτως, παῖδας δὲ περὶ αὐτὴν
τὴν κλίνην ἔμπροσθεν τὸ πάτριον μέλος ἐφυμνεῖν,
καὶ κόρας ἑπομένας ἐξόπισθεν ὅσαι τ᾽ ἂν γυναῖκες
τῆς παιδοποιήσεως ἀπηλλαγμέναι τυγχάνωσι,
μετὰ δὲ ταῦτα ἱερέας τε καὶ ἱερείας ὡς καθαρεύοντι
τῷ τάφῳ ἕπεσθαι, ἐὰν ἄρα καὶ τῶν ἄλλων
εἴργωνται τάφων, ἐὰν καὶ τὸ τῆς Πυθίας οὕτω
τε καὶ ταύτῃ σύμψηφον ᾖ· θήκην δὲ ὑπὸ γῆς
αὐτοῖς εἰργασμένην εἶναι ψαλίδα προμήκη λίθων
ποτίμων καὶ ἀγήρων εἰς δύναμιν, ἔχουσαν κλίνας
E παρ᾽ ἀλλήλας λιθίνας κειμένας, οὗ δὴ τὸν μακά-
ριον γεγονότα θέντες, κύκλῳ χώσαντες, πέριξ
δένδρων ἄλσος περιφυτεύσουσι πλὴν κώλου ἑνός,
ὅπως ἂν αὔξην ὁ τάφος ἔχῃ ταύτῃ [τὴν]¹ εἰς
τὸν ἅπαντα χρόνον, ἂν ἐπιδέῃ² χώματος τοῖς
τιθεμένοις· κατ᾽ ἐνιαυτὸν δὲ ἀγῶνα μουσικῆς
αὐτοῖς καὶ γυμνικὸν ἱππικόν τε θήσουσι.

Τὰ μὲν δὴ γέρα τοιαῦτα τοῖς τὰς εὐθύνας δια-
φυγοῦσιν· ἂν δέ τις τούτων πιστεύων τῷ κεκρίσθαι
τὴν ἀνθρωπίνην φύσιν ἐπιδείξῃ κακὸς γενόμενος
ὕστερον τῆς κρίσεως, γράφεσθαι μὲν τὸν βουλόμενον αὐτὸν ὁ νόμος προσταττέτω, ὁ δ᾽ ἀγὼν
ἐν δικαστηρίῳ γιγνέσθω τοιῷδέ τινι τρόπῳ.
948 πρῶτον μὲν νομοφύλακες ἔστωσαν τούτου τοῦ

¹ ταύτῃ Ast : ταύτην MSS. [τὴν] I bracket.
² ἂν ἐπιδέῃ Hermann : ἐπιδεῇ MSS. : ἀνεπιδεῇ (MSS. marg.)
Zur., vulg.

—they being selected by the relatives of the dead man,—and the procession shall be led by the men of war, all clad in their proper military garb,—cavalry with their horses, hoplites with their weapons, and the rest in like manner; and round about the bier the boys, being in front, shall sing their national anthem, and behind them the girls shall follow singing, and all the women who have passed the age of child-bearing; and next shall follow the priests and priestesses as to a tomb that is sanctified—yea, though they be debarred from approaching all other tombs,—if so be that the voice of the Pythian [1] approves that thus it shall be. Their tomb shall be constructed under ground, in the form of an oblong vault of spongy stone, as long-lasting as possible, and fitted with couches of stone set side by side; in this when they have laid him who is gone to his rest, they shall make a mound in a circle round it and plant thereon a grove of trees, save only at one extremity, so that at that point the tomb may for all time admit of enlargement, in case there be need of additional mounds for the buried. And every year contests of music, gymnastics and horse-racing shall be held in their honour.

These shall be the rewards for those who have passed the scrutiny of examiners. But if any of these examiners, relying on the fact of his election, shall give proof of human frailty by becoming evil after his election, the law shall enjoin on him who wishes to indict him, and the trial shall take place in the court after this manner:—The court shall be composed first of Law-wardens, next

---

[1] The priestess of Apollo at Delphi; cp. *Rep.* 461 E.

δικαστηρίου, ἔπειτα αὐτῶν τούτων οἱ ζῶντες,
πρὸς δὲ τούτοις τὸ τῶν ἐκλεκτῶν δικαστήριον·
γραφέσθω δὲ ὁ γραφόμενος, ὃν ἂν γράφηται,
λέγουσαν τὴν γραφὴν ἀνάξιον εἶναι τὸν καὶ τὸν
τῶν ἀριστείων καὶ τῆς ἀρχῆς· καὶ ἐὰν μὲν ὁ
φεύγων ἁλῷ, στερέσθω τῆς ἀρχῆς καὶ τοῦ τάφου
καὶ τῶν ἄλλων τῶν δοθεισῶν αὐτῷ τιμῶν, ἐὰν
δὲ ὁ διώκων μὴ μεταλάβῃ τὸ πέμπτον μέρος τῶν
ψήφων, τινέτω ὁ μὲν τοῦ μεγίστου τιμήματος
B δώδεκα μνᾶς, ὀκτὼ δὲ ὁ τοῦ δευτέρου, τρίτου δὲ
ἕξ, τετάρτου δὲ δύο.

Ῥαδαμάνθυος δὲ περὶ τὴν λεγομένην κρίσιν
τῶν δικῶν ἄξιον ἄγασθαι, διότι κατεῖδε τοὺς τότε
ἀνθρώπους ἡγουμένους ἐναργῶς εἶναι θεούς,
εἰκότως, ἅτε κατὰ τὸν τότε χρόνον τῶν πολλῶν
ἐκ θεῶν ὄντων, ὧν εἷς ἦν αὐτός, ὥς γε λόγος.
ἔοικε δὴ δικαστῇ μὲν ἀνθρώπων οὐδενὶ διανοού-
μενος δεῖν ἐπιτρέπειν, θεοῖς δέ, ὅθεν ἁπλαῖ καὶ
ταχεῖαι δίκαι ἐκρίνοντ᾽ αὐτῷ· διδοὺς γὰρ περὶ
C ἑκάστων τῶν ἀμφισβητουμένων ὅρκον τοῖς
ἀμφισβητοῦσιν ἀπηλλάττετο ταχὺ καὶ ἀσφαλῶς.
νῦν δὲ ὅτε δὴ μέρος μέν τι, φαμέν, ἀνθρώπων τὸ
παράπαν οὐχ ἡγοῦνται θεούς, οἱ δὲ οὐ φροντίζειν
ἡμῶν αὐτοὺς διανοοῦνται, τῶν δὲ δὴ πλείστων
ἐστὶ καὶ κακίστων ἡ δόξα ὡς σμικρὰ δεχόμενοι
θύματα καὶ θωπείας πολλὰ συναποστεροῦσι
χρήματα καὶ μεγάλων σφᾶς ἐκλύονται κατὰ
πολλὰ ζημιῶν, οὐκέτι δὴ τοῖς νῦν ἀνθρώποις ἡ
Ῥαδαμάνθυος ἂν εἴη τέχνη πρέπουσα ἐν δίκαις.

---

[1] *i.e.* after superannuation.   [2] Cp. 855 C.
[3] Cp. 886 D ff., 891 B ff.

of the living[1] members of the body of examiners themselves, and, in addition to these, of the Bench of select judges;[2] and he who indicts anyone shall state in his indictment that the person in question is unworthy of his distinctions and of his office; and if the defendant be convicted, he shall be deprived of his office and of his tomb, and of the other privileges granted to him; but if the prosecutor fails to gain one-fifth of the votes, he shall pay twelve minas if he be of the highest class,—if of the second, eight, —if of the third, six,—and if of the fourth, two minas.

Rhadamanthys deserves admiration for the way in which, as we are told, he judged cases of law, in that he perceived that the men of his time had a clear belief in the existence of gods,—and naturally so, seeing that most men at that time were the offspring of gods, he himself among others, as the story declares. Probably he thought that he ought not to entrust lawsuits to any man, but only to gods, from whom he obtained verdicts that were both simple and speedy; for he administered an oath to the disputants regarding each matter in dispute, and thus secured a speedy and safe settlement. But nowadays, when, as we say,[3] a certain section of mankind totally disbelieve in gods, and others hold that they pay no regard to us men, while a third party, consisting of the most and worst of men, suppose that in return for small offerings and flatteries the gods lend them aid in committing large robberies, and often set them free from great penalties,—under such conditions, for men as they now are, the device of Rhadamanthys would no longer be appropriate in actions at law. Since,

D μεταβεβληκυιῶν οὖν τῶν περὶ θεοὺς δοξῶν ἐν
τοῖς ἀνθρώποις μεταβάλλειν χρὴ καὶ τοὺς νόμους·
ἐν γὰρ λήξεσι δικῶν τοὺς μετὰ νοῦ τιθεμένους
νόμους ἐξαιρεῖν δεῖ τοὺς ὅρκους τῶν ἀντιδικούντων
ἑκατέρων, καὶ τὸν λαγχάνοντά τῷ τινα δίκην τὰ
μὲν ἐγκλήματα γράφειν, ὅρκον δὲ μὴ ἐπομνύναι,
καὶ τὸν φεύγοντα κατὰ ταὐτὰ τὴν ἄρνησιν
γράψαντα παραδοῦναι τοῖς ἄρχουσιν ἀνώμοτον.
δεινὸν γάρ που δικῶν γ᾽ ἐν πόλει πολλῶν
γενομένων εὖ εἰδέναι σμικροῦ δεῖν τοὺς ἡμίσεις
E αὐτῶν ἐπιωρκηκότας, ἐν ξυσσιτίοις τε ἀλλήλοις
εὐχερῶς συγγιγνομένους καὶ ἐν ἄλλαις συνουσίαις
τε καὶ ἰδιωτικαῖς συγγενήσεσιν ἑκάστων. νόμος
δὴ κείσθω δικαστὴν μὲν ὀμνύναι δικάζειν μέλλοντα, καὶ τὸν τὰς ἀρχὰς τῷ κοινῷ καθιστάντα
949 δι᾽ ὅρκων ἢ διὰ φορᾶς ψήφων, ἀφ᾽ ἱερῶν φέροντα,
δρᾶν ἀεὶ τὸ τοιοῦτον, καὶ κριτὴν αὖ χορῶν καὶ
πάσης μουσικῆς καὶ γυμνικῶν τε καὶ ἱππικῶν
ἄθλων ἐπιστάτας καὶ βραβέας καὶ ἁπάντων
ὁπόσα μὴ φέρει κέρδος κατὰ τὴν ἀνθρωπίνην
δόξαν τῷ ἐπιορκοῦντι· τῶν δὲ ὁπόσα ἐξαρνηθέντι
καὶ ἐξομοσαμένῳ κέρδος μέγα φανερὸν εἶναι δοκεῖ,
ταῦτα δὲ διὰ δικῶν ὅρκων χωρὶς κρίνεσθαι
B ξύμπαντας τοὺς ἐπικαλοῦντας ἀλλήλοις. καὶ τὸ
παράπαν ἐν δίκῃ τοὺς προέδρους μὴ ἐπιτρέπειν
μήτε ὀμνύντι λέγειν πιθανότητος χάριν μήτε
ἐπαρώμενον ἑαυτῷ καὶ γένει μήτε ἱκετείαις
χρώμενον ἀσχήμοσι μήτε οἴκτοις γυναικείοις,
ἀλλὰ τὸ δίκαιον μετ᾽ εὐφημίας διδάσκοντα καὶ
μανθάνοντα ἀεὶ διατελεῖν, εἰ δὲ μή, καθάπερ ἔξω

---

[1] Cp. 934 E.

therefore, the opinions of men about the gods have changed, so also must their laws change. In legal actions laws that are framed intelligently ought to debar both litigants from taking oaths; he that is bringing an action against anyone ought to write down his charges, but swear no oath, and the defendant in like manner ought to write down his denial and hand it to the magistrates without an oath. For truly it is a horrible thing to know full well that, inasmuch as lawsuits are frequent in a State, well-nigh half the citizens are perjurers, although they have no scruple in associating with one another at common meals and at other public and private gatherings. So it shall be laid down by law that a judge shall take an oath when he is about to give judgment, and likewise oaths shall be taken by him who is appointing public officials by voting under oath or by bringing his votes from a sacred spot, and by the judge of choirs or of any musical performance, and by the presidents and umpires of gymnastic and horse-racing contests, or of any matters which do not, in human opinion, bring gain to him who commits perjury. But in all cases where it obviously appears that a large gain will accrue to him who denies stoutly and swears ignorance, all the contending parties must be judged by trials without oaths. And in general, during a trial, the presidents of the court shall not permit a man to speak under oath for the sake of gaining credence, or to imprecate curses upon himself and his family, or to make use of unseemly supplications and womanish sobbings, but only and always to state and hear what is just in proper language;[1] otherwise, the magistrate shall check him for

499

τοῦ λόγου λέγοντος, τοὺς ἄρχοντας πάλιν ἐπανάγειν εἰς τὸν περὶ τοῦ πράγματος ἀεὶ λόγον.
ξένῳ δ' εἶναι πρὸς ξένους, καθάπερ τὰ νῦν,
δέχεσθαί τε ὅρκους παρ' ἀλλήλων, ἂν ἐθέλωσι,
C καὶ διδόναι κυρίως· οὐ γὰρ καταγηράσουσιν οὐδ'
ἐννεοττεύοντες ἐν τῇ πόλει ὡς τὸ πολὺ τοιούτους
ἄλλους κυρίους τῆς χώρας παρέξονται ξυντρό-
φους· δικῶν τε περὶ λήξεως τὸν αὐτὸν τρόπον
εἶναι πρὸς ἀλλήλους πᾶσι τὴν κρίσιν.

Ὅσα τις ἐλεύθερος ἀπειθεῖ τῇ πόλει, μήτ' οὖν
πληγῶν ἄξια μηδ' αὖ δεσμῶν μηδὲ θανάτου,
περὶ δὲ χορείας τινῶν φοιτήσεων ἢ πομπεύσεων
ἢ τοιούτων τινῶν ἄλλων κοινῶν κοσμήσεων ἢ
D λειτουργιῶν, ὁπόσα περὶ θυσίας εἰρηνικῆς ἢ πολεμικῶν εἰσφορῶν εἵνεκα, πάντων τῶν τοιούτων τὴν
πρώτην ἀνάγκην τάττειν εἶναι τὰς ¹ ζημίας, τοῖς δὲ
μὴ πειθομένοις ἐνεχυρασίαν τούτοις οἷς ἂν πόλις
ἅμα καὶ νόμος εἰσπράττειν προστάττῃ, τῶν δὲ
ἀπειθούντων ταῖς ἐνεχυρασίαις πρᾶσιν τῶν ἐνε-
χύρων εἶναι, τὸ δὲ νόμισμα γίγνεσθαι τῇ πόλει·
ἐὰν δὲ ζημίας δέωνται πλείονος, τὰς ἀρχὰς ἑκάστας τοῖς ἀπειθοῦσι τὰς πρεπούσας ζημίας ἐπι-
E βαλλούσας εἰσάγειν εἰς τὸ δικαστήριον, ἕως ἂν
ἐθελήσωσι δρᾶν τὸ προσταχθέν.

Πόλει δὲ ἥτις ἂν μήτε χρηματίζηται πλὴν τὸν
ἐκ γῆς χρηματισμὸν μήτ' ἐμπορεύηται, περὶ ἀποδημίας ἑαυτῶν ἔξω τῆς χώρας καὶ ξένων ὑποδοχῆς
ἄλλοθεν ἀνάγκη βεβουλεῦσθαι τί χρὴ δρᾶν.

¹ τάττειν . . . τὰς : ἰατὴν . . . τῆς MSS. (τακτὴν Winck.)

---

¹ Cp. 850 B ff.

digressing from the point, and shall call him back to deal with the matter in hand. In the case of resident aliens dealing with aliens, it shall be permitted them, as now, to give and receive oaths of a binding character one from another, if so they choose,—for these men will not grow old in the State [1] nor, as a rule, will they make their nest in it, and rear up others like themselves to become naturalised in the country; and in respect of the private actions they bring against one another, they shall all have the same privilege during the trial.

In all cases where a free man disobeys the State, not by acts deserving of stripes, imprisonment or death, but in respect of matters such as attendance at festivals or processions or public ceremonies of a similar kind—matters involving either a sacrifice in peace or a contribution in time of war,—in all such cases the first necessity is to assess the penalty; in case of disobedience, those officers whom the State and the law appoint to exact the penalty shall take a pledge; and if any disregard the pledgings, the things pledged shall be sold, and the price shall go to the State; and if a greater penalty be required, the official proper in each case shall impose on the disobedient the suitable penalties and shall summon them before the court, until they consent to do what they are bidden.

For a State which makes no money except from the produce of its soil, and which does not engage in commerce, it is necessary to determine what action it ought to take regarding the emigration of its citizens to outside countries and the admission of aliens from elsewhere. In giving counsel con-

συμβουλεύειν οὖν τὸν νομοθέτην δεῖ τούτων πέρι
πρῶτον πείθοντα εἰς δύναμιν. πέφυκε δὲ ἡ
πόλεων ἐπιμιξία πόλεσιν ἤθη κεραννύναι παντο-
δαπά, καινοτομίας ἀλλήλοις ἐμποιούντων ξένων
950 ξένοις· ὃ δὴ τοῖς μὲν εὖ πολιτευομένοις διὰ νόμων
ὀρθῶν βλάβην ἂν φέροι μεγίστην πασῶν, ταῖς δὲ
πλείσταις πόλεσιν, ἅτε οὐδαμῶς εὐνομουμέναις,
οὐδὲν διαφέρει φύρεσθαι δεχομένους τ᾽ ἐν αὑτοῖς [1]
ξένους καὶ αὑτοὺς εἰς τὰς ἄλλας ἐπικωμάζοντας
πόλεις, ὅταν ἐπιθυμήσῃ τις ἀποδημίας ὁπῃοῦν
καὶ ὁπότε εἴτε νέος εἴτε καὶ πρεσβύτερος ὤν. τὸ
δ᾽ αὖ μήτε ἄλλους δέχεσθαι μήτε αὑτοὺς ἄλλοσε
ἀποδημεῖν ἅμα μὲν οὐκ ἐγχωρεῖ τό γε παράπαν,
B ἔτι δὲ ἄγριον καὶ ἀπηνὲς φαίνοιτ᾽ ἂν τοῖς ἄλλοις
ἀνθρώποις, ὀνόμασί τε χαλεποῖς ταῖσι λεγομέναις
ξενηλασίαις χρωμένους καὶ τρόποις αὐθάδεσι καὶ
χαλεποῖς, ὡς δοκοῖεν ἄν. χρὴ δὲ οὔποτε περὶ
σμικροῦ ποιεῖσθαι τὸ δοκεῖν ἀγαθοὺς εἶναι τοῖς
ἄλλοις ἢ μὴ δοκεῖν. οὐ γὰρ ὅσον οὐσίας ἀρετῆς
ἀπεσφαλμένοι τυγχάνουσιν οἱ πολλοί, τοσοῦτον
καὶ τοῦ κρίνειν τοὺς ἄλλους, ὅσοι [2] πονηροὶ καὶ
χρηστοί, θεῖον δέ τι καὶ εὔστοχον ἔνεστι καὶ
τοῖσι κακοῖς, ὥστε πάμπολλοι καὶ τῶν σφόδρα
C κακῶν εὖ τοῖς λόγοις καὶ ταῖς δόξαις διαιροῦνται
τοὺς ἀμείνους τῶν ἀνθρώπων καὶ τοὺς χείρονας.
διὸ καλὸν ταῖς πολλαῖς πόλεσι τὸ παρακέλευμά
ἐστι, προτιμᾶν τὴν εὐδοξίαν πρὸς τῶν πολλῶν.

[1] τ᾽ ἐν αὑτοῖς Stallbaum : τε αὑτοῖς MSS.
[2] ὅσοι MSS. marg., Stallb. : οἱ MSS., Zur., al.

---

[1] Cp. 704 E.
[2] By a law of Lycurgus, strangers were forbidden to reside
at Sparta ; cp. Aristoph. Av. 1012 ὥσπερ ἐν Λακεδαίμον
ξενηλατοῦνται.   [3] Cp. Meno 99 B, C.

cerning these matters the lawgiver must begin by
using persuasion, so far as he can. The intermixture
of States with States naturally results in a blending of
characters of every kind, as strangers import among
strangers novel customs:[1] and this result would
cause immense damage to peoples who enjoy a good
polity under right laws; but the majority of States
are by no means well governed, so that to them it
makes no difference if their population is mixed
through the citizens admitting strangers and through
their own members visiting other States whenever
any one of them, young or old, at any time or place,
desires to go abroad. Now for the citizens to refuse
altogether either to admit others or to go abroad
themselves is by no means a possible policy, and,
moreover, it would appear to the rest of the world
to be both churlish and cross-grained, since they
would get the reputation of adopting harsh language,
such as that of the so-called "Aliens Expulsion
Acts,"[2] and methods both tyrannical and severe;
and reputation in the eyes of others, whether for
goodness or the reverse, is a thing that should never
be lightly esteemed. For the majority of men,
even though they be far removed from real goodness
themselves, are not equally lacking in the power
of judging whether others are bad or good; and
even in the wicked there resides a divine and
correct intuition,[3] whereby a vast number even of
the extremely wicked distinguish aright, in their
speech and opinions, between the better men and
the worse. Accordingly, for most States, the exhortation to value highly a good public reputation
is a right exhortation. The most correct and most
important rule is this,—that the man who pursues

PLATO

τὸ μὲν γὰρ ὀρθότατον καὶ μέγιστον ὄντα ἀγαθὸν
ἀληθῶς οὕτω τὸν εὔδοξον βίον θηρεύειν, χωρὶς δὲ
μηδαμῶς, τόν γε τέλεον ἄνδρα ἐσόμενον. καὶ δὴ
καὶ τῇ κατὰ Κρήτην οἰκιζομένῃ πόλει πρέπον ἂν
εἴη δόξαν πρὸς τῶν ἄλλων ἀνθρώπων ὅτι καλλίστην τε καὶ ἀρίστην παρασκευάζεσθαι πρὸς ἀρετήν·
D πᾶσα δ' ἐλπὶς αὐτὴν ἐκ τῶν εἰκότων, ἄνπερ κατὰ
λόγον γίγνηται, μετ' ὀλίγων ἥλιον ὄψεσθαι καὶ
τοὺς ἄλλους θεοὺς ἐν ταῖς εὐνόμοις πόλεσι καὶ
χώραις.

Ὧδε οὖν χρὴ ποιεῖν περὶ ἀποδημίας εἰς ἄλλας
χώρας καὶ τόπους καὶ περὶ ὑποδοχῆς ξένων.
πρῶτον μὲν νεωτέρῳ ἐτῶν τεττεράκοντα μὴ ἐξέστω
ἀποδημῆσαι μηδαμῇ μηδαμῶς, ἔτι τε ἰδίᾳ μηδενί,
δημοσίᾳ δ' ἔστω κήρυξιν ἢ πρεσβείαις ἢ καί τισι
E θεωροῖς· τὰς δὲ κατὰ πόλεμον καὶ στρατείας
ἀποδημίας οὐκ ἐν ἐκδημίαις πολιτικαῖς ἄξιον
ἀγορεύειν ὡς τούτων οὔσας· Πυθώδε τῷ Ἀπόλλωνι καὶ εἰς Ὀλυμπίαν τῷ Διὶ καὶ εἰς Νεμέαν
καὶ εἰς Ἰσθμὸν χρὴ πέμπειν, κοινωνοῦντας θυσιῶν
τε καὶ ἀγώνων τούτοις τοῖς θεοῖς, πέμπειν δὲ εἰς
δύναμιν ὅτι πλείστους ἅμα καὶ καλλίστους τε καὶ
ἀρίστους, οἵτινες εὐδόκιμον τὴν πόλιν ἐν ἱεραῖς τε
καὶ εἰρηνικαῖς συνουσίαις ποιήσουσι δοκεῖν, τοῖς
951 περὶ τὸν πόλεμον ἀντίστροφον ἀποδιδόντες δόξης
παρασκευήν, ἐλθόντες δὲ οἴκαδε διδάξουσι τοὺς
νέους ὅτι δεύτερα τὰ τῶν ἄλλων ἐστὶ νόμιμα τὰ
περὶ τὰς πολιτείας. θεωροὺς δὲ ἄλλους ἐκπέμ-
504

after a good reputation should himself be truly good, and that he should never pursue it without goodness (if he is to be really a perfect man); and furthermore, as regards the State we are founding in Crete, it would well become it to gain for itself in the eyes of the rest of the world the best and noblest reputation possible for goodness; and if it develop according to plan, there is every hope that, as is natural, it (and but few others) will be numbered among the well-ordered States and countries upon which the Sun and all the other gods look down.

In regard, therefore, to the question of going abroad to other lands and places and of the admission of foreigners we must act as follows :—First, no man under forty years old shall be permitted to go abroad to any place whatsoever; next, no man shall be permitted to go abroad in a private capacity, but in a public capacity permission shall be granted to heralds, embassies, and certain commissions of inspection. Military expeditions in war it would be improper to reckon among official visits abroad. It is right that embassies should be sent to Apollo at Pytho and to Zeus at Olympia, and to Nemea and the Isthmus, to take part in the sacrifices and games in honour of these gods; and it is right also that the ambassadors thus sent should be, so far as is practicable, as numerous, noble and good as possible,—men who will gain for the State a high reputation in the sacred congresses of peace, and confer on it a glorious repute that will rival that of its warriors; and these men, when they return home, will teach the youth that the political institutions of other countries are inferior to their own. Also, they ought

πειν χρεὼν τοιούσδε τινὰς τοὺς νομοφύλακας
παρεμένους· ἄν τινες ἐπιθυμῶσι τῶν πολιτῶν τὰ
τῶν ἄλλων ἀνθρώπων πράγματα θεωρῆσαι κατά
τινα πλείω σχολήν, ἀπειργέτω μηδεὶς τούτους
B νόμος. οὔτε γὰρ ἄπειρος οὖσα πόλις ἀνθρώπων
κακῶν καὶ ἀγαθῶν δύναιτ' ἄν ποτε, ἀνομίλητος
οὖσα, ἥμερος ἱκανῶς εἶναι καὶ τέλεος, οὐδ' αὖ
τοὺς νόμους διαφυλάττειν ἄνευ τοῦ γνώμῃ λαβεῖν
αὐτούς, ἀλλὰ μὴ μόνον ἔθεσιν. εἰσὶ γὰρ ἐν τοῖς
πολλοῖς ἄνθρωποι ἀεὶ θεῖοί τινες, οὐ πολλοί, παντὸς δ' ἄξιοι ξυγγίγνεσθαι, φυόμενοι οὐδὲν μᾶλλον
ἐν εὐνομουμέναις πόλεσιν ἢ καὶ μή, ὧν κατ' ἴχνος
ἀεὶ χρὴ τὸν ἐν ταῖς εὐνομουμέναις πόλεσιν
οἰκοῦντα ἐξιόντα κατὰ θάλατταν καὶ γῆν ζητεῖν,
C ὃς ἂν ἀδιάφθαρτος ᾖ, τὰ μὲν βεβαιούμενον τῶν
νομίμων, ὅσα καλῶς αὐτοῖς κεῖται, τὰ δ' ἐπανορ-
θούμενον, εἴ τι παραλείπεται. ἄνευ γὰρ ταύτης
τῆς θεωρίας καὶ ζητήσεως οὐ μενεῖ[1] ποτὲ τελέως
πόλις, οὐδ' ἂν κακῶς αὐτὴν θεωρῶσιν.

ΚΛ. Πῶς οὖν ἂν γίγνοιτ' ἀμφότερα ;

ΑΘ. Τῇδε. πρῶτον μὲν ὁ θεωρὸς ὁ τοιοῦτος
ἡμῖν γεγονὼς ἔστω πλειόνων ἐτῶν ἢ πεντήκοντα,
ἔτι δὲ τῶν εὐδοκίμων τά τε ἄλλα καὶ εἰς τὸν
πόλεμον ἔστω γεγενημένος, εἰ μέλλει τὸ τῶν
D νομοφυλάκων δόγμα[2] εἰς τὰς ἄλλας μεθήσειν
πόλεις· πλέον δὲ ἑξήκοντα γεγονὼς ἐτῶν μηκέτι
θεωρείτω. θεωρήσας δὲ ὁπόσ' ἂν ἔτη βουληθῇ

---

[1] μενεῖ Wagner : μένει MSS.
[2] δόγμα Madvig : δεῖγμα MSS., edd.

---

[1] Cp. *Rep.* 619 A.

to send out other inspecting commissioners (when they have obtained leave from the Law-wardens) of the following kind :—If any of the citizens desire to survey the doings of the outside world in a leisurely way, no law shall prevent them; for a State that is without experience of bad men and good would never be able (owing to its isolation) to become fully civilized and perfect, nor would it be able to safeguard its laws unless it grasped them, not by habit only, but also by conviction.[1] Amongst the mass of men there always exist—albeit in small numbers—men that are divinely inspired; intercourse with such men is of the greatest value, and they spring up in badly-governed States just as much as in those that are well governed. In search of these men it is always right for one who dwells in a well-ordered State to go forth on a voyage of enquiry by land and sea, if so be that he himself is incorruptible, so as to confirm thereby such of his native laws as are rightly enacted, and to amend any that are deficient. For without this inspection and enquiry a State will not permanently remain perfect, nor again if the inspection be badly conducted.

CLIN. How, then, might both these objects be secured ?

ATH. In this way. First, our overseas inspector shall be more than fifty years old ; secondly, he shall have proved himself a man of high repute both in military and other affairs, if it is intended that he shall be despatched into other States with the approval of the Law-wardens ; but when he has passed sixty years of age, he shall cease to act as inspector. When he has been inspecting for as

τῶν δέκα καὶ ἀφικόμενος οἴκαδε εἰς τὸν σύλλογον
ἴτω τὸν τῶν περὶ νόμους ἐποπτευόντων. οὗτος δ᾽
ἔστω νέων καὶ πρεσβυτέρων μεμιγμένος, ἑκάστης
μὲν ἡμέρας συλλεγόμενος ἐξ ἀνάγκης ἀπ᾽ ὄρθρου
μέχριπερ ἂν ἥλιος ἀνάσχῃ,[1] πρῶτον μὲν τῶν
ἱερέων τῶν τὰ ἀριστεῖα εἰληφότων, ἔπειτα τῶν
E νομοφυλάκων τοὺς ἀεὶ πρεσβεύοντας δέκα, ἔτι δὲ
ὁ περὶ τῆς παιδείας πάσης ἐπιμελητὴς ὅ τε νέος
οἵ τε ἐκ τῆς ἀρχῆς ταύτης ἀπηλλαγμένοι. ἕκαστος
δὲ τούτων μὴ μόνος, ἀλλ᾽ ἴτω μετὰ νέου ἀπὸ
τριάκοντα ἐτῶν μέχρι τετταράκοντα, τὸν ἀρέσ-
κοντα αὑτῷ προσλαμβάνων. τὴν δὲ συνουσίαν
εἶναι τούτοις καὶ τοὺς λόγους περὶ νόμων ἀεὶ τῆς
952 τε οἰκείας πόλεως πέρι, καὶ ἐὰν ἄλλοθι πυνθάνων-
ταί τι περὶ τῶν τοιούτων διαφέρον, καὶ δὴ καὶ
περὶ μαθημάτων, ὁπόσ᾽ ἂν ἐν ταύτῃ τῇ σκέψει
δοκῇ συμφέρειν [ἃ][2] μαθοῦσι μὲν εὐαγέστερον
γίγνεσθαι, μὴ μαθοῦσι δὲ σκοτωδέστερα τὰ περὶ
νόμους αὐτοῖς φαίνεσθαι καὶ ἀσαφῆ. ἃ δ᾽ ἂν
τούτων ἐγκρίνωσιν οἱ γεραίτεροι, τοὺς νεωτέρους
πάσῃ σπουδῇ μανθάνειν, ἐὰν δέ τις ἀνάξιος δοκῇ
τῶν παρακεκλημένων εἶναι, τῷ παρακαλοῦντι
B μέμφεσθαι τὸν σύλλογον ὅλον· τοὺς δ᾽ εὐδοκι-
μοῦντας τούτων τῶν νέων φυλάττειν τὴν ἄλλην
πόλιν, ἀποβλέποντας εἰς αὐτοὺς διαφερόντως τε
τηροῦντας, καὶ τιμᾶν μὲν κατορθοῦντας, ἀτιμάζειν
δὲ μᾶλλον τῶν ἄλλων, ἐὰν ἀποβαίνωσι χείρους
τῶν πολλῶν. εἰς δὴ τοῦτον τὸν σύλλογον ὁ

[1] ἀνάσχῃ MSS. : ἀνίσχῃ Zur., vulg.
[2] [ἃ] om. in MSS. : added by MS. marg., Zur., vulg.

---

[1] Cp. 908 A, 909 A.   [2] Cp. 807 ff.

many years out of the ten as he wishes and has
returned home, he shall go to the synod [1] of those
who supervise the laws; and this synod shall be a
mixed body of young men and old which is obliged
to meet every day between dawn and sunrise; [2] it
shall consist, first, of the priests who have gained
the award of merit,[3] and secondly, of the ten senior
Law-wardens; and it shall also include the President of Education who has been last appointed, and
his predecessors in office as well. None of these
members shall go alone, but each of them shall
bring with him a companion—a young man, selected
by himself, between thirty and forty years old.
Their conference and discourse shall deal always
with the subject of laws and of their own State,
and with anything important they may have learnt
elsewhere which bears on this subject, or any
branches of knowledge which are thought likely to
assist in their enquiry, in that the learning of them
helps towards a clearer view of legal matters,
whereas ignorance of them conduces to a view that
is dim and blurred. Whatsoever of these matters
are approved by the elder members the younger
shall learn with all diligence; and should any of
the young men invited to attend be deemed unworthy, the person who has invited him shall be
censured by the whole synod, but such of them
as are held in good repute shall be watched over
by the rest of the citizens, who shall regard and
observe them with special care, honouring them
when they do right, but dishonouring them more
than other men if they turn out worse than most.
To this synod he that has inspected the legal in-

[3] Cp. 946 E.

θεωρήσας τὰ ἐν τοῖς ἄλλοις ἀνθρώποις νόμιμα
ἀφικόμενος εὐθὺς πορευέσθω, καὶ εἴ τινα φήμην
τινῶν περὶ θέσεως νόμων ἢ παιδείας ἢ τροφῆς
εὑρέ τινας ἔχοντας φράζειν, εἴτε καὶ αὐτὸς νενοη-
κὼς ἄττα ἥκοι, κοινούτω τῷ συλλόγῳ ἅπαντι· καὶ
C ἐάν τε μηδὲν χείρων μηδέ τι βελτίων ἥκειν δόξῃ,
χάριν γοῦν τῆς σφόδρα προθυμίας αἰνείσθω· ἐὰν
δὲ πολὺ βελτίων, πολύ τ᾽ ἐπαινείσθω μᾶλλον ζῶν
τελευτήσαντά τε τιμαῖς αὐτὸν προσηκούσαις ἡ
τῶν συλλεγομένων τιμάτω δύναμις. ἐὰν δὲ διε-
φθαρμένος ἀφικέσθαι δόξῃ, μηδενὶ ξυγγιγνέσθω
μήτε νέῳ μήτε πρεσβυτέρῳ προσποιούμενος εἶναι
σοφός. καὶ ἐὰν μὲν πείθηται τοῖς ἄρχουσιν,
ἰδιώτης ζήτω, ἐὰν δὲ μή, τεθνάτω, ἐάν γ᾽ ἐν
δικαστηρίῳ ἁλῷ πολυπραγμονῶν τι περὶ τὴν
παιδείαν καὶ τοὺς νόμους. ἐὰν δὲ ἄξιον ὄντα εἰς
D δικαστήριον εἰσάγειν ἀρχόντων μηδεὶς εἰσάγῃ,
ὄνειδος ἀποκείσθω τοῖς ἄρχουσιν εἰς τὴν τῶν
ἀριστείων διαδικασίαν.

Ὁ μὲν οὖν ἐκδημῶν οὕτω καὶ τοιοῦτος ὢν
ἐκδημείτω, τὸν δ᾽ εἰσεπιδημήσαντα μετὰ τοῦτον
χρὴ φιλοφρονεῖσθαι. τέτταρες δ᾽ εἰσὶ ξένοι ὧν
δεῖ πέρι λόγον τινὰ ποιεῖσθαι. ὁ μὲν δὴ πρῶτός
τε καὶ διὰ τέλους ἀεὶ θερινὸς ὡς τὰ πολλὰ
διατελῶν ταῖς φοιτήσεσι, καθάπερ οἱ τῶν ὀρνίθων
E διαπορευόμενοι, καὶ τούτων οἱ πολλοὶ κατὰ
θάλατταν ἀτεχνῶς οἷον πετόμενοι χρηματισμοῦ

---

[1] Cp. 915 D.

stitutions of other peoples shall repair immediately after his return home ; and if he has discovered any persons able to declare any oracle regarding legislation or education or nurture, or if he has brought back any personal observations of his own, he shall communicate them to the whole synod ; and if it appear that he has come back in no respect worse (nor yet any better) than when he went, still because of his extreme zeal he shall be commended ; while if it appear that he has come back much better, he shall be much more highly commended during his life, and when dead, due honours shall be paid to him by the synod's authority. But if, on the other hand, such an inspector appear to be corrupted on his return, in spite of his pretensions to wisdom, he shall be forbidden to associate with anyone, young or old ; wherein if he obeys the magistrates, he shall live as a private person, but if not, he shall be put to death—if, that is to say, he be convicted in a court of law of being a meddler in respect of education and the laws.   And if, when such an one deserves to be summoned before a court, none of the magistrates summons him, the magistrates shall be censured at the adjudication of awards of merit.

Such, then, shall be the character and the procedure of him that travels abroad.   Next to him we must deal in friendly wise with the visitor from abroad. There are four types of stranger which call for mention. The first and inevitable immigrant is the one who chooses summer,[1] as a rule, for his annual visits, in the fashion of migratory birds—and, like birds, the most of these cross the sea, just as if they had wings, for the sake of making gain by their trading,

χάριν ἐμπορευόμενοι ἔτους ὥρᾳ πέτονται πρὸς
τὰς ἄλλας πόλεις· ὃν ἀγοραῖς καὶ λιμέσι καὶ
δημοσίοις οἰκοδομήμασιν ἔξω τῆς πόλεως πρὸς τῇ
πόλει ὑποδέχεσθαι χρὴ τοὺς ἐπὶ τούτοις ἄρχοντας
τεταγμένους, φυλάττοντας μὴ νεωτερίζῃ τίς τι
953 τῶν τοιούτων ξένων, καὶ δίκας αὐτοῖς ὀρθῶς
διανέμοντας, ἀναγκαῖα μέν, ὡς ὀλίγιστα δ᾽ ἐπιχρω-
μένους. ὁ δὲ δεύτερος, ὄμμασιν ὄντως θεωρὸς ὅσα
τε Μουσῶν ὦσὶν ἔχεται θεωρήματα· τῷ δὴ
τοιούτῳ παντὶ χρὴ καταλύσεις πρὸς ἱεροῖς εἶναι
φιλοξενίαις ἀνθρώπων παρεσκευασμένας, χρὴ δὲ
καὶ τῶν τοιούτων ἱερέας τε καὶ νεωκόρους ἐπιμελεῖσθαι καὶ τημελεῖν, ἕως[1] ἂν τὸν μέτριον
ἐπιμείναντες χρόνον, ἰδόντες τε καὶ ἀκούσαντες
B ὧν χάριν ἀφίκοντο, ἀβλαβεῖς τοῦ δρᾶσαί τε καὶ
παθεῖν ἀπαλλάττωνται· δικαστὰς δ᾽ αὐτοῖς εἶναι
τοὺς ἱερέας, ἐὰν ἀδικῇ τις αὐτῶν τινὰ ἤ τιν᾽ ἄλλον
ἀδικῇ τις τούτων ὅσα ἐντὸς δραχμῶν πεντήκοντα·
ἐὰν δέ τι μεῖζον ἔγκλημα αὐτοῖς γίγνηται, πρὸς
τοῖς ἀγορανόμοις εἶναι δεῖ δίκας τοῖς τοιούτοις.
τρίτον δὲ ξένον ὑποδέχεσθαι χρὴ δημοσίᾳ τὸν
κατά τι δημόσιον ἐξ ἄλλης χώρας ἀφιγμένον· ὃν
στρατηγοῖς τε καὶ ἱππάρχοις καὶ ταξιάρχοις
ὑποδεκτέον ἐστὶ μόνοις, τήν τ᾽ ἐπιμέλειαν τῶν
C τοιούτων μετὰ τῶν πρυτάνεων ποιητέον ἐκείνῳ
παρ᾽ ὅτῳ τις ἂν αὐτῶν τὴν κατάλυσιν ξενωθεὶς
ποιήσηται μόνῳ. τέταρτος δὲ ἄν ποτέ τις ἀφίκη-
ται, σπάνιος μέν, ἂν δ᾽ οὖν ποτέ τις ἔλθῃ τῶν
παρ᾽ ἡμῖν θεωρῶν ἀντίστροφος ἐξ ἄλλης χώρας,

---

[1] ἕως MSS. : ὅπως MSS. marg., Zur.

and fly over to foreign cities during the summer season; this stranger must be received, when he comes to the city, at the markets, harbours, and public buildings outside the city, by the officials in charge thereof; and they shall have a care lest any such strangers introduce any innovation, and they shall duly dispense justice to them, and shall hold such intercourse as is necessary with them, but to the least extent possible. The second type of stranger is he who is an inspector, in the literal sense, with his eyes, and with his ears also of all that appertains to musical exhibitions: for all such there must be lodgings provided at the temples, to afford them friendly accommodation, and the priests and temple-keepers must show them care and attention, until they have sojourned for a reasonable length of time and have seen and heard all that they intended; after which, if no harm has been done or suffered by them, they shall be dismissed. And for these the priests shall act as judges, in case anyone injures one of them or one of them injures anyone else, if the claim does not exceed fifty drachmae; but if any greater claim is made, the trial for such strangers must take place before the market-stewards. The third type which requires a public reception is he who comes from another country on some public business: he must be received by none but the generals, hipparchs and taxiarchs, and the care of a stranger of this kind must be entirely in the hands of the official with whom he lodges, in conjunction with the prytaneis. The fourth type of stranger comes rarely, if ever: should there, however, come at any time from another country an inspector similar to those we send

πρῶτον μὲν ἔλαττον ἐτῶν μηδὲν πεντήκοντα
γεγονὼς ἔστω, πρὸς τούτῳ δὲ ἀξιῶν τι καλὸν ἰδεῖν
τῶν ἐν ταῖς ἄλλαις πόλεσι διαφέρον ἐν καλλοναῖς
ἢ καὶ δεῖξαί τι κατὰ ταὐτὰ ἄλλῃ πόλει. ἴτω μὲν
D νῦν πᾶς ἀκέλευστος ὁ τοιοῦτος ἐπὶ τὰς τῶν
πλουσίων καὶ σοφῶν θύρας, τοιοῦτος ἕτερος
αὐτὸς ὤν· ἐπὶ γὰρ τὴν τοῦ τῆς παιδείας
ἐπιμελουμένου πάσης οἴκησιν ἴτω πιστεύων
ἱκανῶς εἶναι ξένος τῷ τοιούτῳ ξένῳ, ἢ τὴν τῶν
νικηφόρων τινὸς ἐπ᾽ ἀρετῇ· ξυνὼν δὲ τούτων
τισὶ τὸ μὲν διδάξας, τὸ δὲ μαθὼν ἀπαλλαττέσθω,
φίλος παρὰ φίλων δώροις καὶ τιμαῖς πρεπούσαις
τιμηθείς. τούτοις δὴ τοῖς νόμοις ὑποδέχεσθαί τε
χρὴ πάντας ξένους τε καὶ ξένας ἐξ ἄλλης χώρας
E καὶ τοὺς αὐτῶν ἐκπέμπειν, τιμῶντας ξένιον
Δία, μὴ βρώμασι καὶ θύμασι τὰς ξενηλασίας
ποιουμένους, καθάπερ ποιοῦσι νῦν θρέμματα
Νείλου, μηδὲ κηρύγμασιν ἀγρίοις.

Ἐγγύην ἣν ἂν ἐγγυᾶταί τις, διαρρήδην ἐγ-
γυάσθω, τὴν πρᾶξιν πᾶσαν διομολογούμενος ἐν
συγγραφῇ καὶ ἐναντίον μαρτύρων μὴ ἔλαττον ἢ
954 τριῶν, ὅσα ἐντὸς χιλίων, τὰ δ᾽ ὑπὲρ χιλίας μὴ
ἔλαττον ἢ πέντε. ἐγγυητὴς μὲν δὴ καὶ ὁ
προπωλῶν ὁτιοῦν τοῦ μὴ ἐνδίκως πωλοῦντος ἢ
καὶ μηδαμῶς ἀξιόχρεω· ὑπόδικος δ᾽ ἔστω καὶ ὁ
προπωλῶν, καθάπερ ὁ ἀποδόμενος.

---

[1] *i.e.* by forbidding their presence at ceremonial feasts;
or, because (as Grote says) "the Egyptian habits as to eating
and sacrifice were intolerably repulsive to a foreigner."
[2] Cp. 950 A, B.

abroad, he shall come on these conditions :—First, he shall be not less than fifty years old ; and secondly, his purpose in coming must be to view some noble object which is superior in beauty to anything to be found in other States, or else to display to another State something of that description. Every visitor of this kind shall go as an unbidden guest to the doors of the rich and wise, he being both rich and wise himself; and he shall go also to the abode of the General Superintendent of Education, believing himself to be a proper guest for such a host, or to the house of one of those who have won a prize for virtue ; and when he has communed with some of these, by the giving and receiving of information, he shall take his departure, with suitable gifts and distinctions bestowed on him as a friend by friends. Such are the laws in conformity with which they must receive all strangers, of either sex, from another country, and send out their own citizens ; thus doing honour to Zeus, Patron of Strangers, instead of expelling strangers by means of meats and ceremonies [1] (as is now done by the nurslings of the Nile), or else by savage proclamations.[2]

If anyone gives a security, he shall give it in express terms, setting forth the whole transaction in a written record ; and this he shall do before not less than three witnesses, if the amount be under 1,000 drachmae, and before not less than five, if it be over 1,000. The broker in a sale shall act as security for the seller should the latter have no real right to the goods sold or be quite unable to guarantee their possession ; and the broker shall be legally liable equally with the seller.

Φωρᾶν δὲ ἂν ἐθέλῃ τίς τι παρ᾽ ὁτῳοῦν, γυμνὸς
[ἢ]¹ χιτωνίσκον ἔχων, ἄζωστος, προομόσας τοὺς
νομίμους θεοὺς ἦ μὴν ἐλπίζειν εὑρήσειν, οὕτω
φωρᾶν· ὁ δὲ παρεχέτω τὴν οἰκίαν, τά τε σεσημασμένα καὶ τὰ ἀσήμαντα, φωρᾶν. ἐὰν δέ τις
ἐρευνᾶν βουλομένῳ φωρᾶν μὴ διδῷ, δικάζεσθαι μὲν
τὸν ἀπειργόμενον τιμησάμενον τὸ ἐρευνώμενον,
B ἂν δέ τις ὄφλῃ, τὴν διπλασίαν τοῦ τιμηθέντος
βλάβην ἐκτίνειν. ἐὰν δὲ ἀποδημῶν οἰκίας
δεσπότης τυγχάνῃ, τὰ μὲν ἀσήμαντα παρεχόντων
οἱ ἐνοικοῦντες ἐρευνᾶν, τὰ δὲ σεσημασμένα
παρασημηνάσθω καὶ ὃν ἂν ἐθέλῃ φύλακα κα-
ταστησάτω πέντε ἡμέρας ὁ φωρῶν· ἐὰν δὲ
πλείονα χρόνον ἀπῇ, τοὺς ἀστυνόμους παραλαβὼν οὕτω φωράτω, λύων καὶ τὰ σεσημασμένα,
C πάλιν δὲ μετὰ τῶν οἰκείων καὶ τῶν ἀστυνόμων
κατὰ ταὐτὰ σημηνάσθω.

Τῶν ἀμφισβητησίμων χρόνου <ὅδε>² ὅρος, ὃν
ἐάν τις ᾖ κεκτημένος, μηκέτ᾽ ἀμφισβητεῖν ἐξεῖναι.
χωρίων μὲν οἰκήσεών τε τῇδε οὐκ ἔστ᾽ ἀμφισβή-
τησις· τῶν δὲ ἄλλων ὅ τι ἄν τις ἐκτημένος ᾖ, ἐὰν
μὲν κατὰ ἄστυ καὶ κατ᾽ ἀγορὰν καὶ ἱερὰ χρώμενος
φαίνηται καὶ μηδεὶς ἐπιλάβηται, φῇ δὲ ζητεῖν
τοῦτον τὸν χρόνον, ὁ δὲ μὴ ἀποκρυπτόμενος
φανερὸς ᾖ, ἐὰν οὕτω τις ἐνιαυτὸν ὁτιοῦν ἐκτημένος,
D ὁ δὲ ζητῶν διαγένωνται, μὴ ἐξέστω τοιούτου

¹ [ἢ] bracketed by Hermann.
² < ὅδε > added by W. R. Paton, England (δὲ some
MSS.).

¹ Cp. Aristoph. *Nub.* 500, 966.

If anyone wishes to make a search [1] on any man's premises, he shall strip to his shirt and wear no girdle, and when he has first taken an oath by the appointed gods that of a truth he expects to find the object, he shall make his search; and the other man shall grant him the right to search his house, including things both sealed and unsealed. But if, when a man desires to search, the other party refuses leave, the man so prevented shall take legal proceedings, assessing the value of the object sought; and any man thus convicted shall pay as damages twice the value of the object assessed. And if the master of the house happens to be away from home, the occupants shall allow the claimant to search what is unsealed, and he that searches shall counterseal what is sealed, and shall set any man he chooses to stand guard over it for five days; and if the master be absent longer, the claimant shall call in the city-stewards, and so make his search, in which he shall open also what is sealed, and he shall seal this up again in the same way in the presence of the household and of the city-stewards.

In cases of disputed claims there must be a limit of time, after which it shall be no longer possible to dispute the claim of the person in possession. In our State no dispute is possible in respect of lands or houses; but in respect of anything else which a man has acquired, if the possessor be seen to be using it in the city, market, and temple, and if no one lays claim to it,—then if some man asserts that he has been looking for it all this time, while it is plain that its possessor has made no concealment of it, and if this goes on for a year, the possessor still keeping the article and the other man still seeking, at the expir-

κτήματος ἐπιλαβέσθαι μηδένα παρελθόντος ἐνιαυτοῦ. ἐὰν δὲ κατ' ἄστυ μὲν μὴ μηδὲ κατ' ἀγορὰν
χρῆται, κατ' ἀγροὺς δὲ φανερῶς, μὴ προστυχὴς
δὲ ἐν πέντε ἔτεσι γένηταί τις, τῶν πέντε
ἐξελθόντων ἐτῶν μηκέτι [τοῦ λοιποῦ χρόνου]¹
ἐξέστω τούτῳ τοῦ τοιούτου ἐπιλαβέσθαι. ἐὰν δὲ
κατ' οἰκίας ἐν ἄστει τέ τις χρῆται, τριετῆ τὴν
προθεσμίαν εἶναι, ἐὰν δὲ κατ' ἀγροὺς ἐν ἀφανεῖ
Ε κέκτηται, δέκα ἐτῶν, ἐὰν δ' ἐν ἀλλοδημίᾳ, τοῦ
παντὸς χρόνου ὅταν ἀνεύρῃ που, μηδεμίαν εἶναι
προθεσμίαν τῆς ἐπιλήψεως.

Ἐάν τίς τινα δίκῃ παραγενέσθαι κωλύσῃ βίᾳ,
εἴτε αὐτὸν εἴτε μάρτυρας, ἐὰν μὲν δοῦλον εἴτε αὐτοῦ
εἴτε ἀλλότριον, ἀτελῆ καὶ ἄκυρον γίγνεσθαι τὴν
955 δίκην, ἐὰν δ' ἐλεύθερον, πρὸς τῷ ἀτελῆ δεθῆναι μὲν
ἐνιαυτόν, ὑπόδικον δὲ ἀνδραποδισμοῦ τῷ ἐθέλοντι
γίγνεσθαι. ἐὰν δὲ ἀνταγωνιστὴν γυμναστικῆς ἢ
μουσικῆς ἤ τινος ἀγῶνος ἑτέρου διακωλύῃ τις βίᾳ
μὴ παραγίγνεσθαι, φραζέτω μὲν ὁ ἐθέλων τοῖς
ἀθλοθέταις, οἱ δ' εἰς τὸν ἀγῶνα ἐλεύθερον ἀφιέντων
τὸν ἐθέλοντα ἀγωνίζεσθαι. ἐὰν δὲ ἀδυνατήσωσιν,
ἐὰν μὲν ὁ κωλύων ἀγωνίζεσθαι νικήσῃ, τά τε
νικητήρια τῷ διακωλυθέντι διδόναι καὶ νικήσαντα
Β γράφειν ἐν ἱεροῖς οἷς ἂν ἐθέλῃ, τῷ δὲ διακωλύσαντι
μὴ ἐξέστω μηδὲν ἀνάθημα μηδ' ἐπιγραφὴν τοῦ
τοιούτου ἀγωνός ποτε γενέσθαι, βλάβης δὲ
ὑπόδικος γιγνέσθω, ἐάν τε ἡττᾶται ἀγωνιζόμενος
ἐάν τε καὶ νικᾷ.

Ἐάν τις κλεμμάδιον² ὁτιοῦν ὑποδέχηται

---

¹ [τοῦ λοιποῦ χρόνου] wanting in best MSS., bracketed by
England.
² κλεμμάδιον MSS., vulg.: κλέμμα δ' MS. marg., Zur.

ation of the year no one shall be allowed to lay claim to its possession. And if a man uses an article openly in the country—although not in the city or market, —and if no claimant confronts him within five years, after the expiration of the five years no claim to such a possession shall be allowed. And if a man uses an article indoors in the city, the time-limit shall be three years; if he uses it in a concealed place in the country, it shall be ten years; while if it be in a foreign country, there shall be no limit of time set to making a claim, whenever it is found.

If any man forcibly prevent any person from appearing at an action at law—whether it be the person himself or his witnesses,—in case that person be a slave of his own or of another man, the action shall be null and void; and in case the person so prevented be a free man, in addition to the annulment of the action, the offender shall be imprisoned for a year and shall be liable to a charge of kidnapping at the hands of anyone who chooses. And if anyone forcibly prevents a rival competitor at a gymnastic, musical or other contest from appearing, whoso wishes shall report the fact to the Presidents of the Games, and they shall allow him that wishes to contend to enter for the contest free; but should they prove unable, in case he who prevented the competitor wins, they shall give the prize to the man prevented and shall inscribe his name as victor in whatever temples he chooses, whereas the preventer shall be forbidden to put up any tablet or inscription regarding such a contest, and he shall be liable to pay damages, whether he be defeated at the contest or be victorious.

If anyone knowingly receive any stolen article,

γιγνώσκων, τὴν αὐτὴν ὑπεχέτω δίκην τῷ κλέ-
ψαντι· φυγάδος δὲ ὑποδοχῆς θάνατος ἔστω ζημία.
τὸν αὐτὸν φίλον τε καὶ ἐχθρὸν νομιζέτω πᾶς
τῇ πόλει· ἐὰν δέ τις ἰδίᾳ ποιῆται πρός τινας
εἰρήνην ἢ πόλεμον ἄνευ τοῦ κοινοῦ, θάνατος ἔστω
C καὶ τούτῳ ζημία. ἐὰν δέ τι μέρος τῆς πόλεως
εἰρήνην ἢ πόλεμον πρός τινας ἑαυτῷ ποιῆται,
τοὺς αἰτίους οἱ στρατηγοὶ ταύτης τῆς πράξεως
εἰσαγόντων εἰς δικαστήριον, ὀφλόντι δὲ θάνατος
ἔστω δίκη. τοὺς τῇ πατρίδι διακονοῦντάς τι
δώρων χωρὶς χρὴ διακονεῖν, πρόφασιν δ᾽ εἶναι
μηδεμίαν μηδὲ λόγον ἐπαινούμενον ὡς ἐπ᾽ ἀγαθοῖς
μὲν δεῖ δέχεσθαι δῶρα, ἐπὶ δὲ φλαύροις οὔ· τὸ
γὰρ γνῶναι καὶ γνόντα καρτερεῖν οὐκ εὐπετές,
D ἀκούοντα δὲ ἀσφαλέστατον πείθεσθαι τῷ νόμῳ,
μηδὲν ἐπὶ δώροισι διακονεῖν. ὁ δὲ μὴ πειθόμενος
ἁπλῶς τεθνάτω ἁλοὺς τῇ δίκῃ. χρημάτων
εἰσφορᾶς πέρι τῷ κοινῷ, τετιμῆσθαι μὲν ἕκαστον
τὴν οὐσίαν ἕνεκα πολλῶν χρεὼν καὶ τὴν ἐπέτειον
ἐπικαρπίαν ἐν γράμμασιν ἀποφέρειν ἀγρονόμοις
φυλέτας, ὅπως ἂν δυοῖν οὔσαιν ταῖν εἰσφοραῖν,
ὁποτέρᾳ τὸ δημόσιον ἂν χρῆσθαι βούληται,
E χρῆται κατ᾽ ἐνιαυτὸν ἕκαστον βουλευόμενον, ἐάν
τε τοῦ τιμήματος ὅλου μέρει ἐάν τε τῆς γενομένης
ἐπ᾽ ἐνιαυτὸν ἑκάστοτε προσόδου, χωρὶς τῶν εἰς τὰ
ξυσσίτια τελουμένων.

Θεοῖσι δὲ ἀναθήματα χρεὼν ἔμμετρα τὸν μέτριον
ἄνδρα ἀνατιθέντα δωρεῖσθαι. γῆ μὲν οὖν ἑστία
τε οἰκήσεως ἱερὰ πᾶσι πάντων θεῶν· μηδεὶς οὖν

LAWS, BOOK XII

he shall be liable to the same penalty as the thief; and for the crime of receiving an exile the penalty shall be death. Everyone shall regard the friend or enemy of the State as his own personal friend or enemy; and if anyone makes peace or war with any parties privately and without public consent, in his case also the penalty shall be death; and if any section of the State makes peace or war on its own account with any parties, the generals shall summon the authors of this action before the court, and the penalty for him who is convicted shall be death. Those who are performing any act of service to the State must do it without gifts; and it shall be no excuse nor laudable plea to argue that for good deeds a man ought to receive gifts, though not for bad: to decide wisely, and firmly to abide by one's decision, is no easy thing, and the safest course is for a man to listen and obey the law, which says, "Perform no service for gifts." Whoso disobeys, if convicted by the court, shall be put to death once for all. Touching money-contributions to the public treasury, not only must the property of every man be valued, for many reasons, but the tribesmen also must furnish an annual record of the year's produce to the land-wardens, so that the Treasury may adopt whichever it may prefer of the two existing methods of contribution, and may determine year by year whether it will require a proportion of the whole assessed value, or a proportion of the current yearly income, exclusive of the taxes paid for the common meals.

As regards votive offerings to the gods, it is proper for a reasonable man to present offerings of reasonable value. The soil and the hearth are in all cases sacred to all the gods; wherefore no one shall consecrate

δευτέρως ἱερὰ καθιερούτω θεοῖς. χρυσὸς δὲ καὶ
956 ἄργυρος ἐν ἄλλαις πόλεσιν ἰδίᾳ τε καὶ ἐν ἱεροῖς
ἐστιν ἐπίφθονον κτῆμα, ἐλέφας δὲ ἀπολελοιπότος
ψυχὴν σώματος οὐκ εὐαγὲς [1] ἀνάθημα, σίδηρος δὲ
καὶ χαλκὸς πολέμων ὄργανα· ξύλου δὲ μονόξυλον
ὅ τι ἂν ἐθέλῃ τις ἀνατιθέτω, καὶ λίθου ὡσαύτως,
πρὸς τὰ κοινὰ ἱερά. ὑφὴν δὲ μὴ πλέον ἔργον <ἢ>[2]
γυναικὸς μιᾶς ἔμμηνον· χρώματα δὲ λευκὰ
πρέποντ' ἂν θεοῖς εἴη καὶ ἄλλοθι καὶ ἐν ὑφῇ·
βάμματα δὲ μὴ προσφέρειν ἀλλ' ἢ πρὸς τὰ
B πολέμου κοσμήματα. θειότατα δὲ δῶρα ὄρνιθές
τε καὶ ἀγάλματα, ὅσαπερ ἂν ἐν μιᾷ ζωγράφος
ἡμέρᾳ εἰς ἀποτελῇ· καὶ τἆλλα ἔστω κατὰ τὰ
τοιαῦτα ἀναθήματα μεμιμημένα.

Ὅτε δὲ μέρη διείρηται τῆς πόλεως ξυμπάσης,
ὅσα τε καὶ ἃ δεῖ γίγνεσθαι, καὶ νόμοι περὶ τῶν
ξυμβολαίων εἰς δύναμιν τῶν μεγίστων πέρι
πάντων εἴρηνται, τὸ λοιπὸν δὴ δίκας ἂν εἴη
χρεὼν γίγνεσθαι. δικαστηρίων δὲ τὸ μὲν πρῶτον
αἱρετοὶ δικασταὶ γίγνοιντ' ἄν, οὓς ἂν ὁ φεύγων
C τε καὶ ὁ διώκων ἕλωνται κοινῇ, διαιτηταὶ δικαστῶν
τοὔνομα μᾶλλον πρέπον ἔχοντες· δεύτεροι δὲ
κωμῆταί τε καὶ φυλέται, κατὰ τὸ δωδέκατον
μέρος διῃρημένοι, ἐν οἷς, ἂν μὴ διακριθῶσιν
ἐν τοῖς πρώτοις, περὶ ζημίας μείζονος ἰόντων
ἀγωνιούμενοι, ὁ δὲ φεύγων, ἂν ἡττηθῇ τὸ δεύτερον,
τὸ πεμπτημόριον ἀποτινέτω τοῦ τιμήματος τῆς

---

[1] εὐαγὲς Euseb., most edd. : εὐχερὲς MSS.
[2] <ἢ> added by Stallbaum.

---

[1] Cp. Levit. 19. 11 : "He that toucheth the dead body of
any man shall be unclean seven days."

afresh what is already sacred. Gold and silver, which in other States are used both privately and in temples, are objects liable to cause envy; and ivory, which comes from a body bereft of soul, is not a pure offering; [1] while iron and bronze are instruments of war; of wood forming a single piece a man may offer in the public temples whatsoever he wishes, and of stone likewise, and of woven stuff an amount not exceeding a month's output by one woman. For woven stuff and other materials, white will be a colour befitting the gods; but dyes they must not employ, save only for military decorations. Birds and statues make most godlike gifts, and they should be no larger than what one sculptor can complete in a single day; and all other votive offerings shall be modelled on similar lines.

And now that we have stated in detail what and how many the divisions of the State as a whole must be, and have also stated to the best of our power the laws regarding all the most important business transactions,[2] it will be proper to deal next with judicial procedure.[3] Of law courts the first will be composed of selected judges, selected jointly by both plaintiff and defendant, and these will be called " arbitrators," as being a more suitable name than "judges." The second court shall be formed of the villagers and tribesmen (the tribes being divided into twelve parts); and if the cause be not decided in the first court, they shall come before these judges to fight a case involving a greater injury, and if at the second trial the defendant is defeated, he shall pay as an extra penalty the fifth part of the assessed amount of the penalty recorded;

[2] Cp. 922 A.   [3] Cp. 766 D ff.

γραφείσης δίκης. ἐὰν δ' ἐγκαλῶν τις τοῖς
δικασταῖς τὸ τρίτον ἀγωνίζεσθαι βούληται, ἀγέτω
μὲν ἐπὶ τοὺς δικαστὰς τοὺς ἐκλεκτοὺς τὴν δίκην,
D ἐὰν δὲ πάλιν ἡττηθῇ, τὴν ἡμιολίαν τοῦ τιμήματος
ἀποτινέτω. ἐὰν δὲ ὁ διώκων ἡττηθεὶς ἐν τοῖς
πρώτοις μὴ ἠρεμῇ, εἰς δὲ τοὺς δευτέρους ἴῃ,
νικήσας μὲν δὴ τὸ πέμπτον μέρος ἀπολαμβανέτω,
νικηθεὶς δὲ ἀποτινέτω ταὐτὸν μέρος τῆς δίκης.
ἐὰν δ' εἰς τὸ τρίτον ἔλθωσι δικαστήριον ἀπειθή-
σαντες ταῖς ἔμπροσθεν δίκαις, ὁ μὲν φεύγων
ἡττηθείς, ὥσπερ εἴρηται, τὴν ἡμιολίαν, ὁ δὲ
διώκων τὴν ἡμίσειαν τοῦ τιμήματος ἀποτινέτω.
E κληρώσεις δὲ δικαστηρίων καὶ πληρώσεις καὶ
ὑπηρεσιῶν ἑκάσταις τῶν ἀρχῶν καταστάσεις καὶ
χρόνους ἐν οἷς ἕκαστα γίγνεσθαι χρεών, καὶ
διαψηφίσεων πέρι καὶ ἀναβολῶν, καὶ πάνθ'
ὁπόσα τοιαῦτα ἀναγκαῖα περὶ δίκας γίγνεσθαι,
προτέρων τε καὶ ὑστέρων λήξεις ἀποκρίσεών τε
ἀνάγκας καὶ παρακαταβάσεων καὶ ὅσα τούτων
ἀδελφὰ ξύμπαντα, εἴπομεν μὲν καὶ πρόσθεν,
957 καλὸν δὲ τό γε ὀρθὸν καὶ δὶς καὶ τρίς. πάντα
δ' οὖν ὁπόσα σμικρὰ καὶ ῥᾴδια νόμιμα εὑρίσκειν,
πρεσβύτου νομοθέτου παραλιπόντος τὸν νέον
ἀναπληροῦν χρὴ νομοθέτην. τὰ μὲν ἴδια δικαστήρια ταύτῃ πῃ γιγνόμενα μέτρον ἂν ἔχοι·
τὰ δὲ δημόσια καὶ κοινὰ καὶ ὅσοις ἀρχὰς δεῖ
χρωμένας τὰ προσήκοντα ἑκάστῃ τῶν ἀρχῶν
διοικεῖν, ἔστ' ἐν πολλαῖς πόλεσιν οὐκ ἀσχήμονα
ἐπιεικῶν ἀνδρῶν οὐκ ὀλίγα νομοθετήματα, ὅθεν

---

[1] Cp. 766 D ff., 846 B ff.
[2] Cp. 754 C.

and if, dissatisfied with his judges, he desires to fight his case before a court a third time, he shall bring it before the select judges, and if he be again worsted, he shall pay one and a half times the assessed amount. Again, if the plaintiff, when worsted in the first court, does not rest satisfied, but goes to the second court, in case he wins, he shall receive the fifth part, but in case he loses, he shall pay the same fraction of the penalty. And if, through dissatisfaction with the previous verdict, they proceed to the third court, the defendant (as we have said) shall pay, if worsted, one and a half times the penalty, and the prosecutor one-half of it. As regards the allotting of courts, the filling of vacancies, the appointing of serjeants for the several boards of magistrates, the times prescribed for performing each of these duties, the recording of votes, adjournments, and all other necessary judicial arrangements,—such as the fixing by lot of the order of trials, rules about counter-pleadings and counter-attendances, and all matters cognate thereto,— all these we have dealt with previously,[1] but nevertheless it is a proper thing to reiterate twice, —yea, thrice,—the truth.[2] The old lawgiver, however, may pass over all such legal observances as are trivial and easy of discovery, and the young lawgiver shall fill up his omissions. In dealing with the private law courts this method would be reasonable, but in connection with the public courts of the State, and all those which the officials have to use in managing the affairs which belong to their several offices, there exist in many States quite a number of admirable ordinances of worthy men;[3] and from

[3] Alluding, probably, to Athenian law in particular.

νομοφύλακας χρὴ τὰ πρέποντα τῇ νῦν γεννωμένῃ
B πολιτείᾳ κατασκευάζειν συλλογισαμένους καὶ ἐπα-
νορθουμένους, ταῖς ἐμπειρίαις διαβασανίζοντας,
ἕως ἂν ἱκανῶς αὐτῶν ἕκαστα δόξῃ κεῖσθαι, τότε
δὲ τέλος ἐπιθέντας, ἀκίνητα οὕτως ἐπισφραγισα-
μένους, χρῆσθαι τὸν ἅπαντα βίον. ὅσα δὲ περί
τε σιγὴν δικαστῶν καὶ εὐφημίας καὶ τοὐναντίον,
καὶ ὅσα παραλλάττει τῶν [πολλῶν]¹ ἐν ταῖς
ἄλλαις πόλεσι δικαίων καὶ ἀγαθῶν [καὶ καλῶν],²
τὰ μὲν εἴρηται, τὰ δ' ἔτι πρὸς τῷ τέλει ῥηθήσεται.
C πρὸς ἃ πάντα χρὴ τὸν μέλλοντα δικαστὴν ἴσον
ἔσεσθαι κατὰ δίκην βλέπειν τε καὶ κεκτημένον
γράμματα αὐτῶν πέρι³ μανθάνειν. πάντων γὰρ
μαθημάτων κυριώτατα τοῦ τὸν μανθάνοντα
βελτίω γίγνεσθαι τὰ περὶ τοὺς νόμους κείμενα,
εἴπερ ὀρθῶς εἴη τεθέντα, γίγνοιτ' ἄν, ἢ μάτην
τοὔνομα νῷ προσῆκον κεκτῇτ' ἂν ὁ θεῖος ἡμῖν
καὶ θαυμαστὸς νόμος. καὶ δὴ καὶ τῶν ἄλλων
D λόγων ὅσοι τε ἐν ποιήμασιν ἔπαινοι καὶ ψόγοι
περί τινων λέγονται καὶ ὅσοι καταλογάδην, εἴτ'
ἐν γράμμασιν εἴτε καθ' ἡμέραν ἐν ταῖς ἄλλαις
πάσαις συνουσίαις διὰ φιλονεικίας τε ἀμφισβη-
τοῦνται καὶ διὰ ξυγχωρήσεων ἔστιν ὅτε καὶ μάλα
ματαίων, τούτων πάντων ἂν βάσανος εἴη σαφὴς
τὰ τοῦ νομοθέτου γράμματα, ἃ δεῖ κεκτημένον
ἐν αὑτῷ, καθάπερ ἀλεξιφάρμακα τῶν ἄλλων
λόγων, τὸν ἀγαθὸν δικαστὴν αὐτόν τε ὀρθοῦν καὶ
τὴν πόλιν, τοῖς μὲν ἀγαθοῖς μονὰς τῶν δικαίων

¹ [πολλῶν] bracketed by Hermann.
² [καὶ καλῶν] omitted by best MSS.
³ πέρι MSS. : πάρα Steph., Zur.

526

these the Law-wardens must construct a code which is suitable to the polity we are now framing, partly by comparing and amending them, partly by submitting them to the test of experience, until each such ordinance be deemed satisfactory; and when they have been finally approved, and have been sealed as absolutely unchangeable, then the magistrates shall put them into practice all their life long. All rules regarding silence and discreet speech, and the opposite of these, on the part of the judges, and all else that differs from the rules which obtain in the other States concerning justice and goodness,—all these have been stated in part,[1] and in part they will be stated at the end. To all these matters he that purposes to be a righteous and just judge must attend, and that written exposition of them which he possesses he must learn. For of all studies, that of legal regulations, provided they be rightly framed, will prove the most efficacious in making the learner a better man; for were it not so, it would be in vain that our divine and admirable law bears a name akin to reason.[2] Moreover, of all other speeches— whether they be of personal praise or blame, composed in verse or prose, written down or uttered from day to day at some gathering by way of controversy or by way of consent (often of a very futile character),—of all such speeches the writings of the lawgiver[3] will serve as a test; and inasmuch as he possesses these within himself, as a talisman against other speeches, the good judge will guide both himself and the State aright; for the good he will secure both the permanence and the increase of

---

[1] Cp. 766 D, 855 D.   [2] νόμος = νοῦς ; cp. 714 A.
[3] Cp. 811 D, 858 C.

Ε καὶ ἐπαύξησιν παρασκευάζοντα, τοῖς δὲ κακοῖς
ἐξ ἀμαθίας καὶ ἀκολασίας καὶ δειλίας καὶ
ξυλλήβδην πάσης ἀδικίας εἰς τὸ δυνατὸν μετα-
βολήν, ὅσοις ἰάσιμοι δόξαι τῶν κακῶν· οἷσι δὲ
ὄντως ἐπικεκλωσμέναι, θάνατον ἴαμα ταῖς οὕτω
958 διατεθείσαις ψυχαῖς διανέμοντες, ὃ δικαίως εἴη
πολλάκις ἂν εἰρημένον, ἄξιοι ἐπαίνου γίγνοιντ᾽
ἂν τῇ πάσῃ πόλει τοιοῦτοι δικασταὶ καὶ δικαστῶν
ἡγεμόνες.

Ἐπειδὰν δὲ αἱ κατ᾽ ἐνιαυτὸν δίκαι τέλος
ἐκδικασθεῖσαι σχῶσι, ταῖς πράξεσι νόμους
αὐτῶν χρεὼν γίγνεσθαι τούσδε· πρῶτον μὲν ἡ
δικάζουσα ἀρχὴ τὰ τοῦ ὀφλόντος τῷ νικήσαντι
Β χρήματα πάντα ἀποδιδότω χωρὶς τῶν ἀναγκαίων
κεκτῆσθαι, μετὰ τὴν διαψήφισιν ἑκάστην εὐθὺς
ὑπὸ κήρυκος, ἀκουόντων τῶν δικαστῶν· ἐπειδὰν
δὲ ὁ τῶν δικασίμων μηνῶν ἐχόμενος γένηται μήν,
ἐάν τις μὴ ἀπαλλάττῃ τὸν νικήσαντα ἑκόντα
ἑκών, ἡ δικάσασα ἀρχὴ ξυνεπομένη τῷ νικῶντι
τὰ τοῦ ὀφλόντος παραδιδότω χρήματα. ἐὰν δὲ
μὴ ἔχωσιν ὁπόθεν, ἐλλείπῃ δὲ μὴ ἔλαττον
δραχμῆς, μὴ πρότερον εἶναι τούτῳ δίκας πρὸς
ἄλλον μηδένα, πρὶν ἂν ἐκπληρώσῃ τὸ χρέος
C ἅπαν τῷ νικήσαντι· ἄλλοις δὲ πρὸς τοῦτον
ἔστωσαν δίκαι κυρίως. ἐὰν δέ τις ἀφῃρῆται τὴν
ἀρχὴν τὴν καταδικάσασαν καταδικασθείς, εἰσαγόντων μὲν αὐτὸν εἰς τὸ τῶν νομοφυλάκων
δικαστήριον οἱ ἀφαιρεθέντες ἀδίκως, ἐὰν δέ τις
ὄφλῃ τὴν τοιαύτην δίκην, ὡς ὅλην τὴν πόλιν καὶ
νόμους φθείρων θανάτῳ ζημιούσθω.

---

[1] *i.e.* men whose false beliefs are ineradicable, beyond hope
of conversion.

what is just, and for the bad a change as great as possible from their ignorance, intemperance and cowardice, and, in short, from their general iniquity, —that is to say, for all the bad whose opinions are curable ; but for those whose opinions are really fixed by Fate,[1]—if they assigned death as a cure for souls in this condition (a statement that deserves to be often repeated), such judges and leaders of judges would merit praise from the whole State.

When all the lawsuits for the year have been finally adjudged, we must have laws for the execution of the verdicts to this effect :—First, the magistrate who is acting as judge shall assign to the victorious party all the goods of the party convicted, excepting such as the latter must necessarily retain in his possession ; and this he shall do in each case immediately after the voting has taken place by means of a herald's proclamation made in the hearing of the judges ; and unless the loser settle with the victor to their mutual satisfaction by the end of the month next to those in which the courts are sitting, the magistrate who has tried the case shall, at the instance of the victor, hand over to him the goods of the loser. And if the means are not forthcoming, and there be a deficiency of not less than a drachma, the loser in question shall be precluded from suing anyone else until he has paid to the full his whole debt to the victor ; but others may bring valid actions against him. If anyone, when condemned, obstructs the court which condemned him, the officials thus wrongfully obstructed shall summon him before the court of the Law-wardens, and anyone who is cast in such an action, as being guilty of subverting the whole State and its laws, shall be punished by death.

PLATO

Ἀνδρὶ δὴ τὸ μετὰ τοῦτο γεννηθέντι καὶ
ἐκτραφέντι καὶ γεννήσαντι καὶ ἐκθρέψαντι τέκνα
D καὶ ξυμμίξαντι ξυμβόλαια μετρίως, διδόντι τε
δίκας εἴ τινα ἠδικήκει καὶ παρ' ἑτέρου ἐκλαβόντι,
σὺν τοῖς νόμοις ἐν μοίρᾳ γηράσαντι τελευτὴ
γίγνοιτ' ἂν κατὰ φύσιν. περὶ τελευτήσαντας δή,
εἴτε τις ἄρρην εἴτε τις θῆλυς ἦν, τὰ μὲν περὶ τὰ
θεῖα νόμιμα τῶν τε ὑπὸ γῆς θεῶν καὶ τῶν τῇδε,
ὅσα προσήκει τελεῖσθαι, τοὺς ἐξηγητὰς γίγνεσθαι
κυρίους φράζειν· τὰς θήκας δ' εἶναι τῶν χωρίων
ὁπόσα μὲν ἐργάσιμα μηδαμοῦ, μήτε τι μέγα μήτε
τι σμικρὸν μνῆμα, ἃ δὲ δὴ χωρία¹ πρὸς τοῦτ'
E αὐτὸ μόνον φύσιν ἔχει, τὰ τῶν τετελευτηκότων
σώματα μάλιστα ἀλυπήτως τοῖς ζῶσι δεχόμενα²
κρύπτειν, ταῦτα ἐκπληροῦν· τοῖς δὲ ἀνθρώποις
ὅσα τροφὴν [μήτηρ οὖσα ἡ γῆ πρὸς ταῦτα]³
πέφυκε βούλεσθαι φέρειν, μήτε ζῶν μήτε τις ἀπο-
θανὼν στερείτω τὸν ζῶνθ' ἡμῶν. χῶμα δὲ μὴ
χοῦν ὑψηλότερον πέντε ἀνδρῶν ἔργον, ἐν πένθ'
ἡμέραις ἀποτελούμενον· λίθινα δὲ ἐπιστήματα
μὴ μείζω ποιεῖν ἢ ὅσα δέχεσθαι τὰ τοῦ τετελευτηκότος ἐγκώμια βίου, μὴ πλείω τεττάρων
959 ἡρωϊκῶν στίχων. τὰς δὲ προθέσεις πρῶτον μὲν
μὴ μακρότερον χρόνον ἔνδον γίγνεσθαι τοῦ
δηλοῦντος τόν τε ἐκτεθνεῶτα καὶ τὸν ὄντως
τεθνηκότα, εἴη δ' ἂν σχεδὸν ὡς τἀνθρώπινα μέτρον
ἔχουσα τριταία πρὸς τὸ μνῆμα ἐκφορά. πείθεσθαι

¹ δὴ χωρία : ἡ χώρα MSS., edd. (ἡ ᾖ χώρα Hermann).
² δεχόμενα : δεχομένη MSS., Edd.

530

Next, when a man has been born and reared,
and has himself begotten and reared up children,
and has engaged reasonably in the transactions of
business, giving or receiving (as the case may be)
compensation for wrongs done,—when he has thus
duly grown old in a law-abiding life, his end will
come in the course of nature. Touching the dead,
male or female, what the sacred rites are which
require to be performed in respect of the gods
of the underworld, or of this world, shall be
declared by the Interpreters as the final authorities :
no tombs, however, shall be put in places that are
tilled,—whether the monument be small or great,—
but they shall fill up those places where the soil
is naturally fitted for this purpose only,—namely,
to receive and hide the bodies of the dead with
the least hurt to the living; but as regards all
the places which of their own nature desire to
produce food for mankind, of these no one, living
or dead, shall deprive us who are alive. And they
shall not pile up a mound to a height greater
than can be made by five men in five days ; nor
shall they erect stone pillars of a size more than
is required to hold, at the most, a eulogy of the
dead man's life consisting of not more than four
heroic lines. And as to the laying-out of the corpse,
first, it shall remain in the house only for such
a time as is required to prove that the man is not
merely in a faint, but really dead ; and accordingly,
in a normal case, the third will be the proper day
for the carrying out to burial. As in other matters

---

³ [μήτηρ . . . ταῦτα] I bracket (England brackets πρὸς ταῦτα) :
cp. *Rep.* 414 E.

δ' ἐστὶ τῷ νομοθέτῃ χρεὼν τά τε ἄλλα καὶ
λέγοντι ψυχὴν σώματος εἶναι τὸ πᾶν διαφέρουσαν,
ἐν αὐτῷ τε τῷ βίῳ τὸ παρεχόμενον ἡμῶν ἕκαστον
B τοῦτ' εἶναι μηδὲν ἀλλ' ἢ τὴν ψυχήν, τὸ δὲ σῶμα
ἰνδαλλόμενον ἡμῶν ἑκάστοις ἕπεσθαι, καὶ τελευτησάντων λέγεσθαι καλῶς εἴδωλα εἶναι τὰ τῶν
νεκρῶν σώματα, τὸν δὲ ὄντα ἡμῶν ἕκαστον ὄντως,
ἀθάνατον εἶναι ψυχὴν ἐπονομαζόμενον, παρὰ
θεοὺς ἄλλους ἀπιέναι δώσοντα λόγον, καθάπερ
ὁ νόμος ὁ πάτριος λέγει, τῷ μὲν ἀγαθῷ θαρραλέον,
τῷ δὲ κακῷ μάλα φοβερόν, βοήθειάν τε αὐτῷ
μήτινα μεγάλην εἶναι τετελευτηκότι· ζῶντι γὰρ
C ἔδει βοηθεῖν πάντας τοὺς προσήκοντας, ὅπως
ὅτι δικαιότατος ὢν καὶ ὁσιώτατος ἔζη τε ζῶν καὶ
τελευτήσας ἀτιμώρητος [ἂν]¹ κακῶν ἁμαρτημάτων
ἐγίγνετο τὸν μετὰ τὸν ἐνθάδε βίον. ἐκ δὲ τούτων
οὕτως ἐχόντων οὐδέποτε οἰκοφθορεῖν χρή, διαφερόντως νομίζοντα τὸν αὐτοῦ τοῦτον εἶναι τὸν
τῶν σαρκῶν ὄγκον θαπτόμενον, ἀλλ' ἐκεῖνον τὸν
υἱὸν ἢ ἀδελφόν, ἢ ὅντινά τις μάλισθ' ἡγεῖται
ποθῶν θάπτειν, οἴχεσθαι περαίνοντα καὶ ἐμπι-
πλάντα τὴν αὐτοῦ μοῖραν, τὸ δὲ παρὸν δεῖν
D εὖ ποιεῖν, τὰ μέτρια ἀναλίσκοντα ὡς εἰς ἄψυχον
χθονίων βωμόν· τὸ δὲ μέτριον νομοθέτης ἂν
μαντεύσαιτο οὐκ ἀσχημονέστατα. ἔστω δὴ νόμος

---

¹ [ἂν] bracketed by Ast (ἀνιάτων Winck.).

¹ Cp. *Phaedo* 63 B.   ² Cp. 717 E, 719 D.

it is right to trust the lawgiver, so too we must
believe him when he asserts that the soul is wholly
superior to the body, and that in actual life what
makes each of us to be what he is is nothing else
than the soul, while the body is a semblance which
attends on each of us, it being well said that the
bodily corpses are images of the dead, but that
which is the real self of each of us, and which
we term the immortal soul, departs to the presence
of other gods,[1] there (as the ancestral law declares)
to render its account,—a prospect to be faced with
courage by the good, but with uttermost dread by
the evil. But to him who is dead no great help
can be given ; it was when he was alive that all
his relatives should have helped him, so that when
living his life might have been as just and holy
as possible, and when dead he might be free during
the life which follows this life from the penalty
for wickedness and sin. This being so, one ought
never to spend extravagantly on the dead, through
supposing that the carcase of flesh that is being
buried is in the truest sense one's own relative ;
but one ought rather to suppose that the real son
or brother—or whoever else it may be that a man
fancies himself to be mournfully burying—has departed in furtherance and fulfilment of his own
destiny, and that it is our duty to make a wise
use of what we have and to spend in moderation,[2]
as it were on a soulless altar to the gods below :[3]
and what constitutes moderation the lawgiver will
most properly divine. Let this, then, be the law :—

[3] *i.e.* the corpse is like an altar which has no "real
presence" to sanctify it ; hence it is less worthy of costly
fferings.

οὗτος· Τῷ μὲν δὴ τοῦ μεγίστου τιμήματος εἰς
τὴν πᾶσαν ταφὴν ἀναλισκόμενα μὴ πλέον πέντε
μνῶν, τῷ δὲ τοῦ δευτέρου τρεῖς μναῖ, καὶ δύο
τῷ τοῦ τρίτου, μνᾶ δὲ τῷ τοῦ τετάρτου μέτρον
ἂν ἔχοι τῶν ἀναλωμάτων. νομοφύλαξι δὲ πολλά
τε ἄλλα ἀνάγκη πράττειν καὶ πολλῶν ἐπι-
E μελεῖσθαι, τούτων δ' οὐχ ἥκιστα, ὅπως ἂν
παίδων τε καὶ ἀνδρῶν καὶ πάσης ἡλικίας ἐπιμελούμενοι ζῶσι· καὶ δὴ καὶ πρὸς τὸ τέλος
ἁπάντων νομοφύλαξ εἷς γέ τις ἐπιστατῇ, ὃν ἂν
οἱ τοῦ τετελευτηκότος ἐπίσκοπον οἰκεῖοι παρα-
λάβωσιν, ᾧ καλόν τ' ἔστω καλῶς καὶ μετρίως
τὰ περὶ τὸν τετελευτηκότα γιγνόμενα καὶ μὴ
καλῶς αἰσχρόν. πρόθεσις δὲ καὶ τἆλλα ἔστω
μὲν κατὰ τὸν περὶ τὰ τοιαῦτα νόμον γιγνόμενα,
τῷ δὲ πολιτικῷ νόμῳ νομοθετοῦντι παραχωρεῖν
χρὴ τὰ τοιάδε· Δακρύειν μὲν τὸν τετελευτηκότα
960 ἐπιτάττειν ἢ μὴ ἄμορφον, θρηνεῖν δὲ καὶ ἔξω
τῆς οἰκίας φωνὴν ἐξαγγέλλειν ἀπαγορεύειν, καὶ
τὸν νεκρὸν εἰς τὸ φανερὸν προάγειν τῶν ὁδῶν
κωλύειν, καὶ ἐν ταῖς ὁδοῖς πορευόμενον φθέγγεσθαι, καὶ πρὸ ἡμέρας ἔξω τῆς πόλεως εἶναι.
ταῦτα δὴ κείσθω τε οὕτω περὶ τὰ τοιαῦτα
νόμιμα, καὶ ὁ μὲν πειθόμενος ἔστω ζημίας ἐκτός,
ὁ δὲ ἀπειθῶν ἑνὶ τῶν νομοφυλάκων ὑπὸ πάντων
B ζημιούσθω τῇ δοξάσῃ πᾶσι κοινῇ ζημίᾳ. ὅσαι
δ' ἄλλαι γίγνονται περὶ τελευτήσαντας ταφαὶ
534

An expenditure on the whole funeral not exceeding five minas for a man of the highest property-class, three minas for one of the second class, two for one of the third, and one mina for one of the fourth class, shall be held to be moderate amounts. The Law-wardens must of necessity perform many other duties and supervise many other matters, but by no means the least of their duties is to live keeping a constant watch over children and men and people of every age ; and at the end of his life above all everyone must have some one Law-warden to take charge of him—that one who is called in as overseer by the relatives of the dead man ; and it shall stand to his credit if the arrangements about the dead man are carried out in a proper and moderate way, but if improperly, to his discredit. The laying-out of the corpse and the other arrangements shall be carried out in accordance with the custom concerning such matters, but it is right that custom should give way to the following regulations of State law :—Either to ordain or to prohibit weeping for the dead is unseemly, but we shall forbid loud mourning and lamentation outside the house, and we shall prohibit the carrying out of the dead on to the open roads and making lamentation while he is borne through the streets, and the funeral party must be outside the city-bounds before day-break. These shall be the legal regulations regarding such matters : he that obeys them shall be free from penalty, but he that disobeys a single one of the Law-wardens shall be penalized by them all with the penalty adjudged by all in common. All other interments of the dead, or disposal of

εἴτε καὶ ἄταφοι πράξεις, περὶ πατροφόνων καὶ
ἱεροσύλων καὶ τῶν τοιούτων πάντων, εἰρημέναι
ἐν τοῖς ἔμπροσθεν κεῖνται διὰ νόμων, ὥστε σχεδὸν
ἡ νομοθεσία τέλος ἂν ἡμῖν ἔχοι. τῶν πάντων
δ᾽ ἑκάστοτε τέλος οὐ τὸ δρᾶσαί τι σχεδὸν οὐδὲ
τὸ κτήσασθαι κατοικίσαι τ᾽ ἐστίν, ἀλλὰ τῷ
γεννηθέντι σωτηρίαν ἐξευρόντα τελέως ἀεὶ τότ᾽
ἤδη νομίζειν πᾶν ὅσον ἔδει πραχθῆναι πεπρᾶχθαι,
πρότερον δ᾽ ἀτελὲς εἶναι τὸ ὅλον.

ΚΛ. Καλῶς, ὦ ξένε, λέγεις· πρὸς ὅ τι δὲ τὸ
νῦν αὖ ῥηθὲν εἴρηται, φράζ᾽ ἔτι σαφέστερον.

ΑΘ. Ὦ Κλεινία, πολλὰ τῶν ἔμπροσθεν καλῶς
ὕμνηται, σχεδὸν δὲ οὐχ ἥκιστα τὰ τῶν Μοιρῶν
προσρήματα.

ΚΛ. Ποῖα δή;

ΑΘ. Τὸ Λάχεσιν μὲν τὴν πρώτην εἶναι, Κλωθὼ
δὲ τὴν δευτέραν, τὴν Ἄτροπον δὲ τρίτην σώτειραν,
[τῶν λεχθέντων, ἀπεικασμένα τῇ] [1] τῶν κλωσθέν-
των τῷ κύρει τὴν ἀμετάστροφον ἀπεργαζομένην [2]
δύναμιν. ἣν [3] δὴ καὶ πόλει καὶ πολίταις [4] δεῖ
μὴ μόνον ὑγίειαν καὶ σωτηρίαν τοῖς σώμασι παρασκευάζειν, ἀλλὰ καὶ εὐνομίαν ἐν ταῖς ψυχαῖς,
μᾶλλον δὲ σωτηρίαν τῶν νόμων. ἡμῖν δ᾽ ἔτι μοι
φαίνεσθαι δοκεῖ τοῦτ᾽ ἐλλεῖπον τοῖς νόμοις εἶναι,
πῶς χρὴ τὴν ἀμετάστροφον αὐτοῖς ἐγγίγνεσθαι
κατὰ φύσιν δύναμιν.

---

[1] [τῶν λεχθέντων, ἀπεικασμένα τῇ] I bracket, and for πυρί,
I read κύρει (for τῷ πυρί, Herm. ci. σωτηρίᾳ, alii alia).
[2] ἀπεργαζομένην Schmidt, Stallb.: ἀπεργαζομένων MSS.
[3] ἣν Ast: & MSS.
[4] πολίταις: πολιτείᾳ MSS., edd. (πολίταις καὶ πολίτισι
Badh.)

corpses without interment in the cases of parricides, temple-robbers, and all such criminals,—have been previously[1] dealt with and laid down by law, so that our task of legislation has nearly come to an end. But in every case, the full end does not consist in the doing, gaining or founding of an object; rather our view should be that it is only when we have discovered a means of salvation, endless and complete, for our creation, that we are at length justified in believing that we have done all that ought to be done: until then, we must believe, the whole of our creation is incomplete.

CLIN. You say well, Stranger; but explain to us yet more clearly the purport of your last observation.

ATH. O Clinias, many of the sayings of old time have been nobly uttered, and of these not the least, I may say, are the titles given to the Fates.

CLIN. What titles, pray?

ATH. That the first of them is Lachesis, the second Clotho, and Atropos the saviour-third[2]—she that bestows on the dooms ratified by Clotho the quality of irreversibility. She it is that must furnish also to the State and its citizens, not merely health and salvation for their bodies, but also right legality in their souls, or rather the salvation of the laws. And this, as it seems clear to me, is what our laws still lack—namely, a right mode of naturally implanting in them this irreversible quality.

---

[1] Cp. 854 D ff., 873 C f.

[2] Cp. *Rep.* 620 E. Atropos is called "the saviour-third" (cp. τὸ τρίτον τῷ Σωτῆρι) because she completes the work of the other Fates by making the thread of life (doom) spun by them irreversible. (ἄ-τροπος = "unturnable.")

κλ. Οὐ σμικρὸν λέγεις, εἴπερ ἐστὶ μὴ δυνατὸν
εὑρεῖν ὅπῃ γίγνοιτ' ἂν παντὶ κτῆμά τι[1] [τὸ]
τοιοῦτον.

Ε   αθ. Ἀλλ' ἔστι μὴν δυνατόν, ὥς γέ μοι τὰ νῦν
παντάπασι καταφαίνεται.

κλ. Μὴ τοίνυν ἀφιστώμεθα μηδενὶ τρόπῳ,
πρὶν ἂν τοῦτ' αὐτὸ ἐκπορισώμεθα τοῖς εἰρημένοις
νόμοις· γελοῖον γὰρ τό γε μάτην πονήσαντα
ὁτιοῦν εἰς μηδὲν βέβαιον καταβαλεῖν.

αθ. Ὀρθῶς παρακελεύει, καὶ ἐμὲ τοιοῦτον
εὑρήσεις ἄλλον.

κλ. Καλῶς δὴ λέγεις. τίς οὖν δή, φής, σωτηρία γίγνοιτ' ἂν καὶ τίνα τρόπον πολιτείᾳ τε
καὶ τοῖς νόμοις ἡμῖν ;

961   αθ. Ἆρ' οὐκ εἴπομεν ὅτι δεῖ σύλλογον ἡμῖν
ἐν τῇ πόλει γίγνεσθαι τοιόνδε τινά ; δέκα μὲν
τῶν νομοφυλάκων τοὺς πρεσβυτάτους ἀεί, τοὺς
δὲ τἀριστεῖα εἰληφότας ἅπαντας δεῖν εἰς ταὐτὸ
συλλέγεσθαι τούτοις· ἔτι δὲ τοὺς ἐκδημήσαντας
ἐπὶ ζήτησιν εἴ τί που πρὸς τὴν νομοφυλακίαν
γίγνοιτο ἔγκαιρον ἀκοῦσαι, καὶ σωθέντας οἴκαδε
δόξαν τοῦτο[2] αὐτοῖς, διαβασανισθέντας, τοῦ
ξυλλόγου ἀξιοκοινωνήτους εἶναι· πρὸς τούτοις
Β δὲ ἕνα ἕκαστον δεῖν προσλαμβάνειν τῶν νέων, μὴ
ἔλαττον ἢ τριακονταέτη γεγονότα, πρῶτον δὲ
αὐτὸν κρίναντα ἐπάξιον εἶναι φύσει καὶ τροφῇ
τὸν νέον οὕτως εἰς τοὺς ἄλλους εἰσφέρειν, καὶ ἐὰν
μὲν δόξῃ καὶ τοῖς ἄλλοις, προσλαμβάνειν, εἰ δὲ

---

[1] κτῆμά τι Burnet : κτήματι MSS. ; κτήματι τὸ Zur., vulg.
[2] δόξαν τοῦτο W.-Möllendorff : δόξαι τούτοις MSS., edd.

---

[1] Cp. 951 D ff.

CLIN. The point you mention is a serious one,
if it is really impossible to discover a means whereby
everything may acquire some such quality.

ATH. Nay, but it is possible, as I now perceive
quite clearly.

CLIN. Then let us by no means desist until we
have secured this very quality for the laws we have
stated; for it would be ridiculous for us to have
wasted all this labour on an object, and then not
base it on any firm foundation.

ATH. You are right in your exhortation, and you
will find me as ready as yourself to proceed.

CLIN. Very good. Then what is it you say will
prove a means of salvation to our polity and its laws,
and how will it do so?

ATH. Did we not say[1] that we must have in
our State a synod of the following kind:—The ten
senior members, at the moment, of the body of
Law-wardens shall form the synod, in company
with all who have won the award of merit; and,
moreover, those inspectors who have gone abroad[2]
to discover if they could hear of anything pertinent
to the safe-keeping of laws, and who, in the belief
that they have succeeded, have come safely home
again, shall, after undergoing a searching test, be
deemed worthy to take part in the synod? In
addition to these, every member must bring with
him one of the young men, not less than thirty
years old, whom he has first selected as being both
by nature and training a suitable person; after
selecting him, he shall introduce him among the
members, and if they also approve, he shall keep
him as a colleague, but if they disapprove, the fact

[2] Cp. 951 A ff.

PLATO

μή, ἀπόρρητον εἶναι τὴν γεγονυῖαν κρίσιν τοῖς τε
ἄλλοις δὴ καὶ μάλιστ' αὐτῷ τῷ ἀποκριθέντι· δεῖν
δὲ ὄρθριον εἶναι τὸν σύλλογον, ἡνίκ' ἂν τῶν ἄλλων
πράξεων ἰδίων τε καὶ κοινῶν καὶ μάλιστ' ᾖ τις
σχολὴ παντί. τοιοῦτόν τί που λεχθὲν ἡμῖν ἦν ἐν
C τοῖς ἔμπροσθεν λόγοις ;

ΚΛ. Ἦν γὰρ οὖν.

ΑΘ. Τούτου δὴ πέρι τοῦ συλλόγου πάλιν ἀνα-
λαβὼν λέγοιμ' ἂν τὸ τοιόνδε. φημί, εἴ τις
τοῦτον βάλοιτο οἷον ἄγκυραν πάσης τῆς πόλεως,
πάντα ἔχουσαν τὰ πρόσφορα ἑαυτῇ σώζειν ἂν
ξύμπαντα ἃ βουλόμεθα.

ΚΛ. Πῶς δή ;

ΑΘ. Τὸ μετὰ τοῦτο ἡμέτερος ἂν καιρὸς γίγνοιτο
ὀρθῶς φράζοντας μηδὲν ἀπολείπειν προθυμίας.

ΚΛ. Καὶ μάλα καλῶς εἶπες, ποίει θ' ὥσπερ
καὶ διανοεῖ.

D ΑΘ. Χρὴ τοίνυν, ὦ Κλεινία, παντὸς πέρι
νοῆσαι σωτῆρα τὸν εἰκότα ἐν ἑκάστοις τῶν ἔργων,
ὡς ἐν ζῴῳ ψυχὴ καὶ κεφαλὴ τό γε μέγιστον
πεφύκατον.

ΚΛ. Πῶς αὖ φῄς ;

ΑΘ. Ἡ τούτοιν ἀρετὴ δή που παντὶ παρέχει
ζῴῳ σωτηρίαν.

ΚΛ. Πῶς ;

ΑΘ. Ψυχῇ μὲν πρὸς τοῖς ἄλλοις νοῦς ἐγγιγνό-
μενος, κεφαλῇ δ' αὖ πρὸς τοῖς ἄλλοις ὄψις καὶ
ἀκοή. ξυλλήβδην δὲ νοῦς μετὰ τῶν καλλίστων
αἰσθήσεων κραθεὶς γενόμενός τε εἰς ἓν σωτηρία
ἑκάστων δικαιότατ' ἂν εἴη καλουμένη.

540

of his original selection must be concealed from all the rest, and especially from the person thus rejected. The synod must meet at an early hour, when everyone has his time most free from other business, private or public. Was it not some such organisation as this that we described in our previous discourse?

CLIN. It was.

ATH. Resuming, then, the subject of this synod, I will say this:—If one were to lay this down as an anchor for the whole State, possessing all the requisite conditions,—then, I affirm, it would secure the salvation of all that we desire.

CLIN. How so?

ATH. Now will be the time for us to display no lack of zeal in declaring truly what follows.

CLIN. Excellently spoken! Proceed as you propose.

ATH. One ought to observe, Clinias, in regard to every object, in each of its operations, what constitutes its appropriate saviour—as, for example, in an animal, the soul and the head are eminently such by nature.

CLIN. How do you mean?

ATH. Surely it is the goodness of those parts that provides salvation to every animal.

CLIN. How?

ATH. By the existence of reason in the soul, in addition to all its other qualities, and by the existence of sight and hearing, in addition to all else, in the head; thus, to summarize the matter, it is the combination of reason with the finest senses, and their union in one, that would most justly be termed the salvation of each animal.

ΚΛ. Ἔοικε γοῦν.

Ε   ΑΘ. Ἔοικε γάρ. ἀλλ᾽ ὁ περὶ τί νοῦς μετ᾽ αἰσθήσεων κραθεὶς σωτηρία πλοίων ἔν γε χειμῶσι καὶ ἐν εὐδίαις γίγνοιτ᾽ ἄν; ἆρ᾽ οὐκ ἐν νηῒ κυβερνήτης ἅμα καὶ ναῦται τὰς αἰσθήσεις τῷ κυβερνητικῷ νῷ συγκερασάμενοι σώζουσιν αὑτούς τε καὶ τὰ περὶ τὴν ναῦν;

ΚΛ. Τί μήν;

ΑΘ. Οὐδὲν δὴ πολλῶν δεῖ τῶν περὶ τὰ τοιαῦτα παραδειγμάτων, ἀλλ᾽ οἷον περὶ στρατοπέδων νοήσωμεν ⟨ἢ σωμάτων⟩,[1] τίνα θέμενοι στρατηγοὶ σκοπὸν καὶ ἰατρικὴ ὑπηρεσία πᾶσα στοχάζοιτ᾽

962 ἂν τῆς σωτηρίας ὀρθῶς.[2] ἆρ᾽ οὐχ ἡ μὲν νίκην καὶ κράτος πολεμίων, ἡ δὲ ἰατρῶν τε καὶ ὑπηρετῶν ὑγιείας σώματι παρασκευήν;

ΚΛ. Πῶς γὰρ οὔ;

ΑΘ. Ἰατρὸς δὴ τὸ περὶ σῶμα ἀγνοῶν, ὃ προσείπομεν ὑγίειαν νῦν, ἢ νίκην στρατηγὸς ἢ τῶν ἄλλων ὅσα δὴ διήλθομεν, ἔσθ᾽ ὅπως ἂν νοῦν περί τι τούτων ἂν ἔχων φαίνοιτο;

ΚΛ. Καὶ πῶς;

ΑΘ. Τί δὲ δὴ περὶ πόλιν; εἴ τις τὸν σκοπὸν οἷ βλέπειν δεῖ τὸν πολιτικὸν φαίνοιτο ἀγνοῶν, ἆρα ἄρχων μὲν πρῶτον δικαίως ἂν προσαγορεύοιτο,

Β εἶτα σώζειν ἂν δυνατὸς εἴη τοῦτο οὗ τὸν σκοπὸν τὸ παράπαν μηδ᾽ εἰδείη;

ΚΛ. Καὶ πῶς;

ΑΘ. Δεῖ δὴ καὶ τὰ νῦν, ὡς ἔοικεν, εἴπερ μέλλει

---

[1] ⟨ἢ σωμάτων⟩ I add (Baiter adds καὶ νόσων after στρατοπέδων).

[2] ὀρθῶς is assigned by Zur. and most edd. (except Burnet) to Clin.

CLIN. That is certainly probable.

ATH. It is probable. But what kind of reason is it which, when combined with senses, will afford salvation to ships in stormy weather and calm? On shipboard is it not the pilot and the sailors who, by combining the senses with the pilot reason, secure salvation both for themselves and for all that belongs to the ship?

CLIN. Of course.

ATH. There is no need of many examples to illustrate this. Consider, for instance, what would be the right mark for a general to set up to shoot at in the case of an army, or the medical profession in the case of a human body, if they were aiming at salvation. Would not the former make victory his mark, and mastery over the enemy, while that of the doctors and their assistants would be the providing of health to the body?

CLIN. Certainly.

ATH. But if a doctor were ignorant of that bodily condition which we have now called "health," or a general ignorant of victory, or any of the other matters we have mentioned, could he possibly be thought to possess reason about any of these things?

CLIN. How could he?

ATH. What, now, shall we say about a State? If a man were to be plainly ignorant as regards the political mark to be aimed at, would he, first of all, deserve the title of magistrate, and, secondly, would he be able to secure the salvation of that object concerning the aim of which he knows nothing at all?

CLIN. How could he?

ATH. So now, in our present case, if our settle-

τέλος ὁ κατοικισμὸς τῆς χώρας ἡμῖν ἕξειν, εἶναί
τι τὸ γίγνωσκον ἐν αὐτῷ πρῶτον μὲν τοῦτο ὃ
λέγομεν, τὸν σκοπόν, ὅστις ποτὲ ὁ πολιτικὸς ὢν
ἡμῖν τυγχάνει, ἔπειτα ὄντινα τρόπον δεῖ μετασχεῖν τούτου καὶ τίς αὐτῷ καλῶς ἢ μὴ συμβου-
λεύει τῶν νόμων αὐτῶν πρῶτον, ἔπειτα ἀνθρώπων.
εἰ δ᾽ ἔσται τοῦ τοιούτου κενή τις πόλις, οὐδὲν
C θαυμαστὸν ἄνους οὖσα καὶ ἀναίσθητος εἰ πράξει
τὸ προστυχὸν ἑκάστοτε ἐν ἑκάσταις τῶν πράξεων.

κλ. Ἀληθῆ λέγεις.

αθ. Νῦν οὖν ἡμῖν ἐν τίνι ποτὲ τῶν τῆς πόλεως
μερῶν ἢ ἐπιτηδευμάτων ἐστὶν ἱκανὸν κατεσκευασ-
μένον ὁτιοῦν τοιοῦτον φυλακτήριον ; ἔχομεν
φράζειν ;

κλ. Οὐ δῆτα, ὦ ξένε, σαφῶς γε· εἰ δ᾽ οὖν
τοπάζειν δεῖ, δοκεῖ μοι τείνειν ὁ λόγος οὗτος εἰς
τὸν σύλλογον ὃν εἶπες νῦν δὴ νύκτωρ δεῖν ξυνιέναι.

D αθ. Κάλλισθ᾽ ὑπέλαβες, ὦ Κλεινία, καὶ δεῖ
δὴ τοῦτον, ὡς ὁ νῦν παρεστηκὼς ἡμῖν λόγος
μηνύει, πᾶσαν ἀρετὴν ἔχειν· ἧς ἄρχει τὸ μὴ
πλανᾶσθαι πρὸς πολλὰ στοχαζόμενον, ἀλλ᾽ εἰς
ἓν βλέποντα πρὸς τοῦτο ἀεὶ τὰ πάντα οἷον βέλη
ἀφιέναι.

κλ. Παντάπασι μὲν οὖν.

αθ. Νῦν δὴ μαθησόμεθα ὅτι θαυμαστὸν οὐδὲν
πλανᾶσθαι τὰ τῶν πόλεων νόμιμα, ὅτι πρὸς ἄλλο
ἄλλη βλέπει τῶν νομοθεσιῶν ἐν τῇ πόλει ἑκάστῃ.
καὶ τὰ μὲν πολλὰ οὐδὲν θαυμαστὸν τὸ τοῖς μὲν
E τὸν ὅρον εἶναι τῶν δικαίων, ὅπως ἄρξουσί τινες
ἐν τῇ πόλει, εἴτ᾽ οὖν βελτίους εἴτε χείρους

─────────────
¹ Cp. 705 E, 934 B.

LAWS, BOOK XII

ment of the country is to be finally completed, there must, it would seem, exist in it some element which knows, in the first place, what that political aim, of which we are speaking, really is, and, secondly, in what manner it may attain this aim, and which of the laws, in the first instance, and secondly of men, gives it good counsel or bad. But if any State is destitute of such an element, it will not be surprising if, being thus void of reason and void of sense, it acts at haphazard always in all its actions.

CLIN. Very true.

ATH. In which, then, of the parts or institutions of our State have we now got anything so framed as to prove an adequate safeguard of this kind? Can we answer that question?

CLIN. No, Stranger; at least, not clearly. But if I must make a guess, it seems to me that this discourse of yours is leading up to that synod which has to meet at night, as you said just now.

ATH. An excellent reply, Clinias! And, as our present discourse shows, this synod must possess every virtue; and the prime virtue is not to keep shifting its aim among a number of objects,[1] but to concentrate its gaze always on one particular mark, and at that one mark to shoot, as it were, all its arrows continually.

CLIN. Most certainly.

ATH. So now we shall understand that it is by no means surprising if the legal customs in States keep shifting, seeing that different parts of the codes in each State look in different directions. And, in general, it is not surprising that, with some statesmen, the aim of justice is to enable a certain class of people to rule in the State (whether they be really

τυγχάνουσιν ὄντες· τοῖς δ᾽, ὅπως πλουτήσουσιν,
εἴτ᾽ οὖν δοῦλοί τινων ὄντες εἴτε καὶ μή· τῶν δ᾽ ἡ
προθυμία πρὸς τὸν ἐλεύθερον δὴ βίον ὡρμημένη·
οἱ δὲ καὶ ξύνδυο νομοθετοῦνται, πρὸς ἄμφω
βλέποντες, ἐλεύθεροί τε ὅπως ἄλλων τε πόλεων
ἔσονται δεσπόται· οἱ δὲ σοφώτατοι, ὡς οἴονται,
πρὸς ταῦτά τε καὶ τὰ τοιαῦτα ξύμπαντα, εἰς ἓν
δὲ <οὔ,>¹ οὐδὲν διαφερόντως τετιμημένον ἔχοντες
φράζειν εἰς ὃ τἆλλ᾽ αὐτοῖς δεῖ βλέπειν.

963　κλ. Οὐκοῦν τό γ᾽ ἡμέτερον, ὦ ξένε, ὀρθῶς ἂν
εἴη πάλαι τιθέμενον; πρὸς γὰρ ἓν ἔφαμεν δεῖν
ἀεὶ πάνθ᾽ ἡμῖν τὰ τῶν νόμων βλέποντ᾽ εἶναι,
τοῦτο δ᾽ ἀρετήν που ξυνεχωροῦμεν πάνυ ὀρθῶς
λέγεσθαι.

αθ. Ναί.

κλ. Τὴν δέ γε ἀρετὴν τέτταρα ἔθεμέν που.

αθ. Πάνυ μὲν οὖν.

κλ. Νοῦν δέ γε πάντων τούτων ἡγεμόνα, πρὸς
ὃν δὴ τά τε ἄλλα πάντα καὶ τούτων τὰ τρία δεῖν
βλέπειν.

αθ. Κάλλιστ᾽ ἐπακολουθεῖς, ὦ Κλεινία. καὶ
τὰ λοιπὰ δὲ ξυνακολούθει. νοῦν γὰρ δὴ κυ-
βερνητικὸν μὲν καὶ ἰατρικὸν καὶ στρατηγικὸν
B εἴπομεν εἰς τὸ ἓν ἐκεῖνο οἷ δεῖ βλέπειν, τὸν δὲ
πολιτικὸν ἐλέγχοντες ἐνταῦθ᾽ ἐσμὲν νῦν, καὶ
καθάπερ ἄνθρωπον ἐπανερωτῶντες εἴποιμεν ἄν,
Ὦ θαυμάσιε, σὺ δὲ δὴ ποῖ σκοπεῖς; τί ποτ᾽

¹ <οὔ,> added by Stephens, H. Richards.

¹ Cp. 630 E ff.

superior, or inferior), while with others the aim is
how to acquire wealth (whether or not they be
somebody's slaves); and others again direct their
efforts to winning a life of freedom. Still others
make two objects at once the joint aim of their
legislation,—namely, the gaining of freedom for
themselves, and mastery over other States; while
those who are the wisest of all, in their own conceit,
aim not at one only, but at the sum total of these
and the like objects, since they are unable to
specify any one object of pre-eminent value towards
which they would desire all else to be directed.

CLIN. Then, Stranger, was not the view we stated
long ago the right one? We said[1] that all our
laws must always aim at one single object, which, as
we agreed, is quite rightly named "virtue."

ATH. Yes.

CLIN. And we stated that virtue consists of four
things.

ATH. Certainly.

CLIN. And that the chief of all the four is reason,[2]
at which the other three, as well as everything else,
should aim.

ATH. You follow us admirably, Clinias; and now
follow us in what comes next. In the case of the
pilot, the doctor, and the general, reason is directed,
as we said, towards the one object of aim which is
proper in each case; and now we are at the point of
examining reason in the case of a statesman, and,
addressing it as a man, we shall question it thus :—
" O admirable sir, what is your aim? Medical reason

[2] Cp. 631 C ff. : "reason" (or "wisdom") as the most
"divine" stands first, the others being temperance, justice
and courage.

ἐκεῖνό ἐστι τὸ ἕν, ὃ δὴ σαφῶς ὁ μὲν ἰατρικὸς νοῦς
ἔχει φράζειν· σὺ δ' ὢν δὴ διαφέρων, ὡς φαίης ἄν,
πάντων τῶν ἐμφρόνων, οὐχ ἕξεις εἰπεῖν ; Ἦ σύ
γε, Μέγιλλε καὶ Κλεινία, ἔχετον διαρθροῦντες
ὑπὲρ αὐτοῦ φράζειν πρὸς ἐμὲ τί ποτέ φατε εἶναι
C τοῦτο, καθάπερ ὑπὲρ ἄλλων ἐγὼ πρὸς ὑμᾶς
συχνῶν διωριζόμην ;

ΚΛ. Οὐδαμῶς, ὦ ξένε.

ΑΘ. Τί δ'; ὅτι δεῖ προθυμεῖσθαί τε ξυνιδεῖν
αὐτὸ καὶ ἐν οἷς ;

ΚΛ. Οἷον ἐν τίσι λέγεις ;

ΑΘ. Οἷον ὅτε τέτταρα ἐφήσαμεν ἀρετῆς εἴδη
γεγονέναι, δῆλον ὡς ἓν ἕκαστον ἀνάγκη φάναι,
τεττάρων γε ὄντων.

ΚΛ. Τί μήν ;

ΑΘ. Καὶ μὴν ἕν γε ἅπαντα ταῦτα προσαγορεύομεν. ἀνδρίαν γάρ φαμεν ἀρετὴν εἶναι, καὶ
D τὴν φρόνησιν ἀρετήν, καὶ τὰ δύο τἆλλα, ὡς
ὄντως ὄντα οὐ πολλὰ ἀλλ' ἓν τοῦτο μόνον, ἀρετήν.

ΚΛ. Πάνυ μὲν οὖν.

ΑΘ. Ἧι μὲν τοίνυν διαφέρετον αὐτοῖν τούτω
τὼ δύο καὶ δύ' ὀνόματα ἐλαβέτην καὶ τἆλλα,
οὐδὲν χαλεπὸν εἰπεῖν· ᾗ δὲ ἓν ἀμφοῖν ἐπωνο-
μάσαμεν ἀρετὴν καὶ τοῖς ἄλλοις, οὐκ εὐπετὲς ἔτι.

ΚΛ. Πῶς λέγεις ;

ΑΘ. Οὐδὲν χαλεπὸν ὅ γε λέγω δηλῶσαι. δια-
νειμώμεθα γὰρ ἀλλήλοις τὴν ἐρώτησιν καὶ
ἀπόκρισιν.

ΚΛ. Πῶς αὖ φράζεις ;

E ΑΘ. Ἐρώτησόν με τί ποτὲ ἓν προσαγορεύοντες

---

[1] Cp. 893 A.

is able to state clearly the one single object at which it aims; so will you be unable to state your one object—you who are superior, as perhaps you will say, to all the wise?" Can you two, Megillus and Clinias, define that object on his behalf, and tell me what you say it is, just as I, on behalf of many others, defined their objects for you?

CLIN. We are totally unable to do so.

ATH. Well then, can you declare that we need zeal in discerning both the object itself as a whole and the forms it assumes?

CLIN. Illustrate what you mean by " the forms " you speak of.

ATH. For example, when we said that there are four forms of virtue, obviously, since there are four, we must assert that each is a separate one.

CLIN. Certainly.

ATH. And yet we call them all by one name: we assert that courage is virtue, and wisdom virtue, and the other two likewise, as though they were really not a plurality, but solely this one thing—virtue.

CLIN. Very true.

ATH. Now it is not hard to explain wherein these two (and the rest) differ from one another, and how they have got two names; but to explain why we have given the one name " virtue " to both of them (and to the rest) is no longer an easy matter.

CLIN. How do you mean?

ATH. It is not hard to make clear my meaning. Let one of us adopt the rôle of questioner, the other of answerer.[1]

CLIN. In what way?

ATH. Do you ask me this question—why, when

ἀρετὴν ἀμφότερα δύο πάλιν αὐτὰ προσείπομεν,
τὸ μὲν ἀνδρίαν, τὸ δὲ φρόνησιν. ἐρῶ γάρ σοι τὴν
αἰτίαν, ὅτι τὸ μέν ἐστι περὶ φόβον, οὗ καὶ τὰ
θηρία μετέχει τῆς ἀνδρίας καὶ τά γε τῶν παίδων
ἤθη τῶν πάνυ νέων· ἄνευ γὰρ λόγου καὶ φύσει
γίγνεται ἀνδρεία ψυχή· ἄνευ δὲ αὖ λόγου ψυχὴ
φρόνιμός τε καὶ νοῦν ἔχουσα οὔτ' ἐγένετο πώποτε
οὔτ' ἔστιν οὐδ' αὖθίς ποτε γενήσεται, ὡς ὄντος
ἑτέρου.

ΚΛ. Ἀληθῆ λέγεις.

964   ΑΘ. Ἧι μὲν τοίνυν ἐστὸν διαφόρω καὶ δύο,
σὺ παρ' ἐμοῦ ἀπείληφας τῷ λόγῳ· ᾗ δὲ ἓν καὶ
ταὐτόν, σὺ πάλιν ἀπόδος ἐμοί. διανοοῦ δὲ ὡς
ἐρῶν καὶ ὅπη τέτταρα ὄντα ἕν ἐστι, καὶ ἐμὲ δὲ
ἀξίου, σοῦ δείξαντος ὡς ἕν, πάλιν ὅπη τέτταρα.
καὶ δὴ τὸ μετὰ τοῦτο σκοπῶμεν τὸν εἰδότα
ἱκανῶς περὶ ὡντινωνοῦν, οἷς ἐστὶ μὲν ὄνομα, ἔστι
δὲ αὖ καὶ λόγος, πότερον μόνον ἐπίστασθαι
τοὔνομα χρεών, τὸν δὲ λόγον ἀγνοεῖν, ἢ τόν γε
ὄντα τι καὶ περὶ τῶν διαφερόντων μεγέθει τε καὶ
B κάλλει πάντα τὰ τοιαῦτα ἀγνοεῖν αἰσχρόν.

ΚΛ. Ἔοικε γοῦν.

ΑΘ. Μεῖζον δή τι νομοθέτῃ τε καὶ νομοφύλακι
καὶ ὃς ἀρετῇ πάντων διαφέρειν οἴεται καὶ νικητήρια τούτων αὐτῶν εἴληφεν, ἢ ταῦτα αὐτὰ περὶ
ὧν νῦν λέγομεν, ἀνδρία, σωφροσύνη, δικαιοσύνη,
φρόνησις;

ΚΛ. Καὶ πῶς ;

ΑΘ. Τούτων δὴ πέρι τοὺς ἐξηγητάς, τοὺς δι-

---

[1] Cp. *Laches* 196 D ff., *Protag.* 349 B ff.

calling both the two by the single name of "virtue,"
did we again speak of them as two—courage and
wisdom? Then I shall tell you the reason,—which
is, that the one of them has to do with fear, namely
courage,[1] in which beasts also share, and the characters of very young children; for a courageous soul
comes into existence naturally and without reasoning, but without reasoning there never yet came into
existence, and there does not nor ever will exist, a
soul that is wise and rational, it being a distinct kind.

CLIN. That is true.

ATH. Wherein they differ and are two you have
now learnt from my reply. So do you, in turn,
inform me how it is that they are one and identical.
Imagine you are also going to tell me how it is that,
though four, they are yet one; and then, after
you have shown me how they are one, do you again
ask me how they are four. And after that, let us
enquire regarding the person who has full knowledge
of any objects which possess both a name and a
definition, whether he ought to know the name only,
and not know the definition, or whether it is not a
shameful thing for a man worth anything to be
ignorant of all these points in regard to matters of
surpassing beauty and importance.

CLIN. It would certainly seem to be so.

ATH. For the lawgiver and the Law-warden, and
for him who thinks he surpasses all men in virtue
and who has won prizes for just such qualities, is
there anything more important than these very
qualities with which we are now dealing—courage,
temperance, justice, and wisdom?

CLIN. Impossible.

ATH. In regard to these matters, is it not right

δασκάλους, τοὺς νομοθέτας, τῶν ἄλλων τοὺς
φύλακας, τῷ δεομένῳ γνῶναί τε καὶ εἰδέναι ἢ
τῷ δεομένῳ κολάζεσθαί τε καὶ ἐπιπλῆξαι ἁμαρ-
C τάνοντι, πότερον οὐ δεῖ διδάσκοντα ἣν δύναμιν
ἔχει κακία τε καὶ ἀρετὴ καὶ πάντως δηλοῦντα
διαφέρειν τῶν ἄλλων, ἀλλ᾽ ἢ ποιητήν τινα
ἐλθόντα εἰς τὴν πόλιν ἢ παιδευτὴν νέων φάσκοντ᾽
εἶναι βελτίω φαίνεσθαι τοῦ πᾶσαν ἀρετὴν νενικη-
κότος ; εἶτα ἐν τῇ τοιαύτῃ πόλει ὅπου μὴ λόγῳ
ἔργῳ τε ἱκανοὶ φύλακες εἶεν, ἀρετῆς πέρι γιγνώ-
σκοντες ἱκανῶς, θαυμαστόν τι ταύτην τὴν πόλιν
ἀφύλακτον οὖσαν πάσχειν ἃ πολλαὶ πάσχουσι
D τῶν νῦν πόλεων ;

ΚΛ. Οὐδέν γε, ὡς εἰκός.

ΑΘ. Τί οὖν ; ὃ λέγομεν νῦν, ποιητέον ἡμῖν, ἢ
πῶς ; τοὺς φύλακας ἀκριβεστέρους τῶν πολλῶν
περὶ ἀρετῆς ἔργῳ καὶ λόγῳ κατασκευαστέον ; ἢ
τίνα τρόπον τῇ τῶν ἐμφρόνων κεφαλῇ τε καὶ
αἰσθήσεσιν ὁμοιωθήσεται ἡμῖν ἡ πόλις, ὡς
τοιαύτην τινὰ φυλακὴν κεκτημένη ἐν αὑτῇ ;

ΚΛ. Πῶς οὖν δὴ καὶ τίνα τρόπον, ὦ ξένε,
ἀπεικάζοντες αὐτὸ τοιούτῳ τινὶ λέγομεν ;

E ΑΘ. Δῆλον ὡς αὐτῆς μὲν τῆς πόλεως οὔσης
τοῦ κύτους, τῶν δὲ φυλάκων τοὺς μὲν νέους οἷον
ἐν ἄκρᾳ κορυφῇ ἀπειλεγμένους¹ τοὺς εὐφυεστά-
τους ὀξύτητας ἐν πάσῃ τῇ ψυχῇ ἔχοντας περὶ
ὅλην κύκλῳ τὴν πόλιν ὁρᾶν, φρουροῦντας δὲ
παραδιδόναι μὲν τὰς αἰσθήσεις ταῖς μνήμαις, τοῖς
πρεσβυτέροις δὲ ἐξαγγέλους γίγνεσθαι πάντων
965 τῶν κατὰ πόλιν, τοὺς δὲ νῷ ἀπεικασμένους τῷ

---

¹ ἀπειλεγμένους MSS. : ἀπειλημμένους MSS. marg., Zur.,
vulg.

LAWS, BOOK XII

that the interpreters, the teachers, the lawgivers, as the wardens of the rest, in dealing with him that requires knowledge and information, or with him that requires punishment and reproof for his sin, should excel all others in the art of instructing him in the quality of vice and virtue and exhibiting it fully? Or is some poet who comes into the State, or one who calls himself a trainer of youth, to be accounted evidently superior to him that has won prizes for all the virtues? In a State like that, where there are no wardens who are competent both in word and deed, and possessed of a competent knowledge of virtue,—is it surprising, I ask, if such a State, all unwarded as it is, suffers the same fate as do many of the States which exist to-day?

CLIN. Not at all, I should say.

ATH. Well then, must we do what we now propose, or what? Must we contrive how our wardens shall have a more accurate grasp of virtue, both in word and deed, than the majority of men? For otherwise, how shall our State resemble a wise man's head and senses, on the ground that it possesses within itself a similar kind of wardenship?

CLIN. What is this resemblance we speak of, and wherein does it consist?

ATH. Evidently we are comparing the State itself to the skull; and, of the wardens, the younger ones, who are selected as the most intelligent and nimble in every part of their souls, are set, as it were, like the eyes, in the top of the head, and survey the State all round; and as they watch, they pass on their perceptions to the organs of memory,—that is, they report to the elder wardens all that goes on in the State,—while the old men, who are likened to

πολλὰ καὶ ἄξια λόγου διαφερόντως φρονεῖν, τοὺς
γέροντας, βουλεύεσθαι, καὶ ὑπηρέταις χρωμένους
μετὰ ξυμβουλίας τοῖς νέοις, οὕτω δὴ κοινῇ σώζειν
ἀμφοτέρους ὄντως τὴν πόλιν ὅλην. πότερον οὕτω
λέγομεν, ἤ πως ἄλλως δεῖν κατασκευάζεσθαι ;
μῶν ὁμοίους πάντας κεκτημένην [1] καὶ μὴ διη-
κριβωμένως ἔστιν οὓς τραφέντας τε καὶ πεπαι-
δευμένους ;

κλ. Ἀλλ᾽, ὦ θαυμάσιε, ἀδύνατον.

αθ. Ἰτέον ἄρα ἐπί τινα ἀκριβεστέραν παιδείαν
τῆς ἔμπροσθεν.

B   κλ. Ἴσως.

αθ. Ἆρ᾽ οὖν ἧς δὴ νῦν σχεδὸν ἐφηψάμεθα,
τυγχάνει ἂν οὖσα ἧς χρείαν ἔχομεν αὕτη ;

κλ. Παντάπασι μὲν οὖν.

αθ. Οὐκοῦν ἐλέγομεν τόν γε πρὸς ἕκαστα
ἄκρον δημιουργόν τε καὶ φύλακα μὴ μόνον δεῖν
πρὸς τὰ πολλὰ βλέπειν δυνατὸν εἶναι, πρὸς δὲ τὸ
ἓν ἐπείγεσθαι, γνῶναί τε καὶ γνόντα πρὸς ἐκεῖνο
συντάξασθαι πάντα ξυνορῶντα ;

κλ. Ὀρθῶς.

C   αθ. Ἆρ᾽ οὖν ἀκριβεστέρα σκέψις θέα τ᾽ ἂν
περὶ ὁτουοῦν ὁτῳοῦν γίγνοιτο ἢ τὸ πρὸς μίαν
ἰδέαν ἐκ τῶν πολλῶν καὶ ἀνομοίων δυνατὸν εἶναι
βλέπειν ;

κλ. Ἴσως<οὔ>.[2]

[1] κεκτημένην W.-Möllendorff : κεκτημένους MSS., edd.
[2] ⟨οὔ⟩ I add.

---

[1] 962 E, 963 B ff.   [2] Cp. 903 C, D, 961 E.
[3] Cp. Rep. 537 B ff., where the "dialectic" method is

the reason because of their eminent wisdom in many matters of importance, act as counsellors, and make use of the young men as ministers and colleagues also in their counsels, so that both these classes by their co-operation really effect the salvation of the whole State. Is this the way, or ought we to contrive some other? Should the State, do you think, have all its members equal, instead of having some more highly trained and educated?

CLIN. Nay, my good sir, that were impossible.

ATH. We must proceed, then, to expound a type of education that is higher than the one previously described.

CLIN. I suppose so.

ATH. Will the type which we hinted at just now [1] prove to be that which we require?

CLIN. Certainly.

ATH. Did we not say [2] that he who is a first-class craftsman or warden, in any department, must not only be able to pay regard to the many, but must be able also to press towards the One [3] so as to discern it and, on discerning it, to survey and organise all the rest with a single eye to it?

CLIN. Quite right.

ATH. Can any man get an accurate vision and view of any object better than by being able to look from the many and dissimilar to the one unifying form?

CLIN. Probably not.

---

described as a kind of induction (συναγωγή) whereby the mind ascends from "the many" particulars to "the one" universal concept or "idea" : a comprehensive view (σύνοψις) of the whole is what marks the dialectician (ὁ συνοπτικὸς διαλεκτικός).

PLATO

ΑΘ. Οὐκ ἴσως, ἀλλ᾽ ὄντως, ὦ δαιμόνιε, ταύτης
οὐκ ἔστι σαφεστέρα μέθοδος ἀνθρώπων οὐδενί.

ΚΛ. Σοὶ πιστεύων, ὦ ξένε, συγχωρῶ δή, καὶ
ταύτῃ πορευώμεθα λέγοντες.

ΑΘ. Ἀναγκαστέον ἄρ᾽, ὡς ἔοικε, καὶ τοὺς τῆς
θείας πολιτείας ἡμῖν φύλακας ἀκριβῶς ἰδεῖν
πρῶτον ὅ τί ποτε διὰ πάντων τῶν τεττάρων
D ταὐτὸν τυγχάνει, ὃ δή φαμεν ἔν τε ἀνδρίᾳ καὶ
σωφροσύνῃ καὶ δικαιοσύνῃ καὶ ἐν φρονήσει ἓν ὂν
ἀρετὴν ἑνὶ δικαίως ἂν ὀνόματι προσαγορεύεσθαι.
τοῦτο, ὦ φίλοι, εἰ μὲν βουλόμεθα, τὰ νῦν οἷόνπερ
σφόδρα πιέσαντες μὴ ἀνῶμεν, πρὶν ἂν ἱκανῶς
εἴπωμεν τί ποτ᾽ ἐστίν, εἰς ὃ βλεπτέον, εἴτε ὡς ἓν
εἴτε ὡς ὅλον εἴτε ἀμφότερα εἴτε ὅπως ποτὲ πέφυκεν. ἢ τούτου διαφυγόντος ἡμᾶς οἰόμεθά ποτε
ἡμῖν ἱκανῶς ἕξειν τὰ πρὸς ἀρετήν, περὶ ἧς οὔτε
εἰ πολλά ἐστ᾽ οὔτ᾽ εἰ τέτταρα οὔθ᾽ ὡς ἓν δυνατοὶ
E φράζειν ἐσόμεθα; οὐκοῦν ἐάν γε ἡμῖν ξυμβούλοις
πειθώμεθα, ἁμῶς γέ πως μηχανησόμεθα ἐν τῇ
πόλει ἐγγεγονέναι τοῦθ᾽ ἡμῖν· εἰ δ᾽ ἄρα τὸ παράπαν δοκεῖ ἐᾶν, ἐᾶν δὴ [1] χρεών.

ΚΛ. Ἥκιστα, νὴ τὸν ξένιον, ὦ ξένε, θεόν,
ἐατέον που τὸ τοιοῦτον, ἐπεὶ δοκεῖς ἡμῖν ὀρθότατα λέγειν. ἀλλὰ δὴ πῶς τις τοῦτ᾽ ἂν
μηχανήσαιτο;

966 ΑΘ. Μήπω τὸ πῶς ἂν μηχανησαίμεθα λέγωμεν·
εἰ δεῖ δὲ ἢ μή, πρῶτον βεβαιωσώμεθα τῇ ξυνο-
μολογίᾳ πρὸς ἡμᾶς αὐτούς.

ΚΛ. Ἀλλὰ μὴν δεῖ γε, εἴπερ δυνατόν.

---

[1] ἐᾶν, ἐᾶν δὴ Baiter : ἐᾶν ὁρῇι (al. ὁρῃι) MSS. : ἐᾶν Zur.
(ἐᾶν, ὁρᾶν δὴ Winck., Burnet).

ATH.   It is certain, my friend, rather than probable, that no man can possibly have a clearer method than this.

CLIN.   I believe you, Stranger, and I assent; so let us employ this method in our subsequent discourse.

ATH.   Naturally we must compel the wardens also of our divine polity to observe accurately, in the first place, what that identical element is which pervades all the four virtues, and which,—since it exists as a unity in courage, temperance, justice and wisdom,— may justly be called, as we assert, by the single name of "virtue." This element, my friends, we must now (if we please) hold very tight, and not let go until we have adequately explained the essential nature of the object to be aimed at— whether, that is, it exists by nature as a unity, or as a whole, or as both, or in some other way. Else, if this eludes us, can we possibly suppose that we shall adequately grasp the nature of virtue, when we are unable to state whether it is many or four or one? Accordingly, if we follow our own counsel, we shall contrive somehow, by hook or by crook, that this knowledge shall exist in our State. Should we decide, however, to pass it over entirely—pass it over we must.

CLIN.   Nay, Stranger, in the name of the Stranger's God, we must by no means pass over a matter such as this, since what you say seems to us most true. But how is this to be contrived?

ATH.   It is too early to explain how we are to contrive it: let us first make sure that we agree among ourselves as to whether or not we ought to do so.

CLIN.   Well, surely we ought, if we can.

ΑΘ. Τί δαὶ δή; περὶ καλοῦ τε καὶ ἀγαθοῦ
ταὐτὸν τοῦτο διανοούμεθα; ὡς πόλλ' ἐστὶ μόνον
[ὂν]¹ ἕκαστον τούτων, τοὺς φύλακας ἡμῖν
γνωστέον, ἢ καὶ ὅπως ἕν τε καὶ ὅπῃ;

ΚΛ. Σχεδὸν ἔοικ' ἐξ ἀνάγκης δεῖν καὶ ὅπως ἓν
διανοεῖσθαι.

Β   ΑΘ. Τί δ', ἐννοεῖν μέν, τὴν δὲ ἔνδειξιν τῷ λόγῳ
ἀδυνατεῖν ἐνδείκνυσθαι;

ΚΛ. Καὶ πῶς; ἀνδραπόδου γάρ τινα σὺ
λέγεις ἕξιν.

ΑΘ. Τί δαί; περὶ πάντων τῶν σπουδαίων ἆρ'
ἡμῖν ὁ αὐτὸς λόγος, ὅτι δεῖ τοὺς ὄντως φύλακας
ἐσομένους τῶν νόμων ὄντως εἰδέναι τὰ περὶ τὴν
ἀλήθειαν αὐτῶν, καὶ λόγῳ τε ἱκανοὺς ἑρμηνεύειν
εἶναι καὶ τοῖς ἔργοις ξυνακολουθεῖν, κρίνοντας
τά τε καλῶς γιγνόμενα καὶ τὰ μὴ κατὰ φύσιν;

ΚΛ. Πῶς γὰρ οὔ;

C   ΑΘ. Μῶν οὖν οὐχ ἓν τῶν καλλίστων ἐστὶ τὸ
περὶ τοὺς θεούς, ὃ δὴ σπουδῇ διεπερανάμεθα, ὡς
εἰσί τε καὶ ὅσης φαίνονται κύριοι δυνάμεως,
εἰδέναι τε εἰς ὅσον δυνατόν ἐστι ταῦτ' ἄνθρωπον
γιγνώσκειν, καὶ τοῖς μὲν πλείστοις τῶν κατὰ
πόλιν ξυγγιγνώσκειν τῇ φήμῃ μόνον τῶν νόμων
συνακολουθοῦσι, τοῖς δὲ φυλακῆς μεθέξουσι μηδὲ
ἐπιτρέπειν, ὃς ἂν μὴ διαπονήσηται τὸ πᾶσαν
πίστιν λαβεῖν τῶν οὐσίαν πέρι² θεῶν; τὴν δὲ μὴ
D ἐπιτροπὴν εἶναι τὸ μηδέποτε τῶν νομοφυλάκων
αἱρεῖσθαι τὸν μὴ θεῖον καὶ διαπεπονηκότα πρὸς
αὐτά, μηδ' αὖ τῶν πρὸς ἀρετὴν ἐγκρίτων³
γίγνεσθαι;

¹ [ὂν] wanting in MSS.: added by MSS. marg., Zur.
² οὐσίαν πέρι: οὐσῶν περὶ MSS., edd.
³ ἐγκρίτων L. Dindorf, Herm.: ἔγκριτον MSS.

558

ATH.   Very well then ; do we hold the same view about the fair and the good ?   Ought our wardens to know only that each of these is a plurality, or ought they also to know how and wherein they are each a unity ?

CLIN.   It is fairly obvious that they must necessarily also discern how these are a unity.

ATH.   Well then, ought they to discern it, but be unable to give a verbal demonstration of it ?

CLIN.   Impossible !   The state of mind you describe is that of a slave.

ATH.   Well then, do we hold the same view about all forms of goodness, that those who are to be real wardens of the laws must really know the true nature of them, and be capable both of expounding it in word and conforming to it in deed, passing judgment on fair actions and foul according to their real character ?

CLIN.   Certainly.

ATH.   And is not one of the fairest things the doctrine about the gods, which we expounded earnestly,[1]—to know both that they exist, and what power they manifestly possess, so far as a man is capable of learning these matters ; so that while one should pardon the mass of the citizens if they merely follow the letter of the law, one must exclude from office those who are eligible for wardenship, unless they labour to grasp all the proofs there are about the existence of gods ?   Such exclusion from office consists in refusing ever to choose as a Law-warden, or to number among those approved for excellence, a man who is not divine himself, nor has spent any labour over things divine.

---

[1] In Book X.

ΚΛ. Δίκαιον γοῦν, ὡς λέγεις, τὸν περὶ τὰ τοιαῦτα ἀργὸν ἢ ἀδύνατον ἀποκρίνεσθαι πόρρω τῶν καλῶν.

ΑΘ. Ἆρα οὖν ἴσμεν ὅτι δύ᾽ ἐστὸν τὼ περὶ θεῶν ἄγοντε εἰς πίστιν ὅσα διήλθομεν ἐν τοῖς πρόσθεν ;

ΚΛ. Ποῖα ;

ΑΘ. Ἓν μὲν ὃ περὶ τὴν ψυχὴν ἐλέγομεν, ὡς Ε πρεσβύτατόν τε καὶ θειότατόν ἐστι πάντων ὧν κίνησις γένεσιν παραλαβοῦσα ἀέναον οὐσίαν ἐπόρισεν· ἓν δὲ τὸ περὶ τὴν φοράν, ὡς ἔχει τάξεως, ἄστρων τε καὶ ὅσων ἄλλων ἐγκρατὴς νοῦς ἐστὶ τὸ πᾶν διακεκοσμηκώς. ὁ γὰρ ἰδὼν ταῦτα μὴ φαύλως μηδ᾽ ἰδιωτικῶς, οὐδεὶς οὕτως ἄθεος ἀνθρώπων ποτὲ πέφυκεν, ὃς οὐ τοὐναντίον ἔπαθεν ἢ τὸ προσδοκώμενον ὑπὸ τῶν πολλῶν.

967 οἱ μὲν γὰρ διανοοῦνται τοὺς τὰ τοιαῦτα μεταχειρισαμένους ἀστρονομίᾳ τε καὶ ταῖς μετὰ ταύτης ἀναγκαίαις ἄλλαις τέχναις ἀθέους γίγνεσθαι, καθεωρακότας, ὡς οἴονται,[1] γιγνόμενα ἀνάγκαις πράγματ᾽ ἀλλ᾽ οὐ διανοίαις βουλήσεως ἀγαθῶν πέρι τελουμένων.

ΚΛ. Τὸ δὲ δὴ πῶς ἔχον ἂν εἴη ;

ΑΘ. Πᾶν, ὅπερ εἶπον, τοὐναντίον ἔχει νῦν τε καὶ ὅτε ἄψυχα αὐτὰ οἱ διανοούμενοι διενοοῦντο. θαύματα μὲν οὖν καὶ τότε ὑπεδύετο περὶ αὐτά, Β καὶ ὑπωπτεύετο τὸ νῦν ὄντως δεδογμένον, ὅσοι τῆς ἀκριβείας αὐτῶν ἥπτοντο, ὅπως μήποτ᾽ ἂν ἄψυχα ὄντα οὕτως εἰς ἀκρίβειαν θαυμαστοῖς

---

[1] οἴονται, Madvig, Apelt : οἶόν τε MSS., edd.

[1] Cp. 893 B ff.   [2] Cp. 898 C ff.

CLIN. It is certainly just, as you say, that the
man who is idle or incapable in respect of this
subject should be strictly debarred from the ranks
of the noble.

ATH. Are we assured, then, that there are two
causes, amongst those we previously discussed,[1]
which lead to faith in the gods?

CLIN. What two?

ATH. One is our dogma about the soul,—that it
is the most ancient and divine of all the things
whose motion, when developed into "becoming,"
provides an ever-flowing fount of "being"; and the
other is our dogma concerning the ordering of the
motion of the stars[2] and all the other bodies under
the control of reason, which has made a "cosmos"
of the All. For no man that views these objects in
no careless or amateurish way has ever proved so
godless as not to be affected by them in a way just
the opposite of that which most people expect. For
they imagine that those who study these objects in
astronomy and the other necessary allied arts become
atheists through observing, as they suppose, that all
things come into being by necessary forces and not
by the mental energy of the will aiming at the
fulfilment of good.

CLIN. What in fact is the real state of the case?

ATH. The position at present is, as I said, exactly
the opposite of what it was when those who considered these objects considered them to be soulless.
Yet even then they were objects of admiration, and
the conviction which is now actually held was sus-
pected by all who studied them accurately—namely,
that if they were soulless, and consequently devoid
of reason, they could never have employed with such

561

λογισμοῖς ἂν ἐχρῆτο, νοῦν μὴ κεκτημένα· καί
τινες ἐτόλμων τοῦτό γε αὐτὸ παρακινδυνεύειν
καὶ τότε, λέγοντες ὡς νοῦς εἴη ὁ διακεκοσμηκὼς
πάνθ᾽ ὅσα κατ᾽ οὐρανόν. οἱ δὲ αὐτοὶ πάλιν
ἁμαρτάνοντες ψυχῆς φύσεως, ὅτι πρεσβύτερον
εἴη σωμάτων, διανοηθέντες δὲ ὡς νεώτερον,
C ἅπανθ᾽ ὡς εἰπεῖν ἔπος ἀνέτρεψαν πάλιν, ἑαυτοὺς
δὲ πολὺ μᾶλλον· τὰ γὰρ πρὸ τῶν ὀμμάτων
πάντα αὐτοῖς ἐφάνη τὰ κατ᾽ οὐρανὸν φερόμενα
μεστὰ εἶναι λίθων καὶ γῆς καὶ πολλῶν ἄλλων
ἀψύχων σωμάτων διανεμόντων τὰς αἰτίας παντὸς
τοῦ κόσμου. ταῦτ᾽ ἦν τὰ τότε ἐξεργασάμενα
πολλὰς ἀθεότητας καὶ δυσχερείας τῶν τοιούτων
ἅπτεσθαι· καὶ δὴ καὶ λοιδορήσεις γε ἐπῆλθον
ποιηταῖς, τοὺς φιλοσοφοῦντας κυσὶ ματαίαις
ἀπεικάζοντας χρωμέναισιν ὑλακαῖς, ἄλλα τε
D ἀνόητα εἰπεῖν. νῦν δέ, ὅπερ εἴρηται, πᾶν
τοὐναντίον ἔχει.

κλ. Πῶς ;

αθ. Οὐκ ἔστι ποτὲ γενέσθαι βεβαίως θεοσεβῆ
θνητῶν ἀνθρώπων οὐδένα, ὃς ἂν μὴ τὰ λεγόμενα
ταῦτα νῦν δύο λάβῃ, ψυχή τε ὡς ἔστι πρεσβύτατον ἁπάντων ὅσα γονῆς μετείληφεν ἀθάνατόν τε
ἄρχει τε δὴ σωμάτων πάντων, ἐπὶ δὲ τούτοισι δή,
τὸ νῦν εἰρημένον πολλάκις, τόν τε ἡγημένον [1]
ἐν τοῖς ἄστροις νοῦν τῶν ὄντων τά τε πρὸ τούτων
E ἀναγκαῖα μαθήματα λάβῃ, τά τε κατὰ τὴν

---

[1] ἡγημένον : εἰρημένον MSS. (add αἴτιον after ὄντων ci.
Stallb.)

---

[1] An allusion to the saying of Anaxagoras, "All things
were together ; then Reason (νοῦς) came and set them in

precision calculations so marvellous; and even in those days there were some who dared to hazard the statement [1] that reason is the orderer of all that is in the heavens. But the same thinkers, through mistaking the nature of the soul and conceiving her to be posterior, instead of prior, to body, upset again (so to say) the whole universe, and most of all themselves; for as regards the visible objects of sight, all that moves in the heavens appeared to them to be full of stones, earth and many other soulless bodies which dispense the causes of the whole cosmos. These were the views which, at that time, caused these thinkers to incur many charges of atheism and much odium, and which also incited the poets to abuse them [2] by likening philosophers to "dogs howling at the moon," with other such senseless slanders. But to-day, as we have said, the position is quite the reverse.

CLIN. How so?

ATH. It is impossible for any mortal man to become permanently god-fearing if he does not grasp the two truths now stated,—namely, how that the soul is oldest of all things that partake of generation, and is immortal, and rules over all bodies,—and in addition to this, he must also grasp that reason which, as we have often affirmed, controls what exists among the stars, together with the necessary preliminary sciences; [3] and he must observe

---

order." But A. ascribed to Reason only the initiation of a world-order; in all other respects his doctrine was materialistic, and he used purely physical causes and processes in explaining the world, regarding the stars as fiery masses of matter ("full of earth, stones," etc.). Cp. *Phaedo* 97 B ff.

[2] Cp. *Rep.* 607 B, C.

[3] Cp. 818 A ff.

Μοῦσαν τούτοις τῆς κοινωνίας συνθεασάμενος
χρήσηται πρὸς τὰ τῶν ἠθῶν ἐπιτηδεύματα καὶ
νόμιμα συναρμοττόντως, ὅσα τε λόγον ἔχει,
τούτων δυνατὸς ἢ δοῦναι τὸν λόγον [ὅσα τε μή].
968 ὁ δὲ μὴ ταῦθ᾽ οἷός τ᾽ ὢν πρὸς ταῖς δημοσίαις
ἀρεταῖς κεκτῆσθαι σχεδὸν ἄρχων μὲν οὐκ ἄν
ποτε γένοιτο ἱκανὸς ὅλης πόλεως, ὑπηρέτης δ᾽ ἂν
ἄλλοις ἄρχουσιν. ὁρᾶν δὴ χρεὼν νῦν, ὦ Κλεινία
καὶ Μέγιλλε, ἤδη πρὸς τοῖς εἰρημένοις νόμοις
ἅπασιν ὅσους διεληλύθαμεν, εἰ καὶ τοῦτον
προσοίσομεν, ὡς φυλακὴν ἐσόμενον κατὰ νόμον
χάριν σωτηρίας τὸν τῶν ἀρχόντων νυκτερινὸν
σύλλογον παιδείας ὁπόσης διεληλύθαμεν κοινωνὸν
B γενόμενον· ἢ πῶς ποιῶμεν;

ΚΛ. Ἀλλ᾽, ὦ λῷστε, πῶς οὐ προσοίσομεν, ἄν
πῃ καὶ κατὰ βραχὺ δυνηθῶμεν;

ΑΘ. Καὶ μὴν πρός γε τὸ τοιοῦτον ἁμιλληθῶμεν
πάντες. ξυλλήπτωρ γὰρ τούτου γε ὑμῖν καὶ
ἐγὼ γιγνοίμην ἂν προθύμως, πρὸς δ᾽ ἐμοὶ καὶ
ἑτέρους ἴσως εὑρήσω, διὰ τὴν περὶ τὰ τοιαῦτ᾽
ἐμπειρίαν τε καὶ σκέψιν γεγονυῖάν μοι καὶ μάλα
συχνήν.

ΚΛ. Ἀλλ᾽, ὦ ξένε, παντὸς μὲν μᾶλλον ταύτῃ
πορευτέον ᾗπερ καὶ ὁ θεὸς ἡμᾶς σχεδὸν ἄγει· τίς
δὲ ὁ τρόπος ἡμῖν γιγνόμενος ὀρθῶς γίγνοιτ᾽ ἄν,
C τουτὶ δὴ τὰ νῦν λέγωμέν τε καὶ ἐρευνῶμεν.

ΑΘ. Οὐκέτι νόμους, ὦ Μέγιλλε καὶ Κλεινία,
περὶ τῶν τοιούτων δυνατόν ἐστι νομοθετεῖν, πρὶν
ἂν κοσμηθῇ· τότε δὲ κυρίους ὧν αὐτοὺς δεῖ
γίγνεσθαι νομοθετεῖν. ἀλλὰ ἤδη τὸ τὰ τοιαῦτα

---

[1] Cp. *Rep.* 401 D, 500 D, 531 ff.

also the connection therewith of musical theory, and
apply it harmoniously to the institutions and rules
of ethics;[1] and he must be able to give a rational
explanation of all that admits of rational explanation.
He that is unable to master these sciences, in addition to the popular virtues,[2] will never make a
competent magistrate of the whole State, but only
a minister to other magistrates. And now, O
Megillus and Clinias, it is time at last to consider
whether, in addition to all the previous laws which
we have stated, we shall add this also—that the
nocturnal synod of magistrates shall be legally es-
-tablished, and shall participate in all the education
we have described, to keep ward over the State,
and to secure its salvation; or what are we to do?

CLIN. Of course we shall add this law, my excellent sir, if we can possibly do so, even to a small
extent.

ATH. Then, verily, let us all strive to do so.
And herein you will find me a most willing helper,
owing to my very long experience and study of
this subject; and perhaps I shall discover other
helpers also besides myself.

CLIN. Well, Stranger, we most certainly must
proceed on that path along which God too, it
would seem, is conducting us. But what is the
right method for us to employ,—that is what we
have now got to discover and state.

ATH. It is not possible at this stage, Megillus
and Clinias, to enact laws for such a body, before
it has been duly framed; when it is, its members
must themselves ordain what authority they should
possess; but it is already plain that what is re-

---

[2] Cp. 710 A.

κατασκεύαζον διδαχῇ μετὰ ξυνουσίας πολλῆς
γίγνοιτ᾽ ἄν, εἰ γίγνοιτο ὀρθῶς.

ΚΛ. Πῶς ; τί τοῦτο εἰρῆσθαι φῶμεν αὖ ;

ΑΘ. Πρῶτον μὲν δή που καταλεκτέος ἂν εἴη
D κατάλογος τῶν ὅσοι ἐπιτήδειοι πρὸς τὴν τῆς
φυλακῆς φύσιν ἂν εἶεν ἡλικίαις τε καὶ μαθημάτων
δυνάμεσι καὶ τρόπων ἤθεσι καὶ ἔθεσι. μετὰ δὲ
τοῦτο, ἃ δεῖ μανθάνειν, οὔτε εὑρεῖν ῥᾴδιον οὔτε
εὑρηκότος ἄλλου μαθητὴν γενέσθαι. πρὸς τούτοις δὲ χρόνους οὕς τε καὶ ἐν οἷς δεῖ παραλαμβάνειν ἕκαστον, μάταιον ταῦτ᾽ ἐν γράμμασι
E λέγειν· οὐδὲ γὰρ αὐτοῖς τοῖς μανθάνουσι δῆλα
γίγνοιτ᾽ ἂν ὅ τι πρὸς καιρὸν μανθάνεται, πρὶν
ἐντὸς τῆς ψυχῆς ἑκάστῳ τοῦ μαθήματος ἐπιστή-
μην γεγονέναι. οὕτω δὴ πάντα τὰ περὶ ταῦτα
ἀπόρρητα μὲν λεχθέντα οὐκ ἂν ὀρθῶς λέγοιτο,
ἀπόρρητα δὲ διὰ τὸ μηδὲν προρρηθέντα δηλοῦν
τῶν λεγομένων.

ΚΛ. Τί οὖν δὴ ποιητέον ἐχόντων τούτων οὕτως,
ὦ ξένε ;

ΑΘ. Τὸ λεγόμενον, ὦ φίλοι, ἐν κοινῷ καὶ μέσῳ
ἔοικεν ἡμῖν κεῖσθαι, καὶ εἴπερ κινδυνεύειν περὶ
τῆς πολιτείας ἐθέλομεν ξυμπάσης, ἢ τρὶς ἕξ,
φασίν, ἢ τρεῖς κύβους βάλλοντες, ταῦτα [1] ποιη-
969 τέον· ἐγὼ δ᾽ ὑμῖν συγκινδυνεύσω τῷ φράζειν τε
καὶ ἐξηγεῖσθαι τά γε δεδογμένα ἐμοὶ περὶ τῆς
παιδείας τε καὶ τροφῆς τῆς νῦν αὖ κεκινημένης

---

[1] ταῦτα some MSS., Stallb.: πάντα al. MSS., Zur.

---

[1] Cp. *Rep.* 528 B ff.
[2] Cp. *Epp.* 7. 341 C.

quired in order to form such a body, if it is to be
rightly formed, is teaching by means of prolonged
conferences.

CLIN. How so? What now are we to understand
by this observation?

ATH. Surely we must first draw up a list of all
those who are fitted by age, intellectual capacity,
and moral character and habit for the office of
warden; but as regards the next point, the subjects
they should learn,—these it is neither easy to
discover for oneself [1] nor is it easy to find another
who has made the discovery and learn from him.
Moreover, with respect to the limits of time, when
and for how long they ought to receive instruction
in each subject, it were idle to lay down written
regulations; [2] for even the learners themselves
could not be sure that they were learning at the
opportune time until each of them had acquired
within his soul some knowledge of the subject in
question. Accordingly, although it would be wrong
to term all these matters "indescribable," they
should be termed "imprescribable," seeing that the
prescribing of them beforehand does nothing to
elucidate the question under discussion.

CLIN. What then must we do, Stranger, under
these circumstances?

ATH. Apparently, my friends, we must "take
our chance with the crowd" (as the saying is), and
if we are willing to put the whole polity to the
hazard and throw (as men say) three sixes or three
aces, so it must be done; and I will go shares
with you in the hazard by declaring and explaining
my views concerning education and nurture, the
subject now started anew in our discourse; but

τοῖς λόγοις· τὸ μέντοι κινδύνευμα οὐ σμικρὸν οὐδ'
ἑτέροις τισὶ προσφερὲς ἂν εἴη. σοὶ δὴ τοῦτό γε,
ὦ Κλεινία, μέλειν παρακελεύομαι· σὺ γὰρ τὴν
Μαγνήτων πόλιν, ἢ ᾧ ἂν θεὸς ἐπώνυμον αὐτὴν
ποιήσῃ, κλέος ἀρεῖ μέγιστον κατασκευάσας αὐτὴν
ὀρθῶς, ἢ τό γε ἀνδρειότατος εἶναι δόξαι τῶν
B ὕστερον ἐπιγιγνομένων οὐκ ἐκφεύξει ποτέ. ἐάν
γε μὴν οὗτος ἡμῖν ὁ θεῖος γένηται ξύλλογος, ὦ
φίλοι ἑταῖροι, παραδοτέον τούτῳ τὴν πόλιν,
ἀμφισβήτησίς τ' οὐκ ἔστ' οὐδεμία οὐδενὶ τῶν
νῦν παρὰ ταῦθ' ὡς ἔπος εἰπεῖν νομοθετῶν, ὄντως
δὲ ἔσται σχεδὸν ὕπαρ ἀποτετελεσμένον οὐ σμικρῷ
πρόσθεν ὀνείρατος ὡς τῷ λόγῳ ἐφηψάμεθα,
κεφαλῆς νοῦ τε κοινωνίας εἰκόνα τινὰ πως
ξυμμίξαντες, ἐὰν ἄρα ἡμῖν οἵ τε ἄνδρες ἀκριβῶς
C ἐκλεχθῶσι,[1] παιδευθῶσί τε προσηκόντως, παιδευ-
θέντες τε ἐν ἀκροπόλει τῆς χώρας κατοικήσαντες
φύλακες ἀποτελεσθῶσιν οἵους ἡμεῖς οὐκ εἴδομεν
ἐν τῷ πρόσθεν βίῳ πρὸς ἀρετὴν σωτηρίας
γενομένους.

ΜΕ. Ὦ φίλε Κλεινία, ἐκ τῶν νῦν ἡμῖν εἰρημένων ἀπάντων ἢ τὴν πόλιν ἐατέον τῆς κατοικίσεως
ἢ τὸν ξένον τόνδε οὐκ ἀφετέον, ἀλλὰ δεήσεσι καὶ
μηχαναῖς πάσαις κοινωνὸν ποιητέον ἐπὶ τὴν τῆς
πόλεως κατοίκισιν.

ΚΛ. Ἀληθέστατα λέγεις, ὦ Μέγιλλε, καὶ
ἐγώ τε ποιήσω ταῦθ' οὕτω καὶ <σὺ>[2] ξυλ-
D λάμβανε.

ΜΕ. Ξυλλήψομαι.

[1] ἐκλεχθῶσι some MSS., Herm.: ξυμμιχθῶσι al. MSS., Zur.,
vulg.
[2] <σὺ> added by Ast.

truly the hazard will be no small one, nor comparable to any others. And you, Clinias, I specially exhort to take good heed to this matter. For as concerns the State of the Magnesians—or whoever else, by the god's direction, gives your State its name,[1]—if you frame it aright, you will achieve most high renown, or at any rate you will inevitably gain the reputation of being the boldest of all your successors. If so be that this divine synod actually comes into existence, my dear colleagues, we must hand over to it the State; and practically all our present lawgivers agree to this without dispute. Thus we shall have as an accomplished fact and waking reality that result which we treated but a short while ago in our discourse as a mere dream, when we constructed a kind of picture of the union of the reason and the head,[2]—if, that is to say, we have the members carefully selected and suitably trained, and after their training quartered in the acropolis of the country, and thus finally made into wardens, the like of whom we have never before seen in our lives for excellence in safeguarding.

MEG. My dear Clinias, from all that has now been said it follows that either we must forgo the idea of settling the State, or else we must detain this Stranger here, and by prayers and every possible means secure his co-operation in the task of settling the State.

CLIN. That is most true, Megillus; I will do as you say, and do you yourself assist me.

MEG. Assist you I will.

---

[1] *i.e.* if the god should direct the State to be named, not after the Magnetes, but after some other person or place: cp. 704 A, 919 D.　　[2] Cp. 964 D ff.

INDEX

INDEX

INDEX

INDEX

INDEX

INDEX

577

INDEX

INDEX

INDEX

Rule, Ruler, I. 208 *n.*, 211 ff., 237, 275, 279, 283 ff., 289 ff.; II. 273, 401, 479

Running (races), I. 7, 431; II. 141 ff., 163

Rural stewards, *see* Land-stewards.

Sacred line (in draughts), I. 361

Sacrifices, I. 297 ff., 493; II. 55 ff., 73, 113, 125 ff., 241, 307, 383 ff., 497, 501, 505

Safety, *see* Salvation.

Salamis, I. 239, 263 ff.

Sale, II. 191 ff., 397 ff., 515

Salvation (safety, safe-keeping), I. 241, 263, 287, 293; II. 325, 537 ff., 565

Satyrs, II. 93

Sauromatides, II. 59, 63

Saviour, I. xv, 219, 257, 471; II. 537, 541 (cp I. 453)

School, I. 435; II. 57, 75

Science, Scientist, I. 49; II. 315 ff.

Scourging, II. 203, 263, 293 ff., 393

Scrutiny, I. 433, 439 ff., 445; II. 495 (cp. Test)

Sculptor, II. 523

Scythian, I. 45; II. 25

Sea, I. 257

Search, II. 517

Second-best (state, etc.), I. 361, 385; II. 65, 167, 273

Secret-Service, I. 31 *n.*, 431

Security, II. 515 (cp. Surety)

Select judges, II. 207, 237, 433, 471, 491, 497, 525 (cp. I. 445)

Self-defence, II. 287 ff.

Self-inferior (— superior), I. 11 ff., 67; II. 167

Self-love, I. 339

Self-movement (principle of), I. xvi; II. 331 ff., 337

Serious (work, etc.), I. 161; II. 53 ff., 77, 97, 313

Service (military, etc.), I. 429 ff., 501; II. 481 ff., 521

Sex (sexual relations, etc.), I. 495 ff.; II. 149 ff., 157 ff., 163 ff.

Shame, I. 77 *n.*, 81, 153 (cp. Modesty)

Shepherd, I. 229, 349

Ship, I. 55, 259, 415; II. 53

Shrine, II. 189, 203, 385 ff.

Sicily, I. 111

Sileni, II. 93

Silver, I. 175, 371 ff.; II. 47, 105, 523

Simonides, I. 367 *n.*

Simplicity, I. 175

Sin, II. 231 ff.

Singing, I. 127 ff. (cp. Song)

Slave, I. 245 ff., 309, 473 ff.; II. 21, 239 ff.

Sleep, II. 67 ff.

Sling, II. 143

Smerdis, I. 228 *n.*, 229 *n.*

Socrates (alluded to), II. 222 *n.*

Soldier, II. 481, 487

Solid, II. 107 ff., 328 *n.*

Solon, I. 355 *n.*; II. 217, 390 *n.*

Song, I. 127 ff.; II. 49 ff., 129

Soothsayer, II. 389

Sophist, II. 381

Sorcery, II. 455 ff.

Sorrow, I. 341

Soul, I. xiii, xvi, 208 *n.*, 209, 323 ff., 337; II. 335 ff., 365 ff., 533, 541, 551 ff., 561 ff.

Spartan, Spartiate, I. 31 *n.*, 43, 126 *n.*, 218 *n.*, 399, 481; II. 502 *n.* (cp. Laconian)

" Sparti," I. 57 *n.*

Spectators, I. 107, 111

" Sphaeromachia," II. 132 *n.*

Spices, II. 185

Spring, I. 417, 425; II. 181 (cp. Fountain)

Stage, II. 99

Standard, II. 49

Star, II. 113 ff., 349 ff., 367 *n.*, 447 *n.*, 561 ff.

Starting-principle, II., 329 (cp. 333)

State (esp. the Magnesian), I. 165 ff., 208 *n.*, 255 ff., 349 ff., 371 ff., 403 ff., 441, 483 ff.; II. 9, 15, 21, 33, 57 ff., 67 ff., 85 ff., 109 ff., 125 ff., 167 ff., 183 ff., 199 ff., 209 ff., 215 ff., 225, 271 ff., 275, 279, 283, 375, 409 ff., 421 ff., 441, 475, 489 ff., 501 ff., 521 ff., 537 ff., 553 ff., 569 (cp. Polity).—Best State, I. 279, 361 ff.; II. 65 *n.*

Statues, II. 523

Stepmother, II. 445

Story, I. 41, 69, 129, 155, 163, 199, 283 ff.; II. 257, 263, 307, 389, 475 (cp. Myth, Tale)

Stranger, I. 331 ff.; II. 241 ff. 253, 287 ff., 503 ff., 513 ff. (cp. Foreigner)

Strife, I. 15, 267, 353; II. 489 (cp. Faction, Feud)

Substance, II. 335 ff.

INDEX

581

INDEX

PRINTED IN GREAT BRITAIN BY RICHARD CLAY & SONS, LIMITED,
BUNGAY, SUFFOLK.

The Loeb Classical Library

VOLUMES ALREADY PUBLISHED

Latin Authors.

APULEIUS. The Golden Ass (Metamorphoses), W. Adlington (1566).
Revised by S. Gaselee. (*3rd Imp.*)

AUSONIUS. H. G. Evelyn White. 2 Vols.

BOETHIUS: TRACTS AND DE CONSOLATIONE PHILOSO-
PHIAE. Rev. H. F. Stewart and E. K. Rand.

CAESAR: CIVIL WARS. A. G. Peskett. (*2nd Imp.*)

CAESAR: GALLIC WAR. H. J. Edwards. (*4th Imp.*)

CATULLUS. F. W. Cornish; TIBULLUS. J. P. Postgate; and
PERVIGILIUM VENERIS. J. W. Mackail. (*7th Imp.*)

CICERO: DE FINIBUS. H. Rackham. (*2nd Imp.*)

CICERO: DE OFFICIIS. Walter Miller. (*2nd Imp.*)

CICERO: DE SENECTUTE, DE AMICITIA, DE DIVINATIONE.
W. A. Falconer.

CICERO: LETTERS TO ATTICUS. E. O. Winstedt. 3 Vols. *3rd Imp.*

CICERO: PRO ARCHIA POETA, POST REDITUM IN SENATU,
POST REDITUM AD QUIRITES, DE DOMO SUA, DE HARUS-
PICUM RESPONSIS, PRO PLANCIO. N. H. Watts.

CLAUDIAN. M. Platnauer. 2 Vols.

CONFESSIONS OF ST. AUGUSTINE. W. Watts (1631). 2 Vols.
(*3rd Imp.*)

FRONTINUS, STRATEGEMS AND AQUEDUCTS. C. E. Bennett.

FRONTO: CORRESPONDENCE. C. R. Haines. 2 Vols.

HORACE: ODES AND EPODES. C. E. Bennett. (*6th Imp.*)

JUVENAL AND PERSIUS. G. G. Ramsay. (*2nd Imp.*)

LIVY. B. O. Foster. 13 Vols. Vols. I, II and III. (Vol. I *2nd Imp.*)

LUCRETIUS. W. H. D. Rouse.

MARTIAL. W. C. Ker. 2 Vols.

OVID: HEROIDES AND AMORES. Grant Showerman. (*2nd Imp.*)

OVID: METAMORPHOSES. F. J. Miller. 2 Vols. (*3rd Imp.*)

OVID: TRISTIA AND EX PONTO. A. L. Wheeler.

PETRONIUS. M. Heseltine; SENECA: APOCOLOCYNTOSIS.
W. H. D. Rouse. (*5th Imp.*)

PLAUTUS. Paul Nixon. 5 Vols. Vols. I—III. (Vol. I *2nd Imp.*)

PLINY: LETTERS. Melmoth's Translation revised by W. M. L.
Hutchinson. 2 Vols. (*2nd Imp.*)

PROPERTIUS. H. E. Butler. (*3rd Imp.*)

QUINTILIAN. H. E. Butler. 4 Vols.

SALLUST. J. C. Rolfe.

SCRIPTORES HISTORIAE AUGUSTAE. D. Magie. 4 Vols. Vols.
I and II.

SENECA: EPISTULAE MORALES. R, M Gummere. 3 Vols. (Vol.
I *2nd Imp.*)

SENECA: TRAGEDIES. F. J. Miller. 2 Vols. (*2nd Imp.*)

SUETONIUS. J. C. Rolfe. 2 Vols. (*3rd Imp.*)

TACITUS: DIALOGUS. Sir Wm. Peterson, and AGRICOLA AND
GERMANIA. Maurice Hutton. (*3rd Imp.*)

TACITUS, HISTORIES. Clifford H. Moore. 2 Vols. Vol. I.

TERENCE. John Sargeaunt. 2 Vols. (*5th Imp.*)

VELLEIUS PATERCULUS AND RES GESTAE DIVI AUGUSTI.
F. W. Shipley.

VIRGIL. H. R. Fairclough. 2 Vols. (Vol. I *4th Imp.* Vol. II *3rd Imp.*)

Greek Authors.

ACHILLES TATIUS. S. Gaselee.

AENEAS TACTICUS, ASCLEPIODOTUS AND ONASANDER.

AESCHINES. C. D. Adams. [The Illinois Club.

AESCHYLUS. H. Weir Smyth. 2 Vols.

APOLLODORUS. Sir James G. Frazer. 2 Vols.

APOLLONIUS RHODIUS. R. C. Seaton. (*3rd Imp.*)

THE APOSTOLIC FATHERS. Kirsopp Lake. 2 Vols. (Vol. I *4th Imp.* Vol. II *3rd Imp.*)

APPIAN'S ROMAN HISTORY. Horace White. 4 Vols.

ARISTOPHANES Benjamin Bickley Rogers. 3 Vols. [G. R. Mair.

CALLIMACHUS AND LYCOPHRON. A. W. Mair; and ARATUS,

CLEMENT OF ALEXANDRIA. Rev. G. W. Butterworth.

DAPHNIS AND CHLOE. Thornley's Translation revised by J. M. Edmonds; and PARTHENIUS. S. Gaselee. (*2nd Imp.*)

DEMOSTHENES, DE CORONA AND DE FALSA LEGATIONE, C. A. Vince and J. H. Vince.

DIO CASSIUS: ROMAN HISTORY. E. Cary. 9 Vols. Vols. I to VIII.

DIOGENES LAERTIUS. R. D. Hicks. 2 Vols.

EPICTETUS. W. A. Oldfather. 2 Vols. Vol. I.

EURIPIDES. A. S. Way. 4 Vols. (*4th Imp.*)

GALEN: ON THE NATURAL FACULTIES. A. J. Brock.

THE GREEK ANTHOLOGY. W. R. Paton. 5 Vols. (*3rd Imp.*)

THE GREEK BUCOLIC POETS (THEOCRITUS, BION, MOSCHUS). J. M. Edmonds. (*4th Imp.*)

HERODOTUS. A. D. Godley. 4 Vols. [(*2nd Imp.*)

HESIOD AND THE HOMERIC HYMNS. H. G. Evelyn White.

HIPPOCRATES. W. H. S. Jones. 4 Vols. Vols. I and II.

HOMER: ILIAD. A. T. Murray. 2 Vols.

HOMER: ODYSSEY. A. T. Murray. 2 Vols. (*2nd Imp.*)

JOSEPHUS: THE LIFE AND AGAINST APION. H. St. J. Thackeray, 8 Vols. Vol. I.

JULIAN. Wilmer Cave Wright. 3 Vols [ray. 8 Vols. Vol. I.

LUCIAN. A. M. Harmon. 8 Vols. Vols. I to IV. (Vols. I & II *2nd Imp.*)

LYRA GRAECA. J. M. Edmonds. 3 Vols. Vols. I and II.

MARCUS AURELIUS. C. R. Haines. (*2nd Imp.*)

MENANDER. F. G. Allinson.

PAUSANIAS: DESCRIPTION OF GREECE. W. H. S. Jones. 5 Vols. and Companion Vol. Vols. I and II.

PHILOSTRATUS: THE LIFE OF APOLLONIUS OF TYANA. F. C. Conybeare. 2 Vols. (*2nd Imp.*)

PHILOSTRATUS AND EUNAPIUS, LIVES OF THE SOPHISTS.

PINDAR. Sir J. E. Sandys. (*3rd Imp.*) [Wilmer Cave Wright.

PLATO: CRATYLUS, PARMENIDES, GREATER HIPPIAS, LESSER HIPPIAS. H. N. Fowler.

PLATO: EUTHYPHRO, APOLOGY, CRITO, PHAEDO, PHAEDRUS. H. N. Fowler. (*4th Imp.*) [W. R. M. Lamb.

PLATO: LACHES, PROTAGORAS, MENO, EUTHYDEMUS.

PLATO: LAWS. R. G. Bury. 2 Vols.

PLATO: LYSIS, SYMPOSIUM, GORGIAS. W. R. M. Lamb.

PLATO: POLITICUS AND PHILEBUS. H. N. Fowler. ION. W. R. M. Lamb.

PLATO: THEAETETUS AND SOPHIST. H. N. Fowler.

PLUTARCH: THE PARALLEL LIVES. B. Perrin. 11 Vols.

POLYBIUS. W. R. Paton. 6 Vols. Vols. I to IV.

PROCOPIUS: HISTORY OF THE WARS. H. B. Dewing. 7 Vols.

QUINTUS SMYRNAEUS. A. S. Way. [Vols. I to IV.

SOPHOCLES. F. Storr. 2 Vols. (*4th Imp.*)

ST. JOHN DAMASCENE: BARLAAM AND IOASAPH. Rev. G. R. Woodward and Harold Mattingly.

STRABO: GEOGRAPHY. Horace L. Jones. 8 Vols. Vols. I to III

THEOPHRASTUS: ENQUIRY INTO PLANTS. Sir Arthur Ho.

THUCYDIDES. C. F. Smith. 4 Vols. [Bart. 2 Vols.

XENOPHON: CYROPAEDIA. Walter Miller. 2 Vols. Vol. I. (*2nd Imp*

XENOPHON: HELLENICA, ANABASIS, APOLOGY, AND SYM POSIUM. C. L. Brownson and O. J. Todd. 3 Vols.

XENOPHON: MEMORABILIA AND OECONOMICUS. E. Marchant.

XENOPHON: SCRIPTA MINORA. E C. Marchant.